United States Army in Vietnam

Public Affairs: The Military and the Media, 1968–1973

by

William M. Hammond

University Press of the Pacific
Honolulu, Hawaii

Public Affairs: The Military and the Media,
1968-1973

by
William M. Hammond

ISBN: 0-89875-604-9

Copyright © 2001 by University Press of the Pacific

Reprinted from the 1996 edition

University Press of the Pacific
Honolulu, Hawaii
http://www.universitypressofthepacific.com

United States Army in Vietnam

Jeffrey J. Clarke, General Editor

Advisory Committee
(As of October 1994)

John W. Shy
University of Michigan

Col. John F. Connolly
U.S. Army War College

Carlo W. D'Este
New Seabury, Mass.

Brig. Gen. Gerald E. Galloway, Jr.
U.S. Military Academy

Joseph T. Glatthaar
University of Houston

Rose L. Greaves
University of Kansas

Ira D. Gruber
Rice University

Maj. Gen. John P. Herrling
U.S. Army Training and Doctrine
Command

D. Clayton James
Virginia Military Institute

Michael J. Kurtz
National Archives and Records
Administration

Carol A. Reardon
Pennsylvania State University

Brig. Gen. Randall L. Rigby, Jr.
U.S. Army Command and General
Staff College

William A. Walker
Archivist of the Army

U.S. Army Center of Military History

Brig. Gen. John W. Mountcastle, Chief of Military History

Chief Historian
Chief, Histories Division
Editor in Chief

Jeffrey J. Clarke
Col. William T. Bowers
John W. Elsberg

. . . to Those Who Served

Foreword

The U.S. Army in Vietnam series documents the Army's role in the Vietnam War. Most of its volumes deal with the Army's particular military interests: the conduct of combat operations, logistics, engineering, communications and electronics, and advice and support for America's allies. Two, however, depart from that pattern to address a subject unique to recent war, the evolving relationship between the military and the news media. The first of those volumes, *Public Affairs: The Military and the Media, 1962–1968*, appeared in 1988. An account of military-media relations during the early years of the war, it covered the formulation of military policies for dealing with the press in Vietnam and how those policies influenced the conduct of the war prior to the Tet offensive of 1968.

Picking up where that volume ended—just after Tet, as the search for a negotiated settlement to the conflict began—this account carries the story forward through the administration of President Richard M. Nixon to the final withdrawal of American forces from South Vietnam in 1973. It is a tale well worth telling, not only because it draws upon hitherto unavailable sources but because it documents events and precedents that will continue to affect military relations with the news media during future operations. Indeed, many of the book's episodes and themes will have a familiar ring to those who have followed military relations with the media during operations in Grenada and Panama, the war in the Persian Gulf, and a host of subsequent peace operations. I recommend the study for its special insights not only to soldiers, newsmen, and policy makers but to the general public as well.

Washington, D.C.
16 August 1995

JOHN W. MOUNTCASTLE
Brigadier General, USA
Chief of Military History

The Author

William M. Hammond is a graduate of the Catholic University of America, where he earned the M.A. and Ph.D. degrees. He serves as a historian with the U.S. Army Center of Military History in Washington, D.C. In addition to this volume and its predecessor, *Public Affairs: The Military and the Media, 1962–1968*, published in 1988, he is the coauthor of the forthcoming *Black Soldier, White Army: The 24th Infantry Regiment in Korea*. Hammond has also written a narrative on the Normandy invasion for the Center's series The U.S. Army Campaigns of World War II; the Center's history of the selection and interment of the Vietnam War's Unknown Soldier, *The Unknown Serviceman of the Vietnam Era*; and numerous shorter articles in professional journals. He has taught at the University of Maryland, Baltimore County, and at Trinity College in Washington, D.C. In addition to his duties at the Center, he is currently a Lecturer in University Honors at the University of Maryland, College Park.

Preface

This book continues the description of the U.S. Military Assistance Command, Vietnam's efforts to manage relations with the news media during the Vietnam War. Beginning shortly after the Tet offensive of 1968, where its predecessor, *Public Affairs: The Military and the Media, 1962–1968,* left off, it describes the changes introduced into the program by General William C. Westmoreland's successor, General Creighton Abrams, and follows their development through to the end of the war.

Since Washington agencies, especially the White House, throughout the war but particularly toward its end, exerted a major influence over the military's public affairs policies, I have continued to take as broad an approach to the subject as time and available source materials have allowed. Because no *Pentagon Papers* exist to detail official thinking at the highest level during the Nixon administration, I have made extensive use of President Richard Nixon's hitherto unavailable national security files to provide context for the reader but also to flesh out procedures and events that would lack meaning and substance if seen only from the perspective of field agencies. In that way, I have sought to trace the many turns public affairs policies took on issues surrounding such events as the My Lai massacre, the incursion into Cambodia, and LAM SON 719 from the time when they began to take shape in Washington until they found their way through the military bureaucracy to units in the field.

The result, I believe, has been much to the benefit of this study. The controversies that evolved over time between the military and the news media in Vietnam had dimensions far beyond either the press or public affairs officers. Indeed, a careful consideration of the larger record will show that the harsh criticisms leveled by the press often duplicated the positions of responsible members of the Nixon administration itself. On more than one occasion, they even paled in comparison with the anger and recriminations circulating among members of the White House staff. In that sense, the hardening of opinion that set in on all sides as the war ground toward its conclusion, not only between the military and the news media but also between the highest officials of the central government and military officers duty-bound to obey their will, was symptomatic of a malaise far larger than anything the press could have contrived on its own. It went to the heart of the war itself, to the unyielding contradictions that had existed at its core from the very beginning.

Although primarily an analysis of the interactions that developed between military agencies and the news media as the war wound toward its end, the study has of necessity had to build upon conclusions about what the news media are and how they work. In making those judgments, I have drawn upon what I consider to be classic studies in the field. Those include Leon V. Sigal's *Reporters and Officials, The Organization and Politics of Newsmaking*; Edward Jay Epstein's *News From Nowhere, Television and the News*; Daniel Hallin's *The Uncensored War: The Media and Vietnam*; John E. Mueller's *War, Presidents and Public Opinion*; and Herbert Gans' *Deciding What's News*.

In assessing media coverage of specific events, I have made use of the various works of Peter Braestrup, Lawrence Lichty, George Bailey, and others who have had the time or the staff to review the tens of thousands of newspaper pages, journal articles, and filmed news reports that originated during the war. For the rest, I and my assistants, Ann David and Lt. Col. Douglas Shoemaker, have relied on the same sources government officials employed throughout the war years: the close paraphrases of pertinent press and television stories contained in news digests produced by the Department of Defense. In the case of particularly important television news reports, verbatim transcriptions also often appeared in the files of the various military and civilian organizations most affected. We supplemented those sources with news summaries and analyses obtained from White House, State Department, and Department of Defense files when those sources were available and applicable. We also read heavily in the many prominent newspapers and magazines of the day.

On the whole, my selection of topics to treat and news stories to cover has taken its direction from the materials contained in government files, especially the records of the Military Assistance Command, Vietnam; the Office of the Assistant Secretary of Defense for Public Affairs; the Office of the Secretary of Defense; and the White House. In other words, if a news report or commentary generated enough attention on the part of officials to earn mention in their records, it gained much more prominence in my eyes than those stories and editorials, however well- or ill-framed, that never attracted much formal official censure or approval. The presence of that report in the government's files meant, as well, that I had some chance of reconstructing the role it had played in official thinking, the stresses it had created, and the reactions it had sparked.

Straight news reports, whether erroneous or to the point, drew the attention of both officers in Vietnam and officials in Washington, especially when they conflicted with official interpretations of events. As a result, they often compose the points of departure for my case studies. Editorial remarks and the commentaries of syndicated columnists nevertheless also figure in because they sometimes sustained the issues far longer than the news itself would have allowed and provided the spur that prompted some action or reaction on the part of officials. Overall, depending on the issue and its direction, I have attempted to balance the two kinds of reporting in order to create an effect that might approximate what an intelligent reader or viewer of the day might have experienced as he or she encountered the news and the commentaries surrounding an event.

Many people contributed to this study. Although I cannot mention all here, a number at the Center of Military History deserve special thanks. The Chiefs of Military History during the production of this work—Brig. Gens. Harold Nelson, James Collins, and Douglas Kinnard and Maj. Gen. William Stofft—approved the concept of the book and encouraged its completion. The Chief Historian at the Center of Military, a colleague for over eighteen years, Jeffrey Clarke, provided many insights into the nature of the war and its protagonists and was always a resource to be relied on. His predecessors, Drs. Maurice Matloff and David Trask, were likewise unfailingly helpful. The various Chiefs of the Histories Division—Cols. John Jessup, James Ransone, James Dunn, Robert Sholly, and William Bowers and Lt. Col. Richard Perry—also provided essential assistance and support over the years. Ann David and Lt. Col. Douglas Shoemaker contributed valuable background research and deserve special thanks.

The incalculable assistance provided by the former Director of the Nixon Materials Project, James Hastings, and his associates, Frederick Graboski, Joan Howard, Ronald Plavchan, Bonnie Baldwin, and Edith Prise must also be recognized, as must that of David Humphrey at the Lyndon Baines Johnson Library. Charles Mills, Edward McGowan, and Theresa Farrell at the Information Management Section of the State Department's Bureau of Intelligence and Research provided essential documentation. William Heimdahl and Sheldon Goldberg at the Office of Air Force History answered my questions cheerfully, as did Jack Shulimson at the Office of Marine Corps History and Martin Manning at the U.S. Information Agency. The assistance of the CMH librarians, James Knight and Mary Sawyer, was also most appreciated, as was that of Nancy Meenan at the National Security Council. The Chief of the Center's Historical Resources Branch, Hannah Zeidlik, and her associate, Geraldine Harcarik, were similarly generous with their support. Maj. Gen. Winant Sidle, Brig. Gen. Charles W. McClain, Cols. Robert Burke and Robert Leonard, Jerry Friedheim, Peter Braestrup, Stephen Ambrose, Daniel Hallin, Walter Isaacson, Charles Moskos, Stanley Falk, John Schlight, Graham Cosmas, Albert Cowdry, Dale Andrade, John Carland, Alexander Cochran, Vincent Demma, Richard Hunt, Charles Kirkpatrick, George MacGarrigle, Joel Meyerson, Jack Pulwers, and Ronald Spector read all or part of the manuscript and contributed important observations. Isaacson, in particular, allowed me to read in draft those portions of his biography of Henry Kissinger that deal with the Vietnam War.

Special thanks should go to my long-suffering editor, Diane Arms, and her associates, Diane Donovan, Joycelyn Canery, Troy Wolfington, Scott Janes, and LaJuan Watson. I must also recognize the hard work of Beth MacKenzie, who designed the book; Howell Brewer, Jr., who gathered a number of the pictures; Sherry Dowdy, who compiled the maps; Diane R. Gordon, who indexed the book; and Berj Shamigian of the U.S. Army Publications & Printing Command, who carried this project through the printing process. Thanks must go as well to John Elsberg, Catherine Heerin, and Arthur Hardyman who oversaw the entire operation.

My wife, Lilla, and my children, Michael and Elizabeth, provided unfailing encouragement. Their enduring good cheer contributed much more than they will ever know or believe.

I, of course, alone am responsible for the interpretations and conclusions that this book contains and for any errors that appear. In writing it, I have tried to be honest but I must acknowledge, as did reporter Stephen Crane in 1896, that every man is born into the world with his own set of eyes and is ultimately responsible for what he sees. The reader may thus agree or disagree with what I have written. As the famous editor of the *London Times*, John Thadeus Delane, observed in 1854, at the height of the controversy between the military and the news media over the Crimean War, "There is only one rule for improvement and success, whether in peace or in war, and that is to be found in publicity and discussion."

Washington, D.C.   WILLIAM M. HAMMOND
16 August 1995

Contents

Tables

Maps

Illustrations

Public Affairs: The Military and the Media, 1968–1973

Prologue

President Lyndon Baines Johnson's concept of what the American public and Congress would tolerate in Southeast Asia affected not only his handling of the press in South Vietnam but also the way he fought the Vietnam War. Johnson believed that armed U.S. intervention was necessary to stem North Vietnam's ambitions in the region but considered a complete mobilization of America's military might unnecessary and politically unwise. Instead he resorted to a program of gradually increasing pressures against North Vietnam as the means to achieve his ends.[1]

The approach had many benefits from his point of view. Besides leaving room for his domestic agenda to proceed, it promised to reduce the chance of a major confrontation with North Vietnam's allies, the Soviet Union and the People's Republic of China. If it worked, it might persuade the North Vietnamese to abandon their attempt to absorb South Vietnam at relatively small cost to the United States. If it failed, it would still accustom the American people and Congress to war by degrees and allow the military the time they needed to prepare a proper base for action in South Vietnam. Soothing those in Congress who advocated a hard line toward the Communists without giving credence to charges by critics that he was leading the nation into war, it would also preserve options for Johnson that might disappear if a mood favoring outright confrontation gained ascendancy on Capitol Hill.

In line with those goals, Johnson and the members of his administration took pains to avoid alienating the American news media. Although reporters sometimes impeded Johnson's designs by publicizing the widening of the war, the presence of uncensored, sometimes critical American reporters in South Vietnam contradicted enemy claims that the president was somehow luring the American people into an unwanted conflict. The press also provided an excellent means for signaling American intentions to North Vietnam and its allies.

The news media, for their part, basically agreed with Johnson's desire to contain Communist expansionism, especially during the early years of the war. A lone dissenter such as Homer Bigart of the *New York Times* might from time to time sound a warning, but few reporters questioned the legitimacy of the American presence in South Vietnam or doubted

---

[1] Unless otherwise indicated, this section is based on William M. Hammond, *Public Affairs: The Military and the Media, 1968*, United States Army in Vietnam (Washington, D.C.: U.S. Army Center of Military History, Government Printing Office, 1988).

that the United States would in the end prevail. If correspondents such as David Halberstam of the *New York Times* or Neil Sheehan of the Associated Press (AP) thus criticized U.S. policy, it was only to argue for efficiency and effectiveness in the prosecution of the war.

As American involvement in South Vietnam grew, policy makers nevertheless realized that government would have to exercise some sort of control over the press, if only to preserve legitimate military security. Rather than lose the benefits a free press provided, and concerned lest heavy-handed South Vietnamese censors impair already eroding relations between the news media and the American government, the Johnson administration refused to institute full, World War II–style censorship. Instead it opted for a system of voluntary guidelines that promised to protect military secrets without diminishing the independence of the press itself.

Under the arrangement that developed, newsmen agreed to withhold certain categories of information. They were never to reveal future plans, operations, or air strikes; information on rules of engagement; or the amounts of ordnance and fuel on hand to support combat units. During an operation, unit designations, troop movements, and tactical deployments were all to remain secret. So were the methods, activities, and specific locations of intelligence units; the exact number and type of casualties suffered by friendly forces; the number of sorties and the amount of ordnance delivered outside of South Vietnam; and information on aircraft taking off for, en route to, or returning from target areas. The press was also to avoid publishing details on the number of aircraft damaged by enemy antiaircraft defenses; tactical specifics such as altitudes, courses, speeds, or angles of attack; anything that would tend to confirm planned strikes which failed to occur for any reason, including bad weather; the types of enemy weapons that had shot down friendly aircraft; and anything having to do with efforts to find and rescue downed airmen while a search remained in progress. Aerial photographs of fixed installations were likewise to remain off limits. Since it was impossible for a set of rules to cover every tactical situation, the U.S. Military Assistance Command, Vietnam (MACV), provided 24-hour interpretive guidance for reporters concerned about the risk to security of stories they wished to submit.[2]

If a reporter violated those rules, the command, after investigating, had the power to revoke his accreditation as a correspondent. The thirty-day suspension that generally resulted would rescind the newsman's access to the services provided by U.S. official agencies in South Vietnam, including his right to attend news conferences and to use military transportation to reach combat units fighting in the field. Although newsmen received a number of warnings, between 1962 and 1968 at

[2] HQ, U.S. Military Assistance Command, Vietnam (MACV), Command History (hereafter cited as MACV History), 1969, vol. 3, p. XI-6, U.S. Army Center of Military History (CMH) files.

4

most three were disaccredited for infractions against the guidelines. Eleven others were permanently removed from the roster of correspondents for violations of South Vietnamese currency regulations, black market activities, or falsification of their status as employees of news-gathering organizations.[3]

By early 1968 more than 450 accredited correspondents had agreed to the Military Assistance Command's regulations and taken up residence in South Vietnam: 179 Americans, 114 South Vietnamese, and 171 other nationalities. That number grew briefly to 648 after the Tet offensive but stabilized again at about 450 within a few months. Those reporters represented more than 130 media enterprises: *Joon-Gang Ilbo* of South Korea, *Mainichi Shimbun* of Japan, the *London Times*, the American television networks, Agence France Presse, the Associated Press, United Press International (UPI), and all of the world's major newspapers, television networks, and news magazines.

Some of the correspondents had considerable experience as combat reporters or had spent years in South Vietnam: Charles Mohr of the *New York Times*, Merton Perry of *Newsweek*, Peter Braestrup of the *Washington Post*, Peter Arnett of the Associated Press, Wendell "Bud" Merick of *U.S. News & World Report*, John Randolph of the *Los Angeles Times*, to name a few. Others were newcomers with little direct knowledge of war. Still others had limited experience in journalism. Fewer than one-third of all accredited correspondents were true working reporters. A few were the wives of correspondents who had accepted accreditation to gain access to the U.S. Post Exchange in Saigon. The rest were support personnel: cameramen, sound men, stenographers, translators, and secretaries.

Over the years, the U.S. mission in Saigon and the Military Assistance Command developed a sophisticated system for handling the press. An "information czar," the U.S. mission's Minister-Counselor for Public Affairs, Barry Zorthian, advised the MACV Commander, General William C. Westmoreland, on public affairs matters and had theoretical responsibility under the ambassador for the development of all information policy. He maintained liaison between the embassy, MACV, and the press; publicized information to refute erroneous and misleading news stories; and sought to assist the Saigon correspondents in covering the side of the war most favorable to the policies of the U.S. government. In coordination with the Military Assistance Command, he also held weekly background briefings—which meant reporters could use the information but were not to identify its source—for selected correspondents on topics of current interest. Determined to keep the press fully informed and convinced that the newsmen involved would never betray their country's fighting men,

---

[3] It is difficult to determine for the early years of the war who was disaccredited and when because the building in Saigon that housed accreditation records burned during 1966. The names of two are on file. According to contemporary news reports, at least one more was also disciplined. The records for the rest of the war are in better condition.

he would sometimes discuss what the military considered sensitive intelligence information.

The MACV Office of Information, for its part, had day-to-day charge of public affairs relating to military operations in South Vietnam. Besides advising the South Vietnamese armed forces on ways to improve their public image in the United States, it served as the sole point of release for news originating in the war zone, handled all aspects of everyday relations with Saigon correspondents, answered queries, issued press releases, and coordinated morning and evening news briefings.[4] The office also supplied reporters with government transportation to locations throughout South Vietnam and billeted them for a nominal fee at press camps in strategically located operational areas. Those facilities were located at Da Nang, Nha Trang, Qui Nhon, and Pleiku. A very small one also existed at My Tho.

Although the system provided the news media with massive amounts of information without endangering U.S. forces, it never totally satisfied either the press or the government. Dependent on officials for information, the Saigon correspondents tended to distrust their benefactors. Some officials, on the other hand, continued to believe that the success of the American commitment to South Vietnam depended on the wholehearted support of the American news media and questioned news stories that appeared to give the enemy even the slightest advantage. When reports in the press pointed to possible deficiencies in the M16 rifle, the ineptitude of South Vietnamese military units, or the inaccuracy of military measures of progress, many interpreted them as evidence that the press was only interested in sensations.

The Saigon correspondents responded to criticism of that sort by avowing that they were merely portraying the situation as it existed. Yet if the M16 was indeed deficient, progress less than officials asserted, and the South Vietnamese armed forces often poor in performance, that did not exonerate the press from the charge that it had at times distorted the facts during the early years of the war. When AP correspondent Peter Arnett compared the use of tear gas by South Vietnamese forces to the employment of mustard gas in World War I, for example, or when *New York Times* reporter Harrison Salisbury relayed enemy propaganda on the cruelty of American bombing in North Vietnam, they may or may not have given assistance to the enemy, but they assuredly reinforced the arguments of those members of the official community who sought to restrict press reporting of the war.

Senior officials themselves were nevertheless also remiss. Led by President Johnson, who remained concerned that negative reporting might turn the American public and Congress against the war, they attempted to compensate by orchestrating the news. Playing some events

---

[4] Information liaison officers, for example, were stationed at the headquarters of each South Vietnamese corps tactical zone beginning 1964 and at division level after 1968.

in low key while emphasizing others, they mounted public relations campaigns to highlight the effectiveness of programs to win the hearts and minds of the South Vietnamese people, the success of South Vietnamese military operations, and the truth of their continual assertions that the American effort was indeed making progress. In the process, they fell into a vicious circle. For when the promises failed to materialize, the credibility of official statements declined, and the press redoubled its criticism. That prompted more official optimism, leading to more failed promises and to further recriminations in the press.

The American strategy in South Vietnam contributed to the Johnson administration's difficulties. In order to maintain congressional and public support for the war and to keep from provoking the Soviet Union and China, the president had adopted limited goals. Although he would bomb North Vietnam, there would be no extension of ground combat into that country and no attempt to neutralize the enemy's sanctuaries in Laos and Cambodia. On those terms, the initiative rested largely with the enemy. Possessing secure bases and supply lines outside of South Vietnam, he could choose when and where to fight and by so doing control the casualties he suffered. If American forces inflicted a serious defeat, he could withdraw into his sanctuaries to recover. In the meantime, his well-organized sympathizers among the South Vietnamese people could continue to subvert the American and South Vietnamese cause, preparing for the day when the United States would grow tired and depart. General Westmoreland attempted to compensate by adopting an attrition strategy, but more young men came of age in North Vietnam every year than American forces could kill on the battlefield. With China and the Soviet Union providing ample logistical support, the enemy had only to endure to bring the political costs of the war to unacceptable levels for the United States.

As the war continued, doubts about military claims began to arise in the press but also within the Johnson administration itself. By the spring of 1967 skeptics in the Defense Department's office of systems analysis had begun to contend that the losses the Military Assistance Command claimed to have inflicted upon the enemy were insufficient to break his will. The State Department's Bureau of Intelligence and Research avowed that many of the statistics the command cited were incomplete or open to serious question. Secretary of Defense Robert S. McNamara observed during testimony before the Preparedness Subcommittee of the Senate Armed Services Committee that the enemy's supply requirements were so small North Vietnam could carry on the war indefinitely while withstanding almost any attack from the air. Leaked to the press, McNamara's comments caused headlines around the world.

The Johnson administration launched a powerful public relations campaign in the fall of 1967 to counter those criticisms and growing contentions in the press that the war had fallen into stalemate. U.S. Ambassador to South Vietnam Ellsworth Bunker, General Westmoreland, and other senior American officials in Saigon and Washington held press conferences to compare the situation in 1967 to the one that had prevailed in earlier years. Zorthian's directorate, the Joint U.S. Public Affairs Office (JUSPAO) in Saigon, accelerated the release to the press of captured enemy documents in order to underscore enemy failures and to demonstrate that the war was going poorly for enemy forces. At the height of the campaign, Bunker and Westmoreland traveled to Washington, where Westmoreland addressed the National Press Club and testified before the House Armed Services Committee. "It is significant," he told the National Press Club, "that the enemy has not won a major battle in more than a year. In general, he can fight his large forces only at the edges of his sanctuaries. . . . His guerrilla force is declining at a steady rate. Morale problems are developing within his ranks."[5] Bunker repeated the theme, noting that progress would surely accelerate in Vietnam in the coming year. Meanwhile, President Johnson declared in an interview on CBS that although the Communists had yet to win a single battle they continued to search for some way to break the will of the American people.[6]

The enemy retorted on 30 and 31 January, during Vietnam's most festive holiday, Tet. Sending a suicide team to attack the newly constructed U.S. embassy in downtown Saigon, he also struck South Vietnam's 5 largest cities, 36 of the country's provincial capitals, and 64 of its district capitals.

Coming in the wake of the Johnson administration's assertions of optimism, the attacks stunned both the Saigon correspondents and their editors in the United States. Long doubtful of the administration's claims of major progress, they viewed the offensive as evidence that Johnson had been less than honest with the American public. In the weeks that followed, despite continued attempts by Westmoreland and other officials to clarify what had happened, many put the worst possible construction on events. Picking up an assertion by President Johnson that the enemy intended to inflict a psychological defeat upon the United States, they made the point themselves. When General Westmoreland, attempting to put the attacks into context, observed, erroneously but with some reason, that the enemy's main effort was yet to come and would probably occur in the north of the country, the newsmen turned north to focus on the American base at Khe Sanh, which had been under siege by the enemy for nearly a month. In the weeks that followed, their stories built the siege into a symbol of American inability to control the battlefield, a possible repeat of the Battle of Dien Bien Phu, in which the Viet Minh in 1954 had destroyed not only a major French colonial military force but also the will of the French people and government to continue the First Indochina War.[7] All the while, within Congress and the

---

[5] Address by General William C. Westmoreland to the National Press Club, 21 Nov 67, copy in CMH files.

[6] See Msg, State 86286 to Saigon, 18 Dec 67, Central files, U.S. Department of State, Foreign Affairs Information Management, Bureau of Intelligence and Research (FAIM/IR).

[7] The man who is believed to have been in charge of the attack upon Saigon during the Tet offensive, Col. Gen. (then Maj. Gen.) Tran Van Tra, asserted in an interview with CMH

Johnson administration itself, supporters of the war who had earlier begun to waver listened to the press, compared what it was saying with their own reservations, and concluded that the American effort in South Vietnam had been in vain.

The pessimism appearing in the press had more of an effect on Washington officials than it did on American public opinion, which rallied aggressively to the side of the president. Where in January 1968, 56 percent of those queried had considered themselves hawks on the war and 27 percent doves, with 17 percent voicing no opinion, by early February a full 61 percent considered themselves hawks, 23 percent doves, and 16 percent held no opinion. Asked to venture a guess on whether a bombing halt would improve the chances for peace, 71 percent opted for continuing the bombing, an increase of 8 percentage points from the previous October.[8]

The public's reaction had little apparent effect within the Johnson administration. During March McNamara's successor as Secretary of Defense, Clark Clifford, at Johnson's behest, reevaluated U.S. policy in South Vietnam. His prognosis was bleak. The war was becoming a drag upon the United States, he told the president. "We must look at our own economic stability, our other problems in the world, our other problems at home; we must consider whether or not this thing is tying us down so that we cannot do some of the other things we should be doing."[9] Although Johnson was unwilling to disengage from combat, he decided that a fresh approach was necessary.[10] Announcing on 31 March that he intended to halt the bombing of North Vietnam and that he would refrain from running for a second full term in office in order to devote himself entirely to a search for peace, he gave new momentum to the effort to achieve a negotiated settlement.

If the Tet offensive and the decisions following it marked a turn in the direction of the war, press coverage of the issues surrounding the conflict kept step. As an institution, the American news media had always taken their cues from newsmakers, those people in positions of authority, in

historian John Carland that the siege of Khe Sanh was, in fact, a feint designed to draw American forces away from Saigon and other populated areas of South Vietnam. Whether Tra should be taken seriously remains a matter of conjecture. There is a tendency among the representatives of victorious armies to rationalize the outcomes of battles as what they had intended all along, whatever their original ends. See Interv, John Carland with Col Gen Tran Van Tra, 23 Nov 90, CMH files.

[8] Burns Roper, "What Public Opinion Polls Said," in Peter Braestrup, *Big Story: How the American Press and TV Reported and Interpreted the Crisis of Tet in 1968 in Vietnam and Washington*, 2 vols. (Boulder, Colo.: Westview Press, 1977), 1:679–81. The book was reissued in a single abridged volume by Presidio Press, Novato, California, in 1994.

[9] Memorandum for the Record (MFR), 4 Mar 68, sub: Notes of the President's Meeting With His Senior Foreign Policy Advisers, National Security Council (NSC) files, file I, Mar 70, Lyndon Baines Johnson (LBJ) Library, Austin, Tex.

[10] At a 12 April meeting Johnson told Wheeler the operative phrase was "go all out" with the war. See Msg, Wheeler JCS 3965 to Westmoreland, 12 Apr 68, William C. Westmoreland Papers, CMH.

Clifford confers with Johnson.

industry but especially in government, who made things happen. For reporters, access to sources had always been a paramount indicator of solid facts and of accuracy. News was not only what happened but what someone of importance said had happened.[11]

The results of that preference were readily apparent in the pages of the press during the years prior to and just after the Tet offensive. Of 2,850 page 1 stories randomly selected from the *Washington Post* and the *New York Times* between the years 1949 and 1969 by sociologist Leon V. Sigal, 78.1 percent were based on some sort of official pronouncement, news release, or interview. Seventy-two percent of the stories with a Washington dateline, favorable or unfavorable to administration policy, originated with government officials, whether administration spokesmen, program administrators, or congressmen and senators. The same was true for 54 percent of the stories originating in Saigon. The president himself was a magnet for the attention of the press. On any given day, he or one of his close associates could almost always be found holding forth in the press or on television news programs on one subject or another.[12]

When Lyndon Johnson announced a bombing halt above 20 degrees north latitude in North Vietnam and publicly espoused the search for

[11] Leon V. Sigal, *Reporters and Officials: The Organization and Politics of Newsmaking* (Lexington, Mass.: D.C. Heath and Co., 1973), especially table 6-5, p. 124.
[12] Ibid.

peace, the war lost its principal spokesman. With the change in policy, the discipline the president had always exercised over the members of his party—already tenuous in the case of dovish senators and congressmen such as Senator J. William Fulbright of Arkansas—was fatally weakened. It became acceptable even for longtime administration supporters in Congress and elsewhere to criticize events in South Vietnam.[13]

The broadening debate found a ready market in the press, where reporters, cuing to their usual sources and following normal journalistic procedures, replayed what was happening. The result was readily apparent in the case of television news. Prior to the Tet offensive spokesmen for the war predominated over critics in television news reports by 26.3 to 4.5 percent. After Tet and the president's shift in emphasis, critics achieved a rough parity of 26.1 to the supporters' 28.4. Sources other than a newsman were usually responsible. A random sample of 779 television broadcasts between 20 August 1965 and 27 January 1973 has shown that 49 percent of all criticism of administration war policy came from public officials of one sort or another. Thirty-five percent of the rest was attributable to citizens on the street, antiwar activists, and soldiers in the field, while only 16 percent originated from commentaries and interpretations by reporters themselves.[14] Max Frankel of the *New York Times* described the effect. When protest against the war moved "from the left groups, the antiwar groups, into the pulpits, into the Senate . . .," he told an interviewer, "it naturally picked up coverage. And then naturally the tone of the coverage changed. Because we're an Establishment institution, and whenever your natural constituency changes, then naturally you will too."[15]

If the press remained oriented toward the nation's increasingly divided establishment, it nevertheless changed internally throughout the years of the war. Through normal processes of attrition, senior editors and others who had shared the administration's viewpoint on the war retired or took new positions. Their successors, reflecting the climate in a divided Congress and other establishment circles, were less sympathetic. When Russell Wiggins at the *Washington Post*, for example, left that paper's editorial page in 1968 to become the U.S. ambassador to the United Nations, publisher Katherine Graham was willing to give his antiwar successor and onetime deputy, Phillip Geyelin, some leeway. As a result, the *Post*'s editorials became less supportive of the war.[16]

New reporters, recent graduates of America's colleges and universities, contributed to the effect. As the years progressed, they tended to be

---

[13] John E. Mueller makes this point in *War, Presidents and Public Opinion* (New York: Wiley, 1973).

[14] Daniel C. Hallin, "The Media, the War in Vietnam, and Political Support: A Critique of the Thesis of an Oppositional Media," *Journal of Politics* 46 (February 1984): 2–24.

[15] Max Frankel was quoted in Todd Gitlin, *The Whole World Is Watching: Mass Media in the Making and Unmaking of the New Left* (Berkeley: University of California Press, 1980), p. 205.

[16] Chalmers Roberts, *The Washington Post, The First 100 Years* (Boston: Houghton Mifflin, 1977), p. 395.

11

more antiwar than their predecessors and more prone to practice the sort of activist journalism that attempted to convince rather than merely to inform. Over the long run, those individuals either conformed to the proestablishment orientations of the press—whose members cannot appear too radical lest they alienate readers, advertisers, and sources—or they took positions elsewhere, with limited-interest periodicals such as New York's *Village Voice*, which were more in tune with their approach to journalism. Over the short term, however, they caused considerable anxiety within the organizations that had hired them. At the *New York Times*, for example, the director of the editorial page, John Oakes, while implacably opposed to the war almost from the beginning, remained concerned about what he saw as a tendency toward advocacy journalism on the news pages of his paper.[17]

The impact of such reporters on the daily content of the *Times* and other papers is nevertheless difficult to assess. Theories of news that attribute the slant an event receives in the press to a publisher's policies, bias on the part of reporters, or the economic interests of owners, fail to take into account that so many people are involved in the production of a news story that a single point of view has great difficulty coming through. The newsman, indeed, is hardly a soloist. What he does is the product of a range of organizational processes, routines, perspectives, and points of view. Thus, if a few radical reporters were employed at the *Times*, the paper's publisher, Iphigene Sulzberger, a liberal of the Adlai Stevenson stamp, was hardly a threat to the status quo. The foreign editor, James Greenfield, had been an assistant secretary of state for public affairs during the 1960s. The executive editor, Clifton Daniel, was former President Harry S. Truman's son-in-law. The managing editor, Abraham Rosenthal, according to the biographer of the *Times*, Harrison Salisbury, opposed the war but also deplored the lawlessness that occurred on the streets of Chicago during the 1968 Democratic Convention.[18]

Although personnel changes were less apparent at CBS News and the other television networks, something similar happened. As debate on the war became respectable, the definition of what was acceptable on television news programs also broadened. As a result, wherein the past news producers would have found criticism of the American private soldier repugnant, after Tet they could entertain the idea, if only because respectable members of Congress were doing so. Network anchormen nevertheless took pains to alienate as few viewers as possible. They rarely imputed motives, made predictions, or expressed outright doubts about official

[17] Herbert J. Gans, *Deciding What's News* (New York: Vintage Books, 1979), p. 145. Oaks voiced his concerns in an interview with management consultant Chris Argyris. See Chris Argyris, *Behind the Front Page* (San Francisco: Jossy-Bass Publishers, 1974), p. 157. Argyris refused to identify the speaker. Harrison E. Salisbury does so in *Without Fear or Favor* (New York: Times Books, 1980), p. 93.

[18] Gans, *Deciding What's News*, p. 145. Salisbury characterizes the high command at the *Times* in *Without Fear or Favor*, p. 89.

12

statements. If they had opinions, they voiced them on the air with one or two value-laden words rather than in extended arguments. The approach of CBS anchorman Walter Cronkite is instructive. He referred to the enemy as "the Communists" before the 1968 trip to Vietnam that turned him against the war. Afterwards he did so rarely. Overall, according to television news analyst George A. Bailey, interpretive comments that originated with television anchormen tended to be "simple, safe, de facto, and timid."[19]

If the news media changed in step with the viewpoints of the nation's establishment, the manner in which the U.S. government handled the press was also evolving. Convinced that much of what the Saigon correspondents had done and said during and after Tet had been a reaction to exaggerated official optimism during the months prior to the attacks, Secretary of Defense Clifford instructed Chairman of the Joint Chiefs of Staff General Earle G. Wheeler and other members of the Department of Defense (DOD) to adopt a far more conservative approach than they had practiced in the past. Official spokesmen were to refrain from forecasting allied or enemy plans and predicting victory. They were also to avoid any assertion that difficult fighting was in the offing or that the enemy had residual capabilities yet to be committed. In that way, Clifford said, if reverses occurred, there would be no shock, and in the case of victories the credit would be that much the greater. If official spokesmen continued their policy of optimism and the enemy launched a second wave of attacks, he added, the backlash within American public opinion would be so great that the Johnson administration's credibility problems would become virtually unbridgeable. Wheeler transmitted Clifford's instructions to Saigon, where Westmoreland put them into effect.[20]

A change in the way the U.S. embassy viewed the role of the minister-counselor for public affairs paralleled the change of philosophy inaugurated by Clifford. In the past, Minister-Counselor Barry Zorthian had served both as principal public affairs officer for the U.S. mission in Saigon and as the head of the Joint U.S. Public Affairs Office, which coordinated the mission's psychological warfare efforts against the enemy. His role had been controversial. Many in both the government and the press had questioned whether the head of a propaganda organization should also direct official relations with the American news media. Zorthian had been able to overcome those reservations by proving to the press that he could be both fair and candid, but in the process he had alienated some in official circles. The American military in Saigon, in particular, believed

---

[19] George A. Bailey, *The Vietnam War According to Chet, David, Walter, Harry, Peter, Bob, Howard, and Frank: A Content Analysis of Journalistic Performance by the Network Television Evening News Anchormen* (Ann Arbor, Mich.: University Microfilms, 1973), pp. 369–75. For a general treatment of the many influences bearing on television reporters in particular, see Edward Jay Epstein, *News From Nowhere* (New York: Random House, 1973). For the print media, see Gans, *Deciding What's News.*

[20] Msg, Wheeler JCS 2721 to Westmoreland, 8 Mar 68, Westmoreland Papers, CMH.

that he had given far too much sensitive intelligence information to the press at his background briefings, "the family jewels," as the Chief of the MACV Office of Information during most of 1967 and 1968, Brig. Gen. Winant Sidle, put it. Zorthian objected that none of the reporters who participated had ever betrayed his confidence. An uninformed newsman was far more dangerous, he asserted, than one who had an authoritative view of events. If the U.S. mission cut reliable members of the press off from official sources and intelligence briefings, it would, in effect, throw them onto their own devices and remove whatever restraining influence official agencies possessed. The erroneous exposes that would surely result, even if later refuted, could only harm the American public's understanding of the war.[21]

With the support of both Ambassador Bunker and General Westmoreland, Zorthian prevailed over the short term. When his tour of duty ended after the Tet offensive, however, rather than appoint a new head of the Joint U.S. Public Affairs Office with full authority, Bunker split the job in two. A career U.S. Information Agency official who had most recently served as Chief of Public Affairs for the U.S. embassy in Tokyo, Edward J. Nickel, took direction of JUSPAO's psychological warfare activities while an expert in politico-military affairs and former Deputy Chief of Mission at the U.S. embassy in Seoul, Korea, George S. Newman, took control of relations with the news media. Newman had little if any experience in public affairs. "A sophisticated substantive officer of senior rank not a public relations or press affairs specialist," as Bunker put it, he could be expected to represent the official point of view and to side with the press far less than Zorthian had.[22] Shortly after taking office, according to Sidle, Newman declined to host the sort of regular background briefings for the press that Zorthian had found so useful and terminated the practice.[23] From then on, although he coordinated the U.S. embassy's public affairs, he played at best a minor role in the Military Assistance Command's handling of the news media.

The change in philosophy that accompanied Zorthian's departure and Newman's arrival was far more consequential than it might have seemed at first glance. A former newsman who had served as a public affairs officer for many years, Zorthian understood the press and had always been able to balance its interests with those of government. Without releasing anything of value to the enemy, he had satisfied the news media's insistent desire to know as much as possible about the war while safeguarding information of true sensitivity. However well intentioned George Newman might have been, his appointment spelled the loss of that perspective. Civilian officials in Washington—Assistant Secretary of Defense

---

[21] Interv, author with Maj Gen Winant Sidle, 5 Jun 73, CMH files.

[22] Bunker mentioned Newman's qualifications approvingly in 1970, while discussing candidates to take his place. See Ltr, Bunker to Secretary of State, n.d. [Jun 70], Ellsworth Bunker Papers, FAIM/IR.

[23] Ltr, Sidle to the author, 5 Sep 91, CMH files.

for Public Affairs Phil Goulding and his successors—would play a major role in the formation of official public affairs policy in the years to come. General Sidle himself shared Zorthian's point of view and would continue many of his policies. Westmoreland's successor as Commander of the U.S. Military Assistance Command, Vietnam, General Creighton W. Abrams, likewise insisted that his officers deal equitably with the press. Yet over the years to follow, lacking the day-to-day influence a senior civilian of stature could bring to bear on the handling of the press in the field, many of Zorthian's and Sidle's practices would fall into disuse. A bureaucratic mentality less than interested in the requirements of the news media would gradually come to predominate at the U.S. mission in Saigon.

1

"War in a Goldfish Bowl"

If the Tet offensive changed the Johnson administration's approach to the war, the acceptance of negotiations by North Vietnam on 3 April complicated matters for General Westmoreland and his command. Aware that the talks would be long and difficult and that the enemy would try every device to strengthen his position and to appeal to world public opinion, the general was obliged to fight as the peace talks proceeded. His dilemma was obvious. He had to maintain the morale and offensive momentum of U.S. and South Vietnamese forces while doing, as he put it, "as little as possible to give aid and comfort to critics by rocking or appearing to rock the negotiations boat."[1]

Fighting While Negotiating

An example of the difficulties he faced surfaced during March and April 1968. At that time the United States and South Vietnam sought to improve the defense of Saigon by consolidating a number of small, ongoing operations around the city into a single, coordinated effort code-named TOAN THANG (Vietnamese for "Final Victory"). Meanwhile, in the I Corps Tactical Zone, the U.S. 1st Cavalry Division (Airmobile) prepared Operation PEGASUS to open an overland route to the besieged base at Khe Sanh.[2] Mindful that U.S. peacemaking efforts should have center stage, President Johnson instructed Westmoreland to play both operations in low key for the press. (*Map 1*)

Johnson's wishes notwithstanding, there was little Westmoreland could do. Any attempt to open the road into Khe Sanh was important

---

[1] Msg, Westmoreland MAC 4899 to Wheeler, 12 Apr 68, Westmoreland Papers, CMH. Also see Msg, State 141535 to Bangkok, 4 Apr 68, Pol 27 Viet S file, FAIM/IR.
[2] Msg, State 141535 to Bangkok, 4 Apr 68.

INDOCHINA
1969

0   150
Miles

MAP 1

news to reporters who had followed the siege of the base with rapt attention. On the very day that the president's instructions arrived in Saigon, indeed, before Westmoreland could do anything, word arrived at the Military Assistance Command that the Saigon correspondents knew what was going on and that a number were traveling to Da Nang to cover developments. As for TOAN THANG, it had become one of the largest operations of the war to that date. Although the Military Assistance Command announced it to the press without issuing a formal communique and General Sidle attempted to pass it off, quite accurately, as the consolidation of a number of smaller efforts, reporters believed their own eyes and refused to accept the official line. Emphasizing that two major military initiatives were under way, the news stories that followed prompted an outcry both in Congress and the press. Comparing the president's 31 March call for negotiations with what seemed an escalation, critics of the war began to question Johnson's sincerity in calling for peace.[3]

Shortly thereafter, General Wheeler cabled Westmoreland to warn him that careful handling of the news media was from that moment on imperative. The Johnson administration was intent upon prosecuting the war, he said, but those who opposed it would undoubtedly make an issue of the continuing combat. If they succeeded and resistance to the war rose, restrictions would follow "which none of us want and which could be adverse to our negotiating posture." The problem, Wheeler concluded, was "just one more example of conducting a war in a goldfish bowl."[4]

Wheeler underscored his point the next day in a second message to Westmoreland. Learning that the South Vietnamese Air Force had requested permission to participate in air interdiction operations in North Vietnam below 20 degrees north latitude, he warned that the North Vietnamese might seize upon any provocation that resulted as an excuse to back away from the peace talks. They had already begun to stall by suggesting sites for the negotiations that were obviously unsuitable to the United States. One more propaganda advantage in their hands "could well bring the whole effort to naught. I need not emphasize to you that a breakdown in talks attributable to us would be a disaster here in the States."[5]

Although Wheeler might have recommended restrictions on the press, political considerations limited that possibility. The subject came up a few days later, when President Johnson complained to Secretary Clifford that news coverage of the bombing in North Vietnam's lower portions had given opponents of the war a club by citing far too many details of what had happened. Intent on maneuvering Johnson away from the war,

[3] Msg, Westmoreland MAC 4362 to Lt Gen Robert Cushman, Commanding General (CG), III Marine Amphibious Force (MAF), 31 Mar 68; Msg, Cushman to General William Rosson, CG, Provisional Corps, Vietnam (PCV) (later became XXIV Corps), 31 Mar 68; and Msg, Wheeler JCS 3965 to Westmoreland, 12 Apr 68. All in Westmoreland Papers, CMH.

[4] Msg, Wheeler JCS 3965 to Westmoreland, 12 Apr 68.

[5] Quote from Msg, Wheeler JCS 4013 to Westmoreland, 13 Apr 68. Msg, Westmoreland MAC 4893 to Admiral U. S. G. Sharp, Commander in Chief, Pacific (CINCPAC), 12 Apr 68. Both in Westmoreland Papers, CMH.

Clifford was sympathetic but refused to issue restrictions. Any attempt by MACV to curb the release of information about the war would harm U.S. interests, he told the president. The details about targets and missions appearing in the press, he continued, served to contradict wild charges emanating from Hanoi that the United States had been less than faithful to the bombing halt by proving that U.S. attacks were confined to the area below the 20th Parallel. At the same time, the release of details by the press demonstrated that the United States was pursuing the war with vigor, whatever the restrictions on bombing. That would tend to refute claims that the halt risked the lives of American fighting men. A change in the policy governing what the press could say, Clifford concluded, would thus withdraw an important source of comfort from the American people while affording the enemy a major propaganda advantage.[6]

Convinced that official efforts short of outright censorship would have little impact on press reporting, Westmoreland concentrated on ensuring that the Saigon correspondents perceived the continuing combat in the best possible light. Advised by John Daly of the Voice of America that the phrase *search and destroy* had come to connote indiscriminate violence against hapless civilians and villages, he struck the term from his command's lexicon of approved phrases. Large-unit operations were to be described in official communiques as *spoiling attacks* or *reconnaissances in force*, he told General Sidle. Under all circumstances, officials describing operations in the field were to use terms that implied U.S. forces were seeking out and attacking an aggressive enemy before he could attack them.[7]

In the same way, Westmoreland underscored a number of public affairs initiatives that Sidle, with the advice and support of Goulding, had already established within the Military Assistance Command. Senior officers, he emphasized, were to continue to brief so-called responsible newsmen on a background basis. That would open up communications with reporters who could be trusted and provide an opportunity to learn of issues that were bothering newsmen so that information officers could provide credible explanations. The command's historian was likewise to assist "reliable" correspondents when public affairs officers decided additional research on the part of a reporter would help to produce a favorable story.[8]

In the process of promoting good relations with those reporters he considered trustworthy, Westmoreland also attempted to harden his command against the sort of public relations damage that had occurred in the past. Once more following Goulding's and Sidle's lead, he encouraged senior officers to reply "no comment" when the press inquired into sensi-

[6] Msg, Wheeler to Clark Clifford, 16 Apr 68, and Msg, ASD PA 4079 to MACV, 17 Apr 68, citing Msg, Clifford to Wheeler, 16 Apr 68, both in Westmoreland Papers, CMH.

[7] Msg, Westmoreland MAC 4899 to Wheeler, 12 Apr 68; Msg, Westmoreland MAC 4241 to Wheeler, 28 Mar 68; and Msg, Westmoreland MAC 4856 to Wheeler, 12 Apr 68. All in Westmoreland Papers, CMH. Also see Westmoreland History, Notes, bk. 31, p. 2.

[8] Msg, Westmoreland MAC 5344 to Wheeler, 23 Apr 68, Westmoreland Papers, CMH.

tive matters. Newsmen considered "beyond conversion" were meanwhile to receive only the most perfunctory information and to carry on discussions only with public affairs personnel. Believing there was little reason to divulge information the Saigon correspondents had already agreed to withhold, Westmoreland also set severe limits on the practice of releasing on a background basis items banned by the command's guidelines for the press. From then on, although public affairs officers continued to use not-for-release information in briefing the press, they did so only occasionally, in advance of truly major operations.[9]

News Embargo: Operation DELAWARE

The first word of MACV's changes in information policy reached the press toward the end of April, at the beginning of an operation code-named DELAWARE, which was to take place southwest of Hue in the A Shau Valley. A major enemy storage area, vehicle repair depot, and supply route untouched by either American or South Vietnamese forces for years, the valley seemed particularly dangerous to General Westmoreland. Since he suspected that heavy press coverage of PEGASUS had given the enemy considerable information about U.S. dispositions and movements in that case, he decided to embargo news of the new operation for as long as possible. Besides maintaining a margin of security for his troops, the embargo would tend to cover the insertion of a reconnaissance force of up to battalion size into Laos at a point above where the valley entered South Vietnam. Although American aircraft had long operated in Laos, large American units had never crossed the border on purpose and in force. If MACV should give the press an opening to publicize that portion of the operation, the resulting news stories would embarrass the officially neutral government of Laotian Prime Minister Prince Souvanna Phouma, which had been cooperating quietly with the United States. Indeed, if questions from the press arose, the commander of U.S. forces in the region, General William B. Rosson, was prepared to take refuge behind a longstanding policy of avoiding all comment about Laos by responding vaguely that all units involved in DELAWARE were operating in the A Shau Valley.[10]

Westmoreland informed the Saigon correspondents on 26 April that he was imposing an extended embargo on DELAWARE. Although the announcement angered reporters who had spent five tedious days in the field preparing for what they considered a major story, all agreed to go along after receiving assurances that the Defense Department would keep home offices from breaking the news. The situation was nevertheless out

[9] Ibid.; Ltr, Sidle to the author, 5 Nov 90, CMH files.
[10] Msg, Westmoreland MAC 5536 to Phil G. Goulding, Assistant Secretary of Defense for Public Affairs (ASD PA), 26 Apr 68, and Msg, Rosson PHB 561 to Westmoreland, 26 Apr 68, both in Westmoreland Papers, CMH.

of control almost from the start. Filing from Hong Kong, syndicated columnist Joseph Alsop was already revealing that a dangerous operation had just begun in South Vietnam's A Shau Valley. Shortly thereafter, disregarding Westmoreland's restrictions, South Vietnamese information officers announced that their units were involved. In the end, the Saigon correspondents became so incensed by what they considered MACV's lack of faith that Westmoreland, to avoid further controversy, had little choice but to end the embargo. It had lasted only eight days.[11]

The reporters immediately asked whether the general would discredit Alsop, one of the Military Assistance Command's strongest journalistic supporters. When Sidle responded that the reporter had already left for the United States, putting himself beyond the reach of retribution, a few accused the command of favoritism but most dropped the matter. In the same way, many resented the embargo but all had to comply or lose access to their sources. "In the final analysis," Westmoreland later wrote in his diary, "the new policy worked out very well."[12]

Although some reporters suspected that the embargo on DELAWARE had been motivated more by a desire to soft pedal the war than for reasons of military security, secrecy was in fact a major preoccupation for Westmoreland at the time. The Military Assistance Command had just received the results of the first comprehensive survey of U.S. security arrangements in South Vietnam. That investigation had confirmed what many had suspected for some time, that the enemy had almost certainly possessed prior knowledge of virtually every major U.S. air and ground operation to that date.

A grave disregard for security procedures on the part of American forces was often the reason. In the case of B–52 strikes, an unclassified notice required by international agreement was always broadcast from the control tower at Saigon's Tan Son Nhut Airport several hours prior to the arrival of the bombers over their targets. Warning friendly aircraft and possibly the enemy to steer clear of a specified region, that announcement went so far as to broadcast the times the bombers would arrive and depart. The signals were almost as blatant for ground operations. Weeks in advance, the American units involved began ordering supplies by submitting their requests through South Vietnamese clerks employed by the U.S. government, some of whom were almost certainly enemy agents. Those requisitions revealed the code names of operations, unit designations, and delivery points. Meanwhile, U.S. Army engineers coordinated their plans with local South Vietnamese officials whose loyalties were never totally

---

[11] Westmoreland History, bk. 31, p. 11; Msg, Westmoreland MACV 5648 to Cushman et al., 29 Apr 68, in Westmoreland History, bk. 31, tab 76; Zalın B. Grant, "Alsop Lets His Friends Down," *New Republic*, 18 May 68.

[12] Westmoreland History, bk. 31, p. 11. Also see Grant, "Alsop Lets His Friends Down"; George Syvertsen, "8:00 AM World News Roundup," CBS Radio, 29 Apr 68, in *Radio-TV Reports, Inc., Dialog: Detailed Broadcast Log*, DDI B–52 file, hereafter cited as *Radio-TV-Defense Dialog*.

verifiable; engineer units deployed to the target area to prepare communications and landing zones; and all too obvious air reconnaissance missions commenced. Shortly before the start of an operation, convoys converged on the target area, often radioing their positions and intentions in the clear, without resorting to code. At that time, in the case of major deployments, the MACV Office of Information also briefed bureau chiefs and other selected members of the corps of correspondents stationed in Saigon.[13]

Although Westmoreland moved quickly to remedy his command's security lapses, he never seriously considered cutting the press off from information, as the security survey seemed to suggest. The enemy's intelligence analysts had no need for the news supplied to the Saigon correspondents. They were just as capable as any reporter of reconstructing the outline of an operation from unclassified sources. In the case of DELAWARE, for example, even before Alsop had written his column and before public affairs officers had briefed newsmen and imposed the embargo, the Associated Press had published the fact that some sort of operation appeared imminent in the A Shau Valley because B–52 bombers had pounded targets in the area eight separate times over the previous weekend. That the enemy could have missed the cue and might have had to rely on word from American news agencies was unthinkable.[14]

A Change in Command

The controversy over DELAWARE was one of the last Westmoreland had to endure as MACV commander. On 28 March 1968, President Johnson had announced that he intended to nominate the general to become the next chief of staff of the U.S. Army. On 30 May Westmoreland departed South Vietnam to begin preparing for the testimony he would deliver to Congress in support of his nomination. Johnson's announcement gave rise to immediate speculation in the press. At first, there was some talk that Westmoreland was being "kicked upstairs" because of his apparent miscalculation of the enemy's capabilities prior to the Tet offensive. That subject rapidly faded, however, as the question of who his successor would be came to the fore.

Most newsmen agreed that the MACV Deputy Commander, General Creighton W. Abrams, was the logical choice and began to debate whether the general would continue Westmoreland's approach to the war or change it. Many believed that Abrams considered the effort to win the hearts and minds of the South Vietnamese people, the so-called pacification program, the key to victory. If that was so, *U.S. News & World Report* observed, his selection might signal a change in tactics as

[13] MFR, Deputy Assistant Adjutant General (DAAG), 3 Jul 68, sub: Operations Security Briefing, CMH files.
[14] [AP], "Foe Believed Building for Big New Push," *Baltimore Sun*, 8 Apr 68.

General Abrams

well as in command. Pacification required patience, time, and understanding, the magazine noted, a marked contrast to the search and destroy techniques favored by Westmoreland. Others disagreed. *Newsweek*, for one, observed that its sources within the Johnson administration had spoken at length with Abrams in the past and had come away convinced that the general would make few changes. The magazine quoted an unidentified military analyst to the effect that, "All this talk of dropping search-and-destroy operations in favor of clear-and-hold is just a lot of bull." Abrams, for his part, refused to indulge the press. Well known for his directness, a reputation he had won as an armored commander at the Battle of the Bulge during World War II, he demonstrated his talent when interviewers asked whether his appointment was as certain as it seemed. "The White House speaks for itself," he responded laconically. As for a change in strategy he would only say, "I look for more fighting."[15]

On 10 April President Johnson announced that Abrams would indeed become Westmoreland's successor as U.S. commander in South Vietnam. At that time, he also revealed that Lt. Gen. Andrew J. Goodpaster would take his place as Deputy Commander of the Military Assistance Command, Vietnam, and that Admiral John L. McCain, Jr., would succeed Admiral U. S. G. Sharp as Commander in Chief, Pacific. All three appointments were to take effect on 2 July, but since Westmoreland departed on 30 May, Abrams, for all practical purposes, assumed full command of U.S. operations one month early.

The Enemy Attacks: May 1968

During that interlude, problems continued with the press. They centered on one of the highest ranking enemy officers ever to defect to

---

[15] "Tough General With a Rough Job," *U.S. News & World Report*, 8 Apr 68, p. 21; "Man of Action," *Newsweek*, 8 Apr 68, p. 48. Abrams quote from Charles Mohr, "Westmoreland Departure Could Spur War Changes," *New York Times*, 24 Mar 68.

the South Vietnamese, Col. Tran Van Dac. Confirming a suspicion on the part of American commanders that the Communists were planning a second wave of major attacks for sometime near the first week in May, Dac presented the United States with intelligence of such high quality that it opened up an excellent opportunity to inflict a major defeat on enemy forces. For that reason, before leaving South Vietnam, Westmoreland instructed his officers to keep all word of Dac's desertion under close hold. "In particular," he said, "any publication of Dac's defection at this time by the local, U.S., or world press would be unfortunate."[16]

Westmoreland's instructions notwithstanding, someone leaked word of Dac almost immediately to George McArthur of the Associated Press. Putting the news on the wire, the reporter took pains to describe Dac accurately as a North Vietnamese colonel and political commissar who bore the Communist Party name Tam Ha and was attached to the *9th Viet Cong Division*. McArthur added that the colonel had surrendered with the plans for a wave of attacks against Saigon and named the enemy units involved, telling the directions from which each would strike. An extremely serious breach of security, the story prompted a major, if futile investigation by the Military Assistance Command to determine how McArthur had come by his information. Since no infraction of the MACV guidelines for the press had occurred, there was little anyone could do to punish the reporter himself. He went unscathed.[17]

In the end, despite Dac's revelations and McArthur's article, the enemy proceeded with the attack, perhaps because his main objective had less to do with winning a military victory than with harming the morale of the South Vietnamese people and demonstrating his continued ability to strike at will. In all, some 12,000 enemy troops hit Saigon in two attacks, the first commencing on the night of 4 May and the second on the twenty-fifth. Most failed to penetrate defenses set up by the U.S. and South Vietnamese units securing the approaches to the city. Enough, however, got through in each attack to cause fierce fighting in Cholon, where they held out for days, purposely burning buildings to create large numbers of refugees. By the end of May, indeed, over 16,000 dwellings and businesses had been destroyed and more than 125,000 civilians were homeless. Some eleven hundred Americans died in combat during the first two weeks, the highest U.S. toll of any comparable period in the war to that date, including the earlier Tet offensive.[18]

[16] Msg, Westmoreland MAC 5298 to Cushman, 21 Apr 68, Westmoreland Papers, CMH.

[17] Memo, Wheeler CM–3228–68 for Secretary of Defense, 23 Apr 68, sub: Press Report of High-Ranking NVA Rallier, Directorate of Defense Information (DDI) Tet Offensive (7) file; [AP], "Enemy Colonel Is Said To Defect," *New York Times*, 22 Apr 68.

[18] Msg, Saigon 27764 to State, 20 May 68, sub: Assessment of Enemy's May Offensive, DDI May Offensive file; Admiral U. S. G. Sharp and General William C. Westmoreland, *Report on the War in Vietnam (As of 30 June 1968)* (Washington, D.C.: Government Printing Office, 1970), p. 167; Joseph B. Treaster, "2-Week U.S. Toll Is Highest of War," *New York Times*, 24 May 68.

Press Coverage: Concern for Civilian Losses

If the enemy's effort during May paralleled in some respects the Tet offensive, it at least came as no surprise to the Saigon correspondents. Fully a week before the enemy struck, in order to avoid exaggerations of the sort that had occurred during February, General Sidle held an off-the-record briefing for twenty-five bureau chiefs and network correspondents. Insisting that the Military Assistance Command still had a chance to achieve some element of surprise despite McArthur's breach of security, Sidle asked the reporters to refrain from mentioning in their dispatches either U.S. capabilities or the preparations for repelling the attacks. He went on to outline what the command knew about the enemy's intentions, noting pointedly that while the Communists retained the ability to cause severe damage, their assault would be less massive than the one at Tet and would mainly center on Saigon.[19]

When the moment came and the battle developed much as Sidle had predicted, the Saigon correspondents for the most part responded by accepting official statements that the enemy was losing ground and suffering serious casualties. They nevertheless complained—as they had throughout the war—that if American and South Vietnamese forces were killing great numbers of the enemy, U.S. commanders were still exaggerating the body count. They also accused the MACV Office of Information of allowing official communiques to lag too far behind events. So close to what was happening that four of them were wounded and then deliberately executed by an enemy squad on a Saigon street corner, the reporters also made it a point to emphasize how violently U.S. and South Vietnamese forces had responded to the enemy's attack. "With each day of fighting more buildings are burned and destroyed," Lee Lescaze of the *Washington Post* observed. "A handful of snipers in houses around an intersection are wiped out or driven back at the expense of major damage to nearby buildings." In the same vein, reporting the fighting in Saigon's suburbs, Howard Tuckner of NBC described how the many refugees lining the banks of the Saigon River watched as American tanks "poured a rain of fire into their homes. What the tanks missed, helicopter gunships found." Tuckner continued that even though some of the troops involved stood to lose their lives in a deadly game of hide and seek, the real victims were the people lining the riverbank, who would lose, no matter which side prevailed. "When man makes war, he makes refugees," the reporter concluded. "Last week in Saigon he made a lot of both."[20]

[19] Msg, Saigon 25826 to State, Barry Zorthian, Minister-Counselor for Public Affairs, for Dixon Donnelly, Assistant Secretary of State for Public Affairs, 28 Apr 68, DDI May Offensive file.

[20] "The War: Pressures on Saigon," *New York Times*, 12 May 68; Lee Lescaze, "G.I.'s Join Fighting in Saigon," *Washington Post*, 8 Apr 68; Howard Tuckner, "5:00 P.M., The War This Week," NBC-TV, 12 May 68, *Radio-TV-Defense Dialog*.

American tanks seal off Cholon.

Although most of the fighting on the outskirts of Saigon had ended by 14 May, the small but violent battles that continued within Saigon itself remained a theme for the press, which played up the apparent contradiction between MACV's tactics and the desire of the U.S. government to win the allegiance of the South Vietnamese people. Describing conditions within the city's 8th Administrative District, *Newsweek* underscored that the shattered area had once been a showcase for successful civic action programs. In a later article, the magazine told of an incident in which American Cobra helicopters had caused serious damage to an entire city block of low-cost housing originally constructed to demonstrate the South Vietnamese government's concern for social welfare. *U.S. News & World Report* meanwhile described Saigon as a "city of the homeless" and devoted a long article to South Vietnam's 1.5 million refugees.[21]

Although the United States and South Vietnam were once more winning on the battlefield, the enemy again appeared to have gained the political edge. He was not only demonstrating anew his ability to attack Saigon but also generating, according to officials within the pacification program, considerable resentment against the United States among civilian South Vietnamese who had lost relatives and homes to air strikes and artillery. "If the enemy continues to create refugees, to destroy and damage houses and industrial plants, and to impose on friendly forces the

---

[21] "Shattered Symbol," *Newsweek*, 27 May 68, p. 31; "The Forgotten War," *Newsweek*, 10 Jun 68, p. 54; "A City of Homeless," *U.S News & World Report*, 17 Jun 68, p. 14; "Vietnam's 1.5 Million Refugees," *U.S News & World Report*, 3 Jun 68.

need to use air and artillery in a built-up area with resultant civilian casualties," officers of the U.S. embassy in Saigon thus reported in a cable to the State Department on 20 May, ". . . the question is, how long this can be endured without threatening all that has been achieved here."[22]

Public affairs officers at the U.S. embassy attempted to blame the enemy for the destruction, explaining that the Viet Cong could continue the violence in the capital indefinitely for the sake of the psychological impact it had on the South Vietnamese people and world public opinion. "These acts should be seen for what they are," they said, "a Viet Cong effort to keep alive a posture of military strength despite their inability to achieve a significant military objective."[23]

Official explanations notwithstanding, the news stories continued, peaking on 2 June, when an errant rocket launched from an American helicopter killed Saigon Chief of Police Col. Nguyen Van Luan and five other high-ranking South Vietnamese officers. Relying on incorrect preliminary reports, the MACV Office of Information at first denied that American gunships had been involved but reversed itself when the facts became available. The Saigon correspondents meanwhile played the story to the fullest extent possible. They speculated in their dispatches on the possibility that the incident would further harm already strained U.S. relations with South Vietnam. They also passed on rumors circulating in Saigon that the United States was deliberately trying to kill supporters of Vice President Nguyen Cao Ky because Ky had become increasingly anti-American in outlook. Echoes from the affair ran well into August, when the *Nation* published an article by Karl Purnell entitled "Operation Self-destruction" that quoted a comment Luan had reportedly made shortly before his death that "The Viet Cong has no air force of his own so he uses ours."[24]

Prodded by the uproar in the news media and shaken by a report from a U.S. pacification official in Saigon describing the devastation of the city's Cholon district by American forces as "far worse than I had seen in any location in Hue," Secretary of Defense Clifford instructed General Wheeler to determine if there was some way to combat enemy infiltrators without destroying so much private property and so many civilian lives.[25] Wheeler passed the request to Abrams, adding that Clifford wanted the Military Assistance Command to take urgent action on the matter because of "the very real concern here in administration circles and the bad play we are receiving in the news media."[26]

---

[22] Msg, Saigon 27764 to State, 20 May 68, sub: Assessment of Enemy's May Offensive.

[23] Msg, Saigon 28986 to State, 3 Jun 68, Pol 27 Viet S file, FAIM/IR.

[24] Msg, State 175631 to Paris, Donnelly for Jordan, 4 Jun 68, Pol 27 Viet S file, FAIM/IR. Quote from Karl H. Purnell, "Operation Self-Destruction," *Nation,* 26 Aug 68, p. 29.

[25] Memo, Charles Sweet for General Edward Lansdale, 12 May 68, sub: Visit to Districts 6 and 8, covered by Memo, Lansdale for Ambassador Bunker, 2 May 68, sub: Popular Reaction, both in Papers of Clark Clifford, box 5, Abrams, Creighton (1), LBJ Library.

[26] Msg, Wheeler JCS 66117 to Abrams, 4 Jun 68, Papers of Clark Clifford, box 5, Abrams, Creighton (1), LBJ Library.

Rubble litters the streets of Cholon during the May offensive.

Abrams responded that a combined U.S.–South Vietnamese study group had been meeting since 14 May to develop an approach to urban warfare that reduced civilian casualties and property damage. As a result of the incident that had taken Luan's life, he added, he had decided to ban U.S. tactical air strikes, armed helicopters, and artillery fire from the Saigon area unless their use in each instance had his personal approval. Although he would delegate this authority to the II Field Force Commander, Lt. Gen. Frederick C. Weyand, and the commander of the U.S. forces defending Saigon, Maj. Gen. John Hay, he would allow no further delegation. As for the pacification report Clifford had read, Abrams continued, the MACV Inspector General, Col. Robert M. Cook, had confirmed its allegation of serious damage to Cholon but had questioned whether large numbers of civilian casualties had occurred. In fact, two very dangerous engagements had taken place in the suburb, involving some 3,200 of the enemy and generating more than 2,300 friendly and enemy casualties. While Cholon had probably experienced excessive destruction "as a result of the inertia of the combat situation, the tenacity of a stubborn enemy coupled with the inability of commanders on the scene accurately to assess the degree of destruction in progress," the report failed to consider the serious fighting and seemed inaccurate on that account. Abrams concluded by asking whether the transmission of raw, unevaluated data to Washington agencies served the U.S. effort in South Vietnam. "I prefer that such reporting be carefully evaluated," he

29

said, "before it is floated as an official paper. We have nothing to hide but neither should we be constantly on the rebuttal."[27]

Abrams ended with an eloquent plea for understanding.

I feel constrained to point out that while I do not have the benefits of TV and newspapers that are available in Washington, I live here. I ride over the city in a helicopter and see parts burning. I walk in the streets and see the destruction. I walk among refugees overwhelmed with the personal disaster that has been their lot; I visit among the dog tired and grimy soldiers who have survived the fight; I talk with the wounded in hospitals and I visit the bereaved and write letters of condolence. I am fully aware of the extent to which horror, destruction, sacrifice, and pain have risen in this war this year. I have had two sons serving here, one of whom is here now and extending. If somehow a sensing has developed that I have been in too many wars to be concerned and sensitive to its pain or that I am too busy with plans or campaigns or something else to spend time on correcting the destruction of war, let me set the record straight. I recognize all this as my responsibility. I need no urging to look into it, investigate it or explain other ways. I live with it twenty-four hours a day.[28]

Abrams' response incensed Clifford. Avowing that it was important for the secretary of defense, the chairman of the Joint Chiefs of Staff, and the commander in the field to understand one another, he told General Wheeler that he could never accept Abrams' apparent contention that responsible officers within the U.S. embassy in Saigon should wait for clearance from the military before reporting matters of concern to the State Department. In the same way, he said, he failed to see how the submission of a relevant question on the conduct of the war, "a question of great concern to the Commander-in-Chief and to the Secretary of Defense," constituted placing a field commander "constantly on the rebuttal." He wondered as well at Abrams' comment that the Military Assistance Command needed no urging to look into the civilian casualty problem or to investigate alternatives to the tactics then in use. "Am I to interpret this to mean that I am not to ask him to look into an appropriate matter or to investigate a situation or to consider other ways of accomplishing the national purpose?" If that was so, Clifford concluded, alluding to the decision to give Abrams charge of the Military Assistance Command, Vietnam, "it is essential we know this now."[29]

Informed of Clifford's anger, Abrams clarified his meaning in a subsequent message to Wheeler. Admitting that he had been wrong to say that the command was constantly on the rebuttal and to suggest that military commanders ought to review reports from the embassy to the State Department, he explained that he had merely sought to emphasize the feeling he had for the effects of the war on the innocent and that he had

[27] Msg, Abrams MAC 7404 to Wheeler, 5 Jun 68, Papers of Clark Clifford, box 5, Abrams, Creighton (1), LBJ Library.
[28] Ibid.
[29] Memo, Clifford for Wheeler, 8 Jun 68, Papers of Clark Clifford, box 5, Abrams, (Gen. C.W.) (1), LBJ Library.

30

already begun to change tactics and techniques that caused excessive destruction. That being the case, he said, he had still meant to indicate that the news media in the United States seemed to paint a "significantly more gruesome picture of the war than one gets being here."[30]

Although Clifford informed President Johnson of his exchange with Abrams, nothing further came of the matter. The general remained in command and went on to make the protection of Saigon and its civilians one of his most important concerns. When his deputy, General Weyand, later in the month asked for permission to restore the ability of division commanders to call in heavy weapons, he rejected the suggestion out of hand. Paraphrasing Peter Arnett's by-then famous report of the effort to drive enemy forces from the town of Ben Tre during the Tet offensive, he added that the request basically returned authority to where it had been during the periods of greatest destruction in Saigon. "I have tried to make it clear," he said, "that our military forces must find a way to save Saigon without destroying it."[31]

Abrams' Approach to Public Affairs Policy

As soon as it became clear that Abrams would succeed Westmoreland, the Saigon correspondents began to write stories comparing the two generals. Where Westmoreland appeared to have emerged from three decades as a soldier "crisp and untouched," Jack Langguth of the *New York Times* observed, summarizing the opinion of most reporters, Abrams was "worn and scarred," a man who had "decided some time ago that he wasn't going to kid himself about anything." While Westmoreland spoke of progress in Vietnam in "forever hopeful" tones, Abrams qualified every judgment to the point of sometimes sounding disillusioned. After spending more than a year in South Vietnam working to upgrade the performance of the South Vietnamese Army, the reporter noted as an example, Abrams still refused to participate in the campaign to advertise South Vietnamese achievements, preferring to say only, "There's been modest improvement in training," or, "There's slightly better logistics service now."[32]

In basic agreement with Clifford's directive to Westmoreland to let the war in South Vietnam take its own level as far as the press was concerned, Abrams wasted little time before issuing a memorandum on the subject. "Effective now," he told his commanders on 2 June, "the overall . . . policy of this command will be to let results speak for themselves. We will not

[30] Msg, Abrams MAC 7600 to Wheeler, 9 Jun 68, Papers of Clark Clifford, box 5, Abrams, Creighton W. (1), LBJ Library.

[31] Msg, Abrams MAC 8249 to Weyand, 22 Jun 68, Creighton W. Abrams Papers, CMH.

[32] Jack Langguth, "General Abrams Listens to a Different Drum," *New York Times Magazine*, 5 May 68, p. 28.

31

deal in propaganda exercises in any way but will play all of our activities in a low key." U.S. commanders, he continued, were to refrain from revealing future plans and operations of any type because information of that sort not only assisted the enemy but also tended to backfire if the plans went awry, widening the credibility gap. Although Abrams had little objection to contacts with the press, achievements rather than hopes were to be the subject of those encounters. He also ordered his commanders to make "considerably more extensive use" of the phrase *no comment*.[33]

Abrams did everything he could to avoid the difficulties caused by the Saigon correspondents' almost insatiable appetite for news. Immediately upon taking command, he recognized that erroneous and exaggerated news stories were often the result of partial information released to placate the press before all the facts were on hand. He set to work with Sidle and the Defense Department to fine-tune MACV's system for reporting both good and bad news. In the case of bad news—the destruction of an American unit in combat or an embarrassing enemy attack—the first member of the MACV staff to receive word was to inform the MACV chief of staff and the command's Operations Center without delay. While the Operations Center made what Abrams called "a surge effort" to determine what had happened, information officers were to respond to queries from the press by stating that they would have no comment until after a full investigation. If the inquiry confirmed that something bad had occurred or that an error had been made, Abrams said, information officers were to avoid attempting to paper over the truth. As far as good news was concerned, the same process was to apply. Since preliminary reports of favorable events were often badly exaggerated or incorrect, the Operations Center was to examine all incidents of the sort before information officers reported them to the press. Only when the center was absolutely convinced that the facts were correct was an announcement to be made. Abrams recognized that the system was imperfect and that the press might well report whatever information it had despite official no comments. Yet bad news was to his mind far less damaging than the allegation that the command had lied. In the same way, he believed that good news would have a far more favorable effect if reporters discovered it for themselves or if MACV relayed it simply and without embellishment.[34]

Obliged to fight while negotiations were in progress, Abrams had little choice but to take that aspect of the war into account. Prompted by an article Keyes Beech had written for the 27 May *Chicago Daily News*, he issued guidance on the subject almost immediately. Beech had claimed that the Military Assistance Command had circulated a top secret directive to all field commanders ordering them to win the war in the next three months so that U.S. emissaries could exercise a decisive voice at the

---

[33] Msg, Abrams MAC 7236 to All Commanders, 2 Jun 68, sub: Public Affairs Guidance, Abrams Papers, CMH.

[34] Msg, Abrams MACV 7429 to All Commanders, 6 Jun 68, Abrams Papers, CMH.

Paris peace talks. As a result, the reporter had concluded, Americans could expect some of the heaviest fighting of the war after peace negotiations began. Concerned that the article might play into the hands of enemy propagandists seeking to debunk President Johnson's peace initiative, the MACV Office of Information denied that the directive in question had ever existed. Command spokesmen conceded that Beech had seen a message calling on U.S. fighting men to redouble their efforts to deny the enemy the successes he needed to gain a stronger position in the negotiations, but, they said, it had only been a pep talk—the sort commanders continually sent to their subordinates in the field.[35]

Shortly thereafter, Abrams issued a circular message on the subject to all of his commanders. Although the *Daily News* story had been mistaken on some points, he observed pungently, the Military Assistance Command was obviously "as leaky as a sieve" and appeared to be suffering from a form of "diarrhea of the mouth" that was bound to thwart the U.S. effort in South Vietnam. Since the press was hungry for news stories applicable to the Paris peace talks, he continued, reiterating Defense Department guidance first issued on 13 May, members of the U.S. command had to abstain from releasing any information that might have an impact on those negotiations.[36]

The Defense Department issued more specific instructions two weeks later, after the appearance of another article by Beech. The reporter had observed in that report that U.S. aircraft had achieved better results under President Johnson's 31 March bombing limitation than when they were hitting targets throughout North Vietnam. He had then quoted the commander of the U.S. Navy task force stationed off the enemy coast, Rear Adm. Malcolm W. Cagle, to the effect that there was little tactical value in resuming the bombing if the target restrictions that had prevailed before the halt were once more to apply. "Of course," Cagle had said, "if we were allowed to take out Haiphong, that would be a different matter. But that is a political decision." Noting that such observations, however well intentioned, might have the effect of limiting the president's negotiating options, Phil Goulding, after consulting with the State Department, banned all comment and speculation on subjects such as the resumption of attacks on North Vietnam above the 19th and 20th Parallels, the possibility of bombing Hanoi and Haiphong, the effectiveness of the bombing, the chance that the United States might unilaterally escalate or deescalate the war, and the possible withdrawal of U.S. and South Vietnamese forces from the vicinity of the Demilitarized Zone. The listing was by no means complete, Goulding said in closing. What the Johnson administration intended was for everyone concerned with the war, in Saigon and else-

---

[35] Msg, Westmoreland to All Commanders, 6 May 68, cited in Msg, Abrams MAC 7288 to All Commanders, 3 Jun 68, Abrams Papers, CMH; MACV History, 1968, vol. 2, p. 968.

[36] Msg, Abrams MAC 7288 to All Commanders, 3 Jun 68. Abrams alludes to Msg, Clifford Defense 8944 to Commanders of All Unified Commands, ASD PA for Information Officer (IO), 13 May 68, sub: Peace Negotiations, DDI Paris Peace Talks file.

where, "to avoid comment or speculation that could in any way create difficulty for our negotiators in Paris."[37]

American Forces Withdraw From Khe Sanh

Abrams' efforts and Goulding's instructions notwithstanding, it was impossible for the Military Assistance Command to give the war the sort of low profile that the president clearly sought. During mid-June 1968, for example, at about the time when Goulding issued his guidance, the North Vietnamese reinforced their units in the I Corps Tactical Zone by adding at least twelve additional battalions—the equivalent of a reinforced division—to the six divisions already present. Enemy documents captured at the time indicated that the Communists intended to do all they could to cause American casualties. That would establish conditions, as one enemy directive observed, "for the pacifist movements in the United States to expand and the doves to assail the hawks thereby forcing the United States radically to change its Vietnam policy." Recognizing that U.S. forces would have to assume a more flexible posture if they were to counter the threat, Abrams decided to free the units guarding Khe Sanh by dismantling the base.[38]

The move, as Ambassador Bunker observed, posed difficult public relations problems. The enemy was bound to publicize it as an American defeat, a contention that would certainly hold considerable weight because of the adverse press coverage the earlier battle at Khe Sanh had received. The withdrawal was nevertheless essential, Bunker said, concurring with Abrams, because without it the enemy might gain the ability to seize important targets within the I Corps zone, necessitating the sort of hard fighting that could increase American casualties.[39]

On 22 June Abrams informed General Wheeler of the steps he was taking to minimize adverse comment in Congress and the press. To enforce silence among the Saigon correspondents, he said, he intended to impose a news embargo on all word of plans, operations, and troop movements near Khe Sanh until he saw fit to release them. If reporters discovered that the base was closing, MACV would brief Saigon bureau chiefs to gain their cooperation but would otherwise respond with no comment to all questions. When the command announced the operation, official responses to questions by the press would follow scripts prepared in advance. There would be no backgrounding or follow up to questions. Meanwhile, avoid-

---

[37] Msg, Defense 2698 to All Commanders of Unified and Specified Commands, ASD PA for IO, 15 Jun 68, sub: Peace Negotiations, DDI Paris Peace Talks file.

[38] Msg, Abrams MAC 8007 to Wheeler, 17 Jun 68; Msg, Abrams MAC 8128 to Sharp, 19 Jun 68; and Msg, Abrams MAC 8250 to Wheeler, 22 Jun 68. All in Abrams Papers, CMH.

[39] Bunker's comments are in Msg, Saigon 30199 to State, 17 Jun 68, Pol 27 Viet S file, FAIM/IR.

34

Aerial view of the base at Khe Sanh

ing any criticism, expressed or implied, of General Westmoreland's decision to hold Khe Sanh in the first place, information officers were to handle other operations in the region in as normal a manner as possible in order to direct the attention of the press to them and away from Khe Sanh.[40]

Agreeing with Abrams' arrangements, the Defense Department forwarded a number of suggestions to MACV on the wording of the communique announcing the move. Approved by Goulding, Clifford, and other important officials of the department and relayed to Abrams by Wheeler, the proposed news release stated that the United States wanted to reinforce the successes it had already achieved at Khe Sanh by exploiting the enemy's weakness. It thus intended to close the base in order to make the best possible use of the great mobility and firepower of the troops stationed there. Having suffered a debacle at Khe Sanh, the draft statement concluded, the enemy was unlikely to attack the base again. A continued American presence at Khe Sanh was therefore unnecessary.[41]

Abrams responded immediately. Observing that he wanted to avoid being seen with his foot in his mouth, he told Wheeler that the announcement of the closing of Khe Sanh should adhere closely to instructions Secretary Clifford had sent to Westmoreland during the Tet offensive.[42] According to those rules, official spokesmen were never to denigrate the enemy, forecast allied or enemy plans, predict that heavy fighting was in

[40] Msg, Abrams MAC 8250 to Wheeler, 22 Jun 68.
[41] Msg, Wheeler JCS 7043 to Abrams, 26 Jun 68, Abrams Papers, CMH.
[42] Clifford's guidance is in Msg, Wheeler JCS 2721 to Westmoreland, 8 Mar 68, Westmoreland Papers, CMH.

35

the offing, or say that victory was imminent. Rather than impart the impression that the United States was reinforcing success, an assertion that was "not quite true," Abrams continued, the announcement should accept the likelihood of an enemy initiative in the I Corps Tactical Zone, possibly within the month. He preferred, he said, to stick to the real reason for the move, the need to gain a better position to meet the enemy threat.[43] The Defense Department concurred with Abrams' suggestions shortly after they reached Washington. Notifying the general of the decision, Wheeler observed almost apologetically that "Our education is advanced by your low-keyed approach."[44]

Although there seemed some hope at first that the embargo might succeed in downplaying news of Khe Sanh's closing, MACV was, as Phil Goulding told Abrams, "living on borrowed time."[45] On 26 June, indeed, while MACV and the Defense Department were still discussing the wording of their official announcement, John Carroll of the *Baltimore Sun* broke MACV's ground rules to reveal that the base was closing. Goulding attempted to contain the damage by keeping the rest of the press from reprinting Carroll's revelation, yet few of the editors and publishers he contacted were responsive. All argued that secrecy was no longer of concern because Carroll had broken the story. "We will not yield an inch," Goulding told Abrams, "but we have no actual control as long as they only reprint the *Sun* story and they are all most aware of that."[46]

Goulding discussed the situation with Secretary Clifford and General Wheeler. All agreed, Wheeler told Abrams on 27 June, that the Associated Press and the *New York Times* would shortly reprint Carroll's article, giving it credibility and spreading it to radio and television. The longer MACV delayed before making an announcement, Wheeler continued, the greater would be the criticism surrounding the original decision to hold Khe Sanh. Both the enemy and critics of the war in the United States would seize upon the issue, using it to attack the credibility of senior U.S. commanders and to erode public support for the war. All sides would interpret MACV's silence as some sort of delay to formulate excuses to cover up an American defeat. Wheeler observed that the Defense Department would leave final decision on the timing of the news release to Abrams but made it clear that President Johnson himself was concerned.[47]

Abrams made the announcement that day. Following the format he had earlier laid down to Wheeler and Goulding, he noted that enemy forces in the I Corps Tactical Zone had recently increased from six to eight divisions and that MACV intended to close the base at Khe Sanh to free the units there to "attack, intercept, reinforce, or take whatever action is most appropriate to meet the enemy threats." In a separate com-

---

[43] Msg, Abrams MAC 8515 to Wheeler, 26 Jun 68, Abrams Papers, CMH.
[44] Msg, Wheeler JCS 7068 to Abrams, 26 Jun 68, Abrams Papers, CMH.
[45] Msg, Goulding Defense 7083 to Abrams, 26 Jun 68, Abrams Papers, CMH.
[46] Ibid.
[47] Msg, Wheeler JCS 7094 to Abrams, 27 Jun 68, Abrams Papers, CMH.

36

munique issued at the same time, the MACV Chief of Information, General Sidle, announced that Carroll had been disaccredited for an indefinite period. "Mr. Carroll's story revealed a military operation in progress and future plans of the marines in the Khe Sanh area," Sidle said. ". . . The decision as to when to announce an operation and its purpose is a military one; the time of announcing an operation is determined on the basis of not giving the enemy valuable information which may endanger American or other Free World troops. In this case, other correspondents in Vietnam, equally aware of the Khe Sanh activities, honored the ground rules."[48]

The move against Carroll complicated an already difficult situation, for the news media were already analyzing the closing of the base in depth, making many of the points Goulding, Clifford, and Wheeler had predicted. David Brinkley of NBC News and other commentators thus reported North Vietnamese assertions that the withdrawal constituted de facto American recognition of "a most serious American defeat," while newspapers throughout the United States once more dissected Westmoreland's original decision to defend Khe Sanh. Agreeing with a comment by the *Minneapolis Star* that "the nonresults of Khe Sanh's defense do little to enhance the already tattered prestige of U.S. strategists in Vietnam," many journals concluded that Carroll's action was understandable and hardly a violation of military security in any real sense. In a widely reprinted article, military analyst S. L. A. Marshall said that Khe Sanh had never been of enough military value to justify the effort and materiel expended in its defense. Carroll's article had therefore jeopardized little. MACV had "skinned" the reporter "for violating the letter of a ruling." Lee Lescaze of the *Washington Post* questioned the Military Assistance Command's desire to keep the abandonment of the base a secret. "Was it essential to the security of the troops in the area, as MACV said, or was it a politically motivated policy?" Lescaze continued that during the seventy-seven day siege the American military had gone to extremes to assure the American people that the installation could be held and that it was vital to U.S. interests.

Then two months after the enemy threat to Khe Sanh had disappeared, the base was abandoned. If reporters had been allowed to write daily stories . . . there would have been much more public discussion of the evacuation in the United States. It is possible that this would have embarrassed commanders. . . . If Carroll is correct that the enemy could observe the preparations for evacuation from the hills surrounding Khe Sanh and if the news embargo was politically inspired, there was good reason for him to write his story.[49]

[48] Both communiques are quoted in Talking Paper, ASD PA, 27 Jun 68, sub: Inactivation of the Khe Sanh Combat Base, DDI Rose Debriefing file (Khe Sanh) (B).
[49] Huntley-Brinkley Report, NBC-TV, 28 Jun 68, *Radio-TV-Defense Dialog*; "The Defense of Khe Sanh," *Minneapolis Star*, 4 Jul 68; S. L. A. Marshall, "Penalizing of Carroll Dissected," reprinted from *San Antonio Express-News* in *Baltimore Sun*, 29 Jul 68; Lee Lescaze, "Secrecy Over Khe Sanh Questioned," *Washington Post*, 29 Jul 68.

The news media went on to criticize the indefinite length of Carroll's sentence, observing that only a handful of reporters had been disaccredited in the past and none for more than one month. When MACV reduced the suspension to six months, the *Baltimore Sun* responded by petitioning Congress on Carroll's behalf. Maryland's two senators, Daniel B. Brewster and Joseph D. Tydings, rallied to the reporter's defense, Brewster questioning whether MACV had handled the press properly and Tydings condemning Carroll's suspension as vindictive and unjustified. Meanwhile, the Chairman of the House Subcommittee on Government Information and Operations, Congressman John E. Moss of California, asked the Defense Department for a full report. In the end, yielding to the pressure, MACV further reduced Carroll's disaccreditation to sixty days.[50]

The Enemy Attacks Again: August 1968

If Abrams made an example of Carroll to notify reporters that he intended to hold them to their agreement to honor MACV's guidelines for the press, he was equally firm where the Department of Defense was concerned. A case in point occurred during August, when intelligence revealed that the enemy was preparing yet another wave of major attacks in South Vietnam.

The Office of the Assistant Secretary of Defense for Public Affairs drafted an elaborate contingency plan for handling the press. Reminiscent of the plan Goulding had submitted to coordinate information on the evacuation of Khe Sanh, the Defense Department's proposal detailed the steps MACV should take in dealing with the press once the offensive had begun. There were to be frequent briefings and unscheduled news releases during the initial stages of the attack to keep the press abreast of events until MACV could determine whether a full-scale offensive was under way. Having confirmed that the attack had indeed begun, Abrams was to consider briefing the press himself, much as had Westmoreland earlier in the war. He would announce that an offensive was under way, verify that MACV had anticipated it, and confirm that events had occurred as expected. Following that briefing, he might personally conduct a series of backgrounders for selected newsmen, embargoing the information he released if he felt it necessary. After the failure of the enemy effort, the Defense Department suggested that he hold yet another briefing to emphasize that the South Vietnamese armed forces had played a major role in the victory. He might then join Ambassador Bunker in a second, joint press conference designed to stress the stability South Vietnam had

[50] "Carroll Penalty Stiffest of War," *Baltimore Sun*, 28 Jul 68; [AP], "4 Reporters Drew Penalties," *Baltimore Sun*, 29 Jul 68; James MacNees, "Pentagon Asked To Review Carroll's 6-Month Penalty," *Baltimore Sun*, 30 Jul 68; "U.S. Eases Curb on War Reporter," *New York Times*, 31 Jul 68.

38

achieved. Throughout it all, the MACV Office of Information was to issue a running series of up-to-the-minute reports to the press. In that way, the command could keep reporters from writing the sort of erroneous, distorted news stories that had provided propaganda for the enemy during the Tet offensive.[51]

With Bunker concurring, Abrams responded in a 20 August message to Goulding. Barring specific guidance to the contrary, he said, he intended to conduct special backgrounders and briefings only if the news warranted. Otherwise, the normal briefings would suffice. That an offensive was in the offing was already well known to the news media, he continued, so a press conference at MACV seemed unnecessary and might do more harm than good by feeding the inclination of reporters to divine the enemy's future intentions. As for a backgrounder, Abrams said he was willing to hold one, but he noted that sessions of the sort in the past had rarely produced any change in the way the press reported. He preferred, as a result, once more to work through straightforward, day-to-day channels. In general, he concluded, MACV and the Defense and State Departments should avoid overemphasizing the implication that U.S. intelligence agencies had foreseen or predicted the enemy's offensive in detail. Too much could go wrong on the battlefield.[52]

Abrams' comments to Goulding duplicated instructions he had already issued to his command. Observing that facts dispelled rumors, he exhorted his commanders on 18 August to keep their information officers fully informed both about what was happening in the field and on developments they should withhold from the press. "Let our actions speak for themselves," he said. "Avoid speculations that may mislead the press and particularly avoid speculations about the future course of the battle or comment about our future operations. Our capabilities and preparations, together with what has happened and where, and what we have done, provide the soundest basis for comment. . . . Use facts."[53]

The enemy's offensive began even as the discussion of public affairs policy continued, on the night of 17 August, so quietly, General Sidle later observed, that MACV found it difficult to convince reporters a major attack was under way. Although Saigon was once again a target, the Communists concentrated on installations in outlying areas, apparently in hopes of drawing U.S. troops away from the city so that teams of sappers might slip past checkpoints undetected. To prolong the offensive while preserving their strength, enemy commanders also planned to conduct only two battalion-size attacks each day and to rely on mainly mortar and rocket assaults against selected targets. Despite the precautions, by 26 August the halfhearted offensive had failed. Although the enemy continued attacks by fire until well into September, he had no choice but to

[51] Msg, Goulding Defense 9553 to Abrams, 17 Aug 68, Abrams Papers, CMH.
[52] Msg, Bunker and Abrams MACV 11243 to Goulding, 20 Aug 68, Abrams Papers, CMH.
[53] Msg, Abrams to All U.S. Commanders, 18 Aug 68, sub: Public Affairs Activities During Enemy Offensive, quoted in MACV History, 1968, vol. 2, p. 970.

regroup some of his units at new locations in South Vietnam while sending others into Laos.[54]

Overall, press coverage of the August offensive was so restrained that it drew the attention of Secretary of Defense Clifford. Attributing the effect to Abrams' low-keyed approach to public affairs rather than to the fact that reporters had merely reflected a halfhearted effort by the enemy, he cabled his congratulations to MACV on 27 August. In the process, he emphasized his approval of Abrams' basic approach to the press, "particularly," he said, the prescription "that MACV should not predict, claim, or characterize but should point out clearly and promptly the current actions of the enemy and let the actions speak for themselves."[55]

The Military Assistance Command was already doing everything Clifford suggested but the secretary's message put the seal on what would be the U.S. mission in Saigon's basic public affairs policy for the rest of the war. In the months and years to come, information officers at MACV and the U.S. embassy would cut back on the news they released voluntarily to the press. If newsmen saw for themselves, so the reasoning went, they might avoid the sort of mistakes and distortions that had marred their work earlier in the war. At the very least, MACV would experience fewer self-inflicted wounds. Everyone recognized that the system was open to abuse. Abrams himself attempted to counter that possibility by insisting that his commanders could ill afford "to react to press coverage we consider unfair by refusing to meet reporters or by barring them arbitrarily from our areas." What few could foresee was that the approach would fit hand in glove with a hardening of antipress attitudes already developing within the U.S. mission, and that it would, over time, immeasurably complicate official relations with the news media.

---

[54] MACV History, 1968, vol. 1, p. 134; Interv, author with Sidle, 6 May 73, CMH files.
[55] Msg, Secretary of Defense to Commander, U.S. Military Assistance Command, Vietnam (COMUSMACV), 27 Aug 68, sub: Public Treatment of Current Military Situation, quoted in MACV History, 1968, vol. 2, p. 970.

2

The November Bombing Halt

With the fading of the August offensive, the news media's criticism of the war began to cool. Although complaints continued, reporters acknowledged that the government of South Vietnam was growing stronger while the North Vietnamese, as *U.S. News & World Report* observed, continued to spend thousands of lives for no commensurate gain. Beverly Deepe summarized their reasoning in a 13 September article for the *Christian Science Monitor*. The enemy had developed a credibility gap of his own, she said, far deeper than the one that had afflicted the Johnson administration after the Tet offensive. Three major defeats at the hands of American and South Vietnamese forces—at Tet, during May, and again in August—had destroyed the belief of the Communist rank and file in the infallibility of its leaders. Word games at the Paris peace talks, designed to gloss over the heavy involvement of North Vietnamese troops in South Vietnam, had meanwhile done little to enhance Communist standing in international circles. In the past, Deepe concluded, quoting an unidentified American official in Saigon, time had always worked to the benefit of the enemy's forces. With the South Vietnamese growing strong, it could at last begin to incline to the United States. The longer the enemy stalled, the stronger the South Vietnamese would inevitably become.[1]

Doubts Continue

Although the enemy's failed offensives seemed grounds for optimism to some in the press, Secretary of Defense Clark Clifford was more cautious. Agreeing that the enemy had wasted lives and resources, he

[1] Ben Price, "Did U.S. Bungle Victory," *U.S. News & World Report*, 2 Sep 68, p. 25; Beverly Deepe, "Chasing Credibility in Saigon," *Christian Science Monitor*, 13 Sep 68.

41

nevertheless refused throughout the summer to concede that time favored the United States. Despite all the talk about how the South Vietnamese armed forces had improved, he told President Johnson on 19 July after a visit to South Vietnam, better leadership, training, and equipment were still required. Since the Tet offensive, he said, the government of South Vietnam had authorized an increase of 84,000 men in its armed forces. On the surface the development seemed positive. Yet, at the same time, little new equipment beyond M16 rifles was on order for those recruits, and the South Vietnamese bureaucracy clearly remained unprepared to accommodate the influx. More than 4,000 new captains and 1,000 new majors would be needed to command the additional units that would shortly come into being, Clifford noted by way of example, but no one had made provision to find or train them.[2]

Clifford elaborated on his views at a private meeting in Honolulu with Secretary of State Dean Rusk; the president's National Security Adviser, Walt W. Rostow; and the president's Press Secretary, George Christian. Throughout a recent tour of military bases in South Vietnam, he said, he had received the same consistent impression. Although American and South Vietnamese forces were more than able to defend themselves and their areas of operation, "they do not know how they'll win militarily." To defeat the Communists, he continued, the allies would have to shift to the offensive; yet the enemy was building permanent installations just across the border in Cambodia and Laos and could retreat into those positions with impunity when pressed. Meanwhile, the government of South Vietnam had little incentive to bring the war to an end by participating in a negotiated settlement. American troops shouldered the brunt of combat, affording the country relatively complete protection, and American money continued to pour in. A further impediment to progress, Clifford said, quoting a candid conversation with South Vietnamese Prime Minister Tran Van Huong, was the political corruption that continued to eat at the country's institutions like a cancer.[3]

The American public shared Clifford's reservations. Polled by the Gallup organization during August, only a small minority of the people interviewed (13 percent) believed that the peace talks in Paris were making any headway, and more Americans than at any time in the past (53 percent) responded affirmatively when asked if they considered the war a mistake. By a margin of more than two to one, those interviewed also asserted that the Republican presidential nominee, Richard M. Nixon, would do a better job of handling the war than either of the con-

[2] Memo, Clark Clifford for President Johnson, 19 Jul 68, sub: Trip to South Vietnam, 13–18 July 1968, Papers of Clark Clifford, box 2, Memos on Vietnam, Feb–Aug 68, LBJ Library. The United States had ordered the M16s during May 1968.

[3] Handwritten Note, George Christian, 19 Jul 68, sub: Private Conversation, Sharp's Office, Between Rusk, Clifford, Rostow, Christian, Office files of George Christian, box 12, Classified file, 1 of 2, LBJ Library.

tenders for the Democratic nomination, Vice President Hubert H. Humphrey and Senator Eugene J. McCarthy of Minnesota. Nixon's lead, the *New York Times* observed, resulted in part from the Republican Party's campaign promise to de-Americanize the war and in part from public perceptions that Democratic presidents seemed historically to have embroiled the nation in wars while Republican administrations had kept the peace. Although disillusioned, the paper added, the American people clearly disliked any sort of unilateral withdrawal. They wanted, instead, to settle the war in a manner that would preserve the nation's honor.[4]

The president and his advisers were well aware of the public mood. During the months between Johnson's 31 March announcement that he would not run for a second term and the start of the Democratic Convention on 26 August, they did what they could to dampen speculation accompanying almost every lull in the fighting that the enemy was signaling his desire to reach some sort of accord with the United States. On 22 August, for example, Secretary Rusk requested that MACV and the U.S. mission in Saigon do everything possible to stimulate press reporting of the rocket attacks on the city that had accompanied the August offensive. "It is very important," he said, "that people here understand . . . we are not dealing with soft-hearted philanthropists in our talks in Paris. . . . [That will] balance the good deal of reporting back here on the other side."[5]

President Johnson had nevertheless to take account of the divisions growing within his own political party. As the time for the Democratic Convention approached, Humphrey defended the administration's position while McCarthy voiced the concerns of those who opposed the war. In hopes of placating enough antiwar delegates to win the nomination for Humphrey, the president and his advisers attempted to maintain at least the appearance of forward motion in the peace talks. As Clark Clifford observed in his notes of a high-level meeting on 25 May, that seemed the "only way for H.H.H. to make it."[6]

The peace talks remained in session, the convention met in Chicago as planned, and Humphrey won his party's nomination, but only after a week of angry debate on the floor of the convention and violent antiwar demonstrations outside. When security officers within the convention hall and the police on the streets attempted to restore order at the direction of Chicago Mayor Richard J. Daley, they assaulted a number of newsmen and celebrities in the process. News coverage of the event became so harsh as a result that many Democrats concluded they had little chance of winning the November election. Public opinion surveys

[4]"Poll Rates Nixon Best at Handling War," *New York Times*, 25 Aug 68.

[5]Msg, State 226256 to Saigon, Secretary to Ambassador, 22 Aug 68, Inf 6 U.S. file, FAIM/IR.

[6]Clifford, Notes for 25 May 68 Meeting, Papers of Clark Clifford, box 1, Notes Taken at Meetings, LBJ Library.

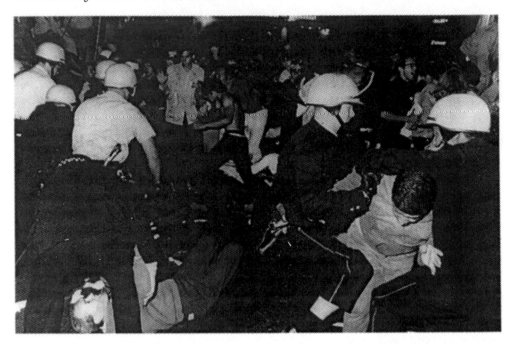

Police clash with demonstrators during the convention in Chicago.

taken shortly thereafter, however, revealed that a majority of Americans had sided with the police against the rioters, despite an impression conveyed by some in the news media that the police had been at fault. Recognizing the opening, Humphrey and other Democrats rushed to Daley's defense. Humphrey, for one, avowed in a widely publicized statement that "We ought to quit pretending . . . Mayor Daley did something wrong."[7]

Political Realities Take Precedence

While President Johnson and his advisers remained preoccupied with the Paris peace talks and the presidential election campaign, General Abrams and his commanders were becoming acutely aware of the enemy's vulnerability. Between 18 and 24 August, the first week of the enemy's third offensive of 1968, the Communists had launched 81 ground assaults and 103 attacks by fire, losing some 5,400 men. Defectors and captured enemy documents later established that even more had died as

[7] "Survival at the Stockyards," *Time*, 6 Sep 68, p. 14; "56% Defend Police in Chicago Strife," *New York Times*, 18 Sep 68; "The Battle of Chicago," *Newsweek*, 9 Sep 68, p. 29. Humphrey is quoted in Betty Beale, "The Other Side of the Chicago Police Story," *Washington Star*, 1 Sep 68, reprinted in *U.S. News & World Report*, 16 Sep 68, p. 60.

the result of air strikes and B–52 attacks and that the morale of many enemy units had sunk low.[8]

Aware that Communist sanctuaries in Cambodia remained an impediment to a secure South Vietnam, Abrams on 1 September attempted to press the American advantage by requesting permission to pursue enemy forces escaping across the Cambodian border. Employing units of up to brigade size and penetrating no more than twenty kilometers into Cambodia, American commanders would resort to the tactic, he said, only when the enemy attempted to use the border to break contact during an attack. When the Johnson administration put the matter under study but made no decision, Abrams repeated the request. He continued to push throughout October and November, if not for authority to pursue fleeing enemy troops into Cambodia at least to bomb lucrative enemy base areas, depots, and training sites in that country. President Johnson again made no formal response. Instead, on 16 October he instructed Abrams to put "constant, relentless, persistent pressure" on the enemy wherever and whenever possible but to avoid any sudden or dramatic increase in out-of-country operations.[9]

The timing of Abrams' requests could hardly have been worse. With the November election in the offing, President Johnson would have caused irreparable divisions within his party by escalating the war. In addition, there was much doubt in official circles that more aggressive military action would work. As Clark Clifford had observed in his notes of the meeting on 25 May, the United States had tried "more men, more bombs, and more killing" to no avail. It seemed time to try something else.[10]

Under the circumstances, the Johnson administration was sorely tempted to expand the partial bombing halt of 31 March into a total cessation of all bombing in North Vietnam. Undercutting enemy contentions at Paris that the United States was the sole aggressor in South Vietnam, a shift in bombing policy would demonstrate anew the president's dedication to peace while galvanizing support for Humphrey and the Democratic Party's candidates in the upcoming election.

A letter from the Premier of the Soviet Union, Alexei Kosygin, to President Johnson on 5 June provided the occasion. Kosygin noted in the message that he and his colleagues had grounds to believe that a cessation of bombing could improve prospects for a peaceful settlement of the war. On 11 September, after a number of exchanges with Kosygin on the subject, Johnson asserted publicly in a speech to the American Legion that

---

[8] Msg, Saigon 37046 to State, 4 Sep 68, sub: Ambassador Bunker's 65th Weekly Message to the President, and Msg, Saigon 38774 to State, 26 Sep 68, both in Pol 27 Viet S file, FAIM/IR.

[9] Msg, Abrams MAC 11819 to Wheeler, 1 Sep 68, sub: Military Actions in Cambodia; Msg, Abrams 16889 to McCain, 10 Dec 68; and Msg, Wheeler JCS 11890 to Abrams, 16 Oct 68. All in Abrams Papers, CMH.

[10] Clifford, Notes for 25 May 68 Meeting.

he would not halt the bombing unless Hanoi agreed to reciprocal military restraints.[11]

Although he said much the same thing in a letter to Kosygin three days later, he nevertheless toyed with the idea of unilateral action. On 19 September General Wheeler thus cabled Abrams to warn that the president might end the bombing of North Vietnam at any time within the next ten days. Since the North Vietnamese had already flatly rejected any quid pro quo, Wheeler said, Johnson might base the move on an assumption that the enemy would refrain from violating the Demilitarized Zone and agree to the seating of the South Vietnamese at the then-stalled peace talks.[12]

Abrams objected. "There exists at this time among our commanders and troops a noticeable sense of confidence both in what has been done and in what lies ahead," he told Wheeler. "To a discernable degree the Vietnamese military are showing this, too." In that light, a bombing halt without a compensating move by the enemy "would come as quite a shock to some of the troops and their commanders." Abrams added in a later message that the absence of some sort of agreement putting the Demilitarized Zone off limits to enemy and friendly personnel alike would allow the Communists to develop within two weeks of a bombing cessation a military capability in the area five times the size of the one they possessed before the halt.[13]

Faced with Abrams' reservations, President Johnson held to his demand that the North Vietnamese agree to mutual restraints. In exchange for a halt to all bombing of North Vietnam, he told the Soviets, the Hanoi regime would have to stop its abuse of the Demilitarized Zone and refrain from attacking South Vietnam's cities, provincial capitals, and major population centers. In addition, the authorities in Hanoi would have to enter promptly into serious political discussions that included the elected government of South Vietnam.[14]

Although Democratic presidential candidate Humphrey affirmed in a 30 September speech that he would consider an unconditional bombing halt "an acceptable risk for peace" but would resume operations if the enemy showed "bad faith," forty-one of sixty-eight senators polled by the Associated Press at the time shared the president's misgivings. The same was true for the American public. A Harris poll published on 7 October reported that if most Americans considered deescalation of the war desirable, a majority still opposed a unilateral bombing halt.[15]

---

[11] Lyndon B. Johnson, Briefing Paper, 28 Oct 68, Papers of Clark Clifford, box 6, Paris Negotiations file 2, LBJ Library. Also see Neil Sheehan, "Johnson Asserts Raids Will Go on Until Hanoi Acts," *New York Times*, 11 Sep 68.

[12] Johnson, Briefing Paper, 28 Oct 68; Msg, Wheeler JCS 10691 to Abrams, 19 Sep 68, Abrams Papers, CMH.

[13] Quote from Msg, Abrams MAC 12743 to Wheeler, 20 Sep 68. Msg, Abrams MAC 13100 to Wheeler, 28 Sep 68. Both in Abrams Papers, CMH.

[14] Unless otherwise noted, this section is based on Johnson, Briefing Paper, 28 Oct 68.

[15] Quote from [AP dispatch], Untitled, 7 Oct 68, CMH files; Louis Harris, "War Issue Sways Votes," *Chicago Daily News*, 7 Oct 68.

With Richard Nixon leading Humphrey in preelection polls, pressure for some sort of action continued to build in Democratic circles. Especially among those who had become convinced that the bombing of North Vietnam was less than worthwhile. Among the advocates of either a bombing halt or a reduction in American demands on the enemy were former presidential adviser McGeorge Bundy, former U.S. Ambassador to the United Nations Arthur Goldberg, former Under Secretary of State George Ball, former Deputy Secretary of Defense Cyrus Vance, and the U.S. Ambassador to the Paris peace talks, W. Averell Harriman.[16]

On 11 October Hanoi's delegation in Paris introduced the issue into official discussions by

North Vietnamese negotiator Xuan Thuy

approaching Ambassador Harriman to ask whether the United States would stop the bombing if it had an answer to the question of South Vietnamese participation in the peace talks. Underscoring the U.S. position on the Demilitarized Zone and the requirement for a cessation of attacks on South Vietnam's cities, Harriman said he would refer the matter to Washington. The State Department immediately contacted Ambassador Bunker and General Abrams for their opinion of the approach. The two responded that the enemy's motives in making the request were far from clear but that the development seemed to indicate the Communists were on the defensive and desired to shift their main effort from the battlefield to the negotiating table. In that light, they said, if the North Vietnamese agreed to American conditions on the Demilitarized Zone and the cities, "We would regard such a response as meeting our essential requirements for a cessation of the bombing."[17]

Abrams' and Bunker's message arrived in Washington at the same time as a cable from the Hanoi delegation in Paris accepting South Vietnamese participation in the peace talks once the bombing of North Vietnam had stopped. Informed of the development by Ambassador Bunker, South

---

[16] Saville Davis, "Pressure Builds To Halt Bombing," *Christian Science Monitor*, 17 Oct 68; Murrey Marder, "Raid Halt Is Urged by Bundy," *Washington Post*, 13 Oct 68.

[17] Quote from Johnson, Briefing Paper, 28 Oct 68, p. 3. Also see Msg, Saigon 40117 to State, from Bunker and Abrams, 12 Oct 68, Papers of Clark Clifford, Meeting Notes file, folder 7, LBJ Library.

Vietnamese President Nguyen Van Thieu agreed to go along, provided that the United States remained prepared to resume bombing if the enemy attacked his country's major cities or violated the Demilitarized Zone. "The problem is not to stop the bombing," Thieu told Bunker, "but to stop the war, and we must try this path to see if they are serious."[18]

Since the Communists had said that substantive discussions could begin on the day following a bombing halt, the State Department requested on 14 October that the first meeting with the South Vietnamese in attendance should convene on the day after the bombing stopped. Informed of the qualification, the North Vietnamese balked. They sought a delay of weeks between the halt and their first meeting with the South Vietnamese and requested a joint communique affirming that the halt was unconditional. The United States refused. Only after fourteen days of strenuous discussions would it consent to a three-day gap between the halt and the first meeting with the North Vietnamese. The Communists, for their part, agreed, at least in the eyes of American negotiators, to a three-part understanding. They would begin serious negotiations that included representatives of the South Vietnamese government; the bombing cessation would depend both on their respect for the Demilitarized Zone and on a halt to attacks against South Vietnam's major cities; and the United States would continue reconnaissance flights over North Vietnam after the bombing ceased. The halt itself was to begin on 29 October at 7 PM Eastern Standard Time.

The South Vietnamese Object

It did not. Instead, South Vietnamese officials decided the time had come for them to balk. Rejecting assurances from General Abrams and Ambassador Bunker that the talks were indeed only two-sided, they declined to associate themselves with the bombing cessation. The Hanoi regime, they contended, portrayed the Communist political organization in South Vietnam, formally titled the National Liberation Front, as a separate and independent party to the negotiations. In fact, it was entirely controlled by North Vietnam and should be part of the North Vietnamese delegation. During the weeks that followed, South Vietnamese diplomats stressed in private conversations with Bunker and others that President Johnson had attempted to drag their country into peace talks just days prior to the U.S. elections in order to improve Vice President Humphrey's prospects.[19]

[18] Quote from Johnson, Briefing Paper, 28 Oct 68, p. 3.
[19] Msg, Wheeler JCS 12492 to Abrams, 30 Oct 68, and Msg, Abrams MAC 14792 to Cushman et al., 2 Nov 68, both in Abrams Papers, CMH. Also see Msg, Saigon 42770 to State, 15 Nov 68, sub: Vietnamese Attitudes Toward War and Peace and the Paris Peace Talks—32nd Report, Papers of Clark Clifford, box 6, Presentation on Paris Peace Talks, Nov 18 [6], LBJ Library.

In a 30 October dispatch to the Military Assistance Command, General Wheeler instructed Abrams to inform Thieu that the president of the United States would never be able to maintain public support for the U.S. effort in Southeast Asia if the American people became aware, after five years of war and months of bargaining, that a move to the negotiating table was being impeded by trivial and unfounded reasons. For himself, Wheeler confided, the situation had become intolerable. He had been a constant, wholehearted supporter of the correctness of the American cause in Southeast Asia. Yet "now and perhaps it is because I am quite tired for the first time I begin to wonder if I have been right for the last five and one-half years."[20]

The next day, acting without the agreement of the South Vietnamese, President Johnson declared the bombing halt. The understanding the United States had reached with the North Vietnamese, he told his advisers, was "precisely the one which as I have told all three presidential candidates we have been seeking in recent months. We have given away nothing. . . . It is wholly consistent with my public statements." Privately, Abrams told his generals that the president and his advisers were all extremely skeptical of the enemy's agreement to keep the Demilitarized Zone inviolate and to refrain from attacking South Vietnam's cities. As a result, he said, rules of engagement had been carefully drafted to permit reaction to attacks and resumption of bombing if that became necessary.[21]

The press guidance accompanying the decision was uncomplicated. Abrams notified his commanders to make certain that they and their civilian and military subordinates avoided making any comment at all to the press. If queried, they were to respond that the president's announcement spoke for itself and that military operations in South Vietnam would continue as originally planned.[22]

The South Vietnamese lacked similar restraint. Galled by the bombing halt, they began an emotional campaign targeted on the American public and designed to sow doubts about the wisdom of Johnson's decision. Keyes Beech of the *Chicago Daily News* told their story. In a widely quoted article published on 31 October, Beech reported that "shocked and angry South Vietnamese had hurled the word *sellout* at their American allies after learning of the halt." One source, he said, had told him that "Your president talks about American casualties. What about Vietnamese casu-

---

[20] Msg, Wheeler JCS 12492 to Abrams, 30 Oct 68.

[21] Quote from Johnson, Briefing Paper, 28 Oct 68; MFR, MACV J3, 4 Nov 68, sub: MACV Commanders' Conference, 4 Nov 68, CMH files. According to Clifford, Abrams made a secret trip to Washington to advise the president on the bombing halt. See Clark Clifford with Richard Holbrooke, "Annals of Government, Serving the President, The Vietnam Years—III," *New Yorker*, 20 May 91, pp. 81–83. For more details of that meeting, see Lewis Sorley, *Thunderbolt: General Creighton Abrams and the Army of His Times* (New York: Simon and Schuster, 1992), pp. 250–53.

[22] Msg, Abrams MAC 14712 to All Commanders, 1 Nov 68, and Msg, Abrams MAC 14710 to All Commanders, 1 Nov 68, both in Abrams Papers, CMH.

President-elect Nixon

alties. They have sold us out as they sold out the Chinese Nationalists twenty years ago."[23]

Primed by South Vietnamese official sources, Beech returned to the subject two days later, when he dutifully visited the U.S. embassy in Saigon to check his facts. To the horror of those present, he leafed through pages of notes, detailing meetings going back to 13 October and reeling off fragments of President Johnson's letters to Thieu and other exchanges between members of the U.S. mission in Saigon and South Vietnamese officials. Although Ambassador Bunker complained that many of the details Beech had received were either slanted or distorted, he conceded that most of the reporter's information was factually correct. It was obvious, Bunker later observed in a cable to the State Department, that someone intimately involved with the negotiations, possibly Thieu or Ky, had briefed Beech. On grounds that the South Vietnamese leaders were leaking material to other correspondents as well and that the facts of the matter ought at least to be clear, Bunker corrected what he termed the "worst distortions and misrepresentations" in Beech's version of events. Although the reporter agreed to refrain from attributing the resulting story to American sources, the article that followed nevertheless suggested that the Johnson administration had made "a deal with Hanoi to halt the bombing five days before the U.S. presidential elections in return for a breakthrough in the Paris talks." Resorting to "high-pressure salesmanship," Beech said, the president and his advisers had then urged the Thieu regime to accept the arrangement.[24]

Numerous reports from Saigon took up Beech's themes. Beverly Deepe emphasized in an article for the *Christian Science Monitor* that the Thieu regime feared the seating of a separate National Liberation Front delegation in Paris because the act would represent a virtual capitulation to the Communists and would probably lead both to a coalition government and to an eventual Communist takeover. *Newsweek* replayed a con-

[23] Beech is quoted extensively in Memo, Daniel Z. Henkin for Secretary of Defense, 17 Nov 68, Papers of Clark Clifford, box 6, Presentation on the Paris Peace Talks [2], LBJ Library.

[24] Ibid. Also see Msg, Saigon 41837 to State, 4 Nov 68, Papers of Clark Clifford, box 6, Presentation on Paris Peace Talks, Nov 18 [1], LBJ Library.

tention of many South Vietnamese that Washington had failed "to keep Saigon abreast of its dealings with Hanoi." Worst of all, the magazine said, "U.S. officials were guilty of a gross miscalculation: they thought they could bring the Saigon regime [around] in time, and they were wrong." *U.S. News & World Report* was even less diplomatic. The Johnson administration's scheme for getting all parties together for talks in Paris had collapsed, the magazine declared, because the South Vietnamese had decided their government was being "dragged to Paris on an equal footing with the Viet Cong," without any guarantee that Hanoi would abide by its agreement.[25]

Despite the publicity and the Saigon government's allegations that the Johnson administration had traded an ally's security for short-term political gains, the American public sided with its president. According to the Harris poll, it agreed by 55 to 28 percent that he had done the right thing. Humphrey benefited. Where in late October, according to Harris, he had trailed his Republican opponent by substantial margins, by 4 November he had narrowed the gap to 2 percentage points, making the election too close to call. In the end, propelled by sentiment that a change was necessary, Nixon won, but by the narrowest of margins in the popular vote, 43.4 to 43 percent.[26]

The impasse between the United States and South Vietnam continued after the election, with little forward motion toward a solution. Sources within the new administration attempted to reassure Thieu that the United States would continue to take strong action against the enemy by leaking word to William Beecher of the *New York Times* and other reporters that American forces would intensify the bombing of enemy infiltration routes in Laos once the halt had gone into effect. Following the same line, *New York Daily News* reporter Joseph Fried revealed on 10 November that the United States had begun hitting targets in Laos with what he termed "the heaviest bombing ever." The administration nevertheless diluted the effect of those revelations by failing to publicize the raids. To save face for the government of Laotian Prime Minister Souvanna Phouma, the U.S. Information Agency instead issued a circular letter on 4 November instructing all of its missions to respond to queries on the subject with a standard answer in use since 1964 that had over the years caused considerable problems with the press: "At the request of the Royal Laotian Government, the United States has since 1964 been conducting reconnaissance flights over Laos by armed aircraft. By agreement with the Lao Government, these escort fighter aircraft may return fire if fired upon."[27]

[25] Memo, Henkin for Secretary of Defense, 17 Nov 68.

[26] "Harris: Bomb Halt Closed Gap," *New York Post*, 4 Nov 68.

[27] William Beecher, "Laos To Be Pounded To Cut Enemy Arms Flow," *New York Times*, 2 Nov 68; Joseph Fried, "Red Laos Bases Hit Secretly," *New York Daily News*, 10 Nov 68; Msg, U.S. Information Agency (USIA) Circular 18311 to All Posts, 4 Nov 68, sub: USG Public Response to Queries, DDI Laos Policy file.

Believing that the South Vietnamese attack on the president was "unwarranted and dishonest," Clark Clifford took action at Johnson's request to refute the allegations. He chose a 12 November press conference at the Pentagon as the occasion. In response to a question on U.S. relations with the Thieu regime he stated that the United States had not failed to inform the South Vietnamese. Instead, President Thieu had concurred with the plan but had later experienced a change of heart. "After all we have done in that country," Clifford continued, and "after the enormous contribution that's been made, with the knowledge that we had gotten to the point where we had the sort of agreement we had been working toward, I believe that the president was absolutely right in not giving Saigon a veto on the plan. . . . I think he owed it to the American people to proceed with the talks." Clifford added pointedly that the United States "should make every reasonable effort to demonstrate to Saigon why it should come in and join the talks. At the same time, if they choose not to, I believe the president has the constitutional responsibility of proceeding with the talks."[28]

The secretary's comments prompted a sharp reaction in Saigon that once more played itself out in the press. South Vietnamese Minister of Information Ton That Thien called a press conference on the morning of 13 November to deny that President Thieu had ever agreed to talks that included the Viet Cong as a distinct entity. The United States had conferred with the Communists for five months and might continue to do so, he continued, but any agreement it entered into affecting the fate or interests of the South Vietnamese people could hardly be binding on the government of South Vietnam. Underscoring the point, Thien's ministry shortly thereafter suspended publication of the *Saigon Daily News* for three months on grounds that the paper had printed Clifford's remarks under a bold headline while relegating Thien's rejoinder to a less prominent position.[29]

The wrangling continued for two more weeks, with the South Vietnamese alternately moving toward accord and then backing off. Finally, on 25 November, faced with Clifford's threat that the United States would go to the talks alone and having received a letter from President-elect Nixon backing Johnson's efforts, Thieu agreed to join the talks. The face-saving communique that announced the development emphasized that the negotiations with Hanoi would be essentially two-

[28] Clifford's papers indicate that he took action on his own authority. See Handwritten MFR, Clifford, n.d. [Nov 68], Papers of Clark Clifford, box 6, Presentation on Paris Peace Talks, Nov 18 [1], LBJ Library. Clifford indicated years later, however, that a request from Johnson himself was behind the press conference. See Clark Clifford with Richard Holbrooke, *Counsel to the President* (New York: Random House, 1991), p. 601; and Clifford, "Annals of Government, Serving the President, The Vietnam Years—III," p. 87. The quotations are from "Secretary Clifford's News Conference of November 12," Department of State *Bulletin*, 59:570.

[29] Msg, Saigon 42770 to State, 15 Nov 68, sub: Vietnamese Attitudes Toward War and Peace and the Paris Peace Talks—32nd Report.

sided and that the delegation of the Republic of South Vietnam would be the main spokesman on all matters of principal concern to the South Vietnamese nation.[30]

Although the agreement with the Thieu regime bolstered hopes that serious discussions with Hanoi might at last begin, little in fact changed in the weeks that followed. Instead, despite the so-called understanding leading to the bombing halt, Communist forces continued to probe the Demilitarized Zone to determine how much provocation the United States would tolerate. By 4 December General Abrams had launched at least one American foray into the zone to eliminate an enemy threat and had requested permission to conduct full-scale operations in the southern portion of the area. President Johnson refused to authorize the attacks because he considered the American position weak. The understanding with the North Vietnamese, he reasoned, had been predicated on the start of negotiations, but the temporizing of the South Vietnamese had frustrated that end. In addition, combat operations in the Demilitarized Zone might engender the sort of large engagements that would jeopardize continuation of the talks. Abrams already had the authority to defend American forces if a major enemy threat developed from across the Demilitarized Zone, Johnson told the general. For the rest, he should make certain he used those powers with the greatest discretion.[31]

As the halt lengthened, MACV intelligence analysts threw the Johnson administration's hope for peace further into doubt by reporting that Communist forces had accelerated deliveries of ammunition, petroleum, and building supplies into Laos and the southernmost portions of North Vietnam. Only two weeks after the beginning of the halt, on 17 November, General Abrams reported that aerial photographs had revealed over 1,000 trucks moving into the area of North Vietnam between the 17th and 18th Parallels and 4,000 more entering the region between the 19th Parallel and the city of Vinh. In addition, hundreds of sampans loaded with ammunition and other cargo were moving freely along canals in those areas, workers were laying a petroleum pipeline, and all of the major roads and bridges had been repaired. Before the halt, on 13 October, Abrams had reported that the enemy's logistical arrangements in North and South Vietnam were in such a shambles that the United States faced a moment of supreme opportunity. By 17 November he had little choice but to withdraw his comment and to observe that the North Vietnamese had reversed the situation. So rapidly was the enemy rebuilding, he told the Joint Chiefs of Staff, that within a few short weeks

---

[30] Handwritten MFR, Clifford, n.d. [Nov 68]; Msg, Saigon 42377 to State, 12 Nov 68, Papers of Clark Clifford, box 6, Presentation on Paris Peace Talks, Nov 18 [7], LBJ Library; Press Release 264, Department of State *Bulletin*, 59:621.

[31] Msg, McCain to Wheeler, 4 Dec 68, and Msg, Wheeler JCS 14235 to Abrams, 4 Dec 68, both in Abrams Papers, CMH. Also see "Saigon's Move," *Washington Star*, 27 Nov 68; B. Drummond Ayres, Jr., "Allies Enter DMZ 1st Time Since Halt," *New York Times*, 27 Nov 68.

Communist forces would be prepared to push their forward supply depots into the northernmost portions of South Vietnam. "This will alter the present strategic equation," he said, "and will give the enemy a logistic option we recently have succeeded in denying him."[32]

It seemed clear in the light of everything that had transpired that the United States intended to end the war and was willing to put up with much more than it had in the past, as long as it saved face. What was not so clear was the effect Lyndon Johnson's decision to halt the bombing and to begin negotiations would have on both the policies of his successor, Richard M. Nixon, and the conduct of the war.

[32] Msg, Abrams MAC 1340 to McCain, 13 Oct 68, Abrams Papers, CMH. Quote from Msg, State 274394 to Moscow, 17 Nov 68, relaying Msg, Abrams to JCS, 17 Nov 68, Pol 27 Viet S file, FAIM/IR.

3

"I Will Not Warn Again"

Richard Nixon took office as president of the United States on 20 January 1969. A seasoned public official who had served in Congress and as vice president under President Dwight D. Eisenhower, he had campaigned quietly in an attempt to divorce himself as far as possible from the controversies that had afflicted his predecessor. The aura of professionalism and quiet competence that settled about him as a result won the admiration of many in the news media. As William H. Stringer of the *Christian Science Monitor* observed, "One of the happiest things about the Nixon administration is its low key approach, its absence of bombast and clamorous claiming, its obvious awareness that these are serious times and that the emphasis must be on responsible problem solving."[1]

The American public was also hopeful. During the first months of 1969, Nixon's popularity in the polls remained well above the level achieved by Lyndon Johnson during the last months of his presidency. Nixon had stated during his campaign that he had a plan to end the war in Vietnam. Most Americans appeared willing to give him time to develop that strategy. In addition, as Tom Wicker of the *New York Times* observed, President Johnson's decision to retire, the opening of the Paris peace talks, the suspension of bombing in North Vietnam, and the change in administrations had at least temporarily stilled the great outpouring of public unrest that had been one of the foremost marks of the previous year.[2]

The mood Nixon set complemented the policy of quiet candor General Abrams had instituted at the Military Assistance Command. "There is little question," wrote Robert Elegant of the *Los Angeles Times*, reflecting on the changes Abrams had set in motion, "that the [public affairs] policy decreed by former President Johnson and executed—often with additional flou-

---

[1] William H. Stringer, "News Slantwise," *Christian Science Monitor*, 19 Mar 69.
[2] *Gallup Opinion Index*, February through August 1969; Tom Wicker, "In the Nation: The Old Merry-Go-Round," *New York Times*, 20 Mar 69.

rishes—in Saigon, contrived a public relations disaster." Elegant went on to contrast Barry Zorthian's regular background briefings for selected members of the press—hailed in their day as a solid improvement over the lack of information that had prevailed before Zorthian's time—with the thoughtful style of the career foreign service officer who had replaced Zorthian, George Newman. Zorthian had held forth regularly on a multitude of subjects, from the attitude of the South Vietnamese government to the interpretation of captured enemy documents, Elegant said, while Newman let reporters find out for themselves or directed them to specialists or South Vietnamese spokesmen who could help. "Except for the few correspondents for whom briefings and 'backgrounders' had displaced reality," he added, "the press corps seems to prefer the new policy. No longer feeling themselves subject to high pressure salesmanship, correspondents are more inclined to take low-keyed official reports seriously."[3]

Secretary Laird Takes Control

Although American public opinion seemed supportive of Nixon, the new Secretary of Defense, Melvin Laird, understood that presidents were always popular early in their terms and believed that limited time remained before the press, the public, and Congress turned completely against the war. He reasoned that a lengthening conflict would inevitably bleed American strength around the world in places far more important to the security of the United States than South Vietnam. In daily touch with friends and political contacts throughout the country, he was also convinced that any attempt to prolong the American role in the fighting would lead to so much controversy and political strife that it would inhibit the president's ability to achieve an honorable settlement. He understood that the war would last into the foreseeable future, but he wanted the involvement of American forces to cease as soon as practical.[4]

A Democrat, Senator Henry M. Jackson of Washington, had rejected the job of secretary of defense before Nixon had offered it to Laird.[5] Laird himself had recognized that retreat from the war would be difficult and that the chief executive might be subject to pressures from many directions. Before deciding to accept the position, he had therefore insisted that

[3] Robert S. Elegant, "Vietnam War Briefings Swing To Quiet Candor," *Los Angeles Times*, 13 Feb 69.

[4] Unless otherwise indicated, this section is based on Interv, author with Jerry Friedheim, Deputy Assistant Secretary of Defense, 1969–73, 3 Oct 86, and Interv, author with Daniel Z. Henkin, ASD PA, 1969–73, 10 Oct 86, both in CMH files.

[5] Msg, NARA 561 to Tokyo, 30 Jun 69, sub: U.S. Ambassadorial Personnel Affairs, National Security Council (NSC) files, Vietnam Subject files, box 67, Cherokee, Richard M. Nixon Papers, Nixon Materials Project, National Archives and Records Administration (NARA), Alexandria, Va. References to the records contained in the Nixon Materials Project will be hereafter cited as the Nixon Papers.

Bunker and Laird

the president sign a letter of agreement stating the length of his term in office as secretary, his authority to pick his Pentagon aides without White House interference, and the Defense Department's position as the lead agency in the process of withdrawing American forces from the war. With that letter in hand, he had taken on the task.[6]

Once in office, he moved swiftly to remedy the credibility problems that had afflicted the previous administration. An experienced politician who enjoyed sparring with reporters and understood how the news media worked, he made it clear to his appointees that the Defense Department would have to build up the confidence of the press by being more forthcoming. Clearly suspicious of some of the individuals working for the president, he instructed his staff to pass all requests for public affairs assistance originating in the White House to him for clearance. In an attempt to make the Defense Department the leading voice on the war, he also established a daily briefing for Pentagon correspondents. Coming early in the morning before the briefings at the State Department and the White House, the session not only built credibility by providing a regular forum for the release of important information to the press, it also set the agenda for the day's discussion of the war.

In the past the Military Assistance Command in South Vietnam had been the point of release for most developments that occurred in the field. Laird left the policy intact but, with General Abrams' concurrence, gave

[6]Interv, author with Friedheim, 3 Oct 86. Also see Sorley, *Thunderbolt*, pp. 332–33.

57

Henry Kissinger

the Defense Department more responsibility for explaining the war. The move created problems for information officers in Saigon, who lost some of their standing with the press when news releases from Washington agencies preempted their own announcements, but the secretary deemed it essential. With critical decisions in the offing, the Defense Department seemed better suited than the Military Assistance Command to set the tone for public affairs on the war, if only because it represented a broader viewpoint. The MACV Office of Information spoke mainly for the U.S. command in Saigon, Laird's Assistant Secretary of Defense for Public Affairs Daniel Z. Henkin later observed, while DOD Public Affairs, in coordination with other Washington agencies, spoke for the government of the United States.[7]

Laird was convinced that information on many aspects of the war was unnecessarily restricted. Although hardly above the practice of leaking when he felt it necessary, he made it a rule whenever possible to avoid off-the-record meetings with reporters. Unlike the president's National Security Adviser, Henry Kissinger, and others at the White House—and much to the chagrin of at least a few correspondents who loved to cultivate a certain cachet about their work—he rarely requested that reporters attribute his remarks only to "high officials" or "official sources."

The approach made good sense as far as public affairs was concerned, but it rapidly came into conflict with the attitude of White House aides such as Kissinger, who considered secrecy essential to the conduct of American policy. A case in point was the air war in Laos. For years the United States had flown attack sorties against portions of Hanoi's main supply route to the south, the Ho Chi Minh Trail, which ran through that country. *(Map 2)* Yet out of deference to the wishes of the Laotian Prime Minister Souvanna Phouma, information officers had replied to all questions with the stock response that the United States had been conducting reconnaissance flights over Laos since 1964 and had only returned fire when fired upon. Since the formulation, as Soviet propagandists took delight in pointing out, bore little resemblance to reality, Laird sought to have it changed.

[7] Interv, author with Henkin, 10 Oct 86.

58

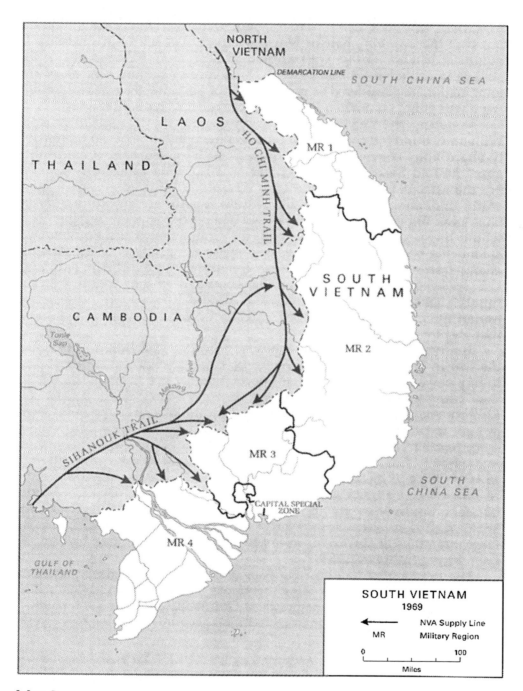

NORTH
VIETNAM

DEMARCATION LINE   SOUTH CHINA SEA

LAOS

THAILAND

HO CHI MINH TRAIL

MR 1

SOUTH
VIETNAM

CAMBODIA

Tonle
Sap

MR 2

Mekong River

SIHANOUK TRAIL

MR 3

CAPITAL SPECIAL
ZONE

SOUTH
CHINA
SEA

MR 4

GULF OF
THAILAND

SOUTH VIETNAM
1969

⟵   NVA Supply Line

MR   Military Region

0   100

Miles

Map 2

He made his move shortly after taking office, through Deputy Assistant Secretary of Defense for International Security Affairs Richard C. Steadman. In a memorandum to the State Department, Steadman pointed out that the bombing halt in North Vietnam had led to an increase in bombing in Laos, a fact well known to newsmen. Since many of the strikes involved B–52 bombers, "which cannot by any stretch of the imagination be considered as reconnaissance aircraft," the attempt to hide what was going on posed a major threat to official credibility.[8]

Assisting the new administration during the transition period, William P. Bundy at the State Department responded. "We do not entirely share your concern that the present policy makes for a credibility gap," he told Steadman. "The bombing is not only completely known, but the reasons for the U.S. and Laos refusal to confirm it . . . are . . . generally understood." A new policy would require an announcement by Souvanna Phouma stating that he had acquiesced to the bombing. That would increase the pressure on both the United States and Souvanna to extend the bombing halt to Laos and make the problem of interdicting enemy traffic along the Ho Chi Minh Trail much more difficult. Although U.S. spokesmen could resort to a "no comment" if they found it easier, Bundy concluded, they would have to continue to respond in the accustomed manner when questioned directly because Souvanna wanted it that way.[9]

Bundy's assurances to the contrary, reporters had little to say about the war in Laos because the policy of no comment had cut off most day-to-day news of the subject. When information became available, however, they could cause a considerable stir. In early March, for example, the Military Assistance Command stationed a company of marines on a hill in Laos to protect the flank of a large U.S. operation in the A Shau Valley code-named Dewey Canyon. Newsmen learned of the event almost immediately from troopers in the field and began to ask questions. The MACV Office of Information responded with the standard formula about reconnaissance flights, conceding only on background that the border between South Vietnam and Laos was extremely ill defined. Official spokesmen then attempted to direct the attention of the reporters to the large quantities of enemy supplies and equipment U.S. forces had uncovered during the operation.[10]

The *Washington Post* and the *New York Times* nonetheless published articles on the subject on 9 March. Rumors meanwhile circulated within the Pentagon that CBS correspondent Don Webster had gone to Laos to fill out the story with his own eyewitness account. In order to keep the

[8] Ltr, Richard Steadman, Deputy Assistant Secretary of Defense for International Security Affairs (DASD ISA), to William P. Bundy, Assistant Secretary of State for East Asian and Pacific Affairs, 4 Feb 69, DDI Laos 69–70 file.

[9] Ltr, William P. Bundy to Richard C. Steadman, 26 Feb 69, DDI Laos Policy file.

[10] Msg, Abrams MAC 2897 to Ambassador William H. Sullivan, U.S. Ambassador to Laos, n.d. [Mar 69], Abrams Papers, CMH.

press from causing major embarrassment to the new administration and Souvanna Phouma, Laird decided to make an immediate statement. Out of deference to policy, he refused to confirm that U.S. troops had been in Laos, but he still found ways to amplify the information available to the press. When reporters raised the issue during a fact-finding trip to South Vietnam, for example, he responded vaguely that "I would not confirm that they were there now, but I would certainly say that there had been operations in which it has been necessary in order to protect American fighting forces that undoubtedly that border, being a very indefinite border, may have been transgressed by American forces in carrying out this responsibility of protecting American fighting forces." Shortly thereafter, confronted by Laird's innovation, the State Department issued instructions to the U.S. embassy in Saigon stipulating that all further responses to questions on the subject were to adhere to Laird's formulation. Confirming that U.S. troops might have crossed the border to protect other American units, official spokesmen were to add that "As you know, we have always recognized that there may be situations where a military commander may have to make a decision to maneuver in the area of the border in pursuance of his right of self-defense." If questioned on who determined when it was necessary to cross the border of another country, they were to reply that they never discussed rules of engagement.[11]

In the end, the story died for lack of nourishment and because the press very obviously sought to give the new president the room he needed to set his policies in motion. Yet if the news media appeared willing to wait, there were indications that, as Laird had perceived, time was limited. During January, 40 percent of the Americans responding to a Gallup poll stated that the war in Vietnam was "the most important problem facing this country today." The figure was 23 percentage points higher than the next most common response: "crime and lawlessness." By March Gallup was reporting that the lack of progress in the war had begun to polarize American public opinion, causing 25 percent of those responding to a recent poll to favor escalation of the war while another 21 percent opted for withdrawal. Although 15 percent recommended fighting on as the Paris negotiations ran their course, that number was balanced by 15 percent who responded simply that they wanted to end the war as soon as possible. A strain of pessimism was also apparent in poll responses. According to Gallup, only 17 percent thought the peace talks were making headway and only 28 percent believed the negotiations would end in an honorable settlement.[12]

---

[11] Msg, State 37093 to Vientiane, 11 Mar 69, sub: Press Guidance on Story U.S. Forces Crossed Lao Border, Pol 27 Viet S file, FAIM/IR.

[12] Quotes from *Gallup Opinion Index*, Feb 69, p. 4. Ibid., Mar 69, p. 11; U.S. Department of State, American Opinion Summary, 26 Feb–12 Mar 69 and 13–27 Mar 69, Vn-Public Opinion file, FAIM/IR; George Gallup, "Favor Extreme Steps To End the War," *Chicago Sun-Times*, 23 Mar 69; MS, Ann David, Study of U.S. Public Opinion, 1 Jun 83, CMH files.

Laird was hardly the only member of the administration to recognize that a problem existed. As early as 5 February William Bundy warned the new Secretary of State, William P. Rogers, that although the heat of the Vietnam issue had lessened for the time being, circumstances could change "rather quickly."[13] Bundy and the Under Secretary of State for Political Affairs, Ambassador U. Alexis Johnson, elaborated on the point in conversations at the State Department with a South Vietnamese emissary, Nguyen Phu Duc. "We would certainly run into serious difficulties over a period of time with American public support," they warned, "if we appeared to be sticking to a position of insisting that political issues must take a complete back seat to the settlement of the military ones."[14]

President Nixon nevertheless intended to weigh all of his options. Refusing to be rushed and counting on the initial period of quiet that always seemed to follow the inauguration of a new president, he rejected suggestions that he make some dramatic gesture to prove his peaceful intentions. Instead, he issued National Security Study Memorandum 1 to all the agencies of the U.S. government involved in the war. A list of twenty-nine questions designed to determine how well the conflict was going, the memorandum was to be the first step in the production of an agreed upon estimate that could become the basis for future policy. Shortly thereafter, to keep from feeding speculation that the United States might begin to withdraw American forces from South Vietnam without concessions from the Communists, he instructed Wheeler and Abrams to confine all discussions with the press on the subject to the question of mutual withdrawals within the context of the Paris negotiations.[15]

In the same way, rather than surrender the least military advantage, he informed Abrams through Wheeler that he believed the United States would come out best in the negotiations if U.S. forces maintained the greatest possible pressure on the enemy. He wanted to know whether Abrams could do more with the resources available. Abrams replied that his command was performing at maximum efficiency. If the president wanted more, he could reinforce the effort to interdict the Ho Chi Minh Trail, accelerate the delivery of new equipment to the South Vietnamese armed forces, reject a Defense Department proposal to reduce B–52 strikes from 1,800 to 1,500 sorties per month, and permit American forces to begin attacking the enemy's base areas in Cambodia.[16]

[13] Memo, William P. Bundy for the Secretary of State, 5 Feb 69, sub: Your Meeting With Nguyen Phu Duc, Talking Points, Pol US-Viet S file, FAIM/IR.

[14] MFR, William P. Bundy, 5 Feb 69, sub: Points Covered With Nguyen Phu Duc by Amb. U. A. Johnson and Mr. Bundy, attachment to Memo, Bundy for the Secretary of State, 5 Feb 69, sub: Your Meeting With Nguyen Phu Duc, Pol US-Viet S file, FAIM/IR.

[15] National Security Study Memorandum (NSSM) 1, Henry A. Kissinger, Special Assistant for National Security, for the Secretaries of State and Defense and the Director of Central Intelligence, 21 Jan 69, DepCORDS Papers, CMH; Msg, Wheeler JCS 1080 to Nazarro, Acting CINCPAC, and Abrams, 25 Jan 69, Abrams Papers, CMH.

[16] Msg, Wheeler JCS 885 to Nazarro, Abrams, 22 Jan 69, and Msg, Abrams MAC 1102 to Wheeler, 24 Jan 69, both in Abrams Papers, CMH.

Nixon Considers Air Attacks on Cambodia

Although the president postponed any decision on Abrams' recommendations, the general's request for a campaign against the enemy's bases in Cambodia was especially attractive to policy makers. Shortly after taking office, to jar the enemy into becoming more forthcoming at the Paris peace talks, Nixon had considered a renewal of the air war against North Vietnam. He had rejected the idea because he believed the move would have served only to confirm the enemy in his obstinacy by sparking vehement antiwar protests in the United States. A campaign of attacks on North Vietnam's sanctuaries appeared much more promising. It contained its own risks to public relations, but it would be easy to defend, if necessary, as a long-delayed response to enemy provocation. Representing a major shift in American policy, it would also signal American resolve to Hanoi much more effectively than a renewal of attacks on North Vietnam itself.[17]

Before Nixon's time, an assault on the enemy's installations in Cambodia had been almost unthinkable. The State Department and the Central Intelligence Agency (CIA) had disagreed with a judgment by Military Assistance Command analysts that the Cambodian port of Sihanoukville was the major conduit for supplies funneling to enemy units in the southern portion of South Vietnam. There was also considerable concern that Cambodia's volatile head of state, Prince Norodom Sihanouk, might formally ally his country with North Vietnam if the United States provided him with an adequate excuse.[18]

By early 1969 those concerns seemed less important than before. Although the State Department and the Central Intelligence Agency continued to dispute MACV contentions that Sihanoukville was an enemy entrepot, ample evidence existed to establish that some supplies were coming through the port and that Cambodia's border areas had become an important sanctuary for enemy troops. Recently captured Communist documents testified that the North Vietnamese considered base areas in Cambodia essential to an eventual victory in South Vietnam. One appraisal, composed as early as 1964, stated that "the rear area is . . . the location of our key agencies. As long as the key agencies exist, the revolution will subsist. Without a base area we cannot develop our mission. Owing to the neutrality of Cambodia and Laos, our base areas can be expanded."[19] In addition, the Communists themselves had become cynical

[17] Memo, Laird for Kissinger, 21 Feb 69; Memo, Kissinger for Laird, 3 Mar 69, sub: Memorandum Enclosing Preliminary Draft of Potential Military Actions Re: Vietnam; and Memo, Dean Moor for Col Alexander Haig, 10 Feb 69, sub: A Scenario of Possible Military Actions Related to South Vietnam, all in NSC files, Vietnam Subject file, box 64, 8F Reappraisal of Vietnam Commitment, vol. 1, Nixon Papers. Also see Henry A. Kissinger, *The White House Years* (Boston: Little, Brown and Co., 1979), pp. 239f.

[18] Msg, Abrams MAC 1166 to Nazarro, 26 Jan 69, Abrams Papers, CMH; Kissinger, *The White House Years*, p. 241.

[19] Msg, CIA 22708 to State, 21 May 64, Papers of Clark Clifford, box 3, SEA Memorandum, LBJ Library.

about their occupation of Cambodian territory. Referring to the Ho Chi Minh Trail in Laos, for example, a second secretary at the North Vietnamese embassy in Vientiane had observed in December 1968, within earshot of a reliable U.S. informant, that "North Vietnam could not possibly move enough equipment to the front . . . if [it] relied only on a small trail through the mountains."[20]

As for Prince Sihanouk, it had become increasingly clear by early 1969 that he was alarmed by the ever more aggressive North Vietnamese presence in his country. As early as December 1968 he had confided to U.S. presidential emissary Chester Bowles that Communist forces operating along Cambodia's border with South Vietnam were a menace and that the United States would be doing his country a favor if it raided those portions of Cambodia inhabited only by such units. Courting resumption of diplomatic relations with the United States—broken off since 1965— Sihanouk repeated his overture during a 6 March 1969 press conference, all but implying publicly that he would welcome American bombing of North Vietnamese sanctuaries within his country as long as no Cambodian civilians came to grief in the attacks. Questioned on the subject by the Australian ambassador to Cambodia, he clarified his meaning several days later. Although he would probably continue to condemn both sides in the war, he said, there would be no repercussions affecting relations with the United States if American forces raided isolated portions of his country. Since Australia had contributed forces to the war in South Vietnam and was clearly an ally of the United States, Sihanouk can have had no illusion that his conversation would remain private. Word of what had transpired passed immediately to the U.S. Department of State.[21]

General Abrams renewed his request for attacks on the enemy's Cambodian sanctuaries in a 9 February message to Wheeler. An enemy defector as well as reconnaissance photographs, he said, had revealed that the main enemy headquarters directing the war in the southern portion of South Vietnam, the Central Office for South Vietnam (COSVN), was located on a nine-acre tract just across the border in the so-called Fishhook area of Cambodia. With enemy preparations for a major offensive in the III Corps Tactical Zone already well advanced, a B–52 strike on so vital a target would inevitably disrupt the enemy's planning and might even forestall the attack. Ambassador Bunker backed Abrams' request, observing that no Cambodians lived in the area of the proposed strike and that the U.S. Air Force had already demonstrated its ability to employ B–52s near population centers without causing harm to civilians.[22]

---

[20] Msg, Abrams MAC 1166 to Nazarro, 29 Jan 69.

[21] Msg, Bangkok 4992 to State, 19 Mar 69, Abrams Papers, CMH; Kissinger, *The White House Years*, p. 250.

[22] Msg, Abrams MAC 1782 to Wheeler, 9 Feb 69, Abrams Papers, CMH. Bunker's comments are in Msg, Saigon 2830 to State, Bunker to Secretary, 12 Feb 69, Pol 27 Viet S file, FAIM/IR.

President Nixon took Abrams' request under serious consideration. Apparently distrusting the ability of foreign service personnel to keep the matter secret and hoping to avoid leaks to the press from that direction, he notified the State Department that he wanted all consideration of the subject dropped in view of a trip he would shortly make to Europe to meet the leaders of the Western Alliance. Shortly thereafter, in a separate message to Abrams transmitted through the Joint Chiefs of Staff, he instructed the general to refrain from discussing the matter further with Ambassador Bunker or any U.S. embassy personnel. Although Bunker had received a message disapproving Abrams' proposition, he said, Abrams was to disregard it and to dispatch a special team to Washington to brief concerned officials as quickly as possible.[23]

The meeting took place on 18 February, with Kissinger, Secretary of Defense Laird, and General Wheeler in attendance. Kissinger advised against unprovoked bombing of the sanctuaries, arguing that the new administration ought to give negotiations a chance. He also suggested that attacks on Cambodia might do more harm than good to public support for Nixon's still evolving policies. In the end the group decided to advise the president to postpone any decision until March, after the trip to Europe had ended.[24]

General Wheeler explained the panel's reservations in a message to Abrams. The attack would have had to occur in one of two ways, he told the general, either of which posed problems. If the United States, on the one hand, simply announced the operation, justifying it with the rationale that an enemy directorate located in Cambodia was masterminding the war against the population of South Vietnam, the admission might spark a violent reaction both at home and abroad. If it used a cover story, on the other hand, averring that a mistake had been made, the excuse would stand little more than twenty-four hours before leaks by knowledgeable sources in Washington exposed it. Violence, again, would surely follow. As it was, Wheeler said, Bunker's message backing Abrams' request had received wide distribution within the State Department, so much so that the department had several times requested copies of Abrams' original message on the subject.[25]

The Tet Offensive of 1969

On the night of 23 February, shortly after Nixon decided to postpone consideration of attacks on the enemy's Cambodian sanctuaries, North Vietnamese and Viet Cong forces in South Vietnam launched their

[23] Msg, State 2385 to Saigon, 14 Feb 69, Pol 27 Viet S file, FAIM/IR; Msg, McConnell JCS 1915 to Abrams, n.d. [Feb 69], Abrams Papers, CMH.

[24] Kissinger, *The White House Years*, p. 242.

[25] Msg, Wheeler JCS 2218 to Abrams, 21 Feb 69, Abrams Papers, CMH.

Enemy rockets on mud ramps

Tet offensive for 1969, shelling or probing by ground attack some 117 military installations and population centers throughout the country. North Vietnamese spokesmen immediately announced that their forces had targeted only military establishments, a proviso of the understanding that had led to the 1 November 1968 bombing halt. The rockets Communist gunners had used were nevertheless so inaccurate and their targets so surrounded by civilian habitations that there seemed little doubt that the enemy had actually indulged in an act of terror against the civilian population of South Vietnam.[26]

General Abrams proposed resumption of the bombing of North Vietnam as the best response. The enemy's rockets had verified the Communist's intentions, he told Wheeler. A failure to take action would invite further provocations to ascertain just how much the United States would tolerate without renewing the bombing or breaking off negotiations. In a separate message, Ambassador Bunker reminded the State Department that the U.S. mission had promised the South Vietnamese government that the bombing halt itself depended on North Vietnamese compliance with the understandings. The morale of the South Vietnamese people would fall, he said, if the United States refrained from bombing the North while civilians in the South reeled under yet another series of terror attacks.[27]

[26] Msg, Abrams MAC 2372 to Wheeler, 23 Feb 69, and Msg, Abrams MAC 2836 to Wheeler, 5 Mar 69, sub: Retaliatory Actions, both in Abrams Papers, CMH.

[27] Msg, Abrams MAC 2836 to Wheeler, 5 Mar 69, sub: Retaliatory Actions; Msg, Saigon 3402 to State, 22 Feb 69, Pol 27 Viet S file, FAIM/IR.

Scheduled to leave for Europe on the day the attacks began, President Nixon was unwilling to jeopardize the success of his first foreign trip as president by bombing North Vietnam, an act that would have caused rioting and protests all along his route. Instead he ordered the bombing of the enemy's Cambodian sanctuaries, instructing the Defense Department to keep the move secret unless Sihanouk protested. Secretary Laird objected that it would be impossible to hide what was happening. The press would be difficult, and public support for the war might falter. Kissinger also recommended against the decision on grounds that it would cloud Nixon's stay in Europe. Faced by so united a front, Nixon relented.[28]

Over the next several weeks, the enemy demonstrated his determination to pursue the war with all the ferocity he could muster. The total of his artillery attacks during March exceeded those he had conducted during the Tet offensive of 1968 by 1½ times. The number of rounds he fired during those attacks was also greater, exceeding Tet 1968 totals by 31 percent. The number of his battalion- and larger-size assaults, meanwhile, came close to equaling those of the earlier offensive. Of even more concern, by mid-March captured enemy documents indicated that North Vietnamese commanders had plans for additional attacks during coming months and for yet another major offensive later on in the year.[29]

On 5 March, in the midst of the developing offensive, Abrams again requested retaliatory air strikes on North Vietnam below 19 degrees north latitude and also suggested extensive ground and air operations against the enemy's sanctuaries in Laos and Cambodia. The North Vietnamese had adopted a high-risk posture, he said, by supporting their entire force in South Vietnam's III Corps Tactical Zone from a limited number of Cambodian bases and a single line of supply through Sihanoukville. They would never have taken that risk unless they believed that political constraints hampered the ability of the United States to respond. In that light, Nixon should strike a blow "of such strategic proportions as would force [the enemy] . . . to reassess his entire strategy."[30]

The enemy's estimate of Nixon's political problems and their effect on his ability to wage war appears to have been more than a little accurate. Although well disposed to Abrams' advice, the president was convinced, as he told South Vietnamese Vice President Nguyen Cao Ky in Paris, that the American people were "very difficult" and that few truly understood the war. Given that perception, the sort of increase in the scope and intensity of the conflict recommended by Abrams appeared out of the question. At best the president might have been able to hold the line. At worst, as seemed more and more the case, he would have to deescalate. Secretary Laird put the matter succinctly in the report of his first trip to South Vietnam. To retain the continued support of the American people,

[28] Msg, Wheeler JCS 259 to Abrams, 23 Feb 69, Abrams Papers, CMH; Kissinger, *The White House Years*, p. 245.
[29] Msg, Abrams MAC 4036 to Wheeler et al., 30 Mar 69, Abrams Papers, CMH.
[30] Msg, Abrams MAC 2836 to Wheeler, 5 Mar 69, sub: Retaliatory Actions.

he told Nixon, the United States would have to withdraw between 50,000 and 70,000 men from South Vietnam by the end of the year, even though the South Vietnamese armed forces had failed to improve as much as had been hoped.[31]

A series of reports appearing in the American news media shortly after the beginning of the offensive underscored the president's and Laird's concern. A number of commentators, speculating on whether the Nixon administration would respond to the enemy's attack by bombing North Vietnam, discussed the dilemmas confronting the new administration. Nixon's need to retain unity at home and his obvious desire to move the negotiations ahead, they said, seemed at odds with his responsibility to keep the Communists from concluding that they had a free hand to attack South Vietnam's cities. A few, notably Marvin Kalb of CBS News, pointed out that ambiguities in the American approach had undoubtedly strengthened the enemy's hand. During November, December, and January, Kalb said, General Abrams had ordered American forces to make an all-out effort against the enemy. "So the question . . . is, who is escalating?"[32]

President Nixon allowed the ambiguities to remain, perhaps on grounds that they could only strengthen the American position in the negotiations. At a news conference on 4 March he thus observed that he could never tolerate continued North Vietnamese violations of the understandings. His spokesmen, however, while repeating his remark afterwards in background sessions for the press, added to the uncertainty by commenting that the president was unwilling to take precipitate action without first weighing all of his options.[33]

As the offensive progressed, allegations surfaced in the news media that the Military Assistance Command was attempting to cover up the effects of the enemy's attacks. Charles Mohr of the *New York Times*, for one, charged on 13 March that investigations by reporters in the field indicated that in case after case official spokesmen had understated the intensity of the enemy's operations and the damage that had resulted. "To longtime observers of the Vietnam scene," he said, "it appeared that an effort had been made to deny the enemy a 'psychological victory' by omitting important details about the attacks from official accounts or even by denying them." Mohr cited a number of examples. On two occasions, he said, official spokesmen had denied that the town of Song Be, eighty-seven kilometers north of Saigon, had been overrun by enemy forces. At Cu Chi, thirty kilometers northwest of Saigon, enemy forces had penetrated an American division headquarters, destroying nine large transport

[31] Msg, Paris 1584 to State, 2 Mar 69, Pol 7 US/Nixon file, FAIM/IR; Msg, Wheeler JCS 3218 to Abrams, 14 Mar 69, Abrams Papers, CMH.

[32] Phillip Potter, "Nixon Haunted by War Problem," *Baltimore Sun*, 8 Mar 68; William Beecher, "Vietnam Dilemma," *New York Times*, 8 Mar 68. Kalb's report is quoted in Msg, State 2313 to Paris, 10 Mar 69, sub: Media Report, Pol 27 Viet S file, FAIM/IR.

[33] Official handling of the press can be seen in Msg, State 2291 to Paris, 7 Mar 69, Pol 27 Viet S file, FAIM/IR.

helicopters. Reporters at the scene had viewed the damage, but MACV had never announced it to the press. In Quang Ngai Province in the northern part of South Vietnam, an enemy force had penetrated the provincial capital. Although suffering twenty-five dead and losing a number of large weapons, it had blown up a Canadian hospital and had inflicted twenty casualties on South Vietnamese troops. Despite the damage, Mohr concluded, official communiques had said nothing about the incident and briefers had confirmed it only in response to questions from the press.[34]

Two days later, Jack Walsh of United Press International leveled more charges. In the first wave of attacks on 23 February, he said, the U.S. 9th Infantry Division's air base at Dong Tam in the Mekong Delta, south of Saigon, had received enemy fire. The U.S. command had alleged that neither casualties nor damage had occurred but in fact two fuel tanks containing 50,000 gallons of gasoline had gone up in a fire visible for many miles. Fourteen helicopters at the airstrip had also received major damage. Walsh continued that military spokesmen had reported only five Americans killed in an attack at Dau Tieng, seventy kilometers northwest of Saigon. In fact, reporters had counted more than twenty-one bodies.[35]

The reporters had most of their facts correct, but official spokesmen were hardly attempting a cover-up. They were merely following Abrams' instructions to allow the war to speak for itself. Questioned by the Defense Department, the MACV Office of Information pointed out that according to rules promulgated after the Tet offensive of 1968, damage specifics were never to be released after attacks by indirect fire in order to keep the enemy from confirming the results he had achieved. Instead, the terms *light, moderate,* or *heavy* were to be used. As for the twenty-one bodies Walsh had reported, information officers said that only five men had in fact fallen at Dau Tieng. The other sixteen bodies had arrived later. Dau Tieng was a brigade base camp and a collection point for casualties incurred in a number of different places.[36]

Bombing Begins in Cambodia

Despite the ambiguities in the American position, as the offensive continued it became clear that Nixon was becoming increasingly impatient with the enemy's probing. Ten days after his 4 March news conference, at a second session with reporters, he observed that American casu-

[34] Charles Mohr, "Field Checks in Vietnam Show Allies Understated Foe's Gains," *New York Times*, 13 Mar 69.

[35] Jack Walsh, "Communist Offensive Not a 'Grade A Fiasco' After All," UPI news dispatch, 15 Mar 69, DDI Misc. Unreliable News Stories file.

[36] MFR, 15 Mar 69, sub: Press Release, and MFR, C. H. Freudenthal, Lt Col, USAF, PADO, 15 Mar 69, both in DDI Misc. Unreliable News Stories file.

alties were still running at between three and four hundred per week. Recalling the comment he had made on the fourth that he would never tolerate continued North Vietnamese violations of the understanding, he added darkly that "We have issued a warning. I will not warn again." Yet rather than inaugurate the combined ground and air attacks Abrams had recommended, he remained interested in bombing the enemy's Cambodian sanctuaries, a move that was easy to defend publicly because it countered an obvious and immediate threat to American forces.[37]

Nixon decided to act on 15 March, after Communist forces fired five rockets into Saigon, a clear violation of the understandings. In order to give the operation he had in mind the lowest possible profile, he instructed the secretaries of state and defense to tell their subordinates to make "absolutely no comment."[38] Then he authorized General Wheeler to notify Abrams to begin planning for a B–52 strike on COSVN's headquarters in Cambodia. Although security was to be stringent and Abrams was to inform President Thieu only an hour before the strike that an attack on an "important" enemy target was about to commence, there was to be no attempt to conceal the escalation behind a cover strike in South Vietnam, as had been the case for some earlier B–52 operations in Laos. If the press inquired, the response was to be a flat "no comment."[39]

Code-named BREAKFAST, the raid occurred during the early morning hours of 18 March. Although it produced some seventy-three secondary explosions, many of them very large, the enemy said nothing about it in public, perhaps to draw as little attention as possible to his own use of Cambodian territory. Prince Sihanouk was only slightly more forthcoming. At a 28 March news conference, after failing to mention the attack, he attempted to emphasize his own noninvolvement by avowing that "no chief of state in the world placed in the same position I am in would agree to let foreign aircraft bomb his own country." Three months later, on 2 July, he resumed formal diplomatic relations with the United States.[40]

Lacking notification from either North Vietnam or Cambodia that an attack had occurred, the American news media also failed to mark the event. Instead, on 25 March, much to the chagrin of a Nixon administration that had long feared a leak, especially from the State Department, United Press International published a report by Jack Walsh in Saigon recounting Abrams' original request to bomb the Cambodian sanctuaries. Based on the testimony of so-called informed American sources, the story received page 1 treatment in the *Washington Star* under a head-

[37] Kissinger, *The White House Years*, pp. 244–45.

[38] Memo, Nixon for Secretaries of State and Defense, 16 Mar 69, sub: March 16 Rocket Attack on Saigon, Pol 27 Viet S file, FAIM/IR.

[39] Msg, Wheeler JCS 3287 to Abrams, 17 Mar 69, and Msg, Wheeler JCS 3297 to Abrams, 17 Mar 69, both in Abrams Papers, CMH.

[40] "Press Conference with Prince Sihanouk," Phnom Penh Domestic News Service, 29 Mar 69, DDI Cambodia 69–70 file.

line that announced "Military Asks To Hit in Cambodia; Presses Nixon To Knock Out Red Sanctuary; Points to Hints by Sihanouk That He Won't Object."[41]

Both the State and Defense Departments refused to comment, with State denying any knowledge of a possible escalation of the war. Meanwhile, General Wheeler cabled Abrams to note that "We all needed this exercise like a hole in the head. I presume you are looking into the possible source of the reporter's information." Abrams responded that the article had been "a disaster bearing directly on the functioning of this command." He was attempting, "with the utmost discretion," to find the source of the leak. "In this regard," he stressed, "I would rather not know than . . . let the press know I'm looking into it."[42]

Although concerned lest the leak further restrict American options, Abrams was convinced that more strikes on the sanctuaries would be of great value. He had already begun a survey to identify future targets in the area, he told Wheeler, adding that he would limit the number of people involved to a very small group of officers and would keep all their papers under the strictest control. Aware that concern was rising in Washington about the Military Assistance Command's ability to keep anything secret, he added that, "I know I can keep this secure. In this manner I hope to edge up on the problem."[43]

President Nixon also saw the value of further attacks. In a conversation with Abrams' deputy, General Goodpaster, on assignment in Washington to assist the new administration on war-related matters, Nixon observed that he would never permit leaks such as the one Walsh had published to control his policies. He was inclined, he continued, to favor more strikes on the sanctuaries, provided the operations were selected and timed carefully.[44]

The Nixon administration took the Walsh article in stride but more jolts followed within the week. On 1 April a UPI report by correspondent David Lamb quoted the 3d Marine Division Commander at Da Nang, Maj. Gen. Raymond Davis, to the effect that "It makes no sense to watch 400 trucks a day moving through Laos with ammunition to kill Americans. . . . The quickest way to shorten this war is to destroy these sanctuaries." Two days later, a report by UPI correspondent Robert Kaylor, citing "military sources," announced that throughout the previous year the U.S. Special Forces, popularly known as the Green Berets, had conducted clandestine forays into Laos and Cambodia. Kaylor's article outlined the command structure controlling the operations and noted that sources in Cambodia had confirmed that Sihanouk had no objection to the penetration of

---

[41] The article and headline are contained in Msg, Wheeler JCS 3659 to Abrams, 25 Mar 69, Abrams Papers, CMH.

[42] Msg, Wheeler JCS 3659 to Abrams, 25 Mar 69; Msg, Abrams MAC 3850 to Wheeler, 26 Mar 69, Abrams Papers, CMH.

[43] Msg, Abrams MAC 3850 to Wheeler, 26 Mar 69.

[44] Msg, Goodpaster JCS 3692 to Abrams, 26 Mar 69, Abrams Papers, CMH.

Cambodia as long as it was done in secret. A second UPI article by Walter Whitehead repeated Kaylor's charges and added that Sihanouk had given tacit approval for the operations. Confusing the situation, a story by Reuters appearing at the same time alleged that the Cambodian government was aware of the attacks and would shortly issue a public protest.[45]

"We are seriously concerned about this cluster of leaks and statements," the State Department cabled Ambassador Bunker, because they "complicate our relations with Laos and Cambodia, cause embarrassment to our delegation in Paris, give propaganda advantage to the enemy, and do absolutely nothing to advance the Allied cause in Vietnam."[46] General Wheeler was also deeply disturbed. The situation was extremely dangerous, he told Abrams. Some of the stories indicated that, besides having well-placed sources in Washington, United Press International might well have managed to penetrate the Military Assistance Command's command structure. He advised Abrams to proceed with a thorough but again discreet investigation.[47]

In the case of General Davis' statement, the command discovered that Lamb had broken faith with the general by publishing a highly simplified version of a background interview never intended for public release. The origin of the other stories was more difficult to determine. The pressure of newsmen in forward areas of the war and the large number of American military and civilian personnel having knowledge of the leaked information made the identities of sources impossible to pinpoint. In the end, Abrams had to content himself with yet another message to his subordinate commanders. Although he was unwilling to suggest that members of his command cut themselves off from the press, he said, as the new administration developed and refined its policies, all would have to refrain from saying anything, even on background, that might be misconstrued as counter to national policy.[48]

On the side, in a separate message, Abrams instructed the teams penetrating Cambodia to avoid killing Cambodian citizens if at all possible, unless the teams' own safety required it. The reason, he said, was that there might be opportunities for "large stakes" in the near future and he had little desire to have those possibilities jeopardized by the Cambodian government's hostility.[49]

With the news media devoting much of its attention to rising speculation that U.S. units would shortly begin departing from South Vietnam,

---

[45] Msg, Wheeler JCS 3787 to Abrams, 27 Mar 69. The articles are excerpted in Msg, Wheeler JCS 4067 to Abrams, 3 Apr 69. Both in Abrams Papers, CMH.

[46] Msg, State 2480 to Saigon, 5 Apr 69, Pol 27 Viet S file, FAIM/IR.

[47] Msg, Wheeler JCS 4067 to Abrams, 3 Apr 69.

[48] Msg, Corcoran NHT 1089 to Abrams, 4 Apr 69, Abrams Papers, CMH; Msg, Saigon 6789 to State, 10 Apr 69, sub: Press Leaks, Pol 27 Viet S file, FAIM/IR; Msg, Abrams MAC 4251 to All Commanders, 4 Apr 69, sub: Public Affairs Guidance and National Policy, Abrams Papers, CMH.

[49] Msg, Abrams MAC 4334 to All Commanders, 6 Apr 69, sub: Attention to Cambodian Citizens, Abrams Papers, CMH.

little stir developed over Kaylor's revelation about the operations of the U.S. Special Forces in Laos and Cambodia. Most reporters in Saigon had long known—or assumed—that the Green Berets were so occupied.[50]

That lack of publicity, together with Sihanouk's reticence, opened the way for more B–52 strikes on the sanctuaries. Between April and August 1969 they occurred intermittently, always with approval from the White House and always, as distinct from the first attack, with a simultaneous cover strike in South Vietnam to throw the press off track. Having proved that the Military Assistance Command could maintain security, Abrams then received general authority to conduct the raids. After that, they became an almost regular feature of the war. To contain leaks, knowledge of the attacks was restricted to the smallest possible number of people and all correspondence on the subject went by backchannel message, a closely held system of private communications used by senior commanders. Code-named MENU, the bombing of Cambodia lasted until April 1970, when overt strikes commenced in support of U.S. and South Vietnamese troops participating in the so-called incursion into Cambodia. In all, the U.S. Air Force flew more than 3,600 sorties into Cambodia.[51]

The press guidance accompanying the strikes was also designed to camouflage the attacks. When a raid occurred, a routine press release referring only to locations in South Vietnam was to state that "B–52 strikes early this morning (or late last night) bombed targets containing enemy activity, base camps, and bunker and tunnel complexes 30 kilometers west of Dak To or 45 kilometers northeast of Tay Ninh City, as appropriate." Official spokesmen were then to list the cover strikes along with the one in question so that it would merge unobtrusively into the mass. If newsmen asked whether the strike had occurred in Cambodia, briefers were to confirm that routine operations sometimes struck near the Cambodian border but that there were no further details. If the press persisted, the spokesman was neither to confirm nor deny but to say that the matter was under investigation. Only if Cambodians protested would the U.S. government acknowledge that a strike had occurred. Then it would apologize and offer compensation.[52] On 27 April, apparently to reduce the visibility of B–52 strikes in general, the briefers for the Military Assistance Command ended their practice of releasing bomb damage assessments for the B–52 strikes they announced.[53]

The Defense Department's public affairs officers disagreed with the guidance they had received. Avowing that the secrecy surrounding the bombing had been designed to protect the administration from a public backlash if the attacks became known, Henkin's deputy, Jerry Friedheim,

[50] Memo, Braestrup for the author, 9 Oct 91, CMH files.

[51] U.S. Congress, Senate, Committee on Armed Services, *Bombing in Cambodia, Hearings, Jul–Aug 73*, 93d Cong., 1st sess., p. 131.

[52] Msg, Wheeler JCS 4818 to McCain et al., 20 Apr 69, sub: Operations BREAKFAST BRAVO, BREAKFAST COCO, and LUNCH, Abrams Papers, CMH.

[53] J. D. Coleman, *Incursion* (New York: St. Martin's Press, 1992), pp. 122–25.

Colonel Hill

observed later that it was all an unnecessary waste of time. If the operations had been handled in a forthright manner, he said, the public would have sided with the president. The only justification required would have been a statement that the bombing was essential to preserve the lives of American troops and to pave the way for safe continuation of U.S. withdrawals. As it was, Friedheim said, Henry Kissinger's view and that of the White House staff prevailed. The Defense Department was overruled.[54]

As was often the case, however, despite all the precautions, the press learned of the raids almost as soon as they began. On 9 May, crediting "Nixon administration sources," the *New York Times* published a detailed account of the strikes by correspondent William Beecher. Other stories in the same vein followed in the *Wall Street Journal*, the *Washington Post*, and *Newsweek*. Confronted by the allegation that the United States had been bombing enemy base camps and supply dumps in Cambodia, the Military Assistance Command's spokesmen followed instructions, volunteering that B–52s had struck areas adjacent to the Cambodian border. When the questions persisted but the Cambodian government once more remained silent, Assistant Secretary Henkin put an end to the discussion by cleverly dismissing Beecher's allegations without telling an outright lie. "This is a speculative story," he told newsmen, "and as such I have no comments on it." Although reporters might have construed Henkin's comment as an affirmation that something was going on, they never pursued the matter. Galled by the leak nevertheless, President Nixon shortly thereafter inaugurated wiretaps on the telephones of some officials he suspected of having informed the press.[55]

At the end of March 1969, just as the bombing was beginning, Col. L. Gordon Hill replaced General Sidle as Chief of the MACV Office of Information. A highly skilled public affairs officer who had served as the

[54] Interv, author with Friedheim, 3 Oct 86.

[55] Msg, Lt Gen Meyer, J–3 (Assistant Chief of Staff for Operations), Office of the Joint Chiefs of Staff (OJCS), JCS/J–3 5706 to Abrams, 9 May 69, Abrams Papers, CMH; [AP], Cambodia Bombing 270, 9 May 69, DDI Unreliable News Stories file; William Beecher, "Raids in Cambodia by U.S. Unprotested," *New York Times*, 9 May 69; Interv, author with Friedheim, 3 Oct 86.

chief of public affairs for the U.S. Army, Europe, Hill had spent a year as special assistant for Southeast Asia at the Office of the Assistant Secretary of Defense for Public Affairs. Arriving in Saigon at a turning point in the war, he faced circumstances far different from the ones that had prevailed during his predecessor's watch. With military institutions hardening to the press and turning inward upon themselves, official spokesmen were doing less than ever before either to sell the war to the American public and Congress or to ensure that the news media had all the information they needed to construct a rounded picture of events.

Meanwhile, even as Washington agencies took a larger hand in explaining the war, the government of the United States seemed increasingly divided against itself. For if Laird and the Defense Department were preoccupied with preserving the credibility of the armed forces by advocating public affairs policies in Laos and elsewhere that allowed all dimensions of the war to speak for themselves, the White House, as with the secret bombing of Cambodia, appeared much less open and much more willing to break rules when political expediency so required.

4

Contradictions

The responses to National Security Study Memorandum 1 that reached the White House during March 1969, just prior to the bombing of Cambodia, revealed startling disagreements among the agencies responsible for the war. The Joint Chiefs of Staff; the Office of the Commander in Chief, Pacific; the Military Assistance Command, Vietnam; and the U.S. embassy in Saigon were all hopeful. Although refusing to forecast victory, they asserted that the South Vietnamese were fighting better than ever before and that the enemy had responded to the pressure by assuming a low profile on the battlefield. The Department of Defense, the Central Intelligence Agency, and, to a lesser extent, the State Department were much more pessimistic. The efforts of the United States and South Vietnam, they said, had at best prolonged a stalemate. The enemy was so far from defeat that a compromise settlement appeared the only feasible outcome for the war.[1]

Although they differed, the two sets of estimates corresponded on a number of points. Both agreed that the South Vietnamese government and armed forces would be unable for the foreseeable future to stand alone against both the Viet Cong and the North Vietnamese. There was also some doubt that the South Vietnamese government would survive a peaceful election if Communist candidates participated. As for the enemy, neither set of estimates suggested that his objectives had changed or that he lacked the strength to pursue them with vigor. Controlling the casualty rates of both sides, he had gone to Paris for political and strategic reasons—to cut costs and to pursue his aims through negotiation—rather than because he faced defeat on the battlefield. Whatever the outcome of those negotiations, it seemed apparent that Hanoi would continue to use its Communist allies for economic and logistical support but would pursue its own ends, independent of both Moscow and Peking.

[1] Unless otherwise indicated, this section is based on MFR, sub: Summary of Responses to NSSM 1, attachment to Memo, Henry A. Kissinger for Members of the National Security Council Review Group, 14 Mar 69, sub: NSSM 1 Vietnam Questions, DepCORDS Papers, CMH.

A memorandum Nixon read shortly after taking office, by an unidentified but knowledgeable expert on South Vietnam, underscored the dilemmas facing the United States. Titling the piece "Vietnam Has the Resources But Lacks the Motivation To Win," the document's author asserted that South Vietnam's problems were so enormous the country could never survive if the United States withdrew too quickly from the war. Major political and social reforms were imperative—to attract and motivate not only the uncommitted but also those who already served in the military—but the nation's leadership seemed as fragmented and corrupt as ever. As a result, while rank-and-file anti-Communists had come to question whether their sacrifices over the years had achieved much benefit, a large part of the nation's ruling faction fought mainly to retain the system of privileges for itself that war had brought. Those individuals, whether from the business, military, or intellectual classes, viewed the conflict as a means to achieve the sort of modernization in South Vietnam that would bring them and their relatives great wealth. They wanted it to continue. "Somewhat like the Communists," they considered the loss of life that resulted unimportant because they felt no obligation toward those of their countrymen who would pay the price. Although the Tet offensive and its aftermath may have convinced some that at least a few social and political reforms would be necessary if the country was to survive, there was little guarantee at that late date that even the most stringent measures would have much immediate effect. Indeed, since a premature withdrawal of American forces would be disastrous and only time and additional effort appeared to offer much hope, the United States had few choices. To avoid exact timetables and to link withdrawals to the progress of political and social reforms, it would have to continue to ensure the integrity of South Vietnam until that nation could stand on its own.[2]

The American Dilemma

Nixon clearly understood the problem that confronted him, as did his national security adviser, Henry Kissinger. He pushed for the sort of reforms that would give South Vietnam a chance at survival, but he also had little choice but to weigh that nation's genuine weakness against both the larger goals he wanted his administration to achieve and the constraints on time that bore so heavily upon Laird.

---

[2] The spelling and syntax of the document indicate that its author spoke and wrote English as a second language. He may therefore have been a South Vietnamese with close ties to the United States. The document is the sole resident of a folder in President Nixon's personal files labeled February 1969. See Unsigned Memo, n.d. [Feb 69], sub: Vietnam Has the Resources But Lacks the Motivation To Win, President's Personal files, box 1, Memos, February 1969, Nixon Papers.

In that sense, although his maximum goal was the survival of South Vietnam, Nixon had no choice but to adopt a minimum fall back position that took into account the clear possibility the country might not endure. Since a precipitous withdrawal—tantamount to defeat—would jeopardize his desire to shape a new foreign policy by tempting America to swing away from post–World War II predominance toward isolationism, he believed he had to create as long an interval as possible between the moment when American forces would depart and the final resolution of the conflict.

Kissinger summarized the approach in a later memorandum. "We recognized from the beginning," he wrote,

the uncertainty that the South Vietnamese could be sufficiently strengthened to stand on their own within the time span that domestic opposition to American involvement would allow. Therefore a negotiated settlement has always been preferable. Rather than run the risk of South Vietnam crumbling around our remaining forces, a peace settlement would end the war with an act of policy and leave the future of South Vietnam to the historical process. We could heal the wounds in this country as our men left peace behind on the battlefield and a healthy interval for South Vietnam's fate to unfold.[3]

Nixon's initial overtures to Hanoi and Moscow underscored the severity of the problem that confronted him. As early as 20 December 1968, a month before taking office, the president-elect had informed Hanoi that he was prepared to undertake serious negotiations based on the self-respect and sense of honor of all parties. The only response he received was a restatement by North Vietnam of a demand that the United States withdraw its forces from South Vietnam and remove the "Thieu-Ky-Huong clique" prior to the start of substantive bargaining. Undeterred by either that response or the knowledge that Hanoi formulated its policies without reference to the wishes of its allies, Nixon tried again after his inauguration. On 14 April 1969, in the belief that the North Vietnamese had little incentive to act, he approached the Soviet Union with an offer that linked the opening of strategic arms limitation talks to an overall settlement of the war. The theory behind the move seemed compelling: tie the conclusion of the war so strongly to Soviet interests that the Soviet Union would take the lead in pressing North Vietnam to make peace. In fact, they may never have approached the North Vietnamese. The only response they made came eight months later, when the Soviet Ambassador to the United States, Anatoly Dobrynin, commented in passing during a conversation with Kissinger that Hanoi refused to talk unless the United States first agreed to a coalition government in South Vietnam.[4]

---

[3] Concern for buying time preoccupied the Nixon administration throughout the war. Kissinger's statement is the clearest expression of that concern yet to come to light. See Draft Memo, Kissinger for the President, n.d. [Sep 71], sub: Vietnam, NSC files, A. M. Haig Special file, box 1013, Gen. Haig's Trip to Vietnam, Sep 71 [1 of 2], Nixon Papers.

[4] Kissinger, *The White House Years*, pp. 260–69.

With the enemy refusing to give Nixon the sort of quick settlement that the president deemed necessary to save face for the United States, an effort to buy time became imperative. Indeed, within weeks of the inauguration, the pressure Laird had foreseen for some sort of accommodation began to build within the United States. Commentators on all sides of the American political spectrum assumed that the president intended to put a swift end to American involvement in the conflict, and their disappointment built as time passed and nothing seemed to happen. For example, as early as 20 March Tom Wicker of the *New York Times* observed that Nixon's first month in office had been singularly unproductive as far as South Vietnam was concerned. "It is almost as if nothing had happened—no election had been held last year, no change of administrations had taken place, no profound public decision to take this country out of a dispiriting and divisive war that can neither be won nor justified. . . . Where are the fresh ideas and the new start—let alone any 'plan' to end the war?"[5]

Syndicated columnists Rowland Evans and Robert Novak responded by attempting to justify the president's silence with an observation that the administration could hardly state its true intentions in public without giving the enemy an advantage in the negotiations. In fact, they said, the president had adopted "an antiwar strategy" that would shortly resolve itself into substantial troop withdrawals. Picking up that theme, other reporters suggested that the administration would redeploy 50,000 men by the end of the year and 200,000 by November 1970. Speculation also appeared in the press on whether the president might abandon the Manila Communique of October 1966 in which President Johnson had pledged that U.S. forces would withdraw from South Vietnam only when the enemy reduced the level of violence, ceased infiltration, and retired to the north. The reports, some of them well founded, so thoroughly agitated the South Vietnamese that they began to doubt U.S. assurances. "You explain these matters to us and we accept what you say," President Thieu's foreign minister thus told U.S. Deputy Ambassador Samuel D. Berger on 11 April, "but our people do not understand."[6]

The Effort To Curtail American Casualties

The mounting tension affected the U.S. Military Assistance Command in South Vietnam. On 3 April General Wheeler told Abrams that the subject of U.S. casualties had become an enormous concern in

---

[5] Tom Wicker, "In the Nation: The Old Merry-Go-Round," *New York Times*, 20 Mar 69.

[6] Rowland Evans and Robert Novak, "Secret Laird Plan Will Allow Early Troop Pullout," *Washington Post*, 24 Mar 69. Quote from Msg, Saigon 6915 to State, 11 Apr 69, Pol 27 Viet S file, FAIM/IR.

the United States. It "is being thrown at me at every juncture," he said, "in the press, by the Secretary of Defense, at the White House, and on the Hill." He was concerned, he said, that if the pressure continued the Nixon administration might have little choice but to adopt a defensive posture in South Vietnam or seek a settlement of the war detrimental to U.S. objectives. To cut off those possibilities, Abrams had to do more to alert the press to the true burdens borne by the South Vietnamese, especially to the fact that casualties among South Vietnamese troops exceeded those of the United States by some 50 percent. In addition, there would have to be an examination of better ways to "get more mileage" out of the South Vietnamese armed forces.[7] Ambassador Bunker put the matter bluntly to Thieu. "There is no question but that as our casualties rise the Communists have an effect on American opinion," he said. "Our people show no interest in enemy casualties but they are very sensitive to ours. President Nixon regards this as one of his most difficult problems."[8]

The enemy, for his part, recognized that the situation developing in the United States worked to his advantage. Beset, by American estimate, with a casualty rate far in excess of 3,000 men per week and with the defection of some 2,600 civilian and military personnel per month, he began to highlight goals in his pronouncements to his troops that were as much political as military. By April 1969 intelligence intercepts, captured enemy documents, and public statements by North Vietnamese leaders all indicated that the Communists intended to exploit the weaknesses they perceived in the American position. Playing upon what they termed "the contradictions in the enemy camp"—American disenchantment with the war, U.S. sensitivity to further American casualties, and South Vietnam's many infirmities—they urged their people to greater levels of sacrifice and exertion. In that way, they sought to tire the American public and to leave Nixon with little choice but to pressure the Thieu regime to make concessions to North Vietnamese demands. When Thieu did that, enemy theorists reasoned, he would so discredit himself in the eyes of his people that the various factions opposing him in South Vietnam would riot in the streets. That, in turn, would prompt more American withdrawals and lead, in the end, to the sort of coalition government in South Vietnam that Communists could control.[9]

Pursuing those goals between January and June 1969, the enemy avoided large-scale ground assaults and conducted artillery, rocket, and sapper attacks in hopes of killing as many Americans as possible while losing no more of his own men than necessary. As a result, where in all of 1968 he had launched only 215 attacks against American installations while concentrating 494 on the South Vietnamese, in the first six months

[7] Msg, Wheeler JCS 4092 to Abrams, 3 Apr 69, Abrams Papers, CMH.
[8] Msg, Saigon 7462 to State, 18 Apr 69, Pol 27 Viet S file, FAIM/IR.
[9] Msg, Abrams MAC 4689 to All Commanders, 13 Apr 69, sub: Hanoi's Strategy, Abrams Papers, CMH.

TABLE 1—ATTACKS UPON ALLIED INSTALLATIONS

Force	1967	1968	Jan–Jun 1969
U.S.	102	215	303
RVN.	469	494	424

of 1969 he nearly doubled his assaults on South Vietnamese installations while tripling the rate of those against Americans. *(Table 1)*[10]

Aware of the enemy's intentions, General Abrams took up the subject at a MACV Commanders Conference on 5 April 1969. After an extensive intelligence briefing, he instructed his generals to continue to put as much pressure as possible on Communist forces but to do so in the awareness that needless American casualties were detrimental.[11] Although the preservation of American lives had always been an important preoccupation of field commanders, Abrams' reemphasis gave the subject even more weight, a fact readily apparent in a 6 April cable from the Commanding General of I Field Force, Vietnam, Lt. Gen. Charles A. Corcoran. Acknowledging that the U.S. 4th Infantry Division had suffered the most U.S. casualties in the II Corps Tactical Zone while attaining the poorest kill ratio, 6.7 enemy dead to 1 American between 22 February and 4 April 1969, Corcoran told Abrams that "We will comply with your guidance . . . at the Commanders' Conference . . . to accomplish our assigned mission with minimum U.S. casualties."[12]

Tentative Reductions Begin

While General Abrams attempted to keep U.S. casualties within limits, the Nixon administration moved to put the increasingly strained finances of the United States in order by instructing the Defense Department to cut its budget by $1 billion in 1970. As a result, Secretary of Defense Laird announced on 1 April that there would be a reduction of U.S. operational capabilities in South Vietnam, including a decrease in B–52 sorties from 1,800 to 1,600 per month. The U.S. Air Force meanwhile began weighing a decrease in the number of squadrons serving in South Vietnam, the Navy proposed cutbacks in destroyer patrols along the

[10] Fact Sheet, Office of the Assistant Secretary of Defense for Systems Analysis (OASD SA), 10 Oct 69, sub: Indicators of Enemy Activity in SVN, folder 127, Papers of Thomas Thayer, CMH.

[11] Msg, Abrams MAC 4689 to All Commanders, 13 Apr 69, sub: Hanoi Strategy.

[12] Msg, Lt Gen Charles A. Corcoran NHT 589 to Abrams, 6 Apr 69, Abrams Papers, CMH.

country's coast, and the Army began preparations to reduce by 2 percent its force of South Vietnamese civilian employees. General Abrams was stunned. Objecting that he saw nothing in the situation to warrant unilateral reductions in U.S. combat power, he told General Wheeler that he wanted only "to be consulted and given a chance as they, the services, cut and run."[13] Wheeler responded that the reductions had come from the White House at the prompting of the Treasury Department. They were, he said, part of a government-wide austerity program designed to cut inflation and to cool the overheated American economy.[14]

By early April, the Nixon administration was also nearing a decision on U.S. troop withdrawals. At a meeting with South Vietnamese Vice President Nguyen Cao Ky, Secretary of State William P. Rogers attempted to win South Vietnamese acceptance by putting the move in the best possible light. Recalling the years of talk about how the South Vietnamese would shortly begin taking responsibility for fighting the war, Rogers observed that, in fact, little progress had thus far occurred. Whatever the mistakes of the past, he continued, the United States and South Vietnam had to show that South Vietnam was indeed taking charge and releasing Americans to return home. Once withdrawals commenced, he said, the administration could promote them in the news media to demonstrate the concrete results President Nixon's policies had achieved.[15]

The Joint Chiefs of Staff greeted the prospect of troop withdrawals with misgivings. On 28 March General Wheeler sent a draft paper to Abrams on the inadvisability of abandoning an offensive strategy in South Vietnam. The point of the study was that the enemy inflicted the greatest number of casualties on American forces when conducting a hit-and-run, harassing sort of war of the kind that would certainly occur if the United States fell into a defensive role. If that happened, the effect on the morale of U.S. fighting men would be considerable. Although U.S. forces remained confident that they could defeat the enemy anywhere, they would rapidly lose heart if they found themselves the victims of enemy attack without the means to strike back aggressively.[16]

American commanders in the field were also troubled. When visiting newsmen passed along rumors that the U.S. 9th Infantry Division would be among the first to go, the division's commander, Maj. Gen. Julian Ewell, contacted Abrams to warn that the South Vietnamese were as yet unready to take control of the areas in the Mekong Delta that his units patrolled. Referring to a commonly held assumption that South

---

[13] Msg, Abrams MAC 4036 to Wheeler et al., 30 Mar 69, Abrams Papers, CMH.

[14] Msg, Wheeler JCS 3939 to McCain, Abrams, 1 Apr 69, Abrams Papers, CMH. Also see Transcript, 1 Apr 69, sub: Laird Interview With the Press, DDI B–52 Policy file.

[15] MFR, 3 Apr 69, sub: Conversation Between Vice President Nguyen Cao Ky, Ambassador Bui Diem, Secretary of State William P. Rogers, et al., Embassy of South Vietnam, Washington, D.C., Pol 27 Viet S file, FAIM/IR.

[16] Msg, Wheeler JCS 3805 to McCain, Abrams, 28 Mar 69, Abrams Papers, CMH.

Vietnamese forces had made an accommodation with the enemy in the region, Ewell underscored his concern by noting that if such an arrangement existed it was quite simple. "The GVN holds the towns, the VC hold the people, and the GVN moves anywhere it wishes in battalion strength and even then gets racked up every few months. Nothing stands still around here, the GVN is either gaining or losing."[17]

Military reservations notwithstanding, as Laird had perceived, political considerations made withdrawals of some sort imperative to the Nixon administration. On 17 April the Joint Chiefs of Staff notified Abrams that the first departure of an American unit would probably occur on 1 July or shortly thereafter. Abrams was astounded. Recognizing that the withdrawals in view represented the virtual abandonment of American goals in South Vietnam, he responded tactfully but emphatically that "I have listened carefully to Ambassador Bunker and Goodpaster report on their meetings in Washington, and while I appreciated from this the pressures for U.S. troop reductions and Vietnamizing the war my impression was that it would be reasonably deliberate so that U.S. objectives here would have a reasonable chance of attainment." The projected date for the initial withdrawals, he said, implied "an acceleration of troop reductions not previously contemplated here in the light of the enemy situation and the anticipated capabilities of the Vietnamese. I feel that the thrust of [that acceleration] . . . also implies a change of mission for MACV." Abrams added that he needed a decision on any particular withdrawal at least forty-five days in advance. The public announcement would have to come shortly thereafter, he said, because the press would quickly deduce from the preparations that departures were imminent and begin to speculate. The 1 July date would therefore require an announcement on 15 May, less than one month away. Before that, coordination would have to begin with the South Vietnamese, who had yet to be informed of MACV's specific plan for troop withdrawals and had yet to come to grips with "the realities of what they must do."[18]

Abrams' comment was relatively mild, but other officers also had their doubts. As General Westmoreland observed in an interview after the war, the drawdown was a politically motivated mechanism to remove American forces from South Vietnam by the end of Nixon's first term in office, whatever the ability of the South Vietnamese to take over on the battlefield. "I knew it was not going to work," he said, "because it was just too arbitrary."[19]

If politics drove the decision, Abrams' objections nevertheless sparked considerable discussion in official circles, with attention focusing on the earliest feasible date for an announcement. On 7 May, with the Military Assistance Command planning for at most a 50,000-man reduction dur-

[17] Msg, Ewell MHU 292 to Abrams, 29 Mar 69, Abrams Papers, CMH.
[18] Msg, Abrams MAC 4967 to Wheeler, 19 Apr 69, referencing DJS/JCS 4690, 17 Apr 69, Abrams Papers, CMH.
[19] Interv, CMH staff with General Westmoreland, 6 Dec 89, pp. 4–9, CMH files.

84

ing 1969, the Joint Chiefs informed Abrams that Secretary Laird believed an announcement might come sooner than anticipated and involve withdrawals larger than expected because of political considerations. By 16 May announcement dates in early June were under consideration with Abrams holding out for 1 July because the enemy appeared to be planning a major offensive in the I Corps Tactical Zone. Laird objected that the president would probably find that date unacceptable because of mounting criticism on Capitol Hill, but General Wheeler told Abrams confidentially that he believed most of the pressure for early reductions was coming from Laird himself. Abrams would have to "call the shots" as he saw them, Wheeler said, but he ought to be aware that he might be overruled.[20]

The Battle of Hamburger Hill

Three days after Wheeler made his comment, the news broke that the U.S. 101st Airborne Division (Airmobile) had engaged a major enemy force at Dong Ap Bia, a small mountain located about two kilometers from Laos near the A Shau Valley. The news stories that followed added to the pressure for withdrawals by turning all eyes once more to the question of American casualties. Code-named Operation APACHE SNOW, the action at Dong Ap Bia (Hill 937) became known almost immediately as the Battle of Hamburger Hill.

APACHE SNOW actually began on 10 May, after intelligence revealed that the enemy appeared to be preparing for an attack on Hue by developing a chain of carefully concealed and fortified positions along routes leading toward the city from the A Shau Valley. When probes into the region established that the *29th North Vietnamese Regiment* had fortified Dong Ap Bia, American commanders decided to attack. During the battle that developed over the next nine days, U.S. air strikes and artillery expended more than 3.5 million pounds of munitions on the mountain. American and South Vietnamese troops meanwhile made some twelve combat assaults, losing, according to official tallies at the time, 56 Americans and 5 South Vietnamese killed in action. Estimates put the enemy's losses at 630 men.[21]

[20] Msg, General John McConnell, Assistant to the Chairman, Joint Chiefs of Staff (ACJCS), JCS 3630, to Abrams, 7 May 69; Msg, McCain to McConnell, 8 May 69; and Msg, Wheeler JCS 5988 to McCain, Abrams, 16 May 69. All in Abrams Papers, CMH.

[21] Combat After Action Report (AAR), The Battle of Dong Ap Bia, reprinted in U.S. Congress, Senate, *Congressional Record*, 29 December 1970, p. S.21403. Also see Msg, Lt Gen Stilwell, CG, XXIV Corps, PHB 936 to Abrams, 21 May 69, Abrams Papers, CMH. The casualty figures are from official reports of the time. Samuel Zaffiri's well researched *Hamburger Hill, May 11–20, 1969*, puts the numbers at 70 Americans dead and 372 wounded. See Samuel Zaffiri, *Hamburger Hill, May 11–20, 1969* (San Francisco: Presidio Press, 1988), p. 272.

Troops charge at Hamburger Hill.

Early news reports of the battle were bland, apparently the product of briefings in Saigon. The interest of the press increased on 16 May, when the fighting reached its peak and an increasing number of reporters arrived at Dong Ap Bia to cover the story. Public affairs officers provided what perspective they could by briefing the reporters on the details of the operation and by making commanders available for interviews.

The reports that followed described the devastation on Dong Ap Bia. The mountain was "almost bare," according to AP reporter Jay Sharbutt, "its heavy jungle cover blasted apart by artillery, rockets, bombs, and napalm," and the anger and frustration of the men fighting to gain the top were unmistakable. "After all these air and artillery strikes," one soldier told Sharbutt, "those gooks are still in there fighting. All of us are wondering why [U.S. forces] . . . can't just pull back and B–52 that hill." Another soldier, badly wounded, told CBS News correspondent Richard Threlkeld that the hill was "absolute suicide." As fighting continued, the term *Hamburger Hill* seemed to appear out of nowhere, the product of some soldier's cynicism or of a reporter's morbid wit.[22]

Senator Edward M. Kennedy of Massachusetts drew national attention to the battle on 20 May. Denouncing President Nixon's policies on Vietnam as "counter to our stated goals and intentions in Paris," Kennedy condemned the Army's tactics at Dong Ap Bia. It was, he said, "senseless and

[22] Jay Sharbutt, "Americans Stained with Blood, Sweat, and Mud—10th Assault on Hill Fails," *Washington Star*, 19 May 69; Richard Threlkeld, CBS Evening News, 23 May 69, *Radio-TV-Defense Dialog*.

Medics assist a wounded paratrooper during the Battle of Hamburger Hill.

irresponsible to continue to send our young men to their deaths to capture hills and positions that have no relation to ending the conflict." American lives were being wasted, he added, merely to preserve military pride.[23]

Kennedy's comments won immediate support from newspapers such as the *Baltimore Sun*, the *New York Post*, the *Boston Globe*, and the *St. Louis Post-Dispatch*, which stressed in their editorials the need to stop the fighting. Other papers—the *Wall Street Journal*, the *New York Times*, and the Hearst syndicate—questioned Kennedy's criticism of military tactics but agreed nonetheless that it was time to lower the level of violence in South Vietnam.[24]

Invoking a policy that kept the Military Assistance Command's spokesmen from commenting on statements by members of Congress, the MACV Office of Information refused to rebut Kennedy directly. It nevertheless made the commander of the operation, Maj. Gen. Melvin Zais, available for questioning. Zais defended his tactics forcefully, observing that the enemy knew how much damage to expect from B–52s and had built bunkers at Dong Ap Bia deep enough to withstand the heaviest air strike. American troops, he said, suffered the most casualties when they waited for the enemy to attack instead of taking the offensive. "It is a myth," he said, ". . . that if we don't do anything nothing will hap-

[23] U.S. Congress, Senate, "Statement of Senator Edward Kennedy," *Congressional Record*, 20 May 69, p. S.13003.
[24] U.S. Department of State, American Opinion Summary, 5 Jun 69, p. 6, Vn-Public Opinion file, FAIM/IR.

pen to us. . . . If we pulled back and were quiet, they'd kill us in the night. They'd come in and crawl under the wire and they'd drop satchel charges on our bunkers and they'd mangle, kill, and maim our men." Of Kennedy, Zais would only say, "He's performing as a senator to the best of his ability . . . [but] I know for sure he wasn't here."[25]

The controversy over the battle continued for weeks. On 23 May television commentator Martin Agronsky refused to criticize either Kennedy or Zais, blaming instead those American decision makers who had committed American forces to an impossible task in South Vietnam. On the twenty-seventh, Ward Just in Washington, contrasted the 101st Airborne Division's assault on Dong Ap Bia with a small-unit operation conducted by Lt. Col. David Hackworth in the Mekong Delta. Where the 101st had lost some 50 men in a frontal assault, Just said, Hackworth had managed to kill 134 of the enemy without losing a single man because he had waited for the enemy to come to him. The reporter made no comment on the validity of Hackworth's body count. On 1 June the *New York Times* noted that the Military Assistance Command had told newsmen only forty-five Americans had been killed at Dong Ap Bia. Reporters at the scene, the newspaper said, had counted sixty. On 11 June David Culhane of CBS News interviewed a survivor who had since left the Army. Although accepting the justice of the war, the man told Culhane that he had felt misgivings about the attack from the beginning. "They just kept sending us up there," he said, "and we weren't getting anywhere. They were just slaughtering us, like a turkey shoot, and we were the turkeys."[26]

When the criticism continued, the Department of Defense counterattacked. In a speech before the Navy League on 4 June, former commander of all marines in South Vietnam, Assistant Commandant of the Marine Corps General Lewis W. Walt, complained that "We Americans tend to crave sensationalism and undoubtedly stimulate this type of reporting." Walt added that he considered news coverage of the war in general "inaccurate and misleading." Secretary of Defense Laird took up the theme at a Pentagon luncheon the next day. "We have our problems and we have many problems, . . . but we'd like to see some of our successes also brought before the public." Shortly thereafter, at a second Navy League function, Chief of Naval Operations Admiral Thomas L. Moorer commented that "Bad news too often attracts the headlines, as do difficulties rather than achievements, and controversy rather than resolution. . . . In my opinion, we sell ourselves short by this mysterious affinity we have for focusing on the bad, the bizarre, and the big."[27]

[25] Sharbutt, "Americans Stained With Blood, Sweat, and Mud"; David Hoffman, "Hamburger Hill, the Army's Rationale," *Washington Post*, 23 May 69.

[26] "Martin Agronsky's Washington," 23 May 69, *Radio-TV-Defense Dialog*; Ward Just, "Guerrilla Tactics and the Body Count," *Washington Post*, 27 May 69; "The Grim and Inaccurate Casualty Numbers Game," *New York Times*, 1 Jun 69; David Culhane, CBS Evening News, 11 Jun 69, *Radio-TV-Defense Dialog*. For a more detailed account of the controversies surrounding the battle, see Zaffiri, *Hamburger Hill*, pp. 273–80.

[27] Richard Homan, "Pentagon Aides Assail Press," *Washington Post*, 7 Jun 69.

The White House took a more indirect approach. Concerned lest the press interpret operations such as the one at Dong Ap Bia as proof that the United States was escalating the war, Henry Kissinger held a background briefing on 26 May to emphasize that if American casualties remained high, enemy-initiated actions rather than American operations were to blame. The number of American battalion-size attacks had remained steady each month since April of the previous year, he said, accounting for up to 150 Americans killed per month. Beyond that, there was a direct correlation between the number of enemy attacks in any given week and the level of American casualties for the same period. Twenty-nine enemy attacks would lead to about 127 Americans killed; fifty-four would push the Americans killed to 197. "The factor that makes for fluctuation," Kissinger said, ". . . is what the enemy does, not what we did." Questioned on whether the battle at Dong Ap Bia was "a case in which we were successful in getting the enemy to engage us on our terms or . . . an enemy initiated action," Kissinger sidestepped the issue. He responded that the battle fell into "a gray area" and that it was one of the "relatively rare cases where we have been able to make [the] opposing force fight when it might not have chosen to fight."[28]

The American Withdrawal Begins

Although Hamburger Hill remained in the news, an announcement from the White House on 21 May that President Nixon would travel to Midway Island on 8 June to confer with President Thieu rapidly overshadowed it as a story. On 14 May Nixon had made a major policy speech calling for mutual U.S.–North Vietnamese withdrawals from South Vietnam, a departure from the so-called San Antonio Formula in which Lyndon Johnson had demanded that North Vietnam withdraw first. He had also called for free elections in South Vietnam, accepting, in effect, the possibility that Communist candidates might gain at least a few offices. Since the change could hardly have set well with the South Vietnamese and since President Thieu commented shortly after Nixon's speech that "the policies of the two nations cannot be solved very easily over 10,000 miles of water," reporters began to speculate that the meeting would result in a confrontation between the two presidents.[29]

In fact, Nixon appears to have considered the conference mainly a backdrop for his first announcement of troop withdrawals. He said as much on 21 May at a meeting with Laird, Wheeler, Goodpaster, and

---

[28] Transcript, Background Briefing at the White House with Dr. Henry A. Kissinger, 26 May 69, CMH files. A second backgrounder to clarify the first was held on 27 May. A transcript of it is attached to the 26 May document.

[29] "How Nixon Is Trying To End the War," *U.S. News & World Report*, 26 May 69, p. 27; "Woe to the Visitors," *Newsweek*, 2 Jun 69, p. 42.

Kissinger, when he acknowledged that he felt he would have to make the disclosure shortly after he saw Thieu. He added that he wanted to base the move on the improvement of South Vietnamese military capabilities as agreed between Thieu and himself rather than on pressures from within the United States. He nodded to those pressures nonetheless by asserting that he believed the number of troops withdrawn should be odd rather than even because a figure of that sort would seem more plausible to the American public. In the same way, although the first units to leave South Vietnam would go mainly to American bases on Okinawa, some portion of them would have to return to the United States for publicity purposes.[30]

General Wheeler had reservations about the plan. In a 24 May message to Abrams, he considered it extremely important for Nixon and Laird to gain a true appreciation of the threat reductions posed to American forces. Laird, he said, had stated before a private group that South Vietnamese "divisions . . . should be able to handle things in I Corps." Yet reports from Abrams, confirmed by intelligence agencies in Washington, indicated that enemy forces were undergoing a buildup in the region. That being the case, Wheeler said, the situation in the area called for reinforcements rather than reductions. He asked Abrams to prepare a briefing on the matter for presentation at Midway.[31]

Whatever his beliefs on the subject, Abrams appears to have recognized that he had little room for maneuver. Outlining his plan for the first American withdrawal in a message to Wheeler on 2 June, he failed to mention either the chairman's objections or his own reservations, preferring, apparently, to take a calculated risk. Outstanding combat units would compose the first increment, he said, to make the reduction credible both to the enemy and to the American and South Vietnamese publics. In order to continue to minimize American casualties by using the superior firepower and mobility of American forces to best effect, reductions in nondivisional artillery, helicopters, and tactical air support would be small. Although removal of the 3d Marine Division from the I Corps Tactical Zone would have a noticeable effect on U.S. casualty rates, no reductions would occur in the III Corps Tactical Zone because Saigon was too important to risk. For the most part, Abrams said, reductions would occur in areas where South Vietnamese forces were strong or where a well-developed pacification program existed.[32]

Planning for Nixon's announcement moved apace, with the White House, the Department of Defense, the Military Assistance Command, and the Joint Chiefs of Staff paying special attention to public relations. Before the Midway conference, information officers in South Vietnam and the United States began to compose special press releases and position papers to counter in advance any possible allegation that the reduction was insignificant or an attempt to assuage American and foreign public

[30] Msg, Wheeler JCS 6206 to Abrams, 21 May 69, Abrams Papers, CMH.
[31] Msg, Wheeler JCS 6337 to Abrams, 24 May 69, Abrams Papers, CMH.
[32] Msg, Abrams MAC 7021 to Wheeler, 2 Jun 69, Abrams Papers, CMH.

90

opinion. An effort also began at each level of command to develop, as Admiral McCain put it, "a coordinated program . . . to ensure maximum political and psychological benefit from this reduction."[33]

Nixon and Thieu met at Midway on 8 June as planned, with Nixon announcing that 25,000 American troops would leave South Vietnam by the end of August. The press immediately began to speculate on the identities of the units that would move, prompting Abrams to request an announcement as soon as possible to cut off leaks and to permit open planning and preparation. On 17 June the Defense Department disclosed that the 9th Marine Regimental Landing Team would relocate to Okinawa while the 1st Brigade of the 9th Infantry Division and the division's headquarters went to Hawaii. The 2d Brigade of the 9th Division along with some 1,200 reservists and national guardsmen called to active duty during the 1968 Tet offensive were meanwhile to return to the United States. They would arrive in Seattle, Washington, on 8 July.[34]

The public affairs guidance accompanying the redeployment was geared to stress both the accomplishments of the departing American units and the ability of South Vietnamese forces to carry on without them. All concerned with the operation were warned to avoid "subjective comments" on the qualifications of the South Vietnamese and to concentrate in their dealings with the press on themes indicating progress. Once the units had arrived at their destination in the United States, they were to parade through the city's streets in order to demonstrate to America and the world that U.S. troops had indeed begun their return from Southeast Asia. Although some heckling was expected, Seattle seemed an excellent choice for an arrival ceremony because of its moderate size and lack of a substantial resident antiwar movement.[35]

The redeployment itself took place as planned. After leave-taking ceremonies at Saigon's Tan Son Nhut Airport, the troops traveled to Seattle, where they participated in a parade attended by General Westmoreland and listened to a welcoming speech by Secretary of the Army Stanley R. Resor. "All the sights and sounds," *Newsweek* later commented, "were of success."[36]

If the ceremonies went well, the news media was nevertheless quick to note disparities. Where most of the returning veterans "felt they had

[33] Msg, McCain to McConnell, Acting CJCS, 25 May 69, and Msg, McCain to Abrams, 3 Jun 69, both in Abrams Papers, CMH.

[34] Msg, Abrams MAC 7512 to McCain, 12 Jun 69, and Msg, McCain to Abrams, 13 Jun 69, both in Abrams Papers, CMH. Also see William Beecher, "U.S. Said To Consider Two New Pullouts of Troops," *New York Times*, 18 Jun 69.

[35] Talking Paper, OASD, n.d. [Jun 69], sub: Redeployment of U.S. Units from Vietnam: Public Affairs Guidance; Talking Paper, ASD PA, 28 Jun 69, sub: Parade of Redeployed U.S. Army Unit; Fact Sheet, OASD PA, 27 Jun 69, sub: Seattle Parade for 3d Battalion, 60th Infantry; and Memo, Fort Lewis, Washington, Office of Public Affairs, n.d. [Jun 69], sub: Information Plan: Redeployment of Troops from Vietnam. All in DDI Redeployments file.

[36] "Beginning of the End?," *Newsweek*, 21 Jul 69, p. 24.

First unit returning from Vietnam arrives in Seattle.

gone to Vietnam to do a job and had done it," *Newsweek* reported, others were "clearly disenchanted." One black soldier waiting to depart Tan Son Nhut, the magazine noted, had thrown a clinched fist salute signifying black power to another driving by in a truck. A second soldier had told newsmen that he considered the ceremonies "just a gimmick." A few had seemed disturbed that they were receiving a victor's send-off before the war itself had been won.[37]

When the troops arrived in Seattle, some fifty antiwar demonstrators who attempted to disrupt the proceedings by waving signs reading "It's a trick, Dick" and "Bring the other 500,000 home" claimed the attention of the press. So did comments by disgruntled bystanders. The *Washington Post* devoted only a small amount of space on page 10 to the ceremonies and then headlined the article with the comment, "Returnees Jeered." *Newsweek* observed that although girls handed out roses and confetti filtered from the windows of surrounding buildings, enthusiasm seemed lacking, as if Seattle, "like the rest of the country," wanted the war to go away. The *New York Times* noted that fewer than 200 of the 814 men in the returning unit had actually served with it in the field. The remainder

[37] Ibid.

were "short-timers" transferred to the unit for the trip out of South Vietnam. The *Times* added that on the same day the troops arrived at McCord Air Force Base in Seattle, one thousand other men departed McCord for duty in South Vietnam. In the end, the Defense Department decided that press coverage of the event had been so negative it would be counterproductive to hold similar receptions for returning troops in the future. The 2d Brigade of the 9th Division thus became the only American unit returning from the war to receive a formal welcome home.[38]

The Battle of Ben Het

Although the press, much to the chagrin of President Nixon, began to speculate on whether Abrams would be able to meet a 31 August deadline for completion of the first redeployment, it was almost equally concerned with determining whether the South Vietnamese armed forces would be able to stand alone once the Americans had gone. The MACV Office of Information attempted to answer the question by publicizing South Vietnamese achievements in battle. It also devoted major attention to the participation of South Vietnamese units in combined operations and encouraged the South Vietnamese Joint General Staff to improve its relations with the Saigon correspondents. Yet if the command succeeded in winning excellent coverage for subjects such as South Vietnam's assumption of responsibility for former American bases and equipment, it never overcame the obvious lack of aggressiveness of the county's military leaders and the preference of the Saigon correspondents for derogatory information.[39]

Shortly before the first American withdrawals, for example, a battle developed at Ben Het, a Civilian Irregular Defense Group camp located some twenty-two kilometers west of Dak To where Laos, Cambodia, and South Vietnam meet. Coming under enemy fire in May, the camp received little attention in the press until mid-June, when enemy pressure against it mounted. By the end of the month the equivalent of an enemy division—six to seven thousand men—had suffered an alleged 1,700 killed while friendly losses amounted to some 300 dead.[40]

---

[38] "Returnees Jeered," *Washington Post*, 11 Jul 69; Steven V. Roberts, "Girls, Bands, and Tickertape," *New York Times*, 11 Jul 69; Talking Paper, OASD PA, n.d. [Jul 69], sub: Redeployment of U.S. Units from Vietnam: Public Affairs Guidance, DDI Redeployments file.

[39] Msg, Wheeler JCS 10285 to McCain, Abrams, 20 Aug 69, and Msg, Abrams MAC 10252 to Wheeler, 8 Aug 69, sub: Publicizing ARVN Achievements, both in Abrams Papers, CMH; Msg, Defense 3402 to COMUSMACV for Military Assistance Command, Vietnam, Office of Information (MACOI), 26 Jun 69, DDI Units Redeploying from Vietnam file.

[40] Msg, Lt Gen Corcoran, CG, I Field Force, Vietnam (IFFV), to Abrams, 27 Jun 69, Abrams Papers, CMH.

Smoke screens shield incoming helicopters from enemy fire at Ben Het.

First reports of the battle were matter of fact. They noted that the enemy had dug deep trenches around the camp and was bombarding it with up to one hundred mortar rounds per day. Only on 26 June did they become critical, when Peter Arnett submitted a report to the Associated Press that became a major source of irritation to both the Nixon administration and the Military Assistance Command.[41]

Since the defense of the camp was entirely in South Vietnamese hands, Arnett concentrated on the American battalion that provided artillery support. The unit, he said, had become the victim of "a logistics foul up that compares with the worst days of the sieges of Khe Sanh and

[41] See, for example [AP], "Enemy Surrounds Besieged U.S. Base," *New York Times*, 24 Jun 69; Joseph B. Treaster, "A Convoy Reaches U.S. Base at Benhet," *New York Times*, 25 Jun 69.

Con Thien in the north." Lacking water for five days, the reporter continued, the troops had been reduced to drinking sodas and dusty rainwater. They were firing three rounds of ammunition for every one they received through resupply channels. The battery's members "not only have to fire the guns, they have to defend their tiny perimeter themselves" because the South Vietnamese had suffered casualties as high as 50 percent. "If we were attached to a U.S. unit we would have at least two infantry platoons giving us security," one artilleryman told the reporter. Yet since the battle was viewed by the U.S. command as a test of the South Vietnamese ability to stand up to the North Vietnamese, Arnett added, "there is a reluctance to interfere. The artillerymen feel they are being sacrificed in an experiment which, from the Ben Het viewpoint, seems to be failing."[42]

Close upon Arnett's allegations, United Press International revealed that on several occasions during the battle U.S. artillery and tactical air support had returned the fire of enemy batteries located across the border in Cambodia. The article underscored the occurrence by noting earlier allegations that U.S. B–52 bombers were already conducting raids against Communist base camps in that country. When information officers at the MACV briefing responded "no comment" to questions on the subject, the assembled reporters hooted in derision.[43]

An immediate investigation by the Military Assistance Command revealed that Arnett, while partially correct, had built his allegations upon the fallible testimony of men at the scene without attempting to flesh out their statements with word from higher commanders who could have provided a broader perspective. During early June, for example, the camp at Ben Het had indeed experienced a water shortage, yet no one had gone thirsty. Beer and soda had been in ample supply, and rainfall had been abundant. Ammunition, on the other hand, had never been a problem except on one or two brief occasions when the battery had temporarily curtailed routine, targetless harassing fire until new supplies arrived. During the week prior to Arnett's report the unit had in fact fired 3,154 rounds while receiving 3,076 replacements. Two thousand rounds had been available at all times. Perimeter defense had also been adequate, involving personnel from the battery itself and some sixty civilian irregulars supported by over 30 artillery tubes, 3 40-mm. cannon, and 1 "quad-50" (a weapon mounting four 50-caliber machine guns in tandem). As for the South Vietnamese, the command believed that their conduct of the battle had indeed been less than commendable, if only because they had dallied before reliev-

[42] Arnett's report was transmitted to MACV in Msg, McConnell JCS 7909 to Abrams, 26 Jun 69, Abrams Papers, CMH. Arnett gives his own version of the episode in his memoirs. See Peter Arnett, *Live From the Battlefield, From Vietnam to Baghdad, 35 Years in the World's War Zones* (New York: Simon and Schuster, 1994), pp. 260–62.

[43] Memo, Office of the Secretary of Defense for Public Affairs (OSD PA) for Col Robert E. Pursley, USAF, Military Assistant to the Secretary of Defense, 5 Jul 69, sub: UPI Story From Saigon, DDI Cambodia file.

ing the base and one of their regiments had come close to collapse. Yet, their casualties had never come near 50 percent, and, while American artillery and air support had played a role, the troops around the base had still managed to keep the enemy from attaining any of his objectives.[44]

Although the Military Assistance Command made its findings available to the press and confirmed, without admitting to B–52 strikes, that American forces had fired into Cambodia, it could do little to counteract the impression that the battle was somehow a test of South Vietnam's ability to fight. Public affairs officers asserted that the 22d South Vietnamese Infantry Division had assumed responsibility for operations in the area four months prior to the battle and had been functioning effectively ever since. But General Abrams himself considered the battle a test of South Vietnamese abilities and had so informed the commander of the U.S. artillery at the scene: his former chief of public affairs, General Sidle. As a result, as every reporter who covered the battle understood, although ample American ground forces were nearby and could have intervened, they never did so. As late as 13 July Drummond Ayres, Jr., of the *New York Times* could thus conclude with some reason that Ben Het demonstrated the inability of the South Vietnamese Army to stand alone, if only because it revealed that South Vietnamese officers lacked aggressiveness and imagination. In the same way, when the South Vietnamese commander in the battle, Col. Nguyen Ba Lien, claimed at a press conference that he had masterminded a brilliant victory by using Ben Het as bait to entice the Communists into a kill zone, *Newsweek* could only react by printing the comment of an angry American adviser who had declared, "Who's he kidding?"[45]

If the press was upset, so were many members of Congress. When Admiral McCain traveled to Washington in late June, he found that interest in the battle on Capitol Hill was at a high pitch. "To put it mildly," he told Abrams,

there is deep serious concern about the ability of the RVNAF to fight the enemy. This, in turn, raises questions about the efficiency of our . . . modernization program and the practicality of the [South Vietnamese] . . . taking over an increasing share of the burdens of war. It underlies congressional questions about the merits of [our] entire basic policy position with respect to Vietnam. It could even impair the ability of the U.S. military commanders to organize, train, and equip allied forces to be really effective.

[44] MFR, National Military Command Center (NMCC), 27 Jun 69, sub: Operations at Ben Het Civilian Irregular Defense Group Camp, DDI Operations file; Msg, Corcoran to Abrams, 27 Jun 69, sub: MACOI Query Re Peter Arnett Story, Abrams Papers, CMH; Fact Sheet, OASD PA, n.d. [Jun 69], sub: Ben Het CIDG Camp, DDI Operations file. Arnett points out in his memoirs that the battery commander, Capt. John Horalek, confirmed that morale among the Americans at Ben Het was deteriorating. See Arnett, *Live From the Battlefield*, p. 261.

[45] Interv, author with Sidle, 21 Nov 90, CMH files; Drummond Ayres, Jr., "The Lull Raises Tricky Questions About Troop Withdrawals," *New York Times*, 13 Jul 69; "Hold Your Breath," *Newsweek*, 14 Jul 69, p. 41.

McCain emphasized that he would never attempt to second-guess Abrams on the conduct of the battle and sought only to inform him that the stakes were very large. "A reverse at Ben Het at this critical time," he said, "as the direct result of enemy action, will raise a hue and cry. The military from General Wheeler on down will be scapegoats. On the other hand, a sound trouncing of the enemy, particularly if it is accomplished by the [South Vietnamese] . . ., even if it is accomplished with U.S. fire and logistic support, would have far-reaching favorable effects."[46]

General Abrams had no intention of losing the battle. Between 5 May and 26 June he authorized some 73 B–52 raids in defense of Ben Het, a number far in excess of what might have been expected. As a result, when MACV Deputy Commander General William B. Rosson visited the base on 29 June, he could report back that American firepower completely dominated the scene. "I think the situation is exceedingly favorable," he told reporters. "We've punished the enemy severely. The camp is intact, fully manned, well supplied, and the morale of forces very high."[47]

Further Restrictions on Information

The controversies surrounding the battles of Dong Ap Bia and Ben Het caused growing concern in official American circles. General Wheeler, in particular, wondered whether the Military Assistance Command was doing enough to promote South Vietnamese military operations. The South Vietnamese armed forces had "participated significantly" in the Battle of Hamburger Hill, he told the director of the Joint Staff, but their effort had received little notice in the press because neither the Defense Department nor the Military Assistance Command had done enough to publicize their role.[48]

Informed of Wheeler's opinion but inclined to let matters speak for themselves and to avoid even the hint of a public relations campaign, General Abrams instructed his chief of information, Colonel Hill, to make the publicizing of South Vietnamese progress and achievements a top priority. On the side, in an attempt to overcome the news media's traditional preoccupation with the American side of the war, he instructed his commanders to play down the role of U.S. forces in large operations in order to make both the withdrawals and South Vietnamese efforts stand out. Shortly thereafter, in compliance with Abrams' wishes, the MACV Office of Information quietly revised its policy of announcing

[46]Msg, McCain to Abrams, 28 Jun 69, Abrams Papers, CMH.

[47]Msg, Corcoran NHT 1089 to Abrams, 29 Jun 69, and Msg, Abrams MAC 8347 to McCain, 29 Jun 69, both in Abrams Papers, CMH. Rosson's comment is in "General Flies to Benhet and Finds Morale 'High,'" *New York Times*, 30 Jun 69.

[48]Memo, Wheeler CM–4446–69 for the Director, Joint Staff, 23 Jul 69, sub: Coordination of Press Treatment of RVNAF and Other Free World Forces, DDI Operations file.

the names of all American operations in progress. From then on, only those that developed "substantial news value" were to be released. In all other cases, briefers were merely to state that fighting had occurred at such and such a place, so many miles from Saigon or some other large city.[49]

The Saigon correspondents recognized the change almost immediately. On 4 August David Lamb of United Press International dispatched a story outlining the new policy and quoting unnamed U.S. officers to the effect that "With the Paris talks now focused on deescalation and troop withdrawals, it does not serve our best interests to ballyhoo a multi-battalion drive in search of the enemy." Another reason for the change, Lamb hypothesized, was that U.S. commanders had occasionally been embarrassed when a highly publicized operation had failed to achieve its goals. He noted by way of example the existence of an operation near Hue several months earlier that had never been revealed to the press because the 101st Airborne Division, during five weeks in the field, had managed to kill only two enemy soldiers.[50]

Lamb's article was so accurate that General Abrams at first suspected the reporter had received classified information from a recent MACV Commanders Conference. Since the article was datelined Da Nang, he cabled the III Marine Amphibious Force to request an explanation. The marines assured him in reply that there had been no breach of security and that Lamb, when interviewed by Da Nang information officers, had been most cooperative in detailing how he had constructed his story. An officer in Saigon had supplied the quotation; the commander of the 101st had personally briefed the reporter and other newsmen on the unsuccessful operation, code-named Bristol Boots; and the rest of the story was built upon very astute observation.[51]

On the day after Lamb's story appeared, information officers at the Military Assistance Command cabled the Da Nang press center to note that the effort to play down U.S. offensive operations hardly meant a change in the policy of releasing significant operations to newsmen and to the public. It signified instead that "we should not go out of our way to publicize them if they do not contain substantial news value. III MAF should continue, as it has in the past, to recommend to MACV that operations (including their nicknames) be released for news coverage. However, in the future, III MAF should be selective about those recommendations. If an operation achieves significant results, and its existence is probably very well known to newsmen, it would not be in our best interest to deny its existence."[52]

---

[49] For a description of the many problems surrounding the South Vietnamese and details of U.S. efforts to remedy them, see Chapter 6. Msg, CG, III MAF, to COMUSMACV, 7 Aug 69, Abrams Papers, CMH.

[50] Msg, Abrams MAC 10176 to Nickerson, CG, III MAF, 6 Aug 69, Abrams Papers, CMH.

[51] Msg, CG, III MAF, to COMUSMACV, 7 Aug 69.

[52] Ibid., quoting the MACV message.

The instruction was a masterpiece of circumlocution. It asserted, on the one hand, that no change had occurred while issuing directions, on the other, that could hardly have been anything but a change. Yet if that was so, it was as much a reflection of the perplexities confronting the Nixon administration as an attempt to dissemble. For the United States in 1969 was beset by contradictions. It had to fight while taking as few casualties as possible, to negotiate with an enemy who remained convinced he could win, and to withdraw from South Vietnam without appearing to abandon the South Vietnamese. All the while, it had to turn the war over to an ally who, as General Abrams had perceived, had yet to come to grips with what he had to do just to survive. Given the enemy's perception of America's problems and his desire to exploit them in any way possible, it was perhaps understandable that the Military Assistance Command would attempt to deny him that advantage by tightening its hold on information about the war. No one recognized at the time that the situation in South Vietnam, as Lamb had demonstrated, was far too open for any effort of the sort to succeed.

5

Vietnamization

When President Nixon had taken office in January 1969, most Americans had given him the benefit of a doubt where the war in Vietnam was concerned. Typical of their attitude was a comment by a retired business executive in Roanoke, Virginia, who told a Gallup poll interviewer, "Nixon can't undo a mess overnight that others have been trying to untangle for the last five years." Of 1,502 adults contacted by the Gallup organization in early April, a majority of 74 percent either approved of the president's handling of the war (44 percent) or suspended judgment (30 percent). A large proportion of the 26 percent who disapproved were waiting for some dramatic step—either an immediate withdrawal of American forces from South Vietnam or an outright escalation to seize victory.[1]

During July and September 1969, the president's rating on the war began to slide. Although his personal popularity remained high and two out of three Americans supported Nixon's decision to turn over more of the fighting to the South Vietnamese, 52 percent of those questioned by the Harris poll in July expressed dissatisfaction with his handling of the war. His ranking fell further in succeeding months. By the end of September, only 35 percent of those interviewed responded positively when asked to rate his handling of the war.[2] There was as yet little sympathy for a precipitate American withdrawal from South Vietnam, even among the harshest critics of administration policy, but also hardly any support for continuation of the war at the levels prevalent between 1966 and 1968. If an obscure poll during October revealed that 52 percent of Americans would support a last-ditch escalation to achieve victory, more telling, in hindsight, were the results of surveys conducted shortly after Nixon's inauguration. They showed that 43 percent of Americans consid-

---

[1] George Gallup, "Nixon Backed on War Handling," *Washington Post*, 10 Apr 69.
[2] Louis Harris, *The Anguish of Change* (New York: W. W. Norton, 1973), p. 69; Harris, "55% Remain Attuned to Nixon But Support on Issues Is Soft," *Chicago Daily News*, 29 Sep 69.

ered the military draft unfair "because it made young men fight in a war they didn't believe in."[3]

The Attitude of the Press

The gradual dissipation of support for the war was apparent in the news media, where important changes in the way reporters gathered and presented information allowed critics greater access to the press than ever before. In the print media, the trend led away from the traditional channels of news gathering—the press conference, official news releases, reports of official proceedings—and toward methods less susceptible to the government's point of view. Reporters were doing more research, conducting more interviews, and publishing more analytical essays. According to a survey by sociologist Leon Sigal, the percentage of news stories based on traditional methods had been dropping gradually for years, from 65.9 percent in 1949 to 50.1 in 1969. Stories based on the newsman's own initiative had meanwhile increased over those years from 21.4 percent to 39.1. Most of that growth had occurred between 1964 and 1969, the period of heaviest American involvement in the Vietnam War, when newsmen's use of those so-called enterprise channels had grown by 13 points.[4]

The trend was even clearer where television coverage of the war was concerned. During 1965 and 1966 researcher George A. Bailey found that ABC broadcast interpretive stories on the war only 13 percent of the time. By 1969 and 1970 that figure had risen to 47 percent. During the same period, the percentage rose from 37 to 48 at CBS and from 28 to 58 at NBC. Few of the stories that resulted were opinionated, according to Bailey, but the change still meant that lower level sources more inclined to criticize the war, especially congressmen, had a better chance than before of being heard. Administration spokesmen still dominated the process, and the opinions of individual members of Congress and antiwar critics rarely if ever outweighed the word of the president of the United States in their ability to generate press coverage. But the broadening of comment that began when Lyndon Johnson espoused the search for peace was clearly apparent.[5]

There were also changes in the amount of coverage television afforded the war. According to Bailey, between August and November 1968 the three network weekday evening news programs covered the war 91 per-

[3] The October poll is mentioned in MFR, 28 Oct 69, sub: Briefing for the Army Policy Council, Analysis of Editorials and Feature Articles by Brig. Gen. Winant Sidle, Chief of Public Information, in Army Policy Council, Meeting Minutes, 28 Oct 69, CMH files. See also Harris, *The Anguish of Change*, p. 69.
[4] Sigal, *Reporters and Officials*, p. 128.
[5] Bailey, *The Vietnam War According to Chet, . . .*, p. 261.

cent of broadcast days. After the presidential election in November 1968 and the advent of an administration pledged to end the fighting, that figure dropped to 61 percent. With the battles of Hamburger Hill and Ben Het and an announcement in July 1969 that President Nixon would conduct protective reaction strikes in North Vietnam in retaliation for enemy attacks on American reconnaissance aircraft, the war gained somewhat in prominence, playing 70 percent of the days between May 1969 and May 1970. Yet even then coverage remained 20 percent below that of earlier years.[6]

It is tempting to speculate that the networks had tired of the war. The producer of the "Huntley-Brinkley Report" on NBC, Robert J. Northshield, told an interviewer in 1974 that by the end of 1968 fatigue was a definite problem for him. "The executive producer sits down every morning to plan his show. He aims at having five segments. He talks to [David] Brinkley in Washington, to other guys. And very often his feeling is, 'Oh, God, not Vietnam again.' By early 1969 that feeling was very marked. The trend was away from Vietnam."[7]

Whatever the value of Northshield's insight, the changing nature of the war itself was also involved. After the November 1968 bombing halt and the beginning of the negotiations, the attention of television news began to point away from combat in South Vietnam and toward subjects that explored the implications of an American disengagement. In March 1969, for example, ABC Evening News executive producer Av Westin issued instructions for his correspondents in South Vietnam to shift their attention away from combat and toward the description of black market activities; examinations of the political opposition to President Thieu; analyses of medical care for civilians; investigative reports on the South Vietnamese government's treatment of ex–Viet Cong; and comparisons of new province chiefs with their predecessors to determine whether the South Vietnamese bureaucracy had become more efficient or if it remained as corrupt and inept as in the past. Executives at NBC issued similar instructions.[8]

In November 1968, shortly after President Johnson halted the bombing of North Vietnam, the network's reporters in the field received word that they should no longer concentrate on combat but on issues relevant to the negotiations. Over the next two months, NBC's producers ran combat footage on the evening news only three times. During the preceding year, with American combat casualties running at about the same rate, stories of that sort had played three to four times per week.[9]

Similar shifts occurred in the print media. The *New York Times*, which had averaged 130 editorials on the war between 1966 and 1968, gradually cut back between 1969 and 1971 to a level of between 60 and 70 per year.

[6] Ibid., pp. 104–16.
[7] Godfrey Hodgson, *America in Our Time* (New York: Vintage Books, 1976), p. 378.
[8] Epstein, *News From Nowhere*, pp. 16–18.
[9] Ibid.

A review by the MACV Office of Information of 265 news stories clipped by the Defense Department and included in news summaries dispatched to Saigon between August 1969 and February 1970 revealed that 87 percent dealt with the effort to turn the war over to the South Vietnamese and other related topics. Assistant Secretary of Defense for Public Affairs Daniel Henkin could only conclude in a year end report to Secretary Laird that the press in general had switched from covering combat to such formerly unpopular subjects as the pacification program and the South Vietnamese armed forces.[10]

An even stronger indication that the news media were changing their approach to the war could be seen in the language television reporters and anchormen used to describe it. Prior to the Tet offensive, most American journalists believed in the justice of American motives even if they disagreed with tactics. According to researcher Daniel C. Hallin, television reporters in particular described the war as "our side" versus "their side." They cast the conflict in terms of the so-called good war, World War II, and quoted statistics liberally. In the process, they made the war seem efficient, rational, and masculine. To them, winning was clearly what counted. Profound if subtle changes set in after the Tet offensive. Reporters still rarely questioned the honesty of American motives, but "our war" became "the war" and references to World War II disappeared. Newsmen also apologized for the coldness of the statistics they continued to use and made the repetitiveness and futility of the war much more of a theme. Its cost to Americans became the important thing, and getting out was what counted. Labeling statements that appeared on television during the post-Tet period by their approach to the war, Hallin found that 42 percent dealt with whether administration policy would help bring an end to the conflict; 23 percent considered related topics such as the cost of continuing American involvement in South Vietnam, the condition of American prisoners of war, and the need to protect American troops; and less than 6 percent referred to the most familiar themes in the pre-Tet period, halting Communist aggression and preserving democracy in South Vietnam.[11]

Although precise figures are difficult to come by, something similar occurred where the print media were concerned. Prior to Tet, despite growing doubts about the credibility of official claims of progress, print journalists tended to interpret the conflict in Vietnam as a circumstance of the Cold War rivalry between the United States and the Communist powers. There were exceptions, but the great majority backed the United

[10] Salisbury, *Without Fear or Favor* (New York: Times Books 1980), p. 89; MACV Office of Information, Report on MACOI Involvement in Reporting on Vietnam Conflict, 10 Feb 70, DDI Correspondence with MACOI (36a) file; Memo, Daniel Z. Henkin for Secretary Laird, 12 Jan 70, 330–76–067, box 99, Viet (South) 320.2 (Jan–Feb) 1970, Melvin Laird Papers, Washington National Records Center (WNRC), Suitland, Md.

[11] Daniel C. Hallin, *The Uncensored War: The Media and Vietnam* (New York: Oxford University Press, 1986), pp. 174–79.

States. After Tet, despite a reluctance to change lest they be accused of inconsistency, a charge that would tend to undermine their own credibility, print journalists began to reappraise the situation. By 1971 they and most of the newspapers in the United States were openly opposed to continuation of the war. Responding to criticisms that had appeared in professional journals, some of them, according to sociologist Herbert Gans, stopped referring to the North Vietnamese as "the enemy."[12]

As 1969 progressed, some of the most telling commentaries dealt with American casualties. The 27 June issue of *Life*, for example, made the magazine's opinion clear by printing the pictures of 242 Americans who had died in

Life *cover, 27 June 1969*

Vietnam during a recent week.[13] Shortly thereafter, NBC News anchorman David Brinkley introduced his report of the latest casualty statistics from Vietnam with the comment that

the president said at his news conference last week that the only thing that had been settled when he came to office was the shape of the table. Well, in the five months since then, they have used the table in the shape agreed on, settled nothing, and in Vietnam the war and the killing continues. Today in Saigon they announced the casualty figures for the week. And though they came in the form of numbers, each one of them was a man, most of them quite young, each with hopes he will never realize, each with families and friends who will never see him alive again. Anyway, these are the numbers. . . .[14]

Although Brinkley had long questioned the war in his televised remarks, his brief comment on casualties was among the strongest he had ever made. More characteristic of television's approach was a report by Richard Threlkeld that appeared on the 30 September 1969 edition of the CBS Evening News. Threlkeld showed several soldiers looking down on three dead friends. Their remarks and reminiscences made up the story. Except in the case of important personages, the bodies never appeared be-

[12] Gans, *Deciding What's News*, p. 201.

[13] "The Faces of the American Dead in Vietnam, One Week's Toll," *Life*, 27 Jun 69.

[14] David Brinkley, NBC Nightly News, 26 Jun 69, quoted in Bailey, *The Vietnam War According to Chet*, . . ., p. 352.

cause, by agreement between the networks and the Military Assistance Command, television cameramen never photographed the face or revealed the name of an American casualty until after notification of the next of kin. Working around the restriction, Threlkeld brought out the loss by defining it in terms of the dead men's friends.[15]

The effect on American public opinion of stories and commentaries of that sort by individual anchormen and reporters is almost impossible to gauge. Brinkley's caustic remarks were few in number, for example, and more than balanced by the less antiwar version of events delivered by Chet Huntley, who cohosted NBC's news program. Covering military developments in Vietnam while Brinkley handled the home front, Huntley read 60 percent of NBC's Vietnam stories and shared responsibility with Brinkley for 13 percent more.[16]

Overall, if all three networks were using more feature material, anchormen themselves remained relatively straightforward and noncontroversial. They rarely evaluated or questioned official interpretations or statements. If, by virtue of the exposure they received, they had more of an impact on audiences than individual newsmen in the field, as seems the case, their reticence may have worked to the advantage of official policy, if only because official agencies and spokesmen continued to be the main sources for news on the war.[17]

Whatever the circumstances, the influence of television coverage on public opinion of the war appears marginal. According to surveys in 1969 by the A. C. Nielsen Company, of 57 million households in the United States that possessed televisions, 30.8 million had their sets turned on at the evening news hour but only 24.3 million had them tuned to the news. An average of two persons per household supposedly watched, but what they retained was much in doubt. A survey undertaken by the National Association of Broadcasters in 1971 found that, when 232 respondents were asked, within an hour of viewing the news, what they remembered, 51 percent failed to recall a single story out of a possible nineteen. Of the 49 percent who remembered at least one, the windup commentaries by such reporters as Eric Sevareid or Harry Reasoner, easily the most opinionated parts of the programs, were the least remembered.[18]

As for the print media, Walter Lippmann, in his book *Public Opinion*, pointed out in 1921 that newspapers might be remarkably successful at telling people what to think about, but they had little influence, whatever they said, over the shape of the conclusions that resulted. Those were the products of a whole range of human interactions beginning in

---

[15] Richard Threlkeld, CBS Evening News, 30 Sep 69, quoted by Hallin, *The Uncensored War*, p. 174.

[16] Bailey, *The Vietnam War According to Chet, . . .*, pp. 369–71.

[17] Ibid.

[18] Marvin Barrett, ed., *A. I. du Pont–Columbia University Survey of Broadcast Journalism for 1971–1972, The Politics of Broadcasting* (New York: Thomas Y. Crowell Co., 1973), pp. 6–7.

childhood and extending throughout the life of a member of the reading audience. In the years since Lippmann made his point, researchers have substantiated his premise, documenting a two-step flow in the process of opinion formation. Individuals receive data from many sources, one of which is the news media. Before forming an opinion they filter that information through a number of "significant others"—parents, supervisors, teachers, and respected associates—before finally reaching a conclusion themselves. The conditioning imposed by society plays an important role in the process, superseding at times even family ties. In one study, researchers found that while those Americans who were related to someone serving in South Vietnam indeed paid more attention to the war, they were far more likely to base their opinion of the conflict on political symbols acquired gradually throughout their lives—whether they were liberal, conservative, ardently anti-Communist, favorably disposed toward the military or suspicious—rather than on their supposed self-interest.[19]

The Nixon Administration's Perceptions

The changes occurring in public opinion and the news media weighed heavily on the Nixon administration as 1969 progressed. For if most of the American people rejected the sort of withdrawals that would spell defeat for the United States, there was little assurance that the mood would last. "Vocal opposition to the war has appeared to diminish," Secretary Laird thus told President Nixon on 4 September 1969, "but I believe this may be an illusory phenomenon. The actual and potential antipathy for the war is, in my judgment, significant and increasing."[20]

Meanwhile, if the rate of American casualties had fallen by one-third during 1969, leading to speculation in the press that the Communists had deescalated in hopes of furthering the negotiations, reports from the field indicated that the enemy's capacity for war had at least doubled in the years since 1966. It seemed clear, in that light, that if the enemy was holding back, he was merely biding his time for some opportunity to strike. Caught between that hard assessment, public distaste for a protracted conflict, and the need to maintain the U.S. government's credibility and leverage both in South Vietnam and around the world, the president sought ardently for some means to enhance the American abil-

[19] Walter Lippmann, *Public Opinion* (Glencoe, Ill.: Free Press, 1921); Bernard Cohen, *The Press and Foreign Policy* (Princeton: Princeton University Press, 1963), p. 13; Elihu Katz and Paul Lazarsfeld, *Personal Influence* (Glencoe, Ill.: Free Press, 1955); Richard A. Lau, Thad A. Brown, and David O. Sears, "Self-Interest and Civilians' Attitudes Toward the Vietnam War," *Public Opinion Quarterly* 42 (Winter 1978): 464.

[20] Memo, Laird for the President, 4 Sep 69, sub: Vietnamizing the War (NSSM 36), Pol 27 Viet S file, FAIM/IR.

ity to give the South Vietnamese a chance at success while shielding the United States from the worst consequences of their possible failure.[21]

Nixon told how he intended to address the problem on 30 July 1969, at a meeting in Bangkok with U.S. chiefs of mission assigned to Southeast Asia. "The way the war ends in Vietnam," he said,

will have an enduring impact upon events, although the domino effect is not necessarily valid. It is easy to feel that we should get out of Asia at all costs. The war plagues us at home, is costly in our relations with the USSR, and offers all kinds of temptations to our politicians. Yet if the Vietnam War goes sour, there would be an escalation of not just get-out-of-Vietnam sentiment but get-out-of-the-world sentiment. And this would be disastrous. Should we abandon Vietnam, there would be far more blood spilled than if we remain steady in our purposes.

Nixon continued that the Communists were "diddling us along" in Paris to extract maximum advantage. He expected little if any assistance from the Soviet Union in promoting a negotiated settlement—"I must say that if I were the Soviets, I would make it tough for the U.S. I would extract everything I could out of America's quandary in Vietnam." Under the circumstances, the question thus became "how to overcome U.S. disenchantment with Vietnam and growing doubts about our involvement in the world."[22]

The solution the president proposed had ramifications far beyond South Vietnam but was intimately linked to the war. Publicized by the White House as the "Nixon Doctrine," it emphasized that the United States would henceforth require the countries of Asia to handle their own subversion and insurgency problems. Nixon believed that once the American people realized "that we are looking to others to maximize their self-help efforts," there would be "better . . . understanding and support for the essential tasks that we must pursue abroad." The countries of Asia "should be under no illusion," he told the chiefs of mission, "that U.S. ground forces will . . . be committed to meeting anything less than a large-scale external attack. If a country can't handle its internal security, it is scarcely capable of being saved."[23]

The public affairs surrounding the portion of the program relating to South Vietnam had been months in preparation. The president's meeting in June at Midway with Thieu and his subsequent announcement of a

[21] Fact Sheet on Vietnam, WH 19588, 10 Oct 69, covered by Memo, Herb Kline for Secretary Melvin Laird, 13 Oct 69, DDI VN Troop Withdrawal file; Memo, Thomas L. Hughes, State Department Bureau of Intelligence and Research, for Acting Secretary of State, 16 May 69, sub: The Coming Summer Offensive, Pol 27 Viet S file, FAIM/IR; Msg, State 206937 to New Delhi, for Secretary Katzenbach, 23 Jul 69, sub: JCS Report of Enemy Initiated Activities, Pol 27–14 Viet S file, FAIM/IR.

[22] Transcript, President Nixon's Comments to Chiefs of Mission, Bangkok, 30 July 1969, attachment to Ltr, William P. Rogers to the President, 29 Sep 69, Pol 1 Asia SE-US file, FAIM/IR.

[23] Ibid.

Nixon meets Thieu during visit to Saigon.

25,000-man troop withdrawal were meant to show that the United States had ruled out a purely American solution to the problem in South Vietnam. So were intimations by Secretary Laird during March, carefully coordinated at the highest level, that the United States had a plan to turn the war over to the South Vietnamese. That American forces would remain heavily involved in the fighting for the time being was clear, as was the president's intention to pull back as soon as he could do so with honor.[24]

The approach had much to commend it from Nixon's point of view. Besides helping to alleviate public concern about an unending war, it would eliminate one possible source of opposition in Congress by keeping the cost of the conflict within tolerable limits. At the same time, it would bolster the self-esteem of the South Vietnamese government and people, the ones who would have to take over as American forces pulled back; demonstrate to the world that the United States could withdraw from the war while honoring its obligations to an ally; and undercut enemy propaganda that the United States intended to remain in South Vietnam forever as a colonial power. On the side, it would also preempt the arguments of the antiwar movement, which was calling for an end to

[24] Talking Paper, OASD SA, 3 Oct 69, sub: U.S. Objectives in Southeast Asia, folder 127, Thomas C. Thayer Papers, CMH files; Msg, Saigon 9723 to State, 19 May 69, sub: Secretary's Meeting With Thieu's Cabinet on 16 May, Pol 27 Viet S file, FAIM/IR; Memo, Daniel Z. Henkin for Secretary Laird, 12 Jan 70.

U.S. military involvement in South Vietnam and a commitment on the part of the administration to a total withdrawal of U.S. forces.[25]

There were likewise disadvantages. As American units withdrew, Henry Kissinger told the president, the morale of those troops who remained would probably decline, as would that of their relatives at home. The first withdrawals would thus increase the pressure for more and diminish the administration's freedom of action. In addition, if the pressure of withdrawals became too great or if the president went too far in stressing them, the United States might lose what advantage it had in Paris by destroying any incentive for the enemy to negotiate on terms favorable to American interests. As it was, analysts with the Defense Department added, the struggle would probably continue for the foreseeable future, if only because the enemy would never agree to a peace treaty that provided for mutual troop withdrawals and the sort of free elections that the United States sought for South Vietnam.[26]

There was also South Vietnam itself to consider. Although President Thieu had managed to keep control of the country's government and had been elected by popular vote in 1967, his regime had little popular support and took what legitimacy it had from its ability to retain the support and approval of the United States. The country's armed forces meanwhile lacked qualified leaders, especially at the platoon and company levels, and still suffered from indiscipline and high desertion rates. They fought well on occasion but just as often badly. The South Vietnamese people, for their part, staggered under the exactions of corrupt politicians and black-marketeers who leached, by Ambassador Bunker's conservative estimate, tens of millions of dollars from the economy every year.[27]

The challenge facing the Nixon administration seemed clear. It had to ease antiwar pressures at home by reducing draft calls, cutting casualties, and withdrawing American combat forces; to persuade President Thieu to broaden the base of his government, reform the military system, and eliminate corruption; and all the while to convince the enemy that the United States was determined to fight the war for as long as necessary to gain an honorable peace. If the task seemed daunting, there were, for Nixon, few plausible alternatives.

The program the administration settled on to turn the war over to the South Vietnamese, officially titled Vietnamization, received the immedi-

---

[25] Memo, Laird for the President, 4 Apr 70, sub: Vietnam, 330–776–076, box 13, Viet 381, Laird Papers, WNRC; Msg, Saigon 9723 to State, 19 May 69, sub: Secretary's Meeting With Thieu's Cabinet on 16 May.

[26] Memo, Henry A. Kissinger for the President, 10 Sep 69, sub: Our Present Course in Vietnam, in Kissinger, *The White House Years*, p. 1480; Talking Paper, OASD SA, 3 Oct 69, sub: U.S. Objectives in Southeast Asia. Also see Kissinger, *The White House Years*, p. 274.

[27] Memo, Laird for the President, 4 Apr 70, sub: Vietnam; Msg, Saigon 1514 to State, 31 Jan 70, sub: Discussion With President Thieu, General Abrams' Personal file 11, CMH. The Personal file is a collection of information copies of State Department cables Abrams received from the U.S. embassy in Saigon.

ate support of the news media. Laird's comments introducing it, the 25,000-man troop withdrawal, and suggestions in public and private that the United States had adopted a policy leading to the total removal of its forces from South Vietnam all produced positive news stories. There were doubts, especially about whether the South Vietnamese were ready or willing to fight on their own, and suggestions that U.S. commanders in South Vietnam were, as columnists Rowland Evans and Robert Novak put it, "tearing their hair" over the policy, but throughout the year a flow of generally favorable commentaries in the press continued. Whatever the problems, the program seemed to many within the press a better way to discern Hanoi's intentions than continued escalation.[28]

As 1969 progressed, the Nixon administration nevertheless remained divided on how much emphasis the American desire to withdraw should receive. Politically oriented officials who agreed with Secretary Laird remained convinced that Congress would shortly begin cutting off financing for the war. Viewing withdrawals as a necessity, they considered public references to them important to reassure both Congress and the American people that the war was ending. Those more concerned with the negotiations, Henry Kissinger in particular, while agreeing on the shortness of time, meanwhile insisted that official references to the subject remain vague and in low key. In that way, they hoped to ensure that the enemy received the impression of an American willingness to stay the course. They also sought to buy time for the South Vietnamese government, which faced collapse if rigid scheduling and hasty decisions forced the pace of withdrawals too fast.[29]

Public affairs policy favored Kissinger's approach but political realities often intruded. Standing procedures stipulated, for example, that administration spokesmen were to stress in conversations with newsmen that even if the United States removed its combat forces, a powerful contingent of Americans would remain in South Vietnam as long as necessary to provide advice and support. There was to be no talk of future plans, deadlines, or timetables for reductions. Instead, the government's public position was to be that all decisions on reductions were based on three criteria: the level of enemy activity in South Vietnam, the rate of improvement of the South Vietnamese armed forces, and whether the peace talks in Paris were making progress. Even so, when former Secretary of Defense Clark Clifford in an article in *Foreign Affairs* called for the unilateral withdrawal of 100,000 men by the end of the year and all combat forces by December 1970, President Nixon felt compelled to retake the high ground by responding, much to

[28] Rowland Evans and Robert Novak, "Secret Laird Plan Will Allow Early Troop Pull Out," *Washington Post*, 24 Mar 69; Memo, Henkin for Secretary Laird, 12 Jan 70.

[29] MFR, OASD SA, 13 Nov 69, sub: Vietnamization Meeting With Secretary Laird, file 75, Thayer Papers, CMH; Kissinger, *The White House Years*, p. 274; Memo, Marshall Green, East Asia desk (EA), for Acting Secretary, 12 Aug 69, sub: The President's Trip, Pol 7 US/Nixon file, FAIM/IR.

Nixon visits American troops in Vietnam.

the chagrin of his national security adviser, that he hoped to improve on Clifford's timetable.[30]

Kissinger was further alarmed when an article in the *New York Times* based on a background interview with General Abrams stated that U.S. commanders in South Vietnam considered a total pullout of American combat forces "feasible" by mid-1971. Although Laird told the president that he was pleased with Abrams' comments because they indicated that the general "understood our objectives and supported them," the national security adviser, according to Laird, was furious.[31] So was the president after hearing Kissinger's reasons. He had strong words to say, Wheeler told Abrams, "about officials who believe they must make statements on this subject at this time."

Shortly thereafter, the president issued new instructions reemphasizing the ban on all talk that linked withdrawals to any particular date.[32]

On the whole, although some officials might have disagreed on the amount of emphasis Vietnamization should receive in public, there was little doubt in anyone's mind that the administration had to keep as much control over appearances as possible. After the president announced the first troop redeployment, for example, news commentaries on television and in the press began to question whether Abrams would be able to reduce his command to 515,000 men by 31 August. Those remarks prompted a reaction from the White House. Aware that the number of American soldiers in South Vietnam varied broadly from day to day as men arrived and departed, the president began to pres-

[30] Msg, Saigon 9723 to State, 19 May 69, sub: Secretary's Meeting With Thieu's Cabinet on 16 May; Msg, State 158482 to Saigon, 18 Sep 89, Pol 27–14 Viet S file, FAIM/IR; Clark Clifford, "Vietnam Reappraisal," *Foreign Affairs* (July 1969); Kissinger, *The White House Years*, p. 274.

[31] Terrence Smith, "U.S. Officers Find Pull Out Feasible by Middle of 71," New York Times, 7 Nov 69. Quote from MFR, OASD SA, 13 Nov 69, sub: Vietnamization Meeting With Secretary Laird.

[32] Quote from Msg, Wheeler JCS 13914 to Abrams, 7 Nov 69, Abrams Papers, CMH. Also see MFR, OASD SA, 18 Nov 69, sub: Vietnam Meeting With Secretary Laird, file 75, Thayer Papers, CMH. The guidance is in Msg, State 192924 to Saigon, 17 Nov 69, Pol 27–14 Viet S file, FAIM/IR.

112

sure Laird and Wheeler to make certain that designated units left on time and that no temporary rebound in troop strength occurred. The president had concluded, Wheeler explained to Abrams and McCain, that "increases after 31 August in our manpower in South Vietnam would risk the same adverse public reactions as failure to reach the target."[33]

In the same way, Nixon warned President Thieu during a visit to Saigon in August that public comments on the war by administration officials might occasionally depart from his own privately expressed assurances to the South Vietnamese. "In this complex war deeply involving public opinion problems," he said, "statements sometimes have to be made which those lacking understanding of public opinion factors can misread. We must trust each other. If we do, there will not be such misunderstanding."[34]

Improving the South Vietnamese Image

As the Vietnamization effort gathered momentum, officials in both Washington and Saigon thus became increasingly sensitive to situations and circumstances that opened either the South Vietnamese government or the Military Assistance Command, Vietnam, to criticism. During June 1969, for example, CBS News televised a report in which Secretary of State Rogers told a news conference that the South Vietnamese were taking over more of the burden of the war "not because we have pushed them but because they are now quite capable of doing so." The network followed the story with a second, filmed in South Vietnam by correspondent Larry Pomeroy, which stated that a South Vietnamese Regional Forces company had panicked under fire and run off in all directions. Galled by Pomeroy's revelation and its proximity to Rogers' comment, President Nixon immediately requested a report on both the incident and the general operational abilities of the South Vietnamese armed forces. He learned in response that the company in question had indeed done poorly but that in a similar operation several days later, unattended by television cameras, several members of the unit had earned the American Bronze Star for heroism.[35]

Agitated by reports of that sort and convinced that the American news media had failed, at Ben Het and elsewhere, to bring out South Vietnamese achievements, General Wheeler began his inquiry into the Defense Department's public relations efforts on behalf of the South

[33] Msg, Wheeler JCS 10285 to McCain, Abrams, 20 Aug 69, Abrams Papers, CMH.
[34] Memo, Marshall Green, EA, for the Acting Secretary, 12 Aug 69, sub: The President's Trip.
[35] Memo, Alexander Butterfield, Deputy Assistant to the President, for Laird, Kissinger, 10 Jun 69, 330–75–089, box 104, Viet (South) 320.2 (Jun) 1969, Laird Papers, WNRC.

Vietnamese. He found that the U.S. mission in Saigon had for months insisted that the South Vietnamese themselves brief newsmen on the operations they conducted. With the American presence declining, so the reasoning went, they would sooner or later have to develop a public relations program of their own, and experience seemed the best instructor. Wheeler concluded that while the policy had merit, conditions in South Vietnam argued against its full implementation at that time. The South Vietnamese lacked well-trained information officers; their commanders resisted the American practice of announcing operations in progress; and the Saigon correspondents put little faith in news releases generated by South Vietnamese public affairs officers.[36] "In our efforts to ensure that the RVNAF story is told by Vietnamese," the general told Abrams, "we may be underplaying our own role. Now that modernization and Vietnamization programs are moving along, I think it is important that we express to the degree possible our public support of the success RVNAF is having in the field, and highlight the manner [in] which they are assuming more combat responsibility."[37]

Wheeler suggested that the Military Assistance Command in Saigon examine its procedures to determine the action it should take to improve the visibility and image of the South Vietnamese armed forces. Official spokesmen might highlight South Vietnamese participation in American operations, the effective use they were making of American advice and support, and examples of the new responsibilities they had assumed as U.S. forces pulled back. The command might also release background information about the program to improve and modernize South Vietnamese units and search for more ways to provide support for South Vietnamese public affairs efforts. On the side, Wheeler also recommended that the command develop a series of periodic reports emphasizing South Vietnamese operations and the effect the Vietnamization program was having on them. "This would give us ammunition to use in our contacts with the press here."[38]

General Abrams responded by pointing out what the Military Assistance Command was already doing to promote the South Vietnamese image. The daily news communique, he said, included South Vietnamese participation in U.S. combat operations. Public affairs officers devoted major attention to aspects of the war that exemplified Vietnamization, especially the turnover of installations and equipment and the expanding combat role of the South Vietnamese armed forces. The command meanwhile maintained close and continuing contact with

[36] Memo, Wheeler CM–4446–69 for Director, Joint Staff, 23 Jul 69, sub: Coordination of Press Treatment of RVNAF and Other Free World Forces, and Memo, Col L. Gordon Hill, Chief of MACV Information, for Col Lee Smith, 19 Jul 69, sub: Procedure for the Release of Information on Free World Forces Operating in Republic of Vietnam, both in DDI Operations file.

[37] RVNAF stands for Republic of Vietnam armed forces. Msg, Wheeler CJCS 9587 to Abrams, 4 Jul 69, sub: Publicizing RVNAF Achievements, Abrams Papers, CMH.

[38] Msg, Wheeler CJCS 9587 to Abrams, 4 Jul 69, sub: Publicizing RVNAF Achievements.

114

the South Vietnamese information organization, seeking any opening it could find to strengthen the program.[39]

Abrams added nevertheless that he would take additional action. While he had no intention of supplanting South Vietnamese news releases with announcements by American briefers, he intended to reestablish, subject to the Saigon regime's concurrence, the practice of reporting in the daily American communique significant South Vietnamese actions involving U.S. artillery or air support. He would also encourage the South Vietnamese to compile and publish monthly and annual summaries of significant operations and to conduct regular background briefings on important subjects, even those that involved problems. As for the South Vietnamese information program, Abrams said that he would attempt to persuade the Joint General Staff to increase the number of billets within the armed forces devoted to public affairs. As it was, he noted by way of example, only five were authorized for the entire South Vietnamese Air Force. In the same way, he would encourage the South Vietnamese armed forces to authorize a larger number of knowledgeable officers to brief the U.S. press in the field and would instruct U.S. commanders to augment South Vietnamese public affairs efforts with U.S. information personnel during significant operations.[40]

Although the Commander in Chief, Pacific, Admiral McCain, concurred with Abrams' suggestions, he insisted that Americans could not continue to provide public relations services for the South Vietnamese. "[A] very recent discussion with top U.S. news correspondents," he told General Wheeler,

. . . disclosed little faith in the ARVN [South Vietnamese Army's] spokesmen in Saigon, or in the statistics provided by RVNAF field commanders. My feelings are that to fully Vietnamize the war, the Vietnamese should establish and operate their own public information program on a professional and credible basis for both the internal Vietnamese and the external world audiences. No matter how fast the process of Vietnamization, an effective public information program is needed to gain not only release and publication of material, but also to gain acceptance by the press and their subscribers. Otherwise our effort for public acceptance of U.S. actions may be made increasingly more difficult.

McCain understood the reluctance of the South Vietnamese government and military to publish unfavorable news but believed that the continuation of long-term American support required that they do so. To that end, he suggested that the Military Assistance Command persuade the Joint General Staff to divorce its public affairs organization from the propaganda agency that had thus far always coordinated its activities. A step of that sort would make it clear that the South Vietnamese government no longer equated public relations with psychological warfare. McCain also

---

[39] Msg, Abrams MAC 10252 to Wheeler, 8 Aug 69, sub: Publicizing ARVN Achievements, Abrams Papers, CMH.
[40] Ibid.

suggested that the Military Assistance Command establish a short, in-country information course for South Vietnamese public affairs officers. Summarizing portions of the curriculum conducted for American personnel at the U.S. Defense Information School at Fort Benjamin Harrison, Indiana, those classes might provide the South Vietnamese with some understanding of the role and functioning of a free press in a free society. At the very least, it seemed reasonable that the effort would impart some feel for how they could successfully and credibly manage their relations with the Saigon correspondents.[41]

The push for improvements in South Vietnam's public affairs activities came at a time of increasing financial stringency for both the Department of Defense and the U.S. mission in Saigon. Shortly after taking office in 1969, reacting to budget cutbacks, Secretary Laird had instructed the Office of the Assistant Secretary of Defense for Public Affairs to decentralize its activities and seek economies. Over the next twelve months, the agency cut its staff by 13 percent and its budget by $5 million. Similar reductions occurred at the 128-man Joint U.S. Public Affairs Office in Saigon, where administrators were under instructions to drop thirteen officers by December and another twelve by the following July.[42]

Retrenchments were under way as well at the MACV Office of Information, but budget cutbacks appear to have been only partly the reason. In a 1 December 1969 memorandum to Henry Kissinger, President Nixon had mandated quiet cuts in the number of military public affairs people serving in South Vietnam. Like their counterparts in the press, he said, they tended to "lean to the left" and posed "particularly difficult" problems for that reason.[43] The Military Assistance Command complied, but only superficially. Although the withdrawal of American units cut 130 spaces from MACV's public information activities during the 1969–1970 fiscal year—a 15.7 percent decrease in personnel—50 percent of that reduction came from command and troop information functions. Secretary Laird and General Abrams deferred most drawdowns in the organization's 53-man central staff until after the end of 1970. In that way they sought to retain adequate resources to tell the Vietnamization story while continuing to furnish advisory assistance to the South Vietnamese armed forces.[44]

[41] Msg, McCain to Wheeler, 17 Aug 69, sub: Publicizing RVNAF Achievements, Abrams Papers, CMH.

[42] Talking Paper, OASD PA, 20 Apr 70, sub: Public Affairs Staffing and Operations, Laird Workbook, Issues of Special Interest, 330–76–076, box 1, 020 D02 (30 Apr 70), Laird Papers, WNRC; Msg, Saigon 13585 to State, Bunker for Ambassador Brown, 31 Jul 69, sub: Civilian Staff Reduction, 74D417, box 2, Bunker Papers, FAIM/IR.

[43] Memo, the President for Henry Kissinger, 1 Dec 69, Vietnam Country files, box 141, V.XIII–1, Nixon Papers, quoted in MS, Graham A. Cosmas, MACV, The Joint Command [Washington, D.C.: U.S. Army Center of Military History].

[44] Memo, Laird for Kissinger, 19 Feb 70, 330–76–067, box 88, Viet 000.7, 1970, Laird Papers, WNRC; Memo, Laird for Kissinger, 20 Dec 69, 330–75–089, box 89, Viet 000.7, 1969, Laird Papers, WNRC; MACV History, 1969, p. XI-2.

Despite the cutbacks, the chief of MACV information, Colonel Hill, had already begun an effort to promote Vietnamization by inaugurating regular background briefings on the subject. Gathering thirty important bureau chiefs and reporters together at the command's headquarters once every two weeks, the sessions dealt with a broad range of topics, from the enemy's COSVN Resolution Number 9 to the South Vietnamese highway construction program. The briefings caused some friction with the State Department, which at first suspected that the resulting news stories had been based on leaks. They nevertheless prompted a number of favorable articles detailing the progress of Vietnamization.[45]

With the arrival of Wheeler's message to Abrams, the program to publicize South Vietnamese achievements gained further momentum. The Military Assistance Command redoubled its efforts to arrange tours by newsmen to sites and special events that highlighted Vietnamization, and military motion picture crews filmed an increasing number of reports on the subject for release to television stations in the United States. Information officers in the field meanwhile made an extra effort to compose feature articles on newsworthy South Vietnamese developments for use by either the civilian news media or official publications. On the side, American public affairs advisers to the South Vietnamese armed forces drew close to their counterparts to suggest ways to improve the Saigon regime's relations with the news media.[46]

Although the South Vietnamese remained suspicious of the press and never divorced public affairs from propaganda, they did bend somewhat to the pressure. The chief of the information directorate sought English-language training for his officers and began to staff his command center on a 24-hour basis in order to keep updated news on hand for the press. Toward the end of the year, the Joint General Staff dropped an irritating requirement that had forced newsmen to submit a letter of introduction from the Directorate of Information every time they sought to visit a South Vietnamese unit in the field. The South Vietnamese also began to coordinate trips by newsmen to visit combat units, a task previously handled entirely by Americans.[47]

In a separate development, the Military Assistance Command secured agreement with the South Vietnamese government for a program to send promising South Vietnamese public affairs officers to the U.S. Defense Information School. The command had approved the attendance of South Vietnamese at the school since 1967, but the training had occurred only on a hit-or-miss basis. With formal procedures in place, there seemed some

[45] MACV Office of Information, Report on MACOI Involvement in Reporting the Vietnam War, 10 Feb 70; MFR, MACOI for the Chief of Staff, MACV, n.d. [1970], sub: MACOI Blue Ribbon Panel on Defense Briefing, DDI Correspondence with MACV (36a) file; MACV History, 1969, p. XI-5.

[46] MACV History, 1969, p. XI-30.

[47] Ltr, Col William Woodside, Chief, Information Advisory Division, MACOI, to Chief, MACOI, 8 Feb 70, attachment to MACOI, Report on MACOI Involvement in Reporting the Vietnam War, DDI Correspondence with MACOI (36a) file.

Promise but also problems—improperly stored supplies and ammunition at a South Vietnamese depot

hope that the South Vietnamese armed forces might at last develop a corps of truly professional public affairs officers.

In fact, results were uneven. The concept of a free press, whether in peace or war, remained alien to most South Vietnamese commanders, and few of the newly trained public affairs officers proved willing to give advice that they knew would be unpalatable to their superiors. As a result, the South Vietnamese armed forces continued to inhibit reporting of the war from their side, especially when things went wrong, and never developed the kind of sophistication in handling the news media that might have furthered their cause with the Saigon correspondents.

That being the case, the Defense Department's program nevertheless produced some short-term gains. Trained South Vietnamese public affairs officers began to take up station at division and corps headquarters, where the perspectives and personal relationships they had acquired in the United States sometimes proved useful. On one occasion, shortly after the U.S. 9th Division relinquished its base at Dong Tam, unfavorable news stories appeared in the American press comparing the lax security in force at the base under the South Vietnamese with the more exacting procedures of the Americans. When the base commander, true to form, responded by closing the installation to newsmen, the Military Assistance Command prevailed upon him to relent by calling up the services of public affairs officers it had trained.[48]

[48] Ltr, Daniel Z. Henkin to Congressman Ogden Reid, 21 Jan 70, DDI Correspondence with MACV (36a) file. Also see Today Show, NBC-TV, 8 Oct 69, *Radio-TV-Defense Dialog.*

Whatever the insufficiencies of the South Vietnamese, the attempt to publicize the progress of Vietnamization went forward. As it did, both the Defense Department and the Military Assistance Command took pains to keep the program in low key. Cautioned continually by Henkin, official spokesmen avoided the sort of overoptimism that had been so damaging during the Johnson years. In Washington, administration sources were quietly optimistic in their assessments but stated repeatedly in speeches, television appearances, and interviews that the enemy retained the ability to take offensive action whenever he wished and that setbacks were bound to occur. The same policy prevailed in South Vietnam, where information officers said no more than necessary on the subject and allowed reporters to see for themselves.[49]

The news dispatches that resulted often pointed up difficulties, but, as Henkin told Laird, "For the most part, criticism and cautioning have been helpful in that they . . . create a realistic picture of the promise as well as the problems in the program." In that way, Henkin said, they helped to allay the concerns and suspicions of some in the United States that Vietnamization was a sham.[50]

Although negative news reports about the South Vietnamese government and armed forces thus remained a feature of the war, from October on the Military Assistance Command's efforts produced a spate of articles and commentaries on South Vietnamese successes.[51] In a long article for the *Washington Post*, Robert G. Kaiser observed that if many problems remained—one South Vietnamese district chief, the reporter said, had used government funds to support ten women in ten different houses—there also seemed to be signs of hope. The Regional and Popular Forces had received new M16 rifles and were showing improvement. Operators of the Chieu Hoi program which sought to encourage enemy defections could boast that a large number of Viet Cong had voluntarily rallied to the government in the previous year. The armed forces were moving steadily into formerly hostile territories, bringing with them "at least a measure of security, and in many places true peace." Kaiser was cautious, noting that the South Vietnamese were far more pessimistic in their assessments than the Americans and that official statistics remained questionable, but he indicated that the enemy appeared to be in decline and that there seemed to be reason to adopt a wait-and-see attitude.[52]

In a story similar to the one by Kaiser, Peter Kann of the *Wall Street Journal* told of how he and three other reporters had rented a 1954 Volkswagen and set off on a 400-mile journey across the Mekong Delta to test

[49] Memo, Daniel Z. Henkin for Brig Gen George S. Blanchard, Director, Vietnam Task Group, OSD ISA, 29 Jan 70, 330–76–067, box 99, Viet (South) 320.2 (Jan–Feb) 1970, Laird Papers, WNRC.

[50] Memo, Henkin for Laird, 12 Jan 70.

[51] Ibid.

[52] Robert G. Kaiser, "Pacification (1969 Style) Seems To Be Working," *Washington Post*, 30 Oct 69.

"if there is no progress at the peace table, is there at least progress on the battlefield." The reporter noted that the trip had offered "glimpses of recent progress and perennial problems," but no grand conclusions. The only observation he would venture was that "three unarmed Americans were able to spend a week driving through rural Vietnam without being shot at. That, perhaps, is progress."[53]

One of the most positive stories came from Wendell Merick of *U.S. News & World Report*. Assigned to evaluate whether the progress officials were pointing to was real, Merick concluded that there had been a significant turn for the better in South Vietnam. Although fighting would continue and the government had hardly done as well as officials had claimed in pacifying the countryside, eliminating corruption, and destroying the Viet Cong infrastructure, "there is discernable momentum toward all of those objectives. Six months ago that could not be reported."[54]

Another favorable report, produced by Charles Collingwood for CBS News and featuring an interview with President Thieu, seemed so balanced and forthright that the U.S. Information Agency purchased it. "Department believes film should be helpful in providing better understanding of our Vietnam policy and programs," the State Department told its chiefs of mission around the world, "both for members of your own official establishment and for foreign officials and opinion leaders."[55]

Despite the growing success of the effort to promote Vietnamization, pressure continued within the Department of Defense for an even more elaborate, worldwide program involving all the agencies of the U.S. government. Henkin opposed the creation of anything of the sort, arguing that so large a program would overemphasize the success of Vietnamization and open the United States to criticism if setbacks occurred. His argument prevailed. As 1970 began, official policy continued to stress candor and perspective and to warn against the dangers inherent in too much optimism.[56]

The decision was, perhaps, fortunate. For as Henkin had clearly perceived, the success of American policy in South Vietnam depended on more than words, and much remained in doubt. Could the South

---

[53] Peter R. Kann, "A Long, Leisurely Drive Through the Mekong Delta Tells Much of the War," *Wall Street Journal*, 10 Nov 69.

[54] Wendell S. Merick, "Behind Optimism About Vietnam," *U.S. News & World Report*, 1 Dec 69, p. 40.

[55] Quote from Msg, State 7081 to All Diplomatic Posts, for Chiefs of Mission, 16 Jan 70, sub: CBS Reports: A Timetable for Vietnam, Pol 27 Viet S file, FAIM/IR. Also see Msg, State 202666 to Saigon, 5 Dec 69, Pol 27 Viet S file, FAIM/IR.

[56] MFR, OASD SA, 5 Jan 70, sub: Vietnamization Meeting With Secretary Laird, folder 75, Thayer Papers, CMH; Memo, Henkin for Blanchard, 29 Jan 70. Also see Talking Paper, OASD PA, n.d., sub: Vietnamization, attachment to Memo, Jerry W. Friedheim, Deputy Assistant Secretary of Defense for Public Affairs, for Daniel Z. Henkin, 30 Sep 69, sub: Request by Vietnamization Group for Draft Public Affairs Suggestions for Vietnamization, DDI Vietnamization (Gen) file.

Vietnamese institute the reforms necessary to create a viable long-term government? Could their armed forces take the initiative on the battle-field? Most of all, if the United States, with all its power and resources, had failed to impose its will on the enemy, would the South Vietnamese—with less power, fewer resources, and more problems—be capable of doing so? The only thing that seemed clear was that the Nixon adminis-tration needed time to achieve its ends and that to gain time, in what was becoming an increasingly dangerous political environment, it would have to control the public images of both the South Vietnamese and the war.

6

Keeping Control: South Vietnam

Although the effort to promote Vietnamization appeared reasonably successful, the Nixon administration recognized that much remained in doubt. The United States might lavish equipment and advice upon South Vietnam but neither the enemy nor the American people would credit administration claims of progress if that nation failed to put the assistance to proper use. In the same way, public and congressional backing for a prolonged American commitment to the war, critical to the negotiated settlement Nixon sought, depended on whether the American people considered the country worth saving and whether the long-term interests of the United States, as perceived by that public, would suffer in the process. If the South Vietnamese allowed their image further to deteriorate or if the United States itself gave the appearance of losing control, pressure might mount for a settlement on any terms.[1]

The challenge seemed manageable on the surface, provided the South Vietnamese cooperated and American fighting forces retained their effectiveness. As 1969 progressed, however, indications began to arise that the task might be more difficult than it appeared. That the Saigon correspondents were prepared to report every development only made matters worse.

The South Vietnamese Image

The government of South Vietnam was the Nixon administration's foremost concern. Beginning with the Diem regime, through all the years of the war to date, it had failed time and again to make the changes neces-

---

[1] Memo, Laird for the President, 4 Sep 69, sub: Vietnamizing the War (NSSM 36), Pol 27 Viet S file, FAIM/IR.

sary to put itself on an effective footing. The result was apparent in the news media's coverage of Vietnamization. Reporters hoped that the program would work and continually relayed information that indicated a turn for the better was in prospect, but the suspicion persisted that the South Vietnamese would ultimately fail to measure up. During June, for example, an article by columnist Jack Anderson appeared in widely circulated *Parade Magazine* detailing the operations of the Saigon black market and highlighting the lifestyles of some of its millionaire operators. On 21 July 1969, Harry Reasoner of CBS News pointed out that junior officers were the ones that fought the South Vietnamese portion of the war and that the upper ranks of the country's armed forces rarely went into the field. The same had been true in President Ngo Dinh Diem's day, prior to large-scale American involvement in the war. On 29 August Robert Keatley of the *Wall Street Journal* observed that South Vietnamese President Thieu continued to resist American advice to broaden his government to include anti-Communist members of the opposition. The appeal of the government thus remained limited. When Thieu appointed a new cabinet in early September, he replaced Prime Minister Tran Van Huong with a right-wing conservative military man, General Tran Thien Khiem, known for his fidelity to the ruling elite. Keatley noted that the new cabinet seemed to have narrowed the government's political base. As a result, Thieu's ability to rally the mass support he needed for an eventual political showdown with the Communists appeared as doubtful as ever.[2]

Time-Life photographer-correspondent Larry Burrows expressed the concerns of many newsmen when he commented during September on the reaction of the South Vietnamese people to the beginning of American withdrawals. "There is a limit," he said, "to the resiliency of spirit of any people, no matter how strong." The Tet offensive, however costly to the enemy, had demonstrated that the Communists could strike anywhere in South Vietnam. During the first six months of 1969, the Viet Cong had kidnapped 4,674 South Vietnamese civilians, 200 more than during the last six months of 1968. Many of those victims were officials of the government, policemen, and teachers.

Of course the Viet Cong, over on the other side, are known to fear the bombs of the unseen B–52's overhead. But it is also true that when darkness falls every local defense militiaman thinks about the V.C.'s seeming ability to go anywhere, and when he thinks about it enough, or is frightened enough, he may be ready to make an accommodation. I asked a friend if he knew of a dedicated and honest village chief. "They are as rare as the autumn leaves," he said. There is no autumn in Vietnam.[3]

---

[2] Jack Anderson, "American Made Millionaires in Vietnam," *Parade*, 8 Jan 69. The Reasoner report is summarized in Msg, McCain to Abrams, 22 Jul 69, Abrams Papers, CMH. Also see Robert Keatley, "Thieu Lagging in Effort To Unite Land, Bar Reds From Post War Power," *Wall Street Journal*, 29 Aug 69; "South Vietnam's Thieu Installs New Cabinet," *Wall Street Journal*, 2 Sep 69.

[3] Larry Burrows, "Vietnam: A Degree of Disillusion," *Life*, 19 Sep 69, p. 67.

More reports along that line appeared during October. On the twenty-seventh *U.S. News & World Report* published an outspoken assessment of the American position in South Vietnam by an unidentified, high-level U.S. military intelligence officer in Saigon. Noting that the government of South Vietnam was a late arrival to the political scene and that it lacked the leadership necessary to challenge the Viet Cong, the author summarized the problems confronting the United States. The effort to eliminate enemy activists among the people, the so-called PHOENIX program, he said, was limping badly. Many captured Viet Cong left confinement within days because they had connections with local politicians or because they had paid off the correct officials. Government forces failed to apprehend other important Viet Cong because those responsible feared enemy retribution or refused to "rock the boat." Meanwhile, corruption was so endemic to the South Vietnamese bureaucracy that it was impossible to wage an effective campaign to ensure a non-Communist government. "We could keep our present troop level another 10 years and not win this war as long as the South Vietnamese Army and Government fail to make the necessary moves to win. . . . As one South Vietnamese colonel said, American aid is like opium: 'Our people have become dependent upon it and have let the Americans do what we ought to be doing for ourselves.'"[4]

Hard on that report came another by John E. Woodruff of the *Baltimore Sun*. Headlined "U.S. Evaluation Shows Saigon Forces Decline in Combat Efficiency," the story was based on one of a series of confidential MACV analyses known collectively as the System for Evaluating the Effectiveness of the Republic of Vietnam Armed Forces, or the SEER Report. Woodruff avowed that the command's own evaluations confirmed a progressive decline in the fighting abilities of the South Vietnamese armed forces over the previous year. The reporter also stated that the information he had uncovered stood in marked contrast to the optimistic private briefings he and other reporters had received from U.S. official spokesmen.[5]

President Nixon and other officials in the United States read the comments appearing in the press with dismay. In the case of the article by Burrows, they questioned the Defense Department closely on the validity of the reporter's conclusions. In reply, Secretary Laird's military deputy, Col. Robert E. Pursley, U.S. Air Force, could do little more than confirm that the reporter had been accurate. The disillusionment afflicting the South Vietnamese people resulted from more than the American withdrawal. It was also tied to the long war, casualties, poor leadership on the part of the South Vietnamese government, and inadequate family benefits for the military. Nonetheless, the problems Burrows had described were real, and there were few short-range solutions. The same was true for the other articles. As Pursley noted in a memorandum to the president's mili-

[4] "State of the War: An Intelligence Report," *U.S. News & World Report*, 27 Oct 69, p. 36.
[5] John E. Woodruff, "U.S. Evaluation Shows Saigon Forces Decline in Combat Efficiency," *Baltimore Sun*, 29 Oct 69.

General Haig

tary assistant, Brig. Gen. Alexander Haig, the SEER Report described by Woodruff contained subjective and unrefined information, but the reporter's description of its contents was correct.[6]

The South Vietnamese themselves did little to remedy matters. Although they had complied with the Military Assistance Command's requests to take over more of the public affairs burden and had on a number of occasions opened their operations to reporters, they insisted on interpreting every news story that criticized the Thieu regime as a threat to national security. Newspapers in Saigon fared the worst. By July 1969 fourteen of thirty-one had been closed for violations of government restrictions, but the foreign press also ran afoul of the government. On 24 June, for example, the bureau chiefs from *Newsweek*, Agence France Presse, and Reuters were all summoned to South Vietnam's Ministry of Information to receive warnings. Reuters had published an apparently erroneous story stating that the Thieu regime was formulating a plan to invite the Communists to join a committee to supervise the next year's general elections. Agence France Presse had passed on allegations that former Prime Minister Tran Van Huong had been forced out of office to make room for Khiem. *Newsweek* had alleged in an article entitled "Vietnam Exodus" that many well-to-do South Vietnamese, including the wife of President Nguyen Van Thieu and other members of the government, were buying villas abroad and making preparations to leave the country in case of a Communist victory. After banning the offending issue of *Newsweek*, the director of the cabinet at the Ministry of Information, Tran Van Phuoc, threatened to expel any journalist who violated South Vietnamese sensitivities. "It is time to end the distinction between the foreign and local press," he told *Time* correspondent Burton Pines. "We have taken no action against foreigners because we considered them as guests. Now that will stop. We

[6] Memo, Col Robert E. Pursley for Col Alexander Haig, 3 Oct 69, sub: Presidential Inquiry, 330–75–089, box 89, Viet 000.7, 1969, and Memo, Pursley for Brig Gen Alexander Haig, 30 Oct 69, 330–75–089, box 103, Viet (South) 320.2, both in Laird Papers, WNRC. Also see Memo, Phil Odeen, OASD SA, for Henkin, 30 Oct 69, DDI Unreliable News Stories file; Msg, Col Joseph F. H. Cutrona, CINFO MACV, MAC 14095 to Col L. Gordon Hill, OASD PA, 30 Oct 69, DDI Unreliable News Stories file.

wish that we could be as hospitable as before, but now we have begun the political battle."[7]

The U.S. embassy in Saigon made the usual representations on behalf of *Newsweek* but could do little more. Seeking to preserve as much of the South Vietnamese image as possible, it then appealed to the Saigon correspondents out of a sense of decency and urged them to play down the incident, because, as embassy spokesmen observed, a nation at war had a right to protect the morale of its citizenry. Privately, Ambassador Bunker and General Abrams nevertheless realized that the tolerance of the press for South Vietnamese inadequacies was exhausted. The Thieu regime would have to curb corruption, improve the leadership of the armed forces, and find a formula to incorporate a political opposition into the life of the country if there was to be much hope for the South Vietnamese image in the United States.[8]

The South Vietnamese Attitude

President Thieu and his associates, for their part, appeared to have little sense of urgency where reform was concerned. One of the most energetic members of the South Vietnamese delegation to the peace talks in Paris, Col. Nguyen Huy Loi, described the regime's attitude during June, in a conversation with a member of the U.S. mission in Paris. Loi had just returned from a trip to Saigon, where he had met with Khiem, Chief of the Joint General Staff General Cao Van Vien, and other high-ranking officers and members of the government. He was concerned about what he considered the failure of South Vietnam's leaders to prepare the army and the people for the exertions that would necessarily begin when the Americans departed. Although the junior members of the military staff were apprehensive about the changes they saw in store, lacking instructions from higher up, they went about their business as though American forces would always be present. Their superiors meanwhile refused to take the negotiations seriously and remained unconvinced that there would ever be an accommodation with the Communists. Little planning had occurred at any level of the government either for Vietnamization or the negotiations. The Foreign Ministry seemed out of touch. Officials everywhere appeared preoccupied with their own personal affairs. Loi concluded that there was little hope. Until his term in Paris was up, he said, he would spend his time studying English composition.[9]

[7] "Vietnam Exodus," *Newsweek*, 23 Jun 69; "Censorship: Ominous Signs in Saigon," *Time*, 4 Aug 69; "Newsweek and Reuters Given Warning by Saigon on Reports," *New York Times*, 24 Jun 69.
[8] Msg, Saigon 1514 to State, 31 Jan 70, sub: Discussion With President Thieu, Jan 30, General Abrams' Personal file 11, CMH; "Newsweek and Reuters Given Warning by Saigon on Reports."
[9] Msg, Paris 9365 to State, 20 Jun 69, General Abrams' Personal file 17, CMH.

South Vietnamese Ambassador to the United States Bui Diem agreed with Loi. Vietnamization could succeed, he told interviewers at the State Department later in the year, only if Thieu united the country by seeking reconciliation with opposition politicians and only if he reformed the armed forces. Yet little serious thought or planning had occurred because Thieu trusted no one and was becoming increasingly isolated from political realities. Diem recognized that these were difficult problems to solve. The mobilization of 80,000 more men to replace departing U.S. troops would spur inflation in South Vietnam and demoralize the country's two most important groups, the military and the civil service. Yet more had to be done. The United States itself had failed, Diem said, to pressure Thieu effectively.[10]

Aware of the problem, Ambassador Bunker had in fact pressed Thieu continually for reforms. South Vietnam's image in the United States, he noted politely during an October meeting with the president, was "decidedly negative," especially in the news media. This resulted from a number of causes: the imprisonment of political opponents, most prominently the opposition candidate who had come in second to Thieu in the previous presidential election, Truong Dinh Dzu; censorship of the local press; the feeling that the country's bureaucracy was rife with corruption and that reform efforts had stalled; and a conviction on the part of many that the recent shuffling of Thieu's cabinet had narrowed rather than broadened the base of the government. Noting that Thieu had often said he wanted "to help the president [Nixon] to help us," Bunker suggested that there were steps he could take to eliminate these criticisms and to improve the image of his government. Thieu responded that he had in fact invited members of the opposition into his administration, only to have them refuse because the jobs he offered lacked the prestige they expected. As for Dzu, he was a hopeless case who would continue to advocate some sort of coalition with the Communists if freed from prison.[11]

Bunker returned to the theme in a meeting with Prime Minister Khiem three weeks later. Referring to a recent visit home, he told Khiem that he needed to speak frankly about the South Vietnamese image in the United States. He had been shocked, he said, "to see how negative that image had become, not only in the communications media but among people generally, including some who follow Vietnamese affairs. . . . Some of the criticism was clearly unfair, . . . but it must also be recognized that some actions of the Government, and some failures to act have contributed to it." Bunker again mentioned the jailing of Dzu, the lagging attack on corruption, and the failure of the government to broaden its

---

[10] MFR, U.S. Department of State, 11 Dec 69, sub: Views of Ambassador Bui Diem on President Thieu and Vietnamization, 330–75–089, box 103, Viet (South) 1969, Laird Papers, WNRC.

[11] Msg, Saigon 20975 to State, 18 Oct 69, sub: Meeting With President Thieu, October 17, General Abrams' Personal file 9, CMH.

base. He went into detail on the problem of the Saigon black market, which was already drawing the attention of Congressman John L. McClellan of Arkansas and would undoubtedly become the subject of future congressional hearings. As the result of recent scandals in the U.S. Post Exchange system, he said, the U.S. Military Assistance Command had already taken steps to control the importation of consumer products into the country. Khiem had to do the same by taking action against sidewalk vendors who openly displayed Post Exchange goods in their stalls and by moving to stamp out the illegal marketing of American currency.[12]

Bunker tried again after the first of the year. By then, McClellan had begun congressional hearings on black market and currency violations, the largest antiwar demonstrations to date had occurred in the United States, and the Nixon administration was clearly concerned about its ability to carry on in South Vietnam. The ambassador was pointed, almost scathing in his remarks. During the hearings, he told Thieu, American, Indian, Chinese, and South Vietnamese violators had been named. All were well known to South Vietnamese authorities. Yet, despite the hundreds of Americans engaging in the traffic and the notorious organized rings operating out of Tan Son Nhut Airport smuggling goods and currency, the South Vietnamese government had done nothing. The losses it had incurred as a result were spectacular—in black market cigarettes alone an estimated 2.5 billion piasters a year. Radical measures were necessary. Criticism in Congress and the news media had become so sharp that the president had established a high-level interagency committee in Washington to investigate. Meanwhile, the morale of the South Vietnamese public, armed forces, and civil service suffered. "A corrupt society is a weak society," Bunker said. "It is a society in which everyone is for himself, no one . . . for the common good."[13]

Thieu and Khiem were cooperative and took many notes of their conversations with Bunker, but nothing of substance ever seemed to happen. Corruption was, in fact, one of the means Thieu used to retain power. As Bunker and other Americans in South Vietnam were well aware, the president employed South Vietnam's inspectorate, controlled by his uncle, Ngo Xua Tich, to maintain dossiers on his generals. When an officer appeared reluctant to support one or another measure that the president wanted, Thieu would produce the information he had and threaten the man with exposure and arrest unless cooperation was forthcoming. The system was hardly perfect. It was common for investigating officers to confront their subjects and offer to destroy part of the information they had learned in return for bribes. Yet everyone appeared to bene-

---

[12] Quote from Msg, Saigon 22753 to State, 13 Nov 69, sub: Improving South Vietnam's Image—Truong Dinh Dzu. Also see Msg, Saigon 22754 to State, 13 Nov 69, sub: Improving South Vietnam's Image—the Black Market Problem. Both in the Bunker Papers, FAIM/IR.

[13] Msg, Saigon 1515 to State, 31 Jan 70, sub: Discussion With President Thieu, 30 January—Corruption, General Abrams' Personal file 11, CMH.

fit. The generals maintained a modicum of independence as well as their lucrative side concerns, and Thieu kept power. There were times when the president would have to replace a particularly corrupt officer to placate the Americans, but the man rarely faced prosecution. Instead he received a transfer to new duties and a promotion.[14]

The wives of important men were often the ones who coordinated corruption. Inseparable from their husbands as far as business was concerned, they used their positions to traffic in assignments, promotions, and transfers and to sell protection to racketeers. The wife of the chief of the Joint General Staff, for example, was widely reputed to be an important vender of military transfers from remote areas to Saigon or other cities. The wife of Prime Minister Khiem, the man in charge of South Vietnam's anticorruption campaign, held extensive shipping, stevedoring, and construction interests at the Port of Saigon and was believed to arrange exit permits for a fee. They and the wives of other prominent politicians and generals had become notorious for the standards of consumption they set, all unattainable on their husbands' salaries without considerable independent wealth or, as seemed the case, graft.[15]

If corruption was rampant at the highest levels of the South Vietnamese government, it reached to the lowest levels of military command in the field, where it affected the ability of some South Vietnamese units to engage the enemy. In many Regional and Popular Force units, for example, up to 20 percent of the men counted as present for duty were, in fact, "ghosts." To repay bribes or to collect the salaries involved, commanders routinely released a percentage of their men from service, especially the sons of important officials or rich merchants. For the same reason, they failed to report some of the deserters who fled their units and the deaths in combat of those men who lacked relatives to apply for death gratuities. American advisers rarely reported on the problem because the organizational chaos within the units they advised was so great that the officers involved seemed able to conjure up, almost at will, large numbers of men who were sick, wounded, on leave, or taking training at other locations. Nevertheless, according to the region's senior pacification adviser, John Paul Vann, a spot check of one battalion serving in the Mekong Delta revealed that of 396 men supposedly assigned, fewer than 200 were present for combat duty. On another occasion, Vann reported, when he visited the 514th South Vietnamese Regional Forces Company in the field, he could account for only 41 of the 80 men he had been told were on duty. A spot check of just one of five Popular Forces platoons serving in the area revealed a similar situa-

[14] Memo, Richard Helms, Director, Central Intelligence Agency, for Secretary Laird, 22 Sep 69, sub: Corruption Within the Inspectorate, 330–75–089, box 88, Viet 000.1, 1969, Laird Papers, WNRC.

[15] Airgram, State A–131, 13 Aug 71, sub: Some Aspects of Personal Relations Among Senior RVNAF Officers, General Abrams' Personal file 32, CMH.

tion. Only 12 of an authorized 35 men were actually present.[16]

Vann continued that over the years he had discussed the problem with a broad range of South Vietnamese officials from the level of lieutenant general on down. All confirmed that it existed and accepted the estimate of 20 percent. "Needless to say," he said, "their acknowledgement of the problem occurred during private conversations and [was] not for published record. . . . I will not be surprised if U.S. officials in the other corps, and for that matter in this corps, would tend to downplay this as a problem. I will point out, however, that there are probably no other officers of my civilian rank and no other general officers who have ever

John Paul Vann

spent a night in a RF/PF outpost or with a night patrol, and hence, must report on the basis of secondhand knowledge, if that." Vann concluded, quoting one of his South Vietnamese informants, that only a genuine determination on the part of President Thieu and his advisers to eradicate the problem could bring the practice to an end. "But, . . . there would be reactions from too many patrons, and this is why nothing is done."[17]

South Vietnamese Sensitivities

In truth, more was involved in the failure to reform than ineptitude and venality. When the United States had entered the war it had relegated the South Vietnamese to a subordinate position in their own country. American troops fought the enemy's main forces while South Vietnamese units were assigned to the tedious task of providing security for pacification. American dollars fueled the South Vietnamese economy. Americans out of military necessity built and repaired roads. Even the graft and cor-

---

[16] Memo, John Paul Vann, Deputy for Civilian Operations and Revolutionary Development Support (CORDS), IV Corps, for G. D. Jacobsen, Assistant Chief of Staff (ACofS), CORDS, MACV, 13 Aug 70, sub: Inquiry From Ambassador Bunker About "Ghosts on the Payroll," Papers of John Paul Vann, U.S. Army Military History Institute (MHI), Carlisle, Pa.

[17] Ibid.

ruption that Ambassador Bunker had fought so hard to eradicate were ultimately the result of the American presence. Official rhetoric put the South Vietnamese first in everything. The role of their forces in military operations received special notice in news releases, and the U.S. embassy in Saigon took care to consult with their leaders on major decisions. The concerns of the Americans nevertheless predominated, and the policies that governed the course of the war almost always took the shape that the United States sought. With the advent of the Vietnamization program the Nixon administration attempted to make the South Vietnamese more independent. Yet it found itself constrained—by attitude, circumstance, and its own conception of what the American people would tolerate—to the sort of role the United States had always played.

The effect on South Vietnamese morale became apparent in the local Saigon press in 1969. Editors and commentators complained bitterly when *Newsweek* alluded in an article to a contingency plan for American troops to fight South Vietnamese forces should that become necessary in connection with the redeployments. They also began to criticize statements in the American press that questioned their country's ability to take over the war. If the United States wanted South Vietnam to do most of the fighting, they asserted, it should give the country more of a say in the basic decisions that would govern its future.[18]

President Thieu shared those sentiments. Sensitive to the U.S. practice of selecting units for redeployment with only a nod to what he conceived as South Vietnam's requirements, he wanted more of an influence over the process. Failing that, he sought at least to give an appearance to his own people that he had an important role to play. The Nixon administration, for its part, clearly believed that the American public and Congress would react vehemently to any indication that South Vietnamese politicians might have some control over decisions affecting American lives.[19]

The issue surfaced during September 1969, when the South Vietnamese became assertive in their relationship with the United States. On the seventh, despite American prompting, Thieu refused to participate in a three-day cease-fire announced by the enemy in observance of Ho Chi Minh's death. On the fourteenth, he became upset with the timing and size of the second installment of U.S. withdrawals and threatened to withhold approval unless General Vien concluded that the reduction would have little effect on combat efficiency, territorial security, and the pacification program. He added that if, as a result of the redeployment, the enemy attacked and overran some city or destroyed the results of pacification, his people would denounce the withdrawals as too fast. Reassured

---

[18] Msg, Saigon 19453 to State, 26 Sep 69, sub: Current Political Mood in Saigon, Pol 27 Viet S file, FAIM/IR.

[19] Msg, Saigon 19453 to State, 26 Sep 69, sub: Current Political Mood in Saigon. Msg, Abrams MAC 12029 to Wheeler, 14 Sep 69, and Msg, Abrams MAC 12080 to Wheeler, 15 Sep 69, both in Abrams Papers, CMH.

by Vien, Thieu approved the plan the next day, but that evening Vice President Ky reasserted South Vietnamese prerogatives by leaking word to reporters at a cocktail party that President Nixon was about to announce another troop reduction totaling 40,500 men. Later in the evening, according to a UPI report that appeared the next day, Ky added that the United States might withdraw as many as 200,000 troops by the end of the year.[20]

General Vien

The leak, especially the assertion that 200,000 men might be withdrawn, caused anguish in Washington by threatening to add to pressures rising in the United States for larger and faster American redeployments. It also affected the administration's nego-
tiating stance in Paris by seeming to indicate that Nixon was prepared to withdraw American forces whether or not the enemy reduced the level of his activities in South Vietnam and contributed to progress in the negotiations. "I literally cannot find words to tell you the problems caused here in Washington by Vice President Ky's statement to the press," Wheeler told Abrams and McCain.

I am sure you will recognize that Ky's mischievous leaking created major problems in the public relations field for President Nixon. In fact, he has spent the better part of the day wrestling with the problem of how to rationalize Ky's statement with the press announcement which you took with you to show President Thieu. This imbroglio and others like it in the past are the reasons . . . that I have an abiding and deep sympathy for presidents of the United States. Of course, Secretary Laird and I were drawn into the public relations maelstrom created by Ky. Very frankly, we have had one hell of a time trying to hold the line.[21]

In the end, the president made the announcement as planned but stressed that, under the newly authorized troop ceiling, approximately 60,000 American fighting men would depart South Vietnam by 15 December. Henry Kissinger added in a later backgrounder for White House correspondents that the United States would replace its forces as

[20] Msg, Abrams MAC 12029 to Wheeler, 14 Sep 69; Msg, Wheeler JCS 11423 to McCain, Abrams, 15 Sep 69; and Msg, Abrams MAC 12096 to Wheeler, 15 Sep 69. All in Abrams Papers, CMH.
[21] Msg, Wheeler JCS 11423 to McCain, Abrams, 15 Sep 69.

rapidly as possible but would not give up the three criteria for continued withdrawals that it had adopted at the beginning of the program. For the rest, he said, the Nixon administration had never established a fixed schedule of withdrawals that it would hold to regardless of the actions of the other side.[22]

In the weeks that followed, Thieu remained truculent. Referring to the three criteria at a meeting with the press on 27 September, he observed that headway in Paris and the level of fighting in South Vietnam were far more important than the progress of the South Vietnamese armed forces in supplanting the Americans. He envisioned making proposals of his own by the end of the year, which would presumably show how many American troops his government thought could be replaced. The next day, on the ABC news program "Issues and Answers," he flatly stated that "we can replace a hundred, a hundred fifty thousand" U.S. troops in 1970, provided that the United States compensated South Vietnam with sufficient funds, arms, materiel, and training facilities. He also called for joint long-range planning on reductions because "we cannot accept surprises when we have war."[23]

Thieu was obviously nervous that he might come under pressure from the United States to accept more reductions than could be justified but saving face was also involved, as became apparent in October, when he began a dispute with the Nixon administration over the use of the word *Vietnamization*. Shortly after President Nixon had come into office, at a meeting of the National Security Council, Secretary of State Rogers had used the term *de-Americanization* to signify the process by which the United States would turn the war over to the South Vietnamese. Secretary of Defense Laird considered Rogers' term awkward and proposed the slightly more elegant expression *Vietnamization*, a term he had used earlier during Nixon's presidential campaign. No one paid much attention to the word at first. It passed into the official vocabulary and from there into the press.[24]

At the beginning, the South Vietnamese themselves appeared unconcerned. With time, however, the term began to rankle. It seemed to suggest that Americans were doing all the fighting when in fact the war had been Vietnamese for many years. Making the word an issue, Thieu expressed his concern on 23 October, when South Vietnamese Foreign Minister Tran Van Lam approached Ambassador Bunker with what he described as a "very delicate" question that he hoped Bunker would present "most tactfully" to the secretary of state. President Thieu had noticed, Lam said, that from time to time high officials in Washington made references to *Vietnamization* as if

---

[22] Ibid.; Msg, State 157599 to Saigon, 17 Sep 69, DDI Units Redeploying from Vietnam file.

[23] Msg, Saigon 19697 to State, 30 Sep 69, sub: Thieu's Latest Pronouncements on U.S. Troop Reductions, Pol 27 Viet S file, FAIM/IR.

[24] Historical Division, Joint Secretariat, JCS, The History of the Joint Chiefs of Staff: The Joint Chiefs of Staff and the War in Vietnam, 1969–1970 (cited hereafter as JCS History), 26 Apr 76, copy in CMH files. Friedheim says Laird used the term *Vietnamization* during the presidential campaign. Ltr, Friedheim to the author, 29 Jul 91, CMH files.

it were an all-encompassing concept embracing every aspect of the war. Thieu had no objection to use of the word to describe military, economic, or even social matters, but he considered the idea that the war had to be Vietnamized in a political sense injurious to South Vietnam. It implied that the country was an American satellite about to be cut adrift.[25]

Bunker agreed. In a message to the secretary of state he suggested that administration spokesmen avoid using *Vietnamization* to refer to political aspects of the situation in South Vietnam. The State Department concurred, as did President Nixon, who issued instructions on 6 November to that effect. The expression itself was nevertheless so broad and circumstances in South Vietnam so tangled that the approach proved unworkable. On 15 November, in a "private note" to Khiem broadly reprinted in the South Vietnamese and American news media, Thieu banned the word from his government's lexicon because, he said, it aided Communist propaganda by making his country seem to be a mercenary employee of the United States.[26]

There was little sentiment in American circles favorable to a change in terminology, if only because the Nixon administration had recently linked *Vietnamization* to another word, *Koreanization*, to form a new concept called *Asianization* that denoted the Nixon Doctrine as applied to the Far East. As a result, the State and Defense Departments for a time debated the tactics they should adopt in their dealings with the South Vietnamese government.[27] State advocated a soft approach. Defense, reflecting Laird's concerns, pushed for a strong line that instructed Bunker to tell Thieu continued semantic wrangling could only harm the public relations surrounding the war. "Both President Thieu and Vice President Ky 'must agree,'" Laird's representatives declared, "that . . . *Vietnamization* is the best available term, particularly when compared with *de-Americanization* and others that were initially used in this connection."[28]

In the end, no message of the kind Laird sought went out, a victory of sorts for the State Department. Yet American official spokesmen continued to refer to *Vietnamization* despite Thieu's objections. Should reporters inquire, the Office of the Assistant Secretary of Defense for Public Affairs stipulated, the Military Assistance Command could affirm blandly that "There is complete understanding and support between Washington and Saigon on efforts to turn over more and more of the U.S. role to the South Vietnamese. *Vietnamization*, of course, refers only to the assumption by the

---

[25] Msg, Saigon 21318 to State, 23 Oct 69, DDI Vietnamization (General) file.

[26] Ibid.; Memo, Henry A. Kissinger for Secretary of State, Secretary of Defense, 6 Nov 69, sub: Public Statements on Vietnamization, DDI Vietnamization (General) file; Msg, Saigon 23006 to State, 17 Nov 69, sub: President Thieu Decries Use of "Vietnamization," Pol 27 Viet S file, FAIM/IR. Also see George W. Ashworth, "Vietnamization's a No-No," *Christian Science Monitor*, 21 Nov 69.

[27] Memo, Marshall Green, EA, for Secretary of State, 21 Nov 69, sub: South Vietnamese Sensitivity Over Term "Vietnamization," Pol 27 Viet S file, FAIM/IR; Ashworth, "Vietnamization's a No-No."

[28] Memo, Robert L. Brown, Deputy Executive Secretary, for Secretary of State, 22 Nov 69, Pol 27 Viet S file, FAIM/IR.

Lawrence Spivak and Bui Diem on "Meet the Press"

Vietnamese of that portion of the war effort carried on previously by the United States. It does not refer to the total war effort in which the South Vietnamese themselves have carried such a large and heavy burden for so many years."[29]

The South Vietnamese were undeterred. Blocked from every direction in the effort to save face, Thieu finally came to the point. On 28 October Ambassador Diem approached the State Department with a proposal. It might be prudent, Diem said, if the next announcement of a redeployment came from President Thieu rather than President Nixon. Thieu would make a public declaration to the effect that the South Vietnamese armed forces were prepared to replace a given number of Americans. Nixon could follow with a statement acquiescing to the suggestion. Secretary Rogers rejected the idea out of hand. He understood, he told President Nixon, "the desire of the Vietnamese Government to leave the impression with their own people that they do have a significant say in these matters which are so fundamental to their own security," but the proposal was "fundamentally unsound." It would "put us in the position of letting the basic decisions be made by the Vietnamese."[30]

---

[29] Msg, Defense 14438 to MACV, Col L. Gordon Hill, Special Assistant for Southeast Asia, for Col Joseph F. H. Cutrona, Chief of MACV Information, 19 Nov 69, DDI Vietnamization (General) file.

[30] Memo, William P. Rogers for the President, 19 Nov 69, sub: Vietnamese Ambassador's Proposal for an Announcement of the Next Troop Redeployment. Also see Msg, Saigon 189884 to State, 10 Nov 69. Both in Pol 27 Viet S file, FAIM/IR.

136

A New Statement of Mission for MACV

If the Nixon administration found it difficult to repair the image of the South Vietnamese government and armed forces, it had its own public relations as well to consider. The president had managed to establish the credibility of his intention to turn the war over to the South Vietnamese, but nothing seemed certain. He had to guard continually against any occurrence in South Vietnam that might force the pace of withdrawals too fast or call into question the sincerity of his well-publicized desire to withdraw. The process required delicate balancing and sometimes painful readjustments.

During August, for example, in an attempt to emphasize to U.S. commanders in the field that American goals had changed, the administration had revised the statement of mission that declared the objectives the Military Assistance Command was to pursue. Where the old statement had indicated an intention to defeat the enemy and to force his withdrawal, the new one emphasized the desire of the United States "to assist the Republic of Vietnam Armed Forces to take over an increasing share of combat operations."[31] There was some resistance within the military at the time to a public announcement of the development. "A publicized change in mission statement," the Joint Chiefs told Secretary Laird, "could jeopardize the credibility of the administration and military because no substantial change in the pattern of operations in South Vietnam would follow." Recognizing the validity of the Joint Chiefs' concern, the president put the statement into effect without notifying the press.[32]

A low-keyed approach might have worked under different circumstances, but in the months that followed the American military in South Vietnam had more than a little difficulty adjusting to the revised objective. According to analysts at the Defense Department, the U.S. headquarters responsible for the northern portion of South Vietnam, XXIV Corps, persisted in following the old attrition strategy. So, apparently, did the U.S. Seventh Air Force, which controlled American air operations in South Vietnam. The attitude of the commander of XXIV Corps, Lt. Gen. Melvin Zais, typified how many American officers seemed to feel. While it was proper to turn the fighting over to the South Vietnamese, Zais told General Abrams during October 1969, American forces "should be departing as victors, proud of their contribution to this valiant people" rather than as the losers they appeared to be in news accounts. "We are winning! Now is the time to go for the jugular. Now is the time to intensify our efforts. Now is the time to up the rent for the VCI [Viet Cong infrastructure] and to raise the price of their

---

[31] Msg, Wheeler JCS 9668 to McCain, Abrams, 6 Aug 69, Abrams Papers, CMH.

[32] Quote from Memo, Wheeler JCSM–474–69 for Secretary of Defense, 30 Jul 69, sub: Statement of Mission of U.S. Forces in Southeast Asia. Msg, Wheeler JCS 9846 to McCain, Abrams, 9 Aug 69. Both in Abrams Papers, CMH.

rice."[33] Even General Abrams appears to have experienced reservations and to have given way only reluctantly. "In reading Abrams' analysis of the military situation in South Vietnam," President Nixon told Henry Kissinger during November, "I get the rather uneasy impression that the military are still thinking in terms of a long war and an eventual military solution. I also have the impression that deep down they realize the war can't be won militarily, even over the long haul."[34]

The difference between the president's announced intention to Vietnamize the war and the attitude of the American military found its way into the press. On 3 November the *Washington Star* published an article by Donald Kirk to the effect that the Vietnamization program had made little difference in the way U.S. forces fought. Referring to a recent avowal by Secretary Laird that American units in South Vietnam had begun to follow a policy of "protective reaction" rather than "maximum pressure," Kirk alleged that as far as the officers and enlisted men of the U.S. 1st Cavalry Division (Airmobile) were concerned the two terms meant exactly the same thing. "I cannot think of a time since we've been in Vietnam," he quoted one officer, "that the real name of our mission has not been protective reaction." That very evening, while General Wheeler hurriedly instructed Abrams to reemphasize to his commanders that Vietnamization was their first priority, President Nixon revealed in a widely publicized address to the nation that he had in fact changed the mission of U.S. forces in South Vietnam several months before.[35]

The Green Beret Affair

The reluctance of American commanders to substitute Vietnamization for the attrition strategy became less important as U.S. withdrawals continued, if only because tactics had to change as the size of the American force in South Vietnam diminished. The good image of the war nevertheless remained at risk, especially where programs that dealt directly with the South Vietnamese government and people were concerned. Most American officials sought to deal equitably with their allies, but there was no accounting for individuals. An ill-advised act by one man or a small group could find its way into the press, harm the administration's public relations, and impair the president's ability to achieve his ends.

[33] MFR, OASD SA, 1 Dec 69, sub: Vietnamization Meeting With Secretary Laird, folder 75, Thayer Papers, CMH. Quote from Msg, Lt Gen Melvin Zais, CG, XXIV Corps, PHB 1984 to Abrams, 1 Oct 69, Abrams Papers, CMH.

[34] Memo, the President for Henry Kissinger, 24 Nov 69, President's Personal files, box 10, Memos, Nov 69, Nixon Papers.

[35] Laird Handwritten Note, attached to copy of Donald Kirk, "1st Cav Finds Mission Unchanged," *Washington Star*, 3 Nov 69, 330–75–089, box 98, Viet 380 Pacification, Laird Papers, WNRC. "The Pursuit of Peace in Vietnam," Address by President Nixon, 3 Nov 69, in Department of State *Bulletin*, 24 Nov 69, p. 437.

An example of what could happen emerged during July, when allegations arose that members of the U.S. Army Special Forces had murdered a South Vietnamese double agent and disposed of his body at sea. When the investigation that followed implicated the commander of the 5th Special Forces Group, 1st Special Forces, in South Vietnam, Col. Robert B. Rheault, and seven members of his command, General Abrams notified the Joint Chiefs of Staff.[36]

The incident was sensitive for a number of reasons. The Special Forces were involved in important highly classified intelligence-gathering operations, many of which might be compromised if court proceedings became too detailed. In addition, the *New York Times* alleged that one of the accused had stated that the victim, a suspected enemy spy, had been murdered at the suggestion of a CIA agent in Nha Trang. Given the dimensions of the case and the obvious intention of the suspects to defend themselves with vigor, General Abrams had little doubt that the Military Assistance Command's decision to prosecute the suspects would shortly become public knowledge. He planned to keep the matter confidential, he told General Wheeler, but all concerned could anticipate that the press would eventually learn of it.[37]

Over the weeks that followed, the case became even more convoluted. The Central Intelligence Agency denied that its representative had either suggested or approved an execution but refused on grounds of executive privilege and the sensitivity of the operations involved to provide documentary evidence to the prosecutors. Abrams, for his part, was angry that members of the Special Forces had taken the law into their own hands and believed that Colonel Rheault, in an interview, had lied to him about the whereabouts of the victim. As a result, he took the highly unorthodox step of placing the suspects in solitary confinement at the American military prison at Long Binh. On the side, the U.S. Navy began a protracted, unavailing search of the waters off Nha Trang for the body of the victim.[38]

---

[36] Msg, Abrams MAC 9072 to Wheeler, 14 Jul 69, Abrams Papers, CMH. For an exhaustive treatment of the Green Beret Affair, see Jeff Stein, *A Murder in Wartime: The Untold Spy Story That Changed the Course of the Vietnam War* (New York: St. Martin's Press, 1992). Sorley, *Thunderbolt*, pp. 269–78, carries a more abbreviated account. For a book written from the defendants' point of view, see John Stevens Berry, *Those Gallant Men: On Trial in Vietnam* (Novato, Calif.: Presidio Press, 1984).

[37] Ibid.; Msg, Resor (Maj Comeau and Capt Sacks) ARV 2270 to Thaddeus Beal, Under Secretary of the Army, 22 Aug 69, sub: United States v. Rheault et al., Abrams Papers, CMH; John Darnton, "Ex-Beret Says He Killed Agent on Orders of CIA," *New York Times*, 4 Apr 71.

[38] Statement by Secretary of the Army Stanley R. Resor to the Press, 29 Sep 69, CMH files; Office of the Judge Advocate General, MACV, Log Maintained by Col Persons, SJA, USARV, 1 Oct 69, Papers of Lt Gen James W. Sutherland, U.S. Army Military History Institute (MHI), Carlisle, Pa. Also see Msg, Abrams MAC 10247 to McCain, 8 Aug 69, and Msg, Mildren, Deputy Commanding General, U.S. Army, Vietnam (DCG, USARV), ARV 2098 to Kerwin, Deputy Chief of Staff for Personnel, Department of the Army (DCSPER, DA), 5 Aug 69, both in Abrams Papers, CMH. Abrams' anger is mentioned in MHI Senior Officer Oral History Interv, James H. Shelton and Edward P. Smith with Gen. Bruce Palmer, 1976, p. 438, MHI.

General Abrams' attempt to hold back news of what had happened succeeded until 4 August, when *New York Times* reporter Juan Vasquez heard rumors of the incident and filed a request for information with the Army's public affairs office in the Pentagon. The Department of the Army passed the query to Abrams, who decided that an announcement was in order but that the Military Assistance Command would release only essentials. He recommended strongly that Washington agencies pass all future questions from the press on the subject to the component of the command most directly involved with the investigation, the U.S. Army, Vietnam (USARV). On 6 August, with the approval of the Defense Department, spokesmen for MACV revealed that Rheault and seven of his subordinates had become suspects in the shooting of a South Vietnamese national. On grounds that any further release of information might infringe upon the rights of the accused, they listed the names of the men involved but revealed nothing more. A similar policy prevailed at the State Department, where the head of the East Asia desk, Ambassador William A. Sullivan, purposely kept himself uninformed of the incident so as to turn away inquiries with an honest plea of ignorance.[39]

The failure of the Military Assistance Command to issue a full explanation led to intense speculation in the press, which immediately labeled the case the "Green Beret Affair." Lacking an authoritative statement, newsmen turned to unofficial sources and began to publish rumors, some of them pernicious. On 9 August, for example, the *Baltimore Sun* quoted "Green Beret personnel" to the effect that the murder had actually been an assassination attempt against a key Saigon government employee. The charge was baseless but it aroused the South Vietnamese government, which sent Ambassador Diem to the State Department to express concern. The department denied the allegation and began to press the U.S. mission in Saigon to release more information on what had happened. The case was too sensitive, Ambassador Bunker responded. Any statement would require the closest coordination in Washington.[40]

The attorneys for the accused added to the confusion. Recognizing that publicity could only assist their clients, they cultivated the news media. A civilian lawyer representing one of the suspects, George Gregory, implied that military authorities were engaged in some sort of vendetta because his client had been subjected to cruel conditions during confinement. "I measured my client's cell very carefully today," he told reporters. "It's 7 by

[39] Msg, Palmer, Vice Chief of Staff of the Army (VCSA), DA, WDC 12882 to Abrams, 4 Aug 69, and Msg, Abrams MAC 1011 to Palmer, 5 Aug 69, sub: *New York Times* query, both in Abrams Papers, CMH. MACV History, 1969, p. XI-15; Msg, COMUSMACV 45193 to AIG 7046, 6 Aug 69, sub: MACV Morning News Release 218-69 of 6 Aug 69, USSF/Rheault Case '69 file, CMH; Msg, State 133837 to Saigon, for Bunker from Sullivan, EA, 9 Aug 69, Def 9 U.S. file, FAIM/IR.

[40] Msg, State 133837 to Saigon, for Bunker from Sullivan, 9 Aug 69; Msg, Saigon 16057 to State, 10 Aug 69, Def 9 U.S. file, FAIM/IR.

140

George Gregory

5, with a tin roof and hot as hell. The metal cot leaves only a foot between it and the wall and there's a foot square peephole. He has to bang on the door if he wants to go to the lavatory."[41] The military lawyers representing the accused also became involved. One issued a press release authored by his client. Another allowed himself to be interviewed on network television, where he alleged that General Abrams had become personally involved in the case. Although the issuance of news releases by civilian counsel was to be expected, the participation of military members of the court in activities of that sort was a violation of Army regulations, which left relations with the press to official spokesmen. MACV judge advocates nevertheless refused to take action against the officers involved because any step of the sort would have seemed an attempt at intimidation.[42]

Public affairs officers in Washington and Saigon, for their part, clarified points of military law unfamiliar to reporters but steadfastly refused to discuss the case in more than the broadest terms. Although the press had a legitimate interest, they said, it was important to protect the rights of the suspects. On top of that, any release of information might inhibit the ability of the military justice system to prosecute the case and to review final sentences. "There's gotta be two sides of the story," the Chief

---

[41] [UPI], "Inquiry Said To Be Suspended in Green Beret Case," *New York Times*, 13 Aug 69.

[42] Office of the Judge Advocate General, MACV, Log Maintained by Col Persons, SJA, USARV, 1 Oct 69. Also see Army Regulation 190–4, *Uniform Treatment of Military Prisoners*, June 1969.

of Information for the U.S. Army, Vietnam, Col. James Campbell, pointed out to newsmen. "Someday you'll know the story and you'll see the Army wouldn't press charges without cause."[43]

On 18 August the U.S. Army, Vietnam, released the suspects from pre-trial confinement, eliminating one cause of controversy. By then, however, the families of the accused had contacted their congressmen, who had immediately sided with their constituents. Congressman Peter W. Rodino, Jr., of New Jersey took the lead. Observing that the confinement of the suspects seemed in contravention of the Uniform Code of Military Justice, which recommended jailing military defendants only if that was necessary to ensure their appearance in court, he told newsmen that he questioned the Army's regard for the rights of the accused. Congressman Albert W. Watson of South Carolina also expressed concern. In a private letter to the secretary of defense he urged Laird to drop all charges. "If these brave soldiers continue to be held," he said, "the morale of the American fighting man, not only in Vietnam today, but for generations to come, will be irreparably damaged."[44]

The Central Intelligence Agency sought to still the clamor by agreeing to hold private background briefings on the case for members of the House and Senate Armed Services Committees, but the effort had little if any effect. On the day following the first of the sessions, Rodino, Carl B. Albert of Oklahoma, and six other members of Congress signed a letter to the secretary of the Army expressing "distress and indignation" over the way the Military Assistance Command had handled the matter.[45]

As pressure mounted within the United States, the lawyers for the defendants attempted to subpoena classified manuals, publications, and instructions on Special Forces activities and operations. They also sought files containing references to the unit code-named B–57, under which Rheault and the other defendants had operated in South Vietnam. When the Central Intelligence Agency continued to refuse to provide documentation under its control, the accused responded that they had been denied materials necessary for an adequate defense. It was clear to all concerned that they expected the Defense Department to drop its charges rather than compromise sensitive intelligence activities.[46]

Although the Military Assistance Command's investigators were convinced that enough evidence existed for a successful prosecution, divisions

[43] Quote from Donald Kirk, "Attorney in Beret Case Puts Blame on Abrams," *Washington Star*, 13 Aug 69. Also see Memo for Correspondents, 14 Aug 69, USSF/Rheault Case '69 file, CMH.

[44] MFR, 14 Aug 69, sub: Gist of Press Interview With Rep Peter W. Rodino, USSF/Rheault Case '69 file, CMH. Quote from Ltr, Albert Watson to the Honorable Melvin R. Laird, 19 Aug 69, USSF/Rheault Case '69 file, CMH.

[45] Ltr, Peter W. Rodino et al., to Honorable Stanley R. Resor, 9 Sep 69, USSF/Rheault Case '69 file, CMH.

[46] Msg, Guy B. Scott, Attorney for Capt Budge E. Williams, to Secretary Laird, 26 Sep 69, 330–75–089, box 95, Viet 250.4, 1969, Laird Papers, WNRC; Msg, Resor ARV 2270 to Beal, 22 Aug 69, sub: United States v. Rheault et al.

grew within the Defense Department over whether to proceed. Secretary of the Army Stanley Resor was inclined to back Abrams on grounds that a full and fair trial was the best course and that the U.S. Army should never condone murder. The office of the Defense Department's general counsel agreed. Except for the pretrial confinement, its analysts said, the command had handled the incident properly. Dismissal of the case would constitute, moreover, a grave failure to observe the Geneva Conventions governing the conduct of war at the very time when the United States was urging North Vietnam to adopt a policy of moderation toward American captives.[47]

Laird, Westmoreland, Wheeler, Deputy Secretary of Defense David Packard, and Director of the Central Intelligence Agency Richard Helms all wanted to drop the case. Under increasing political pressure, President Nixon was also concerned. All suspected that General Abrams had overreacted and that "some emotion," as Westmoreland put it, was involved in the Military Assistance Command's handling of the affair. "They threw them in the worst part of the jug," Westmoreland told the Vice Chief of Staff of the Army, General Bruce Palmer, Jr., in a telephone conversation. "This is not normal handling of an officer when the case hasn't even been investigated formally. You don't normally confine a man until he's tried, convicted and sentenced—you don't demean him. They treated the company and field graders like common criminals. Naturally the press picked it up immediately and that's why they were forced to release them." Westmoreland added a concern of his own that

You have a chain of command involved here and some of their defense is that they carried out their orders. If you use the illegal order theory, the whole Army will start thinking twice about this, particularly the intelligence people, who are risking lives all the time on this. It's a sticky one to handle. The public will raise some flak for a day or two—a few sob sisters. It's almost disappeared in the press now, but will come back if they are tried.[48]

Noting that all of the accused except for Rheault were intelligence officers on assignment to the Special Forces rather than actual members of the Green Berets, Westmoreland for a time considered attempting to change the name of the case from the "Green Beret Affair" to the "Double Agent Case," but by then the matter was almost at an end. On 23 September, with Congressman Rodino claiming on the floor of the House of Representatives that "one of the weirdest—and probably cruelest—trials in the military history of this nation" was about to begin, the Central Intelligence Agency, with the approval of an increasingly beleaguered president, refused for the final time to participate in the case. Convinced

---

[47] Msg, Resor ARV 2270 to Beal, 22 Aug 69, sub: United States v. Rheault et al.; Memo, L. Niederlehner, Acting General Counsel, for the Secretary of Defense, 22 Sep 69, 330–75–089, box 95, Viet 250.4 1969, Laird Papers, WNRC.

[48] Memo, Record of Chief of Staff Telecon with Gen Palmer, 1010, 3 Sep 69, sub: Green Berets and Stano Slot, Westmoreland Papers, CMH. Henry Kissinger mentioned Nixon's concern in an interview with Lewis Sorley. See Sorley, *Thunderbolt*, p. 275.

that a fair trial would be impossible and that further controversy could only harm the military services and the nation, Secretary Resor yielded to the wishes of Laird, Westmoreland, and the others by dismissing all charges against the accused.[49]

Those within the Defense Department who had advocated the move clearly hoped that the affair would go away, but in the weeks that followed the interest of the press held firm. The *New York Times* and the *Los Angeles Times* began to prepare investigative reports on the incident that threatened to spill over into other areas of intelligence gathering. The *Philadelphia Bulletin* charged that "the curtain has been drawn . . . but from behind it comes a whiff of self-corruption dangerous to a democracy." The *New York Times* reported that Congressman Jonathan B. Bingham of New York had introduced a resolution in the House to set up a Joint Congressional Committee on Military Justice in Vietnam. Columnist Carl Rowan observed in the *Washington Post* that "the shrewdest agent in the Soviet Union's 'bureau of dirty tricks' could never have dreamed up a plot that would do so much damage to America's reputation in the world." In South Vietnam reporters documented each development in an attempt by the murdered man's widow to claim compensation from the U.S. embassy. In the United States the press reported the Green Berets' return home and their prospects for the future. Many journals took special care to note that the Army had "served the United States with dedication and distinction for two centuries," but it seemed clear, as Rowan noted, that the case had cost the United States much more than the $6,472 it paid to settle with the victim's widow.[50]

The Attempt To Limit Further Damage

As the Green Beret Affair worked its way toward a conclusion, General Abrams and Secretary Laird became acutely sensitive to any portion of the American effort in South Vietnam that threatened to cause public relations problems in the future. The CIA-assisted PHOENIX pro-

---

[49] Quote from Statement of the Honorable Peter W. Rodino, U.S. House of Representatives, Special Order for September 23, 1969, The Green Beret Case, USSF/Rheault Case '69 file, CMH. Memo, Record of Chief of Staff Telecon with Maj Gen Clifton, 1350, 22 Sep 69, sub: Golf and Green Berets, Westmoreland Papers, CMH; Msg, Resor 16511 to Rosson, Deputy COMUSMACV, 29 Sep 69, Abrams Papers, CMH. Resor dismissed the charges in a statement to the press. See Statement by Secretary of the Army Stanley R. Resor to the Press, 29 Sep 69. Also see Sorley, *Thunderbolt*, p. 277.

[50] "The Shade Is Pulled Down," *Philadelphia Bulletin*, 1 Oct 69; "The Green Beret Case," *New York Times*, 3 Oct 69; Carl T. Rowan, "Green Beret Case Taints Reputations Galore," *Washington Post*, 10 Oct 69; "U.S. Government Paid $6,472 . . .," *Wall Street Journal*, 6 Oct 69; "The Green Berets Come Home," *Newsweek*, 13 Oct 69. The quote on dedication is from "Shadow on Army," *San Diego Union*, 10 Oct 69.

gram came immediately under scrutiny. Established in July 1967 to advise and assist the South Vietnamese armed forces in eliminating the Viet Cong infrastructure, the effort had achieved mixed results. Although it had succeeded in capturing or killing a few enemy leaders, it had put the most pressure on the least important of the enemy's supporters, those who followed the Communists less out of conviction than because they happened to live in areas where the insurgents retained power. South Vietnamese officials in general lacked enthusiasm for it because of the inexact nature of its targeting and the use powerful local bureaucrats made of it to intimidate personal and political opponents.[51]

Americans familiar with the program were little more enthusiastic. Although PHOENIX had supposedly eliminated 12,000 members of the Viet Cong infrastructure during the first eight months of 1969, intelligence analysts questioned the figure and indicated that the enemy had been able to replace whatever losses he had incurred. Numbers of innocent persons meanwhile spent long periods in custody without hearings while dangerous Communists were sometimes allowed to bribe their way to freedom before processing. Of the rest, 75 to 90 percent were released before sentencing or received prison terms of less than one year. Most were thus hardly eliminated for very long. The United States considered ways to improve the score but, as Secretary of the Army Resor noted, the danger always existed that "we may make the program more 'efficient,' without due regard to the social and moral costs which that might entail."[52]

The United States supported PHOENIX because the destruction of the enemy's infrastructure seemed essential to the outcome of the war. It nevertheless attempted to limit possible public affairs problems by formally reminding American participants in the program that they were under the same legal and moral constraints when involved with PHOENIX as they were when participating in regular military operations. If Americans observed activities that failed to comply with the rules of land

---

[51] Talking Paper, 6 Oct 69, sub: The Phoenix Program, PRU Washington Paper file, DepCORDS Papers, CMH; Memo, Col Raymond T. Reid, Chief, Plans and Operations Division, Office of the Secretary of the Army, for Secretary of the General Staff, 24 Nov 69, sub: Fact Sheet on Operation Phoenix, DDI Phoenix Operations file. For more on PHOENIX, see Richard A. Hunt, *Pacification in Vietnam: The American Struggle for Vietnamese Hearts and Minds* (Boulder, Colo.: Westview Press, 1995); and Dale Andrade, *Ashes to Ashes: The Phoenix Program and the Vietnam War* (Lexington, Mass.: Lexington Books, 1990). For more on the Provincial Reconnaissance Units, see William Colby with James McCargar, *Lost Victory: A Firsthand Account of America's Sixteen-Year Involvement in Vietnam* (Chicago: Contemporary Books, 1989), pp. 216–17, 379; Jeffrey J. Clarke, *Advice and Support: The Final Years, 1965–1973*, United States Army in Vietnam (Washington, D.C.: U.S. Army Center of Military History, Government Printing Office, 1992), pp. 379–80.

[52] Talking Paper, 20 Oct 69, sub: The Anti-infrastructure Campaign in South Vietnam, 330–75–089, box 98, Viet 380 Pacification 1969, Laird Papers, WNRC. Quote from Memo, Stanley R. Resor for Secretary of Defense, 20 Oct 69, sub: The Phoenix and Provincial Reconnaissance Unit Programs in Vietnam, PRU Washington Papers file, DepCORDS Papers, CMH.

warfare, they were to refuse further participation, object to what was happening, and report the incident to their superiors.[53]

As the controversy over the Green Beret Affair developed, Laird and Abrams decided that further steps were necessary, especially where one aspect of PHOENIX, the Provincial Reconnaissance Unit program, was concerned. Employing quick reaction forces, composed in part of Viet Cong defectors and advised by the U.S. Army Special Forces, the units were noted for the violence of their methods. Rumor had it that the South Vietnamese government even paid their members a specified amount for the ear of a Viet Cong and more for the head of a leader. Convinced that the program would prove counterproductive to the American effort over the long run, Secretary Laird was anxious to be rid of it, as was General Abrams. Unhappy with his experience in the Green Beret Affair, Abrams told his superiors that he might find it difficult to discipline members of his command who became involved in war crimes while participating in operations that involved agencies outside of his control.[54]

There was some talk, for a time, of a compromise. Under that scenario, some sixty American officers would remain with the program but would divorce themselves from questionable occurrences by declining to take an active part in field operations. General Abrams, however, was adamant. Refusing to fill advisory positions with the units as they fell vacant, he withdrew the members of his command from the program as quickly as possible. By January 1970, as a result, although some American officers continued to participate under severe restrictions, advice and support for the Provincial Reconnaissance Units by American military personnel had for all practical purposes ceased.[55]

The attempts of American officials to preserve the public image of the effort in South Vietnam by convincing the Thieu regime to reform, by changing the mission of the Military Assistance Command, and by withdrawing advisers from the Provincial Reconnaissance Units were fated to disappointment. With the Thieu regime unable or unwilling to change and American public opinion increasingly restive, only one course seemed to hold any promise. The attention of the Nixon administration turned to the home front in search of the solutions that remained elusive in Southeast Asia.

[53] Msg, Abrams MAC 16592 to McCain, Wheeler, Lt Gen Frederick Weyand, 24 Dec 69, sub: Phung Hoang (Phoenix) Program, PRU Washington Papers file, DepCORDS Papers, CMH.

[54] Memo, Laird for Chairman of the Joint Chiefs of Staff (CJCS), 29 Nov 69, sub: Evaluation of U.S. Involvement in Provincial Reconnaissance Unit Program in RVN, and Memo, Wheeler JCSM–752–69 for Secretary of Defense, 8 Dec 69, sub: U.S. Military Involvement in Provincial Reconnaissance Unit Program in the Republic of Vietnam, both in 330–75–089, box 98, Viet 380 Pacification, Laird Papers, WNRC. For an example of the way the news media covered PHOENIX and the Provincial Reconnaissance Units, see "The Rise of Phoenix," *Newsweek*, 12 Jun 70, p. 25.

[55] Memo, Wheeler JCSM–752–69 for Secretary of Defense, 8 Dec 69, sub: U.S. Military Involvement in Provincial Reconnaissance Unit Program in the Republic of Vietnam; "The Rise of Phoenix," p. 25; Andrade, *Ashes to Ashes*, pp. 177–84.

7

The Mood in the United States

When President Nixon took office and pledged to end the fighting in South Vietnam, the antiwar movement in the United States stepped aside to draw breath. By the fall of 1969, however, it was clear that those who opposed the war were losing patience with the administration's policy of gradual withdrawals. During August a coalition of organizations advocating peace began planning for a nationwide day of discussion and protest on 15 October to dramatize public disenchantment with the war. Work also began on a second, larger protest for 15 November that would draw hundreds of thousands of ordinary citizens to Washington, D.C., for a day of peaceful demonstrations at the site of the nation's memorials.[1]

The drive for a "moratorium on business as usual" received financial backing from many of the same individuals who had sponsored the candidacies of Eugene McCarthy and Robert Kennedy during the 1968 presidential primary campaign. More than five hundred college student body presidents and campus newspaper editors endorsed it. So did former U.S. Ambassador to India John Kenneth Galbraith, University of Chicago political scientist Hans Morgenthau, and many other prominent academics. The Roman Catholic Archbishop of Boston, Richard Cardinal Cushing; the President of the Synagogue Council of America, Rabbi Jacob Rudin; and the General Secretary of the World Council of Churches, Reverend Eugene Carson Blake, added their prestige. Two dozen senators and congressmen also lent support, in hopes, as one put it, of turning the day into "an important moral event."[2]

As the moratorium gained in strength and respectability, pressures for change built within Congress. The number of speeches opposing continuation of the war in the House and Senate became so large during Sep-

---

[1] U.S. Department of State, American Opinion Summary, 4–23 Oct 69, Vn-Public Opinion file, FAIM/IR. Also see "Strike Against the War," *Time*, 17 Oct 69, p. 17.

[2] Ibid. For a summary of support for the moratorium, see *Facts on File* (New York: Facts on File, Inc., 1969), 29:626.

tember that the index to the *Congressional Record* required almost a full page to list them. Senator Edmund S. Muskie of Maine termed the president's plans for ending the war "ambiguous"; Senator Edward M. Kennedy of Massachusetts criticized the Saigon government as the main obstacle to peace; Senator Charles H. Percy of Illinois, a moderate, called on the president to halt offensive operations in South Vietnam for as long as the enemy refrained from exploiting the situation; Senator Charles E. Goodell of New York introduced a bill in the Senate requiring the withdrawal of all U.S. forces from South Vietnam by the end of 1970; and Senators Jacob K. Javits of New York and Claiborne Pell of Rhode Island sponsored a measure to revoke the Gulf of Tonkin Resolution. Congressman Allard K. Lowenstein of New York meanwhile announced plans for a national "Dump Nixon" campaign.[3]

Although opposition to the war appeared to be extensive, President Nixon struck a confident pose when dealing with the South Vietnamese. Alluding to the fact that the press, which cued to the Congress, was giving heavy play to the statements of the opposition, he assured South Vietnamese Foreign Minister Tran Van Lam during October that public opinion of the war in the United States bore little resemblance to what was appearing in the news media. He had confidence, he said, in the support of the majority of Americans for his policies. Neither he nor they would ever weaken in their resolve to protect South Vietnam.[4]

Nixon's assessment of the public mood was calculated to assuage South Vietnamese insecurities, but it was still closer to reality than the impression promoted by supporters of the moratorium that most Americans opposed continuation of the war. Many Americans were indeed frustrated with the fighting, so much so that by October six out of ten would consider the war a mistake. Many more believed they knew more about the Apollo effort to land a man on the moon than they did about their nation's policies in Southeast Asia. Relatively few, however, advocated a hasty withdrawal from South Vietnam. Instead, as both the Harris and Gallup polls ascertained during July, most were preoccupied with the antiwar movement and the impact continued civil disobedience would have on law and order in the nation. A majority of adults rated protests by the young the country's largest problem after the war and advocated, by a margin of 84 percent, a government crackdown on student demonstrations.[5]

If most Americans seemed inclined to support the president, a mood of cynicism nevertheless prevailed. According to a *Time*–Louis Harris poll taken during August, neither the press nor the government fared well in

[3] "Vietnam Debate: Will It Help or Hinder," *U.S. News & World Report*, 20 Oct 69, p. 29. For a summary of congressional opposition to the war as viewed from within the White House, see Kissinger, *The White House Years*, pp. 290–303.

[4] Memo of Conversation, President Nixon with South Vietnamese Foreign Minister Tran Van Lam, 6 Oct 69, Pol US-Viet S file, FAIM/IR.

[5] *Gallup Opinion Index*, Jul 69, p. 3; Louis Harris, "College Students Radicalized by Vietnam War," *Philadelphia Inquirer*, 3 Jul 69; "Judging the Fourth Estate: A *Time*–Louis Harris Poll," *Time*, 5 Sep 69, p. 38.

public estimation. Of the nine out of ten who read a newspaper regularly, a clear majority believed that the stories they encountered were "sometimes unfair, partial, and slanted." Although most professed confidence in television news, by a ratio of three to one a majority of viewers also believed that a television camera could lie. As for the government, three out of four asserted that the real story of what was happening in Washington occurred behind the scenes and that only a small portion of the truth ever reached the people.[6]

Despite official protestations to the contrary, the president was clearly unhappy with the support his programs were receiving. He seemed beset by opponents at every turn. Antiwar resolutions appeared almost daily in Congress—eleven alone between 24 September and 15 October. Meanwhile, the President of Yale University, Kingman Brewster, called for an unconditional U.S. withdrawal from South Vietnam, and the presidents of seventy-nine major colleges and universities throughout the United States pressed in an open letter for a firm schedule of redeployments. Aware that the enemy would interpret the rise in antiwar dissent in the United States as a sign of weakness, Nixon began a search for some means to anchor the credibility of his administration's policies, especially its determination to secure the existence of a non-Communist South Vietnam.[7]

At first, according to Henry Kissinger, he toyed with the idea of launching a major air assault on North Vietnam, the sort of initiative that had in the past galvanized American public support while stressing to the enemy the firmness of the country's resolve to see the war through. During September he or his representatives went so far as to instruct General Abrams orally to begin contingency planning for the attack. The operation, code-named PRUNING KNIFE by the Military Assistance Command, was to be designed to inflict major damage on North Vietnam's air defenses, sow tension and anxiety among the country's population, and demonstrate the ability of the United States to enlarge the war at will. On 12 September, indeed, a brief notice in the *Wall Street Journal*'s "Washington Wire" column referred to the possible existence of the highly classified plan. The *Journal* alluded to a suspicion on the part of some skeptics in the press that the president had floated a false rumor in order to jar Hanoi and its allies into making some move toward peace.[8] In the end, given the ferment rising around the country and an increasing likelihood that the Soviet Union would agree to talks on a

[6] "Judging the Fourth Estate: A *Time*–Louis Harris Poll," p. 38.

[7] David E. Rosenbaum, "79 College Heads Bid Nixon Step Up Vietnam Pullout," *New York Times*, 12 Oct 69; Kissinger, *The White House Years*, pp. 284–85.

[8] Kissinger, *The White House Years*, pp. 284–85, 303–06. The plan is detailed in a series of memorandums and messages. See Memo, Kissinger for Secretary of Defense, 24 Oct 69, sub: North Vietnam Contingency Plan, 330–75–103, box 18, file 38, Laird Papers, WNRC; Msg, Abrams MAC 12219 to Wheeler, 18 Sep 69, and Msg, Abrams MAC 12222 to McCain, 18 Sep 69, both in Abrams Papers, CMH. Also see "Washington Wire," *Wall Street Journal*, 12 Sep 69.

strategic arms limitation treaty, the president abandoned the idea. Seeking instead to solidify his base of support in the United States, he moved to preempt the arguments of his domestic opponents while playing on the American public's distrust of both the protest movement and the news media.[9]

Public Affairs Initiative: September–October 1969

The antiwar movement had long been a concern of President Nixon. Shortly after taking office, in May 1969, he had given Attorney General John Mitchell charge of coordinating government activities having to do with civil disturbances. From that time onward, all federal agencies with any sort of police or intelligence function, the Army included, had fed information they acquired on the subject to the Justice Department. With the announcement of the moratorium, the Army had increased its surveillance. The Posse Comitatus Act of 1878 technically forbade military involvement in matters of civilian law enforcement, but it had never been tested in court. Lacking that definition, since many protest demonstrations took place on or near military installations, Army administrators adopted the broadest possible interpretation.[10]

Reasonably certain of what the moratorium's organizers were doing, the Nixon administration took steps to reinforce its position. Turning a strong face to the protesters, the president avowed at a 26 September news conference that he would never allow antiwar demonstrations to sway his determination to end the conflict honorably. In the days that followed, members of his cabinet and other supporters stepped forward with a series of widely publicized speeches and appearances to appeal for public support and to emphasize the administration's continuing efforts to reduce American casualties. To that end, Secretary of Defense Laird confirmed early in October that U.S. commanders in South Vietnam were no longer under orders to keep maximum pressure on the enemy. Shortly thereafter, the secretary of state appeared on the NBC interview program "Meet the Press" to declare that the president had deescalated the war just as he had promised and that troop withdrawals would continue.[11]

---

[9] Kissinger, *The White House Years*, pp. 303–06.

[10] Memo, Col D. Carter, Executive Officer, DA, Directorate for Civil Disturbance Planning and Operations, for Lt Col W. B. Steele, Executive and Senior Aide, Office of the Chief of Staff, U.S. Army, 6 Oct 69, sub: Vietnam Moratorium Committee, 15 Oct 69, Westmoreland Papers, CMH. The Westmoreland Papers contain a number of summaries of antiwar movement activities around the United States during this period.

[11] Orr Kelly, "Unions Back Laird Plea To Support Viet Policy," *Washington Star*, 7 Oct 69; [UPI], "Laird Tells Dual Course To End War," *Chicago Tribune*, 8 Oct 69. For a summary of the administration's efforts, see "Strike Against the War," p. 17; *Facts on File*, 1969, 29: 658–59.

While those efforts proceeded, the president moved to upstage the moratorium. Between 9 and 11 October he held a series of meetings with General Wheeler, who had recently returned from a trip to South Vietnam, and with the U.S. Ambassador to the Paris peace talks, Harriman's successor, Henry Cabot Lodge. The flurry of activity led to speculation in the press that there was more to the administration's efforts on the war than what had thus far appeared in public. On 10 October Nixon also announced the reassignment of the director of the Selective Service System, the outspoken and controversial Lt. Gen. Lewis B. Hershey. Since Hershey had long been a symbol of military service and a target of the antiwar movement, the act was widely interpreted in the news media as an attempt to conciliate young people who would participate in the demonstrations.[12] Playing to that theme, the president three days later released an open letter to a Georgetown University student who had questioned the government's refusal to be swayed by the moratorium's appeal to conscience. "Whatever the issue," Nixon wrote, "to allow government policy to be made in the streets would destroy the democratic process . . . [by giving] the decision, not to the majority, . . . but to those with the loudest voices." Shortly thereafter, three weeks in advance, the White House announced that the president would deliver a major address to the nation on 3 November.[13]

If the president's efforts seemed conciliatory, those of Vice President Spiro T. Agnew were much more heavy-handed. When word arrived in Washington that North Vietnamese Prime Minister Pham Van Dong had released a letter to the American peace movement that concluded, "May your fall offensive succeed splendidly," the vice president seized the opportunity. Calling upon the moratorium's leaders to "repudiate the support of the totalitarian government which has on its hands the blood of 40,000 Americans," he suggested in meetings with reporters that a failure to do so would throw the moratorium's objectives "into severe question."[14]

As the date of the moratorium approached, the administration issued public affairs guidance designed to keep the event in perspective. Observing that the 15 October protests were only an introduction for what promised to be a larger demonstration during November, the State Department instructed all of its posts abroad to play down whatever happened. If concerned Americans appeared outside an embassy or consulate, those in charge were to do everything possible to prevent confrontations. Although each post was to prepare to receive petitions and to avail itself of any opportunity to present the administration's

---

[12] Robert Keatley, "Firing of Hershey Shows Nixon's Concern About Rapid Growth of Antiwar Feelings," *Wall Street Journal,* 13 Oct 69.

[13] John Pierson, "Nixon Letter Seeks To Defuse Protest on Vietnam; Address to Nation Set Nov. 3," *Wall Street Journal,* 14 Oct 69.

[14] "M-Day's Message to Nixon," *Time,* 24 Oct 69, p. 16.

Silent support for the moratorium: soldier with black armband on patrol in Vietnam

viewpoint on the war, all concerned were to discourage press coverage by excluding reporters from meetings and by forbidding photography. "Low-key factual reports of meetings may be made to press subsequently."[15]

Despite official efforts to lessen the import of the moratorium and to discredit its organizers, the members of many communities across the United States observed the day's events. Estimates of participation varied, but most commentators acknowledged that the turnout had been impressive. Over 100,000 people gathered to hear speakers at an afternoon rally on Boston Common. Two hundred thousand or more congregated at various sites in New York City. At Wall Street's Trinity Church, such important members of the establishment as Lyndon Johnson's press secretary, Bill Moyers; former Deputy Secretary of Defense Roswell Gilpatrick; and J. Sinclair Armstrong, an assistant secretary of the Navy under President Dwight D. Eisenhower, read the names of the war dead. In Washington, D.C., Senator George S. McGovern of South Dakota appeared at an American University teach-in; a peace vigil occurred on the steps of the Capitol; the employees of more than twenty federal agencies held quiet ceremonies in their offices; and the widow of Martin Luther King led a candlelight procession from the Washington Monument to the White House. Thousands also participated in demonstrations in Chicago, Denver, San Francisco, and Los Angeles.[16]

In the same way, the event prompted considerable comment in the print media, with warm approval coming from journals that had long advocated an accelerated end to the war such as the *New York Times*, the

---

[15] Msg, State 17347 to All Diplomatic Posts, 13 Oct 69, sub: October 15 Moratorium, Pol 27 Viet S file, FAIM/IR.

[16] U.S. Department of State, American Opinion Summary, 4–23 Oct 69; "Strike Against the War," p. 20.

St. Louis Post-Dispatch, the *New York Post*, the *Boston Globe*, and the *Minneapolis Star*. The *Washington Post* took a middle position, requesting toleration on all sides, not only for the demonstrators but also for the majority that seemed prepared to support whatever approach the president adopted to end the war. A number of journals—the Scripps-Howard syndicate, the Hearst papers, the *Denver Post*, the *Wall Street Journal*—either opposed the moratorium or distinguished between support for the demonstration as an expression of public concern and demands for an abrupt withdrawal of all U.S. forces from South Vietnam. Others opposed undue haste in ending the war but recommended a policy of all deliberate speed. The *Minneapolis Tribune* thus advocated a gradual pullout that would last from twelve to eighteen months. An editorial in *Life* signed by Hedley Donovan suggested much the same thing: a reduction of U.S. forces in South Vietnam to 150,000 by mid-1971.[17]

If magazines and newspapers were both comprehensive and forthcoming in their depiction and interpretation of the event, television seemed timid by comparison. Although the moratorium might possibly have been, as CBS News commentator Eric Sevareid noted, "the biggest . . . popular reaction against an ongoing foreign war that this country has ever experienced," none of the networks covered any part of it live. Both CBS and NBC replaced their late-night talk shows with ninety-minute summaries of the day's action, but coverage of that sort, coming after prime time hours, neither offended anyone nor had much impact. As for the evening news broadcasts, the thirty-minute format of the programs so limited the news that only the barest outline appeared. The CBS Evening News was typical. After a summary of events, brief, impressionistic reports appeared. Reporter Richard Threlkeld described a subdued demonstration in front of the American embassy in Saigon by a small group of American civilian workers. Ike Pappas at Fort Benning in Georgia interviewed a soldier who supported the right of individuals to dissent in a free society but condemned protesters who had painted peace symbols on the headquarters building at the base. Only at the end of the program did any analysis appear, and it seemed uncertain and disjointed. The extent of the protest and the involvement of the middle class, Sevareid commented, were difficult to ascertain. If the demonstrations gave evidence that millions of Americans wanted the United States out of South Vietnam, proposals for a quick and total withdrawal were, from a practical standpoint, impossible. There thus seemed some truth, the reporter concluded, to the claim of a Spanish philosopher "that youth tends to be right in what it opposes and . . . wrong in what it proposes."[18]

[17] U.S. Department of State, American Opinion Summary, 4–23 Oct 69; "An Uncertain Cause," *Wall Street Journal*, 15 Oct 69.

[18] Marvin Barrett, ed., *A. I. du Pont–Columbia University Survey of Broadcast Journalism, 1969–1970, Years of Challenge, Year of Crisis* (New York: Grosset & Dunlap, Inc., 1971), p. 14. Quotes from CBS Evening News, 15 Oct 69, *Radio-TV-Defense Dialog*.

Whatever the comments of the press, public opinion nevertheless sided with the president. As *U.S. News & World Report* observed, although most Americans sought an end to the war as quickly as safety allowed, only a fringe advocated immediate withdrawal. A 16 October telephone poll by Sidlinger & Company found that 68.5 percent of those interviewed believed the president was doing all he could to make peace, an increase of 7 percent over the previous month, when his rating on the subject had stood at 61.5 percent. The Gallup poll said the same thing. Although the weight of opinion tended to favor fast rather than slow withdrawals, where public approval of the president's handling of the war had stood at 52 percent during September, it rose to 58 percent after the moratorium. "From a careful and continuing analysis of public opinion on the war," George Gallup noted, "it is clear that any plan [for ending the war] that receives support from a substantial number of people must be one that calls neither for all out escalation nor abrupt and total withdrawal and one that guarantees the right of the people of South Vietnam to determine their own future."[19]

The president's supporters labored to reinforce the public mood. The White House Director of Communications, Herbert Klein, for one, attempted to be congenial but left no doubt that he considered the protest a mistake. Avowing that most members of the group were "intelligent young people, although there were some misfits among them," he continued that "our hope is that the next time they demonstrate they would do so in a way that would help us—for example, demonstrating to bring the prisoners home from North Vietnam."[20] Secretary of State Rogers also seemed open minded. At a "Family of Man" award dinner for the New York Council of Churches on 21 October, he observed that many of the demonstrators had sought merely to register a "dramatic but dignified expression of their deep concern for peace in Vietnam. And we listened to those voices with respect because we, too, have a deep concern for peace in Vietnam."[21]

If most administration spokesmen seemed conciliatory, Vice President Agnew once again revealed that there was also a deep-running current of anger within official circles. In an appeal to Middle-America's dislike for student protesters and concern for law and order, he told a gathering of Republican Party activists in New Orleans that the moratorium had been sponsored by an "effete corps of impudent snobs who characterize themselves as intellectuals." He warned that "hard core dissidents and professional anarchists" were planning wider, more violent demonstrations in the near future.[22]

---

[19] "Newsgram-Tomorrow," *U.S. News & World Report*, 27 Oct 69, p. 22; U.S. Department of State, American Opinion Summary, 4–23 Oct 69; George Gallup, "3-Part Peace Plan Favored," *Philadelphia Inquirer*, 29 Oct 69; Gallup, "58% Back Nixon War Policy," *Washington Post*, 2 Nov 69.

[20] "Anti-war Offensive, What Comes Next?," *U.S. News & World Report*, 27 Oct 69, p. 30.

[21] James M. Naughton, "White House Discounts Conflict in Officials' Moratorium Views," *New York Times*, 22 Oct 69.

[22] Agnew is quoted in Marjorie Hunter, "Agnew Says 'Effete Snobs' Incited War Moratorium," *New York Times*, 20 Oct 69.

The 3 November Speech

Recognizing that the best way to solidify support would be to convince both the American public and the world that plans to end the war were moving steadily forward, the Nixon administration made heavy preparations for the address the president had scheduled for 3 November. Since newsmen were already speculating about what Nixon would say, the White House instructed official spokesmen to keep public pronouncements on the war to a minimum and to refrain from saying anything that might limit the president's options. If pressed, agency representatives might confirm that Nixon would make "a significant statement of where we stand on Vietnam," but they were to discourage any expectation that he would announce a new negotiating initiative or another troop withdrawal.[23]

Considering international support critical for the success of the speech, the president and his advisers laid careful plans to encourage it. Prior to the event, as a mark of special privilege, the secretary of state was to deliver outlines of the president's remarks to representatives of countries that had contributed troops to the war and to a few others such as Great Britain and Israel that the United States regarded as particularly important. Once the president had spoken, the American ambassadors to those countries were to approach their host governments to request statements of support. The U.S. permanent missions to the North Atlantic and Southeast Asia Treaty Organizations were to do the same by bringing the address to the attention of the secretaries general of those alliances. Meanwhile, the U.S. Information Agency was to prepare to broadcast the speech by satellite around the world and to test international audience reaction by commissioning public opinion polls and analyses of foreign editorial comment. To achieve the widest possible impact, the agency was also to translate the address into every language in the world.[24]

The speech itself played upon the themes that the president considered necessary to answer criticism and to strengthen public support for his policies. He chose its wording carefully. In an attempt to establish that he indeed had a plan to end the war, he first delivered a brief history of the U.S. involvement in Southeast Asia and of all he had done in pursuit of peace. Declaring that "a nation cannot remain great if it betrays its allies and lets down its friends," he then underscored the consequences of precipitate withdrawal by recalling the enemy's massacre of more than 3,000 civilians at Hue during the Tet offensive. "With the sudden collapse of our support," he said, "these atrocities of Hue would become the nightmare of the entire nation—and particularly for the million and a half Catholic refugees who fled to South Vietnam when the Communists took

[23] Msg, State 3362 to Paris, Saigon, 15 Oct 69, sub: Public Statements on Vietnam, Pol 27 Viet S file, FAIM/IR. For an example of the speculation, see "Anti-war Offensive, What Comes Next?," p. 29.

[24] Memo, William P. Rogers for the President, 3 Nov 69, sub: Organizing Support for Your Vietnam Address, Pol 27 Viet S file, FAIM/IR.

Nixon meets with reporters before his 3 November speech.

over in the North." In addition, an American humiliation in South Vietnam would promote recklessness on the part of powers hostile to the United States and spark violence wherever an American commitment helped maintain the peace—"in the Middle East, in Berlin, eventually even in the Western Hemisphere." To emphasize that the United States had always been willing to negotiate in good faith, he then disclosed a number of hitherto secret initiatives he had taken in search of peace, including a letter he had personally written to Ho Chi Minh a few weeks before that leader's death. Ho, he said, had flatly rejected the appeal, making North Vietnam's attitude the chief impediment to a negotiated settlement rather than that of the United States.[25]

Turning to his program for the future, Nixon outlined the American effort to turn the war over to the South Vietnamese. Although much remained to be done, he said, General Abrams had received new orders during July. Under that revised statement of mission, the American force in South Vietnam was to relinquish its role in combat and concentrate on preparing the South Vietnamese to assume full responsibility for the defense of their country. The results of that change were already clear. American casualty rates had begun to decline, and American fighting men were beginning to return home. As for the future, the president said

---

[25] Unless otherwise indicated, this section is based on "The Pursuit of Peace in Vietnam," Address by President Nixon, 3 Nov 69, in Department of State *Bulletin*, 24 Nov 69, pp. 437–43. The point that Nixon paid close attention to the wording of the speech is made in Msg, State 186210 to All Diplomatic Posts, 4 Nov 69, Pol 27 Viet S file, FAIM/IR.

that he had an orderly, scheduled timetable for withdrawals but that he would base each decision to remove troops on the situation in South Vietnam at the time. Hanoi could make no greater mistake than to assume that as American withdrawals continued an escalation of the violence might be to its advantage. "If I conclude that increased enemy action jeopardizes our remaining forces . . ., I shall not hesitate to take strong and effective measures."

The president finished by requesting the support of "the great silent majority" of Americans who understood his desire to end the war honorably. "I pledged in my campaign . . . to end the war in a way that we could win the peace. I have initiated a plan of action which will enable me to keep that pledge. The more support I can have from the American people, the sooner that pledge can be redeemed; for the more divided we are at home the less likely the enemy is to negotiate at Paris. . . . North Vietnam cannot defeat or humiliate the United States. Only Americans can do that."

The speech was a public relations success. Although the Hanoi regime termed it a "perfidious, highly war-like, stubborn, and gunpowder-stinking address [that] had only added to the fire of [antiwar] struggle that is burning intensely throughout the United States," governments around the world extended their congratulations and support.[26] Senator Fulbright and other congressmen and senators who opposed the war questioned the president's sincerity, but 300 congressmen and 40 senators cosponsored resolutions supporting the president's efforts to make peace. Some 59 senators also wrote Ambassador Lodge to commend his and the president's continuing attempt to achieve a negotiated settlement. Meanwhile, a nationwide telephone survey by the Gallup poll on the night of 3 November found that 77 percent of those Americans who had heard the speech approved. A Sidlinger poll said the same thing. Eight out of ten, 79.2 percent, of those interviewed after the speech said they supported the president, an increase of 7 percentage points over the previous high in July. The company's president, Albert E. Sidlinger, observed in a little-noticed side remark that most of the new support had come from young people of college age.[27]

If international and American public opinion appeared to support the president, the reaction of the American print media seemed mixed. The Nixon administration instructed official spokesmen around the world to emphasize that an analysis of thirty-two representative American newspapers showed three out of four in support of the president's position. Yet if newspapers such as the *Cleveland Plain Dealer* and the *Philadelphia Inquirer* considered the speech reasoned and sincere and applauded

---

[26] Memo, Ray S. Cline, Office of Intelligence and Research (INR), for Secretary of State, 6 Nov 69, sub: North Vietnam: Hanoi's Angry Reaction to President Nixon's Speech, Pol 27 Viet S file, FAIM/IR.

[27] Msg, State 194106 to All Diplomatic Posts, 18 Nov 69, sub: Reaction to President's November 3 Address, Pol 27 Viet S file, FAIM/IR; [UPI], "Nixon Support Soars in Poll After Speech," *Washington Star*, 14 Nov 69.

Nixon's intention to follow his private timetable for withdrawals, others expressed disappointment. The *New York Times*, in particular, criticized the president's failure to start any new initiatives and his apparent commitment to defend South Vietnam until it could defend itself. That South Vietnam might succeed in the effort seemed, to the *Times*, "a remote prospect judging by the record of the past fifteen years." The newspaper added that the president had condemned North Vietnam's recalcitrance in the negotiations but had avoided any mention of the South Vietnamese government's failure to democratize and liberalize its institutions. Syndicated columnist James Reston was equally pointed. He remarked that Nixon had mobilized opposition to the antiwar faction by putting "Spiro Agnew's confrontation language into the binding of a hymn book."[28]

In possession of the president's remarks by arrangement with the White House some five hours in advance of the speech, the television networks were equally critical. None supported Nixon's plea for trust or his assurances that he was making progress. In comments that came immediately after the end of the address, Marvin Kalb of CBS questioned the president's interpretation of the letter from Ho Chi Minh. Rather than the flat rejection Nixon had seen, he said, it contained the softest and most accommodating language to appear in a Communist document in years. ABC called on the former U.S. Ambassador to the Paris peace talks and an outspoken critic of administration policy, W. Averell Harriman, for comments. Harriman questioned the president's point of view and called on Senator Fulbright's Foreign Relations Committee to investigate the war once again. ABC's National Affairs Editor, Bill Lawrence, followed with an observation that the speech was "nothing new" politically. It appealed, he said, to those moved by words rather than deeds and would make little difference to voters six months in the future.[29]

The next day's comments on television were less critical but still far from enthusiastic. At ABC, some stories were relatively positive. One contrasted the "silent majority" of Nixon supporters with the "vocal minority" of blacks and antiwar protesters; another, by Howard K. Smith, noted that both Hanoi and the antiwar movement were oriented toward nothing less than a Communist victory. A commentary by Frank Reynolds nevertheless added that the president's forthright stand against his opponents might only contribute to disorder in the United States by adding fuel to the protest movement. At NBC, David Brinkley meanwhile stressed the contention of Senator Fulbright and others that the president had finally made Lyndon Johnson's war his own. CBS News put forward

[28] [UPI], "Nixon Support Soars in Poll After Speech"; "Nixon's Vietnam Timetable," *Cleveland Plain Dealer*, 4 Nov 69; "Mr. Nixon's Plan for Peace," *New York Times*, 4 Nov 69; James Reston, "Nixon's Mystifying Clarifications," *New York Times*, 5 Nov 69.

[29] William E. Porter, *Assault on the Media: The Nixon Years* (Ann Arbor: University of Michigan Press, 1976), pp. 43–44; "Agnew's Complaint: The Trouble With TV," *Newsweek*, 24 Nov 69, p. 88. For transcripts of the 3 November television comments, see James Keogh, *President Nixon and the Press* (New York: Funk & Wagnells, 1972), pp. 171–90.

a theory that General Abrams would shortly resign because he disagreed with the Military Assistance Command's new statement of mission. The administration planned to replace him, according to the broadcast, with a "logistical-type general."[30]

Although the president was elated by the public reaction to his speech—on the day after the address he invited newsmen into his office to see sheaves of laudatory telegrams piled on his desk—he could have had no illusions that public opinion would remain hard and fast in his favor. For if the Gallup poll had found that 77 percent of the public supported his policies, it had also reported healthy skepticism. Only 49 percent, according to the same survey, believed that the president's proposals were likely to bring about a settlement of the war. Twenty-five percent held to the opposite view and a substantial 26 percent remained undecided.[31]

Pollster Louis Harris noted the same finding in a 10 November report on a recent public opinion survey he had done. He had found, he said, that if 45 percent of the American public lacked sympathy for the 15 October moratorium and by a margin of 51 to 36 percent disagreed with the antiwar movement's methods, 81 percent had nonetheless concluded that the demonstrators "are raising real questions which ought to be discussed and answered." Six in ten might agree that the protests hurt the president's chances of achieving peace and gave aid and comfort to the enemy, but by a margin of 50 to 37 percent they also agreed with the demonstrators that the war was morally indefensible and that the United States had erred by becoming involved. In addition, Harris continued, the country was becoming increasingly divided. Support for the antiwar movement centered in the big cities of the East and West—among women, the college educated, blacks, and those under thirty years of age. Southerners, residents of small towns and rural areas, older persons, those with lower incomes, and the less well educated took the opposite point of view. American public opinion was under great strain, Harris concluded. People might hope that the president and his advisers would produce some honorable settlement, but their patience was clearly wearing thin.[32]

The President Moves To Retain the Initiative

Recognizing the divisions growing in the country, the president and his advisers took steps in the days following the speech to reinforce

---

[30] ABC Evening News, 4 Nov 69, and Huntley-Brinkley Report, NBC-TV, 4 Nov 69, both in *Radio-TV-Defense Dialog*. Also see Hallin, *The Uncensored War*, p. 188. The CBS report is mentioned in Msg, Wheeler JCS 13789 to Abrams, 5 Nov 69, Abrams Papers, CMH.

[31] "Nixon Declares 'Silent Majority' Backs His Speech," *New York Times*, 5 Nov 69; "Gallup Finds 77% Support Nixon," *New York Times*, 5 Nov 69.

[32] Louis Harris, "Harris Poll: Viet Protests Gaining With the Public," *New York Post*, 10 Nov 69.

their gains. At the Defense Department, Secretary Laird instructed official spokesmen to avoid any speculation on the timing or number of troop redeployments. Without indulging in further discussion, they were to stand firm on the president's statement that he had a plan. In public appearances they were to stress candor. Although noting that the program to Vietnamize the war was going well, they were to prepare the American public for occasional tactical setbacks by avoiding overly optimistic forecasts. They were also to refrain from leaving any impression that there would be additional U.S. concessions in Paris. General Wheeler meanwhile cabled Abrams to inform him of the CBS allegation about his supposed disgust with the new statement of mission and his putative determination to resign. He suggested that Abrams ignore the broadcast rather than dignify it with any response. In the same way, should newsmen attempt to exploit possible discontent among ranking Americans serving in South Vietnam, all concerned were to emphasize their harmony with official policy and the overriding importance of the attempt to modernize and improve South Vietnam's armed forces.[33]

If military agencies were relatively low keyed in their approach, the White House was much more direct in its dealings with the antiwar movement. Conservative members of Congress, with the backing of the president, attempted to discredit the November march on Washington by releasing a staff report to the effect that if the committee directing the demonstration was not Communist-led the participation of known Communists was still heavy and blatant.[34] Shortly thereafter, the U.S. mission in Saigon released a captured Viet Cong document that called for intense attacks in the region east of Saigon "in support of the struggle campaign for peace which will be initiated by the American people on Nov. 15."[35]

The administration contemplated an even stronger approach to the news media. For months the president and his advisers had grown increasingly disgruntled with what they considered unfair press coverage. Their dissatisfaction broke briefly into public on 25 September, when the Director of the U.S. Information Agency, Frank Shakespeare, charged at the annual convention of the Television News Directors Association that many broadcast journalists showed evidence of a strong, visible liberal bias in their reporting. At first, administration spokesmen attempted to deal with the problem directly, by complaining to editors and news pro-

---

[33] Msg, Wheeler JCS 13857 to McCain, Abrams, 6 Nov 69; Msg, Wheeler JCS 13789 to Abrams, 5 Nov 69; Msg, Wheeler JCS 13830 to Abrams, 6 Nov 69. All in Abrams Papers, CMH.

[34] The report was composed by the staff of the House Committee on Internal Security. See Memo, Jack Caulfield for John Erlichman, 10 Oct 69, White House Special files, President's Office files, box 2, President's Handwriting, October 1 thru 15, 1969, Nixon Papers. See also ABC Evening News, 19 Nov 69, *Radio-TV-Defense Dialog.*

[35] [AP], "Viet Cong Support U.S. War Protest," *Washington Star*, 10 Nov 69; William Grigg, "Capitol Doves Shun Anti-war March; Role of Reds Cited," *Washington Star*, 7 Nov 69.

160

ducers. They found it difficult, however, clearly to define what *unfair* meant where interpretive reporting was concerned. What they considered nuanced, editors seemed to accept as routine. Dissatisfied with the results they were achieving, they began to discuss ways to coerce the press into being more receptive. Suggestions surfaced during October that they should cut offenders off by favoring media outlets that promoted the administration's point of view, that they should use the threat of Internal Revenue Service audits to temper the comments of the worst offenders, or that they should monitor incidents of unfairness and turn the findings over to the Federal Communications Commission for possible legal action.[36]

H. R. Haldeman

President Nixon made the first move. A week before his 3 November speech he instructed his chief of staff, H. R. Haldeman, to establish "an especially effective group" to monitor the three television networks on the night of his broadcast. In addition, "a special strike force" was to examine coverage in the *Washington Post,* the *New York Times,* and the two national news magazines and to contest any critical comment that appeared.[37]

When television newsmen reacted unfavorably to the president's speech, they thus played into his hands. Two days later, at the obvious behest of the White House, the newly appointed Chairman of the Federal Communications Commission, Dean Burch, personally telephoned the heads of the three television networks to request transcripts of the remarks their reporters had made. Since Burch had ready access to official transcripts of news broadcasts, the networks interpreted the move, with its ominous implication that the commission was checking television news broadcasts for possible violations of law, as an unprecedented threat.[38]

One week later the White House notified the three television networks that Vice President Agnew would address the Midwestern

[36] Memo, Jeb Stuart Magruder for H. R. Haldeman, 17 Oct 69, sub: The Shot-gun Versus the Rifle, reprinted in Porter, *Assault on the Media,* pp. 39–43, 244–49.

[37] Memo, the President for Bob Haldeman, 26 Oct 69, President's Personal file, box 1, Memos-Oct 69, Nixon Papers.

[38] Porter, *Assault on the Media,* pp. 39–43.

Spiro Agnew

Regional Republican Conference in Des Moines, Iowa, on 13 November and that the subject would be the unfairness and bias of television news. The notice included a line from the speech that read: "Whether what I've said to you tonight will be seen and heard at all by the nation is not my decision, it's their decision." To make certain that the news media understood the importance of the speech, all three networks received copies in advance, as did the wire services, *U.S. News & World Report*, selected newspapers around the country, and important columnists who might be expected to agree. Confronted by the challenge and by the administration's obvious intention to publicize the speech heavily, the networks decided for the sake of their own credibility to carry Agnew's remarks live, in place of their regular evening news programs.[39]

The speech was emphatic. The vice president complained that since a majority of Americans drew their knowledge of the world from television news programs, a small group of producers, commentators, and anchormen—perhaps fewer than a dozen—controlled the flow of information to the public. That elite exercised a form of censorship over the news by creating symbols where none existed and by elevating individuals from obscurity to national prominence, whether they deserved it or not.

[39] Quote from Memo, Herbert G. Klein for H. R. Haldeman, 12 Nov 69, White House Special files, Staff Member Office files, Klein, Name file 69–70, box 1, H. R. Haldeman-1 [2 of 3], Nixon Papers. "Agnew Demands Equal Time," *Time*, 21 Nov 69, p. 18.

Wielding a free hand "in selecting, presenting, and interpreting the great issues in our nation," it had thwarted "our national search for internal peace and stability" by concentrating on bad news to the detriment of the good.[40]

Agnew continued that the president should have the right to communicate with the American public without having his words and thoughts subject to "instant analysis and querulous criticism." He added that "a raised eyebrow, an inflection of the voice, a caustic remark dropped in the middle of a broadcast can raise doubts in a million minds about the veracity of a public official or the wisdom of a government policy." A distorted image of reality often emerged as a result: "a single dramatic piece of the mosaic becomes in the minds of millions the entire picture." As for the agitators and demonstrators, they had learned to exploit the news media's penchant for controversy. "How many marches and demonstrations would there be," Agnew asked, "if the marchers did not know that the ever-faithful TV cameras would be there to record their antics for the next news show?" He concluded as had Nixon, by appealing to the ordinary American. "The people can let the networks know that they want their news straight and objective. . . . This is one case where . . . the consumer can be the most effective crusader. . . . The great networks have dominated America's airwaves for decades. The people are entitled to a full accounting of their stewardship."[41]

One week later the vice president extended his critique to the print media during a speech in Montgomery, Alabama. A single company in the nation's capital, the *Washington Post*, he said, controlled the city's largest newspaper, one of four television stations, an all-news radio station, and one of the three major national news magazines, *Newsweek*. He deplored the concentration of opinion-making power that the growth of media conglomerates seemed to represent. Meanwhile, he said, "If a theology student in Iowa should get up at a PTA luncheon in Sioux City and attack the president's Vietnam policy, my guess is that you'd probably find it reported somewhere in the next morning issue of the *New York Times*." Yet, when 300 congressmen and 59 senators had endorsed the president's Vietnam policies, even though both the *Washington Post* and the *Baltimore Sun* had played the event prominently on their front pages, the *New York Times* had made no mention of it. Decrying what he perceived as the growing irresponsibility of the press, Agnew concluded that the day when network commentators and the *New York Times* could enjoy a form of diplomatic immunity from criticism had come to an end.[42]

The speeches drew a vehement reaction from the press. After the first, Edward P. Morgan at ABC charged that Agnew's remarks represented a sinister attempt at news management. Chet Huntley at NBC declared that

[40] U.S. Congress, House, "Address to the Midwest Regional Republican Committee Meeting," *Congressional Record*, 115:34043–049.
[41] Ibid.
[42] The speech is excerpted in Porter, *Assault on the Media*, pp. 263–65.

the Nixon administration had embarked on a confrontation with the press that "could get very vicious and very bloody." The President of NBC News, Reuven Frank, observed that "its just another case of the messenger being blamed for the message." *Newsweek* remarked that if television news had problems the vice president's comments contributed little toward a solution. Instead Agnew had exploited the networks' inclination to bend over backwards to assist the government, a tendency exemplified by their decision to cancel the evening news in order to carry his remarks live.[43]

Comments on the second speech merged with those on the first. The *New York Times* immediately pointed out that its late editions had carried a front page story on the congressional endorsement Agnew had alluded to but that the Washington edition, the only one available to the vice president and his speechwriters, had closed too soon for the account to appear. Meanwhile, the *Wall Street Journal*, while avowing that there was a solid core to many of Agnew's arguments, noted that the main defect of television news lay in being too bland rather than too bold. The newspaper implied that greater fault lay with the print media, where some reporters had shown their bias by signing petitions and actively participating in moratorium-day activities when they should have remained aloof observers. The publisher of *Long Island Newsday*, Bill Moyers, who had himself participated in the day's events, conceded that the vice president had legitimate complaints but objected to the tone of his remarks. "There was a meanness in the speech that I think the discussion should avoid."[44]

Time produced one of the most trenchant critiques. While it was true that instant analyses were often feeble, the magazine's editors pointed out, in the case of the 3 November speech, that reporters had received advance White House briefings as well as copies of what the president would say. In the same way, if television was important in the formation of public opinion, the president's ability to command its resources at will gave him a large share in that power. There were those who argued, indeed, that since the president controlled vast public affairs resources of his own and could withhold or release news at will, commentary in the press was necessary in order to balance his official pronouncements with an amplifying point of view. While news producers and editors could certainly alter the shape of reality, the effects of their choices were nebulous. Hundreds of allegations that CBS had distorted the news to make the police the villains had appeared after the 1968 Democratic Convention in Chicago, yet if the influence of television on public opinion was so pervasive, the majority of Americans had still sided with the police. Agnew's most dangerous point, *Time* concluded, was his apparent contention that newscasters ought to reflect majority opinion rather than their own judgment and that this was objectivity. No such thing as objectivity existed.

[43] "Agnew's Complaint: The Trouble With TV," pp. 88–92.

[44] "Beat the Press, Round Two," *Newsweek*, 1 Dec 69, p. 25. Also see Porter, *Assault on the Media*, p. 264; "Winding Down the Rhetoric," *Wall Street Journal*, 15 Nov 69; "The Vice President and the Press," *Wall Street Journal*, 24 Nov 69.

Newscasters and editors had to judge the importance of events on the basis of their own experiences. In doing so, they attempted to be fair but never achieved absolute purity. "We are on guard," the magazine quoted the producer of the ABC Evening News, Av Westin. "We're not infallible. We try."[45]

The News Media Covers the March on Washington

The 15 November march on Washington occurred during the uproar over the vice president's remarks. Involving 250,000 citizens, the largest antiwar demonstration to occur in the nation's capital to date, it received extensive, mostly positive coverage in the print media but, as had occurred with the moratorium, only perfunctory attention from television. Anchormen noted its size and peaceful nature, played films of people marching and singing, and showed brief portions of the comments of speakers such as Senators McGovern and Goodell. Then they switched to the security precautions surrounding the event and incidents of violence in which a small minority of marchers had rioted at Dupont Circle, north of the White House, and on the streets surrounding the Justice Department's downtown offices. Subsequent reports from South Vietnam showed that most of America's fighting men knew about the event, but few were much interested.[46]

The result was contrary to anything Agnew might have predicted. Instead of becoming a platform for the marchers' cause, television news, as the leaders of the march later complained, had distorted it. The substantive remarks of the speakers never appeared, only the sort of platitudes that fit easily into a television format that valued brevity and impact over thought. "This great outpouring of people is not here to break a president or even a vice president," intoned Goodell in the Huntley-Brinkley report of his speech. "We are here to break a war and to begin a peace." Although commentators remarked on the peacefulness of the march, most of the action coverage involved violence or the threat of it. Few watching could have come away with anything but an impression that, for all their protestations of nonviolence, the demonstrators were indeed prone to mayhem.[47]

Although television coverage seemed to coincide with official policy, the phenomenon had nothing to do with the Agnew speech or the administration's efforts to coerce the press. The structure and logic of tele-

[45] "Agnew Demands Equal Time," pp. 18–22.

[46] Barrett, *Columbia University Survey of Broadcast Journalism, 1969–1970*, pp. 15–16; Huntley-Brinkley Report, NBC-TV, 15 Nov 69, *Radio-TV-Defense Dialog*; "Parades for Peace and Patriotism," *Time*, 21 Nov 69; "The Big March," *Newsweek*, 24 Nov 69, p. 30.

[47] Huntley-Brinkley Report, NBC-TV, 15 Nov 69. Also see Gitlin, *The Whole World Is Watching*.

Antiwar marchers rally at the Washington Monument during the November moratorium.

vision news was the reason. Lacking large resources, producers assigned camera crews to events scheduled long in advance that were certain to attract a viewing audience rather than to antiwar rallies that were unpredictable and often impromptu. More important, according to Edward Jay Epstein, who sat in on editorial conferences at NBC News during portions of 1968 and 1969, news producers had taken to heart allegations that the presence of television cameras had contributed to outbreaks of violence at the Democratic Convention in Chicago. Rather than have similar incidents arise in the future, they had forbidden camera coverage of any event where a potential for violence by a crowd existed. Once a disturbance occurred, however, the rules changed. With the need to avoid becoming a cause of violence out of the way and genuine news in the making, reporters and cameramen arrived to record the event.[48]

The effect, a concentration on violent demonstrations to the detriment of hundreds of peaceful actions that never ended in confrontation, distorted the antiwar movement almost as much as television's preoccupation with combat over civic action in earlier years had distorted network coverage of the American role in South Vietnam. Researcher Daniel Hallin found, indeed, that for lack of anything better the protest movement itself became the issue as far as television news was concerned. Eleven percent of the stories on the antiwar movement that he sampled dealt with the

[48] Epstein, *News From Nowhere*, pp. 254–57.

166

effectiveness of demonstrations, 6.2 percent with their bearing upon U.S. or enemy morale, 5.0 percent with the appearance of the demonstrators' hair, 8.8 percent with public support or participation, 7.4 percent with organizing techniques, 4.2 percent with the demographic origins of the participants, 29.9 percent with violence or subjects related to the restoration of order, and 16.6 percent with other minor categories. Only 11 percent of the reports dealt in some way with the political views of the protesters. Even then, the arguments of antiwar leaders rarely received much play. As in the case of the march on Washington, speakers at rallies appeared briefly, when they made statements that were direct and uncomplicated, as befitted television's visual format. Overall, negative statements about the movement by reporters and commentators outnumbered positives by a ratio of 2 to 1.[49]

Although television was hardly as opposed to the administration's point of view as Agnew made it seem, the vice president's charges appeared at first to receive unprecedented support from the American people. In the days following the speech, more than 100,000 television viewers contacted the networks to complain about news coverage, an astronomical number for a medium that could normally count on receiving a few hundred letters and calls in response to an unpopular program. Even so, the public was hardly as opposed to television news as that first response made it appear. When ABC conducted a poll on the subject shortly after Agnew's speech, it found that 51 percent of those who knew of the vice president's objections agreed that television presented the news in a biased fashion, but only one in four accepted Agnew's contention that the news media had been unfair to the Nixon administration. Sixty-six percent, indeed, favored the networks' practice of commenting after a presidential speech. By a wide margin, those interviewed also agreed that network news programs should continue to criticize government.[50] President Nixon was stunned when he learned of the poll's results. "My God!" he noted in the margin of the news summary reporting the finding.[51]

Whatever the beliefs of the public, Agnew's charges and the outcry following them caused considerable soul searching within television news but had little immediate effect on reporting. Although the networks, according to sociologist Herbert Gans, became somewhat more self-critical and reflective after the speeches, they refused to end their instant analyses. There were pressures from affiliate stations, stimulated by the administration itself, for CBS to curtail its commentaries. Rumors also arose from time to time that one or another of the networks had canceled this or that documentary out of deference to the vice president. Even so, if television news producers took any action at all, its effects

[49] Hallin, *The Uncensored War*, pp. 199–201. The figures add to 100.1 because of fractional weighting and rounding.

[50] Barrett, *Columbia University Survey of Broadcast Journalism, 1969–1970*, p. 33.

[51] The summary is contained in the President's Office files, box 31, Annotated News Summaries, Dec 69, Nixon Papers.

were almost imperceptible. According to researcher Dennis Lowry, there was a 9 percent increase in statements that attributed stories to identifiable sources after the vice president made his allegations, but no change at all in the percentage of unlabeled inferences, the so-called nuances Agnew had criticized.[52]

That being the case, Agnew's efforts may still have succeeded over the long term. Although newspapers, secure in their first amendment freedoms, generally refused to back down, a case can be made that television, subject to intimidation because of federal licensing procedures, was much more responsive. Marvin Kalb, who retired from CBS News during the 1980s to become the director of the Joan Schorenstein Barone Center on Press, Politics, and Public Policy at Harvard University, thus asserted in 1988 that the spirit of criticism Agnew's attack set in motion—he called it "Agnewism"—permanently dampened the political commentaries delivered by television news. As a result, subtle modifications occurred in the way the networks presented their material. All continued to provide summaries and commentaries after major speeches and developments, but the product they delivered was hardly as unrehearsed as it seemed. "Instant analysis," Kalb explained, gradually became "a brief, highly produced mini-documentary" in which commentators received advance knowledge of the kinds of questions news anchormen would ask. The appearance of a free-wheeling exchange of ideas remained, but the candor that could sometimes spring from spontaneity was gone.[53]

The Nixon administration's efforts to solidify public support for the president's policies on the war also appear to have achieved their end. On 27 November the Gallup poll reported that no more than one in five Americans supported an immediate withdrawal from South Vietnam, by then one of the main goals of the antiwar movement. Two weeks later the Harris poll revealed that public approval of the president's handling of the war had improved by a margin of 5 percent between September and December.[54]

Those statistics, while heartening to the president, nevertheless told only part of the story. For if a large proportion of the American public had responded favorably to the 3 November speech, a significant reservoir of pessimism remained. At the end of October, according to Harris, the public believed that the war was morally indefensible by a margin of

---

[52] Dennis T. Lowry, "Agnew and the Network TV News, A Before/After Content Analysis," *Journalism Quarterly* 48 (Summer 1971): 205–10, quoted by Gans, *Deciding What's News*, pp. 263–64. Also see "The Vice President and the Press."

[53] Kalb is quoted in Robert J. Donovan and Ray Scherer, *Unsilent Revolution: Television News and American Public Life* (Washington and New York: Woodrow Wilson International Center for Scholars and Cambridge University Press, 1992), p. 118. Also see Marilyn A. Lashner, *The Chilling Effect in TV News* (New York: Praeger Publishers, 1984), p. 5.

[54] George Gallup, "One in 5 Americans Backs Protest's Goal of Quick Withdrawal," *Philadelphia Inquirer*, 27 Nov 69; Louis Harris, "Antiwar Movement Gains Backers After November Protests," *Philadelphia Inquirer*, 4 Dec 69; Harris, "Comparison Shows Gain of 5 Pct. by Nixon on Viet Policy," unattributed clipping, 11 Dec 69, CMH files.

51 to 35 percent. By 55 to 33 percent it rejected claims that the protesters were "hippie, long haired, and irresponsible young people"; and it doubted by 45 to 34 percent that the president's Vietnamization program would work. A solid 45 percent remained in disagreement with the protests during both October and November, but the percentage of those who sympathized with the demonstrators increased over the same period from 39 to 46 percent. If Nixon retained a margin of support on the war, Harris concluded, much still remained uncertain as far as public opinion was concerned. "Flash numbers such as '78 percent support' or '60 percent over-all approval,'" he warned, ". . . should be taken . . . with a grain of salt."[55]

Harris' caution was appropriate. For even as the president strove to strengthen his base of support in the United States, events and circumstances were crowding in on him. Military officers in a position to know—Westmoreland and Abrams, in particular—had become privately convinced that the kind of withdrawals Laird and Nixon had in mind were too arbitrary and inflexible to provide the South Vietnamese with the time they needed to save themselves. Despite their misgivings, those officers adhered to the tenets of their profession, submerged their doubts, obeyed their orders, and pushed ahead to salvage what they could.[56]

The soldier in the field was hardly so compliant. With less and less to do as the president's orders to avoid casualties took effect, he was becoming increasingly restive, just as Kissinger had predicted. Unlike his commanders, however, he was disinclined to bury his feelings. Taking up the sort of pursuits that could only cause nightmares, both for the president and military managers, he brought problems into being that had a far more profound effect on the public image of the war than anything either the press or the antiwar movement could have contrived.

[55] Harris, "Comparison Shows Gain of 5 Pct. by Nixon on Viet Policy"; Harris' conclusion is in Harris, "Antiwar Movement Gains Backers After November Protests."
[56] Interv, CMH staff with General William C. Westmoreland, 6 Dec 89, pp. 9f, CMH files.

8

Race and Drugs

Throughout the early years of the war, the public image of the American soldier in South Vietnam had remained positive. Although incidents of lawlessness had from time to time occurred, both the military and the news media had viewed them as aberrations, the almost inevitable by-products of war itself.

Army magazine stated the military point of view in its October 1967 issue: "These soldiers in Vietnam are tough and battle hardened. But . . . the American trooper's hard image melts when the kids surround him as they do in every village he patrols. He helps build schools, drill wells, and fight disease. . . . He and his buddies 'adopt' orphanages, distribute soap, clothing, school books and food. . . . They're all magnificent. They are soldiers in the finest sense of the word."[1]

The opinion of the press was little different. Although the news media sometimes featured problems, it rarely if ever questioned either the patriotism or the motivation of the American soldier. Analyzing the results of a public opinion survey of the attitudes of young men recently returned from the fighting, pollster George Gallup, for example, concluded that most understood the war and the necessity to defeat communism in Southeast Asia. Writing in the June 1968 issue of *Reader's Digest*, he said that the soldier in Vietnam had grown in self-confidence as a result of his service. By learning both to follow and to lead he had discovered how "to accept responsibility and to be responsible for others." Only 26 percent of the men had wanted to go to Vietnam in the first place," Gallup added, but "94 percent, having returned, say they are glad for the experience."[2]

---

[1] "A Soldier in the Finest Sense of the Word," *Army*, Oct 67, p. 121.
[2] George Gallup, "What Combat Does to Our Men," *Reader's Digest*, Jun 68.

Morale Declines

The confidence of the news media in the ability of the American fighting man never waned, but in the months following the *Digest* article new circumstances became gradually apparent in South Vietnam. For as debate on the war increased in the United States and public support for the conflict weakened, morale among the troops began to decline. It became more and more difficult for many American soldiers to see much sense in the sacrifices they had been asked to make.

Soldiers face to face with the enemy held up well, but President Nixon's decision in 1969 to cut casualties and begin withdrawals drew an increasing number into rear areas. Social tensions were already on the rise in the United States. Drug abuse was growing, and traditional values seemed under siege. Those uncertainties transferred themselves readily to South Vietnam, where troops with time on their hands and only routine chores to perform grew disenchanted. Some inflicted their anger on their fellow soldiers. Others took refuge in drugs they had often become acquainted with before entering military service. More than a few of those who otherwise avoided trouble resolved to do nothing more than what was necessary to get by.

The military services, for their part, were caught unprepared. Laboring under constraints on personnel caused by Lyndon Johnson's decision to impose only a one-year tour of duty in South Vietnam and to refrain from calling up the reserves, they lacked experienced leadership at the squad, platoon, and company levels where much of the trouble occurred. Complicating matters, more and more malingerers were transferred from the front line to units in the rear by officers too harried by the demands of combat to take the time necessary to deal with problem soldiers.[3]

The press caught the mood as it developed. Reporter Georgie Ann Geyer of the *Chicago Daily News*, for one, speculated during January 1969 on the possibility that increasing antiwar sentiment in the United States had begun to affect the soldier in the field. She claimed that half of the troops she had encountered in South Vietnam were to some degree opposed to the war and that few felt much antipathy for the enemy. "The problem with this war," one soldier told her, "is there's nobody to hate, nobody like the Japs and the Germans. Who can hate Ho Chi Minh? I do hate him . . . but he's hard to hate." A second soldier, an officer, shrugged, "I don't hate him." In April, *Newsweek* reported that a growing spirit of dissidence seemed to have appeared among the troops. The magazine noted carefully that outright dissent was rare but added that

---

[3] For a more detailed discussion of the Army's morale problems in Vietnam, see Ronald H. Spector, "The Vietnam War and the Army's Self-Image," in John Schlight, ed., *The Second Indochina War, Proceedings of a Symposium Held at Airlie, Virginia, 7–9 November 1984* (Washington, D.C.: U.S. Army Center of Military History, Government Printing Office, 1986), pp. 169–85.

the men serving in South Vietnam were hardly as single-minded or as clean-cut as their predecessors had seemed to be. The trident-in-a-circle peace symbol seemed ubiquitous, hanging from the necks of enlisted men or inscribed on helmet covers and liners. Four months later, Drummond Ayres reported in the *New York Times* that if the morale of the troops remained high, many of the men serving in South Vietnam had nevertheless become disillusioned. They had ceased to fight for a cause and sought only to stay alive.[4] By November Donald Kirk of the *Washington Star* was alleging that "The worn out cliche of generals and master sergeants that 'morale over here is great' no longer seems to apply to men in the field." Many soldiers believed that the United States should leave South Vietnam as soon as possible, Kirk continued. Others felt a repugnance even for the people they were supposedly fighting to save. "It's a crazy war," one enlisted man told the reporter. "It ain't really worthwhile." Another, a lieutenant, added that only the regulars were enthusiastic about fighting any longer.[5]

Those reports might have seemed the result of growing antiwar and antimilitary bias on the part of the press, but as 1969 progressed, too many appeared by seasoned reporters who had long demonstrated their integrity. A report on 30 October by an old hand in South Vietnam and no enemy of the military, Keyes Beech, was indicative. Beech observed that he had begun to encounter an increasing number of soldiers who asked themselves whether the war was worth more American lives. The answer for many, he said, was no. "The people who are talking up this war," one soldier had told him, "are not the ones fighting it." A second had added by way of explanation that "there are two kinds of Americans over here, those in Saigon and those who are not."[6]

Statistics seemed to bear the reporters out. James MacGregor thus noted in the 18 November 1969 issue of the *Wall Street Journal* that the Army's overall desertion rate was double what it had been during the Korean War and that the 23,000 men missing at that time were enough to constitute a full combat division. He added that unexcused absences were very low among those draftees who supported the antiwar movement, if only because they intended to fight the Army from within. The Army disputed some of the reporter's conclusions, especially an assertion that it was doing little to remedy the problem, but Secretary of the Army Resor

[4] Georgie Ann Geyer, "Viet Foe 'Hard To Hate,' Troops Say," *Chicago Daily News*, 16 Jan 69; "Seeds of Dissidence in the Army," *Newsweek*, 21 Apr 69, p. 36; Drummond Ayres, "Many G.I.'s Disillusioned on War," *New York Times*, 4 Aug 69. Also see Research Report, Ann David, Press Coverage of Military Morale Problems, 1968–1972 [U.S. Army Center of Military History], p. 2, CMH files.

[5] Donald Kirk, "Growing GI Disillusion Casts Doubt on Morale Claims," *Washington Star*, 9 Nov 69. General Sidle notes that Kirk was so negative and inaccurate in his reporting that he caused continual problems for the Military Assistance Command. See Ltr, Sidle to the author, 5 Nov 90, CMH files.

[6] Keyes Beech, "Is War Worth American Lives? Battle Weary GI's Say No," *Philadelphia Inquirer*, 30 Oct 69.

felt compelled to affirm that if MacGregor had slanted his analysis, his facts were still substantially correct.[7]

Another newsman, Donald Tate of the Scripps-Howard syndicate, urged caution in a 12 November report because he believed the morale of most of the men serving in South Vietnam was still high. So did Samuel Jameson of the *Chicago Tribune*. Yet both reporters felt obliged to note at the same time that some of the troops were showing increased signs of discontent. Tate recorded bitter remarks about the failure of American leadership either to win the war or to get out of Vietnam. Jameson told of a soldier who had complained that "seventy-five percent of the Vietnamese don't seem to care. . . . Too many of us have died for no reason at all." *Newsweek* had the final word two months later. In a report on the morale of the so-called new GI, it revealed that the troops had jeered Bob Hope during his annual Christmas tour of the war zone when the usually popular comedian had alluded favorably to President Nixon's plan to end the war.[8]

Some of what the reporters wrote depended upon to whom they had talked and some upon the news media's redirected focus away from combat and toward issues related to the withdrawal. Yet stories questioning military morale had never before appeared so persistently and for so long under the names of reputable newsmen. Clearly, if not the war, at least the men fighting in it were turning slightly sour.

Race Relations

It is difficult to determine when the problems began—the whole complex of morale-related difficulties that would dog public affairs officers in Saigon and Washington from 1968 through to the end of the war. The first indications seemed to arise out of nowhere, in an area, race relations, that both the military and the press had long considered firmly under control. An April 1968 article in the *New York Times* by a black reporter, Thomas Johnson, typified the early attitude of the press. Although admit-

[7] James MacGregor, "Army Worries as G.I.'s Go AWOL and Desert at Record Setting Pace," *Wall Street Journal*, 18 Nov 69; Memo, Stanley Resor for Secretary of Defense, 6 Dec 69, sub: *Wall Street Journal* Article, SEA–RS–265 M, CMH files. The situation would become worse in the years to follow. According to Paul L. Savage and Richard A. Gabriel, overall desertion rates in Vietnam far exceeded those of World War II and Korea, increasing between 1965 and 1971 by a remarkable 468 percent. In 1953, the worst year for desertions during the Korean War, the rate ran at 22.3 per thousand men. The worst year during the Vietnam era was 1971, when the rate ran at 73.5 per thousand. There were few desertions among troops on active service in South Vietnam because disaffected men had nowhere to go. See Paul L. Savage and Richard A. Gabriel, "Cohesion and Disintegration in the American Army," *Armed Forces and Society* 2, no. 3 (Spring 1976): 346f.

[8] Don Tate, "GI Morale Is Good," *Washington Daily News*, 12 Nov 69; Samuel Johnson, "GI Spirits Remain High Despite Demonstrations," *Chicago Tribune*, 17 Nov 69; "A New G.I.: For Pot and Peace," *Newsweek*, 2 Feb 70, p. 24.

174

ting that there were still areas for improvement, Johnson concluded after fourteen weeks of interviews in the war zone that the experience of blacks in South Vietnam was "like a speeded up film of recent racial progress at home. . . . For the Negro . . . Southeast Asia offers an environment almost free of discrimination."[9]

The situation was already changing when Johnson's article appeared. For over a year, reflecting the growth of interracial tensions at home, letters from black servicemen to members of Congress and the chiefs of the various military services had revealed the beginnings of a deterioration in racial harmony in South Vietnam. Drawn from the civilian community, the black soldier had grown up with the civil rights movement in the United states and resented the inequities that had long seemed the lot of his

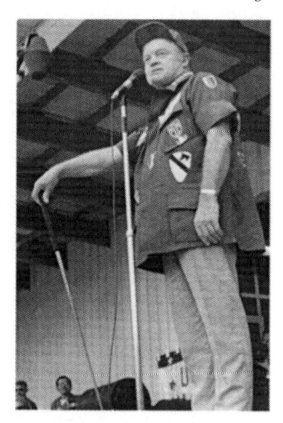

Bob Hope at Long Binh, Christmas 1971

race. He had carried his concern into the Army, where he was less tolerant than ever before of what he considered injustice.

Just one month after Johnson wrote his story, the *Washington Star* thus published a series of stories on the subject by another black newsman, Paul Hathaway, who had also spent several months in South Vietnam interviewing black soldiers. Hathaway reported that from 80 to 85 percent of the men he had talked to, however proud of their service, were troubled by their role in the war and the military's treatment of blacks. He noted that racial integration seemed successful in the combat zone but was much less apparent in rear areas, where black enlisted men all too often encountered relatively uneducated, narrow-minded whites from America's lower socioeconomic classes. Some blacks had concluded as a result of the experience that they were fighting "a white

[9] Thomas A. Johnson, "The U.S. Negro in Vietnam," *New York Times*, 29 Apr 68. Also see Johnson, "Negro Expatriates Finding Wide Opportunity in Asia," *New York Times*, 30 Apr 68. An outstanding account of the early breakdown in interracial harmonies in Vietnam appears in Ronald H. Spector, *After Tet* (New York: Free Press, 1992), pp. 242–59.

man's war" and wondered whether they should be home fighting for their own people.[10]

That the problem was more than a fabrication of the news media became apparent to the military as 1968 lengthened. During August black Marine prisoners rioted at the U.S. Marine Corps brig in Da Nang. Shortly thereafter, a group of black prisoners attacked their guards at the U.S. Army jail at Long Binh. In the melee that followed, blacks clubbed a white prisoner to death and injured many others. In all, thirty-one prisoners and guards required hospitalization. After the violence subsided confusion continued for at least three weeks. Guards confined some 220 of the rioters in an open area of the stockade but could identify few because none volunteered their names and many had replaced their uniforms with makeshift, African-style garb torn from sheets and Army blankets. In addition, fires set by the rioters had destroyed most of the jail's records.[11]

Although incidents as drastic as the one at Long Binh were rare, friction between the races continued during the months that followed. Confrontations occurred at U.S. military facilities throughout Southeast Asia, in Seventh Air Force headquarters in Saigon, at American air bases in Thailand, and on the aircraft carrier USS *America* stationed in the South China Sea. Most were minor but all, together, suggested that a serious problem was developing.[12]

Responding to the rise in tensions, a special team of Defense Department investigators traveled to Europe and South Vietnam to gain a firsthand view of what was happening. After interviewing a large number of black servicemen in private, the leader of the group, a black, L. Howard Bennett of the Office of the Assistant Secretary of Defense for Manpower and Reserve Affairs, wrote an elaborate, disturbing report on the conditions he had found. Paralleling many of Hathaway's observations, he noted that if interracial tensions were little manifest in combat zones, where the need for unity prevailed over prejudice, they had reached disturbing proportions in rear areas. Interracial communication up and down the chain of command in South Vietnam appeared difficult; officials often seemed insensitive to the needs of black servicemen; the majority of blacks lacked confidence in the command's procedures for settling grievances; and many black enlisted men believed that the system of military

[10] Fact Sheet, Racial Tensions and Violence Among the Troops, in Trip Book, sub: Secretary Laird's Trip to Vietnam, 5 to 10 Mar 69, Issues and Problem Areas, tab 25, 330–75–103, box 17, Viet 333 Laird, Laird Papers, WNRC; Paul Hathaway, "The Negro at War: He Asks Himself Some Disturbing Questions," *Washington Star*, 6 May 68. Hathaway's articles appeared in the *Star* between 6 and 10 May. Also see David, Press Coverage of Military Morale Problems, p. 18.

[11] Msg, Wheeler JCS 3231 to Abrams, 14 Mar 69, Abrams Papers, CMH. Also see Carl Rowan, "Racial Strife at U.S. Military Bases Ominous," *Washington Star*, 27 Aug 69; "Army Seeks Clues to Long Binh Riot," *New York Times*, 1 Sep 68; Zalin B. Grant, "Whites Against Blacks in Vietnam," *New Republic*, 18 Jan 69, p. 15. A well-knit account of the riot at Long Binh appears in Spector, *After Tet*, pp. 242–44, 253–56.

[12] Msg, Wheeler JCS 3231 to Abrams, 14 Mar 69.

justice discriminated against them. Advocates of black power and separatism—a growing theme among black activists in America—meanwhile worked among the men, pointedly asking why they should bear arms for a nation that treated them unfairly. Compounding the problem, some white servicemen, besides employing racial slurs, were attempting to maintain in South Vietnam the social segregation they had known at home. There seemed little possibility that blacks as a group would rebel in South Vietnam, Bennett concluded, but "all of the evidence available at this time indicates a proliferating increase in racial tensions, conflict and the incidence of racial violence in Southeast Asia." The repercussions for the United States might be grave. If American military personnel, black and white, returned from duty overseas "agitated, hostile, and in conflict," they would surely add to the potential for disorder in the American community, if only because they brought home with them "all of the murderous skills of combat gained from their training and experience."[13]

Bennett's conclusions were apparently too emphatic to be well received within the Department of Defense, which continued to place reliance on the military's excellent record in matters of race. Bennett's report thus received little if any distribution to working levels of the military services. General Abrams himself only obtained a copy in March 1969, as an afterthought, because Secretary Laird had happened to mention it in passing during a trip to South Vietnam. More than a year later, a talking paper on the subject prepared as background for Laird's second trip noted that the Bennett survey had uncovered serious racial tensions in South Vietnam but that the department had done little initially to get at the root of what was wrong. Only in January 1970, as the result of hearings by a subcommittee of the House Armed Services Committee investigating racial disturbances among marines during the summer of 1969 at Camp Lejeune, North Carolina, did the department begin to develop an educational program on race relations applicable to all of the armed services. Black syndicated columnist Carl Rowan later attributed the delay to arrogance on the part of white liberals within the Johnson administration who believed they knew more about black problems than did blacks themselves.[14]

Whatever the value of Rowan's insight, the public affairs handling of racial tensions at the time reflected the ambivalence of military agencies. Although there appears to have been little inclination on the part of information officers to cover up what was happening, some officials obviously seemed less than willing at first to admit publicly that a problem of possibly major proportions existed. During October 1968, for example, when a black enlisted man at Da Nang went berserk with a gun after a racial confrontation with whites, accidentally killing a black guard, information

[13] Bennett's report is summarized in ibid.

[14] Ibid.; Talking Paper, sub: Racial Tensions and Violence Among the Troops, Annex A to Trip Book, Secretary Laird's Trip to Vietnam, 9–13 February 1970, 330–76–076, box 13, Viet 333 Laird, Laird Papers, WNRC; Richard O. Hope, *Racial Strife in the U.S. Military* (New York: Praeger Publishers, 1979), pp. 40–41; Rowan, "Racial Strife at U.S. Military Bases Ominous."

177

Marines at Con Thien display their black power banner and give the clinched fist salute.

officers were forthright. Announcing new restrictions on the sale of alcohol to American servicemen in the Da Nang area and the closing of the Navy recreation area at China Beach to all but authorized Navy personnel, they made the commander of the installation available to the press.[15] Shortly thereafter, the Deputy Assistant Secretary of Defense for Civil Rights and Industrial Relations, Jack Moskowitz, nevertheless attempted to soften the focus of the news media by reminding the press that the same basic difficulties were prevalent in the United States. Recent confrontations in South Vietnam could never eclipse the fine record the military had achieved in the past, he said, but "the young negro serviceman is expressing his black awareness and wanting to be respected. He is not going to be sloughed off. He is not going to suffer indignities." The lull in the fighting that had followed the advent of the Paris negotiations was a factor in the racial problem, Moskowitz continued, but the special circumstances prevalent in South Vietnam also contributed. Racial incidents had occurred on military property where they were bound to be noticed because most of the country was off limits to the American soldier. When whites and blacks faced combat together, Moskowitz said, the harmony between the races was little short of inspiring.[16]

[15] [UPI], "Racial Rows Force Curbs at Danang," *Washington Post*, 21 Oct 68; John Lengel, "Racial Animosity Among Troops at Danang Worries U.S. Officers," *Washington Post*, 7 Nov 68.

[16] George C. Wilson, "Troop Racial Trouble Is Tied to Lull in War," *Washington Post*, 15 Nov 69.

With the inauguration of Richard Nixon and the continuation of interracial strife in South Vietnam, a greater recognition prevailed that problems existed, but inertia remained. When a second Department of Defense investigating team headed by Bennett visited South Vietnam in November 1969, it found many commanders willing to admit that a greater degree of racial polarization was present than in the year before. Yet it also found that many of the equal opportunity messages it reviewed were dated close to the group's visit and that the signs marking the doors of equal opportunity officers were sometimes freshly painted. General Abrams and other high-level Army and Marine Corps commanders seemed genuinely concerned with finding solutions, one of the group's members, Arthur M. Sussman, observed, but black soldiers continued to assert that the system of military justice favored whites and that the Military Assistance Command was at best marginally attuned to their needs. Officers argued that their doors were open and that the inspector general system was always available to hear the complaints of servicemen, Sussman added, but all too often the noncommissioned officer responsible for a soldier's grievances occupied the space before the commander's door. As for the Office of the MACV Inspector General, it rarely sought out problems on its own but waited for the men to file complaints. Few would do so because most believed that officers who worked for the commander would never conduct a fair investigation of complaints against the command. Instant laughter occurred whenever team members asked, "Why don't you go to the IG?" Overall, Sussman noted, the problem seemed to relate to a lack of communication up and down within the chain of command. The young soldier, black and white, "does not believe he is listened to, and in consequence does not believe what he is told. There is minimal trust at all levels."[17]

Months earlier, when the first reports of racial problems had surfaced at Da Nang, General Abrams had set up watch committees with black representation to monitor conditions and to take appropriate action should potentially dangerous situations arise. Learning of the Bennett team's new conclusions during an interview with Bennett shortly after the group finished its work in November, he amplified that guidance. While MACV conducted an examination of policies and procedures to eliminate unnecessary points of friction between officers and enlisted men, every commanding officer was to take responsibility for the maintenance of communication among the soldiers serving under him. Recognizing that dialogue was essential, Abrams stressed that open forums and discussion groups should receive particular attention as possible means of easing tension and building bridges between the races.[18]

---

[17] Memo, Arthur M. Sussman for Assistant Secretary of the Army (Manpower and Reserve Affairs) (M&RA), 14 Jan 70, sub: Race Relations in the Army, SEA–RS–272, CMH files.

[18] MACV History, 1969, vol. 3, p. XIV-20; Msg, Abrams MAC 14059 to Cushman, 18 Oct 68, Abrams Papers, CMH.

Abrams' efforts were well-intentioned but appear to have been at best only partially successful. Although reporters later noted that officers in South Vietnam who allowed racial prejudice to influence their decisions risked damage to their careers, a May 1970 review of personnel problems within the Military Assistance Command reemphasized that communication among the ranks continued to be difficult and that black enlisted men insisted there was too much talk and too little action where race was concerned. Meanwhile, in practice, the full extent of the problem remained almost impossible for commanders to discern. The chief of one of the Army's most important components in South Vietnam, II Field Force at Long Binh, Lt. Gen. Michael S. Davison, thus notified his superiors during October 1970 that while he was more than willing to move forcefully against racial prejudice, he found it difficult to separate fact from rumor where allegations of discrimination were concerned.[19]

As Sussman had perceived, the Office of the MACV Inspector General was of little help. Acknowledging that "polarization of the races, even though voluntary, is one of the major racial problems confronting commanders in Vietnam," the Chief of the office's Investigation and Complaint Division, Col. William G. Dobson, Jr., indicated in a briefing for his superiors as late as July 1970 that his statistics hardly indicated a serious problem. Of the 2,628 complaints logged by Army inspector generals during the 1969–1970 fiscal year, he said, only 146 had been classed as race-related. "Approximately 96 percent of these cases are unsubstantiated as cases of racial discrimination or prejudice; in fact only about two percent are actually substantiated as cases in which race was the consideration for action or inaction. The remaining cases are partially substantiated, in that there is evidence that race is a factor but discrimination or prejudice were not causes." Dobson continued that the Army command in South Vietnam considered racial tensions fundamentally a problem of leadership amenable to early detection, understanding, and the application of appropriate management techniques.[20]

Whatever the merits of Dobson's argument, the officer failed to note that many aggrieved enlisted men never went to the inspector general and that the classifications of the complaints that did appear depended largely on the points of view of the officers who accepted them. Thus, where one inspector general might see possible racial discrimination, another would feature in his report only an administrative problem. In

[19] [AP], "Tensions of Black Power Reach Troops in Vietnam," *New York Times*, 13 Apr 69; Memo, Roger T. Kelly (Office) for Secretary Laird, 25 May 70, sub: Report on Southeast Asia Trip-2–20 May 70, 330–76–067, box 92, Viet 333 Alpha 1970, Laird Papers, WNRC; Msg, Lt Gen Davison, CG, IIFFV, HOA 2456 to Lt Gen McCaffrey, DCG, USARV, 25 Oct 70, William J. McCaffrey Papers, CMH.

[20] Memo, Col William G. Dobson, Jr., Inspector General (IG), Chief, Investigation and Complaint Division, USARV, for IG, 18 Jul 70, sub: Racial Situation, Vietnam, in Trip Book, Visit of Brig. Gen. Eugene M. Lynch, Dep IG, DA, 13–19 Aug 70, Deputy Assistant Inspector General (DAIG) Historical files, Pentagon (eventually to be transferred to IG Collection, MHI).

that sense, of the 2,628 complaints the command had received on assignments, promotions, demotions, personal services, messing, transportation, unit administration, and discharges, the exact number of those that involved race could never be known.

Complicating the situation was a reluctance on the part of many local commanders to acknowledge that much of a problem existed. "Leaders avoid talking about a war which is being fought every night in barracks and other places where our soldiers gather," Lt. Col. James S. White of the Office of the Deputy Chief of Staff for Personnel told the chief of staff of the Army during a February 1970 briefing in South Vietnam. "Report after report continues to drive home the message that our principal problem is that people don't communicate on this problem to remove the apparent lack of mutual understanding." White added that commanders and noncommissioned officers who failed to acknowledge the existence of racial differences unwittingly allowed interracial tensions to mount. Those who confronted the issue by informing both biased whites and biased blacks that they refused to condone trouble by either side usually had fewer difficulties in their units.[21]

Information officers, for their part, often found themselves caught between the fact of continuing racial tension and their superiors' apparent inability to define the scope of the problem. When Bennett returned from his 1969 tour, for example, they made him available to the press, even though anyone could have predicted that headlines about "pervasive" racial unrest among the troops in South Vietnam would result.[22] Even so, public affairs officers were unwilling to go too far without a better understanding of the problem that confronted them. Learning of an increase in the number of racial incidents during the summer of 1970, the Chief of Information for U.S. Army forces in South Vietnam, Col. Alfred J. Mock, thus argued vehemently against any announcement to the press. "The mere acknowledgement of a rise in racial incidents would serve no useful purpose and be self-defeating," he told the command's deputy commanding general.

We must be prepared to provide facts, statistics, documentation, and other background information to respond to press interest. Most important, we must be able to show clearly that we not only recognize the problem but have comprehensive, effective programs [and] measures which are designed to lessen racial tension and reduce the number of incidents.

It is doubtful that we have sufficient accurate facts and details to document our case. Furthermore, we probably do not at this time have answers to the questions

[21] Lt Col James S. White, ODCSPER, Briefing for Seminars on Racial Tension and Equal Opportunity, attachment to Memo, MACOI-C for Major Commands, 9 Feb 70, sub: Command Information Guidance for 4th Quarter, FY 1970, 334–74–593, box 12, file 413–01, Command Information General files (70), WNRC.

[22] See, for example, Ralph Blumenthal, "'Pervasive' Racial Unrest Is Found in Armed Forces," *New York Times*, 29 Nov 69.

and a solution to the problem convincing enough to satisfy the press, public, and many of our own personnel.[23]

Whether information officers revealed the increase or not, the fact was clear to the Saigon correspondents. They followed the subject avidly and kept up a drumbeat of comment. To make matters worse, Radio Hanoi exploited the situation by beaming bulletins to American troops that described the Communist battle in South Vietnam as yet another front in the American Negro's struggle against white oppression. The allegation appears to have had little effect on the morale of black troops—American soldiers in Vietnam, as in World War II and the Korean War, tended to listen to enemy propaganda broadcasts for the laughs they contained—but it added one more layer of confusion to an already complicated issue.[24]

Drug Abuse

Although both the Saigon correspondents and the military agreed that most members of the various races serving in South Vietnam lived together without violence or measurable difficulty, the two were much further apart where the issue of drug abuse was concerned. When allegations of widespread marijuana usage by American soldiers, sailors, and airmen began to appear in the news media in the fall of 1967, reporters concluded that the practice was widespread. Military spokesmen were much more cautious. Investigating the charges, officials found that marijuana, or "pot," as the troops referred to it, was indeed present wherever American forces were gathered but asserted that the drug was having little impact on the health, morale, and combat effectiveness of the troops. They released statistics indicating that marijuana usage had increased from a rate of slightly less than one man per thousand in 1966 to 2.5 by the end of 1967, but they were also quick to point out in interviews with the press that the figure, while dramatic, was attributable in part to improved efforts at detection and increased command emphasis. "Some of our guys are experimenting," one told newsmen. None were addicted to hard narcotics such as heroin, and none, despite allegations to the contrary, used marijuana in the field, where their lives depended on an ability to think clearly.[25]

If the known involvement rate seemed relatively low, officials in

---

[23] Memo, Col Alfred J. Mock, USARV IO, for DCG, 6 Oct 70, sub: Press Release About Racial Incidents, 73A6994, Decision Papers (70), USARVIO Papers, WNRC. The U.S. Army, Vietnam (USARV), was subordinate to the Military Assistance Command, Vietnam, the joint command.

[24] "Radio Hanoi Has Message Especially for Negro GI's," *Baltimore Sun*, 16 Aug 69.

[25] Quote from David Breasted, "MAC Wars on Dope in Services," *New York Daily News*, 15 Feb 68; MACV History, 1968, vol. 2, p. 839, and 1969, vol. 3, p. XIV-4.

Washington and South Vietnam were convinced that it was still too high. "The use of narcotics, marijuana, and dangerous drugs is inimical to the proper performance of military duties," General Abrams told his commanders. "In a combat theater the user is a danger to himself and to others who must rely on him."[26] On 2 February 1968, therefore, Deputy Secretary of Defense Paul H. Nitze inaugurated a program of enforcement and education to curtail the use of marijuana among the troops. In the campaign that followed, the Defense Department produced films and reading materials on the subject for distribution to officers and enlisted men; special investigators identified and put off limits South Vietnamese business establishments that dealt in illicit drugs; and teams from the MACV Criminal Investigation Division fanned out into the countryside to search for fields

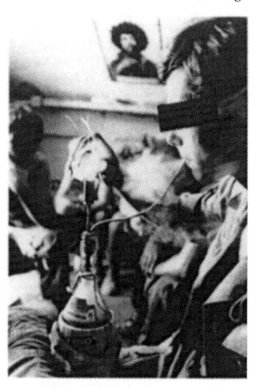

Soldier at Quang Tri lights a home-made drug hooka.

where marijuana was under cultivation. The U.S. embassy in Saigon, for its part, prevailed on the South Vietnamese government to ban the sale and distribution of the drug.[27]

The press followed the effort with interest and even sympathy but also gave full play to developments that cast doubt on the military's point of view. When the Defense Department released its revised drug statistics in February, for example, the *Washington Daily News* took pains to observe that the figures were probably less than accurate because they included only instances of drug abuse that had come to the attention of the authorities. Occasional or cautious marijuana smokers might never become involved in investigations. In the same way, during January 1968 the *New York Times* published an article by Bernard Weinraub on the Australian government's increasing concern about drug abuse among American troops vacationing on Australian soil. Weinraub quoted officers responsible for the MACV Rest and Recreation Program as stating that marijuana

[26] Msg, Abrams MACJ15 to All Commanders, 1 Apr 69, sub: Campaign Against Narcotics, quoted in MACV History, 1969, vol. 3, p. XIV-5.

[27] "Pentagon Fights Troops' Drug Use," *New York Times*, 16 Feb 68; MACV History, 1968, vol. 2, pp. 839–40.

was "somewhat prevalent in this command," and that "what's happening here is a reflection of what's happening in the United States. This pot, you can smell it almost anywhere you go on the streets here, is not against the law in Vietnam and it's easily available." Early in March 1968 the *Washington Star* highlighted testimony before a Senate subcommittee by a veteran of the war, the son of novelist John Steinbeck, John Steinbeck IV. "The result of what I believe to be my sophistication with many aspects of Vietnam tells me," Steinbeck had said, "that about 60 percent of American soldiers between the ages of 19 and 27 smoke marijuana when they think it reasonable to do just that, taking into consideration their responsibilities at the moment." About half, Steinbeck continued, had begun using the substance in the United States, before assignment to South Vietnam, but the Military Assistance Command itself promoted drug abuse by providing for distribution of narcotics such as amphetamines, also known as pep pills, to soldiers in combat.[28]

The *Star* headlined Steinbeck's testimony "Steinbeck's Son Quotes Self as Expert on Drugs, Vietnam," and attempted to balance the story by noting that the witness had admitted to smoking marijuana himself and that he considered laws forbidding possession of the substance "provincial and prejudicial." It also took pains to include the comments of several health care professionals who had testified before the subcommittee that they considered reports of heavy marijuana smoking among the young exaggerated. Military spokesmen in Washington nevertheless characterized the wide play the press had given Steinbeck's remarks as "irresponsible." On the side, they confirmed that the Military Assistance Command had indeed distributed amphetamines in survival kits, but they added that the tablets sometimes spelled the difference between life and death for men who had to stay awake for long periods in the field.[29]

Although the Defense Department and the Military Assistance Command forthrightly admitted that marijuana smoking was, after larceny, the second most widespread criminal offense among U.S. Army troops in South Vietnam, they continued to downplay the extent of the problem. Army spokesmen in Saigon told newsmen in April that only 1,300 of 342,000 members of the U.S. Army in South Vietnam were investigated each year for marijuana possession. "It is very difficult, I would say impossible to cut off the supply," the Deputy Chief of Staff of U.S. Army, Vietnam, at Long Binh, Col. Richard A. Edwards, Jr., told newsmen, "but we are taking steps."[30] At the end of the year, when the Defense

[28] "Drug Use Soars Among Viet GI's," *Washington Daily News*, 15 Feb 68; Bernard Weinraub, "G.I.'s Warned on Taking Marijuana to Australia," *New York Times*, 23 Jan 68; William Grigg, "Steinbeck's Son Quotes Self as Expert on Drugs, Vietnam," *Washington Star*, 6 Mar 68.

[29] Grigg, "Steinbeck's Son Quotes Self as Expert on Drugs, Vietnam"; Breasted, "MAC Wars on Dope in Services."

[30] "Army Lists Marijuana Incidence," *Washington Post*, 25 Apr 68.

Department felt compelled to reveal that marijuana usage had grown to 7.99 cases per thousand men, the Chairman of the Defense Department's drug abuse control committee, Frank A. Bartimo, likewise noted that the figures compared quite favorably with civilian surveys revealing drug use rates as high as 15 and 25 percent at high schools and colleges in the United States.[31] Official news releases at the time added that if Army commanders were concerned about the potential dangers drug abuse posed for U.S. servicemen, there was "virtually no addiction to so-called hard narcotics" such as heroin and that "the rise in marijuana investigations is attributable to an increased awareness of the problem and a more vigorous application of enforcement measures."[32]

As 1969 progressed, the military's contention that drug abuse was an important but relatively minor problem continued to receive its share of attention in the press but so did the opposite point of view. On 21 April, for example, *Newsweek* published an article indicating that drug abuse was so extensive in South Vietnam it had created a subculture among the troops. "A battalion of the U.S. Army's First Cavalry Division trooped into division headquarters at Phuoc Vinh one day recently after a month in the field," the article noted. "The men showered and shaved and ate a hot meal in the mess hall. 'Then when the sun went down,' recalls one GI, 'about 200 of us went into the nearest field and had a damn good smoke.' But the scene was pure marijuana rather than Marlboro Country." Although a count of drug users was difficult to come by, the magazine continued, a recently published preliminary report by an Army psychiatrist estimated that 35 percent of the troops indulged in the practice. The drug rate was highest in units where men hailed from metropolitan centers such as New York City or San Francisco, but it also seemed heavy in mechanized and intelligence units, where the men were supposedly better educated than the infantry. The Army had undertaken a prevention program employing posters and sophisticated radio announcements to combat the problem. Punishment for soldiers convicted of drug-related offenses ranged from a two-week restriction to barracks to five years imprisonment at hard labor. Yet nothing seemed to work. According to one Army psychiatrist: "The lower-level unit commander is reaching an accommodation with pot smokers. If he stopped them all it would decimate his outfit. So he sees no evil and as long as they stay out of trouble he doesn't bother them."[33]

Although the Military Assistance Command attempted to provide what perspective it could for reporters who inquired, it made little effort to refute *Newsweek*'s allegations. Official studies were indeed beginning to indicate that usage levels were much higher than the Defense Department's statistics estimated. As for the stories about the 1st Cavalry Division (Airmobile)

[31] "Pentagon Reports Dope Use Rise," *San Diego Union*, 8 Mar 69.
[32] Talking Paper, sub: Use of Drugs by Servicemen, attachment to Query, Hoffman/AP for Directorate of Defense Information, 12 Mar 69, DDI Drug Abuse file.
[33] "In Vietnam: Mama-san Pushers Vs. Psyops," *Newsweek*, 21 Apr 69.

and the supposed accommodations between marijuana users and junior officers in the field, no one involved was talking. Information officers nevertheless resented the article and the point of view it represented. Believing that the problem was hardly as difficult as *Newsweek* seemed to suggest, one of them observed angrily in an interoffice memorandum that the story was "a fine example of the press focusing on the unfavorable. Note no mention of what the Army is doing to control marijuana problems, how the statistics may be improving, what causes marijuana usage to increase or why there is a problem of marijuana use here."[34]

News stories on marijuana continued in the months that followed. During September Drummond Ayres of the *New York Times* observed that so many soldiers were smoking the plant that it had become a cash crop for farmers in South Vietnam and a major worry for military commanders. He continued that in recent months the Military Assistance Command had seized enough of the substance to make up to five million cigarettes. "A chaplain in the 101st Airborne division . . . estimated that one of every two soldiers in the average company smoked in varying degrees. Yet only a few were apprehended." On 13 October the *Baltimore Sun* reported that according to an article in the *Journal of the American Medical Association* based on materials gathered by two former U.S. Army psychiatrists who had served in South Vietnam, "Some American soldiers in Vietnam are having severe mental disturbances after using marijuana, a condition made potentially more dangerous by the 'environment of the war zone.'" Information officers in Washington confirmed that up to 30 percent of U.S. troops in South Vietnam used marijuana, but once more attempted to provide perspective. According to recent surveys in the field, they said, when current users were asked to indicate how often they smoked marijuana, the average of those who responded three or more times per week was relatively small, only 9 to 11 percent.[35]

Evidence continued to mount nevertheless that marijuana smoking had reached major proportions in the war zone. During November 1969 the office of the U.S. Army surgeon in South Vietnam conducted a controlled survey of 1,000 incoming and 1,000 outgoing personnel at the 22d Replacement Battalion in Cam Ranh Bay. Guaranteeing anonymity to all who participated, he found that approximately 30 percent of the men arriving in South Vietnam and 45 percent of those departing had used marijuana at least once.[36] One month later, as a result of continuing incidents, several involving opium, the Australian government instituted a

[34] Typewritten Note attached to Query, AVHIO for PIO, 1 Apr 69, 72A4722, box 17, folder 17, Historical Inquiry files, WNRC.

[35] Drummond Ayres, "U.S. Military Spurs Campaign To Curb Marijuana in Vietnam," *New York Times*, 21 Sep 69; "Marijuana Effects Noted in GI's," *Baltimore Sun*, 13 Oct 69; Query, Susan Smith, *Reader's Digest*, for Directorate of Defense Information, 28 Sep 69, DDI Drugs 1969–1970 file.

[36] Msg, Lt Col Johnson, IO USARV, Long Binh, USARV 900 to Brig Gen Sidle, Chief of Information, Department of the Army (CINFO, DA), 30 Mar 70, 72A6694, box 8, USARVIO Papers, WNRC.

TABLE 2—RATE OF DRUG ABUSE PER THOUSAND TESTED

Service	1968	1969	1970	1971
MARIJUANA				
Army	8.92	15.63	23.68	13.42
Navy	9.65	8.45	16.21	17.50
Air Force	3.11	4.90	5.67	4.06
Marine Corps	9.06	25.25	29.81	30.75
HARD NARCOTICS				
Army	0.36	0.71	2.51	7.55
Navy	0.06	0.08	1.09	6.02
Air Force	0.11	0.17	1.13	4.12
Marine Corps	0.58	0.60	1.55	29.55

Source Fact Sheet on Durg Abuse, Brıefıng Book, Laırd Trıp to Hawaıı, 6 Nov 71, tab 9, 330–76–207, box 14, Vıet 333 Laırd, 6 Nov 71, Laırd Papers, WNRC

thorough body search of all American military personnel arriving on its territory for rest and recreation tours. The development was disturbing from a public relations standpoint, Admiral McCain told Abrams, and it obviously demoralized the many innocent men who had already submitted to body searches and examinations for venereal disease prior to leaving South Vietnam. Yet it was perfectly understandable and "a commentary on our lack of success in prohibiting narcotics from being transported."[37] A few weeks after McCain made his observation, the Military Assistance Command revealed its drug abuse statistics for 1969. (*Table 2*) The rates for the Army and the Marine Corps, in particular, showed significant increases over the previous year. Those for hard narcotics abuse remained small, but figures for all categories of drug abuse would continue to rise significantly.[38]

Although the evidence seems dramatic in hindsight, officials in both South Vietnam and the United States remained unconvinced. Few outside of the medical community had any knowledge of the study conducted at Cam Ranh, the best and most closely organized to that date. As late as 30 March 1970, indeed, the Army surgeon at Long Binh had lacked access to a computer and so had failed to make more than a preliminary analysis of his data. The study apparently only came to the attention of officials in the Pentagon when a former Army major, the head of a neuropsychiatric team

[37] Msg, McCain for Abrams, 2 Dec 69, Abrams Papers, CMH.
[38] MACV's figures for 1969 are included in the table, which shows the trend in drug abuse over time. The figures were very soft. See Chapter 16 for a more complete picture of the problem. Also see Savage and Gabriel, "Cohesion and Disintegration in the American Army," p. 356.

at Nha Trang between 1968 and 1969, Dr. Joel H. Caplan, testified before the Senate Subcommittee on Juvenile Delinquency that in his experience 50 to 80 percent of all Army personnel in South Vietnam had used marijuana at least once. Anticipating questions from the press, the Chief of U.S. Army Public Affairs, General Sidle, cabled the Army command at Long Binh for information, only to learn that if Caplan's statistics seemed excessive the best figures available in the field were sufficiently worrisome.[39]

As for the increase in the drug abuse rate, officials once more tended to interpret it as the result of improved detection and enforcement rather than as the sign of a deepening problem. The Chief of Staff of the Army, General Westmoreland, for one, asserted at a news conference on 29 January 1970 that drug abuse in South Vietnam had been exaggerated. Challenging a letter to the editor in the *Washington Star* by an Army psychiatrist who had alleged that from 20 to 30 percent of the servicemen in South Vietnam used marijuana, Westmoreland said that his own studies as well as recent reports from the field had convinced him that there was no widespread use of the drug.[40]

The weight of evidence nevertheless continued to increase in the months that followed, making it clear that reports in the press of a rise in drug abuse among the troops reflected more than a desire on the part of newsmen to seek sensations. By October 1970, as the result of a concerted effort to determine whether some hospital admissions and noncombat fatalities in South Vietnam were drug induced, even the comforting thought that the Military Assistance Command had little problem with hard drugs had disappeared. Investigators found that all statistics on the subject had underestimated what was happening because hospital personnel had routinely attributed drug-related illnesses to the primary medical conditions they had treated—hepatitis, pneumonia, or personality disorders—rather than to the ultimate cause, heroin or some other addictive or hallucinogenic substance.[41] The problem was especially acute where deaths were concerned. Since the computer program that tallied the causes of noncombat fatalities made no provision for drug abuse, doctors coded cases of that sort as "unknown" or "accidental self-destruction." Although the Defense Department might modify the program, the agency's comptroller told information officers, a final judgment would still have to await the results of an autopsy, which might take six months to complete. "Even then," he said, "copies of the autopsy report are not always forwarded . . . and the cause of death remains

---

[39] Msg, Sidle WDC 5562 to Lt Col Johnson, IO USARV, 24 Mar 70, and Msg, Johnson ARV 900 to Sidle, 30 Mar 70, both in 72A6694, box 8, USARVIO Papers, WNRC; MACV History, 1969, vol. 3, pp. XIV-4–XIV-8.

[40] John Svicarovich, "Army Chief Disputes Drug Talk," *Norfolk Virginian-Pilot,* 29 Jan 70.

[41] Msg, Abrams MAC 14114 to Secretary of Defense, 28 Oct 70, DDI Drugs 1969–1970 file. For a detailed investigation of the problem, see the testimony of John M. Steinberg before the Senate Subcommittee on Juvenile Delinquency of the Committee on the Judiciary, 30 Oct 70, copy in CMH files.

unknown."[42] The magnitude of the lapse became apparent once official agencies revised their methods. Where the U.S. Army in South Vietnam had been able to identify only sixteen drug-related deaths during all of the 1969 fiscal year, between January and October 1970 it recorded ninety-three. Most of the increase came after 1 August, when the Military Assistance Command began to stress the proper reporting of all cases of drug abuse through medical channels.[43]

Word of the finding came as no surprise to the news media, whose reporting of the subject was impressionistic but still more accurate than that of the military. Official spokesmen contended, with some justification, that problems with race and drug abuse stemmed in large part from the slowing pace of the war and the inactivity and boredom it bred among the troops. They took consolation from the fact that neither racial tensions nor drugs had rendered any unit in the field combat ineffective. Even so, it was clear that as the war wound down the U.S. Army in South Vietnam faced additional enemies, and that the new battles it would fight, like the old, would occur under the harsh eye of the press.[44]

[42] Memo, Jerry E. Bush, OASD/Comptroller (Systems Policy & Information) for Comdr Joseph Lorfano, Southeast Asia (SEA) Desk, Directorate of Defense Information, 11 Dec 70, DDI Drugs 1969–1970 file.

[43] Msg, Abrams MAC 114089 to McCain, 28 Oct 70, DDI Drugs 1969–1970 file.

[44] Msg, Comdr Joseph Lorfano to Col Robert Leonard, Chief, MACV Office of Information, 14 Nov 70, DDI Drugs 1969–1970 file.

9

Discipline and Dissent

From 1968 onward, the Military Assistance Command's difficulties with race and drugs appeared in the press alongside a whole range of other highly publicized problems. The facts in those cases were, at first, equally difficult to discern. Yet all came, with time, to take on significance for the press, either because they served as markers signaling some important turn of events or because they seemed to have a bearing on the meaning of the war itself.

The Club Scandal

The Saigon correspondents had long known, for example, that corruption was rampant in South Vietnam. The list of their articles on the black market seemed endless, and a few reporters, at least, had personal experience of the illegal trade in foreign currencies that the Military Assistance Command had tried for years to halt. The South Vietnamese government, indeed, quietly disaccredited the Saigon bureau chief of an important wire service during 1970 because investigators found his signature on a check in the possession of a major black marketeer. It came as no surprise to newsmen, therefore, when the Defense Department announced during August 1969 that the Army had begun a probe of alleged irregularities at officer and noncommissioned officer clubs in Europe and South Vietnam. What was shocking was the extent of the conspiracy that began to unfold and the importance of the high-ranking officers and enlisted men who were involved.

When it became clear that a major scandal was about to break, official spokesmen handled the announcement carefully. Beyond noting that the Senate's permanent subcommittee on investigations was involved and that a loss of millions of dollars might have occurred, they released few details. Any disclosure would be premature, they told newsmen, and possibly damaging to the rights of the accused. Members of the subcommittee's staff were only slightly more forthcoming. They revealed that the Senate had been investigating since March and that possible bribes and kickbacks in the hiring of entertainers and the purchase of goods and services for the clubs were involved.[1]

General Westmoreland had known of the investigation from the beginning and that the main suspect was one of the most prominent enlisted men in the Army, the principal noncommissioned officer at the Military Assistance Command in Saigon, and, prior to that, the first soldier to hold the rank of Sergeant Major of the Army, Command Sgt. Maj. William O. Wooldridge. When it became clear that there was substance to the charges and that Wooldridge's activities in both Europe and South Vietnam involved prostitution, bribes, and the diversion of purchases by the clubs to businesses owned by the suspect and his associates, Westmoreland had suggested that General Abrams terminate Wooldridge's assignment in South Vietnam. "Appropriate action could then be taken, if merited, in the U.S.," he said, "without attracting undue attention."[2]

There was little possibility of that. In the weeks that followed, the Military Assistance Command substantiated most of the charges against Wooldridge and his accomplices. Meanwhile, the Senate subcommittee began public hearings on black marketing, currency manipulation, and other corrupt activities in South Vietnam. Allegations also began to arise that general officers—the former Provost Marshal of the Army, Maj. Gen. Carl G. Turner, and the head of the Post Exchange system in Germany, Brig. Gen. Earl F. Cole—were somehow involved in a cover-up. Subpoenaed to testify before the subcommittee, Turner admitted that he had attempted to suppress reports linking Wooldridge to irregularities in the operation of service clubs at Fort Benning because he feared that a "witch hunt" was developing that might "blemish the Army."[3] As the scandal developed, reporters chronicled every detail that surfaced. A raft of news stories appeared comparing the activities of Wooldridge and his associates to those of civilian racketeers in the United States and analyzing the effects the subcommittee's probe would inevitably have on the operation of military clubs around the world.[4]

[1] Fred Farrar, "Army Probes Funds Use in Officer Clubs," *Chicago Tribune*, 13 Aug 69.

[2] Msg, Westmoreland WDC 10526 to Abrams, 23 Jun 69, sub: McClellan Committee Investigation, Abrams Papers, CMH.

[3] U.S. Congress, Senate, Report of the Committee on Government Operations, Permanent Subcommittee on Investigations, *Fraud and Corruption in Management of Military Club Systems*, 92d Cong., 1st sess., 1971.

[4] Msg, Abrams MAC 10234 to Westmoreland, 7 Aug 69, Abrams Papers, CMH; Morton Mintz, "GI's Subpoenaed on Club Kickbacks," *Washington Post*, 27 Sep 69; "Ribicoff Says Turner Foiled Exposure of Military Clubs," *Washington Star*, 24 Oct 69; "Khaki Cosa Nostra," *Newsweek*, 13 Oct 69; "Kickbacks, Guns: New Round in Army 'Rackets' Hearing," *U.S. News & World Report*, 20 Oct 69; Jim Lucas, "Army Club Managers 'Scared' in Heat of Worldwide Probe," *Washington Daily News*, 15 Oct 69. Also see U.S. Congress, Senate, Report of the Committee on Government Operations, Permanent Subcommittee on Investigations, *Fraud and Corruption in Management of Military Club Systems*.

Neither the Defense Department nor the Army was inclined to hide anything. Concerned about the well being of the armed forces, policy makers understood that any attempt to dissemble would only postpone the inevitable and complicate the ability of the military to deal with the American public and Congress in the future. When the subcommittee disclosed that Turner had sold for personal profit weapons taken from criminals and donated to the Army, they wasted little time before revealing that, in light of the information, the Army had revoked the general's Distinguished Service Medal.[5] They also issued a statement by Secretary of the Army Resor detailing the many steps the military services were taking to tighten the administration of the club system. Resor conceded that commanders had been lax. "Assignments have sometimes not been made with the kind of care that should be exercised in this sensitive area. As a result, a number of strategically placed enlisted men have apparently been able to abuse their positions."[6] A month later, the Air Force likewise took pains to volunteer that an investigation of its service clubs in Thailand had revealed problems. Secretary Laird noted at the time that the inquiry in Thailand had been the result of a worldwide survey of Air Force clubs begun in June 1968 and that surveillance of that sort would continue.[7]

The Alpha Company Affair

Despite those efforts, the club scandal became a recurring feature in press coverage of the military and the war, to resurface time and again, whenever a politician or a newsman sought to illustrate continuing problems in South Vietnam. If it damaged the public image of the Army, however, it created hardly a stir compared with another incident that surfaced at almost the same time. On 12 August 1969, enemy forces attacked a remote American fire base overlooking the Song Chang Valley some fifty kilometers south of Da Nang. In the battle that followed, a helicopter carrying a battalion commander and seven other persons, one of them AP photographer Oliver Noonan, went down with the loss of all on board. A major effort ensued to reach the site of the crash and to recover the bodies. Over five days of fighting, the 196th Infantry Brigade (Light) accounted for an estimated 524 enemy killed while losing 34 of its own men. One of the American units most heavily engaged, Company A of the 3d Battalion, 21st Infantry, 23d Infantry "American" Division, lost ten killed

---

[5] Interv, author with Jerry Friedheim, Deputy Assistant Secretary of Defense, 1969–1970, 3 Oct 86, CMH files; William Delaney, "Ribicoff Says Turner Foiled Exposure of Military Clubs," *Washington Star*, 24 Oct 69; Lucas, "Army Club Managers 'Scared' in Heat of Worldwide Probe."

[6] OASD PA News Release 821–69, 30 Sep 69, HRC 331.2 NCO and Officers Clubs, CMH.

[7] *Facts on File*, 29:696, 822.

and twenty wounded. When it received orders on the sixth day to move back into the valley, its commander, 1st Lt. Eugene Shurtz, radioed his superior, the battalion commander, Lt. Col. Robert C. Bacon, that the company refused to obey.[8]

Associated Press photographer Horst Faas was within hearing distance of the conversation that followed. He repeated it to his associate, Peter Arnett, who wrote the story and put it on the wire:

"Repeat that, please," the colonel asked without raising his voice. "Have you told them what it means to disobey orders under fire?"

"I think they understand, but some of them simply had enough—they are broken. There are boys here who have only 90 days left in Vietnam. They want to go home in one piece. The situation is psychic here."

"Are you talking about enlisted men or are the NCO's also involved?" the colonel asked.

"That's the difficulty here," Shurtz said. "We've got a leadership problem. Most of our squad and platoon leaders have been killed or wounded."

Quietly the colonel told Shurtz: "Go talk to them again and tell them that to the best of our knowledge the bunkers are now empty—the enemy has withdrawn. . . . Please take a hand count of how many really do not want to go."

The lieutenant came back a few minutes later: "They won't go, colonel, and I did not ask for the hand count because I am afraid that they will all stick together, even though some might prefer to go."

After instructing the lieutenant to take his command post element and move off toward the objective, Bacon told his executive officer, Maj. Richard Waite, and an experienced veteran, Sgt. Okie Blankenship, to fly to the company's position, survey the situation, and reason with the men. "Give them a pep talk and a kick in the butt."[9]

Quoting Blankenship, Arnett described the meeting that followed. The sergeant and the major listened while the men gave their reasons for refusing to go into combat. They were sick of the heat, the sudden fire fights by day and the mortaring by night. "Helicopters brought in the basic needs of ammunition, food, and water at a tremendous risk, but this was not enough for these men. They believed that they were in danger of annihilation and would go no further." Then the sergeant began to argue. When

---

[8] Msg, CG, III MAF, to COMUSMACV, Lt Gen Nickerson to Abrams, 25 Aug 69, Abrams Papers, CMH; Horst Faas and Peter Arnett, "GI Unit Beats Fear, Rejoins Battle in Viet," *Chicago Tribune*, 26 Aug 69; "Incident in Song Chang Valley," *Time*, 5 Sep 69. Also see Memo, Daniel Z. Henkin for Secretary Laird, 12 Jan 70, 330–76–067, box 99, Viet (South) 320.2 (Jan–Feb) 1970, Laird Papers, WNRC.

[9] Faas and Arnett, "GI Unit Beats Fear, Rejoins Battle in Viet." Faas' and Arnett's story was substantiated by Msg, CG, III MAF, to COMUSMACV, Nickerson to Abrams, 25 Aug 69.

Peter Arnett

one soldier shouted that the company had suffered enough, he responded that another company was down to fifteen men but still on the move. He later admitted that the comment had been a lie, but it had achieved the effect he wanted. When someone asked why that unit went on, he replied, "Maybe they have got something a little more than what you have got." One man began to run toward the sergeant with his fists raised. "Don't call us cowards," he howled. "We are not cowards." The sergeant coolly turned his back and walked away. Behind him, the men picked up their rifles and began to fall in. The incident ended. "A company went back to the war."[10]

The Military Assistance Command approached the story in a straightforward manner. Since Arnett had written it as a narrative, without editorial comments, information officers concentrated on verifying the details of what had occurred. They found that most of what the reporter had said was true but denied that the entire company had balked. They told reporters that only five men were involved and that they had yielded to the good leadership of Waite and Blankenship. Leadership was, they said, the problem. The company commander, Shurtz, had been in South Vietnam for only two weeks. Occupying what should have a captain's position, he lacked the experience to handle so difficult a situation. Although no one intended to make him a scapegoat and he remained in good standing as a junior officer, his superiors had

---

[10] Ibid.

relieved him of command even before they had learned of Arnett's dispatch.[11]

In the days that followed, public affairs officers made Shurtz, Blankenship, and the commander of the Americal Division, Maj. Gen. Lloyd B. Ramsey, available to the press. All three supported the official interpretation. Ramsey, in particular, observed that, "When you focus on this very small, insignificant incident involving five men, it detracts from the outstanding contributions and accomplishments of [the] more than 3,000 troops who did their jobs as professionals." Reporters also gained access to the new company commander, Capt. Bernard F. Wolpers, who characterized morale in the unit as "just as good as any company in Vietnam. As a matter of fact, it is rather high right now." Wolpers suggested that the incident was "something that came up on the spur of the moment and nothing that would last."[12]

Seeking to test the truth of those assertions, newsmen went into the field to interview the men of Company A. The soldiers denied that only five of them had balked. Instead, they said, the entire unit had decided to hold back, and the five had emerged more or less as spokesmen. The men were vague about their motives. Some cited fear, others inexperience, but most apparently agreed with one soldier who said that the incident had come about because "morale was at rock bottom."[13]

Reporters perceived that something was wrong, but they were torn between the military's point of view and their own misgivings. Some, Richard Threlkeld of CBS News, for example, and Kenley Jones of NBC, concluded that, as Jones put it,

The American soldier's will to fight is being shaken not so much by enemy gunfire as by the politics of friends. Soldiers, as well as civilians, can perceive the developing strategy of the U.S.: to disengage itself from the war in Vietnam, even though its side has not won and even though the other side has refused to make concessions. That point is not lost on the men in the field, the men who are being asked to gamble their lives until the withdrawal deck is stacked. As the brief revolt of Alpha company suggests, some of them may decide the stakes are too high.[14]

James Reston of the *New York Times* shared that point of view. He noted in a 27 August commentary that since the president no longer said the conflict in South Vietnam was vital to American interests, he was "asking

---

[11] Msg, CG, III MAF, to COMUSMACV, Nickerson to Abrams, 25 Aug 69; CBS Evening News, 26 Aug 69, *Radio-TV-Defense Dialog*; "Incident in Song Chang Valley"; "The Alpha Incident," *Newsweek*, 8 Sep 69.

[12] "General Gives Views," *New York Times*, 29 Aug 69; "Lt. Eugene Shurtz Interviewed," Huntley-Brinkley Report, 29 Aug 69, *Radio-TV-Defense Dialog*.

[13] [AP], "GI Unit That Faltered in Viet Says Entire Company Balked," *Chicago Tribune*, 30 Aug 69.

[14] Quote is from "Lt. Eugene Shurtz Interviewed," Huntley-Brinkley Report, 29 Aug 69. Also see Richard Threlkeld, "A Report From Alpha Company," CBS Evening News, 27 Aug 69, *Radio-TV-Defense Dialog*.

196

Company A to fight for time to negotiate a settlement with Hanoi that will save his face but may very well lose their lives. . . . It is a typical political strategy and the really surprising thing is that there have been so few men, like the tattered remnants of Company A, who have refused to die for it."[15]

Others questioned whether anything important had happened. As Reston's colleague at the *New York Times*, James Sterba, observed, the reason behind Company A's refusal to fight seemed simple to the soldiers he had interviewed, and none of the explanations he had received involved fighting for lost causes, antiwar sentiment, troop withdrawals, or the peace talks in Paris. "Everybody gripes," one soldier had told him. "When guys don't want to go, they just make them go, and once you're out there it's O.K. . . . there's too much to think about." Another observed that the men always complained until the shooting started. Word of it never reached the press or the public because a good company commander would "give you hell and then plead with headquarters to get you some relief. That C.O. must have been new. He didn't know the ropes. And word got out and now there's a big stink. But it's all a lot of bull—it really is."[16]

The *Washington Star* agreed, siding forthrightly with the military. "There have been suggestions from some quarters," it stated in a 30 August editorial, "that Alpha Company's brief 'mutiny' may presage a revolt among young draftees serving in Vietnam who are unwilling to die in an admittedly unwinnable war. . . . There is not a scintilla of evidence to support this, and those who suggest it display little knowledge of what soldiering is all about. There have been similar incidents in every conflict since the Punic Wars." The *New York Post* just as forthrightly condemned the entire military establishment. Referring to Blankenship's avowal that he had dissembled in his confrontation with the men of Company A, the newspaper charged, "Is there anyone associated with this operation, from the battalion sergeant all the way up to the commander in chief, who can justify an attack so perilous that its leaders corrupted their calling and themselves by lying to their troops?" David Lawrence of *U.S. News & World Report* turned on the press. The publication of Arnett's dispatch before the military had a chance to clarify what had happened had left an impression "that the United States had on its hands an incipient rebellion in the ranks of its armed services. Broadcasts by the Viet Cong radio hailed the news and predicted more such incidents would follow." Lawrence suggested that the incident "emphasizes the need for 'voluntary censorship,'" which "should apply even when there is no war in progress. For again and again information is disclosed in the press which could later reduce our military effectiveness."[17]

---

[15] James Reston, "A Whiff of Mutiny in Vietnam," *New York Times*, 27 Aug 69.

[16] James P. Sterba, "G.I.'s in Battle Shrug Off the Story of Balky Company A," *New York Times*, 29 Aug 69.

[17] "Alpha Company," *Washington Star*, 30 Aug 69; "Battle of Words," *New York Post*, 26 Aug 69; David Lawrence, "What's Become of 'Voluntary Censorship,'" *U.S. News & World Report*, 8 Sep 69, p. 92.

197

The *National Observer* sought a middle ground by noting that the incident said more about the politics surrounding the war than it did about the morale of a few twenty-year-old soldiers. Both the hawks and the doves, the journal noted, had seized upon the incident "with varying degrees of unseemly glee" to advance their own viewpoints. Those arguing for quick withdrawals used it to argue that the administration should bring the troops home as quickly as possible, regardless of the blood bath that would follow for the South Vietnamese. Those favoring continuation of the war wielded it just as vehemently to suggest that the process of withdrawal had left the troops vulnerable and with low morale. In fact, whatever either side said or did, the war was ending. For the rest, the men serving in South Vietnam were little different from those who had preceded them. The earlier group had fought bravely in a conflict that lacked strong support at home. The men of Company A, in turn, battled "for a cause their Government has all but officially declared a losing fight, and they, too, eventually moved out."[18]

Although many commentators observed that similar incidents had occurred in earlier conflicts, none, except for veteran correspondent Neil Sheehan, noted that Company A's brief refusal was the first recorded instance of that sort for American troops in the Vietnam War. Earlier, at the Battles of Plei Me and the Ia Drang Valley, Sheehan said, "there had been no doubts. There was fear and anguish for the loss of a buddy, and the riflemen complained about the heat and the dust, yet they seemed to accept their lot as a bitter and necessary duty for their country. They believed the generals and the diplomats and the President who told them that if they did not win here they would have to fight the yellow-skinned Communists, the eternal gooks, at Waikiki or San Francisco." As the war continued and dissent grew at home, the reporter continued, infantry men still seemed free of doubt. The marines cheered as they charged to the tops of the three high hills north of their camp at Khe Sanh, even though 138 of them had died in the attacks leading to the victory. At Dak To, officers shouted "Airborne," and the men called back, "All the way," as they rushed again and again into the enemy's bullets and grenades "until the vocal cords of 158 were permanently silenced and the North Vietnamese were driven from the summit." But, Sheehan said, "there comes a time in some wars when the killing, or just the manner of dying, appears so senseless that even the obedient soldier who is 'not to reason why' begins to question the meaning of his sacrifice." There were many explanations for Company A's refusal, "all of which argued it had nothing to do with the futility of the war. The men were tired, it was said, they had little sleep and little food and no mail. Most of their squad and platoon leaders were casualties. Perhaps these explanations were true and perhaps they were not. What could not be explained away was that men had suffered equally before and had not balked when ordered to endure more."[19]

[18] "The Pain of Withdrawal," *National Observer*, 1 Sep 69.
[19] Neil Sheehan, "Letters From Hamburger Hill," *Harper's*, Nov 69.

Sheehan may have exaggerated the common soldier's sense of frustration with the war but he was correct in asserting that Company A's refusal was a first and that the common soldier had begun to question authority. Small groups of Americans the size of a squad, may have shirked their duty or balked during earlier years of the war, but never an entire company, however worn. If an incident of the sort had occurred, it would almost certainly have become public knowledge. The press seemed sooner or later to learn about everything that happened in South Vietnam, even the president's ultra-secret bombing of the enemy's Cambodian sanctuaries. Some editorial writers, ever supportive of the American soldier, commended Sergeant Blankenship for his leadership and warned that so isolated an incident had little meaning beyond its immediate context. Yet, only nine days later the unheard of happened again, when a second unit refused a lawful order to advance. This time the ringleaders were not green, frightened enlisted men but experienced noncommissioned officers.[20]

Word of what had happened reached the press two months after the event, when UPI correspondent Tom Tiede revealed that a platoon from Company B, 2d Battalion, 27th Infantry, 25th Infantry Division, had refused to move out on a routine patrol. Quoting the company's commanding officer, Capt. Frank Smith, the reporter told how the unit's twenty-one members, all with extensive combat experience, had refused their commander's order because they considered it unfair for them to have to go on another patrol. "I never did get those men to obey me," Smith said. "I tried but they just wouldn't go. I had to bring charges against all of them." Tiede used the incident to highlight the morale problems that had begun to afflict the Military Assistance Command. The men had received very light sentences, he said, leading to complaints on the part of some career officers that the Army had chosen to pamper enlisted men rather than inflict the sort of hard punishments for mass insubordination that would prevent similar outbreaks in the future. The military establishment was so battered by accusations of corruption, so the reasoning went, that it sought to back away from disorders rather than risk crisis confrontations. Although those arguments were only opinions, Tiede cautioned, they nevertheless seemed to reflect a solid worry. Proficiency among the troops was down, grumbling was up, and subtle disobedience seemed endemic at all levels. "You never know any more," the reporter quoted a concerned noncommissioned officer. "If you tell a man to do something, you just never know if he will."[21]

During the investigation that followed Tiede's story, the Army found that the incident was more complicated than the reporter had

---

[20] "Fine Work, Sarge," *New York Daily News*, 27 Aug 69; "Keep 'Mutiny' in Perspective," *Detroit News*, 2 Sep 69.

[21] Unless otherwise indicated, this section is based on Msg, Lt Gen Ewell, CG, IIFFV, HOA 3384 to Abrams, 10 Nov 69, relaying Msg, Maj Gen Hollis, CG, 25th Inf Div, to Lt Gen Mildren, DCG, USARV, CHU 1680, 8 Nov 69, Abrams Papers, CMH.

made it appear. The battalion had lost three of its commanders to wounds in four months and a new company commander had just arrived to replace an officer who had been relieved for cause. The administrative turbulence that had accompanied the shifts in command had given rise to practices in the unit that were contrary to good order and discipline. Soldiers had come to believe, for example, that those serving their last thirty days in South Vietnam were exempt from participation in combat operations. When the new commander attempted to reinstate proper military discipline the men became upset. On the day of their refusal, Captain Smith heard them out but then ordered each one individually to obey. Nineteen once more ignored his instructions. That evening, all nevertheless participated in a dangerous night ambush, demonstrating that cowardice was not the primary motivation for what they had done.

In the end, contrary to Tiede's suggestion, the Army dealt leniently with the men of Company B less because it feared confrontations than because of their exemplary performance in combat during the months prior to the event and the extenuating circumstances surrounding what had happened. Fifteen received fines and reductions in rank during non-judicial (Article 15) proceedings. A court-martial found the ringleaders, two sergeants and two specialists fifth class, guilty of disobeying a lawful order but sentenced them to receive only oral reprimands. The reasons behind the incident spoke for themselves, the judge noted in his opinion. While they hardly justified insubordination, the court had decided in favor of leniency because each man, "except for this one incident," had "served in the highest traditions expected of members of the United States Army."[22]

Company B's refusal received little play in the press. By the time it appeared, the news was stale, and many major stories competed for attention. President Nixon had just delivered his 3 November speech calling for support from the silent majority; antiwar forces in the United States were gearing for the 15 November march on Washington; and Vice President Agnew had begun his campaign to criticize the news media's coverage of Nixon administration policies. In addition, on 13 November the story broke that the Army was investigating allegations that members of the Americal Division had murdered hundreds of South Vietnamese peasants at a village south of Da Nang named My Lai. The incident involving Company A, however, became a staple of the press. Reporters referred to it often, whenever they sought to demonstrate that a decline in morale had occurred. Spurred by the example of Arnett's and Faas' enterprise, they also remained on watch for new incidents capable of demonstrating that the patience of the American soldier with the war was wearing thin.

---

[22] Ibid.

Allegations of Censorship

A case in point occurred during September 1969, when charges arose that the Military Assistance Command was censoring the news it distributed to the troops in the field. The controversy that followed served to confirm suspicions entertained by some in the press that antiwar dissent had found its way into the war zone and that military institutions were hardening to the threat.

The imbroglio had its roots in the contradictions that necessarily arise in time of war between the Army's belief that an informed soldiery fights best, and the concern of commanders in the field that bad news will harm troop morale. Unwilling to leave soldiers serving in combat ignorant of what was happening elsewhere, the American military services had since World War I attempted to supply the troops with word of what was going on both around them and in the world at large. The main means they used were military newspapers and magazines, and, after World War II, the worldwide affiliates of the Armed Forces Radio and Television Service. Problems had arisen periodically during wartime, especially when commanders concluded that the information released to the troops was dangerous to morale, but the censorship of both military and civilian news dispatches had always kept them to a minimum. As a result, most commentators in the civilian press considered officially sponsored military periodicals of broad circulation such as *Stars and Stripes* relatively fair and balanced.[23]

When the United States went to war in South Vietnam, the censorship that had protected military newsmen in earlier wars was unavailable, but few problems at first developed. The Pacific edition of *Stars and Stripes* relied heavily on wire service copy and syndicated columnists but also employed a staff of enlisted reporters to tailor its product to the specific needs and point of view of the American soldier. In South Vietnam those newsmen ranked as accredited correspondents and shared the lot of their civilian counterparts. Observing the Military Assistance Command's guidelines for the press, they sent their work directly to their employer's main office in Tokyo without passing it through official reviewers in Saigon. Their newspaper, in turn, appeared uncensored, with some 125,000 copies going daily to the troops in South Vietnam.[24]

The Military Assistance Command augmented *Stars and Stripes* with broadcasts of radio and television programs through what was called the Armed Forces Vietnam Network. A series of eight radio and television stations scattered across the country, the network was technically under the authority of the Armed Forces Radio and Television Service, a division of the Office of the Assistant Secretary of Defense for Manpower and

[23] For a brief history of military journalism, see Jack Foisie, "The Perils of Military Journalism," *Los Angeles Times*, 19 Oct 69.
[24] Robert Hodierne, "How G.I.'s in Vietnam Don't Learn About the War," *New York Times Magazine*, 12 Apr 70, p. 13.

Star and Stripes *was staple reading for soldiers in the field.*

Reserve Affairs, but the MACV Office of Information set policy and issued guidance. The bulk of the network's programming consisted of music, entertainment, and sports, but news also appeared at specified times each day. In the evening, enlisted announcers broadcast a nightly news program similar to the ones that appeared in the United States. They often retransmitted film reports that had played on the commercial television networks. In theory, the troops received much the same information as the American public at home. In fact, although that was true most of the time, since the Armed Forces Vietnam Network operated in a combat zone and with the permission of the South Vietnamese government, the Military Assistance Command had the power to remove or change those items that it considered inaccurate; dangerous to the safety or morale of the troops; or offensive to the sensitivities of the South Vietnamese people, government, and armed forces.[25]

Over the years the command's policies had never come into question, but in July 1969 a group of nine military broadcasters at the Armed Forces Vietnam Network complained in private to their superiors that

[25] White Paper, Armed Forces Vietnam Network (AFVN) Policies and Procedures [1970], DDI AFVN Censorship file. Also see "Where There Is No Napalm," *Newsweek*, 20 Oct 69, p. 77.

their agency's practices differed significantly from official guidance. They cited a May 1967 Defense Department memorandum prohibiting the calculated withholding of unfavorable news from internal military media and charged that the MACV Office of Information had altered or removed stories and wire service reports that might embarrass the U.S. government, the armed services, or the South Vietnamese. Receiving what they considered unsatisfactory responses, the broadcasters kept their concerns to themselves until the fall, when one of them, Army Sp5c. Michael Maxwell, aired his complaints in an on-camera interview with CBS News reporter Gary Sheppard. Maxwell claimed that the U.S. command was censoring the information the troops received about the war and cited a range of examples. A statement by President Nixon implying that a recent lull in the fighting might allow further troop reductions had never received any mention in military news broadcasts; a recent murder of two U.S. field grade officers by a South Vietnamese sentry had appeared in the South Vietnamese press and even in *Stars and Stripes* but had never aired on the Armed Forces Vietnam Network; Vice President Ky's revelation that President Nixon would reduce U.S. forces in South Vietnam by 40,500 had aired only after a 24-hour delay. "It bothers me," Maxwell concluded, "not being able to tell the whole story."[26]

Shepherd turned to Maxwell's commander, Lt. Col. James Adams, for an explanation. The officer avowed that there were no restrictions, per se. Instead, the command attempted merely to ensure the accuracy of the news that the troops received. Pressed by Shepherd on whether censorship in any form existed, Adams affirmed that he considered the American soldier "the best informed individual in the world" and that "censorship is not applied at any time by anyone." Shepherd noted in his closing commentary that within hours of the interview, Adams had removed Maxwell from his job as war news editor and had reassigned him to cleaning rifles in a back room. The soldier had recently sought a transfer, he said, and now his superiors had granted the request.[27]

Maxwell amplified his remarks in an interview with the print media the next day. He had requested another assignment, he said, because he found it difficult to go on with one-half of the news while deleting the rest. In addition to the stories he had mentioned earlier, he complained that his commanders had ordered him to avoid using commercial television reports on Company A's combat refusal and on the death of Ho Chi Minh. "What we would like to achieve," he said, "is a Congressional investigation: a complete look into the censorship policies of the station here in Saigon, the Vietnam network, and hopefully all of the stations in the Armed Forces Radio and Television Service all over the world."[28]

[26] MACV History, 1969, pp. XI-49f. Quote from CBS Morning News, 19 Sep 69, *Radio-TV-Defense Dialog.*

[27] CBS Morning News, 19 Sep 69.

[28] [UPI], "GI, 21, Leaves News Job, Raps Vietnam Censors," *Washington Star*, 19 Sep 69.

Maxwell's story provoked a flurry of comment in Congress, where the Army's handling of the young soldier received almost as much play as the issue of censorship in the military. Senator Stephen Young of Ohio, for one, complained in outrage that "Our GI's in Vietnam are entitled to hear the news without censorship from some officious Pentagon propagandist. Here is another example of Army brass dealing unjustly with an American enlisted man."[29] The story nevertheless showed signs of dying out when sources within *Stars and Stripes* brought it back to life by revealing during September 1969 that an Army colonel newly assigned to be editor in chief of the publication's Pacific edition had branded the newspaper the "Hanoi Herald."[30]

The episode had occurred during a closed session of a U.S. Pacific Command information officers conference in Taiwan. The officer in question, Col. James Campbell, the Chief of Information for the U.S. Army component command in South Vietnam, USARV, had not attended but had included the remarks in a speech to be read to the group by an aide. Believing that some of *Stars and Stripes'* coverage of American battle casualties had given aid and comfort to the enemy, he cited in particular stories about Company A's combat refusal. "It cannot be argued whether or not this is treason," he was reported to have said. "It was treason."[31] He continued that *Stars and Stripes'* description of another battle and its use of numbers to denote casualties in an infantry company was "absolutely devastating to the morale . . . of all soldiers. It is also my contention that such reporting—in the *Stars and Stripes*, of all publications—is of tremendous aid and comfort to the enemy. . . . Nobody expects *Stars and Stripes* to be a smile sheet and report only tapioca news. But the Army does expect—and is not getting—a fair shake."[32] On the day after Campbell's charges appeared in the press, a second news editor at the Armed Forces Vietnam Network announced to reporters in Saigon that he was resigning to protest continued censorship of news dispatches.[33]

Although Campbell's remarks and those of Specialist Maxwell and the other enlisted men protesting censorship were at opposite extremes, they were emblematic of divisions that were beginning to run deep among the Americans serving in South Vietnam. Campbell, on the one hand, represented those within the U.S. command who objected strenuously to the way the press in general had covered the war, especially its preoccupation with the toll the fighting had taken on the lives of U.S. servicemen. Unable to control what the civilian press reported, they directed

[29] U.S. Congress, Senate, "Outrage," *Congressional Record*, 18 Sep 69, p. S.10795.
[30] Thomas Pepper, "Army Newspaper Termed Disloyal," *Baltimore Sun*, 28 Sep 69.
[31] Ibid.
[32] [AP], "Army Colonel Is Reassigned for Stars and Stripes Blast," *Baltimore Sun*, 29 Sep 69. Campbell referred to an article by Sp4c. Robert Hodierne, "A Weary Company Fights On With Rifles, Grenades, Guts," *Stars and Stripes*, 31 Aug 69.
[33] [AP], "Army Radio Censorship Row in Viet," *New York Post*, 29 Sep 69; "Armed Forces Radio Problems," Today Show, NBC-TV, 30 Sep 69, *Radio-TV-Defense Dialog*.

their anger toward a more accessible target, the Defense Department's continuing toleration of *Stars and Stripes'* independent attitude. "Most *Stripes* reporters are malcontents," one officer complained at the time. "If a guy wants to read anti-establishment trash, he shouldn't get it in *Stripes*."[34] The enlisted men, on the other hand, disagreed with what was, for them, an unrealistic and obvious attempt by the U.S. command to influence the attitudes of their contemporaries. Convinced that they would never receive an impartial hearing from their commanders, they turned to the press to air their views. One of them, in obvious self-defense, had leaked Campbell's remarks to the press in hopes of discrediting a formidable opponent.

The Military Assistance Command, for its part, was bound to lose, however it responded. It could hardly leave Campbell in place without opening itself to charges from the press and Congress that it indeed intended to censor *Stars and Stripes*. Yet there was also little inclination on the part of those in authority to make an example of a respected officer. In the end, the command chose quietly to disavow Campbell's comments as a personal viewpoint and to reassign the colonel to a post far from South Vietnam.[35]

The enlisted men both at *Stars and Stripes* and the Armed Forces Vietnam Network were even more difficult to handle. With antiwar dissent rising in the United States, their complaints continued to receive wide attention in Congress, where various members took offense at allegations that the network had deleted some of their comments from official broadcasts. News stories also continued to draw attention to the subject, with both former and present armed forces reporters coming forward to volunteer observations. One, who had served as a captain, told reporters that he believed an impartial investigation would expose the Armed Forces Vietnam Network as a propaganda effort rather than a legitimate news agency.[36] Another, a reporter for *Stars and Stripes*, Bob Hodierne, revealed that during the fighting around Ben Het in July a dispute had broken out between the Military Assistance Command and the newspaper over the use of the word *siege* to describe what was happening. "They said the word . . . means completely cut off," he charged, "and since they were air dropping supplies, Ben Het could not be said to be under siege."[37]

In recognition of *Stars and Stripes'* semiofficial status, the Defense Department decided for the sake of credibility to allow the paper's editors to speak for themselves. "Our men are under strict instructions to play it straight," Maj. Jimmie Wilson, the Vietnam editor, told newsmen. Contrary to Campbell's charges, "They don't slant the news and they get

[34] "Where There Is No Napalm."
[35] Ibid. Also see [AP], "Army Reassigning Critic of 'Stars and Stripes,'" *Washington Star*, 29 Sep 69.
[36] [AP], "Viet Censorship Laid to Military," *Baltimore Sun*, 2 Oct 69.
[37] "Where there Is No Napalm."

it on the spot whenever they can. One of our reporters has been killed in this war and several have been wounded." As for the allegation that some of the stories appearing in the paper were "treasonous," a *Stars and Stripes* reporter added, "some of us well-meaning guys come up with them periodically. But getting them in the paper is quite the opposite from the push-over that the good colonel implied."[38]

The Armed Forces Vietnam Network was more difficult to defend because of the ambiguity of its position. Official policy clearly stated, on the one hand, that the agency's news would be as objective and complete as possible, "factual, accurate, impartial, and in good taste." News directors in Saigon, on the other, obviously had the right to remove items they considered questionable. In the end, after announcing that the Military Assistance Command would make a full investigation, official spokesmen denied that censorship had occurred and blamed what had happened on the inexperience and immaturity of the broadcasters making the charges. Shortly thereafter, the Director of the Armed Forces Radio and Television Service in Washington, John C. Broger, sent a long letter to Senator Fulbright explaining official news policies in South Vietnam. He noted that his agency attempted to make maximum disclosure of information to the troops except for what was of material assistance to the enemy. He denied that censorship had occurred but made it clear that news the Military Assistance Command considered erroneous or that threatened the well being of the troops was either edited or deleted. He cited as examples two reports on conditions at Ben Het that might have been dangerous to morale and comments by Congresswoman Margaret M. Heckler of Massachusetts indicating that the Army's bulletproof vest was defective. He added that the command also removed stories that might prove offensive to the South Vietnamese government or people, especially when officials considered them unbalanced.[39]

The press, for its part, approached the affair cautiously. *Newsweek* was critical and other journals took pains to cover every aspect of the dissidents' complaints, but many commentators appear to have been less than convinced that the military was in the wrong. Jack Foisie of the *Los Angeles Times* pointed out in a lengthy history of *Stars and Stripes* that the newspaper had always been, in former Chief of Staff General George C. Marshall's words, "a soldier's newspaper, . . . a symbol of the things we are fighting to preserve and spread," a representation of "the free thought and free expression of a free people." High-level commanders had from time to time exerted pressure, he said, but the paper's editors and newsmen had always managed to keep close to Marshall's dictum, main-

[38] Drummond Ayres, "Military in Vietnam Accused of Censoring G.I.'s News," *New York Times*, 14 Oct 69.

[39] [AP], "Viet Censorship Laid to Military"; "Radio Censorship Denied by Army," *Philadelphia Inquirer*, 24 Oct 69; Ltr, John C. Broger, Director, Armed Forces Radio and Television Service (AFRTS), to Senator J. William Fulbright, 18 Nov 69, 330–75–089, box 89, Viet 000.7, 1969, Laird Papers, WNRC.

taining, in the process, a reputation for fairness and balance. As for South Vietnam, the news media in general had experienced problems, "for it is an unpopular war at home, a war we are not winning, and a war with more than the usual proportion of political entanglements." Drummond Ayres of the *New York Times* sided squarely with the disgruntled newsmen in a 14 October survey of the problem but noted that if official agencies monitored news of the war carefully, they were far more liberal when events in the United States were involved. The Armed Forces Vietnam Network, he said, had always broadcast news of antiwar demonstrations, student disorders, and race riots at home. He then quoted Colonel Adams, who had said, "I'm not running ABC or CBS or NBC. This is an armed forces network and our job is to further the mission of the United States military. These censorship charges stem primarily from young men who misunderstand our efforts to avoid broadcasting news that would hurt morale or help the enemy. We can never forget who our audience is." David French of WTOP-TV News in Washington devoted an entire segment of his 27 October broadcast to the comments of Col. Earl Browning, Deputy Chief of Information for the Armed Forces Radio and Television Service. Browning noted that "It's important in Vietnam that we avoid speculation and rumor that may impair morale and may have an injurious effect upon our relationship with our Vietnamese allies. So that it seems quite understandable and proper to me that some speculative stories that might form the basis for a rumor would be held up until they could be verified." An editorial in the *New Orleans Times-Picayune* meanwhile stated forthrightly that, as far as people at home were concerned, questions arose less about how much the soldier in the field knew about the war than about whether he would be able to keep up his morale while reading and hearing so much of the debate at home.[40]

There matters might have remained but for a series of incidents that occurred at the end of December 1969 and during the first week of January 1970. On 29 December officers at the Armed Forces Vietnam Network summarily reassigned a television broadcaster, Air Force Sgt. Hugh Morgan, for what they called editorializing. Aware of Vice President Agnew's recent charge that the electronic news media were indulging in "instant analysis and querulous criticism," Morgan had introduced a commentary by correspondent Eric Sevareid on a speech by the president with a remark that the reporter's thoughts had come "at enough distance not to incur the wrath of Vice President Agnew again." The next morning, Morgan later told the Saigon correspondents, "I was sternly handed my copy from the night before. Did I know I had editorialized on the air? Colonel Adams asked. I was aghast. It had never entered my mind. After all, he is my Vice President." Morgan, who had

---

[40] Foisie, "The Perils of Military Journalism"; Ayres, "Military in Vietnam Accused of Censoring G.I.'s News"; Martin Agronsky's Washington, WTOP-TV, 27 Oct 69, *Radio-TV-Defense Dialog*; "What News to GIs in Battle Zones?," *New Orleans Times-Picayune*, 22 Oct 69.

Specialist Lawrence (left) *and other broadcasters at AFVN*

taught radio and television communications at Midwestern University in Wichita Falls, Texas, and had served as news director for station KTAN in Tucson, Arizona, added that he had written his introduction seriously and with Agnew's criticisms in mind. His superior officer disagreed. "I thought he used a little introduction I thought was editorialization," Colonel Adams told newsmen. "We don't editorialize."[41]

The incident drew out the news media once more. The *New York Times*, for one, commented that while the editing and reporting of military newspapers in a war zone had to be different from that of the uninhibited press in the United States, soldiers who were old enough to serve in South Vietnam were old enough to "read and see all there is to know about what is happening there and in this country."[42]

The controversy might nevertheless have died out again, but for a second dissenting military broadcaster, Sp5c. Robert Lawrence, who announced on the air during a 3 January 1970 news program in Saigon that military newsmen were "not free to tell the truth and, in essence, to tell it like it is." The soldier continued that the Military Assistance Command "has seen to it that all those newscasters who are dedicated to their work are sent away to other areas, in some cases off the air completely." He added that "we have been suppressed and I'm probably in trouble for telling you tonight the truth." A second broadcaster, Marine

[41] Ralph Blumenthal, "Military TV Newsman in Saigon Shifted After Remark on Agnew," *New York Times*, 30 Dec 69.
[42] "Old Enough To Know," *New York Times*, 3 Jan 70.

Cpl. Thomas M. Sinkovitzk, about to begin a sports report, underscored Lawrence's remarks by introducing his segment with the comment, "Thank you, Bob, in more ways than one." Lawrence later told newsmen that his superiors had forbidden him to select and edit war-related film for broadcast because they considered his choices slanted. "For two weeks I was running film just about every night about the Saigon black market . . . and reporting the closing down of newspapers by the Thieu government. They called me up one day and I was told the MACV Office of Information was upset." He noted that most of the film he used had been provided by CBS.[43]

The Military Assistance Command labeled Lawrence's allegations and the entire censorship controversy "a lot of baloney." Official newspapers and magazines were instruments of command information, its spokesmen pointed out, similar to the house organs civilian corporations published for their employees. With the building of morale their main objective, they were "checked for policy and propriety but not really censored at all."[44]

The news media accepted the point in a spate of editorials and commentaries. The *New York Times* professed to understand the military's problem and called on the Department of Defense to clear the air. The *Washington Star* claimed that all sides in the dispute were in error: the broadcasters, because they were soldiers subject to military discipline rather than genuine newsmen representing the free press; and the military, because they should never have assigned newsmen drafted recently from the civilian press to do the sort of reporting required by house organs. In addition, the Pentagon had erred when it had issued directives mandating the free dissemination of information to the troops. Military commanders in South Vietnam, after all, "should be free to edit, censor or reassign the occasional malcontent who gets to a typewriter or a microphone—regardless of how justified the lack of content may be. The uncensored, free and ubiquitous civilian press gives the brass a hard enough time without any help from dissidents within the military establishment." The *Washington Post* accepted the *Star*'s point but added, in line with Marshall's thought, that newscasters in South Vietnam should receive the largest measure of freedom possible, consistent with the welfare and safety of the troops. "The operation of the armed forces TV network loses its whole point," the paper said, ". . . if a commander is needlessly or foolishly or doctrinairely repressive." The newspaper added that "some of the repression, or censorship, in Vietnam looks foolish."[45]

[43] Quotes from [AP], "GI Newsman Assails Curb on Viet TV," *Washington Post*, 4 Jan 70; and, [AP], "2 GIs Relieved of News Jobs Are Silenced in Censor Row," *Washington Star*, 5 Jan 70.

[44] James P. Sterba, "G.I.'s Outburst Widens Censorship Issue," *New York Times*, 4 Jan 70.

[45] "Telling the Troops," *New York Times*, 6 Jan 70; "Tragedy of Errors," *Washington Star*, 8 Jan 70; "Telling It Like It Is-in Vietnam," *Washington Post*, 8 Jan 70.

Although the news media appeared in many instances to agree that the military was within its rights, the situation continued to deteriorate. On 5 January Lawrence told newsmen that the MACV Inspector General, Col. Robert M. Cook, had interrogated him for four hours without the benefit of legal counsel. When he had requested a lawyer, he said, Colonel Cook had replied that since he had yet to be charged with wrongdoing he had no right to representation. After that, he continued, four colonels had attempted to interrogate him in a five-by-seven-foot room furnished with Army blankets nailed to the walls and two tape recorders on a desk. When he refused to cooperate, the colonels yielded to his request and told him to return the next day when a lawyer would be present. Shortly thereafter, the Military Assistance Command announced, apparently without sufficient reflection on the consequences, that it intended to court-martial the soldier for an act of insubordination he had committed during December, before he had made his allegations. The broadcaster immediately charged that the decision was an act of reprisal.[46]

The command denied the allegation. General Abrams' deputy, General William B. Rosson, informed the Joint Chiefs of Staff that Lawrence's superior, a sergeant, had filed charges against the soldier on 30 December, before the 3 January incident. Rosson continued that, in the end, the inspector general had interrogated a total of nineteen members of the Armed Forces Vietnam Network. Out of that number, only Lawrence and three other enlisted men had insisted that the network was censoring the news. They cited its ban on words such as *withdrawals* and *Vietnamization* and its refusal to allow newscasters to play certain stories without first checking for accuracy and authenticity. The inspector general had concluded, Rosson said, that censorship was not the issue. Failures of supervision and communication were the problem, along with the fact that certain of the agency's personnel were obviously unsuited for the positions they occupied.[47]

Despite Rosson's assurances, officials in Washington were sensitive to allegations that Cook had somehow infringed upon Lawrence's rights as an American. Most understood, as did the press, that issues of diplomacy were at stake and that there was a difference between outright censorship and the judgments that both military and civilian editors had constantly to make; yet many also knew that even the lowest private had a right to legal counsel during an investigation. On the theory that Cook had acted improperly, in the absence of General Abrams, the Office of the Inspector General of the Army prevailed upon the Military Assistance Command to assign a brigadier general to investigate Cook's conduct during the affair.[48]

[46] Sterba, "G.I.'s Outburst Widens Censorship Issue"; [AP], "Newsman Suspended by Army," *Washington Post,* 5 Jan 70; [UPI dispatch], 8 Jan 70, Vn-Information Policy file, Air Force News Clipping and Analysis Service, Pentagon.

[47] Msg, General William B. Rosson, Dep COMUSMACV, MAC 380 to Admiral Thomas H. Moorer, Chief of Naval Operations (CNO), JCS, 9 Jan 70, Westmoreland Message file, Jan 70, CMH.

[48] "Telling It Like It Is-in Vietnam"; Interv, Lt Col Joseph Whitehorne, USA, with Col Robert M. Cook, USA (Ret.), 12 Nov 85, to be filed in the Oral History Collection, MHI.

Colonel Cook would later assert that he was within his rights to approach Lawrence as he had and that the soldier had misunderstood the function and purpose of an inspector general inquiry. By statute, the inspector general investigated only to improve the functioning of the military organization. He might direct the Army's Criminal Investigation Command to possible violations of law, but criminal investigators had to make their own cases. None of the evidence his office developed was open to agencies other than his own or admissible in court. As for the tape recorders, they were necessary in an office as busy and controversial as his own. Besides easing the burden of note-taking on his staff, the tapes they produced had proved more than once that his office had maintained the rights of an individual under interrogation. In the end, General Abrams returned, concluded that Cook had been correct, and dismissed the investigation, apparently without a nod to the inspector general in Washington.[49]

The controversy wound on nonetheless. In the press, reporters and commentators chose sides, with liberals condemning the military while conservatives attempted to be supportive. Editors at the *St. Louis Post-Dispatch*, for example, reprinted approvingly a comment by one military reporter that "You are on pretty shaky ground when you can't tell your troops the truth about the war for fear they wouldn't fight if you did." They also published an article by Michael Maxwell in which the former enlisted man purported to give an eyewitness account of news management at the Armed Forces Vietnam Network. A more conservative Keyes Beech of the *Chicago Daily News* took the opposite approach. Distinguishing between news judgment and news management, he attributed the problem to a generation gap between young newscasters and their older superior officers. Charges of censorship to the contrary, he continued, the Armed Forces Vietnam Network had reported in full developments in the noncommissioned officers scandal, the Green Beret trial, and the My Lai case. It also continued to broadcast comments by congressional critics of the war that castigated President Thieu and Vice President Ky. *Time* agreed with Beech but added that if neither side was entirely correct, clumsy counterattacks against the protesters by the military had served only to make matters worse. Herbert Mitgang meanwhile struck a thoughtful pose in a commentary for the *New York Times*. Observing that "it is an unpopular war, fought in a strange land, without battle lines, against an uncertain enemy and for an uncertain ally," he said that news of combat was easy to tell but that the war's political dimension was "hidden and complex and controversial." Because of that, problems of disclosure would continue to nettle the military for as long as the war lasted.[50]

---

[49] Ibid.

[50] "Minimum Disclosure, Maximum Delay," *St. Louis Post-Dispatch*, 10 Jan 70; Michael Maxwell, "GI Describes Censorship Row," *St. Louis Post-Dispatch*, 8 Jan 70; Keyes Beech, "Censorship? GI News in Vietnam Is Same as Heard in U.S.," *Chicago Daily News*, reprinted in *Omaha World-Herald*, 14 Jan 70; "Flack From Officers," *Time*, 19 Jan 70; Herbert Mitgang, "It's Not the War News; It's the Vietnam War," *New York Times*, 12 Jan 70.

Rather than comment at length, reporters for the television networks interviewed soldiers in the field for their opinions. Although most of the men avowed that they were "pretty much aware of almost everything that is going on," a few said they distrusted news broadcast by military stations because "it ain't true." Mike Horowitz of ABC News nevertheless concluded that the censorship issue seemed to reflect mainly internal conflicts within the Armed Forces Vietnam Network. The troops, he said, paid little attention to the news. They were more concerned about the quality of the rock and roll music they received.[51]

In an attempt to regain the initiative, the Military Assistance Command on 26 January released a report on its findings to the press. Dismissing the charges of censorship, investigators for the command denied that the court-martial of Specialist Lawrence for insubordination had anything to do with the soldier's comments on the air. They added that the sensitivities of the South Vietnamese government figured prominently in policies governing the broadcast of news to the troops but continued that stories unfavorable to the military were not prohibited. In fact, the number of unfavorable items appearing on official news programs was so large that it rendered the allegation of censorship "unfounded and unsupported." On the day the report appeared, Walter Cronkite noted wryly during his evening newscast that the Military Assistance Command, after investigating itself, had cleared itself of all charges.[52]

On 6 January the Chairman of the House Subcommittee on Government Operations and Information, Congressman John E. Moss of California, entered the fray by announcing publicly that he would hold hearings on the censorship problem during a forthcoming visit to South Vietnam. Shortly thereafter, he requested a list of people to interview from the Defense Department's office of manpower and reserve affairs.[53]

General Abrams was incensed. He informed Admiral McCain and General Wheeler that his command had already issued a final report on the matter that contained sworn statements. A further inquiry by Congressman Moss would serve little purpose and would "give this group of enlisted men the type of forum they have sought in an attempt to embarrass the military establishment." Abrams requested specific guidance on how to proceed because "Voluntary acquiescence to the request is not contemplated."[54]

Admiral McCain backed Abrams, as did Ambassador Bunker, who pointed out to the State Department that Moss' plans had political ramifi-

---

[51] Quote from Frank Blair, Today Show, NBC-TV, 7 Jan 70. ABC Evening News, 9 Jan 70. Both in *Radio-TV-Defense Dialog*.

[52] The report is quoted in [AP], "Military Report Denies Newscast Censorship," *Washington Star*, 26 Jan 70. Walter Cronkite, CBS Evening News, 20 Jan 70, *Radio-TV-Defense Dialog*.

[53] Frank Blair, "Congress To View Censorship Charges," Today Show, NBC-TV, 6 Jan 70, *Radio-TV-Defense Dialog*.

[54] Msg, Abrams MAC 1262 to McCain, Wheeler, 27 Jan 70, Abrams Papers, CMH.

cations. A full, public congressional hearing outside of the United States, he said, appeared to have little precedent. At the very least, Moss could hardly expect to hold a meeting of that sort without appropriate coordination with the government of South Vietnam.[55]

In the end, faced with the combined opposition of both the State and Defense Departments, Moss backed away from his plan. "Although he contemplates closed hearings and will, no doubt, make press releases, . . ." Wheeler told Abrams, "this is the best compromise that could be reached and it should at least serve to mute the impact which open hearings would obviously have had upon your command." Wheeler added that full cooperation with Moss

Bunker and Abrams confer.

appeared in Abrams' best interests: "Informal discussions indicate that Congressman Moss supports the manner in which you have handled the press problem."[56]

As the threat from Moss receded, the Military Assistance Command began a process of quiet change. In the past, the command's Office of Information had issued guidance but had lacked overall control of day-to-day operations at the Armed Forces Vietnam Network. Recognizing in the light of the Specialist Lawrence affair that the arrangement had failed to allow for sufficiently close supervision, the command turned the network into a staff division under the Office of Information. From then on, professional public affairs officers assumed direct supervisory responsibility for all of the agency's operations. In that way, they could ensure that all broadcasters understood the policies in force and could transfer to other less sensitive assignments those who refused to cooperate. The changes worked. Once they went into effect, the controversies afflicting the Armed Forces Vietnam Network gradually died down.[57]

Stars and Stripes proved more difficult to handle. A number of the reporters who worked for the newspaper were professionals with con-

---

[55] Msg, McCain to Wheeler, 4 Feb 70, relaying Msg, Bunker to State, Westmoreland Message file, CMH.

[56] Msg, Wheeler JCS 1853 to Abrams, 6 Feb 70, sub: Request of Congressman Moss for Investigation of AFVN Censorship Allegations, Westmoreland Message file, CMH.

[57] White Paper, Armed Forces Vietnam Network (AFVN) Policies and Procedures [1970].

213

tacts in the civilian press. Each time the Military Assistance Command attempted to exert an influence, they leaked the move to the Saigon correspondents, who inevitably raised questions. During February, for example, suggestions from the command that the newspaper replace much of its reporting of hard combat with news of pacification, Vietnamization, and civic action programs found their way into the press. In the same way, during April, when the newspaper's editor in chief, Col. William V. Koch, reassigned the head of his Saigon bureau, Patrick Luminello, to Tokyo, Luminello charged in the press that the move was retaliation for comments attributed to him in a yet-to-be-published article by former *Stars and Stripes* reporter Robert Hodierne. Although Koch responded that the transfer was routine because Luminello's tour of duty in Saigon had only a month to run, hardly anyone could have escaped the impression that the Army was once more attempting censorship.[58]

The controversy over *Stars and Stripes* reached a climax when Hodierne's article appeared in the *New York Times Magazine* on 12 April. A wide-ranging, opinionated, yet sometimes perceptive recapitulation of everything that had occurred to date at the Armed Forces Vietnam Network and *Stars and Stripes*, the article affirmed that neither agency had experienced formal censorship in the past, only injudicious, overly cautious, uninformed editing by officers who lacked practical experience in the news media. Hodierne warned nevertheless that *Stars and Stripes*, in particular, might shortly become much more like the house organ many high-ranking officers apparently envisioned it to be. Colonel Koch, he said, had affirmed that he was revising the paper's editorial policies. "It still hasn't become apparent in print but the hints are everywhere. His first act was to put the Saigon reporters back in uniform. . . . The civilian clothes, it was thought, helped them mingle better with civilian reporters and made it easier for them to gather information from sources who often have little respect for enlisted men."[59]

Hodierne's charges made some stir in the press but, lacking further incidents of dissent and preoccupied with breaking news elsewhere, the civilian news media rapidly turned elsewhere. Shortly thereafter, the Assistant Secretary of Defense for Manpower and Reserve Affairs, Roger Kelly, returned to Washington from a visit to Saigon. During an interview with *Stars and Stripes* reporters, he observed that

The quiet good deeds of military people, I am afraid, are going unnoticed and unheralded. With all the anti-military talk to which the military man is exposed, I think he deserves also an exposure to his good deeds. And the good deeds of the military people in Vietnam today are legion.

---

[58] [UPI], "G.I. Publications Asked Not To Stress Fighting," *New York Times*, 13 Feb 70; [AP], "Newsman Fired From Saigon Job; Censorship Cited," *Philadelphia Inquirer*, 5 Apr 70; [Reuters], "Colonel Defends Recall of Editor," *New York Times*, 6 Apr 70.

[59] Hodierne, "How G.I.'s in Vietnam Don't Learn About the War."

Not only are they conspicuous in their valor and in their courage in combat assignments, but the humanitarian reactions of our military people in Vietnam, to the hamlets and villages and their pacification programs, are just a magnificent story of human heroism that needs to be told. And it needs to be told to the military people so they can appreciate the great job they are doing over there. In this respect, I think we have failed.[60]

The Military Assistance Command's official history noted later that following the interview, there was "a perceptible change" in the content of *Stars and Stripes*. Problems received less prominent play and the newspaper devoted more space to reporting the humanitarian deeds of military personnel.[61]

If the military, for the sake of preserving the morale of the troops, thus succeeded in asserting indirect control over *Stars and Stripes*, the effect still had little meaning over the long term. Pentagon spokesmen might argue that discipline remained high and that dissent rarely existed in frontline units, but, as every reporter perceived, something was still wrong and the men in the field knew. If soldiers sporting peace medals and love beads seemed to fight when ordered, the U.S. command's growing problems with morale demonstrated that a malaise of the spirit was spreading among the Americans who served in South Vietnam. As a career naval officer told one *Newsweek* reporter: "I never had to think about morale in the past, it just took care of itself. Now I spend half my time worrying about it."[62]

The Saigon correspondents clearly sympathized with the military services' attempts to solve their problems, but they were aware that an army without discipline lacked the means of survival and remained constantly on the alert for the worst. The military, in turn, resented the attention. As had Campbell with his allusions to the "Hanoi Herald," they put loyalty to the institution they served first and refused to believe that the situation was as bad as some news reports made it seem. The press had already demonstrated, however, that the best reporters, by virtue of their many contacts, sometimes had a better grasp of the war's unmanageable human element than the policy makers supposedly in control.

[60] "Defense Department's Kelly Reviews Far East 'Rap Session,'" *Stars and Stripes*, 3 Aug 70, quoted by MACV History, 1970, vol. 2, pp. XI-13f.
[61] MACV History, 1970, vol. 2, p. XI-14.
[62] "A New GI: For Pot and Peace," *Newsweek*, 2 Feb 70.

215

10

My Lai and Other Atrocities

The Military Assistance Command's difficulties with morale may have threatened President Nixon's effort to rally support for his policies, but they at first had little practical effect. The full extent of the drug problem had yet to become apparent, and racial tensions in South Vietnam were both difficult to define and, in any event, mild in comparison with the rioting and burning that continued to occur sporadically in the United States. Meanwhile, the drop in American casualties that had accompanied General Abrams' deemphasis of large-unit combat operations more than compensated for the bad publicity that accompanied occurrences of indiscipline and dissent that broke out among the troops in South Vietnam.

The Incidents of 3 November

The war nevertheless continued to confound the most astute publicists. On 3 November 1969, for example, shortly before the president issued his appeal to the silent majority, both CBS and NBC ran film reports that purported to show American infantrymen standing idly by while South Vietnamese troops tortured and mutilated enemy prisoners of war. In the same way, two weeks later, on the morning before Vice President Agnew delivered his attack upon television network news, freelance correspondent Seymour Hersh published the first detailed account of charges that American soldiers had massacred hundreds of South Vietnamese civilians at a hamlet near Da Nang named My Lai. In each of those cases, public affairs officers took whatever steps they could to reverse the damage to the public image of the military, but their efforts proved, at best, only marginally successful. With the consensus in the United States in support of the war declining, the unthinkable had become conceivable. The image Americans had always held of the good American soldier had begun to slip into doubt.

On the surface, the two television reports seemed straightforward. NBC "Today Show" anchorman Frank Blair introduced the first by observing that he had "a sidelight this morning on the ugliness of war." Correspondent Robert Hager in Saigon then narrated a film that showed an American major and lieutenant colonel making no move to stop the beating of a Viet Cong prisoner by South Vietnamese interrogators. Hager added a film of a MACV briefer in Saigon who commented, in ignorance of the reporter's story, that the Geneva Convention governing the treatment of prisoners of war prohibited acts of violence or intimidation. The reporter remarked, "It is well known that [the] policy is frequently overlooked under combat conditions."[1]

The second story, narrated by Don Webster, was equally appalling. After showing a South Vietnamese soldier stabbing a North Vietnamese captive while the man lay prone and seemingly defenseless on the ground, Webster claimed that the atrocity had occurred in the presence of U.S. military personnel who witnessed it without making any move to intervene or object.[2]

The two reports were particularly unfortunate from the standpoint of the president and his advisers. For months, they had worked, as Henry Kissinger put it, "to keep the administration on the propaganda offensive" where American prisoners of war in North Vietnam were concerned. Earlier in the year, departing from a policy of silence on the subject designed to protect the prisoners by drawing as little attention to them as possible, the Department of Defense had thus declassified much of what the U.S. government knew about its captured and missing personnel. To dramatize the issue, Defense and State Department spokesmen had then held joint press conferences and briefings in cities throughout the United States with the families of the captives. Finally, on 2 September, a repatriated prisoner had briefed the press for the first time on North Vietnamese torture of captive Americans. By October the initiative seemed to be having some effect. The enemy became defensive when the issue arose during negotiating sessions in Paris, and indications began to appear that he might become more forthcoming on the subject in the future. The appearance of evidence shortly thereafter that the South Vietnamese had abused enemy prisoners in the presence of American advisers threw everything into doubt by reducing the moral standing of the United States before the world and by giving the enemy the excuse he needed to continue to refuse humane treatment to American prisoners of war.[3]

---

[1] Today Show, NBC-TV, 3 Nov 69, *Radio-TV-Defense Dialog.*

[2] Msg, COMUSMACV 67972 to CINCPAC, 10 Dec 69, sub: CBS Allegation of Atrocity Against PW in SVN, and Msg, State 186897 to Saigon, 5 Nov 69, sub: TV Reports of Mistreatment of Prisoners in SVN, both in DDI 33b POW's/Defections file.

[3] Memo, Henry Kissinger for the President, 2 Oct 69, sub: POW Policy in Vietnam, box 3, President's Handwriting, 1–15 Oct 69, and Memo, Alexander Butterfield for the President, 15 Dec 69, sub: POW Campaign Activities, box 4, President's Handwriting, 1–15 Dec 69, both in President's Office files, Nixon Papers. Msg, State 186897 to Saigon, 5 Nov 69.

Citing the concern rising in Washington, the State Department instructed the U.S. mission in Saigon to make a full investigation of the NBC and CBS allegations. The Military Assistance Command complied but immediately encountered difficulties. Neither report gave any worthwhile clue to the American units involved or to where and when the incidents had occurred. The command contacted Hager and Webster for assistance, but both newsmen declined to cooperate on grounds that their sources required protection. Webster, in particular, was adamant. His cameraman had been a South Vietnamese, he said, and might suffer reprisals if the network revealed his name. In the absence of what they felt was adequate evidence, the command's investigators asked the Defense Department to contact Webster's and Hager's employers in New York to request copies of the filmed reports and all footage deleted during editing. "Regarding the CBS film there is general consensus," they said, "that it is a cut and paste job involving different locales and personnel and including an Australian helicopter." Although Webster contended that the film showed one continuous action, they continued, he was not present during the filming. As for the NBC report, "the scene in which alleged advisers are shown seems to be the result of a splicing job rather than part of the central action."[4]

The Defense Department made formal requests to CBS and NBC for the materials. NBC released its film. CBS refused. "Your request raises difficult issues for us," the president of CBS News, Richard S. Salant, responded. "I am sure that you understand that we must jealously guard our roles as journalists, and not perform functions which might inhibit our journalistic responsibilities. . . . I am sure that you know our rule about releasing outtakes . . . [which], like a reporter's notebook, are sacrosanct." Salant concluded that "the Defense Department, with its widespread facilities and means of communications in Vietnam does not have to rely on CBS News in order to carry out its investigation of a field incident involving the Republic of Vietnam Armed Forces at which U.S. personnel were present."[5]

With NBC's films in hand, the Military Assistance Command made rapid progress on its investigation of the incident Hager had reported. On 10 December it revealed that the 25th Infantry Division had been the American unit involved and that the event had occurred as reported on 31 October near the division's headquarters at Cu Chi, some thirty kilo-

---

[4]Quote from Msg, Saigon 22749 to State, 13 Nov 69, sub: TV Reports of Mistreatment of Prisoners in SVN, DDI 33b POW's/Defections file. Also see Msg, Saigon 22371 to State, 7 Nov 69, sub: TV Reports of Mistreatment of Prisoners in SVN; Msg, COMUSMACV 62900 to OASD PA, 11 Nov 69, sub: TV Reports of Mistreatment of PW in SVN; Msg, COMUS-MACV 63204 to OASD PA, 13 Nov 69, sub: TV Reports of Mistreatment of PW in SVN, all in DDI 33b POW's/Defections file.

[5]Quote from Ltr, Richard S. Salant to Norman T. Hatch, Chief, Audio-Visual Division, Directorate of Defense Information, 15 Dec 69. Also see Msg, DA 932798 to CINCPAC, 30 Nov 69, sub: Allegations of Mistreatment of PW and Atrocities in SVN. Both in DDI 33b POW's/Defections file.

meters northwest of Saigon. The U.S. officers present at the scene who had failed to make any protest were disciplined.[6]

In the case of the CBS allegations, nothing further happened for the time being. When Canadian television rebroadcast Webster's report during December, the State Department instructed its consulate in Halifax, Nova Scotia, to reply to queries from the press by stating, "We have seen the television broadcast referred to and are deeply concerned about it. The Department of State and the Department of Defense are attempting to establish the facts. . . . Unfortunately, the television company which produced this film has declined to identify the unit or individuals involved or to provide the date, location, or other identifying information. As a result, U.S. authorities in Vietnam have been limited in their ability to carry forward their investigation."[7] Lacking any evidence to the contrary, the Military Assistance Command reaffirmed its earlier conclusion that the report had been a montage. "Since CBS has refused to provide the facts to establish when and where this incident occurred," the command reported to the Department of the Army, "and local investigation has not repeat not uncovered any additional leads, further action on this investigation is being suspended until more facts are received or developed."[8]

Atrocity at My Lai

The controversy over the two television stories was just beginning when Hersh published his article on the massacre at My Lai.[9] Alerted by a telephone caller who alleged that the Army was "court-martialing some lieutenant in secrecy at Fort Benning" for killing a large number of civilians, Hersh had confirmed the essential facts of the case through sources on Capitol Hill. Traveling to Fort Benning, he had then interviewed the officer accused of the slayings, 1st Lt. William Calley, and had also spoken with the officer's civilian lawyer, George Latimer.[10]

Hersh's report caused an international sensation, but that came as little surprise to the Army. The service had first learned of the incident at My

[6] Msg, COMUSMACV 67978 to CINCPAC, 10 Dec 69, sub: NBC Allegation of Mistreatment of PW and Atrocities in SVN, DDI 33b POW's/Defections file.

[7] Msg, State 203462 to Amconsul Halifax, info Saigon, 6 Dec 69, sub: TV Film of Mistreatment of Prisoners in SVN, DDI 33b POW's/Defections file.

[8] Msg, COMUSMACV 1168 to DA, 8 Jan 70, sub: CBS Allegation of Mistreatment of PW and Atrocities in SVN, DDI 33b POW's/Defections file.

[9] The news media and the Army used a number of names for the hamlet that has come to be called My Lai. Official maps referred to it as My Lai 4 and ranked it as a subhamlet in Tu Chuong hamlet which was a part of the village of Song My. Soldiers and the press often called it Pinkville because some maps colored the area pink to denote its status as enemy-controlled territory. Although spellings varied, the press and television generally used the names My Lai or Song My.

[10] Seymour M. Hersh, "How I Broke the Mylai 4 Story," *Saturday Review*, 11 Jul 70, p. 46.

220

Lai eight months before, during April 1969, when a veteran who had heard of the massacre during his tour of duty in South Vietnam, Ronald Ridenauer, had written letters to General Westmoreland and a number of congressmen and officials describing his suspicions and requesting an investigation. Moving quietly in the months that followed in order to protect the rights of the accused, the Office of the Army Inspector General had confirmed that on 16 March 1968 members of Company C, 1st Battalion, 20th Infantry, 11th Infantry Brigade, of the American Division stationed near Da Nang, while participating as a part of a unit known as Task Force BARKER, had murdered as many as 350 unoffending South Vietnamese

Lieutenant Calley

civilians. What especially disturbed Army investigators was the possibility that a cover-up by the American Division's commanders had occurred. "The Military Assistance Command should have learned of what happened almost immediately," General Westmoreland asserted, "but . . . it was not reported above the division [level]—not even the suspicion."[11]

When Ridenauer's letter arrived and the Army confirmed that there were grounds for suspicion, discussions began immediately at the Defense Department on how best to handle the matter. Should the military drop it, cover it up, or allow justice to proceed and swallow the public affairs problems that would inevitably arise? All concerned rejected the idea of a cover-up. Since the facts were bound to become public, any attempt to hide what had happened would become known sooner or later. When it did, hostile commentators were certain to assert that the U.S. government had condoned an atrocity. That, in turn, would lower the prestige of the nation in the eyes of the world and hand the enemies of the United States a propaganda triumph they could wield to advantage for years. In addition, it would set a precedent that would hinder the enforcement of the laws of war in future conflicts.[12]

---

[11] Westmoreland's comment is in Record of Chief of Staff Telecon with Mr. Frank Pace, 1400, 26 Nov 69, sub: My Lai, FONECON file, Westmoreland Papers, CMH. This analysis of My Lai will be based in part on Research Report, Ann David, Press Coverage of the My Lai Massacre [U.S. Army Center of Military History, 1984], CMH files.

[12] Interv, author with Jerry Friedheim, Deputy Assistant Secretary of Defense, 1969–1973, 3 Oct 86, CMH files.

Ronald Ridenauer

Although full prosecution of all offenders and full disclosure of the details seemed the only recourse, the Defense Department was still determined to avoid self-inflicted wounds. To that end, Assistant Secretary of Defense for Public Affairs Henkin and his advisers waited to make any announcement until September, when the Army was prepared to charge the first of the defendants, Lieutenant Calley. They then released the news at Fort Benning, where the trial was to take place, rather than in Washington, where the major news media congregated. There would be no grounds for any accusation that the department had indulged in a cover-up, Henkin observed later, but there seemed some hope that the impact of the story would be less if it came out of Benning.[13]

The maneuver succeeded almost too well. On 5 September a public affairs officer at Fort Benning responded to a query from David Leonard of Georgia's *Columbus Enquirer* by releasing Calley's name and by stating that the officer had been charged with offenses against an unspecified number of South Vietnamese civilians. Officials at the Defense Department braced for more questions, but none came. The Associated Press picked up the local story, but the rest of the news media paid scant attention. Although the AP story appeared the next day on page 2 of the *Washington Star* and page 11 of the *Atlanta Journal*, the *Washington Post* waited until 7 September to publish it, on page A14, and the *New York Times* carried a shortened version on the eighth, on page 38. ABC was the only television network to report the story. The Huntley-Brinkley newscast carried a brief notice on 10 September, but no other stories on the subject appeared until 13 November, when the article by Hersh detailing the full extent of the charges against Calley finally broke in newspapers across the United States.[14]

---

[13] Interv, author with Daniel Z. Henkin, ASD PA, 1969–1973, 10 Oct 86, CMH files.

[14] The original news release is in Msg, Sidle WDC 20442 to Woolnough, CG, CONARC, et al., 22 Nov 69, sub: Public Affairs Guidance-My Lai Case, Abrams Papers, CMH. Also see Talking Paper, OCINFO, U.S. Army, Early Press Coverage-My Lai, 5 Dec 69, attachment to Chronology of Correspondence Addressed to SEC DEF Concerning My Lai (29 Mar–4 Aug), 330–76–067, box 951, Viet 383 (May) 1970, Laird Papers, WNRC; Seymour M. Hersh, "Officer Charged With Murdering 109 in Viet," *Chicago Sun Times*, 13 Nov 69.

The two-month delay between the announcement at Fort Benning and the moment when the press finally accepted the story is difficult to explain. That the Defense Department had released few details to confirm the suspicions of reporters and editors certainly figured in, but enough information was on the record to at least prompt questions. Four months prior to the Army's first announcement, concerned that official agencies might fail to conduct a thorough investigation, Ridenauer had offered his story through a literary agent to major newspapers and magazines, including *Life, Look, Newsweek, Harper's,* and *Ramparts.* Only *Ramparts* had reacted positively, and Ridenauer had rejected that offer on grounds that the appearance of the story in so radical a journal might discredit the information he had to convey. His proposal to write the story himself for a fee may have weighed against him in the eyes of editors whose sources usually performed gratis. Yet more than enough information was present to spark queries from curious reporters to Army spokesmen. None ever occurred.

A much more established reporter, Hersh also had difficulties. He contacted *Life* and *Look* to no avail before the less well-known antiwar Dispatch News Service agreed to carry his material. He and other reporters later hypothesized that self-censorship on the part of the press was to blame. There was little market, so the theory went, for atrocity stories about American troops.[15] More appropriate may be the comment of sociologist Leon V. Sigal, who observed in his 1973 book on the organization and politics of newsmaking that American editors preferred life in a crowd and disliked making the sort of lone, possibly erroneous stands that could open their publications to criticism.[16]

The American news media were also far more inclined than foreigners to give Americans the benefit of a doubt. Prior to Harrison E. Salisbury's revelation during 1966 and 1967 that the U.S. Air Force had caused major damage to civilian areas in North Vietnam, for example, newspapers in the United States had largely ignored stories on the subject, even though *Le Monde* and other major European periodicals had made a point of them.[17] In the same way, although reporters had long kept a watch for crimes against civilians and Morley Safer of CBS News, for one, had turned the August 1965 burning of Cam Ne by U.S. marines into a cause celebre, most discounted as enemy propaganda allegations that American units had committed mass atrocities in South Vietnam. When Radio Hanoi had thus announced on 17 April 1968 that a brigade of the U.S. 82d Airborne Division had the month before slaughtered 501 women, children, and old people at My Lai, the Saigon correspondents

[15] Seymour M. Hersh, "The Story Everyone Ignored," *Columbia Journalism Review* (Winter 1969/1970): 55–58; Peter Osnos, "My Lai Story Almost Went Unnoticed," *Washington Post,* 1 Dec 69; Richard Strout, "Grim Story May Be Year's Biggest," *Christian Science Monitor,* 29 Nov 69.

[16] Sigal, *Reporters and Officials,* pp. 40–41.

[17] Hammond, *Public Affairs: The Military and the Media, 1962–1968,* pp. 274–79.

223

had accepted out of hand MACV's assertion that the 82d had been nowhere near the area on the date in question and had failed completely to follow up on the allegation.[18] That it should have taken eight weeks for reporters and editors to overcome enough of their inhibitions to take an interest in Calley's trial is thus hardly as unthinkable as it might at first have seemed.

Whatever the reasons for the delay, a flood of sometimes lurid news stories followed Hersh's disclosures. On 14 November the Army announced that a second soldier, S. Sgt. David Mitchell, was being charged with multiple counts of assault with intent to commit murder.[19] Official spokesmen again refused to supply the sort of heavy detail reporters sought, but Ridenauer met with newsmen, and other eyewitnesses also came forward. On 20 November Hersh published a story based on interviews with former members of Calley's platoon stating that the men of Company C had intentionally killed a large number of civilians and that the company's officers had perhaps even ordered the killings. The *Washington Post* incorporated Hersh's interviews into a story of its own alleging that Company C's commander, Capt. Ernest Medina, had told a soldier not to write his congressman about what had happened. The *Post* also reported that the commander of the 11th Infantry Brigade, Col. Oran Henderson, had inquired briefly about indiscriminate killing at My Lai but that nothing had come of the investigation. On 24 November the CBS Evening News ran an interview with a former member of Calley's platoon, Paul Meadlo, who admitted remorsefully that he had personally killed ten or fifteen villagers. CBS was later criticized by the conservative press because it had paid the Dispatch News Service to arrange the interview.[20]

More telling than the eyewitness accounts of the massacre were photographs of the incident that a combat correspondent, Ronald Haeberle, had taken during the assault on My Lai. Published on 20 November by the *Cleveland Plain Dealer*, they showed the fallen bodies of women, children, and old men scattered along the trails surrounding the hamlet. Although required to submit any photographs he had taken in the line of duty to his superiors, Haeberle had used his own camera at My Lai and had kept silent. Taking his pictures with him when he mustered out of the Army, he had sold them to the *Plain Dealer*, *Life*, and a number of European publications when Hersh's story appeared.[21]

---

[18] MACOI Memo for the Press, 4 May 68, sub: Enemy Statements on the War in Vietnam, CMH files.

[19] Richard Homan, "2nd GI Charged by Army," *Virginian Pilot*, 15 Nov 69.

[20] Seymour M. Hersh, *My Lai 4* (New York: Random House, 1970), pp. 136-37; Peter Braestrup and Stephen Klaidman, "Three Vietnam Veterans Tell of Hamlet Slayings," *Washington Post*, 20 Nov 69; [Reuters], "Ex GI Tells of Partaking in Massacre," *Baltimore Sun*, 25 Nov 69; Jim Lucas, "CBS Admits Paying for Meadlo Interview," *Manchester Union Leader*, 1 Dec 69.

[21] "Former G.I. Took Pictures of Dead," *New York Times*, 22 Nov 69. *Life* published the pictures on 5 December. See "The Massacre at My Lai," *Life*, 5 Dec 69, pp. 36–45.

The dead at My Lai

The Effort To Contain the Damage

As the furor over the atrocity increased, the South Vietnamese Ministry of Information added an air of unreality to the situation by avowing in a 22 November statement that allegations of a massacre in Quang Ngai Province were "completely untrue."[22] Asked to explain the discrepancies between the South Vietnamese and American positions on the incident, an anonymous South Vietnamese official replied, "I have no idea."[23] Although the declaration led to some negative comment in the United States, it also apparently prompted Chet Huntley to assert during his 28 November newscast that My Lai was hardly the only massacre in South Vietnam and that the worst had been conducted by the Communists in Hue during the Tet offensive of 1968. South Vietnamese officials had never understood why that atrocity had failed to inflame American public opinion, he said, and the reaction to My Lai had them even more perplexed.[24]

Ambassador Bunker wasted little time before pointing out to President Thieu that his government's apparent disregard for the atrocity strengthened the arguments of critics in the United States who opposed

[22] "Massacre Story False, Saigon Says," *Washington Post*, 23 Nov 69. The full text of the South Vietnamese communique is in Msg, Saigon 23612 to State, 25 Nov 69, sub: Quang Ngai Incident, Pol 27 Viet S file, FAIM/IR.
[23] [AP], "Allies Disagree on Toll in Hamlet," *Baltimore Sun*, 23 Nov 69.
[24] Chet Huntley, Huntley-Brinkley Report, 28 Nov 69, *Radio-TV-Defense Dialog*.

the war. The president remained unimpressed. My Lai was hardly a peaceful stretch of countryside, he told Bunker. It was a fortified Viet Cong area in which men, women, and children engaged in hostile actions against South Vietnamese and American troops. That some of those people might be killed during the course of a military operation seemed, to his mind, perfectly understandable.[25]

Thieu reexamined his position when one of his leading political opponents, a former South Vietnamese commander of the I Corps Tactical Zone serving in the senate, General Tran Van Don, announced plans to go to Quang Ngai Province himself to investigate. Shortly thereafter, Thieu's representatives informed Bunker that the government had, in fact, never closed its books on the case and that the province chief in Quang Ngai was continuing to report any information on the subject that came to hand. Later, Thieu himself emphasized his harmony with the American position on the incident by stressing in a public statement his belief that the American system of justice would prevail.

While Bunker and the State Department dealt with Thieu, the Defense Department moved to contain whatever damage had occurred. After the first Hersh article, official spokesmen had steered clear of acknowledging the number of the dead or details of the legal specifications under consideration to preserve the rights of the accused and to keep from prejudicing through excessive pretrial publicity any case Army prosecutors might present. "These investigations, and the procedures under the Uniform Code of Military Justice which have been initiated, are under the cognizance of the Department of the Army," MACV's information officers told the Saigon correspondents. "Since these actions may result in criminal proceedings . . . information . . . can be released only by the Department of the Army. These procedures are designed to ensure that justice is done." Meanwhile, in Saigon, the Military Assistance Command released a captured enemy report that admitted for the first time that Communist officials were responsible for the Hue massacres.[26]

Official spokesmen in Saigon and Washington held to that line through 14 November, when the Army announced that Mitchell had been charged in connection with the incident. After that they relented. The next day, the Chief of U.S. Army Information, Brig. Gen. Winant Sidle, authorized the release of general details on the status of the various investigations in progress and disclosed that Mitchell had been a squad leader in

---

[25] Unless otherwise indicated, this section is based on Msg, Saigon 23834 to State, 29 Nov 69, sub: Tran Van Don To Investigate Quang Ngai Incident. Msgs, State 3577 to Saigon, 3 Dec 69, sub: Quang Ngai Massacre; Saigon 24034 to State, 3 Dec 69, sub: Quang Ngai Massacre; Saigon 24372 to State, 9 Dec 69, sub: Quang Ngai Massacre; Saigon 24914 to State, Bunker for the President, 19 Dec 69, sub: Ambassador Bunker's 83rd Message to the President. All in General Abrams' Personal file 4, CMH.

[26] Msg, Sidle WDC 19932 to Woolnough et al., 15 Nov 69, sub: Public Affairs Guidance–My Lai Case, Abrams Papers, CMH. The quote is from Memo for Correspondents 323–69, 19 Nov 69, 334–71A374, box 1, 206.02 MACOI, WNRC. The Communist report is mentioned in Joseph Fried, "Hue Massacre Pinned on Reds," *New York Daily News*, 24 Nov 69.

Calley's platoon. At the behest of the Army's criminal investigators, who continued to search out witnesses and new allegations, he nevertheless specified that all local queries dealing with matters beyond that general guidance should be coordinated with his office without informing the inquirer that Washington agencies would be involved.[27]

On 18 November General Sidle cleared for release a statement confirming the names of some of the members of the platoon and revealing that the Army's provost marshal had begun to investigate the matter in early August 1969. Prior to that, the communique affirmed, in response to Viet Cong allegations, the 11th Infantry Brigade had investigated the matter but had failed to turn up enough information to warrant further inquiry. Three days later, the General Counsel of the Army, Robert E. Jordan, held the first high-level news conference on My Lai. At that time he revealed that the Army's Criminal Investigation Division was involved and that nine current and fifteen former members of the Army were under investigation. The next day, 22 November, the Office of the Assistant Secretary of Defense for Public Affairs released an outline of the charges against Calley to both the press and Congress. It confirmed that Ridenauer had played a role in starting the investigation, that earlier investigations had turned up little, and that Calley had been charged with the murder of approximately a hundred South Vietnamese civilians. On 26 November, avoiding any direct comment that might be prejudicial to the upcoming trials of Calley and Mitchell, the secretary of the Army reported in full to the Senate Armed Services Committee on what the Army had learned to date about the events at My Lai. The committee released the text of his remarks to the press.[28]

The information came too late to have much effect on what the news media had to say. Although editorial writers had been reluctant at first to comment on My Lai, by 20 November almost every newspaper in the United States had taken a position. The majority expressed horror at the massacre but refused to put the blame entirely on Calley and the men of Company C. Instead they blamed the brutalizing effects of war and cited the massacre as an important reason for ending the conflict in South Vietnam as soon as possible. A number compared My Lai to mass killings of the past that had occurred at Dresden, Hiroshima, and Lidice during World War II. Most pointed out that there were significant differences between murder as a national policy and the isolated act of a few soldiers, but others noted what they considered disturbing similarities.[29]

---

[27] Msg, Sidle WDC 19932 to Woolnough et al., 15 Nov 69, sub: Public Affairs Guidance-My Lai Case.

[28] David, Press Coverage of the My Lai Massacre, p. 11. Also see Peter Braestrup, "Vietnam Probe Widens," *Washington Post*, 22 Nov 69; Msg, Sidle WDC 20080 to Woolnough, 18 Nov 69, sub: Public Affairs Guidance-My Lai Case, Abrams Papers, CMH; Msg, Sidle WDC 20442 to Woolnough et al., 22 Nov 69, sub: Public Affairs Guidance-My Lai Case; "Official U.S. Report on My Lai Investigation," *U.S. News & World Report*, 8 Dec 69, p. 78.

[29] For a summary of press coverage at the time, see David, Press Coverage of the My Lai Massacre, p. 10.

As comment continued, conservative commentators such as Robert Heinl made much of the fact that Haeberle had sold his pictures to the *Plain Dealer* for $40,000. Others reported that 85 percent of the readers who had called the newspaper afterwards had done so to protest its decision to run such explicit photographs. The drift was nevertheless still unfavorable to the military. The *Chicago Sun Times* likened the Army's handling of the event to the controversies that had surrounded the Green Beret Affair and the denials that had come from official circles during the Salisbury affair almost three years earlier. The *New York Times* termed the incident "an American tragedy" and urged the Army to avoid "foot dragging" and cover-ups in making its investigation. The *New York Daily News* contended that there would be no end to atrocities in Vietnam because a dubious small war had entrapped young Americans in a large moral disaster. Editorial writers across the country also asked again and again why it had taken almost two years for the facts in the case to become known.[30]

The same question was much on the minds of officials within the Army and the Defense Department. Early on, when they had decided to make a full disclosure of what had happened at My Lai, they had realized that they would also have to investigate the possibility of a cover-up. On 24 November Secretary of the Army Stanley Resor and General Westmoreland announced their decision to appoint Lt. Gen. William R. Peers to explore the nature and scope of the original Army investigation into the matter and the adequacy of subsequent reviews.[31]

The credibility of official spokesmen had nevertheless fallen so low by that time that the statement only generated more negatives. There was, for example, clear concern in Congress about the prospect of the Army investigating itself. Shortly after the naming of the "Peers commission," the chairmen of both the House and Senate Armed Services Committees announced that they would hold separate investigations on their own. Meanwhile, the *New York Times* prefaced a commentary by James Reston with the headline, "Who Will Investigate the Investigators?" Cases involving the misdeeds of government officials "have a way of disappearing almost as mysteriously as they appear," Reston then observed. "Almost always there is an investigation. Sometimes it follows through to a satisfactory conclusion, but usually the facts are muffled in the bureaucracy, or hastily dropped, as in the Green Beret murder case, in 'the interest of national security.'" Echoing a comment by Senator Edmund Muskie, *Long Island Newsday* suggested that the inquiry was too impor-

---

[30] Robert J. Heinl, "Witness for the Prosecution Admits He Exploited 'Massacre' at Mi Lai," *Philadelphia Bulletin*, 22 Nov 70. The 85 percent figure is from an undated, unattributed clipping in the My Lai file, Air Force News Clipping and Analysis Service. "No Pinkville Cover Up," *Chicago Sun-Times*, 21 Nov 69; "An American Nightmare," *New York Times*, 22 Nov 69; "The Ultimate Tragedy," *New York Daily News*, 21 Nov 69; "The Dishonorable Song My Episode," *San Francisco Chronicle*, 27 Nov 69.

[31] Interv, author with Friedheim, 3 Oct 86; Msg, Sidle WDC 20471 to Abrams, 24 Nov 69, sub: My Lai Investigation, Abrams Papers, CMH.

(Left to right) *General Peers, Secretary Resor, and General Westmoreland*

tant to be left to the Army and that the president should appoint a blue ribbon panel to study the event in all of its ramifications.[32]

If the news media had concluded that the My Lai massacre was fact, the American public was far less assured. At first, according to the *Wall Street Journal*, people seemed to judge the incident in terms of their own commitment to the war. "To a man," the paper reported, those who sought an immediate end to the conflict affirmed that they were appalled by what had happened. "But a surprising number of persons who support the war disagree, saying, in effect, that's the way war is. An even greater number insist they simply don't believe any mass killings occurred." On 21 December the *Minneapolis Tribune* confirmed the *Journal*'s observation by reporting that 48 percent of the respondents in a statewide Minnesota poll refused to believe that an atrocity had happened. Of the rest, 38 percent accepted press reports of the incident, 2 percent considered them partly true, and 11 percent were undecided. When asked who was to blame if the reports were true—soldiers and officers at the scene, Army leaders, or the brutalizing effects of war—55 percent named the war. By January, according to Harris polls, most Americans had apparently accepted the fact of a massacre, but many still seemed more disturbed by the news media's coverage of the event

[32] Robert Smith, "Army Will Review Study of '68 on Alleged Killings," *New York Times*, 25 Nov 69; Jerome S. Cahill, "Panel Calls for All Data in Army File," *Philadelphia Inquirer*, 26 Nov 69; James Reston, "Who Will Investigate the Investigators?," *New York Times*, 30 Nov 69; "Painful Questions," *Long Island Newsday*, 1 Dec 69.

than by the killings. Sixty-seven percent of those queried believed that the press and television should have avoided interviews with witnesses and participants prior to a trial. By a margin of 55 to 23 percent they also contended that Calley had been made a scapegoat for officers higher in the Army. "Most people are prepared to write off the alleged behavior of some American troops at My Lai," Harris commented, "with the view that 'war is hell' . . . and many things happen which might not be condoned in normal civilian life."[33]

The White House and the Media React

Aware of the public's attitude but concerned that the affair might yet tarnish the Nixon administration, the White House moved early in the crisis to occupy a position that would reassure the American people while insulating the president from what had happened. Queried on the subject, President Nixon's spokesmen thus emphasized that "this alleged incident occurred some ten months before this Administration came into office." The massacre was a direct violation of military law and official policy, they continued, but it "should not be allowed to reflect on the some million and a quarter young Americans who have now returned to the United States after having served in Vietnam with great courage and distinction." Since the matter was moving through the military-judicial process, they concluded, it would be inappropriate to comment further. All questions would have to go to the Department of Defense, which had a better view of what was happening.[34]

With the administration's public posture firmly in place, the president and his advisers began to consider how they would handle the press if unforeseen developments occurred. As Vice President Agnew's attacks on television news had demonstrated, they were inclined to deal with any problem that arose by hitting back from a position of strength. "The greatest mistake we can make [in dealing with the news media]," Nixon told his chief of staff, H. R. Haldeman, at the height of the crisis over My Lai, "is to try to do what Johnson did—to slobber over them with the hope that you can 'win' them. It just can't be done."[35]

Although Nixon preferred a hard line, he and his advisers soon perceived that they had no choice but to bend. When Hersh's story broke, for

[33] "Assessing Songmy, Doves Recoil But Hawks Tend To See 'Massacre' as Just a Part of War," *Wall Street Journal*, 1 Dec 69. The *Minneapolis Tribune* poll is summarized in "Poll Finds Doubters on My Lai," *Washington Post*, 22 Dec 69. Also see [UPI], "Publicity on Mylai Said To Upset U.S.," *Washington Post*, 5 Jan 70; Louis Harris, "66 Percent Against My Lai Court-Martials," *Philadelphia Inquirer*, 6 Jan 70.

[34] Ziegler's statement is quoted in full in Memo, Ronald L. Ziegler for H. R. Haldeman, 5 Dec 69, President's Office files, box 4, President's Handwriting, 1–15 Dec 69, Nixon Papers.

[35] Memo, the President for Bob Haldeman, 6 Jan 70, President's Personal file, box 2, Memos-Jan 70, Nixon Papers.

example, they had been considering a program to reduce the power of their main antagonists within the news media. There would be "no sacred cows," presidential adviser John Ehrlichman wrote at the time, summarizing a meeting with the president. Katherine Graham of the *Washington Post*, David Sarnoff of NBC, William Paley and Frank Stanton of CBS, and Arthur Sulzberger of the *New York Times* would all become the subjects of stringent Internal Revenue Service audits.[36] Meanwhile, the Justice Department would inaugurate antitrust suits against major television networks and newspapers that could be accused of monopolistic business practices.[37]

Although there is no indication of whether the White House went forward with the tax audits, with My Lai in the background, the antitrust suits became much less desirable. "This case could develop into a major trial almost of the Nuremberg scope and could have a major effect on public opinion . . .," White House Director of Communications Herbert Klein told Haldeman at Laird's urging on 21 November. "I called [Attorney General] John Mitchell this morning and suggested that special care be taken that the Justice Department does not move in any actions which might be regarded as intimidation of the media during this particular period of time. He assured me he was aware of the problem and on top of it."[38] The administration postponed its antitrust actions until the fall of 1971, when the furor surrounding My Lai had died down and they were much more politically acceptable. Even then, Klein would contact the presidents of the three television networks to assure them that Nixon, in moving against their organizations, was acting out of a sense of duty to the law rather than because of personal animus toward any of them.[39]

Although the president and his staff considered press coverage of My Lai outrageous, some reporters and commentators still approached the event with caution.[40] Kenneth Crawford of *Newsweek*, for example, warned against any attempt to make generalizations from what had hap-

---

[36] John Ehrlichman, Handwritten Note of Meeting with the President, 23 Nov 69, White House Special files, Ehrlichman, Notes of Meetings with the President, box 3, 1969 JDE Notes [3 of 4], Nixon Papers.

[37] Memo, Herbert Klein for Bob Haldeman, 21 Nov 69, White House Special files, Herbert Klein, Name file 69–70, box 1, H. R. Haldeman I [2 of 3], Nixon Papers. All of the presidents in office since the early 1960s had considered action against the monopolistic practices of news media conglomerates, but all had procrastinated rather than harm their credibility with the public and Congress by appearing to strike at the economic foundations of the press. Also see Memo, Herbert G. Klein for John Ehrlichman, 5 Oct 71, White House Special files, Herbert Klein, Name file 69–72, box 2, Haldeman III [2 of 2], Nixon Papers.

[38] Memo, Klein for Haldeman, 21 Nov 69. Laird's role is mentioned in Ltr, Friedheim to the author, 29 Jul 91, CMH files.

[39] Memo, Herbert G. Klein for H. R. Haldeman, 5 Oct 71, White House Special files, Herbert Klein, Name file 69–72, box 2, Haldeman III [2 of 2], Nixon Papers.

[40] When Senator Peter H. Dominick of Colorado accused the news media of conducting a trial by press in order to cash in "on a hot story before it cools," Nixon wrote "Bravo!" in the margin of the news summary that mentioned the comment. See President's Office files, box 31, Annotated News Summaries, Dec 69, Nixon Papers.

pened at My Lai. "It will be one of the ironies of history if an outrage per-
petrated by U.S. soldiers . . . exposes the whole of South Vietnam to systematic massacre, and that is precisely what can be expected if Mr. Nixon
is forced by the pressure of public opinion to withdraw U.S. forces before
the South Vietnamese Army is prepared to assume full responsibility for
the defense of its country."[41]

The *Wall Street Journal* meanwhile reminded its readers that despite the
isolated actions of individuals, the United States had come to South Vietnam to save a people's freedom while the North Vietnamese, bent on subju-
gating that people, had practiced a policy of atrocity against civilians
throughout the entire war.[42] Without condoning atrocities or necessarily
approving of the president's policies in South Vietnam, John Wheeler of the
Associated Press said the same thing. "Each GI carries with him the knowledge that in any village there may be men, women, and even children . . .
waiting for the time and place to attack him." Yet if Americans sometimes
responded by killing civilians, Wheeler continued, the enemy had pio-
neered the practice, murdering, by some accounts, more than 20,000 noncombatants before the first American ground troops had arrived in 1965. By
1969 the total stood at twice that number, with 3,000 dating from the massacre at Hue alone. Wheeler clearly believed that the way the United States
had fought the war had contributed to the tragedy at My Lai. Many enlisted men, he said, had grown cynical about MACV's prohibitions against
harming civilians because they knew that under the PHOENIX program
enemy civilian officials were sometimes killed. They had also seen the damage American bombers could inflict on civilians. The reporter added, nevertheless, quoting an Army doctor, that part of the brutalization that men
experienced in war was necessary for their psychological survival. "You
can't look war in the face with the kind of emotional responses we use in
the states," the officer had said. "You would go mad."[43]

Although other thoughtful articles and commentaries appeared, news
coverage of the event remained so heavy that by the end of November
many Americans, both within and outside the government, had concluded that the rights of the accused had been irrevocably damaged. Toward
the end of the month, both the prosecutor and Calley's counsel requested
that the military judge in the case, Lt. Col. Reid Kennedy, order the press
to reduce pretrial publicity. Kennedy instructed all potential witnesses to
refrain from speaking to the news media but demurred as far as prepubli-
cation restraints on the press were concerned. Instead, he told reporters,
"This issue will be held in abeyance . . . for a reasonable time . . . [to see
whether the news media] act responsibly." When the press insisted on
interviewing witnesses who were beyond military jurisdiction and news
coverage continued unabated, Kennedy suggested that both the prosecu-

[41] Kenneth Crawford, "Song My's Shock Wave," *Newsweek*, 15 Dec 69, p. 38.
[42] "Atrocities and Policies," *Wall Street Journal*, 1 Dec 69.
[43] John T. Wheeler, "Even Vietnamese Children Could Terrorize the GIs," *Washington
Star*, 5 Dec 69.

232

tion and the defense seek a ban on press coverage from a higher judicial authority. They petitioned the U.S. Court of Military Appeals, which rejected the request on 4 December.[44]

Many members of the news media applauded the decision. The *Denver Post*, for one, avowed that it had "seen no evidence of irresponsible publishing or reporting, but only an aggressive press alert to a significant if highly disturbing chapter in the story of the American involvement in Vietnam and alert to the public's right to know about it."[45] Other members of the press were less certain. On the same day, the more conservative *San Diego Union* termed press coverage of the trial "sensationalism" and claimed that the massacre had been "misused" to "tarnish" the image of the United States. Even if Calley and the others were convicted, the *Union* said, their offense had been solitary and was hardly the result of American policy.[46]

On 10 December the American Civil Liberties Union entered the case by releasing a highly publicized letter to Secretary Laird calling for a dismissal of all charges against Calley because the press, by interviewing potential witnesses and by drawing confessions from men who had been at My Lai, had made it impossible for the lieutenant to receive a fair trial. If the press, to be free, had to make its own decisions about where to draw the line in matters involving civil liberties, the union asserted, it had failed to make sound judgments where My Lai was concerned.[47]

The *Philadelphia Bulletin* took exception. In an editorial on the subject, it pointed out that the American Civil Liberties Union had failed to distinguish between civilian and military juries. Civilian juries were selected at random and might well be influenced by news media accounts. A military jury was different. Composed of professional soldiers, it represented a cross-section of military experience: "combat command, steadiness and heroism under fire, and most importantly a sense of responsibility. It is precisely this sense that would be most resistant to rash judgments and preconceived conclusions that might afflict a civilian jury."[48]

In retrospect, although press coverage of Calley and his codefendants left much to be desired, it is clear that all sides of the case that had anything to gain—the judge, the prosecutors, and Calley excepted—considered the news media an important vehicle for reaching the American

[44] Quote from Peter Braestrup, "Silence Ordered on Mylai," *Washington Post*, 26 Nov 69. Braestrup, "News Stories on Pinkville Upset Judge," *Washington Post*, 29 Nov 69. Also see Winston Groom, "News Curb Ruling Near on My Lai," *Washington Star*, 2 Dec 69; "The News About Mylai," *Boise Statesman*, 4 Dec 69; "Court Right To Reject Media Ban," *Denver Post*, 4 Dec 69.

[45] "Court Right To Reject Media Ban."

[46] Frank Reynolds, ABC Evening News, 28 Nov 69, *Radio-TV-Defense Dialog*; "Sensationalism Perils Justice," *San Diego Union*, 4 Dec 69.

[47] Ltr, John de J. Pemberton, Jr., Executive Director, ACLU, and Melvin L. Wulf, Legal Director, to Secretary Laird, 10 Dec 69, 330–75–089, box 98, Viet 383, 1969, Laird Papers, WNRC.

[48] "The ACLU and Lt. Calley," *Philadelphia Bulletin*, 18 Dec 69.

Captain Medina

public. Some of the defendants, in particular used the press to create sympathy, to foster an impression that they were just simple soldiers, and to build the sort of public support that might exert pressure on Congress and the executive branch for a pardon or some other form of relief. In 1970, one of them, Captain Medina, Calley's immediate superior at My Lai, charged that profiteering publishers had exaggerated the incident and misinformed the public "simply for the monetary value." Yet, prior to Kennedy's restraining order, Medina had made so many statements to the news media—he spoke for more than five hours with *Newsweek*'s Angus Deming alone—that the judge enjoined him specifically from discussing the case with the press.[49] Without Medina's support and that of the other defendants, there would have been a much smaller story for the press to report and far fewer excesses.

Whatever the merits of the way the press handled the story, the affair was hardly without its redeeming aspects, especially where the American image abroad was concerned. Although many foreign commentators were harshly critical, the public debate over My Lai and the U.S. Army's determination to carry out justice accented for others the strength of the American political system. Aldo Rizzo in the Bologna daily *Il Resto del Carlino* expressed appropriate horror at the massacre but noted that the crime was being discussed in the United States with a sincerity and frankness that had "no precedent in the sad history of such things." The respected Turin daily *La Stampa* observed that "the civilization of a people is judged above all by the courage and the severity with which it isolates certain individuals and denounces their crimes. The American press has done and is doing its duty." *Le Soir* of Brussels commented: "The . . . feeling of aversion which the news of the Song My massacre has provoked in the U.S. pleads in favor of American . . . institutions." The *Oslo Aftenposten* remarked that the reaction to the massacre was especially strong in the United States because American soldiers were involved.

[49] Quote from Chuck Green, "Medina: My Lai Misreported," *Denver Post*, 8 Aug 70. "The Captain's Nightmare," *Newsweek*, 16 Dec 69, p. 41; [UPI], "Calley Judge Calls for Inquiry Into Five News Organizations," *New York Times*, 16 Dec 69. Also see "Songmy 1: Will a 'Lynching' Follow a 'Massacre'?," *New York Times*, 7 Dec 69.

"Something else was expected of them because they belong to a civilized nation. However, in Song My, individuals failed—not a nation."[50]

Accolades of that sort were nevertheless the exception. As the My Lai affair ground on, allegations began to arise that other atrocities had occurred. When that happened, the controversy over civilian casualties began to broaden to include not only the isolated act of a single company but also the entire American way of war in Vietnam.

---

[50] *Il Resto del Carlino* and *La Stampa* are quoted in Henry Tanner, "To Much of the World Songmy Signifies an American Tragedy," *New York Times*, 3 Dec 69. *Le Soir* and *Oslo Aftenposten* are quoted in "Realities of Song My," *Baltimore News American*, 2 Dec 69.

11

The My Lai Controversy Broadens

In the weeks that followed the My Lai revelations, stories began to appear in the press that atrocities by Americans and their allies were far more commonplace in South Vietnam than the U.S. government was willing to admit. At first the charges were general. A headline in the 9 December 1969 edition of the *Washington Post*, for example, introduced a commentary by columnists Tom Braden and Frank Mankiewicz by proclaiming that "Mylai Is a Typical Vietnam Battle in a War That's Directed at Civilians." Horst Faas and Peter Arnett likewise submitted a story that highlighted the cruelty of the war. The two reporters noted that if senior military men considered My Lai an unfortunate but understandable consequence of battle U.S. civilians in South Vietnam were far more critical. Blaming the harsh tactics of the American military, those officials contended that they knew of at least fifty incidents susceptible to "similar hysterical recriminations." The brutality, one American contended, was "encouraged by an over-all policy from Saigon that resulted in an overkill."[1]

The Nixon administration was annoyed by the stories. When the Arnett article appeared, the president himself underlined the words *U.S. civilian* in the summary he had received and then wrote in the margin: "Probably AID [U.S. Agency for International Development] and State P.R. types—They never miss a chance to cut the war effort—Can't Bunker do something to get them to be on our side once in a while."[2]

[1] Tom Braden and Frank Mankiewicz, "Mylai Is a Typical Vietnam Battle in a War That's Directed at Civilians," *Washington Post*, 9 Dec 69. The Faas-Arnett article is carried in President Nixon's News Summary for 8 December 69. See President's Office files, box 31, Annotated News Summaries, Dec 69, Nixon Papers. The president's annotated news summary file contains pages marked with marginal comments by the president. While generally identifiable, these pages sometimes lack sufficient information to connect them with the summary for a specific day.

[2] President Nixon's News Summary for 8 Dec 69, President's Office files, box 31, Annotated News Summaries, Dec 69, Nixon Papers.

There was, in fact, little anyone could do. By then, the subject seemed to have a momentum of its own. During the first week in December the *Chicago Sun Times* printed pictures purporting to show an enemy prisoner falling to his death after being thrown from an American helicopter during an interrogation. Congressman Lionel Van Deerlin of California claimed to have learned of an atrocity in which American servicemen had shot a number of civilians near Dong Tam in the Mekong Delta. Robert Kaylor of United Press International alleged that according to American pacification advisers in the Mekong Delta the U.S. 9th Infantry Division, during an operation code-named SPEEDY EXPRESS, had indulged in the "wanton killing" of civilians through the "indiscriminate use of mass firepower."[3]

Meanwhile, in a classified cable, Winthrop Brown of the State Department's East Asia desk warned Ambassador Bunker that a recently completed report by the Rand Corporation suggested that South Korean troops serving in South Vietnam might have performed violent and inhuman acts against civilians. Rand would keep the study confidential, Brown said, but with a subcommittee of the Senate Committee on Foreign Relations about to hold hearings on U.S. support for Korean forces in South Vietnam, the report's findings might leak to the press at any time. "You will readily understand how potentially explosive these charges can be . . ., particularly in view of the fact that it is only our support of the Korean forces . . . that makes their presence in Vietnam possible."[4]

Recognizing that the press and Congress were sensitized to the subject and that allegations would continue to arise, Secretary Laird moved to secure what ground he had left. On 11 December 1969, at Henkin's suggestion, he instructed the secretaries of the military services to investigate expeditiously and thoroughly every atrocity story that surfaced, whatever the source. By candidly acknowledging those that were fact, he hoped to prevent the ones that were mistaken from gaining credence through repetition.[5]

Following Laird's policy, the Military Assistance Command was able to clarify a number of atrocity allegations. Some proved to be true, but many more were false. In the case of the information supplied by Van Deerlin, on the one hand, the command's inspector general confirmed that a platoon leader, acting on orders from his company commander, had ordered his men to fire a "mad minute" across a canal into occupied huts on the far bank. The object of the firing was to expend old ammunition

---

[3] The helicopter story is mentioned in "The Killings at Song My," *Newsweek*, 8 Dec 69, p. 33. Van Deerlin's information is in Msg, Col L. Gordon Hill, SA/SEA OASD PA, Defense 15144 to Col Joseph F. H. Cutrona, 3 Dec 69, DDI Civilian Casualties file. Kaylor's article is summarized in Msg, Lt Gen Ewell, CG, IIFFV, HOA 3671 to Abrams, 10 Dec 69, Abrams Papers, CMH.

[4] Msg, State 205685 to Saigon, 11 Dec 69, Pol 27–14 Viet S file, FAIM/IR.

[5] Memo, Henkin for the Secretary of Defense, 9 Dec 69, sub: Vietnam Atrocity Stories, and Memo, Laird for the Secretaries of the Army, Navy, and Air Force, 11 Dec 69, sub: Atrocity Allegations, both in 330–75–089, box 98, Viet 883, 1969, Laird Papers, WNRC.

before returning to camp, but the act resulted in the death of a woman and the wounding of her nephew. Both officers were charged.[6]

The helicopter story, on the other hand, proved to be distorted. Military spokesmen confirmed after a lengthy investigation that the incident had indeed occurred but that the supposed victim was already dead when loaded into the aircraft. Investigators identified the soldier who photographed the disposal of the body. He had passed copies of his pictures to another enlisted man who had mailed them to his girlfriend along with a fabricated account of how his unit had interrogated a prisoner. She, in turn, had given them to her brother, who had informed the press. Although most of the culprits had left the service and were beyond the reach of the military, the aircraft's commander received a reprimand.[7]

If the military services, for the sake of credibility, were willing to admit to genuine atrocities, they nevertheless felt little obligation when the facts failed to substantiate that war crimes had occurred. In one case that came to the attention of the Military Assistance Command during 1970, the provost marshal determined that, for all the appearance of an atrocity, a simple murder had occurred. Lacking any intense interest on the part of the press or Congress in what had happened and unwilling to wound the good image of the military unnecessarily, General Abrams instructed his information officers to reveal the incident only if newsmen inquired. If that occurred, following standard procedures, they were to release the name of the accused and the charges against him but to withhold all further information until the courts had issued a final ruling.[8]

Although most of the allegations circulating yielded readily to Laird's forthright policy, some were exceedingly difficult to handle. Kaylor's article on the conduct of the 9th Division in the Mekong Delta, for example, made little impression at the time but still raised a major issue: had American tactics in the delta contributed to an inhuman waste of civilian life? If so, who was responsible?

The division's commander, Maj. Gen. Julian Ewell, defended himself with vigor when Kaylor's charges first appeared, even though the press, distracted by My Lai, had failed to make much of them. "This is the biggest collection of malicious innuendo I have ever seen," he told General Abrams.

[6] Rpt of Investigation, MACIG-INV 24–70, 18 Apr 70, sub: Analysis of II Field Force Report of Investigation Concerning Alleged Atrocity by US 9th Infantry Division Unit in June 1969, 334–77–0074, box 1, WNRC. Msg, Hill Defense 15144 to Cutrona, 3 Dec 69, sub: Incident Near Dong Tam. The basic outlines of the incident may be found in *Facts on File*, 13–19 Jun 70, 30: 416.

[7] Memo for Correspondents, 22 Sep 72, Civilian Casualty and War Damages (and War Crimes) file, DepCORDS Papers, CMH.

[8] Msg, Lt Gen Ewell, CG, IIFFV, HOA 108 to Abrams, 12 Jan 70, and Msg, Abrams MAC 542 to Ewell, 13 Jan 70, sub: General Court Martial, 1Lt James B. Duffy, both in Abrams Papers, CMH.

Kaylor of UPI claims he obtained the "information" from both military and civilian advisors at My Tho. I wish these people would keep their big mouths shut when they don't know what they're talking about. . . . Without my beating the inaccuracy of the article to death, it says, "the 9th Division claimed to have killed 33,000 while operating in this area." A rough tabulation shows 6,000 is a better figure. . . . Sources said, "many civilians were killed by indiscriminate use of mass firepower." It is a fact that the 9th used the most restrictive rules of engagement in Vietnam. We used less artillery than any other unit. Our gunships could only fire on contact targets or visually identified enemy armed or in uniform.[9]

Although Kaylor's assertion that 33,000 had been killed was incorrect, Ewell had in fact conceived of his approach in the delta as a manufacturing operation—he called it "mass production guerrilla war"—and had linked recognition for achievement within his command to the number of enemy neutralized.[10] With respect to awards for valor, he had told his officers, "a reasonable rule of thumb is an award for . . . every enemy eliminated. . . . A reasonable guideline for the distribution of valor awards by type is 17% Silver Stars and the equivalent and higher, 33% Bronze Stars and equivalent, and 50% Army Commendation Medals."[11]

The results of such a policy are open to broad interpretation. On the one hand, it may have resulted in an inflated body count. On the other, officers may have resolved to inflict as many casualties on the enemy as possible and, in case of doubt, to shoot first. Pacification reports clearly chose the second interpretation. "It was felt by advisory personnel," one province adviser stated in March 1970, "that the high body counts achieved by the 9th were not composed exclusively of active VC [Viet Cong]. The normal ratio of 3 or 4 enemy KIA [killed in action] for every weapon captured was raised at times to 50 to one; this leads to the suspicion that many VC supporters, willing or unwilling, and innocent bystanders were also eliminated."[12] The U.S. embassy also had its doubts. Reacting to the announcement that the 9th Division would shortly leave the delta, political reporters informed the State Department that if some South Vietnamese would miss the security the division had provided, others, especially farmers and peasants, "will not be particularly dismayed to see . . . [it] go. The massive firepower and

[9] Msg, Ewell HOA 3671 to Abrams, 10 Dec 69, Abrams Papers, CMH.

[10] End of Tour Rpt, Lt Gen Julian J. Ewell, Impressions of a Division Commander in Vietnam, 17 Sep 69, CMH files.

[11] HQ, 9th Infantry Division, AVDE-CG, 16 Jan 69, sub: Awards and Decoration Policy, CMH files.

[12] Pacification Studies Group, CORDS, Redeployment Effects of the 9th U.S. Division from Dinh Tuong and Kien Hoa Provinces, 15 Mar 70, Province Senior Adviser Reports, CMH. During the trial of Lt. James B. Duffey, who was accused of murdering an enemy captive, witnesses from the 9th Division testified that the emphasis on body counts was so strong within the unit that at least one company was informed necessary supplies would be withheld until it killed more enemy soldiers. See "The 'Mere Gook Rule,'" *Newsweek*, 13 Apr 70, p. 30. Records of the trial are in Docket no. CM424795, custody of Clerk of Court, Army Judiciary.

aggressive tactics of the American unit have frequently brought charges that unnecessarily high numbers of civilians were being killed and wounded. . . . In addition, . . . residents complained of being repeatedly rounded up by 9th Division units, even if they had proper identification, and being taken away from their homes for one or two day interrogation sessions."[13]

Whatever the validity of those conclusions, the Military Assistance Command took refuge in the ambiguities surrounding the division's record in the delta. When *Newsweek* reporter Kevin Buckley picked up Kaylor's lead and began to research the story at the end of 1971, General Abrams refused to submit to an interview. The Chief of MACV Information at the time, Col. Phillip H. Stevens, cooperated as far as possible by providing statistics and answering questions but also stressed the "very limited records of the operation in question."[14] When Buckley asked about the low ratio of weapons captured to enemy killed during SPEEDY EXPRESS, an obvious lead into the possibility that many of the dead had actually been unarmed peasants, Stevens confirmed the reporter's statistic: 750 weapons captured to 11,000 killed. He observed nevertheless that the command's investigators had attributed the figure to the nature of the terrain and the tactics Ewell had used. In the delta, so the reasoning went, it was easy for the enemy to dispose of weapons by dropping them in canals, streams, and paddies. A high percentage of casualties had also been inflicted at night or by aviation units, making the retrieval of weapons almost impossible. "In some heavily booby trapped areas, the number of weapons which might have been captured would not have justified the number of casualties that probably would have been sustained to locate them." On top of that, Stevens said, many members of guerrilla units in the region were unequipped with individual firearms.[15]

The excuses eluded Buckley. "The spokesman said he had no way of answering—" the reporter concluded in the article that followed, "a remarkable reply since he had at his disposal 'after action reports,' 'field commanders' reports' and other records of the operation in question." Available evidence proved, Buckley asserted, that the U.S. command knew that a division-size operation in the heavily populated Mekong Delta would make civilian casualties inevitable. "The U.S. Army ignored those assessments both before and after SPEEDY EXPRESS. Indeed, when he promoted the unit's commander, Abrams noted that 'the performance of this division has been magnificent.'"[16]

[13] Msg, Saigon A–368 to State, 18 Jul 69, Pol 27 Viet S file, FAIM/IR.
[14] Ltr, Col Phillip H. Stevens to Kevin Buckley, 13 Jan 72, DDI Incident file, 1972.
[15] Ltr, Col Phillip Stevens to Kevin Buckley, 2 Dec 71, DDI Incident file, 1972.
[16] Kevin Buckley, "Pacification's Deadly Price," *Newsweek*, 19 Jun 72, p. 42. For the most recent scholarly view of SPEEDY EXPRESS, see Guenther Lewy, *America in Vietnam* (Oxford: Oxford University Press, 1978), p. 142, and Andrew F. Krepinevich, Jr., *The Army in Vietnam* (Baltimore: Johns Hopkins University Press, 1986), pp. 254–55.

Buckley's article prompted little reaction when it appeared in June 1972. It not only dealt with yesterday's news, it had to contend for space with the enemy's "Easter" offensive, which was in full swing at that time. The story of Korean atrocities in South Vietnam was a different matter. Embarrassing in the extreme, it caught the United States between the need to preserve official credibility and the possibility that an important ally might lose face.

The situation began to come apart shortly after Brown sent his message on Korean atrocities to Bunker. On 9 January 1970, Terry Rambo of Human Sciences Research, Inc., who had directed a report on Korean atrocities for the Army that paralleled the one by Rand, informed the press that he had uncovered stark evidence that South Korean soldiers had killed hundreds of civilians in South Vietnam. Refugees, he said, had told his researchers of witnessing many slayings. When South Korean troops "passed a village and received sniper fire, they would stop and pull out people at random and shoot them in retaliation. For the Koreans, this was a deliberate, systematic policy." Rambo added that when he had attempted to pursue the matter a general officer at the Military Assistance Command had ordered him to stop investigating the Koreans and to refrain from mentioning the subject in his report.[17]

Investigators were unable to confirm many of Rambo's allegations or whether someone within the Military Assistance Command had ordered the researcher to remain silent. Questioning the methodology of both Rambo's interviewers and those from Rand, the military concluded that the researchers had taken the word of possibly confused or biased refugees without any independent confirmation. "Our general impression is that many of the alleged atrocity charges . . . [are] based on rumor and hearsay that find their origin in unfortunate incidents where civilian casualties have resulted from military operations. In this type of situation it is difficult for us to determine whether killings were in fact unhappy consequences of battle action or were atrocity / war crime."[18]

Ample evidence nevertheless existed to confirm that the Koreans had fought a violent war and that at least some atrocities had occurred. A senior U.S. civilian in South Vietnam volunteered privately to State Department officials that complete reports on the subject existed, some accompanied by gruesome photographs. In one case, the Korean government had admitted fault and had paid an indemnity. In others, despite efforts by the Military Assistance Command, the South Vietnamese government had refused to take action and the Koreans themselves had denied responsibility. There seemed little prospect in this case, Winthrop

[17] Rambo is quoted in *Facts on File*, 15–21 Jan 70, 30: 18. The full report is in MFR, A. Terry Rambo, Dale K. Brown, Human Sciences Research, ARPA-AGILE, May 67, sub: Korean Military Behavior Toward Vietnamese Civilians in Phu Yen Province, HSR–RN–671–Aa, 330–76–067, box 93, Viet 383 (Jan) 1970, Laird Papers, WNRC.
[18] Msg, Saigon 2303 to State, 16 Feb 70, Pol 27–12 Viet S file, and Msg, Saigon 442 to State, 11 Jan 70, sub: Alleged ROK Atrocities, Pol 27 Viet S file, both in FAIM/IR.

Brown indicated in a memorandum to the under secretary of state, despite the outcry over Rambo's revelations, that anything different would happen.[19]

Under the circumstances, the United States had little choice but to retreat behind the technicality that the Korean force in South Vietnam was a separate entity formally unconnected with the U.S. command. On 11 January 1970, during an interview on the ABC news program "Issues and Answers," Secretary Laird thus acknowledged receipt of hearsay information on the subject but avowed that the reports in question were difficult to substantiate legally. In any case, he said, the United States was not involved. South Korea and South Vietnam would handle the matter in their own way.[20]

The effort to disassociate the United States from atrocities by its Korean allies was to little effect. The issue subsided for a time, only to resurface during July, when a former U.S. Army lieutenant who had served in Quang Ngai Province at the time of the incident at My Lai, Frank Frosch, charged in *Playboy* that the South Korean Marine Brigade had caused a staggering loss of civilian life in the area during late 1967. The Koreans thus contributed to the later atrocity at My Lai, Frosch said, by leaving a legacy of hate toward the United States among the peasants of the region that the men of the American Division had inherited. "A third-world force in Vietnam, the Koreans will never be called to account for their actions," Frosch concluded. The Americans, "who walked into the morass in Song My, will—and have been." Queried by the press on Frosch's allegations, the Defense Department declined to comment.[21]

Although the Korean atrocity story was serious, it made at best a minor impression. Far more compelling were the revelations, charges, and countercharges that continued to surround American involvement at My Lai. During February 1970, for example, allegations appeared that a second company from the American Division had committed atrocities in the region surrounding My Lai. During March claims arose before a Senate subcommittee on juvenile delinquency that 60 percent of the men involved at My Lai had been chronic or occasional smokers of marijuana, leading to speculation that drug abuse may have been to blame for some portion of that incident.[22]

---

[19] Msg, State 4219 to Saigon, 10 Jan 70, and Memo, Winthrop G. Brown, EA, for Under Secretary Johnson, 11 Feb 70, sub: Alleged Korean Atrocities–Symington Hearings, both in Pol 27 Viet S file, FAIM/IR. Also see Msg, Saigon 1368 to State, 29 Jan 70, Pol 27–12 Viet S file, FAIM/IR; Msg, Wheeler JCS 624 to Gen Michaelis, Commander in Chief, United Nations Community (CINCUNC), Korea, sub: Allegations of Korean Atrocities in South Vietnam, Abrams Papers, CMH.

[20] Msg, Saigon 442 to State, 11 Jan 70, sub: Alleged ROK Atrocities. Laird is quoted in *Facts on File*, 15–21 Jan 70, 30: 18.

[21] Frank Frosch, "Anatomy of a Massacre," *Playboy*, Jul 70, p. 185. Also see Robert M. Smith, "Ex-Officer Tells of Songmy Data," *New York Times*, 12 Jun 70.

[22] Ted Sell, "My Lai Company Faces Earlier Crime Charges," *Los Angeles Times*, 8 Feb 70; Fred Farrar, "Pot Use by GIs in Viet Told," *Chicago Tribune*, 25 Mar 70.

General Peers in early 1968

The Army denied that drugs were involved at My Lai, but it had earlier charged the commander of the 1st Platoon of Company B within Task Force BARKER, 1st Lt. Thomas K. Willingham, with war crimes in an incident that had occurred two days prior to the one at My Lai, in which as many as ninety women and children may have perished. The charges against Willingham were later dismissed for lack of evidence, but General Peers never doubted that the event had occurred. Disagreeing with the decision to terminate the case and questioning the good judgment of the individual who had made it, he stated that, whatever the outcome, the charges should have been subject to "the most rigorous examination." Word of the event had apparently never risen above company level, Peers said. Information on the operation was thus "more deeply suppressed than even that of Charlie Company. It was an almost total coverup."[23]

Although the dismissal of charges against Willingham and others would later make it seem as though the Army itself was involved in some form of deception, there was, in fact, little inclination on the part of military agencies to hide anything. Once the decision had been made to be as forthright as possible, it was inevitable that everything would come out. What concerned the military was limitation of the damage that might result and preservation of the rights of the accused.[24]

When the Defense Department decided to go forward with a press conference on the Peers commission's findings, semantic wrangling thus began over how the briefers should describe what had happened. "I had drafted a short introductory statement of what I thought the American public should be told," Peers said, "and in it I had used the term *massacre* without being specific as to how many people had been killed. I was requested not to include that portion of my statement." Feeling strongly that any attempt to dissemble would be unfair to the American people,

---

[23] "Pentagon Eliminates Drugs Re: My Lai," ABC Evening News, 25 Mar 70, *Radio-TV-Defense Dialog*. Quotes from Peers are from Lt. Gen. W. R. Peers, USA (Ret.), *The My Lai Inquiry* (New York: W. W. Norton, 1979), pp. 198, 216.

[24] Interv, author with Jerry Friedheim, Deputy Assistant Secretary of Defense, 1969–1973, 3 Oct 86, CMH files.

Peers resisted. The Chief of U.S. Army Information, General Sidle, entered the fray. "I don't know who had given him his instructions," Peers continued,

but it seemed as though they had come from the General Counsel and the Office of the Secretary. He gave us all kinds of reasons why we should not intimate that My Lai had been a massacre—the impact it would have upon the Army's image, its effects upon ongoing and future courts martial and judicial litigation, and on and on. We could not agree on an acceptable alternative, so the meeting ended in a stalemate.[25]

There matters stood until the following morning. Peers remained unwilling to present a watered-down version of his conclusions and, in effect, refused to appear. Shortly thereafter, a member of his staff, Jerome Walsh, observed that there seemed to be little objection to the word *tragedy* since it had been used elsewhere in the statement without comment. He suggested that Peers substitute "tragedy of major proportions" for "massacre." When Sidle agreed, the press conference went forward as scheduled.[26]

The communique and the news conference accompanying it were successful. Noting that an atrocity had occurred, Peers alleged that "serious deficiencies" were manifest in the actions of a number of officers holding command and staff positions in the Americal Division. It went on to name the individuals involved, including two general officers, Maj. Gen. Samuel W. Koster, the former commanding general of the Americal Division, and Brig. Gen. George H. Young, his former assistant commander in South Vietnam.[27]

The reaction of the press was mixed. In the *New York Times*, commentator Edward F. Sherman observed that Peers had revealed a serious "breakdown of proper reporting procedures" that called into question "the values and attitudes inculcated in men by the military." *Los Angeles Times* reporter Ted Sell remarked that the Army, in indicting the generals, had confessed to a failure in its system. Other observers were pleased, however, that the Army had addressed its problems candidly. "Army Acts Wisely," proclaimed the *Milwaukee Journal*. "No Army Whitewash," announced the *Detroit News*. "The Army is probably the last place," Frank Reynolds of ABC News reported, where "those who have lost faith in the establishment . . . would expect to find this kind of soul searching."[28]

---

[25] Peers, *The My Lai Inquiry*, pp. 216–17.

[26] Ibid.

[27] OSD PA News Release, 17 Mar 70, sub: Army Announces Peers-MacCrate Inquiry Findings, 330–76–067, box 93, Viet 383 (Mar) 1970, Laird Papers, WNRC.

[28] Edward F. Sherman, "Army Blows the Lid on Its Own Cover-Up," *New York Times*, 22 Mar 70; Ted Sell, "Army Indicted System by Indicting Generals," *Los Angeles Times*, 29 Mar 70; "Army Acts Wisely," *Milwaukee Journal*, 18 Mar 70; "No Army Whitewash," *Detroit News*, 19 Mar 70; Frank Reynolds, ABC Evening News, 17 Mar 70, *Radio-TV-Defense Dialog*.

The Incidents of 3 November Resurface

If the Army had held its own, it had nevertheless hardly won the contest over atrocities with the press. In the weeks and months that followed, critical stories continued to appear, not only on My Lai but also on other possible violations of the laws of war. On 26 February 1970, for example, a flurry of comment occurred when the Military Assistance Command revealed that five U.S. marines had been charged with the murder of sixteen women and children at a hamlet named Son Thang (4) located some twenty kilometers northwest of the town of Tam Ky in the I Corps Tactical Zone. Although newsmen initially commended the marines for their forthright handling of the event, they turned the case into a cause celebre when political maneuvering began on behalf of the accused. Inquiries by the defendants' congressmen; charges of discrimination and brutality against the one black involved in the incident; and the fact that two lower ranking soldiers were convicted while the team leader, a lance corporal vigorously defended by two of his state assemblymen, went free all complicated the issue.[29]

The marines' case had yet to come to trial when Walter Cronkite resurrected the controversy that had accompanied Don Webster's 3 November 1969 report on the stabbing of the Viet Cong captive. Syndicated columnist Richard Wilson had earlier charged that CBS was under investigation for fabricating horror stories about the war. Cronkite denied the allegation and devoted an unusual fifteen minutes of his 21 May broadcast to the subject. Linking the incident to what he considered continuing attempts by the Nixon administration to browbeat television news, Cronkite accused the president's Special Counsel for Investigations, Clark Mollenhoff, of leaking Pentagon suspicions to receptive reporters and columnists. He then turned the program over to Webster, who attempted to refute Wilson's charges.[30]

Webster replayed the program in its entirety. "Recently," he said, "some Pentagon experts have suggested that the . . . helicopters shown appear to be Australian, not American. . . . Also, says the Pentagon, the so-called fire fight may have been nothing more than a South Vietnamese training exercise. And, . . . it's suggested the enemy soldier may already have been dead." The reporter denied that the helicopter was Australian. Conceding that the vague insignia appearing on the aircraft in the film were similar to those of the Royal Australian Air Force, he noted that the markings resembled even more those of the U.S. 187th

---

[29] For a full account of the incident and its outcome, see Graham A. Cosmas and Lt. Col. Terrence P. Murray, USMC, *U.S. Marines in Vietnam: Vietnamization and Redeployment, 1970–1971* (Washington, D.C.: History and Museums Division, Headquarters, U.S. Marine Corps, 1986), pp. 344–47.

[30] The CBS report is reprinted verbatim in Barrett, *Columbia University Survey of Broadcast Journalism, 1969–1970,* pp. 141–44. Unless otherwise indicated, this section is based on this source. For the syndicated column to which Cronkite referred, see Richard Wilson, "CBS Stand in War News Probe Is Questioned," *Washington Star,* 11 May 70.

Assault Helicopter Squadron based in Tay Ninh Province.[31] He continued that the suggestion that the operation in question may have been a training exercise apparently stemmed from the appearance of a white flag flying from a pole in the background of one scene. Flags of that sort often served as targets during South Vietnamese training exercises, Webster said, but they were also a ubiquitous feature of the countryside, where rice farmers used them as scarecrows. The reporter then identified the place where the incident had occurred as a rice-growing area near the village of Bau Me, about six kilometers north of the town of Trang Bang in Hau Nghia Province.

The Military Assistance Command had claimed that it was unable to determine anything about the men who were supposedly present at the incident, but Webster was more certain. "If you look closely," he said, "this is the patch of the U.S. First Cavalry Division. It is worn on the right shoulder, meaning the adviser formerly served in a war zone with the First Cav. That makes him an American." In the same way, he continued, CBS had readily identified the South Vietnamese soldier who had actually done the stabbing. His name was Sfc. Nguyen Van Mot. "Not only is Sergeant Mot still on duty," Webster said, "but he was named Soldier of the Year for 1969 for all regional forces in III Corps."

The reporter interviewed Mot through an interpreter. The soldier admitted to stabbing his prisoner but claimed he had done so in self-defense, when the man reached for a weapon on the ground beside him. "Those people are very stubborn . . .," Mot said. "Even if they were wounded, . . . they try to grab, you know, whatever around them, weapons or anything they can reach. . . . The last thing they try before they die." Webster conceded that the film showed what appeared to be an enemy rifle on the ground near the victim but added that Mot had stabbed the man a second time, when the prisoner was giving no resistance. He also played one of the outtakes the Defense Department had requested but never received. It showed the prisoner's body being mutilated. "The Pentagon may wish to believe this story never happened," Webster said, "but it did."

Walter Cronkite concluded the piece. "We broadcast the original story in the belief it told something about the nature of the war in Vietnam. What has happened since then tells something about the government and its relations with the news media which carry stories the government finds disagreeable."

Although CBS clearly believed that its story was correct and that officials in the Pentagon and the White House had indulged in a calculated campaign against the news media, both Henkin's deputy, Jerry Friedheim, and Clark Mollenhoff denied the allegation. Friedheim gave a low-keyed statement disavowing any knowledge of an official investigation into the practices of CBS News. Mollenhoff was more emphatic.

---

[31] This was probably the 187th Aviation Company located at Tay Ninh. Army records contain no mention of a 187th Assault Helicopter Squadron.

Writing a series of memorandums and letters to White House Press Secretary Ronald Ziegler and others, he denied that either he or the White House had any part in the news stories that had appeared. Instead, he said, a columnist and war correspondent for the *Des Moines Tribune*, Gordon Grammack, had heard criticism of the 3 November film from military men during a tour of the war zone. Either he or his editors had tipped James Risser of the *Des Moines Register* to the story. Risser had followed through on his own, without ever contacting the White House. The resulting articles had, in turn, drawn the interest of columnist Wilson, who had given Risser's charges a national forum.[32] "It was refreshing to note," Mollenhoff observed in a letter to Walter Cronkite, "that this latest account identified the place of the action, the names of the units, and the name of the man who identifies himself as the wielder of the knife." The story was nevertheless seriously flawed, he continued, because it attempted to implicate the White House in what had been an independent journalistic effort.[33]

Richard Wilson was equally critical. The CBS rebuttal, he said, had filled many gaps, not the least being that Sergeant Mot, contrary to the impression left by the first report, might have acted in self-defense. Even so, the main point still remained at issue. CBS had refused to cooperate with the military effort to move against war crimes involving Americans. Accused of falsifying scenes on a number of occasions—for example, the 1967 episode in which Webster had narrated the severing of a dead enemy soldier's ear—and subject to inquiries from Congress and the Federal Communications Commission on that account, the network had decided to respond publicly and had done so effectively. Yet, Wilson concluded, when it went beyond the matter at hand to imply that its freedom to report was somehow under attack from the Pentagon, the credibility of its conclusion seemed to sag. For it could never have prepared the program containing its rebuttal without the cooperation of the U.S. forces in South Vietnam—"rather a strange way, for government repression to work."[34]

Although Wilson and other commentators accepted the apparent truth of Webster's allegation that an atrocity of some sort had occurred, the Military Assistance Command was less easily convinced. During the months following the May report, it quietly reinvestigated the incident, only to conclude that its original findings had been correct and that

---

[32] Memo, Jerry W. Friedheim, Deputy Assistant Secretary of Defense for Public Affairs, 12 May 70, sub: CBS Being Investigated?????; Memo, Clark Mollenhoff for Ron Ziegler, 22 May 70, sub: Background Presentation on the CBS Matter; Ltr, Mollenhoff to Walter Cronkite, 22 May 70; Memo for the File, 27 May 70, sub: Explanation of CBS Broadcast of May 21, 1970. All in White House Special files, Staff Member Office files, Ronald Ziegler, Numerical Subject files, box 21, Problem Stories 109, Nixon Papers.

[33] Ltr, Mollenhoff to Cronkite, 22 May 70.

[34] Richard Wilson, "CBS Rebuttal on Horror Leaves Central Issue," unattributed clipping, White House Special files, Staff Member Office files, Ronald Ziegler, Numerical Subject files, box 21, Problem Stories 109, Nixon Papers.

Webster's report was a montage drawn from pictures of several occurrences. The command's provost marshal and its inspector general both agreed sufficient evidence existed to support a conclusion that the victim had been dead when Mot had stabbed him and that if American advisers had indeed accompanied the operation in question none had been present when Mot disfigured the body. In addition, the terrain in which the actual event had occurred failed to match that of the area filmed by CBS, and American helicopters almost never accompanied the operations of South Vietnamese irregular troops.[35]

The MACV Inspector General, Colonel Cook, later suggested an explanation for what had happened. Although Webster had supplied a voice-over for the story, he pointed out, the reporter had not been present when the filming itself had taken place. The incident he had narrated in all honesty may thus have been the concoction of a freelance South Vietnamese cameraman who had embellished his material in order to ensure its sale to a major American television network.[36] Indeed, even the Military Assistance Command's sound-on-film production teams were tempted at times to fabricate stories. As Senator Fulbright alleged and General Sidle confirmed, on several occasions early in the war the Defense Department had released films purporting to show combat action that had in fact been staged by soldier-producers in the field.[37]

Whatever the merits of those arguments, the Military Assistance Command had been quick to attribute NBC's 3 November atrocity report to similar manipulation until subsequent information had established beyond a doubt that the incident had occurred. Cook himself would later affirm that by the time the provost marshal had reinvestigated the CBS story, the command's ability to reconstruct what had happened had become limited. Despite the contention of CBS executives that the Army could recall events in almost total detail, he said, the constant churning of personnel that resulted from the policy restricting tours of duty in South Vietnam to one year handicapped investigators in the field. Most of the people involved in an incident departed South Vietnam a short time after an inquiry began, leaving behind an often unreliable substitute, paper records.[38]

In the end, the Military Assistance Command never made its conclusion public, preferring to drop the matter rather than allow the issue to fester. As for the Defense Department, Secretary Laird moved to cut off Mollenhoff's ability to communicate directly with the subordinate ele-

[35] Rpt of Investigation, MAC Provost Marshal, 6 Sep 70, sub: CBS Allegations of Mistreatment and Atrocity Against Enemy PW in SVN, and MFR, Comdr C. H. Lohr, USN, Asst IG, MACV (MIV–61–70–N), 7 Sep 70, sub: CBS Allegations of Mistreatment and Atrocity Against Enemy PW in SVN, both in 334–77–0074, box 1, vol. 6, tab D, WNRC; Interv, author with Col Robert Cook, USA (Ret.), 22 May 87, CMH files.

[36] Interv, author with Cook, 22 May 87.

[37] Interv, author with Maj Gen Winant Sidle, 12 Jun 73, CMH files; J. W. Fulbright, *The Pentagon Propaganda Machine* (New York: Liveright, 1970), pp. 104–06.

[38] Interv, author with Cook, 22 May 87.

ments of his agency. As a matter of practice and form, he told the president's military assistant, Mollenhoff was to work through his office alone when either the military services or the department itself was undergoing any sort of investigation. The White House concurred.[39]

My Lai Remains an Issue

Although the CBS allegations were spectacular, they made little impression compared with the furor surrounding My Lai. Over the next two years, the press continued to follow every bend in the case, documenting the charges against each of the defendants, chronicling the ebb and flow of the various court cases, and speculating about the outcome of the trials that were to follow.

During January 1970 the Chairman of the House Armed Services Committee, Congressman L. Mendel Rivers of South Carolina, called for congressional hearings to probe the massacre at the same time that the Army appointed Peers to head its investigation. A series of clashes ensued between the committee and the Army when Rivers and the chairman of his investigating subcommittee, Congressman F. Edward Hebert of Louisiana, attempted to call witnesses who were also being interviewed by the Army's Criminal Investigation Division. At one point, Hebert threatened to use his power of subpoena if the Army refused to allow certain witnesses to testify. The Army, according to the *Chicago Daily News*, capitulated to the threat.[40]

The controversy intensified on 20 March, when Rivers alleged in public that the subcommittee's report would reveal "lack of leadership at the highest echelon in the U.S. Army." He then termed the Army's effort to investigate the atrocity at My Lai a fiasco.[41]

When the committee's conclusions appeared, they resembled those of the Peers commission but were substantially more critical of the Army's role in the affair. Noting that a tragedy of major proportions had indeed occurred, the probers observed that the cover-up was so extensive and involved so many individuals that it was unreasonable to conclude that this dereliction of duty was without plan or direction. They then questioned whether the men of Company C had been sufficiently trained and in enough emotional control of themselves to judge whether an order was

[39] Memo, Brig Gen James D. Hughes, Military Assistant to the President, for Haldeman, 25 May 70, and Memo, Haldeman for Hughes, 26 May 70, both in White House Special files, Staff Members Office files, Haldeman, box 242, HRH-Staff Memos, May/Jun 70, H-M, Nixon Papers.

[40] William McGriffin, "Lawmakers Plunge Ahead With Own My Lai Inquiry," *Chicago Daily News*, 3 Jan 70. Also see James Doyle, "Politics and Policy in My Lai Probe," *Washington Star*, 14 Dec 69.

[41] [UPI], "Rivers Urges 'Win' Policy in Asia, Decries Latest Mylai Charges," *Washington Post*, 20 Mar 70.

lawful. The report evoked considerable comment in the press, much of it favorable to the subcommittee.[42]

The House Armed Services Committee gathered headlines again in October 1970, during the trial of Sergeant Mitchell, when the judge in the case ruled that under a law known as the Jencks Act, four witnesses for the prosecution would be unable to testify unless defense lawyers received access to their previous comments before the Hebert subcommittee. Hebert refused to release their remarks on grounds that he had made a promise of secrecy to all of his witnesses. Shortly thereafter, Rivers told newsmen that

I think this trial has persecuted these people enough. And I'm not going to contribute to its continuation in any form, in any form. These boys have tasted enough bitterness, they've tasted enough persecution from the "objective press," both TV, radio, and newspapers. And I'm not contributing anything to its continuation. And it's as simple as that—it's as simple as that.[43]

Although the press was scathing in its criticism of the move, whether Hebert's and Rivers' action had any effect on the trial is unclear. What is known is that the prosecutor, confronted by the committee's refusal, called only three witnesses, none of whom could testify with any certainty that Mitchell had actually killed civilians at My Lai. The sergeant went free.[44]

The House Armed Services Committee's dispute with the Army over My Lai tarnished the image of the military, but the effect was small in comparison with the public affairs problems that arose from the handling of the other defendants, especially where General Koster and Lieutenant Calley were concerned. Of the thirteen men charged formally with murder, only Calley was convicted. The commander of Fort McPherson, Georgia, Lt. Gen. Albert O'Connor, who had custody of many of the defendants, dropped the charges against six of the soldiers on grounds of insufficient evidence. The rest were tried by court-martial and declared not guilty. Of the twelve officers accused in connection with the cover-up, none, except for the 11th Brigade commander, Col. Oran Henderson, ever came to trial. Between June 1970 and January 1971, Lt. Gen. Jonathan O. Seaman, Commander, First U.S. Army headquarters at Fort Meade, Maryland, dismissed the charges against them because the allegations were, to his mind, unsupported by the evidence. In the case of Koster, Seaman noted that five of the charges against the general were unsupported but that two seemed to have some foundation. Although he would issue a letter of censure, he said, he had decided to dismiss all charges in

[42] William Kling, "My Lai Probers Allege Coverup Planned by Army," *Chicago Tribune*, 15 Jul 70; Miriam Ottenburg, "Hill Probers Charge My Lai 'Cover-Up,'" *Washington Star*, 15 Jul 70. For comment on the report, see "My Lai Report," *New Orleans Times-Picayune*, 17 Jul 70; "My Lai's Plugged Channels," *Philadelphia Bulletin*, 18 Jul 70.

[43] CBS Evening News, 18 Oct 69, *Radio-TV-Defense Dialog*. For the Jencks Act, see 18 *United States Code (USC)* 3500 (1958).

[44] Douglas Robinson, "Songmy Trial Is Snarled as House Panel Refused To Divulge 4 Men's Testimony," *New York Times*, 16 Oct 70. Also see David, Press Coverage of the My Lai Massacre, p. 34.

General Koster

the case "in the interests of justice," in light of Koster's "long and honorable career," and because the general had never committed any "intentional abrogation of responsibilities."[45]

The Army recognized that the decision posed large public affairs problems, but Seaman was the commander in charge and had final say under military law. Rather than feed the controversy that was bound to develop by appearing either to agree or disagree, official spokesmen therefore made no comment. Later, during May, after a thorough review, the Army registered its unhappiness with Seaman's decision by taking the only action left to it. Secretary Resor demoted Koster to the rank of brigadier general and stripped him of his Distinguished Service Medal.[46]

The Army's failure to take more than token action against the general disturbed General Peers, who was convinced from his own investigation that more than enough evidence existed to bring Koster to trial. He warned General Westmoreland that the Army's inadequate punitive measures would seem a travesty of justice both to supporters and opponents of the military. Given Seaman's decision and the requirements of military law, the alternative, silent acquiescence, was nevertheless equally unacceptable. Unable to reverse Seaman and empowered only to take administrative action, military authorities had done what they could.[47]

Seaman's ruling sparked considerable protest in the press and Congress. The lawyer who had served as Peers' civilian adviser during the Army's investigation of the cover-up, Robert MacCrate, told newsmen that he was shocked by Seaman's decision. It had the effect, he said, of clearing an officer while his subordinates were still under investigation. "I believe that the Commanding General of the First Army has effectively cut off the orderly progress of inquiry up the chain of command. . . . He has done a serious disservice to the Army."[48]

---

[45] David, Press Coverage of the My Lai Massacre, p. 24. Also see [AP], "Gen. Koster Censured in Mylai Incident," *New York Times*, 1 Feb 71.

[46] "Army Acts Against Two Generals," CBS Evening News, 19 May 71, *Radio-TV-Defense Dialog.*

[47] Peers, *The My Lai Inquiry*, pp. 222–23.

[48] MacCrate is quoted in Ibid., p. 224.

One of the congressmen who had served on Hebert's subcommittee, Samuel S. Stratton of New York, also protested. During a long, well-documented speech from the floor of the House, he charged that Seaman had acted in response to pressures from the Pentagon, which seemed to have decided to "let General Koster off the hook." The explanation that the general's long and honorable career had carried heavy weight in the ruling was "absurd," the congressman added in a subsequent article for the *New York Times*. The "steady progression of dropped charges" made it unlikely that the truth about My Lai would ever emerge from the system of military justice.[49]

Stratton's contention that the generals wanted light punishment for a brother officer was understandable. Westmoreland, for example, was himself at first inclined to believe that Koster was the victim of his subordinates' indiscretions.[50] Yet, as Peers observed, "General Westmoreland was very sensitive to the matter of command influence and, knowing the moral code of Secretary Resor, I do not believe he would have had any part of it either. Hence, . . . had there been any collusion within what Congressman Stratton referred to as the West Point Protective Association, it was without their knowledge and approval."[51]

A former chief of information for the Military Assistance Command, Col. Robert L. Burke, took a different approach. The evidence would have had to be overwhelming to convict an officer of Koster's stature and rank, he noted in an interview. General Seaman in all likelihood recognized the ambivalence of the facts and on his own decided against the agony of a formal legal proceeding. Although the decision in the end probably did more damage to the credibility of the Army than any trial would have, Jerry Friedheim added in the same interview, the lines had been laid down long in the past. It was a matter of military law. The judgment on whether to prosecute belonged to the responsible commanding officer—for better or for worse.[52]

The Calley Trial and Its Aftermath

The same was true for Calley, but in that case the commanding officer allowed the court-martial to proceed and the military judge refused, as was his right, to allow the Jencks Act to interfere with the testimony of essential witnesses. As a result, on 29 March 1971, a jury of six officers declared the lieutenant guilty of premeditated murder, and the judge sentenced him to life imprisonment at hard labor. The verdict, along with the

[49] Stratton's speech is quoted in Ibid. Also see Samuel S. Stratton, "The Army and General Koster," *New York Times*, 1 Mar 71.

[50] Record of Chief of Staff Telecon with Mr. Frank Pace, 1400, 26 Nov 69, sub: My Lai, FONECON file, Westmoreland Papers, CMH.

[51] Peers, *The My Lai Inquiry*, p. 225.

[52] Interv, author with Friedheim, 3 Oct 86. Burke participated briefly in the interview.

events that followed, nevertheless caused as much turmoil for the Army as had the Koster affair.

It was clear from the beginning that the American public was deeply troubled by the Army's failure to pursue adequate justice for Koster and other high officers, and divided on the issue of Calley's responsibility for what had happened. Shortly after the jury reached its decision, public opinion surveyors for the Harris organization found that a phenomenal 91 percent of the Americans they interviewed had followed the case closely. By a score of 36 to 35 percent with 29 percent undecided, a plurality disagreed with the court's decision. If 69 percent recognized that the lieutenant had probably shot noncombatants, agreeing that he had been unjustified in killing old men, women, and children, 69 percent nevertheless also considered him a scapegoat. Eighty-one percent asserted that other hidden atrocities on the scale of the one at My Lai had occurred; 76 percent claimed that Calley's platoon had acted on orders; and 43 percent asserted that if they were ordered by superior officers to shoot civilians suspected of aiding the enemy they would do so.[53]

Reflecting the state of public opinion, the judgment caused an uproar across the United States. Callers to military posts throughout the country, some of them sobbing women, protested that the lieutenant had become a scapegoat for men higher up in the Army. Although official spokesmen refused to comment on the verdict, others were less circumspect. A retired general and frequent critic of official policy, James M. Gavin, told newsmen that the conviction was "devastating in its implications for the morale of the Army. Junior officers are bound to feel that they're carrying the terrible burden of the war. That the buck stops with them." Congressman Ronald V. Dellums of California repeated the theme and called for a congressional inquiry into U.S. military policy in Indochina. Senator Abraham A. Ribicoff of Connecticut avowed that Calley had been made to bear sole responsibility for the crimes of many and urged Nixon to overturn the sentence.[54]

As the days passed the pressure mounted. Members of the Illinois legislature introduced a resolution on the floor of that body calling on the president to grant Calley executive clemency and to restore the officer to active duty. Similar measures passed in the Arkansas Senate and the Kansas House of Representatives. Governor George C. Wallace of Alabama, an early contender in the 1972 presidential race, made the release of Calley a campaign theme, attempting, as presidential speechwriter Patrick Buchanan put it, to turn "pro-Calley sentiment into pro-George sentiment—and anti-Nixon."[55] Governor Jimmy Carter of Georgia

[53] Louis Harris, "Public Opposes Calley Sentence," *Washington Post*, 5 Apr 71.

[54] The Gavin and Dellums comments are in "Pentagon Won't Comment on Verdict," *New York Times*, 30 Mar 71. Also see Charles W. Corddry, "Calley Verdict Looses Flood of Protests on Pentagon," *Baltimore Sun*, 30 Mar 71; "Officials, Veterans Groups Ask Clemency for Lt. Calley," *Washington Post*, 1 Apr 71.

[55] Memo, Patrick J. Buchanan for the President, 5 Apr 71, sub: The Calley Situation, White House Special files, Buchanan, Staff Memoranda, box 4, Presidential Memos-1971, Nixon Papers.

meanwhile proclaimed 5 April "American Fighting Men's Day" and asked residents of his state to drive with their headlights on to show support for the soldier in Vietnam, who was bound to have been demoralized by Calley's conviction and sentence.[56]

The situation within the Army was hardly as bad as Carter and other critics of the verdict believed. An unidentified official in the Pentagon, for example, told *Baltimore Sun* correspondent Charles Corddry that, far from being disturbed, professional officers knew that what had happened at My Lai could never be justified. The verdict "will help them to hold their heads high. The moral of an acquittal would have been that anything goes." Another officer, with combat experience in South Vietnam, expressed no sympathy for Calley at all. "There is a clear, defined line between cold-blooded murder and killing in war," he said. "When an individual finds that he is over that line, on orders or not, he must stop."[57]

The furor had its effect on the president nevertheless. Rather than "pass the buck" to a committee, according to White House Assistant Press Secretary Jerry Warren, he decided on 1 April to invoke his constitutional powers as commander in chief to remove Calley from the stockade at Fort Benning and to return him to house arrest on base. Three days later Nixon announced that he would review the outcome of the case himself, once the lieutenant's lawyers had carried the matter as far as they could within the system of military justice.[58]

The news media were cool toward the president's move. Although some newspapers and commentators considered Nixon's declaration a compassionate way to calm public hysteria while avoiding undue interference with the military, others were critical. The *Philadelphia Inquirer* headlined a commentary on the subject by asking, "How Can Justice Be Impartial With Nixon in Calley's Corner?" Columnist Carl Rowan avowed that

Some of the most vehement critics of the conviction and sentence of Calley are people who used to dismiss talk of prosecuting Kluxers and lynchers with the comment: "All he did was kill another nigger." The implication is clear that they are now applying what is known in Vietnam as "the mere gook rule." What Calley shot was merely a bunch of "gooks" and who is going to lock up a good American boy for that?[59]

The *Washington Star* meanwhile took a middle ground. If Calley's sentence was found by an appeals court to be excessive, the newspaper

[56] See "Pro-Calley Supporters Flood Wires," *Washington Daily News*, 31 Mar 71; "Calley Gains Backing in U.S.," unattributed clipping, 2 Apr 71, CMH files; "Officials, Veterans Groups Ask Clemency for Lt. Calley."

[57] Corddry, "Calley Verdict Looses Flood of Protests on Pentagon."

[58] Note, Jerry Warren to Ronald Ziegler, 7 Apr 71, White House Special files, Ziegler, box 18, Calley Case 160, Nixon Papers.

[59] For a comment favorable to Nixon, see "The President and Calley," *New York Daily News*, 6 Apr 71. See, nevertheless, "How Can Justice Be Impartial With Nixon in Calley's Corner?," *Philadelphia Inquirer*, 6 Apr 71; Carl T. Rowan, "Why This Double Standard in Calley's Case?," *Washington Star*, 7 Apr 71.

remarked, or if testimony at the remaining My Lai trials produced new evidence bearing on his guilt, the possibility of commuting his sentence remained open. Even so, "the day this country goes on record as saying that unarmed civilian men, women and children of any race are fair game . . . will be the day that the United States forfeits all claims to any moral leadership of this world."[60]

The Army made no comment on the president's decision to review the case, but, on the side, Secretary Resor's staff composed an eloquent list of arguments against civilian intervention in the matter. Any move by the president in that direction, the talking paper's authors noted, would lead to charges that the lieutenant had acted in accordance with U.S. policy and that Americans considered the lives of all South Vietnamese expendable. It would also serve to repudiate the system of military justice while creating impossible problems where the prosecution of other war criminals was concerned. Overall, the evidence was neither ambiguous nor doubtful. It revealed calculated brutality "of shocking proportions." Thirteen thousand lieutenants had served in South Vietnam since 1965. None had ever done anything approaching the enormity of what had occurred at My Lai. Calley's crime stood "alone in infamy."[61]

Both the military prosecutor in the case, Capt. Aubrey M. Daniel III, and his assistant, Capt. John P. Partin, agreed. In a letter later released to the press, Daniel claimed that Nixon, by injecting political concerns into the processes of military justice, had denigrated the service of the six honorable officers who had found Calley guilty. In the process, he had given encouragement to those in the United States who sought to turn the lieutenant into some sort of military hero, even though the man had murdered at least twenty-one innocent people. Partin was, if possible, even angrier. "At a time when there is an enormous need for respect for the established institutions," he told the president, "it serves nothing to make exceptions of cases due to public pressure. This case could have served as a true vehicle for the respect in the military justice system which is so badly needed. Instead the extraordinary action shows how unrespected it is even within the system."[62]

The White House, for its part, recognized that the president's decision to intervene opened the administration to criticism from all sides. Traditionalists and conservatives, urged on by Wallace and others seeking political gains at the president's expense, Buchanan told Nixon, would continue to push for stronger action on Calley's behalf. At the same time, those opposed to the war would contend that the president had shown disrespect for the law by "siding with the Yahoo elements raising all this

[60] "A Nation Troubled by the Specter of My Lai," *Washington Star*, 4 Apr 71.

[61] Talking Paper, 5 Apr 71, 330–76–207, box 5, file 337-Staff Mtg (SA), 1971, tab G, Laird Papers, WNRC.

[62] Ltr, Capt Aubrey M. Daniel III to the President, 3 Apr 71, and Ltr, Capt John P. Partin to Richard M. Nixon, 4 Apr 71, both in White House Special files, Ronald Ziegler, Alphabetical Subject files, box 18, Calley Case 160, Nixon Papers.

hell in the country." The Army, meanwhile, seemed to view the decision to review Calley's sentence as an attempt by the administration to achieve political benefits at the expense of the military's reputation for total fairness.[63]

Despite those difficulties, Buchanan recommended against any action that indicated the president had decided to retrench. "The disadvantage of this approach—*now*—" he said,

Patrick Buchanan

would be that RN would fly almost into the teeth of national opinion. The country is beginning to turn on the Calley issue. The media is seeing to that. Calley is not going to be a hero in American history. If more revelations come out, he is likely to be back where he originally was. The point is that we should catch opinion as it shifts. Get in front of it—not reaming Calley, but defending the Army, the process of law in this country, our belief that excesses in combat will not be tolerated—and giving a good scourging to the guilt-ridden, war-crime crowd that is on the other side of our fence.[64]

H. R. Haldeman agreed that some sort of presidential statement was necessary but advised that any public pronouncement on the matter at that moment would only inflame the issue further. "Time is on our side," he told Buchanan.

The popular reaction is not sustainable in the absence of further incitement. The task at hand is to undo the damage RN has done and this should be . . . worked out with care and with sensitive regard for timing. In a week, the tide of sustainable opinion is going to be in favor of affirming the verdict while reducing the sentence: we should be in front of this opinion, but not too far in front. To shift now would give the appearance of panic and confusion. Hopefully, if RN has a press conference in the next 10 days he can clear this matter up.[65]

Following his advisers' suggestion, Nixon waited until 29 April to defend his actions. During a news conference, he stated that he considered his intervention proper. Although the system of military justice was impartial, he said, many Americans had been concerned that Calley

---

[63] Memo, Buchanan for the President, 5 Apr 71, sub: The Calley Situation.
[64] Ibid.
[65] Handwritten Note, H. R. Haldeman to Buchanan, n.d., White House Special files, Buchanan, Staff Memoranda, box 4, Presidential Memos-1971, Nixon Papers.

might fail to receive due justice. By announcing his decision to review the matter he had reassured those citizens and had helped to "cool down" the atmosphere surrounding the issue. Later, in response to questions, Nixon added that he had never attempted to influence the reviewing authorities and that he would be fair himself when he considered the final sentence.[66]

The news media reacted to the president's comments with vigor. "Mr. Nixon tried lamely last night to defend his action," the *New York Post* asserted. "His answer explained nothing." The *Washington Post* was only slightly more diplomatic. The provision for the president to review Calley's conviction had always been present, the paper declared, so Nixon had little need to assert it. In that light, the paper continued, "what we are left with, in the starkest terms, is a wholly premature and improper interference in a judicial process which still has a long way to run. . . . 'I believe that the system of military justice is a fair system,' the president said in almost the same breath that he was saying all the other things. . . . That was all he needed to say, and should have said, by way of 'cooling down the country.'"[67]

In the months that followed the president's statement, although concern about the atrocity at My Lai remained constant, public attention shifted away from Calley to the trials of his company commander, Captain Medina, and the 11th Brigade's commander, Colonel Henderson, the only officers other than Calley to face a court-martial because of their actions during or after the incident at My Lai. Both were ultimately cleared of responsibility, Medina on 22 September and Henderson on 17 December 1971.

The Calley case hung on for four more years. On 20 August 1972, the commanding general at Fort Benning reduced the lieutenant's sentence from life imprisonment to twenty years. More than a year later, on 21 December 1973, Calley lost the final appeal of his conviction. With only sentencing reviews remaining, his lawyers took the case into civilian courts to argue that he had never received a fair trial. On 27 February 1974, a U.S. District Court judge freed him on bail pending final determination of his sentence by military authorities and the president. On 16 April, the secretary of the Army, Resor's successor, Howard Callaway, reduced Calley's sentence to ten years, making him eligible for parole in six months. President Nixon in turn announced on 4 May, at the height of the controversy over his administration's role in the burglary of the Democratic Party headquarters in Washington, the so-called Watergate affair, that he had reviewed the sentence and that no further action seemed necessary. Shortly thereafter, Calley entered the federal prison at Fort Leavenworth, Kansas, to begin serving the remainder of his sentence.[68]

---

[66] Nixon's remarks are summarized in *Facts on File*, 29 Apr 70, 30: 330–32.

[67] " . . . The President and Military Justice," *New York Post*, 30 Apr 71; "Lt. Calley and the President (Cont.)," *Washington Post*, 2 May 71.

[68] Unless otherwise indicated, this section is based on the chronology provided by *Facts on File* for the years 1972 (vol. 32), 1973 (vol. 33), 1974 (vol. 34), and 1975 (vol. 36).

There matters might have rested, but for Calley's lawyers and the civilian courts. On 25 September 1974, the U.S. District Court in Columbus, Georgia, overturned Calley's conviction and ordered the lieutenant's release on grounds that massive, adverse pretrial publicity had made a fair trial in his case impossible. The court devoted 85 of 132 pages of its written opinion to criticism of the press and the way newsmen had continued to interview witnesses despite the protestations of the military judge. The Army, for its part, rejected the verdict out of hand, refused to release Calley, and appealed to higher courts.

On 10 September 1975, the U.S. 5th Circuit Court of Appeals in New Orleans found in favor of the Army by a vote of 8 to 5. Any harm that Calley might have suffered from adverse coverage in the press, the majority found, had been more than offset by the trial court's scrupulous attention to detail and its care in selecting a jury. The five dissenting justices agreed with that portion of the verdict but argued that the House Armed Services Committee, by refusing to release the testimony of important witnesses, had withheld the sort of crucial evidence that might have turned the jury against the government's case. By then Calley had served his time in prison and had been released on parole.

Although the courts found in favor of the Army and the press, neither institution came out of the affair unscathed. General Seaman's dismissal of charges against all of the high officers involved in the case except for Henderson harmed the public image of the Army for years to come. Meanwhile, the continuing scramble newsmen made to uncover every aspect of what had happened and to interview witnesses despite the protestations of the judge, made it seem as though the press had abandoned any semblance of impartiality.

In fact, neither institution was all that much at fault. Although more than willing to avoid self-inflicted wounds, the Army had been forthright in its handling of the case. Seaman's failure to prosecute Koster and the other officers may have indicated a degree of personal prejudice on his part, but it is questionable whether the evidence existed to find any of them guilty. The two strongest cases, against Medina and Henderson, proved inadequate. All concerned nevertheless received some sort of retribution. As one knowledgeable old officer noted years afterward, wounds to vanity are sometimes more painful than the worst of legal penalties. Who was to say that Koster, ending a lifetime of honored service in rejection and disgrace, had received no punishment.[69]

As for the press, it had contended all along that adequate safeguards existed to ensure Calley's rights and that the public should have access to the full details of what had happened. There was undoubtedly some self-service in the claim: My Lai was a great story that could only appeal to readers and viewers. Yet, the overenthusiasm of some reporters and the judgmental nature of some commentaries notwithstanding—one televi-

[69] Interv, author with Cook, 22 May 87.

sion report had depicted My Lai as a splotch of blood on the map of South Vietnam—much of what the public read and watched about the case was factual and undistorted. Indeed, with antiwar sentiment running high in the country, the massacre was bound to become a major political issue. No matter what the press said, one side or the other would have been offended.

12

Improving Official Credibility: Laos

The My Lai massacre and its aftermath were hardly the only threat to the Nixon administration's desire to retain public support for a long-term American effort in South Vietnam. Less spectacular but potentially as damaging were public affairs policies that had long sought to disguise U.S. support for the embattled government of Laos. Over the years, State and Defense Department spokesmen had complied with the wishes of Laotian Prime Minister Prince Souvanna Phouma and the dictates of international diplomacy by characterizing U.S. air attacks on enemy infiltration routes through that country as reconnaissance operations. American pilots fired, they said, only when fired upon. In fact, reporters in Indochina recognized early that the assertion was a sham and that the fate of South Vietnam hinged to a great extent on the success or failure of the U.S. effort in Laos.

Prior to 1969 journalists reported only intermittently on the subject. Events in Laos not only seemed remote, they also lacked immediate interest to an American public preoccupied with the war in South Vietnam. Laos gained in the perceptions of the press shortly before the Nixon administration came into office, when President Johnson's November 1968 bombing halt in North Vietnam freed a large number of aircraft for strikes against enemy bases and infiltration routes in that country. The Saigon correspondents had little difficulty deducing that the change had occurred. When the number of military flights departing American bases in Thailand increased while the bombing of North Vietnam had ended and the tempo of operations in the South remained the same, Laos was the only target of any importance that remained. The Soviet Union confirmed reporters' suspicions during January 1969. Breaking a long silence on American activities in Laos, it highlighted the increase in sorties and accused the United States of bad faith in the Paris negotiations.[1]

[1] Ltr, Richard C. Steadman, DASD ISA, to William P. Bundy, Assistant Secretary of State for East Asian and Pacific Affairs, 4 Feb 69, DDI Laos 69–70 file. For a discussion of why the United States had adopted its public affairs approach to the Laotian war, see Hammond, *Public Affairs: The Military and the Media, 1962–1968*, ch. 2.

Pressures Grow for a Change of Policy

The rise in visibility of the Laotian war led to questions from within the new administration. Early in February, with Daniel Henkin's backing, Deputy Assistant Secretary of Defense for International Security Affairs Richard C. Steadman told William P. Bundy at the State Department that a reexamination of the policy of attempting to obscure American air attacks on the Ho Chi Minh Trail in Laos seemed imperative. If the Paris negotiations brought about a complete cessation of bombing in South Vietnam but none in Laos, the event would expose the United States to a public relations disaster. In particular, B–52 bombers could never "by any stretch of the imagination be considered . . . reconnaissance aircraft." At a minimum, Steadman suggested, the United States should resort to a policy of no comment without any elaboration where air strikes in Laos were concerned. A better alternative would be to negotiate a statement with Souvanna that conceded his role in requesting the attacks. The prime minister might agree to the change, Steadman said. During an interview reported by the *Washington Post*, he had openly acknowledged raids by American aircraft and had said that the sorties would have to continue until the North Vietnamese put aside their ambitions in his country.[2]

Although Steadman's approach seemed promising and more news stories appeared suggesting that Souvanna was indeed prepared to make a change, the possibility proved elusive. When United Press International asserted on 12 February 1969 that the prime minister had admitted American aircraft were bombing enemy positions in his country, Souvanna denied ever having made the statement. In the same way, when the State Department asked the U.S. embassy in Vientiane to ascertain whether Souvanna was open to a change, the embassy responded that the prime minister wished to abide by the "usual ground rules."[3]

In the end, the State Department denied Steadman's request. Any affirmation by Souvanna that he had sought American bombing attacks, Bundy observed, would almost certainly force the Soviet Union and other Eastern Bloc nations to denounce him as an American tool. To date, all of those nations, to avoid a broadening of the war that might sap North Vietnam's abilities unnecessarily, had carefully finessed references to Souvanna and his policies, even in their denunciations of the American bombing campaign. In addition, "any official admission of our bombing . . . would considerably increase the pressure on our own government as well as on Souvanna to implement a bombing halt in Laos and, therefore, increase rather than diminish the problem of interdicting what appears to be undiminished traffic along the Ho Chi Minh Trail." For the rest, Bundy said, "We do not entirely share your concern that the present policy

[2] Ibid.
[3] The UPI story is in Msg, State 23069 to Vientiane, 12 Feb 69. Vientiane's response is in Msg, Vientiane 950 to State, 13 Feb 69. Both in Pol 27 Viet S file, FAIM/IR.

makes for a 'credibility gap'; the bombing is not only completely known, but the reasons for the U.S. and Lao refusal to confirm it officially are equally known and generally understood."[4]

Bundy's lack of concern for a "credibility gap" notwithstanding, the problems posed by Laotian involvement would not go away, if only because Souvanna himself seemed to tire of the circumlocutions he had for so long maintained. During June both the *New York Times* and the *Washington Post* thus revealed that the prime minister had acknowledged the bombing in a conversation with a Japanese journalist. Faced with the revelation but unwilling to bend more than necessary, the State Department responded with a half measure. It informed the U.S. embassy in Vientiane that it planned to allow its spokesmen to respond to questions on the subject by saying that they had "no quarrel" with what Souvanna had said but also no comment to add.[5] The line did little to improve official credibility. When a State Department spokesman resorted to it during a 17 June briefing, the assembled reporters laughed in derision.[6]

The department adhered to its position during the months that followed. On 25 July, for example, Souvanna once more alluded to U.S. bombing of North Vietnamese infiltration routes through his country and the agency once more held firm to its policy of no comment. "The DRV [Democratic Republic of Vietnam] continues to deny NVA [North Vietnamese Army] presence in Laos," Under Secretary of State Elliot Richardson explained to Henry Kissinger. If the United States were to admit the bombing, "we would then stand before the world as the sole foreign force there. . . . A change in our public position would [also] be unpropitious following . . . DRV allegations at the Paris talks that we are the aggressor in Laos."[7]

The line might have held if all else had remained steady but the situation in northern Laos began to deteriorate toward mid-1969. By August local Communist forces, the Pathet Lao, supplied and advised by the North Vietnamese, had begun a campaign in the north to put increasing pressure on Souvanna's neutralist government. The development alarmed American policy makers, who had always believed that the Communists intended to save Laos for later and to do no more than necessary to keep the country's feeble armed forces from becoming a threat to their immediate ends in South Vietnam. On 1 August, as a result, Admiral McCain cabled General Wheeler to observe that the enemy could overrun the country at will and that the United States had to come to

---

[4] Ltr, William P. Bundy to Richard C. Steadman, 26 Feb 69, DDI Laos Policy file. Also see Kissinger, *The White House Years*, p. 451.

[5] State's revised response is in Msg, State 97598 to Vientiane, 14 Jun 69, sub: Souvanna's Press Conference. Also see Msg, Vientiane 3900 to State, 15 Jun 69, sub: Souvanna Press Conference. Both in Pol 27 Viet S file, FAIM/IR.

[6] Msg, State 098162 to Saigon, 17 Jun 69, sub: Souvanna Press Conference, 334–71A374, box 1, WNRC.

[7] Msg, State 127323 to New Delhi, 31 Jul 69, sub: Public Position on US Air Operations in Laos, Pol 27 Viet S file, FAIM/IR.

Ambassador Godley

terms with the ambivalence inherent in the way it addressed Souvanna and his problems. The State Department, McCain said, had always believed that diplomatic action provided the best approach to preserving Laotian neutrality. Yet, as American involvement in South Vietnam had progressed, in May 1964, the U.S. Ambassador to Laos, G. McMurtrie Godley, had been forced by circumstances to take charge of a major clandestine military effort in northern Laos to preserve the nation's existence. A reassessment of U.S. policy seemed in order, McCain concluded, to determine whether U.S. forces should assume an overt role in the country.[8]

Two days later, as if to underscore the urgency of McCain's request, Godley withdrew his embassy's long-standing objections to the use of B–52 bombers in the northern portions of the country. Given the Communists' unusual belligerence, he reasoned, the move might serve as a signal to North Vietnam and its allies that the United States was willing to go to great lengths to stabilize the situation.[9]

Ambassador Bunker added his own analysis on 14 August in a chilling message to the State Department. North Vietnam's decision to escalate the fighting in northern Laos, he said, was not tactical and limited as similar operations had been in the past but a direct attempt to influence the course of the war in South Vietnam and the outcome of the Paris negotiations. The enemy intended to exert enough pressure to force the Laotian government to call for a bombing halt along the Ho Chi Minh Trail. If Souvanna refused, North Vietnam intended to establish a government in Vientiane more amenable to its ends.[10]

Bunker drew his conclusion from a number of considerations. Enemy forces in South Vietnam, he said, had little to show for their efforts. The Viet Cong were experiencing high desertion rates and having difficulties with their recruiting. At the same time, the gradual reduction in U.S. forces

---

[8] Msg, McCain to Wheeler, 1 Aug 69, Abrams Papers, CMH.

[9] Msg, Vientiane 4443 to State, 3 Aug 69, Pol 27 Viet S file, FAIM/IR. Also see Kissinger, *The White House Years*, p. 451.

[10] Msg, Saigon 16371 to State, 14 Aug 69, sub: Laotian Developments as Viewed From Saigon, 74D417, box 2, Ambassador's Chron file, Bunker Papers, FAIM/IR.

had led to a belief in some Communist circles that major U.S. contingents would linger in South Vietnam for years. If that was so, any attempt to achieve victory similar to the Tet offensive of 1968 would cost them dearly without changing their prospects. A breakthrough in Laos seemed preferable. If North Vietnam could force Souvanna to call for a stop to the bombing, a qualitative change in its prospects would follow in South Vietnam.[11]

As the United States considered the options available, it also began to plan for the possibility that it would have to adopt a more forthcoming public position on its role in Laos. Queried by the State Department, Ambassador Godley objected strenuously to a change in policy. Any official admission that American bombers had been breaking the Geneva Agreements for years, he said, would embarrass U.S. allies who had served on the International Control Commission overseeing the accord. More important, for reasons of face, the North Vietnamese might well feel compelled to make a negotiated settlement of the war in South Vietnam contingent on an end to the bombing in Laos. In that sense, Godley said, a more open policy would serve mainly to freeze the two sides into positions harder than ever before. "We should keep in mind," he concluded,

that Christian ethic which regards confession as good for the soul has no parallel in oriental value system. Quite the contrary. In this part of the world, as Hanoi's ritualistic emphasis on the 'confessions' of our POW's makes clear, confession is nine/tenths of the law. By admitting the nature of our air operations in Laos, we risk making explicit something the NVN/PL [North Vietnamese/Pathet Lao] may prefer to remain ambiguous, thereby reducing their flexibility as well as ours.[12]

Although the State Department pulled back from the public declaration it had considered, pressure continued to build. During October 1969 the Senate Foreign Relations Committee began closed hearings on Laos. Following the Senate's lead, *Time* printed an article on what it termed the United States' "unseen presence" in northern Laos. Three days later, *U.S. News & World Report* published "More Aid to Laos? A Report on What U.S. Is Doing There." On 24 October newspapers around the world carried word obtained from "informed allied sources" in Saigon that American warplanes in Laos had flown nearly twice the number of sorties logged by their counterparts in South Vietnam (500 daily in Laos; 250 in South Vietnam) during the first fifteen days of the month. Shortly thereafter, the *New York Times* printed a series of three reports by Henry Kamm on what it termed the "twilight war" in Laos.[13]

---

[11] Ibid.

[12] Msg, State 164793 to Vientiane, 27 Sep 69, sub: Change in Public Position on US Air Operations in Laos, and Msg, Vientiane 6653 to State, 29 Sep 69, sub: Some Factors Involved in Changing Public Positions in U.S. Air Ops in Laos, both in Pol 27 Viet S file, FAIM/IR.

[13] "Laos, The Unseen Presence," *Time*, 17 Oct 69, p. 39; "More Aid to Laos? A Report on What U.S. Is Doing There," *U.S. News & World Report*, 20 Oct 69, p. 16; Msg, Vientiane 7409 to State, 28 Oct 69, sub: Press Story on USAF Strikes in Laos, 334–71A374, box 1, WNRC; Henry Kamm, "U.S. Runs a Secret Laotian Army," *New York Times*, 26 Oct 69.

Despite that flurry of attention, the State Department continued to hold firm. When a correspondent for the *Los Angeles Times* requested information from the agency's Bureau of Public Affairs on U.S. defoliation operations along the Ho Chi Minh Trail, officials attempted to evade the question by contending that enemy propagandists had made charges of that sort for years. On one occasion, they said, the Communists had even alleged that the United States was spreading toxic chemicals when in fact crop dusters had been involved in the spraying of insecticides to save a rice crop. The response had no effect on the reporter. His incredulity obvious, he asked if the department actually intended to deny that American aircraft had spread herbicides in Laos. "We replied," the agency told Godley later, "that we had no comment in this regard."[14]

The flow of news stories continued into November. *Newsweek* criticized "amateurish attempts at concealment" during an article surveying the American involvement in Laos. Observing that hundreds of "Green Berets in mufti" played an active role in the fighting, the magazine quoted a U.S. diplomat in Vientiane who asked, "How can you hide all this? . . . It's like trying to hide an elephant under a handkerchief." Late in the month, Souvanna added an ominous note to what the press was saying by commenting publicly that the People's Republic of China had sent some 3,000 workmen and two infantry battalions armed with antiaircraft guns to build an all-weather road from its border, through Laos, toward Thailand.[15]

Nixon Compromises

With U.S. credibility on the subject declining and hard choices in the offing, President Nixon finally decided a change of policy was in order. At an 8 December 1969 news conference in Washington, he stated publicly for the first time that the United States was indeed conducting an interdiction campaign against enemy traffic along the Ho Chi Minh Trail in Laos. Although the American people were entitled to know as much as possible about their country's involvements abroad, he added nevertheless, "I do not think the public interest would be served by any further discussions."[16]

Queried on the development the next day, official spokesmen in Washington refused to elaborate on the president's remarks. The State and Defense Departments instructed the U.S. mission in Saigon to do the same. Should reporters seek additional information, public affairs officers were to

[14] Msg, State 187297 to Vientiane, 5 Nov 69, sub: Memorandum of Conversation With Bob Smith of *Los Angeles Times* Concerning Reports of Herbicides in Laos, DDI Laos 69–70 file.

[15] "Dilemma in Laos," *Newsweek*, 3 Nov 69, p. 43; "Laos, The Chinese Highwaymen," *Time*, 5 Dec 69.

[16] The president is quoted in *Facts on File*, 1969, 29: 791.

allow the president's statement to speak for itself and to avoid any further comment. Although the president had decided to be more forthcoming, the Office of the Joint Chiefs of Staff explained to Col. L. Gordon Hill, who had become director of Defense Information at the Pentagon in September, further admissions would have to wait until the North Vietnamese acknowledged that they were themselves involved in Laos.[17] The Public Affairs Adviser for the State Department's Bureau of East Asian and Pacific Affairs, Paul Neilson, added in a later memorandum to Hill that "As a matter of tactics in handling the press, we have tried to hold the line at stereotyped answers to questions to cut down probing. Our air activities in Laos are known to the press from numerous other sources. The only new facet would be a change in official U.S. government comment."[18]

Whatever the merits of those arguments in the abstract, the problem with Laos was too complicated to yield to half measures. During December 1969, for example, concern that the Nixon administration might attempt to broaden the war had surfaced in the Senate. By a vote of 73 to 17, a bipartisan majority of senators had attached a rider to a $69.3 billion defense appropriations bill forbidding use of the funds to finance the introduction of American ground combat forces into either Laos or Thailand. The legislators had worded the bill so that the stipulation would have no effect on U.S. air operations in Southeast Asia, but it was becoming clear that important members of Congress were unwilling to allow the United States to drift further into war.[19]

While that was happening, on 19 December an enemy surface-to-air missile battalion located in North Vietnam, out of the reach of American gunners, made a serious attempt to shoot down an American B–52 bomber flying over the Ho Chi Minh Trail near the strategic Mu Gia and Ban Karai Passes, the main transshipment points for enemy supplies moving into Laos from North Vietnam. The press never learned of the incident but, given congressional reservations and the sensitivities of Souvanna Phouma, the development so unnerved the Nixon administration that it banned B–52 strikes in Laos within range of North Vietnamese missile sites for over a month. The enemy used the time to increase by eightfold his air defenses in areas affected by the ban.[20]

[17] Msg, State 204579 to Vientiane, 9 Dec 69, DDI Laos Policy file. The new public affairs policy is in Msg, State 206270 to Vientiane, 12 Dec 69, and Memo, JCS for Col Hill, 2 Jan 70, sub: PA Policy on Air War in Laotian Panhandle, both in DDI Laos Policy file. General Abrams passed the policy to his command in Msg, MACV 3146 to All Commands, 19 Jan 70, DDI Laos Policy file.

[18] Memo, Paul Neilson, Public Affairs Adviser, State Department Bureau of East Asian and Pacific Affairs, for Col Gordon L. Hill [sic], Special Assistant for SEA, ASD PA, 14 Jan 70, sub: Proposed Change in U.S. Public Affairs Policy on U.S. Air Activity Over Laos, DDI Laos 69–70 file.

[19] "Senate Tries To Stop Further Involvement in Laos and Thailand," *Wall Street Journal*, 16 Dec 69.

[20] Msg, CINCPAC to Secretary of Defense, 27 Jan 70, sub: Public Affairs Policy on B–52 and KC–135 Operations in SEA, CMH files; Msg, Abrams MAC 1692 to McCain, 5 Feb 70, sub: Request for Strike Authorization, Abrams Papers, CMH.

Jerry Friedheim announces a "protective reaction strike" in North Vietnam.

Rather than lose more momentum, the United States resumed B–52 strikes in the area on 22 January 1970. Shortly thereafter, on 5 February, in order to preserve American freedom of action and the morale of air crews, General Abrams requested permission to begin air strikes against North Vietnamese missile sites and aircraft that constituted an immediate threat to U.S. air operations in Laos. Approved four days later, but only in areas south of 20 degrees north latitude and as a response to clearly defined enemy provocations, the attacks received the name "protective reaction strikes" to emphasize that they were wholly defensive in nature rather than an escalation of the war. In March the secretary of defense amplified the policy further by authorizing air strikes against aircraft control facilities in North Vietnam that had directed attacks by enemy jet aircraft against U.S. air operations outside of North Vietnam. Four conditions were to apply: an attack had to have occurred; the aircraft involved had to have operated from airfields south of 19 degrees north latitude; the target had to have participated in the attack; and the location of the strike itself had again to be south of 19 degrees north latitude.[21]

The possibility that the enemy might succeed in shooting down a B–52 continued to alarm the Nixon administration. A combination of inquisitive newsmen, widespread wreckage, and North Vietnamese victory claims, so the reasoning went, would pinpoint the location of the incident. An enemy propaganda campaign would ensue to censure U.S. infractions of the Geneva Agreements and to emphasize that the United States had never admitted to its operations in Laos. In short order, Daniel Henkin observed, the event would become "a public relations disaster."[22]

[21] Msg, Abrams MAC 1692 to McCain, 5 Feb 70, sub: Request for Strike Authorization; Msg, Wheeler JCS 01970 to McCain, Abrams, 9 Feb 70; Msg, Wheeler CJCS 3318 to McCain, 7 Mar 70. All in Abrams Papers, CMH.

[22] Draft Msg, Secretary of Defense to CINCPAC et al., 30 Jan 70, sub: Public Affairs Policy on B–52 and KC–135 Operations in SEA, DDI Air Incidents Policy file.

Under the circumstances, the Defense Department had little choice but to compose a contingency statement for release to the press as soon as possible after the loss of a B–52. Yet even then the old way of thinking asserted itself. Despite Henkin's avowals that any attempt to dissemble would be counterproductive, the U.S. embassy in Vientiane sought to have the statement amended to read "a U.S. B–52 was shot down . . . over the Vietnam-Laos border" rather than "over the Ho Chi Minh Trail." The Defense Department succeeded in having the change overruled.[23]

New Disclosures Force a Reappraisal

By mid-February 1970 the threat to official credibility presented by U.S. policies on Laos had reached crisis proportions. On the twelfth, alluding to a recent announcement that U.S. aircraft had struck North Vietnamese missile sites, Secretary Laird had attempted to reassure the American public that the policy of protective reaction represented a defensive measure rather than an expansion of the war. He had not gone into detail about how the United States intended to apply the policy, but a so-called ranking military source had immediately amplified his remarks for a *New York Times* reporter. Noting that the policy might include a preemptive attack on an enemy installation that had yet to fire upon American aircraft, the source noted that "If there is activity around an antiaircraft site that could be construed as a demonstrated threat . . . the planes are authorized to take action."[24] The resulting news story and others that followed concentrated on the policy as applied to North Vietnam, but there appears to have been little doubt in official circles that a connection to Laos might occur at any time.

On the same day that the *New York Times* story appeared, General Abrams notified his superiors that Pathet Lao pressure in northern Laos had become so great that Souvanna Phouma's forces could suffer a crippling blow within the next twenty-four to forty-eight hours. If that occurred they would lose control of the strategic Plaine des Jarres. Abrams continued that the Military Assistance Command had already expended a maximum number of tactical air sorties in the region, to no avail. A series of B–52 strikes thus seemed imperative.[25]

An earlier request by Abrams for a B–52 strike on the Plaine des Jarres had triggered, according to General Wheeler in Washington, "the

---

[23] Ibid. Also see Msg, CINCPAC to Secretary of Defense, 27 Jan 70, sub: Public Affairs Policy on B–52 and KC–135 Operations in SEA; Msg, Vientiane 630 to CINCPAC, 28 Jan 70, sub: Public Affairs Policy on B–52 and KC–135 Operations in SEA, CMH files.

[24] Msg, Defense 2226 to MACV, L. Gordon Hill to Col Joseph F. H. Cutrona, 12 Feb 70, sub: NY TIMES Story on SecDef's News Conference/Backgrounder, DDI SecDef Visit to RVN file.

[25] Msg, Abrams MAC 2040 to McCain, 13 Feb 70, Abrams Papers, CMH.

Pathet Lao gunner

most contentious hassle here in my experience."[26] Concerned that if the attack leaked to the press it might kindle more opposition than necessary in Congress, the White House, on that occasion, had refused permission. Yet with the situation in Laos deteriorating by the hour, the president had little choice. He approved the strike for the night of 17 February.[27]

The move caught the Pathet Lao by surprise and stalled their offensive. U.S. bomb damage assessment teams later reported that explosions from the attack had buried or fragmented so many of the enemy that it was impossible to conduct a thorough count of the dead. There was a shortage of drinking water over a broad area in the region, they added, because rotting cadavers had contaminated the region's streams.[28]

Word of what had happened leaked almost immediately to Walter Whitehead of UPI's Saigon bureau. The news stories that followed, citing "informed" or "military sources" in Saigon, so upset President Nixon that the Acting Chairman of the Joint Chiefs of Staff, Admiral Thomas L. Moorer, cabled Admiral McCain to request an investigation. The development, Moorer said, had seriously jeopardized the military's ability to gain approval for similar sensitive operations in the future. The situation seemed so grave by 5 March that General Wheeler informed McCain that

[26] Msg, Wheeler JCS 8843 to McCain, Abrams, 27 Jan 70, Westmoreland Message file, Jan 70, CMH.

[27] Msg, Adm Thomas Moorer, Acting CJCS, JCS 2610 to McCain, 18 Feb 70, Abrams Papers, CMH.

[28] Msg, Godley to McCain et al., 19 Feb 70, Abrams Papers, CMH.

the increasing sensitivity of U.S. operations in Laos had made it difficult to gain approval even for reconnaissance flights in the Plaine des Jarres. Only an urgent military requirement would do and the target under consideration had to constitute a serious threat to friendly forces.[29]

Under the circumstances, the first inclination of officialdom was once more to give as little ground as possible. Shortly after the leak to Whitehead, the State Department cabled the U.S. mission in Saigon to warn against any action on the part of field agencies to modify procedures established by higher authorities. Citing a whole series of recent disclosures in the press having to do with the shift of the preponderance of American air power to Laos, that message's authors emphasized that there had been no change of public affairs policy on the subject.[30]

General Abrams responded by dispatching an immediate circular to all of his commanders requesting "prompt and positive action" to close off information on Laos.[31] In a subsequent joint cable to the State Department that could have been written years before, Abrams and Bunker noted that "We should appreciate that we are confronted with . . . a large, energetic, enterprising and ingenious press corps." Those reporters knew

how to develop a news story and to utilize their organizations for that purpose. Any deviation in the regular pattern of our air operations here as reflected by the daily communique will result in queries to their colleagues in Thailand, Okinawa and Guam as well as to their in-country people near our air bases in Vietnam for a reading on USAF operational activity at those sites. For example, if the daily MACV communique shows none or only a small number of B–52 missions in SVN and a check with their colleagues in areas with B–52 bases reveals substantial number of mission launches, our imaginative press immediately finger Laos as the target. A check with their man in Laos can usually produce advice on the area of greatest military activity and the likely target.[32]

Abrams and Bunker continued that some of their subordinates had added to the problem by providing leaked background information to the press. A few had been motivated by a disagreement with official policy, but most had clearly acted out of a belief that the war in Laos was hardly as sensitive as it might have been in the past. "When our people read that President Nixon has acknowledged at a press conference that we are interdicting the Ho Chi Minh Trail, that Congressional committees are investigating U.S. military activities in Laos, or, . . . that Souvanna Phouma has talked to the press about our air activities in Laos, it is difficult for them to understand why they cannot talk about their personal

[29] Msg, Moorer JCS 2610 to McCain, 18 Feb 70; Msg, Wheeler JCS 3247 to McCain, 5 Mar 70, sub: Reconnaissance in PDJ Area, Abrams Papers, CMH.

[30] Msg, State 25128 to Saigon, 19 Feb 70, sub: Publicity on U.S. Air Operations in Laos, DDI Laos Policy file.

[31] Msg, MACV 9231 to All Commanders, 24 Feb 70, sub: Public Information Guidance on Air Operations, DDI Laos Policy file.

[32] Msg, Saigon 2764 to State, from Bunker and Abrams, 24 Feb 70, sub: Publicity on U.S. Air Operations in Laos, DDI Laos Policy file.

experiences." In that light, "it is most unlikely that further injunctions and reminders to our personnel against talking, despite our pointing out the political and legal implications for our foreign policy objectives, will result in halting leaks to the press."[33]

Bunker and Abrams conceded that there were valid reasons for the public affairs policies governing what official spokesmen could say about Laos. They nevertheless emphasized that the approach "is not capable of being carried out in a meaningful manner and serves only to lessen our overall credibility with the press, the Congress and the American people." At the least, they added, "we should consider the desirability of periodically backgrounding the media on a low-key basis . . . so that press reports are accurate and in proper perspective. . . . If we adhere to our present policy, then we should recognize that there will be press stories and that some of our people, for a variety of reasons, will feed information to the press despite our efforts."[34]

Abrams' and Bunker's message increased pressure for a reexamination of the U.S. government's public affairs policies on Laos, but telling arguments also came from the Air Force. Just a few days later, Secretary of the Air Force Robert Seamans noted in a memorandum to Laird that "If we are to continue our air operations in Laos, even at reduced levels, we are going to require substantial funding from the Congress and the underlying support of the American people. Because of the importance of these operations to our overall posture in Southeast Asia, it thus becomes in the national interest to be more candid publicly; otherwise I question how long we can maintain the necessary public support."[35]

A New Public Affairs Policy for Laos

Although the Nixon administration had ample evidence that a change of policy was necessary, the process of achieving it remained difficult. During the last week of February 1970 Assistant Secretary of Defense for Public Affairs Henkin, at the request of Secretary Laird, composed two different statements for possible release to the press that he felt would "alleviate any public concern over a hidden Vietnam-type war" in Laos. At that time, he told Laird that he suspected "difficulties in coordination." Apparently he experienced them. Neither statement was ever used.[36]

[33] Ibid.
[34] Ibid.
[35] Memo, Seamans for Secretary of Defense, 27 Feb 70, sub: U.S. Position in Southeast Asia, DDI Laos Policy file.
[36] Memo, Daniel Z. Henkin for ASD PA et al., n.d., sub: Proposed Statements on Laos. Henkin's comment to Laird is in Memo, Henkin for Secretary of Defense, n.d., sub: Proposed Statements on Laos. That the statements were never used is mentioned in the memo covering both documents. See MFR, Signed "Ginger," 2 Mar 70. All in DDI Laos 69–70 file.

In the end, on 6 March President Nixon nevertheless issued a public declaration on the U.S. involvement in Laos that achieved much of what the assistant secretary wanted by confirming the raid on the Plaine des Jarres and by acknowledging that American aircraft had been flying sorties against the Ho Chi Minh Trail for years. The level of American assistance to Laos had increased over time, Nixon said, in response to the aggression of North Vietnamese forces, which numbered 67,000, including 13,000 ground combat troops who had arrived in recent months. By contrast, the United States maintained no ground combat forces in Laos and had no plans for introducing them. Nixon continued that no American servicemen assigned to Laos had ever been killed in ground combat operations and that the number of U.S. personnel had remained steady over the previous year. In all, only 616 Americans were employed by the U.S. government in that country, with an additional 424 on contract or subcontract to U.S. agencies. Most of the contractors served as military advisers or in logistical functions. After the president's talk, sources at the White House revealed that U.S. casualties in Laos numbered about 300, with 193 presumed captured or missing. Aircraft losses over the course of the war totaled about 400.[37]

Following the announcement, the Defense Department instructed information officers in Saigon to tell reporters that they had nothing to add to what the president had said. "Any further information . . . will have to come from Washington (not repeat not the Office of the Secretary of Defense) or from the American Embassy in Vientiane."[38] The policy was only an interim measure, Henkin told Admiral McCain. "We will examine the possibility of acknowledging on a day to day basis whether bombing was conducted in Laos, to include services involved and type of aircraft. As you are no doubt aware such a change will in effect be a change in national policy and will require extensive coordination. I will do everything I can to develop an open and candid policy."[39]

The changes came more rapidly than Henkin expected. Shortly after the president's announcement, critics of the war in Congress began to allege that the statement had been a public relations ploy designed to publicize the few casualties that had occurred on the ground in northern Laos while failing to distinguish the many that had resulted from air operations. The president, they said, had also failed to mention casualties that had resulted from secret U.S. combat missions against the Ho Chi Minh Trail that had originated in South Vietnam. Partly in response to those complaints, the administration announced on 9 March that it would begin a new policy of announcing aircraft losses in Laos and any

---

[37] Msg, MACV 11093 to All Commands, 7 Mar 70, sub: Public Information Guidance on U.S. Involvement in Laos, DDI Laos Policy file. Also see *Facts on File*, 5–11 Mar 70, 30: 137.

[38] Msg, MACV 11093 to All Commands, 7 Mar 70, sub: Public Information Guidance on U.S. Involvement in Laos.

[39] Msg, Daniel Z. Henkin Defense 3403 to Adm John S. McCain, 9 Mar 70, sub: Public Information Guidance on U.S. Involvement in Laos, DDI Laos Policy file.

casualties that had resulted from enemy action against American personnel stationed in that country. For reasons of diplomacy, however, since the government of Laos had never received notification that the operations were occurring, casualties resulting from U.S. ground penetrations of Laos that originated in South Vietnam continued to be reported as part of the South Vietnamese total. In the same way, although the Nixon administration was willing to admit publicly that some 50 American civilian support personnel had been killed in Laos over the previous six years, it refused to discuss the details of incidents that had occurred prior to the president's inauguration in 1969. All the agencies concerned, the State Department later told Ambassador Godley, were attempting to develop accurate records on the subject, but information was often incomplete, especially when the causes of air crashes were in doubt.[40]

Seeing little reason to keep the policy secret, the Defense Department informed the press of what it was doing and why. The decision stood the administration in good stead shortly thereafter, when newsmen learned that some twenty American civilians had been killed at Phou Pha Thi in northern Laos during a 1968 enemy attack on a U.S. radar station. Questioned on the subject, White House spokesmen confirmed the incident but were able to divorce the president from what had happened on grounds that it had taken place "before this administration came into office." Reporters grumbled, but, lacking further details, said little more.[41]

Henkin cabled the new policy to the Military Assistance Command on 13 March. Although official spokesmen in Saigon would continue to release overall statistics on American casualties in Southeast Asia, he noted, the U.S. embassy in Vientiane would become the conduit for information on casualties among U.S. military personnel stationed in Laos.[42] As far as the air war in Laos was concerned, little was to be released beyond a series of general statements in the daily MACV communique that "Air Force, Navy, and Marine Corps aircraft yesterday continued interdictions along the Ho Chi Minh Trail in Laos" or, in the case of raids into the Plaine des Jarres or elsewhere, "flew combat support missions in Laos for Laotian forces." When the U.S. Air Force employed B–52s, a

---

[40] Memo, Melvin Laird for Secretary of the Air Force, 23 Mar 70, sub: U.S. Position in Southeast Asia, DDI Laos 69–70 file. The policy for Operation PRAIRIE FIRE is mentioned in Msg, Defense 3101 to CINCPAC, 13 Mar 70, DDI Laos Policy file. That the government of Laos had never been informed is in Msg, Vientiane 2343 to State, 2 Apr 70, Pol 27 Viet S file, FAIM/IR. For background on the positions of antiwar critics, see *Facts on File*, 5–11 Mar 70, 30: 138; Msg, Defense 3156 to MACV, CINCPAC, from ASD PA, 14 Mar 70, sub: Public Affairs Policy—U.S. Casualties in Laos, and Msg, State 39427 to Vientiane, 18 Mar 70, sub: Press Guidance on President's Laos Statement, both in DDI Laos 69–70 file.

[41] Msg, Defense 3156 to MACV, CINCPAC, from ASD PA, 14 Mar 70, sub: Public Affairs Policy—U.S. Casualties in Laos. Also see Excerpt from White House News Conference, 16 Mar 70, DDI Laos 69–70 file.

[42] Msg, Defense 3016 to CINCPAC, COMUSMACV, 13 Mar 70, sub: Public Affairs Policy—U.S. Military Casualties in Laos, DDI Laos Policy file.

statement might add that "B–52's participated in interdiction operations along the Ho Chi Minh Trail in Laos."[43] Air losses were to become public as soon as search-and-rescue operations had ended. The announcement was to include the military service involved; the type and model of aircraft; the date and time of loss, if possible; the approximate location, if possible; the cause of loss; and the number of killed, wounded, or captured. General Abrams passed the guidance to his commanders, with the proviso that none were to provide the press with explicit information on any operation in Laos until the Military Assistance Command had released it in Saigon.[44]

Ambassador Godley in Vientiane objected to Henkin's specifications as soon as he received them. Although he agreed that there was a need to release the names of U.S. personnel killed in Laos, he wanted to maintain as low a profile as possible for the portion of the war he directed. "I fear that press may deduce from breakdown of aerial activity authorized . . .," he said,

some idea of sortie magnitude. Ho Chi Minh Trail area (STEEL TIGER) receives a large number of sorties whereas rest of Laos (BARREL ROLL) receives less numerous sorties. Certain key Lao may have an inkling of the foregoing but we have always . . . fuzzed with knowledgeable Lao the magnitude STEEL TIGER activity lest they compare what we do to protect our men in South Vietnam and what we do to assist Lao soldiers in the rest of the country. I would be placed in a nearly untenable position if it became apparent to the Lao military and political leaders that we might be putting three times more the number of sorties into STEEL TIGER (where there are practically no . . . troops engaged) than we are putting into BARREL ROLL where . . . irregulars are actively engaged and are suffering percentagewise important casualties.

Godley added that revelation of the frequency of B–52 raids on the Ho Chi Minh Trail would increase Laotian pressure for more strikes in the northern portions of the country. "Up to now even the prime minister . . . believes (and is so encouraged) that STEEL TIGER activity is about that of BARREL ROLL. We never lie to him. We just do not . . . volunteer information. Let's leave it that way."[45]

Despite the ambassador's objections, Henkin's approach remained unchanged. Although word went out that "for the present, . . . there can be no announcements as to numbers of sorties or missions," the process of adjusting the policy also continued. On 26 March, for example, the Defense Department went so far as to propose the intermittent release of U.S. Air Force reconnaissance photographs showing enemy traffic on the

[43] Msg, Defense 3015 to CINCPAC, COMUSMACV, 13 Mar 70, sub: Public Affairs Policy—U.S. Air Operations Over Laos, DDI Laos Policy file.
[44] Msg, Defense 3017 to CINCPAC, COMUSMACV, 13 Mar 70, sub: U.S. Military Aircraft Losses Over Laos and Casualties Related Thereto, and Msg, MACV 12410 to All Commands, 15 Mar 70, sub: Public Affairs Guidance on U.S. Operations in Laos, both in DDI Laos Policy file.
[45] Msg, Vientiane 1801 to State, 15 Mar 70, DDI Laos Policy file.

Ho Chi Minh Trail and the results of the U.S. effort to stop it. The program went into effect on 30 April, after a brief delay to obtain the approval of Souvanna Phouma.[46]

Reporters Converge on Vientiane

Although planners at the State and Defense Departments understood that any change in policy on the war in Laos would attract the attention of the press, they failed to anticipate the reaction that developed. In normal times, a total of two correspondents and three stringers covered the news from Vientiane. By 9 March 1970 that number had grown to more than ninety. Within days it exceeded one hundred.

The dislocations that resulted not only strained the capacities of the U.S. embassy at Vientiane but also angered the arriving newsmen. Accustomed to the amenities provided by the U.S. Military Assistance Command in Saigon, the reporters were unprepared for the sometimes spartan arrangements that greeted them.[47] "We believe that majority of newsmen regularly covering Laos war understand we are doing our best," Ambassador Godley reported to the State Department at the time. For the rest, "as Herman Hickman once said of Yale alumni, 'We try to keep them surly but not mutinous.'"[48]

The first reporters who arrived in Vientiane were intent upon dissecting the statistics released by the president during his 6 March statement. They peppered Godley and his staff with questions about the number of American casualties in Laos, the size of the CIA contingent assigned to advise the Laotian armed forces, and the true dimensions of North Vietnam's involvement. They were particularly intrigued by discrepancies between the president's assertion that 67,000 North Vietnamese were present and earlier estimates released to the press that 50,000 were stationed in the country. Following instructions, embassy spokesmen refused to go beyond the president's statement but did point out that the difference between the president's figure and those released earlier was attributable to an enemy buildup, especially the arrival of elements of the *312th North Vietnamese Division*. Agencies in Washington, they added, had the benefit of a broad number of intelligence sources that undoubtedly provided the basis for the president's revised estimate.[49]

[46] Quote from Memo, Laird for Secretary of the Air Force, 23 Mar 70, sub: U.S. Position in Southeast Asia. Msg, Defense 4089 to CINCPAC, 26 Mar 70, and Msg, Vientiane 3069 to State, 30 Apr 70, both in DDI HCM Trail/Photos file.

[47] Msg, Vientiane 1748 to State, 12 Mar 70, and Msg, Vientiane 1659 to State, 9 Mar 70, sub: Press Queries on President's Laos Statement, both in DDI Laos 69–70 file.

[48] Msg, Vientiane 2235 to State, 28 Mar 70, sub: Vientiane Press Corps, DDI Laos 69–70 file.

[49] Msg, Vientiane 1659 to State, 9 Mar 70, sub: Press Queries on President's Laos Statement.

Physical dislocations brought on by the large number of newsmen present compounded the credibility problems that accompanied the embassy's unwillingness to be more forthcoming. To compensate for inadequacies in the local telephone system, for example, Godley had always provided visiting reporters with access to American military communications so that they could contact their bureaus in Hong Kong, Singapore, or Saigon with a minimum of difficulty. The presence of more than one hundred correspondents put an end to the practice. The calls tied up official circuits for hours. In the same way, to give newsmen the best information possible, Godley had at first made his principal assistants available to the press without reservation. With time, that practice also became burdensome and the ambassador began to funnel many of the interviews through his public affairs officers. News stories resulted in each case condemning so-called new restrictions on reporting in Vientiane.[50]

Realizing that journalists tend to suspect any attempt to cut off information, however justified, Godley worked hard to improve his mission's relations with the press. Since the news media would inevitably attempt to dissect U.S. policy in Laos, he strove, as he put it, "to guide the scalpel to the less vital parts of the body politic," but he also sought to satisfy reporters' demands for more and better information. Unable to provide the sort of facilities and access to transportation that the Military Assistance Command supplied the press in Saigon, he sponsored a number of field trips to areas that held a potential for good stories. One group of fifty reporters flew briefly over the road the Chinese were building in northern Laos. Others visited refugee centers and public works projects. A few rode into combat with Laotian Air Force fighter aircraft. Recognizing that the Laotian Ministry of Information was sorely deficient in its ability to deal with the American news media, Godley and his staff also kept in daily contact with the various members of the Laotian government. In that way, they were able to bring about a number of candid background sessions with prominent local military leaders and politicians.[51]

Reporters complained about the quality of the information they received, with Lou Cioffi of ABC News, for one, charging that a military post he had visited on tour was little more than "a Hollywood set."[52] Where some officials might have considered the press a nuisance to be avoided, however, Godley tended to value the insights highly observant reporters could sometimes provide. "One must draw a careful line," he told his superiors at the State Department, "between confining most contacts with journalists to the press officer and his associates and the importance of being able to obtain substantive feedback from the journalists . . .

---

[50] Msg, Vientiane 1748 to State, 12 Mar 70; Msg, Vientiane 1867 to State, 17 Mar 70, sub: Implications of New Disclosures and Press Interest in Laos, DDI Laos 69–70 file.
[51] Msg, Vientiane 2235 to State, 28 Mar 70, sub: Vientiane Press Corps.
[52] Msg, Vientiane 1693 to State, 10 Mar 70, DDI Laos 69–70 file.

The People's Republic of China helped North Vietnam build roads such as this in Laos.

which can be of direct use and pertinence to operational officers."[53] To that end, while attempting to keep newsmen out of areas where American advice and support to the Laotian government were too apparent, he saw little benefit in discouraging reporters from accompanying Laotian military operations into other regions, where the American role was less visible. Although relying increasingly on his public affairs officers, he also attempted to brief reporters personally, when the press of business allowed.[54]

If convinced that the press could be useful, Godley still believed that the corps of correspondents attempting to cover the war in Laos was far too large. Hard news from the battlefront, he told the State Department, tended to be anticlimactic. The only true combat stories that had appeared at all during March, he said, had come because of the ingenuity of two CBS and ABC television news teams. Traveling separately by river from Thailand to Paksé on the Plateau des Bolovens, the two crews had arrived shortly before an enemy attack and had filmed the action. Frequently lacking access to events of that sort because of poor transportation and the irregular nature of the war, Godley continued, most reporters exploited the few unambiguous details of the fighting that were available. The over-simplifications that resulted created a vicious circle in which inflated headlines whetted the appetites of editors for more. That, in turn, put pressure on newsmen in the field to find something else that was new or unique to report. The result, the ambassador concluded, reminded him of the *New Yorker's* tribute to military analyst George Fielding Eliot, "who could make collision of two row boats in Central Park Lake look like Battle of Jutland."[55]

With time, Laos lost some of its attractiveness to the press and the number of correspondents resident in Vientiane declined. Even so, contro-

---

[53] Msg, Vientiane 1867 to State, 17 Mar 70, sub: Implications of New Disclosures and Press Interest in Laos.
[54] Msg, Vientiane 2235 to State, 28 Mar 70, sub: Vientiane Press Corps.
[55] Ibid.

versy persisted. Those reporters who remained continued to complain about the quantity and quality of the news from Laos and to write exposes. *Newsweek*, for one, despite protestations from the Military Assistance Command, published an article during March on U.S. Special Forces penetrations of Laotian territory from bases in South Vietnam. The Nixon administration responded in kind, by continuing its criticism of the way the press reported. On 19 March Vice President Agnew thus made it a point to bring up Laos during a speech, observing that "Pulitzer prizes are not won by exposing the evils of Communism, as readily as by discrediting American elective officials."[56]

The situation was, however, still much improved. Although Godley and the State Department remained sensitive to news stories from Laos, the dire predictions they had made about what the Soviet Union and China would do and say never came to pass. Instead, by changing its policy, the Nixon administration had removed one of the longest standing impediments to official credibility and had enhanced public understanding of an aspect of the war that had been shrouded in secrecy for far too long.[57]

---

[56] Msg, Cutrona MAC 3549 to Hill, 18 Mar 70, sub: *Newsweek* Story on Laos, DDI Laos 69–70 file. Quote from [UPI], "Agnew Hits Media on Laos News," *Washington Post*, 20 Mar 70.

[57] Memo, Laird for Secretary of the Air Force, 23 Mar 70, sub: U.S. Position in Southeast Asia.

13

Cambodia Becomes an Issue

The decision to open up information on the war in Laos came at a moment of increasing anxiety for the Nixon administration. The antiwar movement was relatively quiet in the United States, but there were indications that its leaders had begun a search, as moratorium leader Sam Brown put it, for "something new" to galvanize continuing opposition to the war.[1] Meanwhile, a sense of unease, brought on at least in part by apprehension that the government had failed to control inflation, had come to predominate on Wall Street. A survey of market conditions at the end of April 1970 by White House aide Charles W. Colson showed the results. Mutual fund sales in the United States had come to a virtual halt, Colson told Haldeman, and the number of stock redemptions was so high that neither the New York nor the American stock exchanges could cope with the demand. Word from knowledgeable sources within the financial community was pessimistic. Several major trading firms would probably collapse if a genuine financial panic occurred, and many individual brokers lacked the assets necessary to shield themselves and their investors from more than minor market fluctuations.[2]

The word from South Vietnam was also less than encouraging. The U.S. mission in Saigon asserted in its January 1970 estimate of enemy strategy that, from all available evidence, the Communists remained confident in their ability to prolong the war until they won.[3] After a trip to South Vietnam, Kissinger's assistants at the National Security Council, Brig. Gen. Alexander Haig and Lawrence Lynn, came to the same conclusion. In a confidential briefing for Secretary Laird and others they asserted that progress appeared to have ended in South Vietnam. The enemy

[1] Msg, State 60703 to All Diplomatic Posts, 22 Apr 70, sub: Viet-Nam Highlights, Pol 27 Viet S file, FAIM/IR.

[2] Memo, Charles W. Colson for H. R. Haldeman, 28 Apr 70, White House Special files, Staff Member Office files, Haldeman, Staff Memos, April 1970, A-F, Nixon Papers.

[3] Msg, Saigon 1121 to State, 24 Jan 70, sub: Estimate of Enemy Strategy in 1970, Pol 27 Viet S file, FAIM/IR.

Charles Colson

was rebuilding his base of action; the PHOENIX program had thus far failed to weaken the deeply imbedded network of subversives that continued to support Communist ends; and the main bulwark against the enemy in the countryside, South Vietnam's irregular forces, remained untested and uneven in quality. Meanwhile, Haig observed ominously, the next increment of American withdrawals would cut deeply into the bone and sinew of allied fighting power.[4]

Secretary of Defense Laird repeated many of those conclusions in a 4 April memorandum to the president. If the war had subsided to lower levels of intensity than in the previous year, he observed, the effect was probably more the result of enemy decisions than American efforts. Although some analysts might see the development as a positive reaction to U.S. troop withdrawals, it might just as easily be the product of Hanoi's determination to wait until American forces had departed before launching another major attack. To buttress that conclusion Laird cited assertions by General Abrams that the enemy retained the ability to increase his activities at will. He also noted that the flow of supplies through Laos was undiminished and substantially higher than it had been in previous years. As for the South Vietnamese, they continued to lack effective military and civilian leadership and suffered from chronic instability.[5]

Although assessments such as the ones by Laird, Haig, and the State Department were for internal government consumption only, they found ready counterparts in the reporting of the Saigon correspondents. The 9 February issue of *Newsweek*, for example, made an extensive survey of the Vietnamization program. The magazine's editors emphasized that the United States had turned over 500 gunboats to the South Vietnamese Navy, that the U.S. Air Force was in the process of training 1,200 South Vietnamese pilots, and that 92 percent of the South Vietnamese people, by official estimate, lived in secure areas. Yet, they concluded that until the South Vietnamese armed forces faced the enemy on their own the "report card must remain a blank." Corruption was rampant in the officer corps,

[4] MFR, OASD SA, 5 Mar 70, sub: Meeting w. Sec. Laird, Thayer Papers, CMH.

[5] Memo, Laird for the President, 4 Apr 70, sub: Vietnam, 330–76–076, box 13, Viet 381, Laird Papers, WNRC.

and the individual soldier was so poorly paid that he had to become a proficient pilferer to survive. The results were plain to see in South Vietnam's delta region, where the 7th South Vietnamese Infantry Division seemed reluctant to engage the enemy, and the 21st South Vietnamese Infantry Division faced a serious problem with desertions. American troops filled the gaps, the magazine noted, providing logistics, flying combat support missions, and supplying medical evacuation facilities. The question was what would happen when they were gone?[6]

On 15 February CBS News filed a similar report but added that the situation had taken a toll on both American and South Vietnamese morale. South Vietnamese troops knew that they were "cursed" by their U.S. counterparts privately and "patronized" publicly with terms such as *Vietnamization*. The report so galled President Nixon that he asked the Defense Department to investigate. Laird's military assistant, Air Force Brig. Gen. Robert E. Pursley, responded that there was some truth to the allegation but that any attempt to turn the charge into a generalization affecting all Americans in South Vietnam was clearly a distortion.[7]

The assurances of subordinates notwithstanding, the tensions playing upon the president had their effect. During August 1970 Philip A. Odeen, Deputy Assistant Secretary of Defense for Systems Analysis, drew up a survey of Nixon's public statements on Vietnam since coming into office. He found that at the beginning the president had accentuated the negotiating process. By November 1969, however, that theme had evolved into a stress on Vietnamization, with considerable frustration also evident. By April 1970 the mood was one of anger, with Nixon clearly preoccupied with the need to preserve U.S. credibility before the world.[8]

The president's concern became even more apparent in the weeks that followed, when circumstances arose in South Vietnam laden with both opportunity and danger for the United States. Frustrated by his inability to move in the directions he sought but seeking to mold those developments to his purposes, Nixon made decisions that altered not only the context of the war but also the shape of events in South Vietnam for years to come.

Questions Arise About Cambodia

The situation that developed had its roots in Cambodia but took much of its meaning from the judgments of the U.S. military commanders

[6] "Vietnamization: Will It Work?," *Newsweek*, 9 Feb 70, p. 31.

[7] Memo, Brig Gen Alexander M. Haig for Brig Gen Robert Pursley, 18 Feb 70, sub: Report on Attitude of U.S. Troops Toward the ARVN, and Memo, Pursley for Haig, 2 Mar 70, sub: Report on Attitude of U.S. Troops Toward the ARVN, both in 330–76–067, box 98, Viet (South), Laird Papers, WNRC.

[8] Memo, Phil Odeen for Gen Pursley, 7 Aug 70, sub: Presidential Statements on Vietnam, 330–76–0076, box 12, Viet 092.2, Laird Papers, WNRC.

most concerned with the war, the Commander in Chief, Pacific, Admiral McCain, and General Abrams. Both officers were considerably more optimistic than many of the analysts providing information to the president. McCain, in particular, stressed that the effort in South Vietnam was going as well as could be expected and that Communist strength resulted mainly from "the continuing flow of Soviet aid to NVN, the logistic support available through the Cambodian LOC [line of communications], and the shift of air defenses to the NVN Panhandle." Those undertakings posed a serious threat to Vietnamization, McCain said, unless permission was forthcoming to neutralize them. He added that the United States should take steps to underscore North Vietnam's responsibility for continuation of the war by publicizing the enemy's strength. Besides preparing the American people for possible temporary setbacks, the approach would notify the enemy that the United States was aware of his plans and prepared for any contingency.[9]

Wheeler took no action on McCain's suggestion, apparently because a possibility remained that conditions might change in Cambodia. During Nixon's first year in office, the Cambodian government had overlooked American B–52 attacks on the sanctuaries. It had also quietly reopened diplomatic relations with the United States and had begun to highlight North Vietnamese violations of its neutrality by allowing the local press to publish stories on the subject. The situation seemed so hopeful, indeed, that during January 1970 General Abrams began contingency planning for a relatively modest and predominantly South Vietnamese offensive into the country. The operation was to occur if Cambodia broke formally with the Communists and North Vietnam responded aggressively.[10]

If the situation seemed more positive than in earlier years, the flow of supplies to the enemy through Cambodia's main port at Sihanoukville still continued, with, as McCain observed in a February message to Wheeler, "the knowledge, approval and active involvement of certain key Cambodian officials (both civilian and military). Often munitions are delivered to VC/NVA base areas under supervision of FANK [Forces Armees Nationales Khmeres—the Cambodian Army] officers and with FANK vehicles, drivers and guards." McCain continued that, since diplomatic pressure had failed to slow enemy efforts in Cambodia and the political climate in Southeast Asia and the United States largely precluded the sort of conventional ground attack on the sanctuaries that Abrams was planning, a program of "plausibly deniable, highly selective covert operations" seemed the most feasible course of action. Located near the supply system's primary point of entry into Cambodia and conducted by

[9] Msg, McCain to Wheeler, 28 Jan 70, sub: Vice President Agnew's Visit, Westmoreland Message file, Jan 70, CMH.

[10] See, for example, Msg, State 125290 to Paris, 28 Jul 69, sub: Cambodian Revelations of VC/NVA Presence in Svay Rieng, Pol 27 Viet S file, FAIM/IR; JCS History, 1969–1970, CMH files. Also see Msg, Abrams MAC 2439 to Wheeler and McCain, 22 Feb 70, Abrams Papers, CMH.

clandestine agencies, the effort would include either the bribing or black-mail of selected Cambodian military and civilian personnel; terrorist activities to "eliminate, kidnap, frighten" the people who managed or supported the system; sabotage to damage or destroy shipping facilities, convoys, and storage and transshipment points in Sihanoukville and along the enemy's line of communications; and "a subtle covert . . . pro-gram to develop a world wide adverse publicity and propaganda cam-paign against VC/NVA presence in Cambodia."[11]

When nothing came of the suggestion, McCain returned to the theme later in the month. Repeating his contention that covert operations were imperative, he warned that his analysts were predicting a major Communist offensive in April or May and that the Cambodian sanctuary had become "a primary strategic base essential to the enemy if he is to accomplish his overall objectives against Vietnamization." With Sihanouk at that time out of the country and the government in the hands of an ostensibly pro-American official, Sirik Matak, a timely opportunity for U.S. action existed. All that was necessary was that the move be clearly directed against the Communist North Vietnamese rather than the Cambodians themselves.[12]

Nothing again came of McCain's suggestion, in part because the Central Intelligence Agency refused to agree that the situation was as dras-tic as the admiral believed. Instead the Cambodians themselves took action. In Sihanouk's absence and in response to growing public concern about the extent of North Vietnamese activities on Cambodian soil, Prime Minister Lon Nol and Sirik Matak instituted a currency reform that deprived the Communists of money they had stockpiled to support their resupply effort. Then, on 8 March, with the connivance of the government, demonstrations against the Communists began in five towns located in Svay Rieng Province some fifty kilometers to the west of Saigon. The dis-turbances spread to Phnom Penh on 11 March, where rioters sacked the North Vietnamese and People's Republican Government (Viet Cong) embassies. As the agitation continued, Lon Nol reportedly sent envoys to Paris to present Sihanouk with documents that revealed a Communist plot to assassinate some 400 mid-level Cambodian officers who opposed the prince's policy of granting sanctuary to North Vietnamese forces. The mer-curial prince refused to meet with the emissaries and instead threatened his recalcitrant ministers with imprisonment and death. Shortly thereafter, on 18 March the Cambodian National Assembly voted unanimously to remove him as chief of state and to replace him with Lon Nol.[13]

[11] Msg, McCain to Wheeler, 3 Feb 70, sub: Cambodian Aid to the VC/NVA, Abrams Papers, CMH.

[12] Msg, McCain to Wheeler, 14 Feb 70, sub: Reduction of NVA Sanctuary in Cambodia, Abrams Papers, CMH.

[13] JCS History, 1969–1970, pp. 220–30. The details of the coup may be found in ibid., pp. 230–32. The plot is mentioned in Memo, Theodore L. Eliot, Jr., Exec Sec, for Henry Kis-singer, 29 Apr 70, sub: Daily Report on Cambodia No. 33, Pol 2 Cambodia file, FAIM/IR. Also see William Shawcross, *Sideshow* (New York: Simon and Schuster, 1979), pp. 114–22.

The fall of Sihanouk and the rise of a pro-American government in Cambodia prompted a reassessment by U.S. policy makers. At first, thinking centered on actions the United States could take to assist Cambodia. The provision of American advice, intelligence, air, and artillery support to the Cambodian armed forces came immediately to mind. On 25 March the president took the next logical step by requesting, without informing the State Department, that the Joint Chiefs of Staff draft a plan for an assault into Cambodia by either U.S. or South Vietnamese forces to relieve pressure on Phnom Penh if the city came under attack by the Communists. The Joint Chiefs passed the request to Abrams. On 28 March Admiral McCain took the idea to its logical conclusion by suggesting that, regardless of developments in Phnom Penh, the United States should move against the main threat to Vietnamization, the enemy's sanctuaries along the border. In addition to authorizing commanders to direct artillery fire and air strikes into Cambodia whenever necessary, the policy would provide expanded authority for American and South Vietnamese forces to cross the border in hot pursuit of fleeing enemy units and authorize small spoiling attacks to preempt enemy operations in South Vietnam.[14]

Upon receiving the president's request Abrams submitted the plan his staff had already drafted. On 30 March, again at the president's bidding, he submitted a second set of plans, this time for nearly simultaneous, combined U.S.–South Vietnamese operations against enemy base areas in the so-called Parrot's Beak region of Cambodia, just to the west of Saigon in Cambodia's Svay Rieng Province, and COSVN headquarters in the Fishhook, the region west of Loc Ninh in Cambodia. In the new plan Abrams endorsed the idea of an attack into the Fishhook. An operation in that area, he said, would have a significant impact on any Communist thrust against Phnom Penh. Besides disrupting the enemy's command and control elements and demolishing his logistical installations, it might even, as the president hoped, eliminate COSVN headquarters, the main center of supervision for enemy efforts in the southern portion of South Vietnam.[15]

As talk progressed, Secretary Laird became increasingly concerned. Receiving Abrams' first plan on 26 March, he requested information on the size of the force to be employed, the cost of the operation, its impact

---

In the years since Lon Nol's coup there has been much speculation about the extent of American involvement. What seems clear, if McCain's messages to Wheeler are any indication, is that the United States gave little thought to overthrowing Sihanouk himself but that other Cambodians who were deeply involved in trafficking with the Communists might have been at risk. The names of Lon Nol, for example, and of his brother Lon Nom surfaced frequently in U.S. intelligence reports on the subject. So did those of other prominent government officials. See Department of the Army, Office of the Assistant Chief of Staff for Intelligence, The Role of Cambodia in the NVN-VC War Effort, 1964–1970, 13 Apr 71, pp. 18, 392, 394.

[14] JCS History, 1969–1970, pp. 232–33.

[15] Msg, Abrams MAC 4199 to McCain, 30 Mar 70, Abrams Papers, CMH. Also see JCS History, 1969–1970, pp. 234–35.

on other allied programs, and whether it might impede the progress of Vietnamization. Whatever objections his questions revealed appear to have been lost in the general commotion. The State Department, for its part, received no formal word that the military was planning a possible operation into Cambodia until 27 March, when Abrams obtained authority from Wheeler to inform Bunker. Even then, only the ambassador was authorized to know. In briefing him, Abrams was instructed to stress the need for absolute secrecy and to explain that Secretary Rogers would be informed at an appropriate moment.[16]

Even before Abrams spoke with Bunker he had discussed the combined aspects of the operation with the Chief of the South Vietnamese Joint General Staff, General Cao Van Vien. Vien and his subordinates likewise saw the possibilities inherent in the overthrow of Sihanouk. In the days following the coup they began to meet regularly with their Cambodian counterparts. As they did, an increasing number of reports began to appear in official channels to the effect that units of the two armies were occasionally coordinating operations along the border. At first, the South Vietnamese appear to have confined their activities to providing artillery and air support for Cambodian units in combat with the enemy. With time, however, they became bolder. Their forces, minus American advisers, began to attack across the border. On 27 March a South Vietnamese Army battalion penetrated some three kilometers into Cambodia, where it claimed fifty-three enemy dead.[17]

The operation alarmed the White House, which immediately cabled Ambassador Bunker to warn that continued South Vietnamese cooperation with Cambodian forces might play into the hands of those in Congress and elsewhere who claimed that the United States was being drawn into an expanded war. In that sense, the risk of losing domestic support for the president's Vietnam policies might outweigh the benefits to be gained from cross-border operations. Shortly thereafter, Secretary Rogers instructed Bunker to urge Thieu to curtail further attacks until all concerned could formulate an agreed-upon policy. Thieu immediately complied with the request. In the negotiations that followed, the Nixon administration agreed to withdraw its objections to cross-border operations by the South Vietnamese if they would abide by two restrictions: they were to make certain that their efforts remained at the levels prevalent prior to 29 March and they were to continue to coordinate their activities with the Cambodians. Thieu agreed. The new policy went into effect on 1 April.[18]

The South Vietnamese reestablished their operations in Cambodia shortly thereafter, but the restrictions Nixon laid down appear to have carried little weight. On 5 April a South Vietnamese armored cavalry contingent charged into Cambodia along with two battalions of infantry and close air support. The operation occurred at the request of Cambodian

[16]JCS History, 1969–1970, pp. 234–35.
[17]Ibid., pp. 235–37.
[18]Ibid., p. 328.

military leaders and uncovered a large cache of enemy documents and weapons but still agitated Secretary Laird. Apprehensive that continued high profile attacks into Cambodia would fire opposition at home, he sent a memorandum to the Joint Chiefs complaining that the South Vietnamese had gone too far. He had agreed to limited border operations, he said, because failure to allow them might have proved "detrimental to our own forces and the US goal in SVN." Even so, "we must tread a narrow line between the Scilla and Charybdis of permitting the South Vietnamese to do too little . . . and of encouraging them to do too much."[19]

Laird requested that Wheeler inform General Abrams of his concern. Abrams responded immediately that the South Vietnamese appeared to have handled their activities in Cambodia with "sensitivity to the political forces involved." To avoid embarrassment to the government of Lon Nol, which occupied a position advantageous to the United States because of the problems it caused for the Viet Cong and North Vietnamese, he advised nevertheless that "we should not talk with press about these operations."[20]

Managing Relations With the News Media

If Abrams believed that a policy of silence would succeed in obscuring the operations, he was mistaken. For although the number of newsmen resident in South Vietnam had diminished as the pace of American withdrawals had increased, the Saigon correspondents remained, as Col. L. Gordon Hill put it in a 1 April briefing for the Army Policy Council at the Pentagon, "as pervasive and aggressive as ever." They and their publishers seemed to be paying less attention to the war, Hill continued, recalling his own experience as chief of the MACV Office of Information during 1969, but the appearance of anything out of the ordinary had the effect of "throwing a few pounds of raw meat to a pack of starving hyenas." The press corps in South Vietnam was "a diverse bunch" that ranged from scrupulously honest newsmen to those who would write "anything for a buck." Even so, certain types of incidents still seemed to unite them all against the government. "Anytime it appeared to newsmen that they were prevented from going into a particular area, such a situation was a loser all the way. . . . Anytime a commander, a headquarters, or a unit would not talk with a newsman who had questions about something, the resulting press story was invariably worse than it would have been." None of this was new, Hill concluded. It happened in the United States as well. "But we continue to re-learn old lessons."[21]

[19] Memo, Laird for Wheeler, 6 Apr 70, sub: South Vietnam/Cambodia Border Operations, OCJCS 091 Cambodia, 1 Jan–20 Apr 70, quoted in JCS History, 1969–1970, p. 239.

[20] Msg, Abrams MAC 4587 to McCain, 8 Apr 70, Westmoreland Message file, CMH.

[21] Presentation by Col L. Gordon Hill, Jr., OASD PA, to the Army Policy Council, 1 Apr 70, sub: The Press in Vietnam, copy in CMH files.

The soundness of Hill's warning became clear in the days that followed, as the press began to devote major attention to the situation in Cambodia. So many newsmen flocked to Phnom Penh and moved into the countryside in search of action that at times, according to Glenn Currie of the *Washington Daily News*, "there seemed . . . to be as many foreign newsmen and photographers as Cambodian soldiers." Vying for stories but lacking the protection provided by the Military Assistance Command in South Vietnam, which had always briefed newsmen on battle conditions and allowed them to travel in the relative safety of U.S. helicopters, the reporters took many chances. The only alternative, as American involvement in Cambodia grew, was an uninformative daily briefing by Cambodian government spokesmen who passed along little news of value but were delighted to receive updated word of events from those reporters who had just returned from the field. Two freelancers on assignment for *Time* and CBS News, Sean Flynn and Dana Stone, were the first to vanish. They disappeared into the hands of Communist forces while traveling alone by motorcycle along a remote country road. Fifteen more followed during the next month. Among the few ever to return were Richard Dudman of the *St. Louis Post-Dispatch* and Elizabeth Pond of the *Christian Science Monitor*. By the end of the war in 1975, a total of twenty-five correspondents would be listed as missing or dead in Cambodia.[22]

Although under pressure from both the Communists in the field and Cambodian censors in Phnom Penh, the reporters had no problem in constructing an outline of what was happening. Interviewing a variety of sources in many locations across the country, they learned almost immediately that the South Vietnamese were conducting major attacks into Cambodia. Correspondents, for example, spoke with a district chief in Svay Rieng Province who expressed great happiness that the operations were occurring and avowed that American aircraft and artillery were participating. The inquiries that revelation sparked prompted a cable from the U.S. interest section in Phnom Penh to the State Department requesting information. "I have received virtually no info from Saigon about what is happening," the concerned charge, Lloyd Rives avowed. "(Perhaps there is no frontier, perhaps there is no info)." If the United States had, in fact, decided to intervene, Rives warned, the move might "place Cambodian Government in embarrassing position where it may well have to protest. News will also be most welcome to Sihanouk, CHICOMS and other friends," who were bound to use it to justify their own depredations.[23]

---

[22] Glen Currie, "Censors Hard on Newsmen," *Washington Daily News*, 1 May 70; "Beyond the Checkpoint," *Newsweek*, 15 Jun 70; "A Bad Trip," *Newsweek*, 20 Apr 70; "Cambodian Perils High for Newsmen," *New York Times*, 17 May 70. For a list of the lost reporters, see Braestrup, *Big Story*, 1:iii.

[23] Msg, Phnom Penh 423 to State, 4 Apr 70, retransmitted in Msg, Paul M. Kearney, OCJCS, JCS 4624 to McCain, Abrams, 4 Apr 70, Abrams Papers, CMH. Also see Msg,

In the same way, when the Cambodians, in an outburst of xenophobia and fear, massacred some of the 600,000 ethnic Vietnamese resident in their country and began to drive many of the remainder away from their homes and into South Vietnam, correspondents counted the bloated bodies of more than four hundred dead floating in the Mekong River and reported the event in their dispatches. The news infuriated the South Vietnamese government, which was involved in a sensitive transfer of captured enemy arms to the Cambodian armed forces. In the end, General Abrams persuaded Thieu to continue the operation, but only after making the point that South Vietnam's own best interests were at stake.[24]

The Military Assistance Command had less difficulty dealing with suspicions that American forces might participate in the attacks. Newsmen accompanying American units on the border of South Vietnam could see for themselves that U.S. forces were under strict orders to refrain from entering Cambodia and that the aircraft crossing the border were South Vietnamese in origin. Their dispatches reflected that fact. On 17 April, for example, the Associated Press reported a massive South Vietnamese and American military buildup along the Cambodian border but observed pointedly that there was no evidence of armed American forays.[25]

Although the Military Assistance Command managed to quell many of the misgivings of the press, officials remained reluctant to say anything more than necessary, apparently in response to Lon Nol's desire to preserve at least a facade of neutrality for his government in case the Communists proved willing to make some sort of accommodation. Thus, when the South Vietnamese decided to make a major incursion into Cambodia on 14 April, the American commander in the adjoining region of South Vietnam, Lt. Gen. Julian Ewell, specified that the members of his command were to discourage press coverage. In the same way, when General Wheeler authorized a lengthy series of B–52 strikes in Cambodia, he stipulated that all official reporting was to be transmitted by backchannel and ordered public affairs officers to respond to queries from the press with a cover story describing the operation as a "protective reaction" to threats against American forces in South Vietnam. As late as 22 April, when the III Corps commander, Lt. Gen. Do Cao Tri, expressed concern about negative press coverage and asked what to do, American military advisers counseled against any form of harassment but still advised him to deny that his forces were engaged in cross-border operations. When newsmen discovered that the South Vietnamese were shipping captured enemy arms to Cambodia and applied at the U.S. mission in Phnom Penh

Phnom Penh 447 to State, 7 Apr 70, retransmitted in Msg, State 52067 to Saigon, 9 Apr 70, General Abrams' Personal file 27, CMH.

[24] JCS History, 1969–1970, p. 243.

[25] [AP], "Viet Allies Mass Near Cambodia," 17 Apr 70, unattributed newspaper clipping, CMH files; JCS History, 1969–1970, p. 243.

290

for further information, official spokesmen at the scene took the same approach. They denied the allegation.[26]

With time, the South Vietnamese government, the Nixon administration, and the Military Assistance Command began to give ground for the sake of credibility. Instead of denying outright that they were operating in Cambodia, South Vietnamese spokesmen gradually adopted a far more suitable policy of no comment on the subject. In the same way, White House Press Secretary Ron Ziegler admitted on 23 April that deliveries of captured enemy arms had gone to Cambodia with U.S. knowledge. He justified the move as an attempt to cope with an emergency. Meanwhile, U.S. field commands near the South Vietnamese border handled newsmen with the utmost propriety. They indicated that correspondents were welcome at U.S. fire bases in the area and offered helicopter transportation to move them there. Those advances were hardly satisfying to newsmen. The Nixon administration and the South Vietnamese government released little further information, and reporters who traveled to fire bases learned immediately upon arrival that any attempt to leave an American compound might result in detention by the South Vietnamese, who controlled the roads.[27]

The consequences of the policy were readily apparent in the news media, where the attempt to give the operations a low profile became, as Hill had warned, almost as much of a story as anything occurring in the field. During the 17 April edition of the CBS Evening News, for example, a filmed report appeared in which a newsman seeking permission to enter Cambodia confronted an American military policeman who barred the way. "ARVNs can go into Cambodia but no GI's, no civilians, no Americans," the soldier said. "But we have ARVN press cards," the reporter responded. "That doesn't mean anything. You are an American citizen. They [the South Vietnamese] don't want anybody near the border. They don't want anybody in there right now."[28] In another story, an AP reporter described the military buildup on South Vietnam's border and the passage of dozens of armored personnel carriers and tanks into Cambodia. The newsman then inserted a statement that "The U.S. command in Saigon has sent a message to all subordinate commands and province and district advisers ordering them to make no comments on the Cambodian situation."[29]

---

[26] Msg, Lt Gen Ewell, CG, IIFFV, HOA 843 to Maj Gen Bantz, CG, 25th Inf Div, 12 Apr 70; Msg, Wheeler JCS 5405 to Abrams, 20 Apr 70; and Msg, Lt Gen Davison, CG, IIFFV, HOA 939 to Abrams, 22 Apr 70. All in Abrams Papers, CMH. Msg, Phnom Penh 613 to State, 23 Apr 70, retransmitted in Msg, State 60712 to Saigon, 23 Apr 70, General Abrams' Personal file 27, CMH.

[27] Msg, State 61525 to Phnom Penh, 24 Apr 70, sub: Delivery of AK–47 Rifles to Cambodia, General Abrams' Personal file 27, CMH. Also see MFR, U.S. Department of State, n.d., sub: Chronology, Cambodia, 7/7/70–8/7/70, Pol 27 Camb file, FAIM/IR; Msg, Abrams MAC 5493 to Wheeler, McCain, 25 Apr 70, sub: Press Guidance for Operations in Cambodia, Abrams Papers, CMH.

[28] CBS Evening News, 17 Apr 70, *Radio-TV-Defense Dialog.*

[29] [AP], "Viet Allies Mass Near Cambodia."

The President Weighs His Options, April 1970

Publicly, the Nixon administration remained on the upbeat. During a 20 April television address on the war, the president said little about Cambodia. Instead he asserted that gains in training and equipping the South Vietnamese had "substantially exceeded our original expectations." Communist activity had increased in a number of areas, especially in Laos, but enemy force levels had declined in South Vietnam. With Vietnamization going so well, the removal of an additional 150,000 American troops from South Vietnam by the spring of 1972 thus seemed well justified. Nixon finished by commenting that there were, of course, risks: "If I conclude increased enemy action jeopardized our remaining forces in Vietnam, I shall not hesitate to take strong and effective measures to deal with that situation."[30]

Privately, the information reaching the White House was much more somber. Intelligence reports indicated that the enemy had responded to the rise of Lon Nol by systematically cutting all of the major roads and waterways leading into Phnom Penh. Few analysts believed that the Communists intended to take physical control of the city. Instead, they appeared to be cultivating the countryside with a view to developing an indigenous force that would ultimately compel the government of Lon Nol to capitulate. The American charge in Phnom Penh, Lloyd Rives, was particularly pessimistic. On 21 April he cabled the State Department to suggest that his superiors consider what the United States should do if the city fell. With Communist forces closing in, he questioned whether it was wise to continue installing expensive communications equipment in the U.S. embassy. Only massive intervention by the United States and South Vietnam, he said, seemed likely to save the situation.[31]

The Chief of Staff of the Army, General Westmoreland, was equally concerned. The Cambodian armed forces were untrained for operations above the platoon level, he told Secretary Laird, and apparently unable to stop the advances of even small enemy units. In that light, the captured AK47 rifles the United States and South Vietnam were providing would do little good. Outright division-size attacks into Cambodia seemed the only solution. When the North Vietnamese and Viet Cong had moved out of their sanctuaries into the Cambodian countryside, they had exposed themselves to attack from the rear, probably in the belief that the United States would do little to deter them. The South Vietnamese armed forces might exploit the vulnerability that resulted by launching immediate attacks into enemy base areas to destroy headquarters and com-

[30] White House News Release, 20 Apr 70, sub: Statement by the President of an Update Report on Vietnam, DDI Cambodia Opns Backup file.

[31] Kissinger, *The White House Years*, p. 487. See, for example, Memo, Westmoreland CM–5063–70 for Secretary of Defense, 21 Apr 70, sub: Courses of Action With Regard to Cambodia, Westmoreland History file 37, CMH; Msg, Phnom Penh 582 to State, 21 Apr 70, Abrams Papers, CMH.

munications facilities, to seize supplies, and to break up remaining enemy troop concentrations. It would be unnecessary for American forces to cross the border with the South Vietnamese. All that was required, Westmoreland said, was a relaxation of a few political restraints to allow for limited American logistical and artillery support for the operation.[32]

Admiral McCain supported Westmoreland's position. Time was short, he told Wheeler. Although there were political problems, the United States had within its grasp an opportunity both to shore up Lon Nol and to break Hanoi's hold on its Cambodian bases. Those moves would have a decisive impact on the enemy's aggression in South Vietnam. The Communists could never sustain their war in the southern portions of the country without the supplies and shelter that Cambodia's ports and border areas provided.[33]

President Nixon had apparently already reached the same conclusion. On the morning before he gave his optimistic television speech, his chief of staff, H. R. Haldeman, remarked in his notes of a morning meeting at the White House that "P [the president] really pushing on strong moves in Laos & Cambodia [—] hit all the sanctuaries."[34] By 22 April General Westmoreland could inform Abrams and McCain that the president was so concerned about the situation in Cambodia that he might relax some of the constraints under which the military had thus far operated. "If this happens," he said, "we should be prepared to take advantage of the opportunity."[35]

Nixon authorized shallow cross-border attacks by division-size South Vietnamese forces on the same day that Westmoreland's message arrived in Saigon. He permitted U.S. tactical air and artillery support for those operations but backed away from any commitment of U.S. ground combat units. "As you are well aware, there are some strong dissenting opinions in high levels of our government as to the extent of U.S. involvement," the Acting Chairman of the Joint Chiefs of Staff, Admiral Moorer, told Abrams and McCain. "However, highest authority [the president] feels very strongly that a Communist takeover of Cambodia will place Vietnamization program in serious jeopardy."[36]

The South Vietnamese were at first disinclined to commit troops to areas in Cambodia that posed little direct threat to their forces, but Abrams succeeded in overcoming their reluctance. On 23 April the general submitted a plan for a large-scale South Vietnamese attack into the Parrot's Beak. President Nixon approved the operation the same day, with

[32] Memo, Westmoreland CM–5063–70 for Secretary of Defense, 21 Apr 70, sub: Courses of Action With Regard to Cambodia.

[33] Msg, McCain to Wheeler, 22 Apr 70, Abrams Papers, CMH.

[34] Handwritten Note, H. R. Haldeman, 20 Apr 70, White House Special files, Staff Member Office files, Haldeman, box 41, H Notes [April 1–May 5, 1970] part 1, Nixon Papers.

[35] Msg, Westmoreland JCS 5495 to McCain, Abrams, 22 Apr 70, Abrams Papers, CMH.

[36] Msg, Moorer JCS 5634 to Abrams, McCain, 23 Apr 70, quoted in JCS History, 1969–1970, p. 250.

a proviso, as Moorer put it, that "our objective is to make maximum use of ARVN assets, so as to minimize U.S. involvement, and to maintain lowest possible U.S. profile. . . . U.S. advisors in Cambodia will be restricted to those required to control U.S. aircraft if and when introduced."[37]

Press guidance went to Abrams two days later, but only after considerable deliberation and much jockeying between the president and his advisers, on the one hand, and public affairs professionals, on the other. "The first order at the meeting this morning with our number one boss was," Wheeler explained to Abrams, "no press, no photographers, no public relations personnel to observe these operations. Of course this is an order that is impossible to execute and we are trying to get it boiled down simply to maximum effort to achieve minimum press exposure. We recognize that a flurry of activity aimed at completely eliminating press coverage would be counter productive."[38]

Public affairs officers succeeded in moderating the president's wishes but only to a degree. The guidance that went out to the Military Assistance Command avoided the Draconian measures Nixon and his advisers had contemplated but was clearly designed to tell no more about the operation than absolutely necessary. "It is hoped," Admiral Moorer told Abrams, "that publicity can be handled in as low key as possible, keeping . . . within pattern heretofore followed with respect to more shallow cross border operations. . . . It is hoped that all practicable will be done to prevent public media representatives from accompanying forces." Once the extent of the operation became evident, Moorer continued, Thieu and his government were to be prepared to make a forthright statement emphasizing that they had no intention of occupying Cambodian territory and were taking steps to assure the humane treatment of the country's population. As for the government of Cambodia, "We cannot and should not expect Lon Nol to state that he asked for or welcomed the operation, but would hope he would say that, while he regretted this incursion into Cambodian territory, he recognized the necessity that brought it about."[39]

General Abrams responded to the guidance by noting that the South Vietnamese were taking action to keep correspondents out of border areas. "We have not participated in this and should not change our position," he said, "because it would introduce a new factor and thus indicate something different." Instead, reporters would be allowed to travel by helicopter to U.S. fire bases in the region but would continue to find it difficult to enter zones controlled by the South Vietnamese. If they asked about American participation in the operation, command spokesmen would respond with a no comment. That would cause speculation but would fail to confirm their suspicions. Once the South Vietnamese

[37] JCS History, 1969–1970, p. 250; Msg, Moorer JCS 5623 to McCain, Abrams, 23 Apr 70, sub: Operations in Cambodia, Abrams Papers, CMH.
[38] Msg, Chief of Naval Operations (CNO) to COMUSMACV, CINCPAC, Moorer to Abrams and McCain, 25 Apr 70, Abrams Papers, CMH.
[39] Msg, Moorer JCS 5636 to Abrams, 25 Apr 70, Abrams Papers, CMH.

Moorer and Nixon

government issued its statement and the United States followed with one of its own, Abrams concluded, the press would have a relatively complete picture of what was going on.[40]

The Idea of a Combined Operation Takes Shape

Although the president had decided in favor of the Parrot's Beak operation, he remained troubled. The attack, from his viewpoint, possessed political dangers of large proportion. "I have been enjoined," General Wheeler thus told Abrams privately, alluding to the abortive U.S. attempt to launch an invasion of Cuba in 1961, "to reiterate the president's concern that, if the operation fails, he will be subjected to the same kind of criticism evoked by the Bay of Pigs." Wheeler did not question Abrams' abilities, but he doubted those of some of the South Vietnamese commanders involved. Those officers had been "timid and slow in their reactions to tactical situations," he said. "I trust that you and your U.S. commanders will be able to help them overcome these faults."[41]

If the president was apprehensive, however, he was even more intrigued by the idea of somehow dealing a telling blow to the enemy. "I

[40] Msg, Abrams MAC 5493 to Wheeler, McCain, 25 Apr 70, sub: Press Guidance for Operations in Cambodia.
[41] Msg, Wheeler JCS 5711 to Abrams, 25 Apr 70, Abrams Papers, CMH.

have been queried several times in the last couple of days," Wheeler told Abrams, "regarding my views as to the usefulness of an operation against Base Area 352/353 [the Fishhook]. I have consistently responded that I favor the operation because it is targeted against the normal operating area of COSVN, and I can imagine no greater help to us than the disruption of their command and control of operations in South Vietnam, not to mention the very substantial logistic and administrative base located within the target area."[42] Basing his assessment on his own conversations with the president and those of others, Wheeler believed that there was "better than a so-so chance that the COSVN operation, using both ARVN and US forces, will be ordered at an early date." He told Abrams that

During the course of our discussions, on several occasions the highest authority spoke of: the need to get the job done using whatever is necessary to do so; these operations absolutely must succeed; at last the military has a chance to do it their way; operations must be fast and surgical; use all the force necessary; if we get caught with our hands in the cookie jar we must be sure to get the cookies, etc. He suggested, partly in jest, that Abe "act as a Patton rather than a Montgomery."[43]

In the end, concerned that the objective was too important to place sole reliance on the South Vietnamese, who appeared more and more reluctant to enter COSVN's dangerous redoubt in the Fishhook without American participation, President Nixon decided to gain as much as he could by launching a double incursion. South Vietnamese forces would conduct the attack into the Parrot's Beak as planned, he noted in his 26 April decision, but a combined U.S.–South Vietnamese force would penetrate Base Area 352/353. The president sought to deflect criticism by specifying that the American attack would penetrate no more than thirty kilometers into Cambodia and by insisting, in the days that followed, that Military Assistance Command spokesmen place as much stress as possible on the South Vietnamese portions of the operation. There was likewise to be a strong public affairs offensive and no negative talk. "Even if ARVN screw up," Haldeman paraphrased the president in his notes of a meeting on 27 April, "keep word out of success."[44]

The decision was nevertheless controversial from the start. Although Westmoreland supported the idea of South Vietnamese and American incursions into Cambodia, he opposed the commitment of large numbers of American troops because that hardly seemed necessary. General Abrams appears to have been more open to the idea, but, if he favored the use of American forces, he wanted them employed selectively and against only the most lucrative targets. Rogers and Laird, meanwhile, opposed

[42] Ibid.

[43] Msg, CNO to COMUSMACV, CINCPAC, Moorer to Abrams and McCain, 25 Apr 70.

[44] JCS History, 1969–1970, pp. 254–55. Quote from Haldeman, Handwritten Note of Meeting With Kissinger, 0915, 27 Apr 70, White House Special files, Staff Member Office files, Haldeman, box 41, H Notes [April 1–May 5, 1970] part I, Nixon Papers.

the idea emphatically. Both men had argued vehemently against, as Moorer put it, "introducing even a single U.S. soldier into Cambodia."[45] Laird had gone along with the Parrot's Beak operation with so much reluctance, indeed, that the president had instructed Kissinger as early as 20 April to send correspondence on the subject by backchannel rather than through the secretary. He refused, as Haldeman recorded in his notes of the meeting, "to let Laird kill this by pulling out too fast." Apparently for the same reason, the president also neglected to inform Laird and Rogers of his decision to enter the Fishhook until the day after he made it.[46]

Learning of the decision in favor of a joint operation, Rogers took the lead in attempting to change the president's mind. The secretary was unconvinced that the situation in Cambodia was as dangerous as it seemed to McCain and others. His analysts at the State Department contended that the alternative was perhaps worse and that the Communists would prefer to preserve their source of supply in Cambodia through an accommodation with Lon Nol rather than risk overthrowing the general by force. "A significant expansion of the scale of South Vietnamese operations would tighten the bind in which the Communists find themselves," they said, "and increase the prospects of radical Communist action vis-a-vis Phnom Penh." If South Vietnamese operations were restricted to border areas, the Communists would adapt by shifting their zone of control farther to the west but would do little more to destabilize the Cambodian government. Extensive allied operations into Cambodia, however, would give the Communists an opportunity to make propaganda throughout the world about American imperialism. Meanwhile, they would use the occasion to draw South Vietnamese forces farther and farther away from populated areas at home, expand their operational zones in Cambodia, throw their full weight behind indigenous Cambodian Communists, and rally their Soviet allies against Lon Nol in the diplomatic arena.[47]

At a stormy 27 April meeting with Nixon, Laird, and Kissinger, Rogers built on those arguments to accuse Kissinger of having failed to provide the president with adequate information about the consequences of an attack into Cambodia. An incursion, he said, would offer very little

[45] Memo, Westmoreland CM–5063–70 for Secretary of Defense, 21 Apr 70, sub: Courses of Action With Regard to Cambodia; Msg, Abrams MAC 5364 to Westmoreland, 22 Apr 70, 330–76–076, box 6, Cambodia 381 (Jan–Apr) 1970, Laird Papers, WNRC. Quote from Msg, CNO to COMUSMACV, CINCPAC, Moorer to Abrams and McCain, 25 Apr 70.

[46] Quote from H. R. Haldeman, Handwritten Note of Meeting With the President, 20 Apr 70. Handwritten Note, H. R. Haldeman, 27 Apr 70, sub: Meeting Between the President, Rogers, Laird, and Kissinger in the President's Executive Office Building Office. Both in White House Special files, Staff Member Office files, Haldeman, box 41, H Notes [April 1–May 5, 1970] part I, Nixon Papers. Also see Memo, Kissinger for the President, 26 Apr 70, sub: Meeting on Cambodia, Sunday, April 26, 1970, Nixon Papers.

[47] Memo, Ray S. Cline INRB–94 for Secretary of State, 13 Apr 70, sub: Cambodia: Possible Communist Reactions to South Vietnamese Border Operations, Pol 27 Viet S file, FAIM/IR.

gain at the risk of severe U.S. casualties. As for the suggestion that the operation target the enemy's headquarters, the Central Office for South Vietnam (COSVN), that organization never stayed in one place for long. Indeed, even a knockout blow against it would fail to have much effect. Rogers concluded that he was slated to testify before Congress the next day. If inquiries surfaced on whether the president had decided to commit American military units to Cambodia, he did not intend to lie.[48]

Laird seconded Rogers but added a number of points of his own, both at the meeting and in a later memorandum to the president. The first of his objections was procedural. The directive authorizing the assault into Cambodia made the Washington Special Actions Group, a high-level committee composed of close advisers to the president, responsible for implementing the operation. Rather than do that, Laird said, the administration should follow established chains of command and give the secretary of defense responsibility. That said, Laird launched into a critique of the concept behind the operation. The enemy, he said, was flexible in adjusting his base areas and could replace combat losses quickly. In that light, an incursion into Cambodia would hardly be decisive to the conflict in South Vietnam and might only give the Communists an excuse to delay serious negotiations, especially if the attack aroused strong popular and congressional opposition in the United States. Other risks were even greater. The operation might jeopardize the support of the American people for the effort in Southeast Asia and might constitute the beginning of operational patterns that went beyond the U.S. government's budgeted resources. Both eventualities would have dire consequences for the outcome of the war. In addition, the plan for the attack had already leaked to the enemy, giving him the sort of advantage that might lead to many U.S. combat deaths. Laird added, in conclusion, that Abrams himself opposed the idea of going after the enemy's headquarters.[49]

Making use of Abrams' ambivalence, Kissinger challenged Laird's assertion that the general opposed a strike against COSVN. The president, for his part, adopted a more neutral stance, in an obvious attempt to soften the confrontation between his advisers. Ignoring the arguments against the operation itself, he concentrated his attention on objections that had been raised to launching an attack on the enemy's central office. The South Vietnamese operation into the Parrot's Beak was hardly an adequate action by itself, he explained. It had to be combined with a move of greater significance. He was willing to consider any objective the group proposed, but all of the alternatives he had studied still required the presence of U.S. troops and were much lower in value than COSVN. In that sense, although the casualties resulting from an attack into a different area might be fewer, the United States

---

[48] Handwritten Note, H. R. Haldeman, 27 Apr 70, sub: Meeting Between the President, Rogers, Laird, and Kissinger in the President's Executive Office Building Office.
[49] Ibid.

would pay much the same political price for whatever course it chose but profit less.[50]

It is clear from the context of the discussion and all that had gone before that the president was convinced that if Cambodia fell South Vietnam would surely follow.[51] He understood the insignificance of COSVN as a target but sought the strongest possible justification for a move that would inevitably spark controversy. To that end, he wanted to be able to tell the American public and Congress that his objective was nothing less than the enemy's Pentagon, the Central Office for South Vietnam. That the office was composed of many small bureaus spread over a large geographic area and that each of its most important cells had a backup in case of disaster made little difference to him. The name was what he wanted. With it, he felt he would be able to save Lon Nol while dealing a telling blow against the enemy's logistical base. Without it, neither objective would appear to make much sense to either the public or Congress. Both would reason, as had Laird and Rogers, that neither the enemy's supplies nor Lon Nol was worth an increase in American casualties and an extension of the war farther into Southeast Asia.

That morning's edition of the *New York Times* contained a foretaste of what policy makers could expect if they failed to convince the public and Congress that the operation was necessary. Contemplating the South Vietnamese Army's limited attacks into Cambodia, the paper's editors charged emotionally that any effort to involve American or South Vietnamese troops in Cambodia would provoke a Communist attempt to destroy Lon Nol and spark intense opposition in Congress by compromising the negotiations to end the war. Besides endangering the process of deescalation, the move would draw the United States into "as indecisive a quagmire" as the war in South Vietnam had already proved to be. "Military victory in Indochina has always been a mirage," the paper's editors concluded, "receding as rapidly as it is pursued. Lyndon Johnson learned that to his sorrow and it is inconceivable that President Nixon would set off at this late date on a similar chase. For once it is perceived that neither the Vietnam War nor the Communist sanctuary can be finished off in Cambodia, the stakes there can be seen to be marginal and hardly worthy of major risks."[52]

The president postponed the operation for twenty-four hours, but nothing came of the delay. He appears to have made the move mainly to quiet further opposition from within the administration by giving all sides time to calm down. Commenting on a conversation he had held with Kissinger shortly after the meeting with Laird and Rogers, Haldeman noted that "K. [Kissinger] takes whole deal as test of P's [president's] authority and I think would go ahead even if plan is wrong just to

---

[50] Ibid.

[51] Kissinger discusses this in *The White House Years*, p. 485. Also see pp. 483–505 for his view of the discussions leading up to the attack on the sanctuaries.

[52] "Cambodian Quandary," *New York Times*, 27 Apr 70.

South Vietnamese forces advance into Cambodia.

prove P. can't be challenged. P. recognizes maybe need another look & that if we change plan but still do two [operations] his authority is maintained but we show we're willing to listen." In the end, on 28 April, having received assurances from Abrams and Bunker that they indeed backed the attack, Nixon affirmed his decision to go ahead.[53]

Countering the Opposition

The South Vietnamese portion of the attack commenced on the evening of the twenty-eighth, with the Military Assistance Command under instructions to withhold all information from the press until as late as possible after Thieu and Washington agencies had issued statements. "Since I understand that MACV normally holds a press conference at 1630 hours every afternoon," Wheeler told Abrams, "it may be that the MACV briefer will be placed in a difficult position of having to 'stonewall.' . . . We are sorry, but these are our instructions."[54]

The press releases by Thieu and the Department of Defense that appeared after the incursion began stated that the attack was designed to save South Vietnamese and American lives by destroying important

---

[53] Quote from Handwritten Note, H. R. Haldeman, 27 Apr 70, sub: Meeting Between the President, Rogers, Laird, and Kissinger in the President's Executive Office Building Office. Kissinger, *The White House Years*, pp. 501, 1484n.

[54] Msg, Wheeler JCS 5835 to McCain, Abrams, 28 Apr 70, Abrams Papers, CMH.

enemy bases in Cambodia. The South Vietnamese, in particular, specified that the units participating were under orders to preserve Cambodian lives and property and to return to South Vietnam upon completion of the operation.[55]

The communique released by the Military Assistance Command was written in Washington and closely resembled the one released by the Department of Defense. The United States, it said, was providing supplementary support for the operation—"advisors, air, logistics, medical and artillery support, as required"—in response to requests from the South Vietnamese government. At the direction of the president, who wanted the televised speech he planned for the evening of 30 April to set the tone for all discussion of the subject, no other comments, conjecture, or backgrounders accompanied the announcement. In response to queries from the press, official spokesmen in Saigon limited their answers to the information contained in the statements released by Thieu and the Department of Defense.[56]

General Abrams recognized that the Saigon correspondents were resourceful and that the main effect of so restricted a policy would be to force them to rely on less than fully informed sources. To guarantee that newsmen received at least a modicum of factual information, he proposed that his spokesmen issue periodic statements confirming, without specifics, the number of American casualties and the type of support his command was providing to the South Vietnamese. The same thing, he said, was already being done in the case of operations in Laos.[57]

Although the Defense Department apparently never ruled on Abrams' request, it did attempt to reassure newsmen that it had their interests in mind by issuing a memorandum to correspondents shortly after the South Vietnamese entered Cambodia. The communique noted that pool arrangements would probably be necessary and that the South Vietnamese would continue to have jurisdiction over areas under their control, but it also explained that Secretary Laird had advised the Military Assistance Command to give newsmen access to the activities of American personnel supporting the operation. The South Vietnamese commander, General Tri, for his part, issued letters of authorization to thirty newsmen. As a result, American reporters accompanied the forces that entered the Parrot's Beak, with some penetrating as far as sixteen kilometers into Cambodia.[58]

[55] Msg, Abrams MAC 5752 to Wheeler, McCain, 29 Apr 70, sub: Statement of the Ministry of Defense Concerning RVNAF Operations in Parrots Beak Area of Cambodia, Abrams Papers, CMH; ASD PA, Statement on Cambodian Operation by Daniel Z. Henkin, 29 Apr 70, DDI Cambodia Opn Background file.

[56] Msg, Wheeler JCS 5836 to Abrams, 28 Apr 70, sub: Press Guidance for Operations in Cambodia, Abrams Papers, CMH.

[57] Msg, Abrams MAC 5739 to Wheeler, McCain, 29 Apr 70, sub: Press Guidance for Operations in Cambodia, Abrams Papers, CMH.

[58] Msg, OASD PA 7461 to MACV, 29 Apr 70, DDI Cambodia Opn Background file; Undated Note attached to Msg, OASD PA 7461 to MACV, 29 Apr 70, DDI Cambodia Opn Background file.

The reaction of the press to the development was predictable. "In connection with the Parrot's Beak operation," a State Department survey of the news media reported on 29 October, "the press has largely ignored the GVN statement that the ARVN units participating have received orders to return to the territory of Vietnam after completion of the operation. . . . News reports have persisted in describing the operation as an invasion."[59] The *New York Times*, in particular, was critical. Referring to pledges earlier in the month by American military spokesmen that U.S. forces would not become directly involved in Cambodia, the paper observed on the morning of 30 April that

The American public can have little confidence in such assurances. The Saigon command and the administration in Washington have been less than candid in the recent past concerning the degree of American involvement in Cambodia, and in Laos before that. If the current American-supported invasion of Cambodia is necessary to protect American and other "free world forces" in Vietnam, how long will it be before we are told that American troops must move into Cambodia to protect the American advisers and the "free world forces" that are now there?[60]

The administration's decision to support a South Vietnamese operation into Cambodia also produced a vehement reaction in the Senate, where leading members of both parties vowed to cut off funds for American military operations in Cambodia. Although conservative senators spoke out in favor of the move, even some of them were cautious. Senator John Stennis of Mississippi, for example, told newsmen that the destruction of the enemy's sanctuaries in Cambodia was essential to the continuing American withdrawal but still made it clear that he opposed the provision of extensive military aid to the Cambodian government.[61]

Aware that important segments of the news media and the Congress would be even more critical when they learned that a large American force would be involved, the president and his advisers worked anxiously in the days prior to the American entry into Cambodia to prepare public support for the move. On 29 April, the night before the president was to announce the event, General Wheeler instructed Abrams to take "all possible steps" to "dampen the expected efforts of . . . critics . . . and the impact which these efforts will have on the American people. Specifically, . . . U.S. participation should be played down and the press should be encouraged to focus on the RVNAF contribution." Wheeler added that the Military Assistance Command should emphasize the importance of the sanctuaries to the enemy and the magnitude of the contribution those bases made to his designs. "To that end, I would appreciate you insuring

[59] Memo, Theodore L. Eliot, Jr., Exec Sec, for Henry Kissinger, 29 Oct 70, sub: Daily Report on Cambodia No. 4, Pol 2 Cambodia file, FAIM/IR.

[60] "Escalation in Indochina . . . ," *New York Times*, 30 Apr 70.

[61] John W. Finney, "Senators Angry, Some Seek To Cut Off Funds for Widened Military Action," *New York Times*, 30 Apr 70.

302

thorough pictorial coverage of these base areas once we get into them, to include condemning pictures of enemy installations, caches, captured materiel, documents, etc., which can be used to validate the impression we wish to convey."[62] Wheeler added in a subsequent message that he had received reports that the South Vietnamese had already uncovered several substantial caches of enemy weapons and rice in Cambodia. "If any worthwhile pictures of this material have been taken," he said, "I can use them to good advantage back here as the first evidence to what we have found."[63]

The morning before the speech, members of the White House staff called all cabinet officers to request that they urge their assistant secretaries to listen closely to the talk so that, as White House Director of Communications Herbert Klein put it, "a government-wide line" would go forth. Meanwhile, James J. Kilpatrick, Holmes Alexander, Roscoe Drummond, Ralph de Toledano, and other conservative syndicated columnists received advance notification that the president's speech that evening would be important, and staff members laid plans to follow up with them after the broadcast to ensure that they understood the significance of what Nixon had said. The White House staff also arranged for Vice President Agnew to appear on the CBS Sunday interview program "Face the Nation" and to tape a ninety-minute conversation with talk show host David Frost. It likewise drafted a fact sheet for distribution to editors and opinion makers who might support the operation, prepared advertisements for placement in newspapers across the country, compiled a list of prominent newsmen who were to receive calls after the speech, and readied a mass mailing to 300,000 Americans who had supported administration programs in the past. Senators John G. Tower of Texas, Thomas J. Dodd of Connecticut, and Peter H. Dominick of Colorado, among others, promised to tape statements for release on the next morning's news programs. Even Secretary Rogers agreed to go on television, but with the stipulation that his appearance be postponed, as Klein phrased it for the president, "until after tomorrow," in order to distance himself from the effort to promote the operation.[64]

The president's speech itself was carefully crafted to justify the incursion to the widest possible cross-section of the American public. Although the bulk of the fighting would be in the hands of the South Vietnamese, Nixon said, a combined American–South Vietnamese operation would be necessary in the Fishhook to "attack the headquarters for the entire Communist military operation in South Vietnam. This key control center has been occupied by the North Vietnamese and Viet Cong for 5 years in blatant violation of Cambodia's neutrality." Nixon insisted that his move into Cambodia was "not an invasion" but a necessary extension of the

---

[62] Msg, Wheeler JCS 5859 to Abrams, 29 Apr 70, Abrams Papers, CMH.

[63] Msg, Wheeler JCS 5864 to Abrams, 29 Apr 70, Abrams Papers, CMH.

[64] Memo, Herbert Klein for the President, 30 Apr 70, White House Special files, Haldeman alpha, box 116, Cambodia [part II], Nixon Papers.

Nixon announces the attack into Cambodia.

Vietnam War designed to protect American lives and to guarantee the successful completion of the Vietnamization program. Asserting that he had made his decision without regard to the political consequences, he stated his belief that the majority of Americans favored the withdrawal of American forces and that his action would further that end. "Whether my party gains in November is nothing compared to the lives of 400,000 brave Americans fighting for our country and for the cause of peace and freedom in Vietnam."[65]

Both before and after the speech, Daniel Henkin and other official spokesmen stressed that the main justification for the operation was the threat the sanctuaries posed to American lives. Aware that the importance of the Central Office for South Vietnam was capable of being distorted, they also attempted to counteract the president's emphasis on destroying that headquarters by noting delicately that the facility was an elusive target whose personnel rarely occupied any fixed position for long.[66] "We are not interested in the personnel," Henry Kissinger told newsmen during a backgrounder prior to the speech. "We are interested in the supply depots and in the communications equipment." Disavowals of that sort notwithstanding, the concept of an attack on COSVN so appealed to the press that newsmen made the effort to find the headquarters an important

[65] "The Cambodia Strike: Defensive Action for Peace," Address by President Nixon, in Department of State *Bulletin*, 18 May 70, p. 617.

[66] See, for example, Statement by Gen John Vogt, Commander, U.S. Pacific Air Forces, 2 May 70, DDI Cambodia file.

304

gauge of the incursion's success. The first question a reporter asked during Kissinger's backgrounder, indeed, had to do with the central office and its distance from the South Vietnamese border.[67]

President Nixon apparently believed that, whatever the press and his opponents said, he would still be able to do significant damage to the enemy. Yet in that area likewise, he may have oversold what he could accomplish. On the morning after he made his speech, he traveled to the Pentagon to brief the Joint Chiefs of Staff on his decision. After the meeting, Westmoreland approached him. The general had long advocated limited American involvement in Cambodia but had been at best marginally involved in planning for the operation at hand. Learning that the president intended to "clean out" the sanctuaries once and for all, he became concerned. The goal seemed far larger than anything he, after years of experience in Southeast Asia, would have considered possible. "I pointed out that there was a great deal of real estate involved," he later noted in a memorandum for the record,

that the number of days with good weather were numbered, and that General Abrams is limited by his resources in terms of troops, helicopters, sorties, and logistics. . . . All of these factors led me to emphasize that it was practically impossible to accomplish the mission of cleaning out all of the bases as he had indicated. I did make the point that certainly in each of the base areas it would be possible to bomb, send patrols, and for about five of the base areas to employ sizeable numbers of U.S. troops. Vietnamese troops could invade others. The president said he understood these limitations and realized that the commander on the scene would have to do the best he could.[68]

Westmoreland's comment had little more effect on the president than the arguments of Laird and Rogers. Spurred by the fall of Sihanouk and the enemy's aggressive attempt to secure lines of supply through Cambodia, Nixon was determined to go through with his plan. In some ways, from a military point of view, the move was long overdue. Yet as the comments of Rogers, Laird, and Westmoreland had all indicated, it was probably also too late. Nixon would learn within the week that what might have been possible and logical two years earlier was no longer politically feasible, if only because the step required—from the American public, Congress, and news media—an act of faith in the credibility of government that too few were any longer willing to give.

---

[67] Background Briefing at the White House with Dr. Henry A. Kissinger, 8:14 P.M., 30 Apr 70, DDI Cambodia Operations, Background Through 2 May 70 file. Also see Robert B. Semple, Jr., "Not an Invasion," *New York Times*, 1 May 70.

[68] MFR, William C. Westmoreland, 6 May 70, sub: Meeting of Joint Chiefs of Staff With the President on Friday, 1 May 70, Westmoreland History file 37, CMH.

14

Incursion Into Cambodia

Shortly after President Nixon announced the move into Cambodia on 30 April 1970, Secretary Laird met with the leaders of the House of Representatives and Senate to explain the decision. None were "enthusiastic or overjoyed," Haldeman's assistant Charles Colson reported later. Instead, they asked "difficult, penetrating" questions. The Republicans, in particular, seemed concerned. Many had gone on record three days earlier to assure their constituents that American ground forces would never enter Cambodia.[1]

The president's strongest allies in Congress stood by him as the operation began, but others were less firm. While Senate Minority Leader Hugh D. Scott, Jr., of Pennsylvania told reporters, "There has never been a time when it is more important to hold one's emotional fire and to trust the president," the ranking Republican on the Senate Foreign Relations Committee, Senator George D. Aiken of Vermont, broke with the administration over the issue.[2] Senator Robert J. Dole of Kansas meanwhile asserted that "I just can't see anything but an increase in wounded and killed, and this will cause a sharp downturn in support of the president's policies." Bipartisan opposition in the Senate grew so vigorously, indeed, that within days of the president's announcement it became clear that the Senate might pass a measure proposed by Senators John Sherman Cooper of Kentucky and Frank F. Church of Idaho to cut off funding for further American involvement in Cambodia.[3]

[1] Memo, Charles Colson for Lawrence Higby, 30 Apr 70, sub: Report From Timmons on the Leadership Meeting, White House Special files, Haldeman alpha, box 116, Cambodia [part I], Nixon Papers.

[2] Quote from [UPI], Untitled news clip, 30 Apr 70, CMH files. John W. Finney, "Nixon Promises To Quit Cambodia in 3 to 7 Weeks," *New York Times*, 6 May 70.

[3] Quote from "Nixon's Gamble: Operation Total Victory," *Newsweek*, 11 May 70. John W. Finney, "U.S. Aids Saigon Push in Cambodia With Planes, Artillery, Advisers; Move Stirs Opposition in Senate," *New York Times*, 30 Apr 70.

Much of the press in the eastern United States also voiced concern. The *New York Times* had already gone on record to oppose involvement of any sort in Cambodia. *(Map 3)* When Nixon announced the incursion, the newspaper labeled as a "military hallucination" his assurances that the step would save lives and hasten the withdrawal of American forces from South Vietnam.[4] The *New York Post* added that the president was leading the nation into "another dangerous dead-end road," and *Long Island Newsday* termed the move "utterly pointless."[5]

In the South, Midwest, and Far West, according to a quick tabulation by the *New York Times*, the reaction was somewhat more supportive of administration policy, but many newspapers still expressed opposition. *Chicago Today* commended Nixon for having the courage to take a "politically suicidal step" to save American lives; the *Atlanta Journal* declared that the move was the "only honorable course" open to the United States; and the *Detroit News* indicated that, if the president's decision entailed some risks, "inaction in the face of the new North Vietnamese build up could be regarded as even more dangerous." Yet, the *Cleveland Plain Dealer* labeled the president's speech a "maudlin appeal to patriotism"; the *Arkansas Democrat* declared that Nixon's decision to enter Cambodia ran "counter to the attitude of the average American, who does not care whether we win the war in Southeast Asia"; and the *Milwaukee Journal* termed the operation an unjustified counterweight to the enemy's own illegal activities in Cambodia.[6] Even the normally hawkish *Chicago Tribune* appears to have been uncomfortable. According to a commentary in *Newsweek*, the paper had earlier supported bombing in Cambodia but had also expressed doubts that the American people would agree to an expanded war in Southeast Asia. When the president announced his move into Cambodia, its editors thus appear to have been torn between their own misgivings and a desire to back administration policy. They welcomed the incursion on 2 May as an attempt "to protect the lives of our men," but on the day the attack began they failed to say anything.[7]

Military leaders, for their part, were pleased with the development but also were acutely aware that the move into Cambodia posed considerable political risks. In a candid interview with *New York Times* correspondent William Beecher, several unidentified high-ranking officers in Washington asserted that if a successful attack on the sanctuaries could only improve the American position in South Vietnam, they were still uncomfortable with the inconsistency between their accustomed role as fighting men and the political requirements circumstances had imposed. "We're supposed to base our advice on purely military concerns," one officer explained. "But anyone who has followed the course of this war

[4] "Military Hallucination-Again," *New York Times*, 1 May 70.
[5] "Editorial Comments on Move in Cambodia," *New York Times*, 1 May 70.
[6] Ibid Also see "Twisted Trail in Cambodia," *Milwaukee Journal*, 3 May 70.
[7] Quote from "The President Would Rather Be Right," *Chicago Tribune*, 2 May 70. "Nixon's Gamble: Operation Total Victory."

INCURSION INTO CAMBODIA
May–June 1970

⟵ Axis of Attack

△ Area of Operations
(Informal Designation)

MR Military Region

0 ————————— 100
Miles

MAP 3

knows how vital the attitude in the Congress and among the electorate is to the basic character of our strategy. If the casualty rate suddenly shoots up, political dissent could rise meteorically."[8]

President Nixon understood the point. In the weeks that followed, he would muster all of the considerable resources at his disposal to marshal support to his side. He would find, however, as had his predecessor, that public relations had its limits and that the American public and Congress, seemingly dependent upon the central government for guidance, often have a direction of their own.

The Press

As the incursion developed, the task that confronted the president and his public affairs advisers seemed daunting. On the day that Nixon announced the move into Cambodia, at least 450 accredited print and television journalists and support personnel were resident in Saigon. Within the week that number would begin to swell, reaching 497 by the end of May. Thirty-six of those reporters were freelancers. The rest represented 8 wire services, 17 radio and television organizations, 26 newspapers, 9 news services, 8 major magazines, and 2 newsreel services. Besides a large contingent of Americans and South Vietnamese, 21 nationalities were present. Thirty-two of the reporters were from Japan and Korea, 21 from Great Britain, 17 from France, and 7 from Australia. The rest hailed from nations as diverse as Belgium, Canada, Greece, India, Ireland, and Singapore, among many others. The American television and radio networks employed by far the largest staffs. At the beginning of the incursion, CBS News had on hand about 46 reporters and staff members. ABC had 30 and NBC 24. The major news bureaus were next, with the Associated Press and United Press International fielding 24 and 21, respectively.[9]

As in the past, the corps of correspondents encompassed a broad range of journalistic expertise. Some of the newsmen were only learning their trade but a number of old hands were either present in Southeast Asia or returned quickly to report the story: Peter Arnett of the Associated Press, for example, William Beecher of the *New York Times*, Morley Safer and Mike Wallace of CBS News, and Richard Dudman of the *St. Louis Post-Dispatch*. Others, such as freelancers John Hohenberg and Jeffrey Race, were journalists but also scholars and writers of books. A few, such as Hubertus, Prince of Lowenstein, although accredited to news organizations of one sort or another, were present mainly to gain impressions and

---

[8] William Beecher, "Military Planners View Nixon Decision as Sound," *New York Times*, 2 May 70. Also see Robert G. Kaiser, "Generals Planned Smaller Offensive," *Washington Post*, 8 May 70.

[9] MACV History, 1970, vol. 3, p. XI-1.

to depart. Perhaps one-third of those accredited were true working journalists. The rest, as always, were secretaries, technicians, and spouses.[10]

Whatever their backgrounds, those reporters, as a group, were far more opinionated on the subject of the war than ever in the past. Although a majority remained concerned with telling all sides of the story as clearly as possible, the views of some were very strong, both in support of the president's decision to enter Cambodia and against it. An influential minority—journalists, in particular, with lengthy service in South Vietnam and strong connections with the military command—had long before concluded that the practice of allowing the enemy sanctuary in Cambodia was detrimental to the well-being of American forces. They were elated when the United States finally took action and tended to see events in that perspective. The reporters for *U.S. News & World Report*, while often dispassionate in their appraisals, were certainly to be numbered among that group.[11] Offsetting that point of view was one held by newcomers such as James McCartney of the Knight newspaper chain, who arrived in South Vietnam during February 1970, but also by correspondents such as Peter Arnett, who had served in South Vietnam for years. More negative and sometimes more finely attuned to the dissent spreading in the United States, those reporters tended to question the long-term value of the attack into Cambodia and to point up the contradictions present in the president's Vietnam policies. Whether they agreed or disagreed with the president's decision, however, most reporters followed Nixon's lead and judged the operation by its success in finding COSVN. With reports continuing to circulate about drug abuse and combat refusals and with the My Lai massacre and Cambodian atrocities against innocent Vietnamese fresh in the news, they also kept watch for signs of poor morale among the troops and for any indication that crimes against humanity might have occurred.[12]

Public Affairs Policy in the Field

General Wheeler and other officials in Washington were well aware of the news media's concerns and moved from the very beginning of the operation to warn the MACV Office of Information to be on the alert. In the case of the Central Office for South Vietnam, for example, Wheeler cabled Abrams on 2 May to advise that the press was beginning to use the subject as a measure of progress. In that light, he said, "It would be highly

---

[10] U.S. Army Center of Military History, Database of Vietnam War Correspondents, Cambodian Incursion List, 15 Mar 88 (hereafter cited as Correspondents Database), CMH files.

[11] Wendell Merick made the point in Interv, author with Wendell Merick, 16 Apr 79, CMH files.

[12] "Beyond the Checkpoint," *Newsweek*, 15 Jun 70, p. 65.

Colonel Cutrona

desirable . . . to maximize the possibilities of dealing COSVN a damaging blow if it is within the realm of your capabilities during this present campaign."[13]

Other suggestions followed, with both Wheeler and the Office of the Assistant Secretary of Defense for Public Affairs carefully advising Abrams on steps he might take to reduce the impact of the operation on the American public. Although American newsmen would have to accompany the campaign to guarantee that the people received full information about what was happening, Wheeler noted in a series of messages that conveyed thinking within the Department of Defense, it was still important that the South Vietnamese receive the maximum exposure possible. To that end, MACV public affairs officers were to deemphasize U.S. participation where they could. Abrams was likewise to see to it that his men avoided atrocities and to attempt to ensure that the South Vietnamese, in particular, followed proper procedures where the civilian population of Cambodia was concerned. On the side, the Defense Department recommended that Abrams hold a formal news conference to explain the operation. In that way, he could convey the government's position to the Saigon correspondents in a clear and effective manner.[14]

The Director of Defense Information, Colonel Hill, amplified those themes in a 2 May cable to the MACV Office of Information. Since undue emphasis on casualties could only have an impact on American public opinion, he said, public affairs officers in Saigon should refrain from releasing statistics on American killed and wounded in Cambodia. "If you announce casualties for the operation as for any other . . ., irrespective of which side of the border they occur, maybe we can get by." As for insinuations that were beginning to arise in the press that some of the troops were less than enthusiastic about entering Cambodia, Hill continued, the new Chief of MACV Information, Col. Joseph Cutrona, might see

[13] Msg, Wheeler JCS 6056 to McCain, Abrams, 2 May 70, sub: COSVN Headquarters, Abrams Papers, CMH.
[14] Msg, Wheeler JCS 5971 to McCain, Abrams, 30 Apr 70, sub: Press Guidance; Msg, Wheeler JCS 5859 to Abrams, 29 Apr 70; Msg, Wheeler JCS 5828 to Abrams, 28 Apr 70; and Msg, Abrams MAC 5871 to Wheeler, 1 May 70. All in Abrams Papers, CMH.

312

to it that commanders in the field quietly informed newsmen, "to the extent of the facts," that the president's announcement of the incursion had "buoyed the spirit of the troops" by demonstrating the concern the nation's leaders held for their well-being.[15]

Overall, the messages stressed that an image of success was to prevail. While publicizing the importance of the sanctuaries to the enemy, Wheeler told Abrams, the Military Assistance Command was to assist Washington agencies in their public affairs efforts by forwarding pictures of captured enemy installations and materiel "which can be used to validate the impression we wish to convey."[16]

As Wheeler had suggested, Abrams exerted every effort to destroy the enemy's central office. One of his B–52 strikes came close to catching an important portion of the office in a vulnerable position, but, to the dismay of President Nixon, the enemy received at least seven hours' advance notice and escaped. Enemy soldiers captured in Cambodia would later reveal that Communist forces often received word of B–52 strikes up to twenty-four hours in advance, long before the bombers had even left the ground.[17]

Abrams likewise complied with most of the other instructions he received by dispatching regular couriers to Washington with pictures of captured enemy installations and materiel and by attempting as far as possible to make the South Vietnamese the center of attention. As the Defense Department had suggested, he refrained from maintaining cumulative casualty statistics for Cambodia, but he took care to preserve his credibility by handling the figures as he would have in any other operation. Reporters thus received intermittent tallies for the campaign as a whole, whether the losses had occurred in South Vietnam or Cambodia. Should they question the practice, Abrams instructed command spokesmen to make the point that since operations in Cambodia were one aspect of the war in South Vietnam, it made sense to include all statistics in the totals for that war.[18]

For the rest, the general followed his usual no-nonsense approach to the news media. Although some South Vietnamese commanders operating in the Parrot's Beak barred the press from accompanying their forces, he provided reporters with as much access to the operation as he could. At his instruction, the Military Assistance Command organized special flights to move correspondents to command posts near the fighting and arranged for couriers to transport television news film to Saigon. In that

---

[15] Quotes from Msg, Col L. Gordon Hill, Director of Defense Information, OASD PA, Defense 6064 to Col Joseph F. H. Cutrona, 2 May 70, DDI Cambodia file. Msg, Col L. Gordon Hill Defense 6023 to Cutrona, 1 May 70, DDI Casualty file.

[16] Msg, Wheeler JCS 5859 to Abrams, 29 Apr 70.

[17] Memo, the President for Henry Kissinger, 25 May 70, President's Personal file, box 2, Memos, May 1970, Nixon Papers; Msg, Maj Gen Bautz, CG, 25th Inf Div, CHU 714 to Lt Gen Davison, CG, IIFFV, 14 May 70, sub: PW-COSVN Signal Unit, Abrams Papers, CMH.

[18] Msg, Cutrona MAC 5912 to Hill, 2 May 70, DDI Cambodia Policy file.

way, at least, there would be no complaints that the Military Assistance Command was somehow attempting to restrict access to the operation. As far as circumstances permitted, units in the field meanwhile provided visiting newsmen with daily briefings, local transportation, communications, food, and temporary lodging.[19]

As the incursion progressed, Abrams also attempted to impose as much common sense as he could upon the suggestions he was receiving from Washington agencies. He thus refused to participate in the on-the-record news conference the Defense Department had requested because so radical a departure from his usual practice of avoiding public statements would have put the press on notice that he was attempting to "enhance" their acceptance of the operation. Instead, he allowed his chief of intelligence to hold a background briefing on the sanctuaries and instructed the members of his command to emphasize the threat those facilities posed to American lives. In the same way, neither he nor Cutrona appear to have taken action on the suggestion to emphasize the high morale of the troops. There was, in fact, little need to do so. Moving into the field, reporters encountered instances of dissatisfaction but also noted the presence of soldiers who genuinely believed, as Frank Reynolds of ABC News put it, that the United States was at last "doing something that will really shorten the war."[20]

Abrams likewise managed to put an end to a potential conflict over the name of the operation that might have harmed official credibility if the press had learned of it. Shortly after the incursion began, officials in Washington had noticed that the South Vietnamese had chosen to call their portion of the incursion TOAN THANG 43, a term that translated to "Final Victory" in English and seemed to indicate a desire for some sort of total conquest over the North Vietnamese rather than the negotiated settlement the United States sought. "It is becoming evident," Colonel Hill thus told Cutrona, ". . . that the use of *Toan Thang* . . . creates a situation . . . for some to make derisive comments on the name alone." In that light, Hill suggested that the Military Assistance Command attempt quietly to change the term to something innocuous such as "the Fish Hook Operation." Abrams, with Wheeler's backing, advised against any move of the sort. The South Vietnamese not only had a right to name their operation anything they chose, he told Wheeler, a change hardly seemed necessary. The Saigon correspondents had taken little notice of the phrase *Toan Thang* even though they understood its meaning. They found such descriptions

[19] Msg, Cutrona MAC 6197 to Hill, 7 May 70, sub: First Withdrawal of Units from Cambodia, Abrams Papers, CMH; Msg, Abrams MAC 5871 to Wheeler, 1 May 70. For an example of the way field units treated the press during the operation, see Combat After Actions Rpt, 1st Cavalry Division (Airmobile), Cambodian Campaign, 6 Jul 70, annex I, 334–72A870, box 9/12, WNRC.

[20] Msg, Abrams MAC 5871 to Wheeler, 1 May 70. The J–2 briefing is in Msg, Maj Gen W. G. Dolvin MAC 5898 to Lt Gen John W. Vogt, Dir, J–3, OJCS, 2 May 70, sub: Request for Background Information, DDI Cambodia Policy file. Quote from Frank Reynolds, ABC Evening News, 10 May 70, *Radio-TV-Defense Dialog*.

as the "Fishhook operation" and the "Parrot's Beak" more suitable to their purposes.[21]

The Situation in the United States

The Nixon administration's care in orchestrating the public relations surrounding the incursion might have achieved tangible benefits earlier in the war, but by 1970 patience had begun to run thin in the United States. According to a study by public opinion researcher Hazel Erskine reprinted in the *Washington Post* on 10 May, contrary to popular belief, opposition to the war had become more widespread among older Americans than among the young. By October 1969, indeed, 63 percent of those over fifty years of age termed the war a mistake, while only 54 percent of those under forty-nine and 58 percent of those under twenty-nine said the same. The study's findings were particularly striking, Erskine said, because older Americans were usually hesitant to reveal their opinions to interviewers.[22]

That the American public was beginning to have profound reservations about the war was clearly visible in the polls that appeared in the weeks following the beginning of the incursion. As was usually the case, a majority of citizens rallied to the president's side once Nixon had announced his decision to expand the war. According to a preliminary Gallup poll published on 5 May, 51 percent of those interviewed said they approved of what the president had done. Yet, when pollsters rephrased the question to omit the role of the president, it became obvious that most Americans preferred to send arms and materiel rather than fighting men to Cambodia. Fifty-three percent agreed that the dispatch of weapons would be proper, but by a margin of 58 to 28 percent a strong majority disapproved of sending troops. Harris poll results were less specific but revealed similar reservations. Fifty-six percent of those interviewed believed the president was justified in making the move, but most also asserted that American troops would become bogged down in Cambodia. A plurality avowed that it believed Nixon had started another Vietnam War.[23]

Discontent was also spreading rapidly among the young. By April 1970 many of the nation's college campuses seethed with resentment and indignation, not only at the war but also because progress in the civil rights movement appeared to have stalled and because university

[21] Msg, Hill to Cutrona, 2 May 70, sub: Popular Name for Toan Thang 43, DDI Cambodian Policy file. Also see Msgs, Wheeler JCS 6076 to Abrams, 2 May 70, and Abrams MAC 5985 to Wheeler, 4 May 70, both in Abrams Papers, CMH.

[22] Hazel Erskine, "Most War Foes Are Over 50," *Washington Post*, 10 May 70.

[23] "The Gallup Poll-51 Pct Support Nixon on Cambodia Venture," *Washington Post*, 5 May 70; Harris, *The Anguish of Change*, p. 71.

administrations seemed unresponsive to student demands for curriculum reform and free speech. A Harris poll of college students taken during May 1970 revealed that half of all students had been involved in some sort of public protest during their time in school. By a score of 76 to 22 percent the group criticized the president's handling of the war; by 66 to 22 percent it questioned his credibility on the subject; and by 67 to 30 percent it asserted that his administration was out of touch with the mood of America.[24]

More than two-thirds of the American population under the age of thirty was not enrolled in college, according to Harris, but many members of that group, if they sometimes frowned upon student activities, were still clearly sympathetic to the students themselves. Their reaction to an incident that occurred on 1 May, when Nixon visited the Pentagon to brief the Joint Chiefs of Staff on the incursion, demonstrated the depths of their concern. Encountering a group of federal employees near the entrance to the building, the president had remarked within earshot of a reporter that the men serving in South Vietnam and Cambodia represented the cream of America while student protesters were little more than "bums." When asked to react to the president's comment, the young, as a group, whether enrolled in college or not, rejected the claim by a score of 60 to 36 percent. The rest of the population was more evenly divided, perhaps in reaction to the violence that was occurring on many college campuses. According to polls published by Harris on 1 June, Americans rejected Nixon's characterization of students as "bums" by only the slightest of margins, 47 to 43 percent. Fifty-two percent meanwhile condemned student protests, but 53 percent also opposed any ban on demonstrations against the war.[25]

Harris later observed that the findings reflected growing ambivalence on the part of Americans in general toward the war. That may have been so, but the response may likewise have indicated an unwillingness on the part of a majority of Americans to repudiate a system of values that prized the right to protest peacefully. In that sense, the reply resembled the reaction that had followed Agnew's criticism of the news media the year before, when many Americans had sympathized with the vice president's opinions but had rejected any official attempt to limit the news media. That Americans, whatever their personal opinions, were disinclined to repress the honest beliefs of their children goes without saying.

During the week that followed Nixon's announcement, all of those discontents came into focus, especially in the universities. Arsonists set minor fires at Ohio State University in Columbus and at Case Western Reserve University in Cleveland. Twenty major fire-bombing incidents

---

[24] Harris, *The Anguish of Change*, pp. 217–20.

[25] Quote from Juan De Onis, "Nixon Dubs 'Bums' Label on Some College Radicals," *New York Times*, 2 May 70. Ibid., p. 219; Louis Harris, "52% Condemn Protests But Oppose Ban," *Philadelphia Inquirer*, 1 Jun 70.

316

National guardsmen prepare to fire at Kent State.

occurred at the University of Wisconsin in Madison, where police arrested 83 students. At New York University, some 200 students seized the campus' main computer and held it for a $100,000 ransom. Several state governors responded to the turmoil by ordering Army National Guard units to occupy university campuses. On 4 May one of those units at Kent State University in Ohio reacted in panic and anger to the taunts of protesters by firing into a crowd of bystanders. Four students were killed, none of them demonstrators. The deaths contributed to the chaos that seemed to be swelling in the country. By 7 May student strikes had occurred at 441 college campuses across the United States, and additional demonstrations were planned around the country. By the end of the week, California Governor Ronald Reagan had closed the state's university system, the nation's largest, and demonstrators were converging on the nation's capital for what they hoped would become a major antiwar protest.[26]

Violent antiwar rallies and angry reactions by the president's supporters gained headlines in the days that followed. On the evening after the incident at Kent State, Vice President Agnew fanned the flames by launching what the *Washington Star* termed "a prepared rhetorical bom-

---

[26] This description is drawn from Memo, Alexander P. Butterfield, Deputy Assistant to the President, for Members of the Cabinet, 7 May 70, sub: Briefing Material, 330–70–067, box 67, Cambodia 381 (1–10 May) 1970, Laird Papers, WNRC. Also see "At War With War," *Time*, 18 May 70, p. 6; "Kent State Martyrdom That Shook the Country," *Time*, 18 May 70, p. 13.

317

bardment of 'elitists who encourage traitors, thieves and perverts . . . in our midst.'" He went on to dismiss student protesters as "tomentose exhibitionists who provoke more derision than fear." The comment, while ill advised, expressed the feelings of at least some Americans. Two hundred construction workers gained wide attention shortly thereafter by chasing antiwar marchers through New York's financial district in a wild melee that injured seventy.[27]

The disorders and polarization that occurred after the announcement of the incursion led some to question whether the nation could survive. Reflecting on the disturbances, the *Wall Street Journal*, for one, noted on 4 May that the Vietnam War had taken a "cruel toll in destruction of the bonds of consensus and authority" in the United States and that "the danger of disintegration here is far more serious than any military threat in Indochina."[28]

Many peaceful protests nevertheless also occurred. "Clean cut, often freshly barbered students in ties and jackets swarmed over Capitol Hill," *Time* thus reported on 18 May, "visiting sympathetic Congressmen, obtaining audiences with willing members of the Administration." Some students, rather than riot, pledged to boycott popular soft drinks until the war had ended or donated university cap and gown fees to a fund for antiwar candidates.[29] Hardly noticed in all of the commotion were the tens of thousands of students and faculty members at the nation's colleges and universities who, whatever their personal feelings about the war, either remained on the periphery of the protests or chose to avoid them altogether.

As disorders spread across the country, a bill to repeal the Gulf of Tonkin Resolution appeared in the House of Representatives along with an amendment to pending legislation that would have cut off military authorizations for Cambodia immediately and for South Vietnam by the end of the year. Both were too radical to gain much of a following, but the Cooper-Church Amendment to cut off funds for the incursion by 1 July seemed to gain momentum.

The administration opposed those measures vigorously but lost face when it allowed Senate Minority Leader Hugh Scott to pledge on one day that the United States would avoid resumption of the bombing of North Vietnam and then announced on the next that it had conducted a series of heavy protective reaction strikes on enemy antiaircraft sites located in North Vietnam near the border with Laos. Coordination on the subject was apparently so poor between the Office of the Commander in Chief, Pacific, and that of the Office of the Secretary of Defense that Henkin had to go on record the day after the raids to apologize for a statement Laird

[27] "Time To Stop the Dialogue of Invective," *Washington Star*, 10 May 70; Homer Bigart, "War Foes Here Attacked by Construction Workers," *New York Times*, 9 May 70; "At War With War," p. 10.

[28] "The President's Gamble," *Wall Street Journal*, 4 May 70.

[29] "At War With War," p. 10.

had made to newsmen admitting to three raids when ample evidence existed that four had occurred.[30]

The president, for his part, had little choice but to attempt to dampen down the passions that were beginning to rise. Although inclined to keep his intentions secret from the enemy and to cut as broad a path through Communist base areas in Cambodia as possible, he announced publicly on 5 May that he had, in fact, made a firm commitment to congressional leaders to establish time and distance limitations for the operation. American forces would penetrate no more than thirty kilometers, about nineteen miles, into the Cambodian countryside, he said, and would withdraw within three to seven weeks. On the side, he quietly instructed Agnew to say nothing about student unrest in a forthcoming speech in Atlanta.[31]

If the president saw the necessity for compromise, he still remained inclined to give no more ground than necessary. During a series of meetings with his closest advisers on the day before he met with the congressional leadership, he thus stated that, as Haldeman quoted him, "The need now [is] to mobilize Congress to stand up. Don't waffle under student riots. Resist govt. by demonstrators."[32] In the days that followed, indeed, his staff conducted a far-reaching public relations campaign to bolster support for the incursion. Speakers traveled across the country to brief patriotic organizations. Administration representatives cultivated labor groups such as the American Federation of Labor–Congress of Industrial Organizations in an attempt to gain endorsements. Full-page advertisements appeared in major periodicals. Telephone calls and letters went out to concerned state legislators. Even so, the president understood that much of his ability to firm up support depended on whether the troops in the field uncovered the evidence he needed to justify his action. In the end, he told his advisers on 3 May, all concerned would "have to hold . . . 'til they find something."[33]

Mixed Signals

G eneral Abrams and his officers, as a result, often found themselves paying as much attention to the political requirements that accompa-

[30] Laird made the comment on 4 May. See Transcript, 4 May 70, sub: Secretary of Defense Melvin R. Laird Interviewed by Newsmen Following Appearance Before Defense Subcommittee of the House Appropriations Committee, copy in CMH files. Henkin's retraction is in Msg, Defense 8073 to COMUSMACV et al., 6 May 70, DDI Cambodia file.

[31] Msg, Moorer JCS 6037 to McCain, 1 May 70, Abrams Papers, CMH; Finney, "Nixon Promises To Quit Cambodia in 3 to 7 Weeks"; Handwritten Meeting Note, H. R. Haldeman, 6 May 70, White House Special files, Staff Member Office files, Haldeman, box 41, H. Notes, April–June 70 [May 6–June 30, 1970] part II, Nixon Papers.

[32] H. R. Haldeman, Note of 3 May [70], White House Special files, Staff Member Office files, Haldeman, box 41, H. Notes, April–June 70 [April 1–May 5] part I, Nixon Papers.

[33] Memo, Charles Colson for H. R. Haldeman, 13 May 70, White House Special files, Staff Member Office files, Haldeman, box 116, Cambodia, Nixon Papers. Quote from H. R. Haldeman, Note of 3 May [70].

nied the incursion as they did to their strictly military duties. Some of the requests that arrived from Washington were relatively minor. On 5 May, for example, Wheeler cabled Abrams to inform him that "higher authority" hoped an additional operation into Base Area 354, straddling the Cambodian border along South Vietnam's Tah Ninh Province, would "sort of blend into other operations in the Parrot's Beak and that you will not find it necessary to make an announcement at its inception." Abrams could only respond that the press was well aware of the move and that he had already received four requests for information.[34]

Other demands had more serious implications. Abrams, indeed, had hardly begun to search the sanctuaries when Wheeler had notified him on 4 May that both the press and opposition groups in the United States were developing the theme that American and South Vietnamese forces would be "bogged down forever in Cambodia." Since "words alone will not be convincing enough," Wheeler continued,

it would be very much to our advantage to be able to announce . . . the withdrawal of some forces back to Vietnam as soon as this is operationally feasible and desirable. . . . I do not wish to imply that we would want you to prematurely terminate an operation or in any way jeopardize it just to gain a press advantage. However, it would be highly desirable for higher authority to be in a position to exploit fully the termination of an operation or withdrawal of at least some of the forces engaged in Cambodia.[35]

Abrams objected. "After the low tempo of friendly offensive operations during the past several months," he told Wheeler, "it took some doing to get people back into the offensive spirit. We have recaptured it and don't wish to create impression we are slowing down by premature announcement of troop withdrawals from Cambodia." As a matter of fact, he continued, a total of eight separate operations were planned, so there would be no units to spare for even a token withdrawal. Several, in fact, would even have to do double duty.[36]

Abrams' comments notwithstanding, the secretary of defense was intent on reducing the American presence in Cambodia. On 12 May he therefore announced that several thousand American troops had already left the country and that more would depart within the week. Only the timely arrival of General Haig from Washington slowed the withdrawal. As Haig later explained to Kissinger,

Saw General Abrams. . . . He was as you suspected very disturbed by mixed signals from Washington. He has been told to reduce US presence in sanctuaries

---

[34] Quote from Msg, Wheeler JCS 6224 to Abrams, 5 May 70, sub: Attack on Base Areas in Cambodia. Msg, Abrams MAC 6126 to Wheeler, 6 May 70. Both in Abrams Papers, CMH.

[35] Msg, Wheeler JCS 6139 to McCain, Abrams, 4 May 70, sub: Completion of Individual Operations, Abrams Papers, CMH.

[36] Msg, Abrams MAC 6065 to Wheeler, 5 May 70, sub: Completion of Individual Operations, Abrams Papers, CMH.

320

and to provide comfortable cushion to ensure all forces are out by June 30. I gave him clear picture of President's thinking. This guidance arrived just in time since he was preparing response to SecDef containing specific plan for withdrawal of all US forces. He will now be less precise in response while avoiding head-on confrontation. He will also adjust to ensure maximum effort in sanctuaries consistent with weather and actions of enemy not artificial restrictions imposed by OSD. Discussions with Abrams's staff also confirms they were under impression US forces should be withdrawn as early as practicable. One example of this was that they had already prepared for OSD charts showing that the total US strength in Cambodia had declined continuously since the first week of cross-border operations.[37]

If Laird's concern for early withdrawals caused problems for Abrams, officers in the field were also encountering pressure, both of their own making and from the Saigon correspondents. The experience of the U.S. commander in the II Corps Tactical Zone, Lt. Gen. Arthur S. Collins, Jr., is a case in point. Informed abruptly that units of his command were to enter Base Area 702 west of Kontum in Cambodia's Rôtânôkiri Province, Collins was elated. Yet, with opposition already on the rise in the United States, he also recognized that the president might have little choice but to pull the troops back before they could accomplish anything worthwhile and decided to take immediate action. "I believed . . . we had to move fast," he later recalled, "or we'd never get to go." He thus pushed his commanders to cross the border before all preparations were complete but instructed them as well to be careful. "There was so much furor . . . at home," he said, "I did not want to have a lot of U.S. casualties. . . . I told the 4th Division commander to avoid hot landing zones, to just back off [if enemy firing commenced] and look for an open LZ."[38]

Although Collins had little doubt that controversy would dog his entrance into Cambodia, he clearly hoped he would be able to accomplish his mission without encountering more problems than necessary. In his haste, however, he caused his troops to outrun their fuel supplies at the very moment when a large group of reporters had arrived to cover the operation. "Well," he related afterwards, "with those reporters scurrying around for a good story, and all these soldiers lying around the airstrip with their gear off . . . [the newsmen] just had a field day. 'What are you waiting for? When are you going into Cambodia?' Naturally the soldiers told them that we didn't have enough fuel." Adding an air of crisis to the situation, one of the few platoons from the 4th Division to arrive in Cambodia on schedule lost several men when it came under enemy fire

---

[37] "Laird Says Thousands Have Already Left Cambodia," *New York Times*, 13 May 70. Also see James P. Sterba, "More Americans Out of Cambodia," *New York Times*, 14 May 70. Quote from Msg, Haig 592 to Kissinger, 21 May 70, NSC files, A. M. Haig Special file, box 1010, Vietnam/Cambodia, Gen Haig's Trip May 19–26, 1970 [I of III], Nixon Papers.

[38] Interv, Col Chandler P. Robbins with Lt Gen Arthur S. Collins, Jr., 1982, U.S. Army Military History Collection, Senior Officer Oral History Program, copy in CMH files.

shortly after landing. The resulting news stories, describing swirling clouds of red dust, casualties, and U.S. troops unable to move because of fuel shortages, prompted Abrams to travel to Collins' headquarters at Pleiku, where he arrived, according to the general, in a billow of cigar smoke, "grim and glowering."[39]

Difficulties With the Press

The Saigon correspondents, for their part, missed little that occurred. Not only was an American reporter present in North Vietnam to hear the air strikes that had embarrassed the Department of Defense, but Lon Nol himself informed newsmen that the United States had failed to consult with his government before committing troops to his country. Max Frankel of the *New York Times* meanwhile revealed that both Rogers and Laird had expressed serious misgivings about the incursion.[40]

Laird attempted to refute Frankel's allegation by issuing a carefully worded statement to the effect that he had always supported operations to destroy the enemy's sanctuaries, but the response had little effect. Reports persisted that he had opposed committing U.S. troops to Cambodia. To put an end to the issue, the secretary finally conceded on 14 May that he had at first argued against the operation. Even then, however, he minimized the vehemence of the position he had taken by stating that he had changed his mind quickly once he had become convinced there was little risk of high American casualties.[41]

If Laird thus managed to draw attention away from his own attitude toward the operation, other officials were less compliant. Correspondents learned almost immediately, for example, that the incursion had caused profound divisions within the U.S. embassy in Saigon. Hardly anyone was ready to speak for attribution, *Baltimore Sun* correspondent John Woodruff reported, but "men who usually limit themselves to a circumspect silence when they disagree with major government policies already are freely criticizing the decision in private conversations with their colleagues, and even with correspondents. Sharply worded criticisms reach even as high as certain members of the Mission Council." Although the ambassador, his closest associates, and most of the military supported the

[39] Ibid. Also see Msg, McCown CTO 486 to Abrams, 1 May 70, Abrams Papers, CMH; "In Search of an Elusive Foe," *Time*, 18 May 70.

[40] Msg, Hill Defense 6087 to Cutrona, 2 May 70, sub: Public Affairs Items, Saturday, 2 May 1970, DDI Cambodia file; Henry Kamm, "Phnompenh Given No Prior Notice," *New York Times*, 2 May 70; Max Frankel, "Rogers and Laird Termed Doubtful," *New York Times*, 6 May 70.

[41] Msg, OASD PA Defense 8161 to COMUSMACV, 6 May 70, 330–70–067, box 67, Cambodia 381 (1 May–10 May) 1970, Laird Papers, WNRC; William Beecher, "Doubt on Policy Denied by Laird," *New York Times*, 7 May 70; Fred Farrar, "Laird Admits He Had Doubts on Cambodia," *Chicago Tribune*, 15 May 70.

president, Woodruff continued, many civilian officials appeared to agree with the views of a U.S. mission council member who avowed that of all the possibilities open to the United States "this was probably the worst." Another civilian told Woodruff that the move into Cambodia was an obvious attempt to shore up Lon Nol. Without adverting to the fact that the military had pressed for just such an attack for years, he then asked, "How can we say with a straight face that it's the sanctuaries that we're worried about when we showed every sign of planning to live with them forever until March 18."[42]

The president's news analysts believed that he had made some headway during the week of 4 May in obtaining favorable press coverage of his contention that the incursion was limited in time and place. A number of reports also appeared on the military's success in uncovering the enemy's supplies and ammunition. One, by George Syvertsen of CBS News, depicted a vast enemy complex in Cambodia filled with tons of weapons and ammunition. The effect of such stories was, however, often ruined by other reports that brought the reader or viewer back to the controversies that had come to surround the incursion. On the same evening that Syvertsen's story appeared, for example, a second showed Gary Sheppard interviewing a soldier about to go into Cambodia. The trooper indicated that he would follow orders only because his father wanted him to avoid a bad conduct discharge.[43]

In the same way, there seemed some hope at the beginning of the week that themes of Nixon's courage and willingness to face up to his responsibilities might receive more play in the press than they had to that point. Yet, on the evening of 6 May, in another CBS interview, a soldier about to depart for Cambodia once more denied the administration and its supporters the satisfaction they sought. Responding to a query from a newsman on whether he might refuse to accompany his unit into Cambodia, the soldier remarked that any action he took would depend on what the rest of his unit did. The story prompted a call from Senator John Stennis to General Westmoreland. Stennis believed that the interviewer had asked a leading question designed to incite fear and disobedience. In addition, the soldier's response had appeared in "countless thousands of living rooms" across the United States and was bound to leave a bad impression. "I just don't see," the senator said, "why you have to let those men go into there with those cameras."[44]

[42] John R. Woodruff, "Drive Splits U.S. Embassy," *Baltimore Sun*, 3 May 70.

[43] Memo, Patrick Buchanan for the President, n.d. [mid-May], attachment to Memo, Herb Klein for H. R. Haldeman, 18 Jun 70, White House Special files, Staff Member Office files, Haldeman, box 242, HRH-Staff Memos (May/June 1970), H-M, Nixon Papers.

[44] Memo, Mort Allen for Jeb Magruder, Lyn Nofziger, Chuck Colson, 11 May 70, sub: Major Stories of Week of May 4th, White House Special files, Staff Member Office files, Haldeman, box 129, Major News Stories, May–Sept 1970 [part I of II], Nixon Papers. Quote from Record of Chief of Staff Telecon with Sen. Stennis, 1515, 7 May 70, sub: Cronkite Show, FONECON file, Westmoreland Papers, CMH.

Westmoreland passed the complaint to Henkin with a recommendation that the Military Assistance Command consider withdrawing the reporter's accreditation. Henkin responded that he would be willing to talk to CBS about the story and might even consider placing restrictions on interviews prior to the commencement of an operation but that disaccreditation would be "the worst thing we could do. . . . If we withdraw, they would replay it hour by hour. . . . We've got to wince and let it fly by."[45]

Although Westmoreland favored disaccreditation, there were no grounds for action in that case. A breach of military security was required to suspend a reporter's credentials, and none had occurred. Far from being an attempt to provoke disobedience, indeed, the reporter's question, however ill advised, was perfectly logical in context. For if violent protests were taking place in the United States, at least a few genuine combat refusals were occurring in South Vietnam. In one, at the U.S. 4th Infantry Division's headquarters at Pleiku, an infantryman protested the decision to enter Cambodia by binding himself with a rope and sitting down in the middle of a heavily traveled road. In another, widely reported by the press, six 4th Division infantrymen announced their refusal to obey an order to go into combat but later reconsidered their position and joined their unit in the field. A similar incident occurred while units of the U.S. 25th Division were preparing for operations in the Angel's Wing region of Cambodia. A strong case can be made that reporters have no business bringing up subjects such as combat refusals during interviews just prior to a military engagement, when soldiers are most fearful. Under the circumstances prevailing during the incursion into Cambodia, however, that they would avoid the question was almost unthinkable.[46]

Conditions were different on 7 May, when George Esper of the Associated Press broke the MACV's guidelines for the release of information by revealing that a flotilla of American and South Vietnamese gunboats was preparing to move up the Mekong River into Cambodia. Esper's article not only divulged that the attack would occur, it went so far as to reveal the precise number of ships involved and the armament they would carry. Although the reporter would later contend that South Vietnamese Foreign Minister Tran Van Lam had in fact announced the operation, the MACV Office of Information insisted on suspending his accreditation for thirty days. "It is difficult to see an excuse," Colonel Cutrona told Esper's superiors, "for going beyond . . . [Lam's] information (which was bordering on a violation in itself) to the specific number and armament of the American (and South Vietnamese) boats involved."[47] The ruling made little difference

---

[45] Record of Chief of Staff Telecon with Henkin, 1515, 7 May 70, sub: Cronkite Interview, FONECON file, Westmoreland Papers, CMH.

[46] James P. Sterba, "New U.S. Thrusts in Cambodia Open Two More Fronts," *New York Times*, 7 May 70; "Carrot and Stick," *Newsweek*, 25 May 70.

[47] Ltr, Cutrona to David Mason, Bureau Chief, Associated Press, Saigon, n.d., MACOI Correspondent Accreditation files, 334–74–593, box 14, Bad Guy file, WNRC. Also see George Esper Disaccreditation 1970 file, 72A821, box 1, WNRC.

American forces enter Snuol.

to Esper. By the time the Military Assistance Command had finished the reviews and paperwork necessary to impose the penalty, the reporter had departed for the United States on home leave.

If the Military Assistance Command could discipline Esper for breaking its ground rules, there was little it could do about Peter Arnett of the Associated Press and Leon Daniels of United Press International, who revealed how troops from the U.S. 11th Armored Cavalry had looted the Cambodian town of Snuol. Alleging that several civilians had been killed in air strikes preceding the incident, Arnett observed that "One GI ran out of a Chinese grocery clutching a bottle of brandy. Another broke into a watch shop and came out with a handful of wrist watches, while another GI lashed a Honda [motorcycle] to the top of his A–CAV [armored personnel carrier] before his troop moved off down the road."[48]

The event received wide play in the press. Although some reporters dealt with it unemotionally—Henry Kamm of the *New York Times*, for one, noted that the Viet Cong had long before turned Snuol into a major transshipment point for rice and supplies—most viewed it as an American intrusion upon the rights of the Cambodian people. After describing the looting, Jed Duvall of CBS News thus charged dramatically that the United States had made "no friends in Snuol today."[49] Interviewing some of the town's inhabitants, an NBC newsman concluded that all concerned wanted

[48] Arnett is quoted in "Spiking the Loot," *Newsweek*, 18 May 70, p. 76. Arnett tells the story in his memoirs. See Arnett, *Live From the Battlefield*, pp. 264–68.

[49] Henry Kamm, "Viet Cong Long a Fixture at Snuol, Deputy Says," *New York Times*, 30 May 70. The Duvall quote is from Memo, Buchanan for the President, n.d. [mid-May], attachment to Memo, Herb Klein for H. R. Haldeman, 18 Jun 70.

the Americans to go away and never come back. *New York Times* correspondent Gloria Emerson reported that the villagers were perplexed about the necessity for the American attack. Although the Military Assistance Command insisted that enemy forces had put up a stiff resistance, witnesses at the scene asserted that the enemy had, in fact, sought mainly to draw U.S. fire in order to force the troops to destroy civilian habitations. Emerson then quoted an eighteen-year-old American enlisted man who had said that the Scotch whiskey he had looted from the town "wasn't bad at all."[50]

MACV public affairs officers issued an immediate statement to emphasize that the U.S. government never condoned looting, but they could do little to contradict the allegations circulating in the press. The command's inspector general later confirmed the outlines of what had happened but contended nevertheless that reporters had exaggerated the situation. Although soldiers had indeed taken a motor scooter and a backhoe, he reported, both were later restored to their owners. Meanwhile, squad leaders and junior officers had quickly stopped whatever pilferage had occurred. As for allegations that the men had taken alcoholic beverages or other commodities, the inspector general asserted that they remained unsubstantiated.[51]

The reporters insisted that their stories were true. Arnett, for one, repeated his allegations to investigators from the Senate Foreign Relations Committee on 10 May, avowing that he had witnessed U.S. troops looting in Snuol and Cambodian civilian casualties caused by U.S. air strikes and napalm. In the end, his report and those of the others appear to have differed from the conclusions of the inspector general less in substance than in emphasis. The military considered the incident a matter to be dealt with in due course, while the press deemed it, as the *Washington Post* observed, "an instant editorial" on the war.[52]

There the matter might have ended, but for the Associated Press, which chose at first to soft-pedal what had happened by running Arnett's report unedited in its international dispatches while cutting all mention of the looting from the version it sent to its 500 U.S. clients. In a cable informing AP's Saigon bureau of the decision, the organization's general manager, Wes Gallagher, explained that the political situation in the United States appeared so dangerous that he had decided to exercise caution before running "inflammatory stories" of that sort.[53]

The move was controversial at the time but hardly extraordinary. The publisher of the *Washington Post*, Katherine Graham, was similarly cau-

[50] "Beyond the Checkpoint," p. 65; Gloria Emerson, "Ruined Town Can't Understand Why," *New York Times*, 23 May 70.

[51] Memo, Statement on Looting, 7 May 70, DDI Cambodia file; Ltr, Col S. F. Jillson, IG, to Honorable Howard W. Robinson, 15 Jun 70, 330–70–067, box 66, Cambodia 000.1–099, 1970, Laird Papers, WNRC.

[52] Msg, J. Lowenstein and R. Moose Saigon 7214 to State, for Carl Marcy, Senate Foreign Relations Committee, 11 May 70, General Abrams' Personal file 34, CMH; "The Battle for Snuol: An Instant Editorial," *Washington Post*, 7 May 70.

[53] "Spiking the Loot," p. 76.

tious about some of the stories her paper ran during the period. On one occasion, she even asked her editors to "cool down" coverage of the slayings at Kent State lest the *Post*'s reporting somehow contribute to the disorders that seemed to be spreading across the country.[54]

Gallagher's decision electrified AP's correspondents in South Vietnam, especially since United Press International had approved and released Daniel's account of the incident without question. Many protested by declining briefly to go into the field. A ten-year veteran of reporting the war and the recipient of a Pulitzer Prize, Arnett was himself so offended that he contemplated resigning. Deciding that the act would have little long-term impact, he concluded that he at least needed to clarify the record and leaked details of what happened to *Newsweek*'s Kevin Buckley. Questioned by the magazine shortly thereafter, Gallagher stifled the budding controversy by reevaluating his stand and admitting publicly that he had erred.[55]

The Attempt To Establish Success

If some within the news media were prone to caution, a mood of anger and bitterness over the way the press was covering the incursion still prevailed at the White House. President Nixon was particularly concerned. Believing that he had failed to make clear his thinking on the necessity for the operation, he began to search for a way to demonstrate the success of his decision to enter Cambodia.[56]

The course he chose presented itself when American and South Vietnamese forces began almost immediately to find large quantities of food and ammunition stockpiled by the enemy in the sanctuaries. Nixon immediately instructed General Wheeler to have the Military Assistance Command report the development in the most concrete manner possible in order to make it meaningful to the American public. "We should report ammunition in terms of rounds of various types," Wheeler told Abrams shortly thereafter, ". . . rather than tons. . . . In certain significant caches it might be possible to not only report . . . by type and quantity but also . . . in terms of days of supply for the enemy."[57]

The approach alarmed Secretary Laird, who believed that an emphasis on captured enemy supplies and the destruction of installations and facilities would serve mainly to open administration spokesmen to all the

---

[54] Sigal, *Reporters and Officials*, p. 32.

[55] "Spiking the Loot," p. 76. Arnett described his role in the episode during a talk to University of Maryland Honors students on 14 October 1992.

[56] See, for example, Memo, Buchanan for the President, n.d., attachment to Memo, Klein for Haldeman, 18 Jun 70. Also see Memo, the President for H. R. Haldeman, 11 May 70, White House Special files, Staff Member Office files, Haldeman, box 140, H. Presidential Memoranda To and From HRH (Steps Taken) [1970] [folder 2], Nixon Papers.

[57] Msg, Wheeler JCS/CJCS 6172 to Abrams, McCain, 5 May 70, Abrams Papers, CMH.

Cambodians fill bags with captured enemy rice.

ambiguities and uncertainties of battlefield reporting. He warned the president in a lengthy memorandum that the technique also ran the risk of turning the operation into a statistical exercise that might backfire if the gains suggested by official spokesmen proved illusory or suspect. The procedure might even open the president to the charge that he had bargained the lives of American soldiers for commodities that the Soviet Union and China could replace with little difficulty.[58]

Laird continued by commending the way Nixon had thus far justified the operation, in terms of the American withdrawal and as an effort to avoid further American casualties. He suggested that the president should dwell on broad issues of that sort, as well as on the possibility that the incursion might prompt the enemy to begin serious negotiations in Paris. To that end, he said, White House officials might leak word to the press of a U.S. willingness to consider "certain proposals." There might then be a show of ambassadors returning to the United States for consultations and lengthy meetings with the National Security Council and various Vietnam working groups. All of those activities would find their way into the press, where they would underscore Nixon's goodwill and his desire to end the war. Laird concluded that he had begun a series of daily briefings for congressmen and senators from both parties on the situation

[58] Memo, Laird for the President, 7 May 70, sub: Cambodian Operations, 330–76–076, box 6, Cambodia 381 (May–June) 1970, Laird Papers, WNRC.

in Southeast Asia. During the course of those sessions, friends of the administration had assured him that a six-week duration for the operation was about right and that both they and the American people would support the incursion if the president could demonstrate that it had furthered American withdrawals.[59]

Nixon rejected Laird's suggestions. They lacked, in his eyes, the qualities necessary to mount the hard-hitting public relations campaign that he considered necessary. What he wanted, he told Haldeman, was

a positive, coordinated administration program for getting across the fact that this mission has been enormously successful. . . . Above all Laird must get the instructions out to the field so that all commanders in Saigon and everybody in Saigon and Vietnam who talk to the press do not just reflect on what the situation is in their area. All of them should talk optimistically, confidently and particularly backing the decision on the basis of the enormous success it has had in capturing enemy equipment.[60]

The Military Assistance Command was already doing most of what the president required. Information officers in Saigon had made it a point to release as much as they could about what allied forces had found in the field, from routine body counts to minutely detailed lists of the number of rounds of small arms ammunition uncovered in enemy caches. A case in point occurred on 14 May, when a MACV communique detailed the contents of an enemy supply dump uncovered by the U.S. 25th Division: "87 individual weapons, 13,600 rounds of small arms ammunition, 167 60-mm. mortar rounds, 159 120-mm. mortar rounds, 66 75-mm. recoilless rifle rounds, one bicycle, three typewriters, and two 7 hp. generators."[61]

The command's spokesmen, as General Wheeler had requested, also evaluated the success of the operation in terms that emphasized the huge quantities of equipment and supplies allied forces were uncovering in Cambodia. According to the system of accounting they adopted, by the middle of May, U.S. and South Vietnamese forces had captured 10,898 rifles, enough to equip at least an entire Communist division; more than 2,700 tons of rice, a stock sufficient to feed the 90,000 enemy regulars serving in the lower half of South Vietnam for forty-one days; and 1,505 tons of ammunition, an amount that would supply 126 enemy battalions for up to four months in the field.[62]

Army photographers validated those statistics by documenting enemy supply caches and rushing their film to Saigon for developing and transmission to Washington. Information officers at the Military Assistance Command meanwhile attempted to steer the Saigon correspondents toward the most lucrative stories. At first, until major supply

[59] Ibid.
[60] Memo, the President for Haldeman, 11 May 70.
[61] Fact Sheet, Impact on the Enemy of the Cambodian Operations, 14 May 70, with attachment, FOL Released in Saigon, 14 May 70, CMH files.
[62] "Cambodia: Now It's 'Operation Buy Time,'" *Time*, 25 May 70, p. 28.

"The city" received heavy play in the press.

dumps could come to light, they set up a collection point for enemy weapons so that newsmen could see the broad range of enemy armaments that was coming to light as the incursion proceeded. Later, when American units uncovered a huge depot honeycombed with large, heavily camouflaged bunkers overflowing with arms, ammunition, and rice, they rushed newsmen to the scene. The reporters responded by dubbing the area "the city" and giving it heavy play in their dispatches. Information officers likewise took pains to inform the press that American and South Vietnamese agencies had begun to distribute large quantities of captured enemy rice to the many refugees who had fled Cambodia. They even transmitted moving pictures of the effort by costly telecommunications satellite so that the gesture received timely play in the United States.[63]

Those depictions of success notwithstanding, U.S. intelligence analysts in both Saigon and Washington were considerably more cautious in their assessments than official releases to the press might have indicated.

[63] Msg, Abrams MAC 6017 to Wheeler, 4 May 70, Abrams Papers, CMH. For a somewhat jaundiced description of military public affairs efforts at the time, see Terence Smith, "Results Uncertain in First Cambodian Forays," *New York Times*, 10 May 70. "The city" is mentioned in Msg, Abrams MAC 6264 to Wheeler, 8 May 70, Abrams Papers, CMH. The effort to publicize rice distribution is covered in Memo, Bill Safire for H. R. Haldeman, 18 May 70, sub: Humanitarian Distribution of Rice, White House Special files, Staff Member Office files, Haldeman alpha, box 116, Cambodia, Nixon Papers. Also see Msg, MAC JO3 for MACV Staff, 22 May 70, sub: Weekly Chief of Staff Conference Notes-18 May 70, 72A370, 5/12, 228.02, Staff Council Action Memo file, WNRC.

Intelligence officers at the Military Assistance Command, for example, were convinced that the operation had disrupted the enemy's system of supply, impeded the infiltration of his forces into South Vietnam, delayed the deployment of weapons yet to be used against allied forces, and bought time for the pacification program to work. Even so, they were reluctant to predict what the long term effects of the operation. When Henry Kissinger's military assistant, Brig. Gen. Alexander Haig, visited Cambodia to gain a firsthand view of the situation, they thus confirmed in briefings that the operation had limited Communist capabilities in the lower portions of South Vietnam but cautioned that the enemy's activities were politically motivated and that he retained the ability to launch attacks at will. They also warned against placing too much reliance on reports that purported to tabulate captured enemy equipment because they were based on battlefield estimates that might prove "grossly and embarrassingly misleading" when subjected to review and verification.[64]

Caution of that sort was hardly appreciated in Washington. When the Military Assistance Command attempted to reduce its estimate of the amount of ammunition captured in Cambodia, General Wheeler immediately warned that the move would produce credibility problems in the United States by contradicting the far more optimistic information Washington agencies had already released to the press.[65]

If MACV's analysts were guarded in their assessments, the Office of the Assistant Secretary of Defense for Systems Analysis in Washington was blunt in the appraisals it delivered to the White House. On 16 May, in response to continuing requests for information, its representatives warned Kissinger that it was far too early to estimate the operation's impact upon the enemy's ability to continue the war. Rice was by far the largest component of the materiel captured to date, but it was easy for the enemy to replace. Approximately 80,000 tons of the commodity were present in the portions of Cambodia under Communist control and much of that supply was available through purchase or confiscation. In the same way, the effect of captured ammunition on the enemy's ability to operate depended on stockpiles already in position in Laos and South Vietnam. If current estimates were even roughly correct, the supplies seized in Cambodia during the first two weeks of the operation amounted to at best 15 percent of the total stockage available, and what remained "would be enough to meet VC/NVA needs for one-and-one-half to four years." Although that estimate seemed extreme, the analysts warned, studies of enemy logistical practices indicated that the Communists attempted to maintain large reserves, often in excess of one year. Whether it was correct or not, the most important consideration in judging the effect of the

---

[64] Msg, Abrams MAC 7169 to Wheeler, 26 May 70, Westmoreland Message file, CMH; Msg, Abrams MAC 7018 to Wheeler, 23 May 70, sub: General Haig Visit, Abrams Papers, CMH; Memo, Maj Matthew P. Caulfield for Comdr Howe, White House Situation Room, date illegible [Jun 70], DDI Cambodia Opns file.
[65] Msg, Wheeler JCS 7115 to Abrams, 21 May 70, Abrams Papers, CMH.

operation was how long it would take the North Vietnamese to rebuild. While they would certainly have to disperse their supplies and alter their routines to compensate for the incursion and the continuing threat the South Vietnamese would pose to the sanctuaries after American troops had withdrawn, they were more than capable of making those adjustments. Between November 1969 and April 1970, indeed, they had moved over 100 tons of ammunition and supplies per day through Laos into South Vietnam. During peak weeks in February 1970, they had increased that amount to over 280 tons per day. The coming of the rainy season would degrade their ability to continue at that pace, but even if they managed to ship only 25 tons per day, they would be able to replace all of their ammunition and equipment losses within sixty days.[66]

The advice had little effect. Instead, the White House staff continued to insist that the Defense Department translate raw statistics into examples that would, as Haldeman put it, "hit home to the American people."[67] The department produced the information but declined to revise its judgment that the approach risked major public relations problems. "As you know," Deputy Assistant Secretary of Defense for Systems Analysis Philip Odeen told General Pursley on 2 June, referring to a White House request for yet another statistical analysis, "such comparisons are misleading and could prove embarrassing to the president."[68]

General Abrams, for his part, appears to have contributed little to the discussion. Convinced that the operation was going well and that its effects would be positive, he chose instead to concentrate on those aspects of the situation that he considered encouraging. Responding on 14 May to a request from the president for information on the performance of the South Vietnamese units in Cambodia, for example, he noted that those troops had reacted so vigorously to the opportunity to strike directly at their enemy that some Americans had expressed concern they might seek independence from U.S. advice and support. If that occurred, he said, it would be of considerable benefit to the Vietnamization program. In the same way, during a 26 May message to Wheeler and Moorer, he cautioned that substantial amounts of food and materiel remained to be discovered in the sanctuaries but that U.S. and South Vietnamese forces had uncovered at least 40 percent of the enemy's logistical base.[69]

---

[66] Fact Sheet, Impact on the Enemy of Supply Losses in Cambodia, 16 May 70, attachment to Memo, OASD SA for Comdr Howe, White House Situation Room, sub: Request for Information, DDI Cambodia Opns file. The fact sheet went initially to Kissinger but Laird also saw it. See 330–70–067, box 66, 381 (11–30 May) 1970, Laird Papers, WNRC.

[67] Memo, Haldeman for Klein, 19 May 70, White House Special files, WHCF–Subject files, Confidential Oversize files 1969–1974 [CF]ND 18/30 26 [Wars] [1969–70], Nixon Papers.

[68] Memo, Philip A. Odeen for General Pursley, 2 Jun 70, sub: Impact of Cambodian Operations, 330–70–067, box 67, Cambodia 400–499 1970, Laird Papers, WNRC. Also see Memo, Caulfield for Howe, White House Situation Room, date illegible [Jun 70].

[69] Msg, Abrams MAC 6676 to Moorer, 14 May 70; Msg, Abrams MAC 7134 to Wheeler, 26 May 70. Both in Abrams Papers, CMH.

The News Media React

The Saigon correspondents appear at first to have fallen in with the president's desire to illustrate the concrete benefits that had resulted from the incursion. During the first two weeks of the operation, their reports relayed U.S. accounts of heavy enemy casualties and the huge quantities of arms and ammunition that were beginning to appear. Orr Kelly of the *Washington Star*, for example, noted on 12 May that a failure by enemy units to obey orders to stand and fight had left "the city" undefended and had resulted in a far smaller U.S. casualty rate than expected. By official estimate, he said, some 4,543 of the enemy had died, one-eighth of the force the Communists employed in Cambodia. On the same day, Joseph Fried reported in the *New York Daily News* that the allied push into Cambodia had already resulted in the seizure of more Communist munitions than ever before in the war. He then relayed numbers supplied by the Military Assistance Command. Gary Sheppard of CBS News did the same two days later, quoting an unidentified American soldier to the effect that a recently discovered enemy depot represented "at least six months worth of supplies and perhaps more." Meanwhile, the editors of *U.S. News & World Report* asserted that the incursion had deterred the enemy from launching an offensive in South Vietnam for at least the next six months; the *Washington Star* applauded the success of the attack and criticized those who would prefer to see the operation fail in order to have their own dire prophecies fulfilled; and J. Regan Kerney of the *Philadelphia Bulletin* termed the vast stores of enemy arms uncovered in Cambodia "an astonishing sight."[70]

Reports of that sort continued in the weeks that followed, but many correspondents came to question the statistics they were receiving. Laurence Stern and Robert G. Kaiser of the *Washington Post* were among the first to do so. Observing that the incursion was strikingly similar to Operations CEDAR FALLS and JUNCTION CITY in 1967, they underscored statements by General Westmoreland at the time that the campaign had deprived the enemy of enormous stores of supplies while denying him the use of vital communications facilities and bases. Whatever the truth of those assertions, the two reporters noted, the enemy's losses appeared to have had little effect. The Tet offensive occurred just eight months later.[71]

Time took up the theme a week after that story appeared. According to its sources, the magazine said, enemy forces were far from crippled,

[70] Orr Kelly, "Red Units Rebelled in Fishhook," *Washington Star*, 12 May 70; Joseph Fried, "Cambodia Arms Yield Sets Record for War," *New York Daily News*, 12 May 70; Gary Shepard, CBS Morning News, 13 May 70, *Radio-TV-Defense Dialog*; "Fighting in Cambodia-The Real Meaning," *U.S. News & World Report*, 18 May 70, p. 37; "Smashing Red Sanctuaries: The Gains So Far," *U.S. News & World Report*, 25 May 70, p. 31.
[71] Laurence Stern and Robert G. Kaiser, "'Zero Contact' Offensive Falls Short of Goals But Turns Up Tons of Booty," *Washington Post*, 10 May 70.

despite the large quantities of rice, arms, and ammunition seized by allied forces. "Food is as close as the nearest paddy field. There is ample evidence, too, that the Communists, anticipating an assault, carted off substantial supplies. . . . Even now they are knitting together a river network that will supplement the Ho Chi Minh Trail."[72]

The 25 May issue of *Newsweek* appeared on the same day as the story in *Time*. Leading off the magazine's main article on Cambodia, boxed and in large type, was a purportedly top secret cable from Secretary Laird to General Abrams. "Dear Abe," it said, "In light of the controversy over the U.S. move into Cambodia, the American public would be impressed by any of the following evidence of the success of the operation: (1) high ranking enemy prisoners; (2) major enemy headquarters, such as COSVN; (3) large enemy caches. . . ."[73] Jerry Friedheim immediately contacted *Newsweek*'s Pentagon correspondent and its Washington bureau chief. Both were upset that their superiors had failed to check the item with them. On that basis, the Defense Department shortly thereafter denied that Laird had ever signed a cable of that sort. "No such message was dispatched from this building by anybody to anybody," Friedheim told reporters at the Pentagon. "I am personally aware that the story did not originate in this building, nor do I think it originated in Washington. The whole affair is phoney."[74] On the side, Colonel Hill cabled the Military Assistance Command to determine whether Abrams had ever received a message similar to the one that had appeared. Although Abrams was well aware of the mood in Washington and had received a number of messages asking him to promote the success of the incursion in various ways, he was able to state honestly that he had never received one similar to the item *Newsweek* had quoted. Noting that the story had probably originated in Saigon, Colonel Cutrona responded on Abrams' behalf that Friedheim's answer to the magazine's allegation had been sufficiently strong and that a broadening of the discussion to cover messages received from many sources would only weaken the Defense Department's position.[75]

Although *Newsweek* denied that the story was a fabrication and claimed that it had "double checked" before going to press, a message with wording similar to what the magazine had quoted has never appeared in official files.[76] Given the instructions Abrams had already received, indeed, a notification of that sort was probably unnecessary. The general knew what he had to do. In any event, with Abrams unwilling to enter into an open dispute with *Newsweek* and with other stories breaking, the affair died from lack of nourishment.

---

[72] "Cambodia: Now It's 'Operation Buy Time,'" *Time*, 25 May 70, p. 28.
[73] The article is quoted in Msg, Col L. Gordon Hill OASD PA 6916 to Col A. Lynn, USAF, CINCPAC PAO, 18 May 70, sub: *Newsweek* Dtd 25 May 1970, DDI Cambodia file.
[74] Msg, Wheeler JCS/CJCS 6172 to Abrams, McCain, 5 May 72.
[75] Msg, Cutrona MAC 6794 to Hill, 19 May 70, sub: *Newsweek*, dated 25 May 1970, DDI Cambodia file.
[76] [UPI], "Laird's 'Secret Cable' Denied by Pentagon," *Washington Post*, 19 May 70.

The controversy over the broader issue of MACV's statistics nonetheless continued. On 29 May John Woodruff of the *Baltimore Sun* remarked that, whatever the value of military assertions of progress, the United States and South Vietnam were pursuing an operation calculated to pay off in months while the enemy was strengthening his position in the Laotian hinterlands and launching "a combined political and military program conceived in terms of years and probably decades." *Time* meanwhile noted that the numbers military spokesmen cited to prove the progress of the operation were at times "downright misleading." That the 11,805 rifles, pistols, and submachine guns captured to date could arm 33 Communist battalions was true, the magazine noted, but most of the 126 battalions in the lower half of South Vietnam were already fully armed and most of the rifles the Military Assistance Command had found were dated SKS models replaced by the AK47 two years before. In the same way, much more than the 3,334 tons of rice taken in Cambodia had been captured in South Vietnam during each of the three preceding years, with no apparent effect on the enemy. As for the 1,700 tons of ammunition claimed by military spokesmen, the haul was indeed huge, but two-thirds of it was large-caliber antiaircraft ammunition rather than the small arms type employed by Viet Cong units in South Vietnam. Although many of the magazine's points were little different from criticisms appearing in official circles, the capture of so much antiaircraft ammunition may have been of major benefit to U.S. forces in South Vietnam. In making the comment, *Newsweek*'s editors apparently failed to reflect on the possibility that the presence in Cambodia of huge stocks of antiaircraft ammunition may have indicated that the enemy was planning major new initiatives against American and South Vietnamese aircraft and helicopters.[77]

Even more telling was a 30 May article by James Sterba in the *New York Times*. Conceding that the amount of captured materiel was impressive, Sterba replayed most of the objections that had appeared in other accounts of the operation. He then addressed assertions by military spokesmen that, as a result of the incursion, the enemy had postponed or canceled a number of short-term operations in South Vietnam and that the morale and coordination of some of his units had begun to break down. In fact, Sterba said, his own military sources indicated that the drop in enemy activity might have been the result either of an effort on the part of the Communists to conserve supplies or, more simply, of prudence. "There have been signs of sagging morale, food shortages, and a breakdown in coordination for five years, including the months just prior to the 1968 Lunar New Year offensive." Sterba concluded that it was the belief of many of the military men he had talked to "that the operation was oversold because of political considerations and is being undercut because of political considerations. They are being required to

[77]John E. Woodruff, "Communists Forming Base for Long Cambodia Struggle," *Baltimore Sun*, 29 May 70; "Just How Important Are Those Caches?," *Time*, 1 Jun 70, p. 27.

hail it publicly as a tremendous strategic victory while they privately believe that the most they have gained is a short-term tactical advantage."[78]

The Administration Attempts To Regroup

The criticism rising in the press angered the president's advisers. They began to consider ways to respond. A few, such as Charles McWhorter and Daniel Patrick Moynihan, urged caution. Inappropriate statements by Agnew and others, they said, might only foster a crisis of national unity or lead to violence by antiwar zealots against the president or the families of his staff. Others, Patrick Buchanan in particular, agitated for action by emphasizing the poor performance of the news media. Ignoring attempts at restraint by individual editors and publishers such as Gallagher, they stressed what they considered the many violations against objectivity and fairness that they saw appearing in newspapers and on television. Over the first two weeks in May, Buchanan thus told President Nixon, CBS News had failed to screen the kind of footage that might have demonstrated the logic behind the move into the sanctuaries. Instead, the network had concentrated on "fumbling South Vietnamese troops, shattered and burning hideouts, a few soldiers who bad-mouth America, some pitiful refugees of war and a few looters." It was an example, Buchanan said, of "how the media can manipulate public information and opinion without appearing to do so."[79]

The president shared Buchanan's anger. Convinced that only the most emphatic measures would force his presumed enemies in the press into submission, he instructed his staff on 11 May to cut off the *New York Times* and the *Washington Post* from all but the most routine contacts with the White House. Under no circumstances, he told Haldeman, was Ziegler or any other member of the presidential staff to grant interviews to reporters employed by those papers or to return their calls. Instead, the *Washington Star*, the *Washington Daily News*, the *New York Daily News*, the *Chicago Tribune*, the *Los Angeles Times*, and other publications that competed with the *Post* and the *Times* were to become the recipients of special private interviews and other signs of presidential favor. The president took no action at the time against CBS or the other television

[78] James P. Sterba, "Cambodian Foray After a Month: From Arms and Rice to Buttons," *New York Times*, 30 May 70.

[79] Memo, Charlie McWhorter for Ehrlichman, Haldeman, Klein, Garment, and Keogh, 6 May 70, White House Special files, Staff Member Office files, Haldeman alpha, box 116, Cambodia, Nixon Papers; Memo, Daniel P. Moynihan for the President, 9 May 70, President's Office files, box 6, President's Handwriting, May 70, Nixon Papers. Quote from Memo, Buchanan for the President, n.d. [mid-May], attachment to Memo, Klein for Haldeman, 18 Jun 70.

networks. An obvious, heavy-handed attempt to ban television reporters and camera crews from White House functions would have risked an angry confrontation with the press while cutting the administration off from a valuable source of day-to-day publicity. As a substitute, the president appears to have contented himself with continuation of efforts by his staff to notify network news managers emphatically but confidentially of White House objections when particularly offensive stories appeared.[80]

The president carried out his moves against the *Post* and the *Times* in private, but he recognized that a public effort was also necessary. He therefore began preparations for a televised 3 June speech on the progress to date of the operation in Cambodia. Meanwhile, his staff enlisted conservative business executives such as the president of the Marriott Corporation, J. Willard Marriott, Sr., and celebrities such as actor Bob Hope and evangelist Billy Graham to begin planning for a special "Honor America Day" that would occur in Washington on 4 July. Attracting tens of thousands of Americans to the nation's capital for a day of patriotic entertainment and peaceful demonstrations, the event would exhibit the continued support of the silent majority for the president and his aims.[81]

On the side, the vice president gave expression to the president's anger by renewing his criticism of the administration's opponents. During a speech at a 22 May Republican fund-raising dinner in Houston, Texas, he expressed scorn for the "liberal news media . . . who would like to run the country without submitting to the elective process as we in public office must do." Naming editorial writers at the *Washington Post*, *New York Times*, *Atlanta Constitution*, and the *New Republic*; columnists James Reston, Carl Rowan, and Tom Wicker of the *Times*, and Hugh Sidey of *Life*; *Post* editorial cartoonist Herblock; and a number of other journalists as particularly reprehensible, he then went on to characterize the antiwar movement as a "small hard core of hell-raisers" on college campuses and "isolationists" in the U.S. Senate.[82]

The president's 3 June report on the incursion appears to have gone over well. Although commentators in the *New York Times*, among others, noted that Nixon had presented little evidence that the operation would prove any more effective in shortening the war than many earlier so-called successes, White House news analysts were overjoyed with the reaction the speech received. "Relatively light response to RN's speech (1

[80] Memo, the President for Haldeman, 11 May 70. See, for example, Memo, H. R. Haldeman for Klein, 11 Jun 70, White House Special files, Staff Member Office files, Haldeman, box 242, HRH-Staff Memos (May/June 1970) H–M, Nixon Papers.

[81] MFR, n.d. [Jul 70], sub: Follow-up Action on the Administration, Week of June 29th, attachment to Memo, Mort Allen for Jeb Magruder, Chuck Colson, Lyn Nofziger, 6 Jul 70, sub: Major Stories of Week of June 29, White House Special files, Staff Member Office files, Haldeman, box 129, Major News Stories, May–Sept 1970 [part I of II], Nixon Papers. Also see Memo, Jim Keogh for Bob Haldeman, 24 Jun 70, White House Special files, Staff Member Office files, Haldeman, box 141, Press and Media 1 [part II], Nixon Papers.

[82] Agnew is quoted extensively in *Facts on File*, 28 May–3 Jun 70, vol. 30.

General Dzu guides VIP tour of Communist sanctuaries in Cambodia.

paragraph in *Time*)," one of them noted, "but next day's headlines domi-nated by 'success,' 'all objectives reached,' etc."[83]

On the day of the speech, as part of the effort to counter the allega-tions of critics and to establish the success of the incursion, a special deputation of governors, congressmen, senators, and White House aides departed Washington to conduct an inspection of the war zone. The presi-dent's Director of Communications, Herbert Klein, had at first resisted the idea of the trip, on grounds that it would have to include opponents of the operation to be credible, and that they would certainly raise objec-tions. In addition, Klein noted, according to President Johnson's Press Secretary, George Christian, a similar tour during the Johnson adminis-tration to observe the 1967 South Vietnamese elections had ended badly because the participants had been unable to see everything they had desired. "There is a possibility, with the dwindling supplies and predic-tion of increased fighting, that we might run into the same kind of prob-lem."[84] Klein's reservations notwithstanding, the president had dis-

[83] See, for example, "The Other War in Cambodia," *New York Times*, 5 Jun 70. For the speech itself, see News Release, Office of the White House Press Secretary, Radio and Television Address by the President on the Cambodian Sanctuary Operation, 3 Jun 70, DDI Cambodia Opns file. Quote from Memo, Mort Allen for Jeb Magruder, Chuck Colson, Lyn Nofziger, 8 Jun 70, sub: Major Stories of Week of June 1, White House Special files, Staff Member Office files, Haldeman, box 129, Major News Stories, May–Sept 1970 [part I of II], Nixon Papers.

[84] Memo, Jeb Magruder for H. R. Haldeman, 12 May 70, sub: Follow-up on Our Cambodian Program. Quote from Memo, Klein for Haldeman, 20 May 70. Both in White House Special files, Staff Member Office files, Herbert Klein, Name file, 69–70, box 1, H. R. Haldeman, II [I of V], Nixon Papers.

patched the delegation, with all but one of its members, Senator Thomas J. McIntyre of New Hampshire, clearly well disposed to the incursion.

Klein's expectations proved accurate. Although the delegation, with only McIntyre dissenting, reported favorably on the operation, an incident described by Jack Laurence of CBS News during the course of the tour created just the sort of cause celebre that Klein had suspected would discredit the group's findings. It occurred when the party visited units of the 3d Brigade of the U.S. 9th Infantry Division in Cambodia, at a location identified by Laurence only as "Shakey's Hill." Prior to the team's arrival, the reporter noted, the division had taken extreme steps to police its base camp, a place that was normally littered, as were most combat areas in Southeast Asia, with the garbage and clutter of war. "Captured enemy weapons were polished, clean white linen was placed on the tables that were especially lifted to Shakey's Hill for the inspection of the captured arms. The military exercise in showmanship went as far as haircuts for the soldiers, three barbers having been flown into the fire base. Some of the men were given clean fatigues and combat boots, which they normally get less often." The committee inspected a carefully prepared display of captured weapons, the reporter continued, before each member met with "carefully chosen, dressed, shaved and briefed" soldiers from his home state. "Finally, the visitors were led down a jungle path that had been carefully chosen for them, to inspect two of the bunkers that had held some of the captured weapons. . . . They were not told that the weapons they were looking at down in the hole had been put there, having once been removed, to give them the impression of reality." The visitors were impressed, Laurence noted. Senator John Tower stated afterwards that "You could question the political effects of the offensive into Cambodia, but you could not question the military achievement." The soldiers had a different reaction. "We live like animals," one told the reporter, "until someone comes. . . . Sleep in the mud, rain. Now, we get all dressed up."[85]

The report galled the Nixon administration, which used it internally to illustrate Buchanan's contention that television news was biased against the president and his policies. Yet even journals that had adopted a relatively balanced stance toward the incursion were critical of the trip, for many of the same reasons Laurence had suggested. The *Washington Star*, for one, printed a forthright summary of the group's conclusions but then insisted in an editorial that the fact finders should have stayed home. Summarizing Laurence's report point by point, the paper charged that the trip had been a waste of taxpayer dollars because the group had seen at best a sanitized version of what was happening in Cambodia.

[85] Transcript, n.d., sub: John Laurence Report, Cronkite News, June 8, 1970, attachment to Memo, Haldeman for Klein, 11 Jun 70, White House Special files, Staff Member Office files, Herbert Klein, Name file, 69–70, box 1, H. R. Haldeman, II [I of V], Nixon Papers. Since the transcript was drawn from an oral report, the author has added several commas and broken up a run-on sentence for clarity.

"That is the way the fact-finders learn the things they come home and tell us about. And that is why hawks and doves retain their accustomed feathers after such trips. The scene on Shakey's Hill, that day, had nothing to do with the real war."[86]

Other papers such as the *Washington Daily News* were even more uncomplimentary. They emphasized the necessarily tentative nature of the group's conclusions, quoting, among others, a Republican governor, Raymond P. Shafer of Pennsylvania, who observed that if the incursion had indeed been a short-term military success, "Lord only knows about the long term." In the same way, negative remarks by McIntyre came in for heavy quotation. Reflecting on an observation by Nixon during the 3 June speech that the South Vietnamese would base their decision to withdraw from Cambodia upon "the actions of the enemy," an indication that they would probably choose to stay on after American forces retired, the senator had expressed profound reservations. "What do we do if the defense of Cambodia by Asian forces runs into trouble?" he had remarked at a news conference. "Do we go back in to save them? Or do we keep our word not to when the alternative may be the collapse of the Lon Nol regime and the conversion of all of Cambodia into one vast communist sanctuary from which attacks can be launched?" McIntyre then revealed that presidential counselor Bryce Harlow, rather than a member of the delegation, had written the majority's favorable report. Harlow had done the work during a stopover in Honolulu, the senator said, after consulting with each member of the task force but while most of the party had "hit the pool for a couple of hours."[87]

In the end, neither the Nixon administration nor the Military Assistance Command made any attempt to refute either McIntyre's comments or Laurence's story. The damage had been done. Any attempt to explain would have made matters only worse by opening the issue to further examination. As a special assistant to the president, James Keogh concluded in a memorandum to Haldeman later in the month that the White House staff had spent too much time fabricating "gimmicks" to the detriment of the president's policies. In each instance, suspicious newsmen had been "waiting at the entrance to the alley," where they had made all concerned "look more devious than we are." That, in turn, had created the sort of credibility problems that served to make the press only "more suspicious . . . than ever."[88] Deputy Secretary of Defense David Packard agreed. Noting a proposal that defense use the large quantity of captured enemy documents taken during the incursion for public relations purposes, he recommended against the idea for the same reason that Keogh had given: "The less we use any of this material for public affairs the better off

---

[86] Memo, Haldeman for Klein, 11 Jun 70. The summary is in "Cambodia Drive Success Cited by 'Fact-Finders,'" *Washington Star*, 10 Jun 70. Quote from "Fact-Finders: Stay Home," *Washington Star*, 10 Jun 70.

[87] Ted Knap, "Cambodia Report Glows," *Washington Daily News*, 11 Jun 70.

[88] Memo, Keogh for Haldeman, 24 Jun 70.

we are," Phil Odeen paraphrased him. "The recent Herb Klein trip to Southeast Asia had done no good and had caused all sorts of problems."[89]

American Forces Withdraw

In the days that followed the delegation's return, the president and his staff began preparations for the departure of American forces from Cambodia. On 3 June, Nixon had assured his listeners that he would meet the 30 June deadline. He was resolved to do so, but neither he nor the South Vietnamese had any intention of leaving Cambodia to the enemy. Instead, as early as 24 and 25 May, both the State and Defense Departments had indicated quietly in public statements that the United States would probably not oppose the wish of the South Vietnamese armed forces to continue operations in Cambodia after the American departure. The president's 3 June speech had repeated the point.[90]

Those comments, along with the decline in American activities that began as U.S. troops retired well in advance of the target date, prompted the Saigon correspondents to pay more attention than ever to South Vietnamese activities in Cambodia. The articles that resulted often dealt with South Vietnamese successes, but they still asked difficult questions and drew unflattering parallels. Both *Newsweek* and *Time*, for example, noted that the South Vietnamese armed forces had developed a new confidence, but *Time* still observed that those units seemed to fight better in Cambodia than they had at home, if only because there were fewer snipers and booby traps. "Not even the intense euphoria of the Cambodian excursion," the magazine explained, "can overcome low pay, corruption and lackluster leadership." In the same way, James Sterba of the *New York Times* observed that if the South Vietnamese had gained in morale and confidence, many Americans still questioned whether they had learned much that would be of use in South Vietnam, where the enemy remained more difficult to identify than in Cambodia.[91]

Within the government itself, Secretary Laird was even less confident. He agreed emphatically with a decision by Abrams to use the conclusion of the incursion on 30 June as an excuse to push the South Vietnamese armed forces to accept a greater share of the combat burden in their own country, but he doubted that they were operating as effectively in Cambodia as Abrams seemed to think. After years of hearing

[89] MFR, Phil Odeen, 11 Jun 70, sub: Vietnamization Meeting With Mr. Packard, Thayer Papers, CMH.
[90] "Vietnamizing Cambodia," *New York Times*, 24 May 70; Peter Grose, "Rogers Hints U.S. Won't Curb Ally," *New York Times*, 25 May 70.
[91] "A Different Scene," *Newsweek*, 8 Jun 70, p. 35; "Cambodia: A Cocky New ARVN," *Time*, 8 Jun 70, p. 30; James P. Sterba, "Cambodian Incursion by U.S. Appears To Unite Foe," *New York Times*, 29 Jun 70.

how inept and cautious those forces tended to be, he told his staff as early as 15 May, he was now reading about "the tigers of Southeast Asia." In fact, he said, there was a genuine danger that the enemy would trap and maul one of those units deep in Cambodia. If that happened, it would cause severe damage to public opinion in the United States.[92]

In the end, the South Vietnamese never suffered the sort of defeat that both Laird and McIntyre had considered possible, but shortly after U.S. forces withdrew from the country they managed to cause public relations problems nonetheless, by looting the Cambodian town of Kompong Speu, a major enemy depot prior to the incursion. The event found its way into the press, where Peter Kann of the *Wall Street Journal* quoted Cambodian General Southenne Fernandez as saying that if the South Vietnamese had liberated the town they had also ravaged it. "It is regrettable, no?" the officer had told the reporter. "The population is very discouraged with our South Vietnamese allies. I am also discouraged."[93]

General Abrams, for his part, while pleased with the renewed confidence of his confederates, was concerned about the restrictions the Nixon administration intended to impose on American operations in Cambodia after the 30 June deadline. The rules of engagement to take effect on that date barred American ground forces from entering Cambodia under any circumstances except self-defense. American aircraft might fly interdiction strikes against enemy supply routes in Cambodia, but they were to leave close air support of South Vietnamese units operating in the country to the South Vietnamese Air Force. Abrams had few problems with most of those rules, but the one covering American ground forces precluded the insertion of U.S. ground intelligence teams into Cambodia. If that restriction went into effect, Abrams told McCain, it would force the United States to place "unprecedented reliance" on questionable South Vietnamese sources.[94]

The Acting Chairman of the Joint Chiefs of Staff, Admiral Thomas Moorer, who would succeed Wheeler as chairman on 1 July, backed Abrams in a memorandum to Laird, but the Defense Department's office of international security affairs objected. Any attempt to continue the operations—code-named SALEM HOUSE—along lines that had prevailed in the past, by assigning American advisers to accompany reconnaissance teams, the agency's analysts said, would be inconsistent with the president's promise to remove all U.S. troops from Cambodia. Earlier in the war, only a few press reports had dealt with those operations and

[92] MFR, Phil Odeen, 27 May 70, sub: Meeting With Secretary Laird on Vietnam. Quote from MFR, Phil Odeen, 15 May 70, sub: Meeting With Secretary Laird on Vietnam. Both in folder 75, Thayer Papers, CMH.

[93] Peter Kann, "Vietnamese Alienate Cambodians in Fight Against Mutual Enemy," *Wall Street Journal*, 2 Jul 70. Also see Sidney Schanberg, "Looting by Saigon Units Stirs Cambodian Hatred," *New York Times*, 2 Jul 70.

[94] Msg, Abrams MAC 7652 to Davison, 6 Jun 70, and Msg, Abrams MAC 7292 to McCain, 29 May 70, both in Abrams Papers, CMH.

there had been few if any diplomatic or political repercussions. After 30 June, however, the world would pay close attention to whether U.S. forces were still entering Cambodia. Any attempt on the part of the United States to hedge on its promises could thus result in serious consequences. When Henry Kissinger concurred with that opinion and the State Department offered no objection, Laird decided against any attempt at compromise. From then on, although extralegal exceptions may have occurred, clandestine cross-border operations into Cambodia became, to Abrams' dismay, a largely indigenous South Vietnamese operation.[95]

Public affairs officers at the Military Assistance Command were happy to see the operation end on 29 June, when some fifty newsmen and five congressmen greeted the last American units to withdraw from Cambodia. Even so, the event was hardly without controversy. Morley Safer filed a report for CBS stating that the command had brought out a band and refreshments to greet the returning troops but that only those soldiers within the view of the press and assembled dignitaries had participated in the festivities. The event, the reporter indicated, was obviously a public affairs extravaganza designed to emphasize to the American public, Congress, and press that American units had indeed departed from Cambodia. In fact, while some sort of celebration had obviously occurred, it appears to have been instigated by the U.S. 1st Cavalry Division (Airmobile) rather than MACV's Office of Information. Informed of the report years later, the chief of MACV information at the time, Colonel Cutrona, could recall only that he would never have organized an event of that sort to mark the end of the incursion. Because of the controversies that had already occurred, he said, he and his officers had sought to extract American forces from Cambodia quietly and with as little fanfare as possible.[96]

Whatever the validity of the report, Safer's comments were indicative of public relations failures that had dogged the incursion into Cambodia from the very beginning. As *U.S. News & World Report* correspondent Wendell Merick had observed, the operation itself, while controversial, had considerable military justification, both as a long overdue stab at the enemy's sanctuaries and as a means to save American lives. The president and his advisers had determined, however, that explanations of that sort were too nebulous to attract the heavy public support they deemed necessary. Understanding that the move into the sanctuaries would cause

[95] Memo, Adm Thomas Moorer CM–5266–70 for Secretary of Defense, 16 Jun 70, sub: SALEM HOUSE Operational Authorities, and Memo, ASD ISA for Secretary of Defense, n.d. [29 Jun 70], sub: SALEM HOUSE Operating Authorities, both in 330–76–076, box 4, 337 SD/JCS, Laird Papers, WNRC. Also see Memo, Moorer CM–405–70 for Secretary of Defense, 8 Dec 70, 330–76–076, box 4, Cambodia 381 (Oct–Dec) 1970, Laird Papers, WNRC.

[96] CBS Evening News, 27 Jun 70, excerpted in Marvin Barrett, ed., *A. I. du Pont–Columbia University Survey of Broadcast Journalism, 1969–1970, Years of Challenge, Year of Crisis* (New York: Grosset & Dunlap, Inc., 1970), p. 145. Also see Interv, author with Gen Joseph F. H. Cutrona, USA (Ret.), 28 May 87, copy in CMH files.

opposition but miscalculating the degree of antagonism it would evoke in the United States, they had thus sought to rationalize their decision by citing simple, concrete explanations that the so-called silent majority could comprehend. When the search for COSVN headquarters proved as futile as Laird and Rogers had predicted and when the importance of the arms, ammunition, and rice uncovered in Cambodia failed to measure up to intense scrutiny, they were left with little to fall back on. They resorted to more of the same. The real story thus became, in the eyes of the press, not the operation itself—most reporters conceded that it had indeed harmed the enemy—but its long-term results and the attempts at justification that both the military services and the president had made.

Patrick Buchanan and others on the president's staff claimed that the press, by highlighting the contradictions inherent in the president's policies, was acting out of a profound bias. Those opinions to the contrary, it was hardly exceptional that stories critical of the operation would receive heavy play in the news media. With political elites in the United States in disagreement over the event and an air of deep concern pervading the nation, reporters in both South Vietnam and the United States were bound to cover the debate over the operation as it developed and bound to keep a watchful eye for anything that went wrong.[97] That the resulting news stories were little more pointed than many of the critiques appearing in official memorandums spoke more to the controversial nature of the president's decision to enter Cambodia than it did to some putative intention on the part of the news media to manipulate the American public.

White House news analyses for the period, moreover, if hardly favorable to the press, tend to suggest that news coverage of the incursion, taken as a whole, was often more balanced than either the president or his advisers were willing to accept. Although the ombudsman of the *Washington Post* would later conclude that his own newspaper's coverage of the operation was "one-sided and unfair" to the Nixon administration and criticism abounded on the editorial pages of many other American newspapers, the official point of view came across well, both in the news and through the other vehicles of expression open to the president and his staff.[98] Almost every important statement and communique the White House issued during the period received extensive news coverage. In addition, during the week of 4 May alone, Vice President Agnew defended the president's position on the popular "David Frost Show." White House Director of Communications Klein joined with evangelist Billy Graham to do the same on the "Dick Cavett Show." Ambassador Bunker appeared on "Meet the Press," Under Secretary of State

[97] To obtain a sense of the mood of the press, see, for example, "The President's Gamble."
[98] See, for example, Memo, Allen for Magruder, Nofziger, Colson, 11 May 70, sub: Major Stories of Week of May 4th. Also see Hallin, *The Uncensored War*, p. 189. Quote from Memo, Richard Harwood for the editors of the *Washington Post*, 26 Jan 71, in Laura Langley Babb, ed., *Of the Press, by the Press, for the Press (and Others, Too)* (Washington, D.C.: Washington Post Co., 1974). Also see Braestrup, *Big Story*, 1:708.

Elliot Richardson on "Issues and Answers," and Admiral Moorer on "Face the Nation." Meanwhile, the administration-sponsored "Tell It To Hanoi" Committee launched a major radio campaign budgeted at $100,000; the Veterans of Foreign Wars conducted a post-to-post campaign to gather backing for the incursion; the AFL-CIO began a major effort to rally its membership behind the president's action; administration supporters in the House and Senate appeared daily on network radio news programs; and sympathetic reporters and columnists received a series of officially authored position papers and background reports in support of the president's decision. Similar activities followed the next week and for all of the weeks thereafter until American troops departed from Cambodia. The result was plain to see. As James McCartney noted in the *Philadelphia Inquirer* on 16 May, for at least several days during the first week of the incursion, "the essential points in the Administration case . . . dominated the news."[99]

One of the president's advisers, Raymond K. Price, Jr., summarized the president's public affairs problems during the incursion in a forceful memorandum to H. R. Haldeman. "It is impossible to divorce our media relations from the substance of our operations," he told the president's chief of staff on 24 June.

There seems to have been a fairly prevalent attitude around here in recent months that anything can be sold if only it's sold skillfully enough—and this simply isn't so. A "game plan" can help sell something that's inherently salable—but even this is true only up to a point. Whenever we tip over into transparent (or discoverable) contrivance, we spend a part of our credibility capital. *And nothing is more important to us in the long run than maintaining our credibility—even if we lose the opportunity to make a few points in the short run.*

Price concluded that the mood within the administration had changed since the early days of the Nixon presidency. The attitude of the White House staff had once been zestful, creative, and optimistic. "We were trying to unite a divided people, not to profit a few points in the next month's Gallup [poll] by playing to its discontents."[100]

As for the success of the incursion, it remained open to debate. Over the next year, the president and his staff would time and again refer to the great advantages it had brought, from the huge amount of weapons it had produced to a decline in enemy activity in South Vietnam that appeared to have been one of its most important benefits. By February 1971 the

[99] Fact Sheet, Follow-up Action on Indochina, Week of May 4th, attachment to Memo, Allen for Magruder, Nofziger, Colson, 11 May 70, sub: Major Stories of Week of May 4th. White House Special files, Staff Member Office files, Haldeman, box 129, Major News Stories, May–Sept 1970 [part I of II], Nixon Papers, contains a number of memos on the same subject covering the rest of the incursion. James McCartney, "Nixon Using Big Guns To Plug for Cambodia," *Philadelphia Inquirer*, 16 May 70.

[100] Memo, Raymond K. Price, Jr., for Bob Haldeman, 24 Jun 70, sub: Your Memo of June 22 on Press and Media, White House Special files, Staff Member Office files, Haldeman, box 141, Press and Media 1 [part II], Nixon Papers.

Defense Department's office of systems analysis could nevertheless still report to Laird that the enemy's logistical units had survived in the border regions. As a result of the incursion, indeed, a wider war had come into being. East of the Mekong River in Cambodia, some sixty to seventy enemy battalions operated as a rear base for future moves into South Vietnam. To the west and south, enemy units had isolated Phnom Penh both from the sea and from its western provinces while seizing the territory they needed to extend their Laotian infiltration routes southward. Meanwhile, the morale of Lon Nol's poorly trained and equipped army continued to fall as Communist forces severed the land routes between Cambodia and South Vietnam and continued to develop an indigenous "Liberation Army" to take over the Cambodian portion of the war.[101]

In hindsight, the situation in the United States was probably as ominous. On the very day that the incursion ended, the Senate passed the Cooper-Church Amendment. The legislation allowed for continued support of American servicemen in combat but prohibited the expenditure of public funds for any future introduction of U.S. ground forces into Cambodia. It marked a portent for the future. In 1975 Congress would once more exercise its power over the purse by cutting off, finally and definitively, American support for the war.

---

[101] MFR, OASD SA, 4 Feb 71, sub: The War in Cambodia-An Overview, 330–76–207, box 1, file 020 SD 1971, Laird Papers, WNRC.

15

A Change of Direction

Although the incursion into Cambodia showed some promise of improving the situation in South Vietnam, in the months that followed the operation even normally optimistic officials felt constrained to admit that progress in many areas of the war remained elusive. Ambassador Bunker, for one, could tell the president with great sincerity on 26 August 1970 that the results of the incursion had been "widespread and advantageous" yet just as sincerely report to the vice president on the same day that circumstances still remained "troublesome." South Vietnam, he told Agnew, seemed to rely on the United States not only for military support but also for the basic economic commodities that sustained its life. Overwhelmingly dependent on imports, most of which were financed through U.S. aid or American military purchases of piasters at a subsidized rate of exchange, it thus continued to procure more than $750 million in goods and services per year abroad while exporting at best $15 million in locally produced merchandise. Those circumstances, the ambassador said, demoralized honest South Vietnamese by contributing to the spread of graft and corruption.[1]

Despite his misgivings, Bunker clearly believed that few absolutes were possible in human affairs and that major opportunities still existed for the United States in South Vietnam. Other officials in both Saigon and Washington were less certain. The authors of a compendium on pacification completed for the Defense Department's Vietnam Special Studies Group during May 1970, for example, contended that whatever progress that program had achieved over the previous five years had resulted primarily from U.S. large-unit operations rather than attempts by the South Vietnamese government and military to win the hearts and minds of the people. The enemy's infrastructure meanwhile remained intact, and the

---

[1] Quotes from Msg, Saigon 13850 to State, Bunker to the President, 26 Aug 70. Msg, Saigon 13886 to State, Bunker to the Vice President, 26 Aug 70. Both in Bunker Papers, FAIM/IR.

influence of that shadow government seemed sufficiently strong to nullify the overall impact of the American effort. The study concluded that in the light of those deficiencies and the continuing inability of the South Vietnamese government to identify willing, capable leaders, any cease-fire in the near future would be more advantageous to the enemy than to the United States.[2]

An information briefing during August by members of the Army Staff for the Joint Chiefs was even more pessimistic. Time was running out, the authors of that analysis noted. When the United States finally relinquished the conduct of the war to South Vietnam, the South Vietnamese armed forces would find themselves so preoccupied with providing security for the people that they would find it almost impossible to carry on the fight against the enemy's conventional forces, a task thus far borne by Americans. Meanwhile, the country's territorial and paramilitary forces would lack the time and resources necessary either to assume a satisfactory role in pacification or to make much progress toward neutralizing the Viet Cong infrastructure. Although there was some hope that the destruction of enemy base areas in Cambodia and Laos might forestall a collapse, the net effect would probably be an eventual Communist victory.[3]

Each of those analyses had its opponents. One commentator observed, for example, that the "all is lost" theme was hardly supported by the recent experience in Cambodia or by the statistics that continued to emerge from the pacification program. Yet the weight of the war was clearly becoming heavy for many within the U.S. government. The United States would spend $2,343,100,000 on ammunition to fight the war during the 1970 fiscal year, apparently to no long-term effect, while the best estimates indicated that the Soviet Union and the People's Republic of China would spend only $102 million on such supplies for North Vietnam, a ratio of over twenty-two to one. To exist at bare subsistence levels, indeed, the enemy required only 99 short tons of supplies per day from sources outside of South Vietnam, less than twenty truck loads, and his ability to resupply his forces was almost proverbial. During a January–February 1970 "supply offensive," he shipped enough equipment and ammunition into South Vietnam to continue the war for seven months at the relatively low level then prevailing. His manpower pool also seemed unlimited. According to General Abrams, he could send 110,000 men south every year without faltering and could provide as many as 235,000 in a peak year. The U.S. Air Force insisted that its interdiction campaign in Laos was having a demonstrable effect on enemy activities in South Vietnam, and General Wheeler argued that the U.S. goal was only to impose a ceiling on enemy effectiveness to buy time for the South Vietnamese. Yet the conclu-

[2] Memo, Brig Gen Robert E. Pursley for Secretary Laird, 20 May 70, sub: Vietnam Special Studies Group, 330–76–067, box 93, Viet 3809 Pacification (Jan–May) 1970, Laird Papers, WNRC.

[3] Point Paper, Vietnam Briefing, Annex to Fact Book, 3 Aug 70, sub: JCS Meeting, 330–76–076, box 13, Viet 381, Laird Papers, WNRC.

sion seemed inescapable to a growing body of opinion within U.S. official circles that the war had become a bottomless hole.[4]

As 1970 lengthened, the strains imposed by the inconclusive nature of the conflict began to take their toll. As they did, military and civilian information officers both in South Vietnam and the United States found themselves confronting controversies unlike any they had encountered in the past.

Institutional Debility

The problems that confronted the public affairs program in South Vietnam had their roots in the same pressures that had given rise to the drug abuse, combat refusals, dissent, and interracial tensions among the troops that had begun to occur in 1969. The length of the war, its unpopularity at home, the lack of satisfaction many officers felt with a task that seemed interminably unproductive, pure institutional debility—all had their effect. Their influence was at first difficult to see in the case of the MACV Office of Information, which kept up with its routines and met its deadlines. Even so, the difficulties they caused became a source of increasing aggravation to General Abrams and his staff as the war progressed.

The first sign that something was wrong occurred during February 1970, when reporters learned that two U.S. Army intelligence agents had received credentials as correspondents from the MACV Office of Information. Alarmed, they notified their superiors immediately that, as NBC's bureau chief in South Vietnam put it, "Federal investigators have infiltrated the press corps in Saigon."[5] Shortly thereafter, news stories appeared chastising the Military Assistance Command for attempting to spy out newsmen's sources, and concerned members of Congress contacted the Department of Defense for an explanation.[6]

[4] Ibid.; Fact Sheet, 19 Oct 71, sub: Ammunition Shipped to Southeast Asia During CY 1970, covered by Memo, Brig Gen A. P. Hanket, Director, Industrial Preparedness and Munitions Production, OSD, for Pursley, 19 Oct 71, 330–76–197, box 87, Vietnam 400–499, 1971, Laird Papers, WNRC; Issue Paper, OSD SA, May 70, sub: Effectiveness of U.S. Interdiction Efforts in Southern Laos, 330–76–067, box 76, Laos 385.1 (May) 1970, Laird Papers, WNRC; Msg, Saigon 19962 to Bangkok, 19 Dec 70, sub: SEACORDS Meeting, Saigon, Dec 17, 1970, General Abrams' Personal file 37, CMH; Talking Paper, U.S. Air Force, Office of the Assistant Chief of Staff for Studies and Analysis, May 70, sub: Investigation Into the Relationship Between Supply Throughput and Level of Enemy Activity in South Vietnam, and Memo, Wheeler JCSM–216–70 for Secretary of Defense, 8 May 70, sub: Study of Effectiveness of U.S. Air Operations in Southern Laos, both in 330–76–067, box 67, Laos 385.1 (May) 1970, Laird Papers, WNRC.

[5] Msg, Abrams MAC 1319 to Wheeler, 27 Jan 70, sub: Alleged Press Accreditation of Intelligence Agency, Abrams Papers, CMH.

[6] [AP], "2 U.S. Agents in S. Viet Pose as Reporters," *Chicago Tribune*, 29 Jan 70; Msg, Lt Gen Bennett, Dir, DIA, DIADR 2267 to Abrams, 12 Feb 70, sub: Alleged Press Accreditation of Intelligence Agents, Abrams Papers, CMH.

The facts were less dramatic than reporters presumed. Two military intelligence agents had indeed received accreditation as correspondents, not to spy on the news media but to conduct close surveillance of a militant antiwar activist who had booked passage on a flight to Saigon. Even so, the investigators had never needed to use their press cards and had returned them to the Office of Information within days. The Military Assistance Command, for its part, dampened the speculation that was beginning to arise in the press by forthrightly admitting the error and by revealing that Colonel Cutrona had reprimanded and reassigned the officer who had made the mistake. To fill in details that might otherwise have raised questions, General Abrams then conducted a personal, off-the-record background briefing for those reporters who remained concerned.[7]

Although the Military Assistance Command in that way softened the impact of what had occurred, the incident was hardly as unimportant as it appeared. Since both of the intelligence agents had identified themselves and their purpose while applying for credentials, they should never have received official recognition as reporters. Perceiving that members of the press would resent any hint of official interference, the authors of the guidelines that governed accreditation of correspondents had, at the very beginning of the war, prohibited the distribution of press cards to anyone but bona fide reporters. The officer who decided to break that rule had obviously done so with good intentions, to further what he considered proper enforcement of the law. Yet by taking that action, he had indicated his own lack of understanding and sympathy for the larger purposes of the organization he served. Members of the intelligence directorate had many ways to accomplish their ends, but every action that diminished the credibility of the Military Assistance Command hampered the ability of the United States to achieve its goals in Southeast Asia.[8]

By itself, the episode would probably have been little more than an isolated example of poor judgment. During the months that followed, however, other patterns of activity within the MACV Office of Information also began to break down, revealing difficulties that went to the very heart of the Military Assistance Command's public affairs program. Many of those problems seemed purely administrative in nature, but they revealed, deep down, a failure of purpose and of spirit that was becoming all too familiar among the Americans serving in South Vietnam.

By mid-1970, for example, the military services had begun to find it increasingly difficult to identify experienced public affairs officers to

[7] Msg, Abrams MAC 1319 to Wheeler, 27 Jan 70, sub: Alleged Press Accreditation of Intelligence Agency; Msg, Abrams MAC 1735 to Wheeler et al., 6 Feb 70, sub: Background Press Briefing Reference Press Accreditation of Investigators, Westmoreland Message file, CMH. Also see [AP], "Reprimand Given in Saigon Incident of False Newsmen," *New York Times*, 7 Feb 70.

[8] Msg, Abrams MAC 1319 to Wheeler, 27 Jan 70, sub: Alleged Press Accreditation of Intelligence Agency.

replace those who departed South Vietnam at the end of their tours of duty. Captains, as a result, sometimes filled jobs designed for majors and lieutenant colonels. There were also problems of continuity. The carefully crafted system of on-the-job training the Defense Department had set into place during the early days of the war, under which an officer served a year as special assistant for Southeast Asia in Washington before becoming the chief of MACV public affairs, was a case in point. It had disappeared in 1969, the victim of a Defense Department reorganization. Colonel Cutrona's replacement, Col. Robert Leonard, as a result, had served at Da Nang as an adviser to the South Vietnamese during 1958 and 1959

Colonel Leonard

and again in 1962 and 1963 but had no direct public affairs experience relating to the war. He found himself confronting major responsibilities after spending only a few weeks in preparation reading background files at the Defense Department's Directorate of Defense Information.[9]

In any bureaucratic situation, General Sidle would later note, men with experience usually serve alongside those lacking it and, to an extent, compensate for the deficiencies that occur. By 1970 and 1971, however, too few officers of that sort remained in the field. George Newman's replacement as chief of public affairs at the U.S. embassy in Saigon, John E. McGowan, had served as Barry Zorthian's assistant earlier in the war and undoubtedly provided some perspective. But by late 1970 he mainly concentrated on issues involving the U.S. embassy and had little practical say over MACV's relations with the news media. As the chief of information for the entire U.S. Army, Sidle himself provided occasional assistance and advice to Leonard, but his concerns extended far beyond South Vietnam. He could do little on a day-to-day basis. The same was true for another former chief of MACV information, Col. L. Gordon Hill, who continued to direct public affairs programs in Washington but was too far from South Vietnam to have much impact. To make matters worse, the director of the Office of Information's Public Information Division, an Air

---

[9] Ltr, Leonard to the author, 17 Oct 90, CMH files. Unless otherwise indicated, this section is based on Interv, author with Comdr Joseph Lorfano, Special Assistant for Southeast Asia, 22 Aug 73, CMH files. General Sidle confirmed the details of the analysis in Interv, author with Maj Gen Winant Sidle, USA (Ret.), 26 Oct 88, CMH files.

Force colonel, was senior to Leonard in date of rank. Leonard immediately asserted his prerogatives, citing a 1965 agreement between the Air Force and the Army specifying that the chief of information would always be an Army officer and the equivalent of a brigadier general. But the arrangement still clearly provoked the Air Force officer and can only have impeded the efficient operation of the office.[10]

Hampered by problems of that sort and the fading of institutional memory, the public affairs officers at MACV tended more and more as 1970 progressed to take refuge in the formal rules that governed the material they released to the press. Meritorious from the standpoint of those who considered the news media an opponent, the approach lacked the flexibility necessary to preserve official credibility, especially in a time of stress. The MACV guidelines and the methods of dealing with the press that had grown up around them, while adequate for most circumstances, had always required considerable fine-tuning to meet the needs of the moment. During 1967 and 1968 Sidle had been willing to bend regulations when he had considered that necessary to preserve official credibility. His successors, Hill and Cutrona, who later both became general officers, had done the same. By 1971, however, Leonard and his associates were less disposed to the practice than in the past. Leonard, according to one information officer, often "bent over backwards" to assist the press and of necessity at times bent the rules himself to make a point. Nevertheless, the proverbial "book," Sidle asserted, came more and more to define the limits of what was acceptable for many public affairs officers.[11]

An example of what happened occurred in late 1970, when a U.S. Air Force jet crashed in Laos near the South Vietnamese border and American troops went in to protect the pilot until an evacuation helicopter could arrive. Reporters learned of the incident and asked about it at the MACV briefing. Policy dictated that in cases of that sort official spokesmen should refrain from admitting that U.S. forces had entered Laos and attempt to make it appear that South Vietnamese forces had been the ones involved. The officer briefing the newsmen, however, Capt. James Meir, USAF, recognized that the press knew everything and that he would lose his credibility if he appeared to dissemble. He therefore answered the question by noting blandly that if he had been the one shot down he would almost certainly have wanted U.S. forces to back him up. The reply satisfied the press but it upset Leonard, who shortly thereafter took the

[10] Interv, author with Maj Gen Winant Sidle, 12 Jul 73, CMH files; Ltr, Bunker to William H. Sullivan, Deputy Assistant Secretary for East Asian and Pacific Affairs, 1 Mar 70, 295 74D417, box 2, Chron files, Bunker Papers, FAIM/IR. Leonard observed that the problem of command was resolved after one or two weeks and ceased to matter to him. Whether that was so or not, it was a subject of comment within the Defense Department's Office of the Special Assistant for Southeast Asia three years after it had supposedly ended, and, nearly twenty years later, General Sidle himself recalled it as a controversy of some note. Ltr, Leonard to the author, 17 Oct 90; Interv, author with Maj Gen Winant Sidle, 3 Dec 90, CMH files.

[11] Interv, author with Lorfano, 22 Aug 73; Interv, author with Sidle, 12 Jul 73.

briefer to task. A note from Secretary of Defense Laird arrived in Saigon several days later, commending Meir for his candor.[12]

The Saigon correspondents complained bitterly during 1970 and 1971 that the Military Assistance Command had become unsympathetic to their needs and was attempting to cover up some of its activities. In a report widely distributed during January 1971, United Press International cited charges by Joseph Fried that repression of the news media was the worst he had seen in the 7½ years he had reported the war. The news service continued that official spokesmen had stopped arranging briefings from intelligence or operations officers shortly after the incursion into Cambodia and that they had failed to pass on requests for interviews with high-ranking officers. In addition, they had declined on occasion to confirm or deny information that had been made public in Washington and had even refused to respond to questions about their policies on grounds that, as Leonard had apparently told reporters, "The policy has not changed, so there is no point in discussing it."[13]

Public affairs officers explained the slowdown as the necessary by-product of reductions in personnel within the Office of Information, the practice of allowing the South Vietnamese to tell their own side of the war, and the unwillingness of the briefers to deliver "instant confirmation," without checking, of possibly controversial developments in the field. Even so, changes had, in fact, occurred in the way the U.S. command dealt with the press.[14] Old hands such as Fried noticed them and were bound to interpret them as restrictions on the flow of information. Earlier in the war, for example, MACV's intelligence directorate had held formal, off-the-record briefings to keep the press up to date on enemy dispositions and other matters that might have a bearing on the news. By 1970 that was no longer the case. Angry with the press and disinclined to deal directly with reporters, the command's chief of intelligence had ceded the task entirely to the Office of Information, which held background briefings on the subject for selected newsmen and responded to individual requests for information. Whatever the candor of those presentations, however, they carried little weight with reporters who preferred meetings with trained intelligence officers to sessions with less-informed public affairs officers who might have a line to sell.[15]

A vicious circle came into being. Increasingly distrustful of the military, newsmen confirmed the apprehensions of some officers that the press was against them by filing reports critical of the war. Already suspicious of the news media, most of those officers responded by avoiding reporters whenever possible and by declining to give interviews, but a

[12] Interv, author with Maj Charles Johnson, USMC, a former MACV briefer, 2 Aug 73, CMH files.
[13] [UPI], 22 Jan 71, DDI Press file.
[14] Interv, author with Lorfano, 22 Aug 73; Ltr, Leonard to the author, 17 Oct 90.
[15] Quotes from Ltr, Leonard to the author, 17 Oct 90. Interv, author with Maj Gen Winant Sidle, 26 Nov 90, CMH files.

few of the more vehement actively retaliated by discriminating against reporters they disliked or by cutting off the flow of information from their commands. The negative news reports those actions prompted closed the circle and began the process of recrimination anew.[16]

A case in point occurred during 1970 and 1971 in the Mekong Delta, where the U.S. public affairs adviser to the 9th South Vietnamese Infantry Division was a captain serving in a lieutenant colonel's slot. Encountering several uncooperative, "seedy" reporters at the beginning of his tour of duty in July 1970, that officer decided to have as little as possible to do with the press from then on. Aware that his superior, the Chief of the Delta Military Assistance Command, Maj. Gen. Hal D. McCown, harbored little sympathy for the press, he began, on his own authority, a quiet program to reduce the number of reporters that normally arrived. To that end, he never revealed that he had access to a helicopter when a visiting correspondent requested transportation. He also pushed to have his division's press camp closed so that reporters would have to use less acceptable South Vietnamese accommodations. By the spring of 1971, he noted, the number of reporters visiting the 9th Division had fallen from three to four per week to one every two weeks. To ensure that matters stayed that way after he departed from South Vietnam, without informing Leonard, he then recommended that McCown eliminate the position he had occupied as information adviser to the 9th Division. That would remove much of the American influence over South Vietnamese public affairs in the region and discourage the press even more. All this occurred at a time when the Military Assistance Command was attempting to interest the Saigon correspondents in reporting the increasingly secure conditions that had begun to prevail in the delta.[17]

The situation might have declined further if General Abrams had yielded to requests from Admiral McCain in October 1970 that he accompany the phase down of U.S. forces in South Vietnam with drastic reductions in the services the Military Assistance Command provided newsmen. By that time, however, the Nixon administration was nearing decision on a possible cross-border operation into Laos, a development that, if it occurred, would almost certainly spark controversies larger than those that had accompanied the move into Cambodia. Since the MACV Office of Information had already cut its staff by 16 percent, Abrams decided to avoid more complications with the press and put off any further action.[18]

---

[16] Interv, author with Sidle, 26 Nov 90. The attitude of high-ranking officers toward the news media is well portrayed in Douglas Kinnard, *The War Managers* (Hanover, N.H.: University Press of New England for the University of Vermont, 1977), pp. 124–35. Also see "Newsmen Say U.S. Reduces Viet Reports," *Baltimore Sun*, 17 Jan 71.

[17] Interv, author with Maj Michael Davidson, 5 May 81, CMH files.

[18] Msg, McCain to Abrams, 13 Oct 70, sub: News Media Accreditation and Support; Msg, Abrams MAC 14147 to McCain, 30 Oct 70, sub: News Media Accreditation and Support; Msg, Abrams MAC 14914 to McCain, 19 Nov 70. All in Abrams Papers, CMH. Also see Memo, Col Joseph F. H. Cutrona for Daniel Z. Henkin, 10 Feb 70, DDI Correspondence with MACOI (36a) file.

The Saigon Correspondents

By the end of 1970, the news media were themselves beginning to experience the consequences of the war's length. The effect was most obvious in Cambodia, where support for the press was virtually nonexistent, but there were also parallels in South Vietnam.

In the case of Cambodia, about twenty-five correspondents remained of the more than one hundred who had congregated in Phnom Penh at the beginning of cross-border operations. The U.S. embassy had done what it could to assist them by providing air transportation for filmed reports and by presenting background briefings on developments, but conditions were still spartan. As 1970 lengthened, fatigue had thus set in.[19]

The reporters found coverage of Cambodia frustrating because the government of Lon Nol remained unconvinced that the provision of adequate transportation and facilities for the press lay at all in its best interest. Lacking the sort of official assistance that had become the norm in South Vietnam but obliged to go into the field to provide the coverage their employers expected, the correspondents continued to suffer casualties and became increasingly concerned about their own safety. They took what steps they could to protect themselves, many declining to wear clothing that resembled military garb lest soldiers on either side mistake them for combatants. Others, according to Denis Cameron of *Time* and Kate Webb of United Press International, refused unequivocally to take personal risks. Henry Kamm of the *New York Times*, for one, according to embassy officials, declined to cover the war from anywhere outside of Phnom Penh's city limits.[20]

By December 1970 a consensus had grown, as one reporter put it, that all the news media were "losing money on Cambodian coverage." The *New York Times*, the *Baltimore Sun*, *Time*, and other leading journals had already chosen to leave that portion of the war to their regional bureaus, which assigned reporters to Phnom Penh on an irregular basis. During December, when John Wheeler left, the Associated Press failed to replace him. His assistant, Robin Mannock, took charge. The same thing occurred when UPI's Frank Frosch was killed. No new reporter arrived to take his place. His assistant, Kate Webb, carried on. United Press International also made no effort to replace Kyoichi Sawada, a cameraman who had also been killed. Meanwhile, on 13 December, Francois Sully closed the *Newsweek* bureau. Two days later, ABC withdrew its personnel, and word began to spread that NBC, which employed a cameraman but no correspondent, would soon pull out.[21]

---

[19] Memo, Theodore Eliot for Henry Kissinger, 23 Jul 70, sub: Biweekly Report on Cambodia No. 2, Pol 2 Cambodia file, FAIM/IR; Msg, Phnom Penh 07 to State, 30 May 70, sub: May Activities, copy in CMH files.

[20] Unless otherwise indicated, this section is based on Msg, Phnom Penh 3419 to State, 15 Dec 70, DDI Cambodia, 69–70–71.

[21] Ibid.

Freelance reporter Sean Flynn was one of many who disappeared in Cambodia.

The U.S. mission in Phnom Penh, for its part, was ambivalent about the development. The exodus of professional, resident correspondents would have both favorable and unfavorable results, the embassy's public affairs officer told the State Department. Although the incidence of sensational and contrived reporting might decrease, he said, the reporters serving in Cambodia had at least attempted to convey the facts as they saw them. The stringers and freelancers who would replace them might well be less responsible.[22]

Many of the trends observable in Cambodia were apparent in South Vietnam, where the press was likewise undergoing change. The stress experienced by the Saigon correspondents was less than in Cambodia because reporters could visit units in the field without great fear for their own safety, but fatigue was still a factor. Peter Arnett provides an example. He returned home shortly after the incursion. Few reporters had ever been able to take more than two years of the war without burning out, he later explained, and he had served eight, much of that time in the field.[23]

A number of correspondents of long experience remained in South Vietnam at the time: Wendell Merick of *U.S. News & World Report*; Francois Sully who freelanced for *Newsweek*; George McArthur of the Associated Press; Arnett's partner at the Associated Press, photographer Horst Faas; and *Time-Life* photographer Larry Burrows, to name a few. As in Cambodia, nevertheless, the war was becoming a financial drain on news organizations. Although the number of correspondents continued

[22] Ibid.
[23] Interv, author with Peter Arnett, 6 Sep 88, CMH files.

to hover near 400, with between 150 and 160 Americans always in attendance, by the end of 1970 many small news outlets and some large ones had begun to place greater reliance on freelancers, reporters who were less expensive than staff correspondents because they provided their own subsistence and were paid by the piece.[24]

A new sort of reporter, although definitely in the minority, had also begun to appear, one who was more opinionated and more attuned to the sentiments of the young in the United States than his predecessors had been. A few of those individuals were close in age to the draftees fighting the war. They sported the same hairstyles, spoke with the same slang, and, in the case of television correspondents, even used rock and roll music as background in their reports. Sympathetic to the antiwar movement at home, some went so far as to participate in antigovernment political activities. Michael Morrow was thus disaccredited by the South Vietnamese in November 1970 for wearing a black armband and addressing a meeting of anti–Thieu regime demonstrators. John Steinbeck IV, a stringer for CBS News, narrowly escaped the same fate when the South Vietnamese police photographed him participating in a Saigon political rally. Don Luce, a correspondent for the U.S. Conference of the World Council of Churches who freelanced at various times for the *Christian Century* and the *Progressive*, was suspected of serving as liaison between antiwar groups in the United States and similar organizations in Saigon.[25]

Although often opposed to the war, the reporters who took up station in Saigon after 1969 could still sometimes boast of considerable experience in South Vietnam. Luce had served as director of the International Volunteer Services organization in Vietnam for six years prior to 1967, when he had resigned to protest the war. Ronald Ridenauer of the Dispatch News Service, while hardly a professional reporter, had served a tour of duty in the war and was the Vietnam veteran who had first brought the My Lai massacre to light. Phil Brady, who joined NBC News in 1971 as a correspondent, had worked in the pacification program under John Paul Vann.[26]

---

[24] The figures are drawn from a series of weekly summaries that the MACV Office of Information dispatched to the commander in chief, Pacific, and the Office of the Secretary of Defense between 5 January and 23 November 1970. See MACV Historical Summaries, 334, 72A870, box 11, 14–2 MACOI 4d, WNRC. Also see Ltr, Jerry Friedheim to Senator Edmund S. Muskie, 8 Aug 70, 330–76–067, box 88, Viet 000.73 1970, Laird Papers, WNRC; Msg, McCain to Abrams, 13 Oct 70, sub: News Media Accreditation and Support.

[25] Barry L. Sherman, "The Peabody Collection: Vietnam on Television, Television on Vietnam, 1962–1975," *1987 American Film Institute Video Festival* (Los Angeles: American Film Institute, 1987), pp. 28–31; Msg, Saigon 19213 to State, 6 Dec 70, sub: Luce and Morrow Cases, General Abrams' Personal file 37, CMH; Msg, Saigon 838 to State, 19 Jan 71, sub: Don Luce, and Msg, Saigon 6918 to State, 6 May 71, sub: Don Luce, both in Abrams Papers, CMH.

[26] Msg, Saigon 3302 to State, 4 Jul 70, sub: CODEL Montgomery-Visit to Con Son Prison, General Abrams' Personal file 35, CMH. Brady's background is mentioned in Neil Sheehan, *A Bright Shining Lie* (New York: Random House, 1988), p. 819. Also see Robert G. Kaiser, "U.S. Denies Responsibility for 'Tiger Cages' at Conson," *Washington Post*, 8 Jul 70.

Whatever their qualifications, as the war lengthened, the freelancers came to pose far more problems to public affairs officers than the regularly employed correspondents that made up the bulk of the press corps. Staff reporters had deadlines to meet and could hardly afford to alienate the official sources who provided much of the routine material they used. Although most guarded their independence assiduously, they were thus open to correction and would sometimes even test their conclusions on knowledgeable officers within the Military Assistance Command to ascertain their accuracy and to see what reaction they would evoke. Possessing at least a modicum of financial security, they considered themselves professionals, and, however they viewed the war, usually attempted to round out their work with some allusion to the opposite point of view.[27]

Freelance correspondents, on the other hand, had few obligations and less security. Many practiced a high degree of craftsmanship and a number of regular correspondents served intermittently as stringers when the bureaus that employed them suffered reductions in staff. A highly visible minority, according to the manager of the MACV press center at Da Nang during 1971, Lt. Col. Perry G. Stevens, nevertheless lived day-to-day and for the moment. Depending for subsistence on post exchange privileges and the inexpensive press camp accommodations provided by the Military Assistance Command, those individuals, according to Stevens, sometimes dealt in black market currency and drugs as well as words. Whether they did or not, some of them were capable of gross distortions of fact if that was what it took to sell a story.[28]

The MACV Office of Information attempted to remedy the problem by reducing its support for reporters who rarely submitted work to publications and by requiring each freelancer to present letters from established news outlets firmly committing those agencies to publish his work. Those rules, however, had hardly any effect. Although the number of so-called occasional correspondents decreased, the work they produced had never amounted to much. Meanwhile, the majority of freelancers went about their business unimpeded. With nothing to lose, bureau chiefs in Saigon, according to Stevens, continued to give out letters of reference to anyone who showed the slightest promise of being able to draft a news dispatch.[29]

[27] Interv, author with Col Perry Stevens, PAO, XXIV Corps, Military Region 1 (MR1), 1970–71, 1983, 25 Apr 89, CMH files.

[28] Ibid. Also see Interv, author with Lt Col Charles McClean, IO for the 101st Airborne Division during 1971, 1983, CMH files.

[29] Memo for the Press, Col Joseph F. H. Cutrona, 14 Oct 69, 72A5121, box 226, Correspondents file, 1969, JUSPAO Papers, WNRC; MACV Directive 360–1, 15 May 72, DDI Policy file, 1972.

A Case Study in Change

Problems with the news media had occurred in the best of times, but the fatigue and declining morale afflicting both the MACV Office of Information and the press began to have a cumulative effect, endowing the controversies that occurred after 1970 with a hard edge of confrontation. The stories reporters submitted were about as accurate or inaccurate in detail as before. Yet the conclusions they contained seemed to allow little room for that benefit of a doubt that had earlier distinguished the work of the Saigon correspondents.

A story that broke during July 1970, when Don Luce and a congressional aide, Thomas R. Harkin, revealed substandard conditions at a South Vietnamese prison, provides a case in point. The expose appeared at the worst possible moment for the United States. Declaring that the South Vietnamese government was employing U.S. aid in the mistreatment of both civilian inmates and captive Viet Cong sympathizers, it not only endangered the American negotiating posture in Paris but also reinforced the growing reluctance of some in Congress to continue spending for the war. Meanwhile, it threatened to dilute the impact of a major drive begun by the Nixon administration in 1969 to counter North Vietnam's effort to use its American captives to extract concessions in Paris.[30]

At the moment when Luce and Harkin made their charges, the United States was preparing two initiatives affecting prisoners of war. The first was an effort to assist the South Vietnamese government in the repatriation of sixty-two sick and disabled North Vietnamese captives. Although few expected North Vietnam to reciprocate, the move promised to contrast that country's ruthless treatment of American prisoners of war with the humanitarian policies in effect in the South. The second had to do with planning for a clandestine thrust into North Vietnam to rescue dozens of American pilots imprisoned in a compound at Son Tay, a village located forty-five kilometers northwest of Hanoi. That operation likewise possessed public relations potential. Whether it succeeded or failed—and Nixon understood from the beginning that the prisoners might be moved before the rescuers could arrive—it would highlight the continuing concern of the United States for its captive personnel while emphasizing North Vietnam's unwillingness to abide by international treaties that governed the handling of prisoners in time of war.[31]

---

[30] Msg, State 119666 to Saigon, 25 Jul 70, sub: Treatment of Prisoners, General Abrams' Personal file 28, CMH; Msg, Saigon 13816 to State, 9 Jul 69, sub: Discussion of Prisoners in Private Meeting, General Abrams' Personal file 7, CMH. For a resume of U.S. efforts on behalf of the prisoners, see Memo, G. Warren Nutter, ASD ISA, I–25620–70 for Secretary of Defense, 17 Nov 70, sub: PW/MIA-Efforts and Results Since January 1969, DDI PW file.

[31] Msg, State TOSEC 186 to Saigon, Acting Secretary to Berger, 8 Jul 70, sub: Con Son, General Abrams' Personal file 28, CMH. Also see Ltr, Melvin Laird to William P. Rogers, 31 Jan 71, Pol 27–7 Viet S file, FAIM/IR; Memo for Ron Ziegler, 24 Nov 70, sub: Operation Chop Chop, NSC files, Vietnam Subject files, box 87, North Vietnam Raid, 21 Nov 70, Nixon Papers.

One of the tiger cages at Con Son

The problem began to take shape on 2 July, when Luce visited a prison on Con Son Island, located one hundred kilometers off the Mekong Delta in the South China Sea. He did so without permission but with the connivance of Harkin, who was escorting Congressman Augustus F. Hawkins of California and William R. Anderson of Tennessee on a tour of the facility. During the course of the visit, in violation of rules in effect at prisons around the world and over the protest of the facility's commandant, Harkin photographed some of the prisoners. The party then chanced upon what were known as tiger cages, maximum security cells with iron grills for tops that were used to hold particularly dangerous prisoners, "tigers" in local parlance. Harkin and Luce, again over the protest of the commandant, questioned some of the inmates. The prisoners claimed that when they were disobedient, the guards sprinkled them from above with powdered lime that burned their flesh and eyes. The commandant denied the allegation on the spot, asserting that the lime in evidence around the site was used only to whitewash walls. The Chief of the Public Safety Directorate of the Office of the Assistant Chief of Staff for Civilian Operations and Revolutionary Development Support (CORDS) Frank E. Walton, who was present, later contradicted that assertion, observing that powdered lime was evident on the top of the grillwork covering the cages. In all, Walton said, between four and five hundred hard core Communist civilian prisoners, 350 of them females, appeared to occupy the cells. From nine and ten thousand prisoners were present in the camp.[32]

---

[32] MFR, MACCORDS-PS, Frank E. Walton, 2 Jul 70, sub: Congressional Visit to Con Son Island, copy in CMH files. Also see Msg, Saigon 10622 to State, 4 Jul 70, sub: CODEL Montgomery-Visit to Con Son Prison, General Abrams' Personal file 35, CMH.

Walton and the members of the Public Safety Directorate that had accompanied the tour stressed throughout the visit that South Vietnam rather than the United States had responsibility for Con Son, and that, despite all appearances to the contrary, the nation was making progress in improving its prison facilities. Later, either they or someone on the CORDS staff passed that point to Congressman G. V. "Sonny" Montgomery of Mississippi, who had not visited the island but who had chaired the delegation, along with word that Harkin and Luce had taken liberties. As the congressman departed from Tan Son Nhut Airport at the end of the group's stay, he told Ambassador Bunker that he regretted the incident and that he would do what he could to keep it from getting out of hand.[33]

Montgomery was as good as his word. The report that his committee filed on 6 July spent considerable time on other aspects of the situation in South Vietnam but devoted only a single paragraph to Con Son. The delegation, it stated, had uncovered conditions on the island that required remedial action but had received assurances from the South Vietnamese government that an investigation would occur.[34]

Luce and Harkin were hardly as forbearing. Soon after the report appeared, Luce briefed the Saigon correspondents on what he had seen in the camp. Harkin, in Washington, meanwhile dramatically resigned his position as a congressional aide. At a news conference, he then accused Montgomery of settling for a generalized military briefing in Saigon rather than attempting to ferret out the facts for himself. Describing conditions within the tiger cages, he charged that the abuses had occurred with the assistance of American foreign aid and under the eye of American advisers. Anderson and Hawkins also spoke. Anderson claimed that several prisoners had indicated to him that because of beatings, malnutrition, and long periods of forced inactivity they had lost the use of their legs. Hawkins declared that the facility at Con Son was "a symbol of how some American officials will cooperate in corruption and torture because they want to see the war continued and the government they put in power protected."[35]

Those statements received wide play in the press both in the United States and around the world. Robert Walters in the *Washington Star* alleged that "some of the shackles which hold the legs of prisoners in the 'tiger cages' . . . are made of iron bars provided by the U.S. aid program." An article by Gloria Emerson in the *New York Times* asserted that a fact sheet prepared for Anderson and Hawkins by Walton's staff had

[33] MFR, MACCORDS-PS, Walton, 2 Jul 70, sub: Congressional Visit to Con Son Island; Msg, Saigon 10622 to State, 4 Jul 70, sub: CODEL Montgomery-Visit to Con Son Prison.

[34] The report's conclusions are summarized in *Facts on File*, 9–15 Jul 70, 30:494.

[35] Msg, State 107856 to Saigon, 7 Jul 70, sub: Press Reports Re Con Son Island Prison Conditions, General Abrams' Personal file 28, CMH. Also see George C. Wilson, "Viet Prison Whitewash Is Charged," *Washington Post*, 7 Jul 70; Kaiser, "U.S. Denies Responsibility for 'Tiger Cages' at Conson"; Robert Walters, "U.S. Supplied Aid for S. Viet Prisons," *Washington Star*, 8 Jul 70.

described Con Son as a "correctional institution worthy of higher ratings than some U.S. prisons." Unwilling to accept that the remark may have been as much a commentary on prison conditions in some areas of the United States as in South Vietnam, the *Washington Post* called on 21 July for Walton's resignation.[36]

The comment in the fact sheet notwithstanding, the U.S. embassy in Saigon had little sympathy for the abuses Harkin, Luce, and the congressmen had described. When the story became public, it thus readily confirmed that American advisers had been aware of the tiger cages and had discussed the problem with South Vietnamese officials. Even so, embassy officials attempted to put as much distance as possible between the United States and South Vietnam's civil prisons by stressing that "control of this system rests with the Ministry of the Interior. . . . There is no [American] public safety adviser stationed at Con Son." On 9 July Walton himself held a background session for a group of profoundly skeptical correspondents. Making the same point, he affirmed that conditions in South Vietnamese civil prisons in general left much to be desired but denied that prisoners at Con Son had been abused.[37]

Whatever the truth of that assertion—Walton admitted to reporters that American observers visited the facility only once a month and never at night—the State Department considered the charges that had surfaced serious enough to inform the U.S. mission in Saigon that immediate corrective action was necessary. "Congressional, public, and press reaction here continues to be severely critical of US and GVN for tolerating alleged conditions, especially in light of [the U.S. government's] . . . strong criticism of NVN treatment of US . . . [prisoners of war]. We recognize that Con Son is civil prison, not PW facility, but this distinction is technical one and . . . does not excuse what has been depicted as grossly inhumane treatment of detainees, many of whom are reportedly interned for political offenses."[38]

The Nixon administration was likewise somber. Although affirming that Harkin's and Luce's allegations had political overtones, Herbert Klein, for one, told his associates in the White House that "we came out of the . . . committee story amazingly well." For the rest, Con Son had become "legitimate news." In that sense, there seemed little value in denying what the congressmen had seen. Instead, "Our approach should be . . . to get our people to charge that the peaceniks seize on any excuse to try to force the President out of South Vietnam, that they have not

---

[36] Press reporting is summarized in Msg, State 107856 to Saigon, 8 Jul 70, sub: Press Reports Re Con Son Island Prison Conditions; Msg, State 112530 to Saigon, 15 Jul 70, General Abrams' Personal file 28, CMH. Also see "Conson: A Case History of Deceit," *Washington Post*, 21 Jul 70.

[37] The statement is quoted in Kaiser, "U.S. Denies Responsibility For 'Tiger Cages' at Conson." Msg, Saigon 10963 to State, 9 Jul 70, sub: Press Developments Re Con Son Case, General Abrams' Personal file 38, CMH.

[38] Msg, State 108819 to Saigon, 9 Jul 70, sub: Con Son, General Abrams' Personal file 28, CMH.

shown similar concern for those mistreated by the North Vietnamese, or for our men who are POW's. In other words, we need to turn this into a political issue instead of a moral one."[39]

Following Klein's recommendation, the Nixon administration made little attempt in the weeks that followed to refute Harkin's and Luce's allegations. Instead, at its urging, the South Vietnamese government publicly declared that it would remedy conditions at Con Son. Meanwhile, the U.S. embassy in Saigon counseled President Thieu to peg all statements on the subject to specific corrective actions, and, if at all possible, to make certain that independent eyewitnesses gave public testimony to any progress he claimed. Shortly thereafter, Congressman Philip M. Crane of Illinois visited Con Son, where the commandant observed pointedly that most of the problems at the camp could be traced to South Vietnam's inadequate financial resources rather than to a deliberate policy of repression. On that occasion, the prisoners in the tiger cages were clean and well groomed. No lime was in evidence.[40]

The United States took pains in the months that followed to investigate some of the more outrageous charges aired by Anderson and Hawkins. Physicians from the Military Assistance Command were thus able to establish that those prisoners who had complained of paralysis were, in fact, either malingering or suffering from hysteria. Enough was still clearly wrong at Con Son to prompt the International Commission of the Red Cross to take a hard stand on conditions at the strictly military South Vietnamese prisoner-of-war camps that fell under its purview. When one of those facilities, located on Phu Quoc Island off the coast of Cambodia in the Gulf of Thailand, came in for special censure, the development seemed particularly ominous to General Abrams. He complained bitterly that the Red Cross had applied Western standards to an Asian environment and that the South Vietnamese armed forces would resent any attempt to provide better medical care and living conditions for enemy prisoners than the rank and file in their own army received.[41]

Those objections to the contrary, Abrams nevertheless pressed Thieu for reforms. To have done otherwise might have created conditions that would have forced the Military Assistance Command to take direct con-

---

[39] Memo, Herbert G. Klein for John R. Brown III, 14 Jul 70, sub: Action Memorandum P–483, White House Special files, White House Action Memos 1970, box 6, White House Action Memos II [I of II], Nixon Papers.

[40] Msg, Saigon 12063 to State, 28 Jul 70, sub: Treatment of Prisoners in Viet-Nam, General Abrams' Personal file 35, CMH; MFR, J. Nach, 21 Jul 70, sub: Visit to Con Son Island, copy in CMH files.

[41] Msg, Saigon 353 to State, 9 Jan 71, General Abrams' Personal file 37, CMH; Msg, Moorer CJCS 13955 to McCain, 14 Oct 70, sub: ICRC Inspection of Phu Quoc PW Camp; Msg, McCain to Abrams, 15 Oct 70, sub: ICRC Inspection of Phu Quoc PW Camp; Msg, McCain to Moorer, 16 Oct 70, sub: ICRC Inspection of Phu Quoc PW Camp; Msg, Abrams MAC 13649 to McCain, 16 Oct 70, sub: ICRC Inspection of Phu Quoc PW Camp. All in Abrams Papers, CMH.

trol of prisoners it had long before released to South Vietnamese custody. To guarantee that nothing went amiss, the Defense Department then made certain that the Red Cross replaced the inspector who had raised questions with one more amenable to the American point of view.[42]

South Vietnam's reluctance to remedy conditions at Con Son was at least in part the product of circumstances beyond anyone's control. An effort had begun almost immediately to build a new hospital at the camp and to purchase necessary supplies. Yet the buildings took many months to complete and the government had difficulty hiring additional guards, a necessity if greater freedom of movement for prisoners was to be possible. The inmates at Con Son themselves refused to cooperate. By the end of December, claiming that they were well on their way to rebellion, the facility's commandant threw some 1,900 of them back into shackles. The United States argued vehemently in conversations with South Vietnamese administrators that the situation both at Con Son and other penal institutions could only create bad publicity, but in the end it could do little more than attempt to limit the damage. When CBS News sought permission during May 1971 to photograph South Vietnam's prisons, the Defense Department thus advised the South Vietnamese to reject the request. As Laird's aide Phil Odeen observed at the time, quoting the president's special consultant on public affairs, former ABC correspondent John Scali, "Anybody that let a group of reporters go out and photograph those prisoner-of-war camps was out of his mind."[43]

In the end, the Con Son episode had few of the dire effects that the State Department and others had foreseen. The negotiations in Paris continued unimpaired. The prisoner-of-war release went ahead as scheduled on 11 July, making only a modest ripple in the press. The Son Tay raid, as it came to be called, probably had a beneficial effect even though it failed, by demonstrating to the families of the prisoners that the Nixon administration had their best interests at heart.[44]

Con Son might, indeed, have subsided as an issue but for the South Vietnamese, who ensured that problems at the camp remained in the public eye long beyond their time by moving during October to expel Luce from their country. When they took that step, canceling Luce's visa and press accreditation, Ambassador Bunker protested but won only token concessions. The Thieu regime extended the reporter's visa until May but refused to reinstate his credentials to cover the war. As the contro-

[42] The replacement of the inspector is mentioned in MFR, 9 Nov 70, sub: Vietnamization Meeting With Secretary Laird, Thayer Papers, CMH.

[43] MFR, Phil Odeen, OASD SA, 9 Nov 70, sub: Vietnamization Meeting With Secretary Laird, Thayer Papers, CMH; MFR, Phil Odeen, OASD SA, 17 Dec 70, sub: Vietnamization Meeting With Secretary Laird, 330–76–067, box 88, Viet 092 (Sep–Dec) 1970, Laird Papers, WNRC; Msg, Saigon 20218 to State, 26 Dec 70, General Abrams' Personal file 37, CMH. Quote from MFR, Phil Odeen, OASD SA, 19 May 71, sub: Vietnamization Meeting With Secretary Laird, folder 77, Thayer Papers, CMH.

[44] For an extensive treatment of the raid and its effects, see Benjamin F. Schemmer, *The Raid* (New York: Harper & Row, 1976).

versy escalated, influential members of Congress concluded that the South Vietnamese were penalizing the reporter for aiding a congressional investigation. Senator Fulbright, indeed, lectured Secretary Rogers on the subject during an 11 December hearing on a supplemental aid appropriation for South Vietnam.[45]

Recognizing that the incident continued to pose a grave threat to American ends in South Vietnam, the State Department instructed the U.S. embassy in Saigon to use Fulbright's concern to press the Thieu regime to reconsider. Legislation vital to the future of South Vietnam was at stake. Deputy Ambassador Samuel D. Berger made that point during subsequent conversations with Thieu, adding that a few vocal legislators in the United States had even construed the move against Luce as an act of retaliation against Congress itself.[46]

Berger's arguments had little effect. Viewing Luce as a major opponent, Thieu refused to reinstate the reporter's privileges. That left the Military Assistance Command with little latitude. Since standard procedure required South Vietnamese approval as a prerequisite for American press accreditation, the information officers had no choice but to inflame the situation further by terminating all American assistance to Luce. The lack of transportation into the field and of admission to official briefings made little difference to the reporter. He had abundant sources of his own. Much more damaging was the loss of access to the U.S. armed forces postal system, a development that forced him to use South Vietnamese facilities and that subjected his personal correspondence to the possible scrutiny of Thieu's intelligence agents. He complained to Senator George Aiken, who kept the confrontation alive between Luce and official agencies by contacting the State Department for an explanation.[47]

Luce himself appears to have done nothing to placate his adversaries. Toward the beginning of 1971, he took part in a NET-TV public affairs program in which he argued in favor of allowing Viet Cong representation in the South Vietnamese government. Then, during April, he escorted antiwar Congressman Paul N. McCloskey, Jr., of California on a visit to a joint U.S.–South Vietnamese prisoner-of-war interrogation center. Both incidents galled the Thieu regime. On 26 April the South Vietnamese Ministry of Foreign Affairs notified the reporter that his visa would expire on 16 May.[48]

Luce informed the Associated Press, the *New York Times*, and other sympathetic media outlets, noting angrily that the government had failed

[45] Msg, State 201553 to Saigon, 11 Dec 70, sub: Status of Don Luce, Pol 27–7 Viet S file, FAIM/IR.

[46] Msg, Saigon 20296 to State, 29 Dec 70, sub: Don Luce, General Abrams' Personal file 37, CMH.

[47] Msg, Saigon 19213 to State, 6 Dec 70, sub: Luce and Morrow Cases; Msg, State 53095 to Saigon, 30 Mar 71, sub: Don Luce, General Abrams' Personal file 31, CMH.

[48] Msg, Saigon 6518 to State, 29 Apr 71, sub: Alleged Expulsion of Don Luce, DDI Vietnam 1971 file; Msg, Saigon 1079 to State, 23 Jan 71, sub: Don Luce, General Abrams' Personal file 37, CMH.

to give any explanation beyond a vague avowal that it was taking action "for specific reasons."[49] In the days that followed, as one commentator within the U.S. embassy observed, a "one-sided campaign portraying Luce as [a] victim of GVN press repression" came into being in both the news media and Congress.[50] Reinforcing that theme, the U.S. Conference of the World Council of Churches issued a resolution on 28 April commending his efforts on behalf of "all prisoners, military and political, . . . throughout Indochina" and his role "in disclosing the inhuman 'tiger cage' dungeons of South Vietnam's political prison on Con Son Island."[51] Senator Fulbright then invited him to Washington to testify on the plight of prisoners in South Vietnam.

As the controversy continued, official spokesmen attempted to point out that the order against Luce was more the result of the reporter's political activities than of anything he had done as a newsman. Most of the 412 foreign correspondents resident in Saigon had written stories critical of the South Vietnamese government, they said. A raft of articles had even appeared on conditions at Con Son, with none of the writers but Luce experiencing any retribution.[52]

On the day before Luce was to testify, in an attempt to upstage his appearance before Congress, public affairs officers in Saigon underscored those points by planting a question with Maggie Kilgore of United Press International for use at the evening briefing. During that session, the reporter asked for the "special reason" alluded to in the notice that had informed Luce of his expulsion. The South Vietnamese spokesman present, Nguyen Ngoc Huyen, responded that the reporter's activities had been inconsistent with the role of either a journalist or a social worker because he had served as a contact between antiwar groups in the United States and South Vietnam. In addition, his employer had notified the government months before that it intended to replace him with someone else. He thus lacked any further reason to remain in South Vietnam.[53]

There matters might once more have rested. Instead, Huyen turned the session into a debacle by flourishing a handful of papers and offering to show proof that Luce had been guilty of improprieties. The documents he presented, however, were mimeographed copies of Viet Cong and North Vietnamese news articles, one of which had originally appeared in the *Washington Post*. During the chaotic give-and-take that ensued, Jeff Williams of NBC News pointed out that someone had stolen a number of papers during a burglary at Luce's apartment just two weeks before.

---

[49] Msg, Saigon 4143 to State, 29 Apr 71, sub: Alleged Expulsion of Don Luce, DDI Vietnam 1971 file.

[50] Msg, State 6918 to Saigon, 6 May 71, sub: Don Luce.

[51] Msg, Saigon 77428 to State, 5 May 71, sub: Don Luce, General Abrams' Personal file 31, CMH.

[52] Msg, Saigon 6518 to State, 29 Apr 71, sub: Alleged Expulsion of Don Luce.

[53] Msg, Saigon 7348 to State, 12 May 71, sub: Don Luce, PPB 7 Viet S file, FAIM/IR.

Where, he asked, had Huyen gotten the materials he had shown. The spokesman refused to answer. Correspondents never divulged their sources, he said, and neither would he.[54]

From that point on, the Con Son tiger cages entered into the expanding lore of the Vietnam War, to resurface time and again, as would My Lai and the Green Beret Affair, whenever an antiwar activist sought to portray the alleged injustice of the American involvement. In fact, although conditions at Con Son were indeed cruel, the incident probably said as much about the fragmenting American consensus on the war as it did about the nature of the conflict itself. For Con Son, or something like it, had long existed in South Vietnam, with neither the U.S. government nor the Saigon correspondents paying much attention.[55] Only with the advent of American withdrawals and the decline in support for the war on the part of Congress and the news media had the issue come to matter.

Even so, in combination with the intelligence agent affair, the episode highlighted the loss of vision that had occurred in South Vietnam on the part of both the American military and the news media. For if Don Luce had used the privileges and advantages of a correspondent to promote his antiwar cause, an information officer had done something similar, by allowing official investigators to use the press as cover for a police operation. In earlier years, incidents of the sort had never been allowed to occur, on either side. For the correspondents and their bureau chiefs, the maintenance of at least an air of detachment from events had been a matter of professional pride. Government officials, meanwhile, had placed a high premium on the independence of the press in order to preserve their best means for communicating credibly with the American public.

So much seemed wrong in South Vietnam, however, that the controversy over the tiger cages soon passed. Even as Luce and Harkin made their revelations, the Saigon correspondents were turning to a far more compelling subject, the decline in morale that had begun to afflict American forces in South Vietnam as the U.S. role in ground combat decreased and withdrawals continued.

---

[54] Ibid.

[55] For a thorough discussion of this subject, see Clarke, *Advice and Support: The Final Years,* p. 170.

16

Morale Becomes an Issue

Although influencing the military's public image, the controversies surrounding Don Luce were hardly more than irritations to General Abrams
and his staff. Of far more importance was a series of stories that began to
appear in the press about the same time as the tiger cages affair, having to
do with combat refusals, drug abuse, and race. Over the months to come,
those disclosures and others like them would contribute to a series of running controversies between the officers of the Military Assistance
Command and the Saigon correspondents that would leave few on either
side unscarred.

Signs of Crisis Appear

Reporters had begun to document the problems spreading within the
Military Assistance Command during 1969, but hardly anyone within
either the press or the armed forces was prepared for the situation that
evolved after the incursion into Cambodia, as the American role in combat
declined and unit withdrawals began in earnest.[1] By the fall of 1970, however, there was no mistaking that morale problems of major proportions
existed, if only because officers in the field themselves took the initiative to
inform their superiors in Washington. On 1 September, indeed, the Chief
of Staff of the Army, General Westmoreland, received word from his
Deputy Chief of Staff for Personnel, Lt. Gen. Walter T. Kerwin, Jr., that
forty young officers representing all the services in Vietnam had gone outside the chain of command to inform their commander in chief, the president, of the condition of their morale. The letter they sent carried heavy
weight because none of the men were substandard performers, none had
refused to do their duty, and none had taken their complaints to the press.

[1] See Chapters 8 and 9 for the early reporting of these issues.

Those officers asserted in their letter that the public reaction to the My Lai massacre, the Green Beret Affair, and all of the limitations imposed on the way the military conducted the invasion of Cambodia indicated to them an unwillingness on the part of the United States either to face the brutal facts of war or to carry the effort in South Vietnam to victory. Contending that, in many cases, the "protesters and troublemakers" President Nixon had referred to in his speeches were "our younger brothers and friends and girlfriends and wives," they continued that

We, too, find continuation of the war difficult to justify and we are being asked to lead others who are unconvinced into a war in which few of us believe. This leaves us with nothing but survival—"kill or be killed"—as a motivation. . . . Those who force us into this position . . . are perceived by many soldiers to be almost as much our enemies as the Viet Cong and the NVA. . . . It seems very possible that if the war is allowed to continue much longer, young Americans in the military will simply refuse en masse to cooperate. . . . This day is coming quickly. You must have us out of Vietnam by then.[2]

Similar concerns clearly affected higher officers. One, "a West Pointer and a professional" of field grade rank, according to Assistant Secretary of Defense for Administration Robert F. Froehlke, wrote of his own frustrations in a letter to his superiors. With the war winding down, he said, "we at troop level are getting the worst of both the combat and garrison worlds. Troops are very reluctant to seek out the enemy when they know that combat troops will be withdrawn in the near future. With the name of the game still being body count, I am sure you can imagine the pressures." The officer continued that he was very disillusioned.

It is the total lack of satisfaction that I now have. The feeling that we don't know what we're doing—that our role is now purposeless. I am tired of troops that refuse orders to go to the field; fed up with the Army's new judicial system that stacks the deck against the commander and adversely affects good order and discipline. I am tired of arrogant blacks who feel they can violate every regulation with impunity and do. Most of all, I am fed up with senior commanders who never question our reason for being, our mission, or the changing nature of [the] environment both socially and tactically. . . . A good infantryman should take delight in staying with the troops. But I have had it.[3]

It is difficult to determine how deeply senior officers perceived the challenges that were developing. Many appear to have adopted a middle course, recognizing that problems of serious magnitude existed but contending, as did the Deputy Commander of the U.S. Army, Vietnam, Lt.

---

[2] Msg, Lt Gen Walter T. Kerwin, DCSPER DA, WDC 16087 to Westmoreland, 1 Sep 70, Westmoreland Message file, CMH.

[3] Memo, Robert F. Froehlke, ASD Admin, for Secretary of Defense, 8 Dec 70, 330–76–067, box 92, Viet 330.11, 1970, Laird Papers, WNRC.

Gen. William J. McCaffrey, that the troops continued to stand up well to a demanding situation. A very thin margin of leadership held most troop units together, McCaffrey told Kerwin during October, reacting to an article by John Saar in *Life* that had depicted many of the problems afflicting commanders. "The average rifle company will be lucky to have one regular officer and two to four regular Army sergeants." Even so, and "despite the violence and virulence of the anti-Vietnam clamor," the record over the previous six months continued to show substantial accomplishments in combat.[4]

Other high officers were less optimistic. Reflecting on a tour of duty as commanding general of I Field Force, the central portion of South Vietnam, between February 1970 and January 1971, Lt. Gen. Arthur S. Collins, for one, marveled that the American soldier performed in combat as well as he did, given the adverse coverage of the war by the news media and the hostility of Congress. That being the case, he continued, the U.S. Army in Vietnam had begun to deteriorate badly.

Bizarre uniforms, shirts and helmets not worn in combat situations that warranted them, the excessive number of accidental shootings—too many of which appeared other than accidental—and the promiscuous throwing of grenades that lent new meaning to the expression *fragging* should leave us all with an ill-at-ease feeling. Add to this the number of incidents along LOC's [lines of communication] resulting from speeding, shooting from vehicles, or from hurling miscellaneous items at Vietnamese on the roads. When these indicators of lower standards are combined with the number of friendly casualties caused by our own fire due to short rounds or misplaced fire, or by other accidents caused by carelessness, it appears to me that we have a serious disciplinary problem which has resulted in operational slippage.[5]

The situation continued to decline in the months following Collins' report. By April 1972 the U.S. commander in Military Region 3, the area around Saigon, Maj. Gen. James R. Hollingsworth, could only declare that he was appalled at the appearance of his troops in public. "It is very common to observe U.S. soldiers driving and riding in trucks along the roads and highways in the Long Binh–Bien Hoa–Saigon area who are a disgrace to the Army and to the United States," he told McCaffrey.

Seldom does one see such a soldier with a proper haircut wearing a complete and proper uniform. Frequently, they wear no headgear and are in their undershirts. Many times they are bare to the waist. Further, many of our soldiers wear defaced hats and jackets with unauthorized embroidered and stenciled symbols and sayings, pins, buttons, and other items that give them a hippie like appearance. In addition, these soldiers often operate their vehicles in an equally careless manner.

---

[4] Msg, McCaffrey, DCG, USARV, WDC 19450 to Kerwin, 29 Oct 70, William J. McCaffrey Papers, CMH. Also see John Saar, "You Can't Just Hand Out Orders," *Life*, 23 Oct 70.
[5] Debriefing Rpt (RCS–CSFOR–74), 7 Jan 71, Debriefing Report by Lt. Gen. Arthur S. Collins, 330–76–197, box 84, Viet 381 (Feb–Apr) 1971, Laird Papers, WNRC.

A soldier wearing long hair, love beads, and a peace tattoo.

. . . Standards (observed off post) merely reflect standards practiced on post.[6]

The conditions that Collins and Hollingsworth described were extreme but hardly unique to South Vietnam. By the time Collins made his report, grave morale problems had begun to become apparent among American forces stationed around the world. Meanwhile, by September 1970 antiwar sentiment had reached such proportions in the United States that a few draft boards had even begun to exempt persons eligible to serve in the Army on the basis of simple, unsupported statements by those individuals that they were conscientious objectors.[7]

With the American effort in South Vietnam fading and public support for the war diminishing, the decline in military morale became a staple for the Saigon correspondents. As in earlier years, reporters showed considerable respect for the abilities of those soldiers who remained on duty in the field. "As much as they complain," *Newsweek* reporter Kevin Buckley thus observed, "they also boast about their work." Journalists were nevertheless also quick to point out that the United States was spending vast sums in support of a large military commitment in South Vietnam at a time when the soldiers involved frequently had little more to do than cause trouble.[8]

---

[6] Msg, Hollingsworth, CG, TRAC/ZONE Coordinator, MRIII, ARV 890 to McCaffrey, 16 Apr 72, McCaffrey Papers, CMH.

[7] Msgs, Maj Gen Woolnough, CG, CONARC, MRO 1269 to Westmoreland, 10 Sep 70, and General Bruce Palmer, VCSA, WDC 16495 to Westmoreland, 9 Sep 70. Both in Westmoreland Message file, CMH. Also see Msg, Gen Haines, CINCUSARPAC, to Westmoreland, 11 Sep 70, Abrams Papers, CMH.

[8] Kevin Buckley, "'You Can Have Your Own Little Castle,'" *Newsweek*, 11 Jan 71, p. 31. This analysis on boredom in the rear areas is based in part on Research Rpt, Ann David, Press Coverage of Military Morale Problems, 1968–1972 [U.S. Army Center of Military History], CMH files.

In addition, the reporters noted, the U.S. Army in South Vietnam was developing cracks that were beginning to divide not only the "grunts" at the front from support troops in the rear, but also career members of the military from draftees. While some soldiers preferred life in the field to the tedium and regimentation prevalent in base areas, others at the front frequently resented what they considered the easy life of the many who never saw combat. Meanwhile, the conflict seemed to have become "a lifer's war" in which draftees rather than volunteers suffered the combat casualties and in which some officers pushed their troops to engage the enemy in order to earn medals, promotions, and prestige assignments for themselves.[9]

Many writers noted that a new kind of soldier had come into being in South Vietnam, one who questioned his orders more than his predecessors and was sometimes reluctant to risk his life in battle. His attitude seemed to be, remarked reporter John Saar at the time, "that since the U.S. has decided not to go out and win the war, there's no sense in being the last one to die." More sympathetic to the antiwar movement than infantrymen of the past, the new soldier sometimes allowed his hair to grow long and wore "love beads" and peace medallions on his uniform. Whether he conformed outwardly to military standards or not, he seemed to assume that the United States had lost the war and that the American people considered his efforts in Southeast Asia a failure. "There's nothing good about us being here," one soldier thus told Buckley. Another added, "A lot of our buddies got killed here but they died for nothing."[10]

Professional officers were inclined to dismiss stories such as those by Saar and Buckley. "We must accept the fact that coverage like the *Life* article will continue to be published," McCaffrey thus told Kerwin. "The writers reflect their own life style. It makes them more comfortable to define the 'lifers' as eccentrics and the pot-smokers as normal." Although sometimes couched in lurid language and perhaps more sweeping than the situation in South Vietnam required, the reporters' conclusions nonetheless paralleled the views that Collins, Hollingsworth, and others within the Army were expressing privately. Even the assertion that some officers had callously risked the lives of their men to enhance their careers had counterparts in official studies of the time. One, an inquiry into the status of military professionalism composed by the U.S. Army War

[9] "Who Wants To Be the Last American Killed in Vietnam?," *New York Times*, 19 Sep 71. Many of the themes related to the lifer's war are exemplified in Buckley, "'You Can Have Your Own Little Castle,'" p. 31. Also see "Defense Report: Draftees Shoulder Burden of Fighting and Dying in Vietnam," *National Journal*, 15 Aug 70; "Of Lifers, Grunts and Morale in This 'Crummy' War," *Philadelphia Inquirer*, 5 Jan 71.

[10] Saar, "You Can't Just Hand Out Orders." On the subject of the new soldier, see, for example, Buckley, "'You Can Have Your Own Little Castle.'" Also see Haynes Johnson and George C. Wilson, *Army in Anguish* (Washington, D.C.: Washington Post, Pocket Books edition, 1972). The "Army in Anguish" series ran in the *Washington Post* during September and October 1971. Buckley, "'You Can Have Your Own Little Castle.'"

College, indicated that mid-level officers were becoming disenchanted with superiors who sometimes rode to high rank on the swollen backs of heavily overworked subordinates.[11]

If some generals disagreed with the views of the press, moreover, others were willing to admit publicly, if only for the sake of credibility, that the war had done serious damage to the armed forces as an institution. While hardly inclined to conclude with some in the press that the military services should abandon the war to save themselves, most within that group agreed with a comment by General Westmoreland, who told Haynes Johnson and George Wilson of the *Washington Post* in 1971 that the conflict had become "a very traumatic experience for us." The Commander in Chief, U.S. Army, Europe, General Michael S. Davison, for one, observed in an interview with the same two reporters that "When you look at the attitudes reflected in the country today, it is really hard to say that [the price of Vietnam] has been worth it. . . . The Army has paid an enormous price and the country has paid a tremendous price."[12]

Although most officers were thus more than willing to acknowledge that major problems existed, the news media's affinity for stories that depicted the military in the worst possible light became an increasing source of irritation to them and a running problem for public affairs officers. From 1970 onward, indeed, the press portrayed the decline in discipline Collins and Hollingsworth described as an important feature of the war. Commanders in the field and public affairs officers at the Military Assistance Command sometimes disagreed, but they found themselves at an increasing disadvantage in making their case.

Herbicides

Complicating matters, the situations depicted by the press were sometimes the result of changes in the rules governing the way soldiers fought in South Vietnam. Almost from the beginning of the war, for example, the United States had employed herbicides in South Vietnam to defoliate the trees that hid the enemy's base areas and logistical routes. Although a few scientists in the United States had questioned the program after 1965, the press had raised hardly any questions. The agents in question were generally accepted even in the United States, and most reporters considered the denial of food and cover to enemy forces a legitimate military objective. During 1970, however, when antiwar members of Congress adopted the issue and the Nixon administration suspended the

---

[11] Quotes from Msg, McCaffrey ARV 3063 to Kerwin, 29 Oct 70, McCaffrey Papers, CMH. U.S. Army War College, *Study on Military Professionalism* (Carlisle Barracks, Pa.: U.S. Army War College, 1970).

[12] Johnson and Wilson, *Army in Anguish*, p. 83.

use in South Vietnam of the most efficient weed killer, known as agent orange, because it contained a chemical suspected of causing birth defects, reporters began to keep careful watch on the issue. As a result, commanders in the field very shortly found themselves caught between their own concept of what was necessary to preserve the lives of their men and the evolving requirements of public relations.[13]

The problem became acute during October 1970, when *Time* discovered that members of the U.S. Americal Division, lacking less toxic but much slower acting weed killers known as agents white and blue, had deliberately used agent orange in Quang Ngai and Quang Tin Provinces both to destroy crops in enemy-controlled areas and to clear foliage around the perimeters of base camps. Confirming the magazine's allegations and learning that chemical officers both within the division and at the Military Assistance Command had known of the development but had done nothing, General Abrams had little choice but to accelerate steps to put all remaining stocks of orange under centralized control and to limit the use of the small amounts of agents blue and white that remained within his command to remote areas and to the fringes of installations where the jungle provided a threat to security. On 29 December the White House announced "an orderly phase out of . . . herbicide operations to be completed by next Spring."[14]

Those steps should have eliminated any cause for concern that the Military Assistance Command would face further criticism for its handling of herbicides, but, in fact, they opened up a whole new field of potential controversy. As stocks of agents blue and white dwindled in South Vietnam, tensions began to build among soldiers in the field. To many, the lush jungle growing around their base camps invited attack, a threat that was obviously more immediate than the genetic damage herbicides supposedly caused. By the spring of 1971, the time targeted for the end of all herbicide operations, well-founded rumors thus began to circulate within both the Military Assistance Command and the Defense Department that soldiers who had taken rest and recreation leave outside of South Vietnam were returning to their units with commercial weed killers they had purchased on the open market for use around their fire bases.[15]

[13] Unless otherwise indicated, this section is based on William A. Buckingham, Jr., *Operation Ranch Hand: The Air Force and Herbicides in Southeast Asia, 1961–1971* (Washington, D.C.: Department of the Air Force, Office of Air Force History, 1982), pp. 157–84.

[14] Memo, David Packard for CJCS, 16 Oct 70, and Memo, Moorer CM–461–70 for Deputy Secretary of Defense, 24 Dec 70, both in 330–76–067, box 93, Viet 370.64, 1970, Laird Papers, WNRC. Also see Msg, Abrams MAC 13747 to Moorer, 19 Oct 70, Westmoreland Message file, CMH. The White House statement is quoted by Buckingham, *Operation Ranch Hand*, p. 175. For a basic chronology of the herbicide question, see Talking Paper, OASD ISA, Vietnam Task Force, 10 Jan 72, sub: Herbicides, War Crimes, ROE-Vn file, Westmoreland Papers, CMH.

[15] MFR, Phil Odeen, 10 Aug 71, sub: Vietnamization Meeting With Secretary Laird, folder 77, Thayer Papers, CMH. Also see Msg, Brig Gen L. Gordon Hill, CINFO Saigon, MAC 7218 to Henkin, 27 Jul 71, 330–76–197, box 84, 370–64 (Jul–Aug) 1971, Laird Papers, WNRC.

While visiting South Vietnam in June 1971, Colonel Hill stated the dilemma confronting the military in a message to Henkin. If the herbicide program had become an emotional issue with both environmentalists and the antiwar movement, he said, "Imagine, the story impact of an attack on a fire base wherein several Americans are killed and some distraught soldier on the scene charges that if they'd been permitted to defoliate around the perimeter the attack either would not have happened or would not have been successful. If the story were to blow hard, developments could be a minor disaster."[16]

Although Secretary Laird requested authority to continue to use approved herbicides to protect U.S. installations as early as 13 May and General Abrams himself argued that the lack of defoliants was costing the lives of South Vietnamese and American soldiers, it took until 18 August for President Nixon to overcome his reluctance to face the issue. Approving the use of agents white and blue when essential for the protection of U.S. and allied personnel, he then specified that public affairs officers in Saigon were to refrain from announcing his decision to the press. If the subject arose, they were to say only that the ban on agent orange remained in effect and that American forces were continuing to phase out herbicides in South Vietnam. The policy had the desired effect. Although herbicide usage in South Vietnam remained a subject of concern for the press, the sort of horror stories Hill had envisioned never came to haunt the Military Assistance Command.[17]

Combat Refusals

Not so for the growing reluctance of some American soldiers to risk their lives for what seemed a lost cause. As the war lengthened, the Saigon correspondents asserted repeatedly that a malaise of the spirit had begun to spread among the troops in South Vietnam and that combat refusals were beginning to take place with alarming frequency. The Military Assistance Command had little choice but to admit that the phenomenon indeed occurred but refused to concede that it was anything more than a minor nuisance, the normal give-and-take between officers and enlisted men that sometimes occurred on the battlefield. Reporters could see for themselves, however, and the string of reports that they composed proved a continuing source of embarrassment and irritation to officers in the field.

Peter Arnett's discovery during September 1969 that members of Company A, "Alpha Company," of the 3d Battalion, 21st Infantry, 196th Infantry Brigade (Light), had refused orders to recover bodies from a

---

[16] Msg, Hill MAC 7218 to Henkin, 27 Jul 71.
[17] MFR, Phil Odeen, 10 Aug 71, sub: Vietnamization Meeting With Secretary Laird; Buckingham, *Operation Ranch Hand*, pp. 181f.

downed helicopter appears to have first sensitized the press to the subject. The refusals that accompanied the 4th Infantry Division's entry into Cambodia during May 1970 also sparked interest, but none of those reports produced more enduring images than one by Jack Laurence that played on the CBS Evening News during April 1970.[18]

Laurence had joined Company C, "Charlie Company," of the 2d Battalion, 7th Cavalry, 1st Cavalry Division (Airmobile), while the unit operated in War Zone C, a region some eighty kilometers northwest of Saigon in Tay Ninh Province, near the Cambodian border. His purpose had been to document in a series of reports the daily life of an American military unit in the field. During the days that followed he had done so, recording not only such mundane events as mail call, meals, and resupply missions but also the unit's reaction to the loss of experienced company and battalion commanders and its tentative adjustment to the new officers who took charge. Highly attuned to the morale of the soldiers who were his subjects, the reporter showed little sympathy for the officers taking command. "*Flaky* was the word heard most often now," he noted. The term, he explained, was "a GI expression meaning that the company and the battalion did not seem to be operating as efficiently as before."[19]

The reporter played upon that theme in describing an incident he witnessed on 6 April, when brigade and battalion commanders had discovered that the unit was operating in the area of a forthcoming B–52 strike and instructed the company's commander to clear the zone as quickly as possible. Since the transmission was uncoded, the reason for the command was not revealed. Following orders, the commander instructed his company to walk down an unsecured road to a clearing where helicopters could land. He met immediate resistance. As the reporter's cameraman filmed the scene, the men in the lead platoon explained to their commander that their old officers had taught them to avoid unsecured roads because the enemy often used them for ambushes. At length, after explaining the tactics the company would use and the necessity to comply with orders from above, the company commander once more issued his command. The men complied grudgingly but had to go only a short distance down the road before battalion headquarters diverted them to a smaller, more secure pick-up zone.[20]

In all likelihood, the episode would never have received any attention at all but for the presence of Laurence's cameras, which recorded it as it happened. Laurence dramatized the moment in his report by emphasizing the objections of the enlisted men while paying little attention to the point of view of their commanders. "What's the problem?" he asked one soldier.

---

[18] See Chapter 9 for details of the Alpha Company affair.

[19] Jack Laurence, CBS Evening News, 9 Apr 70, *Radio-TV-Defense Dialog*.

[20] Msg, Maj Gen Roberts, CG, 1st Cav Div (Airmobile), FCV 490 to Lt Gen Ewell, CG, IIFFV, 7 Apr 70, Abrams Papers, CMH. Also see J. D. Coleman, *Incursion* (New York: St. Martins Press, 1992), pp. 208–11. Coleman was a public affairs officer assigned to the 1st Cavalry Division at the time.

"Well," the man responded, "we just don't want to walk down the road—this is one of the things I told you about when we were wondering what the new CO was going to be like. . . . These are the kinds of things you don't want him to be like." Another soldier called the road "a shooting gallery." A third asserted that "I don't think [the captain] . . . knows his stuff; he hasn't been a captain but maybe two weeks—maybe three weeks." A fourth avowed that "We've heard too many companies, too many battalions want to walk the road. They get blown away." At the end, the reporter termed the incident a "rebellion" but refused to blame the men who had participated. Instead, he suggested that the war had taken on a new dimension that kept "normally brave and obedient" American fighting men from risking their lives without reason. "Veteran soldiers who are not afraid of combat," he said, had thus refused to walk a road that had become for them "symbolic of the way 40,000 other GI's had gone before."[21]

Since the incident had occurred on the spur of a moment in front of a television camera, MACV public affairs officers handled it in as forthright a manner as they could. There was nothing to deny. Instead, on grounds that the truth was normally less sensational than the suppositions that grew in the absence of solid facts, they met with Laurence to inform him of the impending B–52 strike. They also made the soldiers involved in the incident available to the Saigon correspondents and provided reporters with access to knowledgeable officers who could explain what had happened from a military point of view.[22]

During the interviews that followed, the officers of the 1st Cavalry Division criticized Laurence's use of the term *rebellion* and questioned his suggestion that the incident was symbolic of larger trends in the war. In fact, they said, the men on the road had shown good sense. They were seasoned combat veterans while the battalion, company, and platoon commanders were all new. "There hasn't been a war in which the troops didn't question certain judgments," observed the deputy commander of the 1st Cavalry Division's 1st Brigade, Lt. Col. Robert L. Drudik. "It happens time and again—it's nothing new."[23]

The approach had some effect. Verifying the imminence of the B–52 strike with the Pentagon, CBS apparently toned down Laurence's story before broadcasting it. Meanwhile, if *Newsweek* would later observe that "extreme caution, even to the point of disobedience, may become the watchword in a war that the U.S. says it no longer seeks to win," the rest of the press gave the episode far less coverage than the Alpha Company incident of the year before.[24]

As time lengthened, the story nonetheless achieved a kind of symbolism, in part because television cameras had filmed it as it had occurred,

---

[21] Jack Laurence, CBS Evening News, 9 Apr 70. Also see "'Just Downright Refusal,'" *Newsweek*, 20 Apr 70.

[22] Coleman, *Incursion*, p. 210.

[23] [AP], "GI's Who Defied Order Praised by the Army," *Washington Star*, 13 Apr 70.

[24] Coleman, *Incursion*, p. 210; "'Just Downright Refusal.'"

and in part because the 1st Cavalry Division refused to allow the matter to rest. Indeed, two weeks after the incident, in response to continuing reports by Laurence on Charlie Company's poor morale, the division's commander resurrected the issue by barring the correspondent from any further visits to Company C. In announcing his decision, he explained that the efficiency of the unit had been impaired by the continued presence of the television crew, which had "portrayed the men as other than disciplined and well trained soldiers." As the troops had become aware of the slanted treatment they were receiving, he continued, their officers had become concerned about the impact the characterization might have on morale and combat effectiveness.[25]

It was well within a battlefield commander's prerogative to make that decision, but the move needlessly angered the press at a time when the armed forces required all the public support they could muster. Shortly thereafter, Walter Cronkite complained on the air that the Army had forced CBS to terminate "one of the most productive news assignments of a long war." Then letters from congressmen and senators began to arrive at the Department of Defense expressing concern that the Army had, in effect, embarked on a program to repress the news media.[26]

Over the year that followed, as disillusionment with the war spread and a scattering of combat refusals occurred similar to the one Laurence had reported, the press criticized the Army for the way commanders handled those incidents. That was the case during March 1971, when an exhausted, under-equipped and -manned armored unit near Khe Sanh refused to make a dangerous nighttime thrust into enemy territory to retrieve secret documents and equipment aboard an abandoned armored personnel carrier.

As the episode evolved, the commander of the 1st Brigade, 5th Mechanized Division, Brig. Gen. John G. Hill, Jr., relieved the captain in charge for a failure of leadership but refused to take action against the men involved. The move was controversial, even among the military, because the officer Hill replaced had been a popular and proficient troop commander. Even so, the general's superiors supported his decision. As the U.S. commander in the XXIV Corps region, Lt. Gen. James W. Sutherland, Jr., told General Abrams, Hill had acted in light of the tactical situation as he had perceived it and out of a necessity to return the troop to combat effectiveness as quickly as possible. The move, Sutherland added, appeared to have succeeded. The unit performed well under its new leaders.[27]

Hill himself made those points in an interview with the press soon after the incident. In describing his attitude toward the fifty-three men

---

[25] DDI Talking Paper, 8 May 70, DDI Cambodia file.

[26] Walter Cronkite, CBS Evening News, 24 Apr 70, *Radio-TV-Defense Dialog*; Ltr, Jerry Friedheim to Senator Lowell P. Weicker, 15 Jun 70, 330–76–067, box 88, Viet 000.3, 1970, Laird Papers, WNRC.

[27] Msg, Lt Gen Sutherland, CG, XXIV Corps, QTR 582 to Abrams, 29 Mar 71, McCaffrey Papers, CMH.

who had refused to take the mission, however, he added a comment that, for all of its humor, expressed both his own sense of futility and the dilemmas confronting the military in South Vietnam. "What do you want me to do," he asked the reporters, "take them out and shoot them?"[28] The remark offended those conservatives within the news media who had begun to look askance upon what they considered an increasing reluctance on the part of the U.S. Army to discipline rebellious soldiers. As a result, without adverting to the fact that Hill had made a difficult on-the-spot decision, ABC News anchorman Howard K. Smith, for one, charged that "in a non-sequitur rapidly becoming typical in Vietnam, today the commander was replaced, but the Army announced no charges will be filed against the men because 'they're back in the field doing their duty.'" In the same way, the military analyst for the *Detroit News*, retired Marine Corps Col. Robert D. Heinl, Jr., rebuked the Army for its "supine" response to the incident and called a comment by Hill to the effect that the event had been blown out of proportion "a funeral oration on the U.S. Army in Vietnam."[29]

Although some commentators condemned military commanders for their failure to exert maximum discipline, most of the press attempted to handle combat refusals in an even-handed manner. During October 1971, for example, when five members of a platoon stationed at Fire Support Base PACE, located northwest of Saigon near the Cambodian border, told freelance reporter Richard Boyle that they were unwilling to go on patrol, reporters reacted to the news by scrutinizing all sides of the event. They listened attentively, on the one hand, when MACV public affairs officers gave them access to the men involved and faithfully relayed the soldiers' objections that the mission meant virtual suicide and that the operation was offensive in nature when the Nixon administration had promised that American forces would assume a defensive role in South Vietnam. On the other, they also interviewed officers who noted that the so-called mutiny reported by Boyle had never occurred because the company commander had withdrawn his order upon learning that a South Vietnamese unit had already assumed the mission. The reporters then relayed comments by the U.S. commander in Military Region 3, Maj. Gen. Jack Wagstaff, admitting that genuine combat refusals sometimes occurred but were so rare that he had never encountered one.[30]

---

[28] Ibid.

[29] Howard K. Smith, ABC Evening News, 22 Mar 71, *Radio-TV-Defense Dialog*; Col. R. D. Heinl, Jr., "Troop B's Mutiny Signals Downfall of Army in Viet, *Detroit News*, 25 Mar 71.

[30] The Military Assistance Command changed the term *corps tactical zone* to *military region* on 30 April 1971. Since this chapter spans that period, it will use the term *military region* to keep from confusing the reader. See, for example, Harry Reasoner, ABC Evening News, 11 Oct 71, *Radio-TV-Defense Dialog*; "South Vietnam: A Question of Protection," *Time*, 25 Oct 71; Craig Whitney, "Army Says Some G.I.'s Balked Briefly at Patrol," *New York Times*, 12 Oct 71; Peter Jay, "Combat Refusals Called Rare," *Washington Post*, 25 Oct 71. For an official description of the incident, see Fact Sheet, Fire Support Base PACE Incidents, attachment to Memo, Lt Gen Walter T. Kerwin, Jr., DCSPER, for Chief of Staff, United States Army, 22 Oct 71, sub: White House Fact Sheet, copy in CMH files.

While almost never critical of the enlisted men who had participated in the incident, some of the reports that appeared sketched the dilemmas confronting U.S. forces serving in regions near the Cambodian border, where the episode had occurred. *Time* observed that South Vietnamese units were supposedly responsible for protecting U.S. fire support bases in the area, but their commanders insisted that they lacked the strength to do the job. "Every time we move out," one soldier had thus told reporters, "we get our asses kicked off." As a result, the United States relied on artillery, a scattering of B–52 strikes, and assaults by helicopter to keep the enemy off balance but still had to send American units out on patrols. At that point, the magazine observed, as at Fire Support Base PACE, "the 'I don't want to be the last man shot' syndrome" sometimes showed itself.[31]

NBC News anchorman David Brinkley had little sympathy for explanations of that sort. Siding squarely with an enlisted man who had termed the operation "senseless suicide," he noted that officials in Washington said little publicly on the subject but deep down appeared to agree that "there's nothing left in Vietnam worth any more American lives."[32] Nicholas Proffitt of *Newsweek* was more dispassionate. Although critical of efforts by some in the Pentagon to depict press coverage of the incident as "scavenger" journalism, the reporter observed that the episode might never have gained much attention at all but for Boyle. A radical journalist who had entered South Vietnam illegally from Cambodia after being expelled during 1969 for participating in an antigovernment demonstration, the reporter had turned an embarrassing but hardly unusual situation into a major controversy by offering to deliver to Senator Edward Kennedy a letter of protest signed by some sixty-six members of the unit. After "peddling" his version of the event to Agence France Presse, which dramatized the incident by labeling it a mutiny, Proffitt said, Boyle had indeed contacted Kennedy, who had responded by issuing a call for a congressional investigation. In the end, Proffitt noted, once the incident had begun to fade, Kennedy had reconsidered. When Boyle later asked for an interview to pursue the subject, "the senator's staffers . . . replied that their boss was unavailable."[33]

Although Proffitt was careful to cover all sides of the question, his report nevertheless reflected themes that had begun to preoccupy both conscientious journalists and the military. The incident at PACE, he said, may have been only a minor example of what happened in many U.S. units in South Vietnam, but it was still significant.

For an increasing number of GI's, there is a feeling of being forgotten men. Fewer and fewer journalists get into the field these days, and long ago, the U.S. public stopped thinking of Vietnam grunts as heroes. But there is more to it than that. For today, the GI's fear of death is accompanied by a seemingly even more into-

---

[31] "South Vietnam: A Question of Protection."
[32] David Brinkley, NBC News, 13 Oct 71, *Radio-TV-Defense Dialog.*
[33] Nicholas C. Proffitt, "Soldiers Who Refuse To Die," *Newsweek*, 25 Oct 71.

lerable thought that his death will be anonymous. In a time of "acceptable" casualty figures (the latest weekly U.S. toll was eight dead and 72 wounded), more and more U.S. soldiers serving in Vietnam are understandably concerned that they may be among the last to die in a war everybody else considers over.[34]

Problems With Race Relations and Fragging

The condition of military morale in the field remained a concern for the Saigon correspondents. But with the American role in combat declining, most reporters found their best opportunities in areas away from the fighting, where soldiers suffered less from a fear of dying than from boredom and all of the social ills that accompanied it. The problems the military faced in the rear, especially with race relations, assaults against officers, and drug abuse thus became a staple for them, and a continuing source of trouble for public affairs officers.

By mid-1970 and 1971, the press treated MACV's difficulties with race relations as a standard feature of the war. Most articles that dealt with military discipline and morale mentioned the issue, often in a manner sympathetic to the Army. "Considering the explosive potential involved in molding large numbers of black and white Americans into one fighting force," *Newsweek* thus observed on 29 June 1970, "there have been encouragingly few overt racial incidents among the U.S. troops in South Vietnam. And when confrontations do occur, the military usually takes great pains to settle them quickly, informally—and quietly." In the same way, Wendell Merick of *U.S. News & World Report* observed in January 1971 that while racial tensions existed among the troops in South Vietnam they were often difficult to identify as such. Although a thoughtless racial comment, even in jest, might cause a brawl at any big base, the problem seemed slight in the field, where black and white soldiers appeared to work in harmony. "Given beer, whisky or drugs, mixed in with a crowd of blacks and whites, and you can have trouble," the reporter said, quoting an unidentified officer. "But you never know which came first—the booze, the drugs, or racial disagreements."[35]

If some reporters thus attempted to dispel the idea that the U.S. Army in South Vietnam was a hotbed of racial tensions, others still contended that problems involving race had become so widespread that black enlisted men had, in some cases, attempted to kill their officers. "In Vietnam," noted Bruce Biossat of the *Washington Daily News* in January 1971, "the practice of 'fragging officers'—tossing fragmenting grenades into their offices, messes, or living quarters, has evidently become fairly com-

---

[34] Ibid.

[35] "The Evans Nine," *Newsweek*, 29 Jun 70; Wendell S. Merick, "Sagging Morale in Vietnam: Eyewitness Report on Drugs, Race Problems and Boredom," *U.S. News & World Report*, 25 Jan 71.

monplace. What evidence there is—men observed running from the scene, the Army grapevine, etc.—points to black soldiers."[36]

A year after Biossat made his report, Eugene Linden of *Saturday Review* took up the same theme. Interracial tensions continued unabated, the newsman noted.

During the week I was up north at Danang and Hue, two race riots erupted in the Danang area alone. When MP's were called in to quell the riot at Camp Baxter, they found that whites and blacks had sequestered about the camp stocks of frags [fragmentation grenades], ammunition, and even a couple of M–60 machine guns. A few days later at a detachment of engineers, a breach of unwritten mess hall etiquette set off two days and two nights of skirmishes in which five GI's were injured.

Blacks and whites were united by common needs in the field.

Linden went on to describe the attempted murder of an officer who black enlisted men believed had discriminated against them. In an attempt to contain the problem, he continued, many units had denied their men weapons in rear areas. Others had set up forums to improve communication between officers, noncommissioned officers, and the enlisted ranks, "but so far the Army has had scant success in stemming the lethal fad."[37]

Reports such as those and others charging that the system of military justice favored whites, that the frequency of punishment for blacks was greater than for whites, and that violence between the races in the war zone was inevitable prompted the Military Assistance Command to conduct a major investigation of the subject during 1971. In January 1972 the command's inspector general, Colonel Cook, informed General Abrams that many of the allegations circulating in the press seemed exaggerated. In all of the cases studied, he said, no instances of inequity in punishment between blacks and whites had occurred. Instead, a field inquiry into 248 specific cases where relations between blacks and whites had seemed an

[36] Bruce Biossat, "'Fragging' Officers," *Washington Daily News*, 21 Jan 71.
[37] Eugene Linden, "The Demoralization of an Army, Fragging and Other Withdrawal Symptoms," *Saturday Review*, 8 Jan 72, p. 12.

issue had shown that proportionally more whites than blacks had been disciplined, despite the fact that whites had been the aggressors only 17 percent of the time, versus 83 percent for the blacks. In most confrontations between soldiers of different races, he continued, race was not an element. Although the incident Linden had reported at Camp Baxter had indeed occurred during December 1970, the inexperience of young company commanders, inadequate attention to the morale and welfare of the troops, an indulgent attitude toward drug abuse by junior officers, poor communications up and down the chain of command, and the overly permissive enforcement of rules and regulations were as much an element in the disturbance as racial animosities. In most cases, drug trafficking, prostitution, and gambling, "controlled by hoodlums, predominately black," had caused the violence. Considering the total picture, Cook concluded, it appeared that only 33 out of 5,200 incidents that had occurred within the command during 1971 were attributable to race alone. "This hardly paints a picture of widespread serious racial confrontations."[38]

Whatever the validity of Cook's estimate that the press had exaggerated the situation, newsmen at least had grounds for their concern. Both the testimony of black chaplains who had served in South Vietnam during 1971 and 1972 and an evaluation of the situation by the Chairman of the Joint Chiefs of Staff, Admiral Moorer, during July 1971 highlighted the problem. In oral history interviews, the chaplains asserted that racial tensions were severe throughout South Vietnam. Commenting, for example, on an assignment during 1971 with the 5th Transportation Command, the unit involved in the incident at Camp Baxter, one chaplain asserted that "It was death all over the place. . . . At nightfall most of the camp was divided . . . blacks over here, whites over there. [The commander] didn't go out at night . . . he had his own trailer and he had guards all around it." Another black chaplain commented on the situation at Long Binh depot during his tour of duty in 1971. The men, he said, would "go out on missions and the racism would drop . . . and they'd come back to the compound and kill each other. I didn't understand it."[39]

Admiral Moorer was equally emphatic. Commanders tended to underestimate their problem with race, he told Secretary Laird. They had no experience in dealing with the subject, and they found it difficult to find out what was happening beneath them in the chain of command. Some of their subordinates seemed more interested in creating flawless records for themselves than in allowing information to go forward that might somehow prove disadvantageous to their careers. Meanwhile, the centralization of messing, pay, and logistics had reduced the respon-

[38] Memo, Col Robert M. Cook for Chief of Staff, MACV, 31 Jan 72, sub: Result of MACIG Field Inquiry Into Alleged Racial Incidents, copy in CMH files.

[39] Both quotes from MS, Henry F. Ackerman, He Was Always There: The U.S. Army Chaplain Ministry in the Vietnam Conflict [U.S. Army, Office of the Chief of Chaplains, 1988], pp. 311–14.

sibility of commanders for their men and had impeded the formation of esprit de corps within units; the frequent shifting of commanders had tended to induce anxiety and frustration among all the ranks; and the permissiveness that seemed to pervade American society as a whole had bred a spirit of cynicism and hostility toward authority among the men that only served to accentuate the problems commanders faced.[40] Under the circumstances and despite the ambiguities Cook had uncovered, it should have been no surprise that significant problems with human relations had arisen among the troops in South Vietnam.

In attempting to explain what was happening, public affairs officers could do little more than compromise between the direct testimony reporters gave and the inconsistencies Cook and others noted. Hoping to do as little damage to the Army's image as possible, they thus conceded that problems existed but also pointed out that many incidents of violence involving Americans in South Vietnam had nothing to do with race. Overall, they said, the Army "has a race problem because our country has a race problem."[41]

They took the same approach where fragging was concerned. Although they encouraged reporters to use the term *assault with explosives* because they felt that *fragging* trivialized a serious offense, they acknowledged that the phenomenon occurred, that white troops also indulged in the practice, and that it was a major concern to the Military Assistance Command. Even so, in an attempt to provide some perspective, they cautioned newsmen that the extent of the problem was difficult to track. "After the incident is first reported, there simply is no evidence except that an explosion has occurred. Because of the small number of injuries, it appears that in the majority of cases the intent is to intimidate or to scare."[42]

Drug Abuse

If public affairs officers encountered difficulties with race relations and crimes of violence against officers, their problems were far larger where drug abuse was concerned. By 1970 and 1971 the press could contend with considerable justification that experimentation with marijuana and narcotic agents such as heroin and barbiturates had reached epidemic proportions among American forces in South Vietnam. As correspon-

---

[40] Memo, T. H. Moorer for Secretary of Defense, 20 Jul 71, sub: Discipline in the Armed Forces, 330–76–201, box 2, 250, 1971, Laird Papers, WNRC.

[41] The Army released a report to the press that made these points on 24 January 1970. *Facts on File*, 5–11 Feb 70, vol. 30. Also see Biossat, "'Fragging' Officers."

[42] Talking Paper, 17 May 71, DDI Fragging file. Quote from Talking Paper, USARV IO, 31 Dec 70, sub: Reply to AP, 72A6994, box 8, News Media and Release files, USARVIO Papers, WNRC.

dent Peter Arnett observed after the war, the situation was obvious. On one occasion, he said, during a temporary assignment to South Vietnam to report on drugs, he had driven to Newport, the U.S. Army port on the Saigon River that handled military cargoes. Approaching the gate, he met no challenge. The guard was "stoned" on drugs and semi-conscious within his booth. "Everywhere you stepped inside the facility," the reporter continued, "you encountered empty vials littering the ground and crunching under foot. I spoke with the captain in charge. He confirmed that at any one time close to half of his men were stoned on drugs."[43] Arnett's description paralleled circumstances that existed at the 5th Transportation Command's headquarters near Da Nang during at least part of 1971. "All over the place you could find these little vials," one chaplain recalled, "little plastic things laying around all over the place."[44]

At first, officials in Washington felt confident in asserting, as they did in a report released to Congress in September 1970, that the news media had exaggerated the extent of drug abuse in South Vietnam. By printing poorly substantiated allegations, some members of the press promoted that attitude. Syndicated columnist Jack Anderson, for one, charged during August 1970 that the Military Assistance Command had consistently attempted to cover up the true dimensions of the drug problem in Southeast Asia. The situation had become so difficult, he said, that troops "stoned" on extra-strength marijuana had in one instance attempted to shoot down a helicopter gunship. The aircraft had defended itself with a storm of machine gun fire, leaving several of its assailants dead. The bodies of the men were found later, Anderson avowed, strewn with the remains of marijuana cigarettes. Launching an immediate investigation, Colonel Cook was able to refute Anderson's allegations. Beyond the kind of unsubstantiated rumors that often circulated near battlefields, he said, they had no basis in fact. If a fight of the sort the reporter had indicated had indeed occurred, it would almost certainly have left some trace in official reporting as a result of the stringent investigating that always accompanied American deaths by friendly fire. Nothing of the sort existed.[45]

Although Anderson's account of the helicopter incident was incorrect, that fact, in the end, proved of little consolation to officials. Over the months that followed, the problem with drugs increased, and the press continued to report that the situation was far worse than many officials appeared to believe. "GI Pot Smoking Called 'Epidemic,'" observed the *Washington Daily News*. "G.I.'s Find Marijuana Is Cheap and Plentiful,"

---

[43] Interv, author with Peter Arnett, 6 Sep 88, CMH files.

[44] Ackerman, He Was Always There, p. 313.

[45] Felix Belair, Jr., "Pentagon Unit Finds Drugs 'Military Problem' in Asia," *New York Times*, 4 Jan 71. The Anderson report is summarized in Msg, Frank Bartimo AGC M&RA 4127 to Brig Gen Greene, J1 MACV, 10 Aug 70, retransmitted in Msg, Greene to Maj Gen Bowers, C/S USARV, 13 Aug 70, copy in CMH files; Msg, MACV 42154 to CINCPAC, 17 Aug 70, sub: Anderson Article, *Washington Post*, 9 Aug 70, 334–72A870, box 11, 14–2 DISC 9-Drugs, WNRC.

noted the *New York Times*. "Does Our Army Fight on Drugs?" asked *Look* magazine.[46]

One of the most galling of those reports appeared on 13 November 1970, when CBS broadcast a story by correspondent Gary Sheppard in which the newsman interviewed members of the 1st Cavalry Division (Airmobile) while they participated in a "pot party" at a fire support base code-named ARIES in War Zone D, some sixty kilometers northeast of Saigon. Observing that the war had reached its lowest ebb in five years and that marijuana was "as plentiful in Vietnam as C–rations," the reporter asked one of the men, "Aren't you worried about maybe getting attacked and not being able to react properly?" The soldier responded, "No, nobody usually seems to worry. . . . We're worried—more worried—about lifers. I think we're constantly on the guard for lifers when we smoke." One soldier proceeded to use his shotgun barrel as a pipe. "Do you do that very often?" Sheppard asked. "Whenever, Vito's around," came the response. "Vito is a 20 year old . . . squad leader," Sheppard explained, "responsible for the lives of a dozen men." The reporter then observed that "Fire Base ARIES is not unique. What's happening here is also happening to some extent at virtually every other American installation in Vietnam. Recent surveys estimate that well over 50 percent of the soldiers in Vietnam use marijuana."[47]

Unlike Anderson's story, Sheppard's report, filmed as it happened, was almost impossible to deny. Rumors circulated for a time that the reporter had staged the event, but an extensive investigation by the Military Assistance Command produced no evidence to confirm the allegation. Instead, a series of failures in command came to light. The officer supposedly assigned to escort Sheppard, one day short of returning to the United States, had passed the duty to another, who had departed after a time to pursue his own responsibilities. In the absence of any escort, the reporter had fallen in with an enlisted man who had invited him to participate in some "live action." Sheppard had gone reluctantly, apparently because little else was happening. The squad leaders responsible for the group that held the "party" were young and inexperienced. Probably aware of what was taking place but more inclined to be "buddies" with their soldiers than to lead, they had done nothing to interfere. As Sheppard had reported, one had even participated in the party.[48]

---

[46] [UPI], "GI Pot Smoking Called 'Epidemic,'" *Washington Daily News*, 18 Aug 70; James Sterba, "G.I.'s Find Marijuana Is Cheap and Plentiful," *New York Times*, 2 Sep 70; Joel H. Kaplan, M.D., as told to Christopher S. Wren, "Does Our Army Fight on Drugs?," *Look*, 16 Jun 70.

[47] Msg, Defense 15220 to Leonard, CINFO MACV, 13 Nov 70, sub: CBS News Story, DDI Drug file.

[48] Msg, Brig Gen J. R. Burton, CG, 1st Cav Div (Airmobile), OHFCV 1520 to Lt Gen McCaffrey, DCG, USARV, 15 Nov 70; Msg, Lt Gen Collins, CG, IFFV NHA, NHT 2228 to McCaffrey, 15 Nov 70, sub: CBS Telecast of 1st Cav Div "Pot Party"; Msg, Lt Gen McCaffrey, DCG, USARV, ARV 3276 to Lt Gen Kerwin, DCSPER, 16 Nov 70. All in McCaffrey Papers, CMH.

Jerry Friedheim at the Defense Department refused to comment on the specifics of the story until all the facts were clear but affirmed shortly after it played that it underscored a matter of deep concern to the military services. "We have not denied that there is a problem," he said; "we have acknowledged . . . [that we] share it with the rest of society." Defense Department spokesmen then confirmed that marijuana usage in South Vietnam continued to increase and that up to 50 percent of the soldiers were probably smoking the substance.[49]

In the end, the Military Assistance Command apparently decided the best it could do was to keep Sheppard's story within bounds. When Bruce Dunning of CBS News thus attempted to travel to Fire Support Base ARIES to interview officers and to film the men of the unit as they watched a tape of the report, the chief of MACV information, Colonel Leonard, recommended that the 1st Cavalry Division refrain from showing the tape and refer all questions on drug abuse to higher authorities. Leonard was disinclined to hide anything, but he clearly intended to contain whatever damage had occurred.[50]

Officers in the field were less scrupulous. While some were relatively open to the press and made it a point to admit to reporters that the drug problem was real but difficult for commanders to track, others attempted to protect their careers by shielding themselves and their commands from inquiring newsmen. As a result, during the weeks following the incident, charges began to appear in the press that a number of units had strengthened their escort policies to ensure that information officers accompanied visiting newsmen at all times. The Associated Press even claimed that the U.S. 101st Airborne Division (Airmobile) had set up a rating system for correspondents and was checking to determine whether those who visited it were favorable or unfavorable to the military. The unit's information officer later denied the allegation, but he did confirm that for a time during mid-November, after an unusually large influx of newsmen, the division's chief of staff had ordered an acting information officer to gather information about future visitors. That officer was to determine the names of those correspondents, their employers, anticipated lengths of stay, and whatever background information existed on whether their work had been favorable or unfavorable to the military.[51]

---

[49] Msg, Lorfano Defense 15268 to Leonard, 13 Nov 70, sub: Statement Re: Marijuana at Fire Base Aries, and Talking Paper, 13 Nov 70, both in DDI Drugs, 69–70 file.

[50] MFR, Lt Col Charles A. Gatzka, Deputy IO, USARV, 18 Nov 70, sub: FONECON Between COL Leonard and LTC Gatzka at 181350 Nov 70, 72A6994, box 8, News Media & Release files-70, USARVIO Papers, WNRC; Msg, Brig Gen Ursano, DCS, P&A USARV, to Maj Gen Davis, ODCSPER DA, 21 Dec 70, sub: CBS Report on Heroin; *Newsweek* Story on Morale in USARV, 72A6994, box 8, Backchannel file, USARVIO Papers, WNRC.

[51] See, for example, Merick, "Sagging Morale in Vietnam: Eyewitness Report on Drugs, Race Problems and Boredom"; Msg, Leonard MAC 15689 to Lorfano, 9 Dec 70, sub: AP Story on 101st Div "Rating System," DDI Misc. Background Messages file.

Those stories and others like them made it seem as though the Military Assistance Command, as Anderson had charged, was bent on covering up the extent of drug abuse in South Vietnam. Although reluctant to inflict more wounds than necessary upon the military services and considerably less pessimistic than some within the press, General Abrams and his public affairs officers were, in fact, inclined to take the opposite approach, if only as a means of self-defense. The Military Assistance Command thus stipulated that when questions about drug abuse arose it was official policy for all concerned to deal honestly with reporters. While attempting to direct the attention of newsmen to the effort to alleviate the problem, everyone had to realize that, as the Chief of USARV Public Affairs during 1971, Col. Alfred J. Mock, put it, "failure to respond to queries and refusal to allow the press to interview . . . staff officers . . . would likely . . . create the impression that we are trying to conceal an overwhelming problem with which we are unable to cope."[52]

Following that reasoning, both the Defense Department and the Military Assistance Command sought to provide the press with the best information they had on the subject. On 30 October 1970, the MACV Office of Information thus issued a communique that confirmed Abrams' belief that drug abuse was "a matter of grave concern." While failing to ratify without proper scientific evidence the impressions reporters had gained about the extent of the problem, the release noted that the number of drug-related hospital admissions within the command had increased from 527 during all of 1969 to 746 during the first nine months of 1970. It added that 241 of those cases had occurred in August and September alone. Acknowledging that figures for the previous years were probably defective, the command then revealed that there had been a marked increase in the availability of high potency heroin in South Vietnam and that the number of deaths due to drug abuse was far larger than anyone had earlier expected.[53]

Although Abrams and the Defense Department recognized that candor was far more constructive than either deceit or half-truths, they were caught between that judgment, their own inability to measure the extent of drug abuse accurately, and a whole series of requirements imposed by the political nature of the war. On the one hand, the number of hard-core drug abusers among the American troops in South Vietnam was not known and difficult even to estimate. As the Principal Deputy Assistant Secretary of Defense for Manpower and Reserve Affairs, Lt. Gen. Robert C. Taber, noted in congressional testimony during July 1971, much depended upon the perspectives of those who gave evidence. If interrogators interviewed drug abusers, the numbers came in high. Yet when they

[52] Memo, Col Alfred J. Mock, USARV IO, for DCG, USARV, 22 Aug 70, sub: Response to Press Queries Concerning Drug Usage in USARV, 73A6994, box 8, Decision Papers (70), USARVIO Papers, WNRC.

[53] Fact Sheet, untitled but with notation, "Released in Saigon," 30 Oct 70, DDI Drugs, 69–70 file.

By the end of American involvement in the war, more soldiers were being evacuated to the United States for drug problems than for wounds.

spoke to nonusers, the estimates proved low. Each group's view was limited and both tended to interpret the world in terms of what was most familiar to them.[54] On the other hand, General Abrams and his staff could hardly avoid the demands of the Nixon administration, which desired to put the best face it could on the war to deny issues to its critics and to forestall those in Congress who sought to end the conflict at any price. There was also the South Vietnamese government to consider. Its morale and good standing before the world were essential if Vietnamization was to succeed. Yet, as the press was quick to suggest, some of its members were obviously involved in sheltering those who sold drugs to American troops.

The attitude of the Nixon administration became apparent in June 1971, when sources within the Defense Department began to acknowledge that up to 10 percent of the American servicemen in South Vietnam had tried heroin and that 5 percent were addicted. The claim was conservative in comparison with stories appearing in the press to the effect that the use of heroin had risen to 20 percent in some units and that hard drugs had begun to cause almost as many casualties as the enemy, but it sparked the anger of White House aide Charles Colson.[55] "Is it the party line," Colson asked another aide, Egil Krough, Jr., on 22 June, "that we acknowledge that 10% of the GI's in Vietnam are on heroin, half of them addicted? It seems to me that this is a staggeringly high figure. . . . If it is somebody's guess, it seems to me the Pentagon should be told to stop guessing. I think it

---

[54] Statement Before Defense Subcommittee of Senate Appropriations Committee, Lt Gen Robert C. Taber, USA, Principal Deputy Assistant Secretary of Defense (Manpower & Reserve Affairs), 9 Jul 71, DDI Drugs, 1971 file.

[55] Memo, Charles Colson for Bud Krough, 22 Jun 71, White House Special files, Staff Member Office files, Scali, Subject files, box 1, Colson Action Memos [3 of 7], Nixon Papers. See, for example, Frank Blair, Today Show, NBC-TV, 27 Jan 71; Gloria Emerson, "G.I.'s in Vietnam Get Heroin Easily," *New York Times*, 25 Feb 71.

would be very damaging to have this statistic continually cited by our critics." Colson sent a copy of the note to the president's adviser on public affairs, John Scali, with a handwritten instruction appended to the margin: "Scali—Please turn DOD off!"[56]

General Abrams did nothing to alter his basic guidance that members of his command should deal candidly with the press, but he put drug statistics under strong control. Within two weeks of Colson's instruction to Scali, he forbade the public release—"without my personal approval"—of figures revealing the population of MACV's drug detoxification centers, the results of drug tests applied to soldiers returning home, and the number of those who were evacuated from South Vietnam for habitual drug abuse.[57]

Although Abrams' strictures resulted in part from a concern that the selective release of statistical data might lead to distortions and misinterpretations, they clearly paralleled the Nixon administration's desires. Shortly after the general announced the policy, indeed, the head of a recently announced presidential antidrug offensive, Jerome H. Jaffe, attempted to dampen public concern that huge numbers of American servicemen were using illegal drugs. Jaffe told reporters that if some military estimates had suggested an addiction rate among American soldiers of perhaps 14 percent or 33,000 men, that was an "upper limit." In fact, he said, the rate of heroin addiction in South Vietnam was declining.[58]

Although some officers, on their own, backed Jaffe in interviews with the press, knowledgeable high-level military officials such as the Chief of Naval Operations, Admiral Elmo R. Zumwalt, Jr., asserted publicly that the extent of the problem was difficult to measure but still very great. Within three months of Jaffe's statement, the concerns of the White House notwithstanding, information officers at the Military Assistance Command had no choice but to reveal that of the more than 2,500 soldiers evacuated from South Vietnam for medical reasons during September 1971, almost 55 percent had been drug abusers rather than battle casualties. To put those statistics into context, reporters then noted that at the height of the Tet offensive in 1968, with a larger American force present than in 1971 and much heavier fighting, the U.S. Air Force had evacuated for medical reasons no more than 5,000 men per month.[59]

[56] Memo, Colson for Krough, 22 Jun 71.

[57] Msg, Abrams MAC 6527 to Gen L. D. Clay, Comdr, Seventh AF, et al., 7 Jul 71, sub: Drug Abuse Counter Offensive, Abrams Papers, CMH. Abrams' first instructions appeared in Msg, Abrams MAC 6460 to Gen L. D. Clay, Comdr, Seventh AF, et al., 4 Jul 71, sub: Drug Abuse Counter Offensive

[58] "Nixon Adviser on Drug Abuse Ends 3-Day Survey in Vietnam," *New York Times*, 14 Jul 71.

[59] "Drug Problem Exaggerated, Says Colonel Back From Viet," *Chicago Tribune*, 14 Jul 71. See a comment by the Chief of Naval Operations, Admiral Elmo Zumwalt in [Reuters], "Navy Announces Amnesty on Drugs," *New York Times*, 30 May 71. Msg, Col Phillip H Stevens, Deputy Chief of Information, MACV, MAC 10148 to Lorfano, 23 Oct 71, sub: Release of Statistics on MEDEVAC of Drug Abusers, and Msg, Lorfano to Stevens, 28 Oct 71, sub: Medical Evacuation of GI Addicts, both in DDI Drugs, 1972 file.

Those figures seemed drastic but they still gave a very inexact impression of the extent of drug abuse in South Vietnam. Researchers working for a Special Action Office for Drug Abuse Prevention within the Executive Office of the President would establish within the year, too late to do much good for official credibility, that at the very time when the Military Assistance Command was releasing its statistics on medical evacuation flights, many more Americans were using drugs than most officials could apparently bring themselves to believe. Interviewing a random sample of soldiers leaving South Vietnam during September 1971, they found that almost 69 percent had at least experimented with marijuana, a number nearly 20 percent above the 50 percent figure the Defense Department had released to the press when the incident at Fire Support Base ARIES had occurred. The researchers also found that 45 percent of the soldiers they interviewed admitted, under promises of immunity from prosecution, that they had used unauthorized narcotics, barbiturates, or amphetamines at least once during their tours of duty; 29 percent said they had used them regularly (more than ten times and more than weekly); and 20 percent reported that they had been addicted. Thirty-eight percent had tried opium, 34 percent heroin, 25 percent amphetamines, and 23 percent barbiturates. Those figures were far in excess of the 5 percent that tests in the field identified as drug abusers and that official spokesmen often referred to in dealing with the press. Despite General Abrams' efforts at candor and the evaporation of the wishful thinking that had been the mark of early public affairs policies on drug abuse, American officials thus seemed almost foreordained to fall behind in their dealings with the news media on the subject.[60]

The South Vietnamese Connection

By mid-1971 with press coverage of drug abuse in South Vietnam increasing along with pressure from the Nixon administration for remedial action, Ambassador Bunker and General Abrams turned their attention to the South Vietnamese government in hopes of making some headway against the problem. Both were aware that members of the Thieu regime were involved either in coordinating the sale of narcotics to American troops or in condoning the practice for political reasons. They seem to have believed that those individuals would respond to American requests for action once they understood, as Bunker put it in a conversation with Thieu, that the American public and Congress might turn against South Vietnam if the country's leaders remained inattentive to the

[60] Kaplan, as told to Wren, "Does Our Army Fight on Drugs?," p. 21; Lee N. Robbins, Ph.D., Executive Office of the President, Special Action Office for Drug Abuse Prevention, Final Report, *The Vietnam Drug User Returns* (Washington, D.C.: Government Printing Office, 1973), pp. vii–ix, 29–44.

involvement of their subordinates in the sale of drugs to American troops.[61]

A report on drug abuse in South Vietnam by NBC correspondent Phil Brady underscored Bunker's and Abrams' concern. It appeared on the night of 24 January 1971 and told of conditions at Landing Zone ENGLISH, a U.S. base north of Qui Nhon in Binh Dinh Province that housed the men of the U.S. 173d Airborne Brigade. Noting that the 173d was an elite organization composed almost entirely of volunteers, Brady contended that when it came to drugs, the unit was "no different" from any other. The reporter then played a film showing soldiers purchasing drugs at a house located within the confines of the base. He explained that the American military police had no control over the situation because the house was the property of a South Vietnamese citizen, who also owned the land upon which the landing zone stood. "But that's not all," he added. "There are Vietnamese Army barracks on the base and Vietnamese soldiers also sell drugs to the GI's. When a Vietnamese commander was confronted with evidence of this by the Americans, he was furious and he complained to his superiors and not long after the U.S. commander had to write the Vietnamese a letter of apology."[62]

Although the Military Assistance Command denied that it had ever forced an American commander to apologize to the South Vietnamese for having complained about drug-related activities at Landing Zone ENGLISH, it had little choice, as in the case of Fire Support Base ARIES, but to confirm most of the details in Brady's story. American military policemen had, in fact, made controlled purchases of heroin at the house and during November 1970 had even requested that the South Vietnamese commander at the base close the dwelling and relocate its inhabitants. They were also well aware that South Vietnamese troops sold drugs to American troops. A line of succeeding American commanders at the landing zone had discussed the problem with their South Vietnamese counterparts, but beyond token gestures had apparently received little satisfaction. Indeed, almost two months elapsed between the end of November 1970, when the American commander at ENGLISH had received promises that the house would close, and 24 January 1971, when Brady's report appeared. The South Vietnamese moved only when NBC publicized the situation. Then they managed to demolish the house within the week.[63]

Both in their internal communications on the subject and in their dealings with the press, the military tended to make excuses for the South Vietnamese. The commanding general of I Field Force, which had charge

[61] Msg, Saigon 6693 to State, 3 May 71, sub: Specific Problems and Actions To Be Taken To Reduce Smuggling and Traffic in Narcotics, 295–74D417, box 2, May 70–71 Chron files, Bunker Papers, FAIM/IR.

[62] Msg, Lt Gen McCaffrey ARV 261 to Maj Gen Brown, CG, IFFV, 26 Jan 71, copy in CMH files.

[63] Msg, Maj Gen Brown, CG, IFFV, NHT 217 to Abrams, 27 Jan 71, sub: NBC News Story: "Drugs, White House LZ English," Abrams Papers, CMH; Msg, Leonard MAC 888 to Sidle, 28 Jan 71, sub: NBC News Story on White House, DDI Drugs, 69–70 file.

of Landing Zone ENGLISH, Maj. Gen. Charles P. Brown, contended in messages to General Abrams that if the local commander seemed always to leave the initiative in antinarcotics operations to American forces, "coordination and cooperation between U.S. and ARVN military police throughout MR [Military Region] 2 have been good and are improving." In responding to questions on Brady's story, public affairs officers said much the same thing. They then directed the attention of the Saigon correspondents to various joint efforts by American and South Vietnamese military police to suppress the drug trade.[64]

Neither General Abrams nor Ambassador Bunker were much moved by the optimism of their subordinates. With reporters such as Brady continuing to charge that some officers refused to enforce drug regulations out of fear for their lives, they watched the situation carefully and received almost daily reports on the decline of U.S. morale and the role South Vietnamese corruption played in it.[65] In a long, detailed talk with President Thieu on 3 May, both men thus emphasized the danger of continued inaction where the smuggling of illicit goods and the traffic in narcotics were concerned. "You are well aware," Bunker asserted,

that the American press is now filled with articles about the heroin traffic . . . and the involvement of high officials. . . . I must tell you in all frankness that no one can assure that the American people will continue to support Vietnam or [that] the Congress will vote the hundreds of millions required for economic assistance next year, and in the following years, if this situation continues. I think you might consider bringing Ambassador [to the United States] Bui Diem back on consultation to give you the full picture of public and Congressional feeling which is rapidly developing in the United States over the heroin traffic in Vietnam."[66]

Bunker and Abrams continued that in a few celebrated instances cooperation between U.S. and South Vietnamese agents had yielded spectacular results. On one occasion, customs officers had managed to capture a ship laden with 1,900 barrels of brass shell casings worth millions of dollars, "40% of which were new . . ., with the primers intact." More often, however, after a flare of publicity, the prosecution of offenders had slowed to a halt, punishment had never occurred, and both cases and culprits had disappeared.

At the end of the meeting, Bunker delivered a lengthy aide-memoire to Thieu that listed concrete instances in which the South Vietnamese government had failed to take action. Well-known smugglers had complete access to aircraft and customs sheds at Tan Son Nhut, the ambassador said, because customs officers feared the smugglers' powerful political contacts. In the same way, the U.S. embassy sometimes received

---

[64] Ibid.

[65] Phil Brady, NBC Nightly News, 25 Jan 71, and Brady, Today Show, NBC-TV, 26 Jan 71, both in *Radio-TV-Defense Dialog*.

[66] Msg, Saigon 6693 to State, 3 May 71, sub: Specific Problems and Actions To Be Taken To Reduce Smuggling and Traffic in Narcotics.

information about illegal transactions involving important Vietnamese or their wives, but customs and narcotics officers were afraid to join forces with American officers to investigate or seize the contraband. Also, military vehicles crossed Cambodia's border with South Vietnam without search or check, and customs and narcotics officers were often barred from approaching official aircraft and naval vessels that arrived in South Vietnam from abroad; despite its large size, the port of Da Nang was so open to smuggling on a large scale that it made little contribution to South Vietnam's customs revenues; and Indian, Chinese, and Korean black market currency operators who serviced smugglers and narcotics dealers continued to flourish. Bunker concluded that time was of the essence not only because American aid was at stake but also because the easy availability of huge quantities of heroin put South Vietnam's people themselves at risk. "There are already protests from Vietnamese parents that their children are experimenting with drugs."[67]

President Thieu seemed to respond well to the ambassador's admonitions. Several days after meeting with Bunker and Abrams, he told American visitors that he believed the abolition of the drug trade required as much attention as he had earlier given to the conduct of the war and the pacification program. Agreeing that officials within his government were involved in the problem, he promised to take action and set about organizing a task force within his administration to do so. In the weeks that followed, among other measures, he replaced his director general of customs and transferred other customs officials, including a brother of the prime minister, to less sensitive positions. He likewise tightened customs and security measures at Tan Son Nhut Airport and removed all of the police, customs, and military security personnel that had formerly served at the facility. Meanwhile, police forces began to seal off airports and harbors throughout South Vietnam, the Ministry of Health banned the sale of dangerous drugs without prescription, a joint U.S.–South Vietnamese customs group began checking parcels and third- and fourth-class mail leaving South Vietnam, and the government established a system of tax-free rewards for those who provided information on narcotics.[68] Ambassador Bunker was so pleased by the reaction that he told President Nixon he believed the government of South Vietnam had begun to move "with a sense of greater urgency on this problem than it has on any since I have been here."[69]

The press was less confident. On 15 July Phil Brady charged on the NBC Nightly News that both President Thieu and Vice President Ky were

[67] Ibid.

[68] Msg, Saigon 7007 to State, 7 May 71, sub: Drugs and Smuggling; Visit of BNDD Director Ingersol, General Abrams' Personal file 59, CMH; Aerogramme, Saigon A–113 to State, 21 Jul 71, sub: Significant Events and Activities in Vietnamese Efforts To Suppress Drug Traffic, copy in CMH files.

[69] Msg, Saigon 9075 to State, Bunker to the President, 9 Jun 71, sub: Herewith My Ninety-Fourth Message, Bunker Papers, FAIM/IR.

financing their reelection campaigns with the proceeds from the sale of drugs. He added that one of Thieu's personal advisers, Lt. Gen. Dang Van Quang, had for years been notorious for his dealings in the narcotics trade. During August Mark Gayn of the *Chicago Daily News* began a four-part series on drugs in which he declared that the profits from the trade in opium had come to permeate the politics of South Vietnam and the entire region, corrupting state leaders, generals, and border policemen alike. On the next day, barely three months after Thieu's campaign had begun, Henry Kamm of the *New York Times* charged that "Heroin remains as readily available to Americans in South Vietnam today as it was before the widely publicized measures against its sale and use were initiated early this year." Although Thieu had replaced a number of important officials and had made other arrangements to stop the flow of illicit drugs, American and South Vietnamese officials familiar with the program believed that most of those changes had been "little more than gestures in response to American urging." The state of mind of those officials was such, Kamm said, that charges implicating specific South Vietnamese dignitaries in the drug trade were rarely denied. Instead, "the standard reply is to say only that no proof is available."[70]

Although it was highly unlikely that Thieu himself would have risked personal involvement in the commerce in drugs, the suspicion lingered because of the way he handled his political affairs. During the South Vietnamese election campaign of 1971, for example, he bribed enough of the South Vietnamese National Assembly, according to Ambassador Bunker, to pass a bill effectively barring his main opponent, Ky, from running. He then sent secret written instructions to loyal province chiefs throughout the country to do whatever was necessary to guarantee his victory. The money to finance that maneuvering was clearly far greater than his own personal resources would have allowed.[71]

That Brady at least had reason for his suspicions could also be seen in the fate of the antidrug campaign. By August, as Kamm had alleged, due to bureaucratic inertia and the obvious reluctance of South Vietnamese leaders to press the program vigorously, the effort had begun to falter. "Arrests are concentrated in Saigon and most of those apprehended are small peddlers or addicts," Bunker thus informed Thieu in January 1972. "There are signs that big smugglers and drug traffickers are being protected by people in positions of power." Meanwhile, the South Vietnamese Air Force "and to some extent the Army and Navy" had

---

[70] Phil Brady, NBC Nightly News, 15 Jul 71, *Radio-TV-Defense Dialog*; Mark Gayn, "Drugs: Sordid Fuel for Kings and Wars," *Chicago Daily News*, 29 Aug 71; Henry Kamm, "Drive Fails To Halt Drug Sale in Vietnam," *New York Times*, 30 Aug 71. Also see Alfred W. McCoy et al., *The Politics of Heroin in Southeast Asia* (New York: Harper and Row, 1972), p. 189.

[71] Msg, Bunker Saigon 198 to Kissinger, 18 Sep 71, NSC files, Alexander M. Haig Special file, box 1013, General Haig's Trip to Vietnam, Sept 71 [1 of 2], Nixon Papers.

declined to cooperate in drug suppression efforts, customs officials continued their failure to search Vietnamese air force aircraft, the courts remained unwilling to move at more than a glacial pace in trying and punishing offenders, and the government had never disbursed the funds marked for the reward program. "As a result," Bunker said, "heroin is still easily available in most parts of Vietnam and addiction to hard drugs is increasing."[72]

Whatever the involvement of Thieu, there was little the United States could do to remedy the situation without at the same time forswearing all it had attempted to accomplish over the years in Southeast Asia. As Henry Kissinger put it in a message to Bunker during April 1971, the political implications in the United States would have been "incalculable, particularly if it is confirmed or even suggested that members of the GVN [government of South Vietnam] are directly or indirectly implicated in the [drug] traffic."[73]

American officials thus continued to make excuses for their South Vietnamese counterparts. In some cases, Bunker told Kissinger, "the difficulty is to get evidence that will substantiate what we believe to be facts." In others, it seemed better to allow a miscreant to remain in power because he was less corrupt than his replacement might have been, or more amenable to American advice. When charges thus arose in Congress during July 1971 that the South Vietnamese commander in Military Region 2, Maj. Gen. Ngo Dzu, was deeply involved in the drug trade, the American adviser in the area, John Paul Vann, defended the officer. Vann acknowledged forthrightly that Dzu was corrupt and that, whatever his interest in drugs, his lifestyle far exceeded his legal income. Yet he was, said Vann, so amenable to American instruction that, to maintain respect for him within the South Vietnamese Army, his American advisers had even on occasion warned him to be more independent. On that account, said Vann, "Despite some obvious shortcomings, I would rate Ngo Dzu as second . . . [among] the eight corps commanders I have worked with." With Vann's rejoinder on record, the U.S. mission in Saigon dropped the issue and never pursued the allegations against the officer.[74]

[72] Msg, Saigon 587 to State, 13 Jan 72, sub: Narcotics-Aide Memoire Given President Thieu, General Abrams' Personal file 59, CMH.

[73] Msg, Kissinger WHS 1040 to Bunker, 27 Apr 71, NSC files, Backchannels, box 412, Amb. Bunker, Saigon, 1971, Nixon Papers.

[74] Quote from Msg, Bunker Kathmandu 654 to Kissinger, 20 Apr 71, NSC files, Backchannels, box 412, Amb. Bunker, Saigon, 1971, Nixon Papers. Dzu was alleged to have been involved in the diversion of brass. Bunker and Abrams alluded to that in their conversation with Thieu. See Memo, Brig Gen Alexander M. Haig for the President, 6 May 71, sub: Contraband Brass in South Vietnam, and MFR, 4 May 71, sub: Meeting on Contraband in Brass in Vietnam, White House Situation Room, both in NSC files, H. A. Kissinger Office files, Country files, Vietnam, box 103, Brass, Contraband in South Vietnam, Nixon Papers. Memo, Lorfano for Henkin, 9 Nov 71, sub: Response to Congressman Steele Re: Allegations of Gen. Dzu's Complicity in Narcotics Traffic, DDI Drugs, 1972 file; Msg, Vann MRT 680 to Abrams, 20 Sep 71, sub: RVNAF Leadership, Abrams Papers, CMH. Also see Sheehan, *A Bright Shining Lie,* pp. 758f.

The dilemmas the United States Army faced over drug abuse and all of the disciplinary problems that came to exist in South Vietnam as the American role in the war wound down would have been painful even if the Saigon correspondents had not been present. That they were only added another layer of complication to an already difficult situation. Under other circumstances, like the officer at Camp Baxter who shut his problems out at night by posting guards and withdrawing into his quarters, military commanders might have attempted to turn the best face they could to the world by paying no more attention than necessary to the distressing realities around them. With the press in attendance that was hardly possible.

Suffering from great personal and institutional stress, expecting support but encountering criticism, many officers responded by hardening their opinions and fixing their anger upon their tormenters. Their attitude was obvious not only in the steps the 101st Airborne Division had taken after the incident at Fire Support Base ARIES to gather information on reporters attempting to visit the command but also in an incident that occurred elsewhere in South Vietnam during April 1972, when a group of young infantrymen from the 196th Infantry Brigade (Light) temporarily refused, in the presence of newsmen, to move out on an operation. One soldier even shouted melodramatically, "It's not our war. Why fight if nobody back home cares?" After bringing the men under control by telling them that other Americans might die if they refused to go, the battalion commander turned on the reporters and accused them of causing the incident. "All you press are bastards," he said. "I blame you for this and you can quote me on it."[75] In fact, while the troopers might have expressed their opinions far more subtly in the absence of the press, there were few American combat infantrymen left in South Vietnam by that late date, and none of those who remained, as the soldier's comment indicated clearly, saw a useful purpose in their exertions and sacrifices.

An exchange of views that occurred as early as a November 1970 meeting at the Pentagon between Secretary Laird and Ambassador Bunker exemplifies the complexity of the issue. Bunker observed that with the American role in combat declining the Saigon correspondents had too little to write about. Desperate to find stories that would sell, they gravitated toward any incident that provided the conflict and tension their editors desired. Distorted descriptions of drug abuse, racial unrest, and combat refusals became the inevitable result. Laird, for his part, refused to deny that problems existed. Underscoring the hard choices that confronted the Nixon administration, he responded that if idle troops meant disciplinary problems idle journalists could fasten upon, the effect

---

[75] [AP], "GI Unit Balks," *Washington Star*, 11 Apr 72; "Colonel Assails Newsmen," *New York Times*, 13 Apr 72. Also see White House News Summary, 13 Apr 72, President's Office files, box 40, April 12–25, 1972, Nixon Papers. The incident occurred during the Easter offensive of 1972 and receives more extensive treatment in Chapter 21.

was preferable to the large number of American casualties that would surely occur if the United States returned to a policy of all-out war.[76]

[76] MFR, Phil Odeen, 18 Nov 70, sub: Vietnamization Meeting With Secretary Laird, folder 76, Thayer Papers, CMH.

17

Embargo—DEWEY CANYON II

As the end of 1970 approached, the Nixon administration appeared to have achieved impressive gains in South Vietnam. Although problems with the morale of American forces continued, the cost of the war for the United States had declined, and U.S. casualty rates were low. Meanwhile, the South Vietnamese armed forces seemed to have the enemy on the run. Newly equipped with modern arms and inspired by success in Cambodia, they had achieved at least a semblance of improved security throughout the country. As for the enemy, he had abandoned the large-unit tactics he had adopted prior to the Tet offensive of 1968 and had returned to a more economical form of combat that emphasized terrorism and guerrilla warfare.

Profound doubts nevertheless lingered within Washington agencies. After eighteen months of effort, one Defense Department analyst told Secretary Laird, Vietnamization remained at best "a half-caste program." Despite great effort, the United States had failed to change North Vietnam's basic objectives or to decrease the countrywide scope of its activities in the South. It had likewise failed to create a military structure in South Vietnam that the nation could afford or long support; there remained no substitute for U.S. air power in the attempt to stop enemy resupply efforts along the Ho Chi Minh Trail; and the PHOENIX program for neutralizing the enemy infrastructure in the countryside continued to limp. In addition, American military managers had never devised a credible plan for the South Vietnamese either to end the war on a favorable basis or to win the peace that would follow a negotiated settlement. Criteria were even lacking to determine when the war had ended.[1]

How to put an end to the war remained the question, the analyst continued. Two alternatives presented themselves: negotiation or force. Since

[1] This section is based on Memo, An Unsolicited Talking Paper (or "Think Peace"), sub: Vietnamization . . . Still Only a Half-Caste Program, 330–76–067, box 98, Viet (South) 320.2 (Aug–Dec) 1970, Laird Papers, WNRC.

A Studies and Observations Group team reconnoiters the Ho Chi Minh Trail in Laos.

the Paris peace talks showed little promise of deterring North Vietnamese aggression in the South, coercion seemed the best approach. Yet neither the bombing of North Vietnam nor the attrition strategy followed during the early years of the war had succeeded. Under the circumstances, a ground attack on enemy infiltration routes through Laos seemed the most promising alternative, as long as South Vietnamese troops carried the burden of the fighting and the United States contributed only air support. If North Vietnam chose to resist, a conventional engagement much to the benefit of the South Vietnamese would ensue along a relatively narrow front open to the full force of American air power. The analyst concluded that the most opportune moment to make the move would arrive after November 1970 and during 1971, because no national elections were scheduled for that period in the United States. The administration would thus be able to carry out the attack with less than the normal political risk.

The Idea for a Raid Into Laos Takes Shape

Although more optimistic than Laird's analyst, President Nixon and his advisers were also concerned. They believed that the South Vietnamese had gained in confidence and expertise, but they understood that much remained to be done and that the enemy would never stand still. In fact, by November 1970 intelligence reports indicated that North Vietnamese leaders were intent upon rebuilding their sanctuaries in Cambodia and were putting the government and armed forces of Lon Nol under increasing pressure. They were also accelerating an effort to shift supplies southward along the Ho Chi Minh Trail in Laos, in obvious preparation for a major offensive that, given the long lead times they habitually observed, would probably come early in 1972. By then, fewer than 45,000 first-line American combat troops would remain in South Vietnam and a presidential campaign would be in full swing in the United States. The enemy was bound to reason that the South Vietnamese were more vulnerable than ever to attack and that Nixon, facing a multitude of political uncertainties, might have difficulty formulating an adequate response.[2]

Convinced that the South Vietnamese armed forces, in combination with the American combat units that remained at the beginning of 1971, would be sufficient to preempt the enemy's plans, Nixon began a series of studies during November 1970 to determine the next moves he should take. The idea for a series of major South Vietnamese strikes into Cambodia and Laos rapidly emerged. If successful, so the reasoning went, the forays would interrupt the North Vietnamese buildup, buy six months or more for the Vietnamization program to proceed uninterrupted, ensure the continued progress of American withdrawals, and provide a strong deterrent to subsequent enemy adventures. There was even a possibility, Nixon stressed in a meeting with his advisers on 18 January, that the operations might "prove decisive in the over all conduct of the war."[3] At the least, Admiral Moorer observed in a memorandum to Laird, it would be the last opportunity the South Vietnamese would have for a major operation against the enemy's sanctuaries while American forces were strong enough to provide backing.[4]

While convinced that an operation into Laos was necessary, with funds for the war more thinly stretched than in the year before and Congress increasingly restive, President Nixon lacked the freedom of movement he had possessed when he had sent American troops into Cambodia. During May, he had developed a program to provide Lon Nol with what he considered enough military assistance to keep Communist forces at bay. In doing so, he had managed to avoid the need for congressional approval by withdrawing resources from other recipients of American military aid. Reporting to the country at the end of June, he had then promised that he would avoid involving the United States deeply in the permanent direct defense of Cambodia and had renounced any suggestion that his administration would provide massive American assistance to that government.[5]

---

[2] MFR, 19 Jan 71, sub: Meeting Between the President, Secretary Rogers, Secretary Laird, the Chairman of the Joint Chiefs of Staff, Henry Kissinger, Richard Helms, et al., 18 Jan 71, NSC files, Vietnam Subject files, box 83, Special Operations file, Jan 16–25, 1971, vol. 1, Nixon Papers.

[3] Talking Paper, Feb 71, sub: Lam Son 719: February 1971, White House Special files, Haig, General Special file [5 of 5], Nixon Papers. Also see Msg, Moorer CJCS 16390 to Abrams, 10 Dec 71, Abrams Papers, CMH. Quote from MFR, 19 Jan 71, sub: Meeting Between the President, Secretary Rogers, Secretary Laird, the Chairman of the Joint Chiefs of Staff, Henry Kissinger, Richard Helms, et al., 18 Jan 71.

[4] Moorer's observations are in JCS History, 1971–1973, p. 19.

[5] This section is based on William P. Bundy, untitled draft manuscript on American foreign policy during the 1970s and 80s, ch. 3, p. 15.

The pledge proved overly optimistic. During the months that followed, conditions in Cambodia deteriorated so drastically that by October Nixon felt constrained to call upon Congress for the very assistance he had promised to avoid. His request set off a vehement debate in the Senate. Only in December did the legislators agree to release $250 million in aid, and then they exacted a heavy price. To receive the money, Nixon had to accept a new version of the Cooper-Church Amendment that prohibited the use of American ground forces and advisers not only in Cambodia but also in Laos. Passed into law during January 1971, the measure allowed for only one loophole. To ensure the security of American forces still serving in South Vietnam, it placed no restriction on the use of American air power in either Cambodia or Laos.

The debate over aid to Cambodia did nothing to deter the president's plans for large-scale operations. On 6 December Admiral McCain thus notified Abrams that the administration was contemplating ground offensives against enemy targets in Cambodia and southern Laos and possible diversionary activities against the North Vietnamese panhandle. Abrams responded the next day that President Thieu and other South Vietnamese leaders favored the approach. A plan already existed for the Cambodian portion of the operation. As for Laos, Thieu believed that an attack involving up to two divisions should center on the region around the town of Tchepone, located in the Laotian panhandle some 35 kilometers up Highway 9 from the border with South Vietnam and 50 kilometers from the old American base at Khe Sanh.[6]

During the weeks that followed, Abrams refined the plan into a two-part campaign that involved an initial attack into Cambodia followed by a move into Laos. In Cambodia, South Vietnamese forces would attempt to destroy the enemy's newly established sanctuaries by conducting operations in and around a Communist stronghold known as the Chup Plantation, some 40 kilometers west of the South Vietnamese border near the city of Kompong Cham. The Laotian portion of the operation would have four phases. Beginning during late January, an American brigade would secure Highway 9 up to the Laotian border, establish an advance supply depot at Khe Sanh, and position artillery where it could best support troops operating in Laos. During phase two, beginning between 6 and 13 February, South Vietnamese forces would move overland into Laos along Highway 9 to the accompaniment of B–52 strikes and the insertion by helicopter of blocking forces to the north and south of the avenue of attack. When the ground assault had reached its midpoint, a South Vietnamese task force would launch a helicopter-borne attack against the airfield at Tchepone and then move to link up with the forces on the highway. Phase three, commencing in mid-February, would see the inauguration of search-and-destroy operations near Tchepone and in

[6] Msg, McCain to Abrams, 6 Dec 70, and Msg, Abrams MAC 15603 to McCain, 7 Dec 70, both in Abrams Papers, CMH.

404

the region to the south, where the bulk of the enemy's supplies were stored. Those operations would continue until the start of phase four, a period of withdrawal and retrenchment beginning in mid-April. After the operation had ended, South Vietnamese commando units would remain behind to keep the enemy off balance by conducting harassing attacks.[7]

Abrams and other high-level officers backed the plan because it struck the enemy where he was most vulnerable, but Abrams himself understood that it posed considerable risk.[8] On that account, he refused to relinquish any margin of assurance. When a suggestion thus arose during January that the United States might keep Laotian Prime Minister Prince Souvanna Phouma from protesting the attack by conducting the campaign solely as a South Vietnamese endeavor, without the presence of American helicopters, he refused even to consider the idea. Rather than advance into Laos with less than a full commitment, he informed Admiral Moorer that he would cancel the operation. He even set a date to do so unless he received word that he could proceed unimpeded by political restrictions. In the end, a pledge from Souvanna that he would protest vigorously but would not expect the South Vietnamese to leave his territory immediately appears to have sufficed. Although delaying the actual decision on the move into Laos until the last moment, the president instructed Abrams to continue preparations for the operation and made it clear that any cancellation would come from Washington.[9]

If Abrams was cautious, many of the president's advisers in Washington were less than enthusiastic. All concerned supported the Cambodian portion of the plan on grounds that it was necessary and hardly a departure from precedents set the previous year, but some had doubts about the campaign in Laos. Secretary Laird, for one, appears to have been ambivalent. He conducted a spirited defense of the attack at an 18 January White House meeting with the president, arguing that it might free South Vietnamese forces to concentrate on the security of their own country by lessening their concern about Cambodia and its problems. In private, however, he remained unconvinced that the attack

[7] Memo, Haig for Kissinger, 29 Jan 71, sub: Meeting With the Vice President, et al., 1 Feb 71, NSC files, A. M. Haig Chron file, box 976, Haig Chron, Jan 25–31, 1971, Nixon Papers.

[8] Msg, McCain SPECAT to Moorer, 27 Jan 71, sub: Planning for Laos, Abrams Papers, CMH. After January 1971, to maintain security and to reduce message traffic on backchannel circuits, military agencies in Washington and the Military Assistance Command conducted most of their sensitive message traffic on what were called SPECAT, or "special category," channels. Most of those communications are filed in chronological order on microfilm in the Center of Military History. Duplicates are often present in the National Security Council files of the Nixon Papers.

[9] Msg, JCS SPECAT 2075 to Abrams, 26 Jan 71, and Msg, Abrams SPECAT to McCain, 27 Jan 71, sub: Planning for Laos, both in Abrams Papers, CMH; JCS History, 1971–1973, p. 23.

was all that necessary. The Vietnamization program appeared to be making good progress, he told his associates. A major setback in Laos could only threaten that success. The U.S. government's intelligence analysts were also cautious. They noted quietly that the operation would be extremely risky because the enemy was clearly aware it was coming. In addition, Communist forces not only possessed ample resources to protect their interests in southern Laos, their antiaircraft defenses were so well developed that they could inflict heavy casualties upon the American aircrews that would of necessity have to fly in support of the South Vietnamese.[10]

Secretary of State Rogers was by far the most outspoken of those who opposed the operation. At a meeting with the president on 29 January, he avowed that his own support for the attack hinged on whether the move into Laos had a reasonable chance for success. If it did, he said, it might be worthwhile, but failure seemed by far the more likely prospect, if only because intelligence reports indicated that the enemy had fairly complete knowledge of the plan. Besides the international repercussions that might follow the attack, with either the Soviets or the Chinese revoking their support for Laotian neutrality or resorting to other extremes, the operation might have a devastating effect upon the Thieu regime. If it failed, that development might not only shatter the confidence and resilience of the South Vietnamese people and armed forces but also produce the sort of backlash that could result in a defeat for Thieu in the coming South Vietnamese presidential election. In addition, Rogers said, the support of the American public was critical, yet most Americans would question why the United States was disturbing the balance in Southeast Asia. The president himself had promised only the year before that the Cambodian incursion would be enough. As for Congress, opponents of the war were bound to charge that the operation was contrary to the spirit, if not the letter, of the Cooper-Church Amendment.[11]

President Nixon had already considered most of Rogers' objections. He conceded that "we will get some real heat" from Congress and the press but considered the political risks acceptable if he could blunt the enemy's ability to damage U.S. forces as they drew down to less than 100,000 men. To the warning that the enemy had anticipated the attack and was preparing an all-out response, he and the others who favored the operation placed great store in the promise of American firepower. If the enemy stood and fought, Kissinger thus observed at the meeting on 18

[10] Memo for the President's file, 18 Jan 71, sub: Meeting Between the President, Rogers, Laird, Moorer, Helms, and Kissinger, White House Special files, President's Office files, box 83, Memoranda for the President, Jan 17, 1971, Nixon Papers; Memo, Haig for Kissinger, 29 Jan 71, sub: Meeting With the Vice President, et al., 1 Feb 71; Memo, Kissinger for the President, 26 Jan 71, sub: Possible Reactions of Various Concerned Parties to Operations in Laos, NSC files, Vietnam Subject files, box 83, Special Operations file, vol. II, Jan 26–29, 1971, Nixon Papers.

[11] Rogers arguments are contained in Memo, Haig for Kissinger, 29 Jan 71, sub: Meeting With the Vice President, et al., 1 Feb 71.

January, so much the better. He would become vulnerable to massive air attacks. The result would set his timetable back by up to a year.[12]

Warnings that failure would be costly both to Thieu and the United States drew an especially pointed response from the president. Taking a lesson from advice he had received and ignored prior to the incursion into Cambodia, Nixon stressed at the meeting on 18 January that even if the operation achieved less than satisfactory results it could not be allowed to come out as a defeat. Official spokesmen had to package it simply, he said, as a raid into the enemy's sanctuaries rather than a major invasion. The goals they announced for it had thus to be limited and all claims of success modest. Only when the attack had ended were members of his administration to "crow" about accomplishments.[13]

Handling the Press

Although President Nixon believed that a careful public relations program could dampen criticism if the operation began to lag, he took little account of the increasing skepticism of the Saigon correspondents. For months, reporters had taken each significant westward movement of U.S. and South Vietnamese troops in Military Region 1 as an indication that the United States was planning an incursion into Laos to cut the Ho Chi Minh Trail. In the same way, shortly after Congress had ratified the new version of the Cooper-Church Amendment, they had begun to look for violations and to imply that the U.S. effort in support of Lon Nol broke at least the spirit, if not the letter, of the law. To the chagrin of General Abrams, one newsman had even photographed an American officer standing near a clearly marked Cambodian school building and next to a parked helicopter that bore distinct American insignia. Informed of the picture by the U.S. Ambassador to Cambodia, Emery Swank, Abrams had little choice but to admit that an inadvertent error had occurred and that the officer in question had disobeyed standing orders.[14]

That incident, along with continuing coverage in the press of MACV's problems with discipline and morale, led to a mood of increasing caution

---

[12] This section is based on MFR, 19 Jan 71, sub: Meeting Between the President, Secretary Rogers, Secretary Laird, the Chairman of the Joint Chiefs of Staff, Henry Kissinger, Richard Helms, et al., 18 Jan 71. Also see Talking Paper, Feb 71, sub: Lam Son 719: February 1971. Kissinger's opinion is also mentioned in H. R. Haldeman, *The Haldeman Diaries, Inside the Nixon White House* (New York: G. P. Putnam's Sons, 1994), entry for 26 Jan 71, p. 239.

[13] MFR, 19 Jan 71, sub: Meeting Between the President, Secretary Rogers, Secretary Laird, the Chairman of the Joint Chiefs of Staff, Henry Kissinger, Richard Helms, et al., 18 Jan 71.

[14] Msg, Abrams SPECAT to McCain, Moorer, 28 Jan 71, sub: Planning for Laos-Lam Son 719; Msg, Swank Cam 058 to Abrams, 9 Jan 71, sub: U.S. Military Ground Forces in Cambodia; Msg, Abrams MAC 628 to Swank, 20 Jan 71. All in Abrams Papers, CMH.

on the part of military planners as preparations for the operation in Laos progressed. Since the South Vietnamese would be doing most of the fighting, General Abrams insisted that they assume responsibility for public affairs. The Military Assistance Command would keep newsmen informed about the American portion of the operation and provide airlift assistance from Saigon to Khe Sanh, but the South Vietnamese were to handle all briefings on their own activities and to coordinate transportation for reporters in the field. Abrams emphasized in particular that reporters were to ride South Vietnamese rather than American helicopters into Laos. That would highlight the South Vietnamese role and keep the newsmen from seeing and photographing American aircrews on the ground in Laos recovering damaged helicopters.[15]

If Abrams was disposed to do as little as possible to assist newsmen, he still understood that any overt attempt to cut the press off from what was happening would result in speculation far more damaging than the facts. He therefore planned to embargo all news reports that dealt with the movement of troops in Military Region 1 but at the same time to brief at least selected members of the press shortly before the first phase of the campaign began and at regular intervals thereafter until he lifted the ban. By taking reporters into his confidence, he told Moorer, he might have a chance to achieve basic cooperation with the press and might then be able to hold back news of the event until he wanted it to surface.[16]

The Commander in Chief, Pacific, Admiral McCain, endorsed Abrams' plan. Although he was highly dissatisfied with what he termed the "tendency toward muckraking" of the Saigon correspondents, he believed that the incursion provided an excellent opportunity to demonstrate the progress of the Vietnamization program and that the South Vietnamese could, with proper U.S. assistance, conduct complex operations on their own. He thus suggested that Abrams conduct the initial briefing for the press personally, both to emphasize those points and to increase the probability that newsmen would comply with official constraints. He likewise insisted that MACV inform reporters of the plans it developed for press coverage and that it devise a "foolproof" system for lifting whatever restrictions on reporting it devised. That would leave less likelihood for premature disclosures and less chance for misunderstandings to develop. In making his points, McCain emphasized that a continuation of negative news stories from the field might lead Congress to place further limits on the military's ability to conduct the war and might even have an unfortunate impact upon that year's entire military budget.[17]

---

[15] Msg, CINCPAC to Secretary of Defense, 22 Jan 71, and Msg, CINCPAC to CJCS, 14 Feb 71, both in 330–76–207, box 5, file 337, WH (18 Feb 71), Laird Papers, WNRC.

[16] Msg, Abrams MAC 775 to Moorer, 24 Jan 71, sub: Cross Border Operation, Abrams Papers, CMH.

[17] Msg, McCain SPECAT to Moorer, 26 Jan 71, sub: Cross Border Operations, Abrams Papers, CMH.

408

Abrams and McCain originally hoped that they would be able to keep their plans secret until 30 January, when American units would begin the move toward the Laotian border along Highway 9. At that time they intended to impose their embargo. By 28 January, however, it had become evident to all concerned that the scenario would never hold. The logistical effort surrounding the operation was so great and the equipping of South Vietnamese forces so obvious that neither the press nor the enemy could ignore the fact that a major attack was in the offing. Abrams therefore cabled McCain to inform him that a change would be necessary. Although prohibited from revealing troop movements in advance by the MACV guidelines for the press, he said, reporters would make every effort to cover the event from any available source. Since the area of operations was relatively accessible from Da Nang, any attempt to narrow the access of the press to what was happening would be impossible and would only lead to speculation. Immediate invocation of the embargo thus appeared the only recourse. That would permit reporters to cover the incursion from the beginning yet allow enough time prior to publication for perspective to develop and for the story to settle down. Admirals Moorer and McCain both concurred with Abrams' plan, but McCain again cautioned that "objective coverage of this operation will be dependent upon press view of candor and cooperation display[ed] by the military. Any indication of press restrictions will detract from the . . . results desired."[18]

With that warning in hand, on 29 January, spokesmen at the Military Assistance Command in Saigon announced an embargo on all information about operations in Military Region 1 except for those described in the daily MACV communique. Public affairs officers scheduled a background briefing for selected newsmen the next evening to describe what was going on and then explained that the embargo would remain in effect until further notice but would end when military security permitted. Requesting the cooperation of the reporters, they then added that "This announcement constitutes a part of the embargo and is not for publication."[19]

The embargo on the embargo appeared an afterthought, but it was as the chief of MACV information, Colonel Leonard, later explained, essential to the prohibition Abrams had set in place. "If the second embargo had not been put into effect," Leonard said, "there would have been no point to the first . . . as the press would have . . . filed stories about a news blackout on the Laotian frontier. Speculation would have overturned any surprise military security achieved."[20]

---

[18] Msg, Abrams SPECAT to McCain, Moorer, 28 Jan 71, sub: Planning for Laos-Lam Son 719. Msg, Moorer SPECAT 2394 to McCain, 29 Jan 71. Quote from Msg, McCain SPECAT to Moorer, Abrams, 29 Jan 71, sub: Planning for Laos-Lam Son 719. All in Abrams Papers, CMH.

[19] Msg, Abrams SPECAT to McCain, 29 Jan 71, sub: Planning for Laos-Lam Son 719, Abrams Papers, CMH.

[20] Ltr, Leonard to the author, 17 Oct 90, CMH files.

The press guidance that accompanied the announcement attempted to harmonize Abrams' concerns with McCain's admonition that overt restraints upon the press would be counterproductive. Although American commanders were to refrain from providing South Vietnamese reporters with assistance and information because those individuals were subject to their own nation's regulations rather than the embargo, the other MACV accredited correspondents were to receive billeting and messing privileges at the American headquarters nearest the action and "all practicable assistance" within the limits of military security. Even so, to reduce the number of newsmen in operational areas, information officers were to discourage travel by single correspondents and to form press pools whenever possible. As a further check, escorts were to accompany those groups of reporters that traveled into the field.[21]

"Speculation Is Rampant"

Reporters and editors surmised that an invasion of Laos was imminent almost as soon as the Military Assistance Command announced the embargo. A comment by Secretary of State Rogers at a news conference on 29 January fed that suspicion. Noting that Laos was a source of major concern to the Nixon administration, Rogers refused to rule out the possibility that an allied strike might occur at some time in the future against enemy supply and communications facilities in the region.[22]

Tantalized by the comment but lacking anything more solid, news agencies besieged the State and Defense Departments and the White House for answers. Receiving little satisfaction, they turned to Senator Fulbright. Fulbright called Secretary Rogers, who responded that Abrams was responsible for the embargo and that troop movements entirely within South Vietnam were involved. When Fulbright then asked whether the operation was preliminary to an invasion of Laos, Rogers took refuge in the fact that the president had yet to decide formally on whether to proceed. "I said if you are talking about [American] ground troops going in the answer is no," he later reported to Kissinger. "But I said . . . that when a decision is made I'll get in touch with you. . . . I can't give out any information before the decisions are made."[23]

Recognizing that the pressure from Congress might be intense, Kissinger shortly thereafter informed the Defense Department that the president had approved the release of a private statement advising mem-

[21] Msg, MACOI SPECAT to CG, 101st Abn, et al., 29 Jan 71, sub: Press Guidance-Lam Son 719, Abrams Papers, CMH.

[22] Terence Smith, "U.S. B–52's Strike Foe's Laos Bases Around the Clock," *New York Times*, 1 Feb 71. Also see "Some Daylight on the Blackout," *Washington Daily News*, 4 Feb 71.

[23] Transcript, 29 Jan 71, sub: Telephone Conversation Between Rogers and Kissinger, Nixon Papers.

bers of Congress in advance that troop movements were indeed occurring in South Vietnam near the Laotian border. The department was to explain to any congressman or senator who inquired that the move was the result of continuing needs associated with the success of Vietnamization and the withdrawal of American forces.[24]

Colonel Leonard held the background briefing Abrams had promised the next day. Specifying that all of the information involved remained under embargo until released by the Military Assistance Command, he introduced an intelligence specialist from the MACV staff. That officer linked the movement of U.S. forces into Military Region 1, code-named Operation DEWEY CANYON II, to the enemy's continuing buildup in Laos and total dependence upon the Ho Chi Minh Trail for supplies. He noted that North Vietnamese logisticians had improved and extended roads leading around the western end of the Demilitarized Zone and eastward into South Vietnam and that they appeared to be stockpiling food and equipment for a major offensive in South Vietnam. In the process, they had brought together elements of nine infantry regiments, one artillery regiment, significant numbers of rear service troops, and antiaircraft units. Located just across the border in Laos, those forces and the buildup that sustained them constituted an obvious danger to continued American withdrawals.[25]

A summary of U.S. and South Vietnamese plans to block the enemy's efforts followed. Avoiding any mention of a possible incursion into Laos, a briefer from MACV's Operations Directorate noted that the U.S. 101st Airborne Division intended to reopen the old American base at Khe Sanh, secure Highway 9 up to the Laotian border, and establish fire bases throughout the surrounding region. In an attempt to underscore the need for an embargo, the briefer then emphasized that security and surprise were essential to the accomplishment of the mission.[26]

By the end of the session the reporters present were seething. Most could see little reason for the kind of secrecy the Military Assistance Command was attempting to impose. The movement of huge bodies of troops in Military Region 1 had been obvious to anyone who had taken the time to travel to Da Nang. That those troops might move into Laos had, indeed, been an open topic of conversation among the local South Vietnamese for at least a week. The enemy himself could hardly have missed so obvious a signal.[27]

The reporters pressed Leonard for an explanation. Did American or South Vietnamese forces intend to go into Laos? Under orders, Leonard

[24] Memo, Kissinger for Secretaries of State and Defense, 29 Jan 71, sub: Congressional Notification of Free World Troop Movements, Nixon Papers.

[25] Msg, MACV SPECAT to CINCPAC, 30 Jan 71, sub: Press Briefing, Abrams Papers, CMH.

[26] Ibid.

[27] Interv, author with Terry McNamara, U.S. Consul General in Da Nang during 1971, 22 Mar 81, CMH files. Also see Ralph Blumenthal, "U.S. News Blackout in Saigon Tried To Keep Even Its Existence Secret," *New York Times*, 5 Feb 71.

Reporters could see U.S. forces moving toward the border with Laos.

refused to discuss future operations. The reporters then wanted to know whether they could speculate in print about that possibility. Leonard again declined, warning that since the embargo covered the session they were attending they were not to use the information they had received in any manner until the Military Assistance Command terminated the restriction. "In spite of our continued emphasis that we could not 'permit' speculation," Leonard later reported in a message to the Joint Chiefs, "the point seemed to materialize that . . . neither could we prevent it."[28]

The reporters' observation was on target. As Fulbright's call to Rogers had shown, the situation was already out of control. "Speculation is rampant," Moorer told Abrams on the day after the embargo went into effect "that we are embarked on extensive campaign and high officials are being pressed to comment on U.S. and GVN intentions." Recognizing that an outcry in the press was inevitable and that it might limit the president's ability to carry through with the operation if it sparked increased opposition in Congress and around the country, Moorer suggested that Abrams lift the embargo on at least the portion of the operation that involved the movement of U.S. troops into Military Region 1. In that manner, he said, "factual news can begin to flow from source and help dampen rumors which could adversely affect future decisions."[29]

[28] Msg, MACV SPECAT to CINCPAC, 30 Jan 71, sub: Press Briefing, Abrams Papers, CMH.
[29] Msg, Moorer JCS SPECAT 2614 to McCain, Abrams, 30 Jan 71, sub: Planning for Laos-Lam Son 719, Abrams Papers, CMH.

Abrams declined. "I have been reviewing in detail, daily all . . . intelligence on North Vietnam, Laos and SVN MR 1 [South Vietnamese Military Region 1]," he responded. "I am convinced from this that as of now the enemy suspects many things but at this point is uncertain as to where, when and in what force allied forces will strike. I consider it absolutely imperative for the safety and security of this command and the success of operations underway that the strict embargo . . . now in effect be held."[30] Admiral McCain agreed. In a separate message to Moorer he noted that "from the viewpoint of the enemy we have many options including the element of surprise. We must not lose this advantage."[31]

Lacking any move by the Military Assistance Command to lessen restrictions on the press, the embargo began to crumble of its own weight. A few reporters alerted their home offices to what was going on and kept them abreast of developments as they occurred, often with cryptic or coded cables. On the evening of 30 January both a Reuters reporter and Tammy Arbuckle of the *Washington Star* thus contacted the U.S. deputy chief of mission in Vientiane to pass on queries from their employers about the validity of reports that an invasion was imminent. The Reuters inquiry even indicated that the size of the force involved would be larger than two divisions. The deputy chief put the reporters off by dismissing the story as the product of unfounded rumors, but his response had little long-term effect. The next day, Souvanna Phouma received a visit from an Agence France Presse reporter seeking his reaction to a dispatch from Washington indicating that "local observers of Indochina" had predicted an American–South Vietnamese attack into southern Laos within the week.[32] That same day, the *New York Times* wire service carried a lead story printed originally in the *London Observer* that speculated brazenly on the information supplied by Leonard's background briefing. A wholesale violation of the embargo, it observed that the Military Assistance Command had imposed a strict news blackout on military activities in the northern portion of South Vietnam and that the embargo was probably linked to plans for an invasion of Laos. Shortly thereafter, the command learned that the Defense Department had managed only at the last moment to suppress a similar Associated Press report, by dealing directly with the news service's management. The embargo continued to disintegrate that evening, when an article by *Washington Star* correspondent Orr Kelly containing comments on the news blackout in Saigon and possible troop movements in Military Region 1 also appeared. In that case, no violation of MACV's ground rules by a correspondent based in South Vietnam had occurred. Instead,

[30] Msg, Abrams SPECAT to McCain, Moorer, 30 Jan 71, sub: Planning for Laos-LAM SON 719, Abrams Papers, CMH.

[31] Msg, McCain SPECAT to Moorer, 30 Jan 71, sub: Planning for Laos-Lam Son 719, Abrams Papers, CMH.

[32] Ralph Blumenthal, "U.S. News Blackout in Saigon Tried To Keep Even Its Existence Secret," *New York Times*, 5 Feb 71; Msg, Vientiane 561 to State, 31 Jan 71, Nixon Papers.

Kelly's editors had inserted the banned material into an otherwise unoffending report when they saw that the *Times* and other papers were printing the news.[33]

Unable to link the *London Observer* story clearly to any individual (the paper's correspondent in Saigon, Leonard noted, "had always been a man of integrity") and uncertain that every member of the far-flung corps of correspondents in South Vietnam had received word that an embargo was in effect, Colonel Leonard could do little more than notify the Saigon correspondents that he would respond to further breaches of MACV's restrictions by disaccrediting the offending parties. Although his strictures appear to have had some effect in South Vietnam, where reporters remained dependent on the goodwill of the Military Assistance Command, they had little impact on reports originating outside of the country, where speculation continued unabated.[34]

By the next day, 1 February, little semblance of the embargo remained. Reports on the news blackout in Saigon appeared in the *Washington Post* and the *Baltimore Sun*. Meanwhile, the *New York Times* printed articles by Tillman Durdin and Terence Smith dealing with the possibility of a strike into Laos. Durdin reported accurately from Vientiane that Laotian leaders might protest a South Vietnamese incursion into their country but would do so only as a matter of form because Laos needed the strike to relieve North Vietnamese pressure on its army. Smith noted from Washington that speculation on the possibility of an assault into Laos had become so widespread that clandestine Viet Cong radio stations were citing Western news reports to denounce the expected invasion. He then quoted a statement by White House Press Secretary Ronald Ziegler as an example of the coy manner in which officials in Washington continued to avoid the issue. "The President is aware of what is going on," Ziegler had told newsmen. "Not to say there is something going on."[35]

Circumstances continued to deteriorate that afternoon. The senior Republican on the Senate Foreign Relations Committee, George Aiken, and Senate Minority Leader Hugh Scott issued statements that attracted the attention of the press. Aiken advised newsmen that he had received word of the troop buildup in Military Region 1 from Nixon administration officials the previous Friday and that the operation was shrouded in "the tightest censorship since World War II." Scott followed with reassurances that no U.S. troops would cross into Laos. Informed of the statements, official spokesmen at the State and Defense Departments once more refused to comment, but a declaration by Soviet Premier Alexei

---

[33] MFR, NMCC, 31 Jan 71, sub: News Media Leak, DDI Vietnam-1971 file; Ltr, Charles B. Seib, Managing Editor, *Washington Star*, to Laird, 1 Feb 71, 330–76–197, box 79, Vietnam 000.73, 1971, Laird Papers, WNRC.

[34] Ltr, Leonard to the author, 17 Oct 90. Also see MACV History, 1971, p. X-47.

[35] "News Blackout Continues in Indochina," *Washington Post*, 1 Feb 71; "Viet Moves Shrouded in Secrecy," *Baltimore Sun*, 1 Feb 71; Tillman Durdin, "Laotians Report No Word of an Incursion by Saigon," *New York Times*, 1 Feb 71; Smith, "U.S. B–52's Strike Foe's Laos Bases Around the Clock."

414

Ron Ziegler

Kosygin denouncing "the outrageous invasion of the southern provinces of Laos" received wide play.[36] A comment by Jerry Friedheim during a news conference at the Pentagon also did little to dampen speculation. Asked to remark on the prospects for an invasion of Laos, the deputy assistant secretary of defense for public affairs responded that he would have no comment on matters that General Abrams had "embargoed" in Saigon, a "no comment" that he said was also embargoed under General Abrams' rules.[37]

More disclosures came on 2 February. The *Washington Post* published an article on the embargo and the Laotian campaign drawn from UPI sources and the Kyoda news agency in Japan. The *Baltimore Sun* commented on the silence in Saigon and interpreted Friedheim's remark as an acknowledgment that a news blackout was in effect. The *New York Times* printed a galling report from Saigon by correspondent Ralph Blumenthal dealing with the history of news embargoes in general in South Vietnam. Although readers who followed events could hardly have missed the story's larger meaning, Blumenthal never once mentioned that an embargo was in effect and thus ingeniously avoided any infraction of MACV's restrictions.[38]

[36] Robert Dobkin [AP], news clip on Laos, 1 Feb 71, copy in CMH files.
[37] Chalmers Roberts, "Laos Border Activities Still a Secret," *Washington Post*, 2 Feb 71.
[38] Ibid.; Charles Corddry, "U.S. Silence Persists on Activities in Laos," *Baltimore Sun*, 2 Feb 71; Ralph Blumenthal, "Security Termed Blackout Reason," *New York Times*, 2 Feb 71.

Not so a report by *Times* correspondent Terence Smith appearing at the same time. Basing his information on leaks by anonymous "U.S. officials" in Washington, Smith confirmed that a major military operation was under way near Khe Sanh. Although avowing that a decision had yet to be made on whether to enter Laos, the reporter singled out the town of Tchepone as the probable target of any incursion that might develop.[39]

More leaks followed, some of them clearly originating deep within the Nixon administration, either among opponents of the operation who hoped to kill it or, more likely, among those who sought to counteract some of the adverse effects that the embargo might have on official credibility. A radio report that morning by CBS diplomatic correspondent Marvin Kalb thus cited "reliable sources" to disclose that 25,000 South Vietnamese and 9,000 American troops supported by massive U.S. air power were moving up Highway 9 toward the Laotian border. "Both American and South Vietnamese soldiers are fighting in this part of the operation," the reporter said.

Then the South Vietnamese are supposed to continue along Highway 9 in Laos towards the Communist controlled town of Sepone [Tchepone] a focal point for North Vietnamese men and supplies moving from North to South. There is no telling whether the South Vietnamese intend to remain in Sepone if successful or leave after causing heavy damage. The point of this operation is two-fold. First to try to reduce enemy supplies flowing into Cambodia on the Southern part of South Vietnam, thus easing the problem of a step-up rate of U.S. troop withdrawal over the next three months. The second point is to head off an expected Communist attack against the Northern part of South Vietnam. . . . President Nixon under Pentagon pressure gave his final approval [for the operation] last Wednesday.[40]

CBS returned to the topic that evening with a report by Dan Rather indicating that "a live offensive has been underway several days in the northwest corner of South Vietnam, but . . . no decision has been made on whether to continue it on into Laos." Citing "sources in positions to know," Rather continued that Nixon had met that afternoon with his top advisers to discuss the invasion, and that "a high ranking administration official who declines to be identified told CBS News that a decision one way or another may be made this evening."[41]

The next morning William Beecher of the *New York Times* quoted "senior strategists" in Washington, "primarily military but with a sprinkling of well placed civilian officials," who asserted that the logic for an attack into Laos had become compelling. The South Vietnamese had never received the sort of bombers capable of striking the Ho Chi Minh Trail on a sustained basis, those officials had noted. They therefore had to demonstrate to the enemy that his lifelines were vulnerable by proving

[39] Terence Smith, "U.S. Officials Say Allied Drive Is on in Area Near Laos," *New York Times*, 2 Feb 71.

[40] Marvin Kalb, CBS Radio Broadcast, 8:30 AM, 2 Feb 71, Nixon Papers.

[41] Dan Rather, CBS Evening News, 2 Feb 71, Nixon Papers.

that they could strike into Laos at will. "Whether the current operation in the northwest corner of South Vietnam involves a move into Laos or not," Beecher said in token compliance with the embargo, "there are growing indications that the Nixon Administration may well approve limited forays into Laos as it did last spring into Cambodia."[42]

The Chairman of the Joint Chiefs, Admiral Moorer, put the best face he could on those stories and others that appeared by telling administration officials who inquired that the Military Assistance Command had accounted for security breaches in its planning and that he was confident the operation would succeed in spite of them. General Abrams himself seemed unfazed. "I propose to hold the existing embargo . . . until substantial contact has been made with the enemy in Laos," he told McCain and Moorer. "We recognize that holding the embargo is becoming increasingly difficult in view of Washington statements today. However, lifting it at this time in my judgment would jeopardize the safety of our men."[43]

Abrams' wishes notwithstanding, by 3 February the demise of the embargo appeared imminent. That morning the *Philadelphia Inquirer* complained about the confusion that had resulted from Abrams' no-news policy. A bitter *St. Louis Post-Dispatch* termed MACV's restrictions "a disgraceful piece of business" and accused the president of attempting to hide what was happening in South Vietnam from the American public and Congress until it was too late for them to protest. The *Chicago Daily News* criticized the president for excluding the public from information that was common knowledge to the rest of the world and for failing to comprehend "the how or why of treating the American people like adults."[44]

Jerry Friedheim at the Pentagon attempted to hold the line. "If we at any point have to sacrifice immediate or instant credibility to protect the safety and security of troops," he told newsmen, "then the safety and security of troops will prevail."[45] By the end of the day, nevertheless, the anger appearing in the press had prompted such deep concern at the White House that media analyst Mort Allen told H. R. Haldeman: "From a PR standpoint the Indochina situation is very damning. The stories in the papers are . . . the most serious credibility gap articles yet in this administration."[46]

As pressure on the embargo increased, the president wavered on whether to approve the second phase of the operation, but in the end, he

[42] William Beecher, "The Incursion Issue," *New York Times*, 3 Feb 71.

[43] Msg, JCS SPECAT 3106 to Abrams, 2 Feb 71, sub: Lam Son 719. Quote from Msg, Abrams SPECAT to McCain, 2 Feb 71, sub: Press Guidance LAM SON 719 and TOAN THANG 01-71NB. Both in Abrams Papers, CMH.

[44] James McCartney, "Mum's the Word on Secret War in Laos, *Philadelphia Inquirer*, 3 Feb 71; "Concealing the Facts on Laos," *St. Louis Post-Dispatch*, 3 Feb 71; "Blindfolding the Public," *Chicago Daily News*, 3 Feb 71.

[45] The Friedheim quote is from [UPI], "Some Daylight on the Blackout," *Washington Daily News*, 4 Feb 71.

[46] Memo, Mort Allen for H. R. Haldeman, 3 Feb 71, sub: Notations for Feb. 2–3 News Summaries, White House Special files, Buchanan, Chron files, box 1, Feb 71, Nixon Papers.

Jerry Friedheim briefs the press.

decided to go ahead. Convinced that much of the speculation appearing in the press was based on leaks from sources within the State and Defense Departments, he reasoned that he would lose any hope of controlling the bureaucracy if he allowed its members to dictate his decisions by playing to the press.[47]

With that, on 4 February, just prior to the beginning of the Cambodian portion of the operation, Admiral Moorer issued new public affairs guidance. According to the plan he cabled to McCain and Abrams, as stipulated by an earlier agreement with President Thieu, South Vietnamese information officers were to issue a routine notification at their regular afternoon news conference that an operation had begun in Cam-

bodia. In that way, the move would tend to merge with earlier cross-border operations and attract less attention than it would if preceded by a formal backgrounder. As for DEWEY CANYON II, Moorer said, with word of the strike into Cambodia already beginning to appear in the press and with concern rising in Congress, so much pressure had developed from all sides that there was little choice but to lift the embargo. "This pressure," he continued,

is bursting at the seams and the public affairs experts feel that . . . [the embargo] will be broken before too many hours regardless of what we do. . . . Films and tapes are already poised in major studios across the nation, and remarkably accurate information is somehow becoming public knowledge in Washington. A total embargo is no longer productive. In short, it could become unmanageable. . . . I assure you once again that your views have been strongly put forward at the highest level and that this decision . . . was made only after a most careful review. . . . We do not wish the embargo as such to be the single factor which prevents us from proceeding with the remainder of the operation. The way news is flying around in Washington there is a strong possibility that just such a thing can happen.[48]

---

[47] Haldeman, *The Haldeman Diaries*, entry for 3 Feb 71, p. 242.

[48] Msg, Moorer SPECAT 3224 to McCain, Abrams, 4 Feb 71, sub: Press Guidance for TOAN THANG 01-71 NB and LAM SON 719, Abrams Papers, CMH. Also see Msgs, MACV SPECAT to CJCS, 3 Feb 71, and McCain SPECAT to Moorer, 2 Feb 71, both in Abrams Papers, CMH.

Shortly thereafter, the Military Assistance Command issued an advisory to the Saigon correspondents terminating the embargo. As suggested by Moorer, information officers reminded the reporters that they were to discuss the operation "only as far as it has progressed to date," without identifying unit designations below the level of division and brigade and without revealing the number of troops at individual locations. "The embargo has served its purpose," the notice concluded, "in that our casualties have been at an absolute minimum."[49]

On the surface, as Moorer's message seemed to indicate, the embargo appeared to have failed. Yet it may still have served at least part of General Abrams' purpose. The welter of conflicting information, speculation, and opinion that accompanied it in the American news media can have served only to obscure President Nixon's final intentions from the enemy. As one National Security Council analyst observed in a 4 February news summary: "Confusion reigns in wire service reports as far as objective of operation is concerned. One says Thieu has left decision to enter Laos up to president, another that no decision has been made, a third that Acting Ambassador [Samuel D.] Berger has informed Thieu of decision during a meeting on this date." Meanwhile, as Leonard noted, other news reports were circulating to the effect that South Vietnamese units had already crossed the border and that paratroopers had landed on the Bolong Plateau in southern Laos.[50]

Whether any of that made much difference to the enemy must remain a matter of conjecture. North Vietnam had sources of information of its own at that time, some so well placed within the South Vietnamese bureaucracy and Army that it learned almost immediately of every major decision involving the incursion. Its leaders had, indeed, decided long before that just such a drive into Laos was inevitable and had begun preparations as early as October 1970 to repel it. By the beginning of February 1971 they had moved their most critical supplies southward, begun construction of a road to bypass the area in Laos most open to attack, and prepared defensive positions along Highway 9. In that light, as the *New York Times* would later note, even if military security had justified a period of news suppression, the embargo had probably continued far longer than necessary.[51]

As it was, the end of the embargo opened the Nixon administration to a flood of criticism in the press. For although a few newspapers such as the *Jacksonville Journal* and the *Chicago Sun-Times* either supported the expedient as a military necessity or, as in the case of the *New Orleans Times-*

[49] MACV Advisory, 4 Feb 71, DDI DEWEY CANYON II file.

[50] Quote from Memo, Dave Clark for Dave McManis, 4 Feb 71, sub: Morning Cable Summary for 4 Feb 71, NSC files, Subject files, box 386, Situation Room Cable Summaries, 2/1/71–3/31/71, vol. V, Nixon Papers. Ltr, Leonard to the author, 17 Oct 90.

[51] Msg, Sutherland QTR 306 to Abrams, 10 Mar 71, Abrams Papers, CMH; Maj. Gen. Nguyen Duy Hinh, Indochina Monographs, *Lam Son 719* (Washington, D.C.: U.S. Army Center of Military History, 1979), p. 82. ". . . Increases the Credibility Gap," *New York Times*, 24 Mar 71.

Picayune, failed to mention that it had occurred, newspapers as diverse as the *Dallas Morning News,* the *Miami Herald,* the *Louisville Courier-Journal,* the *St. Paul Pioneer Press,* and the *Fresno Bee* all commented that Abrams' restrictions had increased the anxiety of the American people, widened the credibility gap, and undermined support for the war.[52]

Congressional opinion appeared to mirror that of the press. Senator Mike J. Mansfield of Montana charged that the embargo had created "a very difficult situation." Senator Aiken told reporters that his office was receiving a heavy flow of mail from constituents alarmed by reports of a possible attack into Laos. "So long as the blackout continues," he said, "they fear and expect the worst." Senator Robert C. Byrd of West Virginia was among the most critical. A steady supporter of the administration's Vietnam policies, he termed the embargo "inexcusable bungling" that had created "an entirely unnecessary credibility gap." The *Washington Star* meanwhile reported that a number of senators were threatening to introduce legislation to prevent similar occurrences in the future.[53]

Free at last to speak, the Saigon correspondents were especially vehement both in their denunciation of the embargo and in their criticism of the other rules Abrams had imposed to accompany the incursion. Some months before, with the cooperation of the MACV Office of Information, they had formed an association to represent their interests. With the conclusion of the embargo, they used that organization to file a widely reported protest that termed MACV's handling of DEWEY CANYON II "incomprehensible." Although the Military Assistance Command had held daily briefings in Saigon to keep the press informed of the operation's progress to date, the reporters refused to give that effort much credence and charged instead that the command had in fact declined to provide enough background on developments to allow them to fulfill their professional responsibilities. Not only had the Military Assistance Command failed to respond to the protests of the press, they said, it had also sought to bar reporters from important news sources, and, through its escort policies, it had attempted to monitor interviews with soldiers in the field. Most damaging of all in the eyes of the newsmen was the command's refusal to allow them to make any mention of the embargo in their reports and broadcasts while Jerry Friedheim, Ronald Ziegler, and other official sources in Washington had all but acknowledged its existence.[54]

---

[52] "Behind the Laos News Blackout," *Chicago Sun-Times,* 5 Feb 71; "The Hue and Cry," *Jacksonville Journal,* 8 Feb 71; "Who's Widening the War," *New Orleans Times-Picayune,* 5 Feb 71; "News Blackout Ends on War," *Dallas Morning News,* 5 Feb 71; "The People Deserve To Know What Is Going on in Laos," *Miami Herald,* 4 Feb 71; "What Did Saigon News Blackout Accomplish?," *Louisville Courier-Journal,* 6 Feb 71; "Apt Questions For Mr. Laird," *St. Paul Pioneer Press,* 7 Feb 71; "Strange News Embargo on Laos," *Fresno Bee,* 4 Feb 71; "Vietnam, The Communications Breakdown," *Washington Post,* 5 Feb 71.

[53] "Senators Assail Secrecy," *New York Times,* 4 Feb 71; James Doyle, "Some Senators Chafe at War News Blackout," *Washington Star,* 4 Feb 71.

[54] [UPI], "Writers Rap U.S. Curb on Viet News, *Chicago Tribune,* 6 Feb 71.

420

Given U.S. awareness that the attack into Laos had been compromised almost from the start and the mounting toll the embargo had taken on official credibility, General Abrams' stated reason for continuing restraints on the press—that they served to preserve American and South Vietnamese lives by keeping the enemy off balance—appears to have provided only a partial explanation for his decision. The general may have been seeking to trick the enemy into believing that a feint occurring at that time toward North Vietnam's coast by elements of the U.S. Seventh Fleet was much more than a diversion.[55]

Then again, the bad blood that seemed increasingly to characterize military-media relations in South Vietnam may have been the cause. For months, the press had criticized almost every aspect of Abrams' command, from the morale of his troops to possible violations of the Cooper-Church Amendment. Goodwill between the military and the Saigon correspondents had fallen so low, as a result, that individual members of the two groups had on occasion nearly come to blows. One incident, in which NBC News correspondent James Bennett had verbally assaulted the XXIV Corps public affairs officer, Lt. Col. Perry G. Stevens, had led not only to the disaccreditation of the reporter but also to the closing of the Da Nang press center. The reason cited for the shutdown, that the facility was no longer economical to run, was merely an excuse. In fact, the command's inspector general, Colonel Cook, and his investigators had concluded that the reporters in residence there constituted little more than a public nuisance.[56] In that sense, the embargo may have been a manifestation of a deeper misunderstanding. As Leonard noted,

The press refused to believe there was a military reason for the embargo while MACV couldn't believe that a few days delay in publication would represent a terrible infringement on the public's right to know. It was a classic confrontation as to which was most important: military security or the public's right. . . . As an old infantryman, my sympathies will always lie with the soldier . . . who always has to fight the war, not [with] the reporter who writes about it. If the embargo saved one life it was worth it.[57]

Whatever Abrams' reasons, the decision to continue restrictions on the press in the face of intense opposition was unfortunate. For if the enemy had failed to attack the troops converging on Khe Sanh, he still appears to have possessed a relatively clear idea of American intentions and could have attacked if his best interests had so required. Instead he chose to wait and to marshal his forces for the assault he knew would

---

[55] For details of diversion, see Graham A. Cosmas and Lt. Col. Terrence P. Murray, USMC, *U.S. Marines in Vietnam, Vietnamization and Redeployment, 1970–1971* (Washington, D.C.: History and Museums Division, Headquarters, U.S. Marine Corps, 1986), pp. 207–09.

[56] Interv, author with Col Robert Cook, USA (Ret.), 22 May 87, CMH files. Also see MACVIG Rpt of Investigation, 28 Jan 71, sub: Report of Investigation Concerning Unprofessional Conduct of Mr. James P. Bennett, NBC News (MIV–1–71), 334–77–0074, box 1, vol. V, WNRC.

[57] Ltr, Leonard to the author, 17 Oct 90.

421

come. In that sense, the embargo added nothing but an extra layer of complication to a situation that, given the increasing willingness of the press to believe the worst of the military, was already certain to become one of the most controversial and problematic of the war.

18

LAM SON 719

Within hours of lifting the embargo on DEWEY CANYON II, President Nixon approved the execution of the operation's Laotian phase, the move toward Tchepone along Highway 9. As soon as the attack began on 8 February 1971, in order to underscore the role of the South Vietnamese armed forces, the Military Assistance Command terminated all references to DEWEY CANYON II in its communications with the press. From then on both the military and the news media called the operation by its South Vietnamese name, LAM SON 719.[1] *(Map 4)*

Still uncertain about the value of entering Laos and apparently concerned that Abrams might refuse to pull back if the attack became a political liability, Secretary Laird, over the objections of Admiral Moorer, sanctioned U.S. support for the South Vietnamese in Laos only through 5 April, a date that cut almost a month from the time planners had expected the operation to last. Notifying General Abrams of the decision, Moorer emphasized that if the Military Assistance Command desired to extend that authorization it should submit the request as far in advance as possible. He warned, however, that continued support in various quarters in Washington might be contingent upon limiting the campaign to the six to eight weeks Laird's ruling appeared to contemplate.[2]

[1] Msg, State 19640 to Saigon, 4 Feb 71, NSC files, Vietnam Subject files, box 84, Special Operations file, vol. 4, 4–8 Feb 1971, Nixon Papers. Moorer suggested the change in Msg, Moorer JCS SPECAT 2788 to McCain, Abrams, 31 Jan 71, sub: LAM SON 719, Abrams Papers, CMH.

[2] Msg, Moorer SPECAT 3244 to McCain and Abrams, 4 Feb 71, NSC files, Vietnam Subject files, box 84, Special Operations file, vol. 4, 4–8 Feb 1971, Nixon Papers. Moorer mentioned his objections in a telephone conversation with Kissinger. See Extracts from Telephone Conversations Between Dr. Kissinger and Defense Department Officials, Admiral Moorer (tab N), March 9, covered by Memo, Jon Howe for Kissinger, 24 Mar 71, sub: White House View of Laotian Planning (February 8–March 20), NSC files, Jon Howe Chron files, box 1077, Mar 71, Nixon Papers. This document will be cited hereafter as Telephone Extracts: White House View of Laotian Planning. The covering memo also refers to Laird's "enigmatic role."

The stipulation seemed only a bureaucratic annoyance at first, but it came to weigh heavily upon South Vietnamese commanders during the weeks that followed. They brought it up on a number of occasions after their attack had begun to falter, each time as an indication that their American ally was less committed to the operation than they. That was hardly the case, but the deadline nevertheless showed the growing unease of Laird and others within the Nixon administration and their desire to preserve as much room as possible for political maneuver and damage control.[3]

Public Relations Scenarios

If Laird seemed increasingly apprehensive, many of his colleagues within the Nixon administration appear to have been preoccupied mainly with the public image of the attack. Informed in advance of what Souvanna Phouma planned to say in condemning the incursion, for example, the State Department drafted a response that sought to dilute any allegation that South Vietnam was an aggressor. The carefully crafted comment, designed to accompany a U.S. pronouncement on the American role in the attack, took note of Souvanna's objections but underscored a point he intended to make as well, that "primary responsibility" for the raid rested upon the North Vietnamese, who remained in "scornful violation of international law and . . . the neutrality and territorial integrity of [Laos]."[4]

The Washington Special Actions Group, composed of high-level representatives of all the agencies concerned with the war, also devoted considerable attention to public relations. As soon as Nixon decided in favor of the attack, it drafted a plan to make certain that the announcements accompanying the operation created an impression of South Vietnamese competence and American resolution. Although Nixon had final say on whether the operation would proceed, the group insisted that President Thieu release first word of the event and take public responsibility for the decision to enter Laos. Those moves would enhance the South Vietnamese image and deemphasize the U.S. role. In the same way, Thieu was to allay concern that the move was an act of imperialistic aggression against Laos by issuing a communique that affirmed the limited nature of the attack and South Vietnam's desire to uphold the independence and territorial integrity of the Laotian state. The U.S. mission in

[3]South Vietnamese concerns are clear in the telephone conversations Kissinger held with Moorer and Laird as the incursion progressed. See, for example, his telephone conversations between 9 and 11 March in Telephone Extracts: White House View of Laotian Planning.
[4]Msg, State 21021 to Saigon, 7 Feb 71, NSC files, Vietnam Subject files, box 80, Vietnam: Operations in Laos and Cambodia, vol. 2, Nixon Papers.

424

Saigon, for its part, would issue a simple statement shortly after Thieu made his remarks to confirm that no U.S. ground forces or advisers would enter Laos and that American forces would supply only air combat and logistical support. Assistant Secretary of Defense for Public Affairs Daniel Henkin would repeat that theme in Washington but would likewise shy away from any comment that added to or subtracted from Thieu's declaration. From then on, American spokesmen would keep to the background, supplying information about the American portion of the effort but leaving the South Vietnamese to become the primary source for news of events in Laos.[5]

While the Washington Special Actions Group refined its plan, officers at the State and Defense Departments worked with Thieu to draft an announcement for the operation. Paying special attention to Nixon's advice that official spokesmen were to state only minimal goals for the attack, they encouraged Thieu to avoid any mention of Tchepone as a target. They also insisted that he substitute the word *disrupt* for *destroy* in his description of what he hoped his forces would achieve when they reached the enemy's depots in Laos.[6]

Thieu accepted that advice but balked at other suggestions that had to do with the handling of the Saigon correspondents. When the Defense Department proposed that he allow his public affairs officers to convene a background briefing for the press shortly after he had announced the operation, he declared his intention instead to postpone any session of the sort for at least a day. With General Abrams concurring on grounds of military security, he also declared that he would prohibit reporters from accompanying his troops into Laos for the same period of time, until all danger of compromise had passed.[7]

Confusing the Issues

The scenario U.S. agencies had devised played itself out as planned on 8 February, when the South Vietnamese armed forces began their move into Laos. Thieu made his statement; the U.S. mission issued its brief confirmation of the American role; and Henkin followed in Washington with an unemotional news release that stressed the limited nature of the

[5] Msg, State 19640 to Saigon, 4 Feb 71; Msg, Moorer JCS SPECAT 3369 to McCain, Abrams, 6 Feb 71, Abrams Papers, CMH; Memo, Ron Ziegler for Henry Kissinger, 5 Feb 71, sub: Public Relations Scenario for Phase II, NSC files, Vietnam Subject files, box 80, Vietnam: Operations in Laos and Cambodia, vol. 2, Nixon Papers. Also see Msg, McCain SPECAT to Moorer, 5 Feb 71, Abrams Papers, CMH.

[6] Msg, JCS SPECAT 3397 to McCain, Abrams, 6 Feb 71, retransmitting Msg, Saigon 1709 to State, 5 Feb 71, Abrams Papers, CMH; Msg, State 20549 to Saigon, 5 Feb 71, NSC files, Vietnam Subject files, box 80, Vietnam: Operations in Laos and Cambodia, vol. 2, Nixon Papers.

[7] Msg, State to Saigon, 6 Feb 71, General Abrams' Personal file 69, CMH.

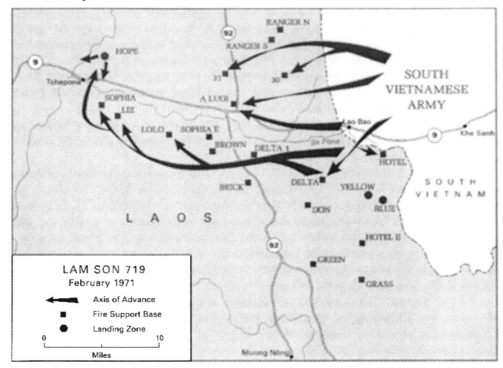

MAP 4

operation. Souvanna deplored the fact that "once again . . . foreign troops . . . have deliberately chosen [Laotian] . . . territory as a battlefield." The State Department responded by charging quietly that the primary responsibility for what had occurred rested solely with North Vietnam.[8]

Over the days that followed, administration spokesmen conducted a broad campaign to explain what the president hoped to accomplish in Laos both to the press and opinion leaders throughout the United States. Charles Colson contacted Howard K. Smith of ABC News to elicit a commentary in favor of the operation. Herbert Klein called the Associated Press to arrange for a backgrounder on the subject. Henry Kissinger briefed friendly reporters and columnists. Special assistant to the president Jeb Stuart Magruder began to generate letters to the editor praising the president's courage in making a difficult decision. Efforts likewise went forward to distribute fact sheets on Laos, to gain the endorsement of the American Federation of Labor–Congress of Industrial Organizations, and to generate as much favorable comment as possible from friendly congressmen and senators. In each case, administration spokesmen highlighted the success of the previous year's operation in Cambodia, the president's commitment to ending the war honorably, and the bankruptcy of those who criticized

[8] Msg, USIA 2041 to All Diplomatic Posts, 8 Feb 71, and Msg, USIA 2075 to All Diplomatic Posts, 8 Feb 71, both in DDI LAM SON II–Laos file.

administration policy. On the side, at the president's suggestion, they also explained that if the embargo of the week before had inconvenienced newsmen it had still confused the enemy and saved American lives.[9]

Only one small mistake appeared in the carefully orchestrated program. The communique the Military Assistance Command released to the Saigon correspondents failed to use the word *disrupt* and instead affirmed that South Vietnamese forces were involved in "interdiction operations" in southern Laos. Since *interdict*, as a word, vaguely connoted an act of cutting, it appeared to violate the president's stipulation that official spokesmen should link the operation to the narrowest goals. It passed unnoticed at the time, partly because Thieu had used the word *disrupt* in his statement and partly because the president and his advisers were intent upon stressing in private meetings with congressional leaders that long-term results rather than short-term tactical advantages were what mattered. Its use by MACV nevertheless diluted the effect of Thieu's careful phrasing and may have contributed to an impression, already prevalent among reporters, that the United States and South Vietnam intended to stop all traffic on the Ho Chi Minh Trail.[10]

Whatever the effect of that oversight, the president and his advisers were themselves hardly immune to error. As early as 9 February, during a meeting with congressional leaders, the president, for one, had stressed how competent the South Vietnamese had become by contrasting their aggressive attitude in undertaking the attack with what he believed had been that of General Westmoreland earlier in the war. "Back in 1965," he said, "when I recommended this [operation] to Westmoreland, he didn't think we could accomplish it with American troops. Now ARVN troops are conducting . . . operations outside South Vietnam right now; ARVN troops are the ones responsible for cutting the Ho Chi Minh Trail."[11] Although the president conceded that there were going to be some "hairy days" ahead because the enemy would undoubtedly stand and fight, his comments still tended to undermine his desire to accentuate minimum goals. They not only reinforced the idea that the South Vietnamese were in Laos to *cut* rather than disrupt supply lines, they also set up expectations that the operation would somehow demonstrate the success of Vietnamization.

[9] Memo, Charles Colson for H. R. Haldeman, 11 Feb 71, sub: Getting Our Line Out on Laos and Cambodia, White House Special files, Buchanan, Staff Memoranda, box 3, Haldeman [2 of 2], Nixon Papers; Memo, Jeb S. Magruder for Staff Secretary, 12 Feb 71, sub: Action Memo P1362, White House Special files, Klein, Action Memoranda 1970–1971, box 8, White House Action Memos P1210H–1434H, Nixon Papers.

[10] MACOI Memorandum for Correspondents 39–71, 8 Feb 71, 334–74–593, box 12, file 413–05, Newspaper files (71), Weekly Summaries, WNRC. See, for example, Alvin Shuster, "Saigon Viets Drive Into Laos To Strike Enemy Supply Line," *New York Times*, 8 Feb 71; Richard Dudman, "Drive in Laos May Last 4 Months, Scott Says," *St. Louis Post-Dispatch*, 8 Feb 71.

[11] This is a close paraphrase of the president's comment. The word *cut* figures so prominently that Nixon probably used it. See Memo, Patrick Buchanan for the President, 10 Feb 71, sub: Notes From Leadership Meeting, February 9, 1971, White House Special files, Buchanan, Chron files, Feb 71, Nixon Papers.

South Vietnamese forces enter Laos.

Administration spokesmen attempted the next day to correct the idea that the South Vietnamese would choke off the trail. "That would be attempted," they told newsmen, "only if South Vietnam were prepared to put as many as three to five divisions along it and keep them there."[12] The president himself, however, once more confused the issue. At a 17 February news conference, he prefaced a remark that the South Vietnamese were in Laos only to disrupt enemy communications with a comment that civilian and military experts had long agreed "the way to stop North Vietnamese infiltration into South Vietnam was to cut the Ho Chi Minh Trail." The South Vietnamese, he added dramatically, "have already cut three major roads."[13]

Other exaggerations occurred below the presidential level. On 10 February, for example, Secretary Laird held a background briefing for twenty-five members of the Pentagon press corps. During the session, he stressed the ability of the South Vietnamese armed forces to execute major military operations and asserted that they alone had conceived and planned LAM SON 719. When the United States finally relinquished the war to the South Vietnamese and their Cambodian allies, he said, it would leave more than a million men under arms, a force more than equal to the threat Saigon faced. As for the operation in Laos, U.S. forces were providing only air support, more than 30 B–52 and 300 tactical air and helicopter sorties per day. Thus far, losses had been relatively small. Laird concluded that it was his judgment, "and I could be wrong," that if everything went well "a very, very dramatic change" would occur in the overall situation in Southeast Asia. "The enemy would have sustained a major loss, a major loss. Just as those cross border operations in Cambodia . . . put them out of business in the lower . . . areas of South Vietnam, so this will begin to

[12] William Beecher, "U.S. Aides Believe Thrust May Cost Foe Year or More," *New York Times,* 10 Feb 71.
[13] "Transcript of President's News Conference," *New York Times,* 18 Feb 71.

428

drastically nibble away at his effectiveness in Cambodia and South Vietnam, and assure that we will be able to get . . . [our] forces out."[14]

Laird's comments drew a vehement protest from the Military Assistance Command. The optimistic picture the secretary had presented, General Abrams told Admiral McCain, was a distortion of the facts. If the South Vietnamese were indeed improving and had assisted on a number of details, he continued, they had not planned LAM SON 719. The concept for the operation had come from his command, as had much of the initial groundwork. In the same way, although the Cambodian armed forces had improved, they were hardly a match for the North Vietnamese without major assistance from their allies. As for the sortie rates Laird had released, the MACV Office of Information had withheld those numbers from the Saigon correspondents on grounds that they were of value to the enemy. That Laird had mentioned them, even on background, could only strain the command's relations with the press. Newsmen would never understand how information officers in the field could hold the line on statistics of that sort while Washington agencies released them. The comment on aircraft losses was equally ill advised. "The enemy is capable of inflicting substantial losses to helicopters as flights are made deeper into Laos. If the public is misled in believing losses are unexpected, the conclusion could be made that the operation is not proceeding according to plan." Abrams concluded pointedly that if press coverage was essential for operations such as the one in Laos, the accuracy of the news officials released to reporters was also important. He crossed off a final sentence as, perhaps, too pointed. It read, "Inaccuracies, intentional or unintentional, tend to foster . . . belief in the credibility gap."[15]

According to Jerry Friedheim, who had helped to prepare the backgrounder, Abrams' objections had little effect upon Laird. The secretary wanted the American withdrawal from South Vietnam to continue on schedule and did not want the president or Kissinger to have any reason to change the timetable. He understood that if LAM SON 719 failed withdrawals would continue, possibly at a rate even faster than before. "The danger was," Friedheim said, "that if 719 *succeeded* Nixon would be tempted to stay longer. Thus Laird cast it all that *victory* by South Vietnamese troops would 'assure that we will be able to get our forces out.' . . . [In that way,] *whatever* happened in 719 made U.S. withdrawal on schedule possible. He also did not want the White House (Kissinger) to increase the sortie rates or mission profiles. So he set a 'ceiling' on background. . . . [The phrase] *'I could be wrong'* was very deliberately said, so he could be optimistic, as the White House insisted, but also . . . realistic— as later proved right." Laird, in other words, had used the backgrounder to set up expectations within the news media that would tend to restrain

---

[14] Msg, Defense 3781 to Unified and Specified Commands, 11 Feb 71, sub: Background Briefing by Senior Defense Official, 319–84–051, box 9, WNRC.

[15] Msg, Abrams SPECAT to McCain, 14 Feb 71, sub: Backgrounder Briefing, Abrams Papers, CMH.

the president and Kissinger rather than allow them the free rein they might otherwise have sought.[16]

Arrangements in the Field

Hoping to avoid problems with the press, MACV public affairs officers at MACV took what steps they could to assist the Saigon correspondents. Since they had little control over the information newsmen received from the South Vietnamese, they planned from the beginning to solidify their own relations with the press by being as forthcoming as possible about American casualties.[17] For the same reason, they did what they could to prepare accommodations and assistance for correspondents in the field.

At the beginning of DEWEY CANYON II, the public affairs officer for XXIV Corps, Lt. Col. Perry G. Stevens, established a press camp at Quang Tri City. It included billeting and sleeping quarters for newsmen and a liaison office where reporters could receive briefings and communiques. With the Da Nang press center closing, that facility quickly became a hub for newsmen attempting to cover the incursion. The reporters shuttled into Quang Tri from Saigon and Da Nang aboard official American aircraft and from there to Khe Sanh and other forward positions in South Vietnam. Once in the field, they had to request accommodations from the units they were visiting, but that was a formality. In almost all cases, as had been the custom from the beginning of the war, they received billeting and food at nominal cost. When they returned to Quang Tri, the Military Assistance Command provided them with rapid air transport and telephone and teletype circuits to move their copy and film to Saigon as quickly as possible.[18] The system was so efficient that on 8 February, when South Vietnamese troops arrived at the Laotian border to begin the cross-border portion of the operation, they found a number of American newsmen waiting to interview them.

If MACV's attempt to provide for the physical needs of the press proved successful, Abrams and his public affairs officers nevertheless failed to supply the one thing newsmen wanted most, access to what was happening. Although reporters experienced little difficulty traveling up to the Laotian border, they discovered upon arrival that official fog obscured the subject they had come to see, the fighting.

[16] Quotes from Memo, Friedheim for the author, 26 Jul 91, CMH files. The punctuation has been altered slightly to make the reading flow. Interv, author with Friedheim, 12 Aug 91, CMH files.

[17] Memo, Daniel Henkin for Dr. Dennis Doolin, OASD ISA, 11 Feb 71, DDI LAM SON II–Laos file.

[18] Memo, Lorfano for Henkin, 12 Feb 71, sub: Press Facilities/Services for DEWEY CANYON II/LAMSON 719, DDI DEWEY CANYON II file. Also see Hinh, *Lam Son 719*, p. 65.

Shortly after the operation began, at the urging of Colonel Stevens, the South Vietnamese corps commander, Lt. Gen. Hoang Xuan Lam, moved to remedy the problem by setting up a press center of his own near that of the Americans at Quang Tri and by promising to station a senior South Vietnamese public affairs officer there. He also agreed to provide daily briefings for the press and to make transportation available for reporters who wished to accompany his troops into the field.[19]

Those assurances notwithstanding, Lam and his commanders—partly on the advice of President Nixon, who had urged them to strengthen restrictions on the news media—had no intention of giving the Saigon correspondents the true story of the battle or of allowing reporters to cross into Laos. They thus took three days to dispatch the promised briefer to Quang Tri and announced almost immediately that they would prevent the press from accompanying their troops into the field until those forces had established a secure situation.[20]

The credibility of American spokesmen suffered as a result. When reporters attempted on the first day of the operation to accompany the units entering Laos, for example, they found the way barred by American military policemen who had little choice but to support Lam's orders. In the same way, according to Colonel Stevens, when a South Vietnamese briefer finally arrived at Quang Tri, he lied so blatantly and without reservation during his first session with the press that the reporters turned on the American information officers present and accused them of condoning untruth. The session was particularly unfortunate, Stevens said, because the briefer had told the reporters that South Vietnamese units had thus far suffered few casualties in Laos when almost every man present had, in fact, seen helicopters returning continually from the field laden with the bodies of the dead.[21]

The antipathies that some members of the military harbored toward the press did nothing to remedy matters. When James Bennett of NBC News disguised a South Vietnamese cameraman as a military photographer and sent him to join a unit bound for Laos, an American crewman on the helicopter transporting the troops discovered the ruse. In an excess of enthusiasm, he threw the newsman's expensive camera out the aircraft's open door. The comment that he made in doing so, "I've got my orders," did little to improve MACV's relations with the press.[22]

[19] Msg, Sutherland QTR 45 to Abrams, 7 Feb 71, Abrams Papers, CMH; Interv, author with Col Perry Stevens, 25 Apr 89, CMH files.

[20] MFR, 1 Mar 71, sub: Meeting Between Kissinger, Laird, Haig, Pursley, 18 Feb 71, NSC files, Presidential/HAK Memcon files [Jan–April 1971], box 1026, Nixon Papers; Msg, Sutherland QTR 45 to Abrams, 7 Feb 71; Interv, author with Col Perry Stevens, 25 Apr 89.

[21] Interv, author with Col Perry Stevens, 25 Apr 89.

[22] Quote from "Curtain Kept Over Laos Drive," *Washington Post*, 10 Feb 71. "Information Freeze," *Newsweek*, 1 Mar 71. Col. Perry Stevens confirmed the incident involving the cameraman. See Interv, author with Col Perry Stevens, 25 Apr 89. Also see Research Rpt, Douglas Shoemaker, Press Reporting of DEWEY CANYON II and LAM SON 719 [U.S. Army Center of Military History], p. 8, CMH files.

Larry Burrows (right) *of* Life

The South Vietnamese command eased its restrictions on 10 February by allowing a helicopter to carry newsmen into Laos. To its chagrin and that of the Saigon correspondents, the aircraft strayed, blundered into an enemy machine gun position, and went down with the loss of all on board. Among the casualties were Larry Burrows of *Life*; Henri Huet of the Associated Press; Ken Potter of United Press International; Keisaburo Shimamoto, stringing for *Newsweek*; and Sgt. Vu Tu, a South Vietnamese Army photographer. The South Vietnamese tried again on 13 and 16 February, when their helicopters ferried some seventeen newsmen into the battle zone. Another ten reporters managed to make the trip overland by convoy. Yet in all, no more than twenty-seven newsmen entered Laos between 8 and 20 February.[23]

Despite the poor performance of the South Vietnamese, the credibility of the MACV Office of Information had by then fallen so low that the Saigon correspondents could hardly resist an invidious comparison. The reporters began to charge that Lam and his officers were more forthcoming in their treatment of the press than the Military Assistance Command because they had given reporters at least some access to Laos while American public affairs officers had done nothing.[24]

---

[23] Msg, Abrams SPECAT to McCain, Moorer, 12 Feb 71, sub: Lam Son 719, Abrams Papers, CMH; Talking Paper, Newsmen Entering Laos, n.d., DDI Press Support for Lam Son 719 file.

[24] Laird made this observation at a meeting in the White House. See MFR, 1 Mar 71, sub: Meeting Between Kissinger, Laird, Haig, Pursley, 18 Feb 71.

Public affairs officers were thus trapped between the Saigon correspondents' bitter complaints about the lack of regular transportation into Laos and General Abrams' continuing demand that they bar reporters from riding American helicopters. In the end, after the deaths of Burrows and Huet, they could do little more than cite as justification a Defense Department regulation that prohibited military aircraft from carrying civilians across international boundaries. The credibility of MACV spokesmen declined further as a result. As Craig Whitney observed in the *New York Times*, the rule had been written to keep military flights from competing with commercial airlines during times of peace and had little application to accredited correspondents covering combat. The Military Assistance Command had, indeed, broken it with abandon the year before, when American forces had entered Cambodia.[25]

Reporters were also less than satisfied with official American responses to their requests for information. When they asked about what was happening in Laos, Whitney complained, public affairs officers replied, "Americans do not comment on Vietnamese operations. . . . It's a Vietnamese show." The South Vietnamese, meanwhile, "still do not say how long they intend to stay in Laos, where they are trying to go or where they are now."[26]

If the South Vietnamese were uncommunicative, Whitney continued, American authorities were themselves little more forthcoming about their own side of the operation. They refused to give any information on how many American helicopters were flying in Laos or how far they had gone into that country. When U.S. aircraft accidentally dropped antipersonnel bombs on a South Vietnamese unit, killing six and wounding fifty-one, no one announced the event until newsmen discovered that an unusually large number of medical evacuation flights had occurred and began to ask questions. On another occasion, Whitney said, an American briefer had announced that "'I have nothing to report on American activities today. . . . Everything was quiet. . . .' That day American helicopter pilots who have been flying over Laos . . . were coming back breathless, with bullet holes in their craft. One said: 'Every time we've gone out, we've had our aircraft shot to hell.'"[27]

If the Nixon administration agreed with columnist Ralph de Toledano that the Saigon correspondents were better disposed toward the enemy than to their own side, it could still see that the news media's complaints about transportation were tarnishing the public image of the effort in Laos. It therefore suggested that Abrams rescind his ban on allowing newsmen to ride in American helicopters. Abrams once more refused to yield. If the Military Assistance Command allowed newsmen to fly in its helicopters, Admiral McCain argued on his behalf, reporters would

[25] Craig R. Whitney, "Big Gap at the Briefings on Laos," *New York Times*, 13 Feb 71.
[26] Ibid.
[27] Ibid.

almost certainly highlight the role of American air crews in Laos. That would detract from the impression the United States sought to convey of a South Vietnam increasingly responsible for its own defense.[28]

Reduced to fending for themselves, reporters wasted little time in developing their own leads. The news stories that resulted were, as Admiral Moorer put it, "unusually rapid and complete." Because of the uninformed nature of the sources, however, they were also at times unreliable. A number of newspapers, for example, began to report as early as 11 and 12 February that the South Vietnamese had reached Tchepone, even though those forces had covered only half the distance to that goal. In the same way, trusting the word of American infantrymen over that of South Vietnamese and American public affairs officers, correspondents for United Press International alleged on 11 February that at least 100 American infantrymen had engaged in combat in Laos while protecting work crews retrieving damaged helicopters. ABC and CBS likewise reported that U.S. troops, some wearing South Vietnamese uniforms, were on the ground in Laos.[29]

The press itself appears to have corrected the assertion that the South Vietnamese had reached Tchepone. By 16 February the subject had all but disappeared from news dispatches. The allegation, however, that U.S. troops were fighting in Laos was so explosive that it prompted concerned queries from the Washington Special Actions Group and special attention from the White House, General Abrams, and the State Department. All concerned denied that U.S. troops in disguise were operating in Laos. Observing that the unit referred to by United Press International appeared to be part of the 2d Squadron of the 17th Cavalry, General Abrams took pains to point out that the unit had indeed operated near Laos and that some of its soldiers probably believed they had crossed the border. The impression was incorrect, he said. A special South Vietnamese combat team provided security for the crews that recovered helicopters in Laos. American troops served that function only on South Vietnamese soil.[30]

Although Abrams and his staff were candid in their attempt to calm public apprehension, the larger problem underlying the errors of the Saigon correspondents went unrecognized, or, at least, unrepaired. For in the environment of suspicion that had come to surround the incur-

[28] Ralph de Toledano, "Furor in Washington Perils GI Lives," *San Diego Union*, 16 Feb 71, p. 23; Msg, McCain SPECAT to Moorer, Abrams, 14 Feb 71, Abrams Papers, CMH.

[29] Quote from Msg, Moorer SPECAT 4057 to McCain, Abrams, 14 Feb 71, sub: Lam Son 719, Abrams Papers, CMH. See, for example, "Airstrip Being Rebuilt," *New York Times*, 11 Feb 71. The report is quoted in Msg, Moorer SPECAT 3769 to McCain, Abrams, 11 Feb 71, Abrams Papers, CMH. Also see [UPI], "Newsmen Report Seeing U.S. Troops Inside Laos," *Washington Star*, 12 Feb 71; *New York Times*, 12 Feb 71, sec. 4, p. 5; *New York Times*, 13 Feb 71, sec. 3, p. 3.

[30] Msg, Abrams SPECAT to McCain, Moorer, 12 Feb 71, sub: Lam Son 719. For a public statement on the subject, see Msg, State 25754 to All Consular Posts, 16 Feb 71, 319–84–051, box 9, WNRC.

sion, as the *Washington Post* observed, the effort to obscure what was happening had succeeded only in fanning "the darkest speculations." As a result, where the Nixon administration had sought to depict LAM SON 719 as a strictly limited attempt to buy time for Vietnamization, many reporters had come to believe just the opposite, that the president intended to expand the war. While a number of newspapers accepted the official point of view, so many more questioned the evasions and circumlocutions that seemed to dog the operation that a large portion of the American public itself apparently came to believe the worst. A nationwide opinion poll taken shortly after the attack began showed that of the more than 1,000 persons questioned, 46 percent had concluded, despite vigorous official denials, that American ground forces were definitely operating in Laos.[31]

Public and Editorial Opinion

When the South Vietnamese first entered Laos, the response both around the world and in the United States nevertheless seemed mild to members of the Nixon administration, especially in comparison with the outcry that had occurred the year before, at the start of the incursion into Cambodia. Many foreign governments viewed the attack as a logical extension of the earlier cross-border operation and reacted with private expressions of approval. As expected, the People's Republic of China pledged to support North Vietnam against the "U.S. aggressor and its running dogs." The Soviet Union's official press agency, TASS, termed the attack "imperialist piracy."[32] And the Secretary General of the United Nations, U Thant, condemned the event as "one more deplorable episode in the long history of the barbarous war in Indochina."[33] Of the Western European nations, however, only Denmark and France expressed strong opposition, the one repeating a contention it had made earlier that negotiation was the only way out of Indochina and the other alleging that the invasion would merely prolong the war. Great Britain, in particular, supported the attack because it seemed likely to further the progress of Vietnamization and American withdrawals. So did the countries fighting along side the United States in South Vietnam: Australia, South Korea, and New Zealand. Japan was one of

[31] "Laos: Rear Guard or Third Front?," *Washington Post*, 9 Feb 71; Memo, Joe Shergalis for Dave McManis, 9 Feb 71, sub: Overnight Reaction to LAM SON 719, NSC files, Subject files, box 386, Situation Room Cable Summaries, 2/1/71–3/31/71, vol. V, Nixon Papers.

[32] This section is based on Memo, Theodore Eliot, Jr., Exec Sec, Department of State, for Kissinger, 8 Feb 71, sub: Foreign Reaction to Operation Lam Son; Memo, Theodore Eliot for Kissinger, 9 Feb 71, sub: U.S. and Foreign Reactions to Operation Lamson, both in Pol 27 Viet S file, FAIM/IR.

[33] Msg, U.S. Mission United Nations 379 to State, 8 Feb 71, Pol 27 Viet S file, FAIM/IR.

the few American allies to strike a middle course. Mindful, perhaps, of its own painful history in Southeast Asia but also of its close ties to the United States, it called for the withdrawal of all foreign troops from Laos but noted as well that North Vietnam had increased its military activities in that country.

Congressional reaction in the United States also appeared muted. Critics of the war in the Senate such as William Fulbright and Stuart Symington of Missouri opposed the operation and a number of Democrats expressed reservations, but Congress, as a whole, seemed prepared to give the president the benefit of a doubt as long as the incursion enhanced American withdrawals. As Max Frankel observed in the *New York Times*, hardly anyone on Capitol Hill was willing to question the president's judgment that it was desirable to choke off enemy supply lines, and all conceded that Nixon had observed the letter of the law by keeping American ground forces out of Laos. Similarly, few were willing to quarrel with the administration's use of the concept that the invasion of neutral territory was permissible in self-defense, when the government of the nation in question proved incapable of curbing the activities of a menacing belligerent. The Speaker of the House, Congressman Carl B. Albert of Oklahoma, summarized the mood. Advised by Secretaries Laird and Rogers that U.S. action in Laos would be limited to air and logistical support, he told reporters, "if that is true, I think it is prudent action on the part of our government."[34]

The press in the United States appears to have been more apprehensive than Congress, but its initial reactions fit the trend. State Department news analysts observed on 9 February that a majority of news media outlets around the country appeared to accept the validity of U.S. actions in Laos, even though many criticized the public affairs policies that continued to muddle the issue and many questioned the long-term implications of the move. Editors for the Scripps-Howard papers and the *Chicago Tribune*, normally strong supporters of administration policy, were characteristically approving, and those who opposed it such as the *St. Louis Post-Dispatch* and the *New York Times* just as adamant in their opposition. Yet many of the rest of those who were critical seemed reserved. While the *Times* thus struck a defiant pose, claiming that the operation was a "significant escalation of the war . . . that points . . . toward a wider, unending conflict," the comments of the *Baltimore Sun* and *Washington Post* seemed more typical of what most of the press was thinking. Both newspapers expressed concern that the incursion might open, as the *Post* put it, a "third war front" rather than remain a "strictly limited rear guard action." The *Sun* nevertheless accepted the president's reasons for entering Laos as valid, and the *Post* avowed that the operation made some sense, "if you believe that

[34] Max Frankel, "Purpose in Laos: A Shorter War," *New York Times*, 9 Feb 71. Quote from Memo, Eliot for Kissinger, 9 Feb 71, sub: U.S. and Foreign Reactions to Operation Lamson.

436

Vietnamization will proceed." Neither, according to the analysts, had expressed outright opposition.[35]

If portions of the press seemed willing to go along with the president as long as American ground forces stayed out of Laos, the Nixon administration had few illusions that the mood represented wholehearted support for the incursion. During the first week of the operation, State Department analysts kept a running tally of where the most newspapers in the United States stood on the issue. Time and again they pointed out that if supporters supposedly outnumbered opponents by a ratio of twelve to six, much of the support was conditional and even grudging. William Randolph Hearst, Jr., had thus swung his newspaper chain into line with administration policy, they observed, but the influential *Christian Science Monitor* was far more tentative. "Every effort should be made," the paper had asserted, "to ensure . . . that the strike does not hamper America's withdrawal plans or result in a significant widening of the war." In the same way the *Wall Street Journal* had backed the operation, but with the proviso that its decision to do so was based upon an unhappy choice that balanced "the risk of deeper involvement [in the war] against the need for an orderly withdrawal and periodic military ventures to facilitate it." So doubtful were many periodicals that, as late as 11 February, eight out of twenty-six tallied by the State Department had failed to come down for or against the operation. Since their attitude appears to have been that of the *Chicago Sun-Times*, which told its readers it hoped the attack would prove to be the last U.S. "rear-guard action" in Indochina, they probably belonged in spirit more with the opponents than they did among the twelve that had expressed support.[36]

The public reaction in the United States was as flat as that of the press. Shortly after the operation began, antiwar leaders called for mass protests around the country. The demonstrations that followed, however, failed to match the ones that had accompanied the incursion into Cambodia. According to reports in the press, where tens of thousands of Americans had marched in April 1970, only 2,000 attended rallies in New York City during the first week after the attack, and 3,000 in Boston. One thousand briefly took control of a science building at the University of Wisconsin in Madison, but only seventy occupied a computer center at Stanford University in California. In Washington, D.C., a mere 2,000 demonstrators marched on the White House while a few more threw rocks and broke windows in the city's downtown business section. Later, during May, the antiwar movement would be able to orchestrate a protest in Washington large enough to result in thousands of arrests, but by then winter had passed and enough time had elapsed to marshal support from all across

[35] Memo, Eliot for Kissinger, 9 Feb 71, sub: U.S. and Foreign Reactions to Operation Lamson.

[36] U.S. Department of State, Operations Center, Status Rpts 1, 4, and 5, for 10, 11, and 12 Feb 71, sub: Status Report on Operations in Laos and Cambodia, NSC files, Vietnam Subject files, box 80, Vietnam: Operations in Laos and Cambodia, vol. 1, Nixon Papers.

the country. That was hardly the case in February. As Donald Graham of the *Washington Post* observed, the marchers appeared to be the sort of die-hard activists "who can be turned out for a demonstration in 20-degree weather on a day-and-a-half's notice."[37]

It would be interesting to speculate that the failure of the American public to support the protests was some sort of patriotic response to a highly publicized telegram from the head of the Viet Cong delegation at the Paris peace talks, Mme. Nguyen Thi Binh, to antiwar groups in the United States. "Earnestly call you mobilize peace forces your country," the envoy had urged. "Check U.S. dangerous ventures Indochina." Earlier in the war, the Hanoi regime had inadvertently helped to divert public attention in the United States from the possible bombing of civilian targets in North Vietnam in just the same way. Attempting to make propaganda, it had insulted American sensitivities by releasing photographs of a mob in Hanoi jeering a parade of captured American pilots.[38]

Enemy support for antiwar protests in the United States, however, hardly ranked with the prisoners of war as a cause for concern to the American public. The disinterest most Americans showed for the protests, as *Time* observed, was thus probably little more than a demonstration of the president's shrewdness in calculating that it would be difficult to argue with a policy that had steadily reduced U.S. troop levels in South Vietnam. The lack of participation of American ground forces in the fighting in Laos was another obvious factor. If Americans seemed unresponsive to the antiwar movement, moreover, that was hardly an indication that they agreed either with continuation of the war, even at reduced levels, or with the effort in Laos. Over the ten months that had elapsed since the operation in Cambodia, their support for the conflict had softened progressively. By 31 January 1971, indeed, Gallup polls had revealed that 73 percent of them favored a proposal to end all U.S. troop involvement in South Vietnam by the end of the year, an increase of 18 percent from the previous September.[39]

A second poll taken after the incursion had begun was equally revealing. Presidents earlier in the war had been able to rely upon a brief surge in public support whenever they had made a difficult decision. By 1971 that was no longer the case. The new finding showed that public approval for President Nixon had actually declined 5 percentage points after the move into Laos, falling from 56 to 51 percent. The figure hardly equaled the 63 percent that had disapproved of Lyndon Johnson's han-

---

[37] Martin Weil, "Antiwar Leaders 'Outraged' Over Laos, Protests Planned," *Washington Post*, 9 Feb 71; Martin Arnold, "Thousands in U.S. Protest on Laos," *New York Times*, 11 Feb 71; Donald E. Graham, "War Protest Calls on Young," *Washington Post*, 11 Feb 71.

[38] Quote from "Indochina: The Soft-Sell Invasion," *Time*, 22 Feb 71, p. 26. See Hammond, *Public Affairs: The Military and the Media, 1962–1968*, p. 272.

[39] "Indochina: The Soft-Sell Invasion," p. 26; George Gallup, "Sentiment Grows Markedly To Quit Vietnam Before '72," *Baltimore Sun*, 31 Jan 71.

dling of the war after the Tet offensive of 1968, but it was still telling. As public opinion analyst Michael Wheeler later observed, the incursion seemed so inconsistent with the desire of most Americans to end the war that many could no longer bring themselves to muster even a token show of support. The editors of the *Omaha World-Herald* were equally pointed in their appraisal. The main difference, they said, between the "hawks," who earlier in the war had favored strong action in Vietnam, and the "doves," who had opposed American involvement, had become mostly a matter of speed. "A Hawk wants to get out of Vietnam a little more slowly than the Dove."[40]

The press continued to complain about the "mist" obscuring the incursion, but the campaign against the enemy's sanctuaries, especially in Cambodia, nevertheless appeared to be going well. On 12 February, commenting on the attack toward the Chup Plantation in Cambodia, Mike Miller of the *Washington Daily News* thus observed that South Vietnamese forces had won several significant battles, causing 600 enemy killed for 61 of their own. In the process, he said, they had driven more than sixty-four kilometers into Cambodia and had begun clearing enemy caches and supply depots.[41]

Coverage of the fighting in Laos was much more confused but, at least during the first days of the operation, hardly unfavorable to the official point of view. Focusing upon the experiences of American helicopter crews because the airmen were the only credible eyewitnesses available to newsmen, reporters carried on a running controversy with the Military Assistance Command over the number of helicopters lost in Laos. Even so, it took time for the enemy to marshal his resources and to mount a counterattack. In the interim, official South Vietnamese and American claims of progress appeared regularly both in newspapers and on television in the United States. On 12 February, for example, Walter Cronkite termed the helicopters supporting the operation "sitting ducks" for Communist gunners and claimed that some twenty-six had been destroyed or damaged during the first five days of the attack while MACV's spokesmen admitted to only ten. But, he also repeated claims by South Vietnamese President Thieu that the operation was succeeding. The *Washington Star* likewise spent considerable time reporting on helicopter losses—the highest, it said, since 1967—but also relayed South Vietnamese claims that during the first five days of the operation 759 of the enemy had died in both Laos and Cambodia to 107 South Vietnamese. The newspaper then listed the quantities of tanks, trucks, mortars, heavy

[40] Roper, "What Public Opinion Polls Said," in Braestrup, *Big Story*, 1: 687. The poll is quoted in Michael Wheeler, *Lies, Damn Lies, and Statistics: The Manipulation of Public Opinion in America* (New York: Liveright, 1976), p. 147. "Hawks Still Flying," *Omaha World-Herald*, 18 Feb 71.

[41] See, for example, Gloria Emerson, "A 'Mist' Hangs Over the Laotian Campaign," *New York Times*, 21 Feb 71, sec. 4, p. 1. Mike Miller, "Cambodia Drive Scores Too," *Washington Daily News*, 12 Feb 71.

machine guns, and ammunition that South Vietnamese forces claimed to have destroyed or captured.[42]

As the operation progressed, some reporters complained that public affairs officers had instructions to soft-pedal American support for the incursion and had failed, in particular, to acknowledge casualties among the U.S. troops supporting the attack. The majority nevertheless understood that General Abrams was adamant in his refusal to doctor casualty statistics, if only because any attempt to lie about them would lead to exposes far worse than the controversies that could result from the release of honest figures.[43] As a result, as late as 17 February, a White House news summary could report cheerfully that administration efforts to win endorsements for the success of the operation had achieved some success. According to the summary's author, ABC News anchorman Howard K. Smith had quoted official sources to the effect that the South Vietnamese had cut about half of the enemy's supply routes in Laos. Dan Rather on CBS had repeated a similar claim while also relaying a view of the situation that was well attuned to the administration's interpretation. On the same program, Marvin Kalb had broadcast, as the summary's author put it, "the Admin message circulating on . . . [Capitol] Hill; to wit: There is great military success so far, leading to greater success in the political sphere. . . . Republicans, like [Senator Robert] Dole are 'gleefully' predicting political damage to the Dems who have attacked the incursion. The only ones who may escape are those like [Senator Henry] Jackson and Kennedy who have held their verbal fire." Of the American television networks on 16 February, the summary's author noted, only NBC appeared particularly negative in its reporting. In a comment that President Nixon later underlined on his copy of the day's news summary, David Brinkley quoted unidentified sources to report that the North Vietnamese had apparently stopped the incursion "dead in its tracks" and that from 50,000 to 75,000 men would be required to close the Ho Chi Minh Trail permanently.[44]

Brinkley's comments were much closer to reality than many within either the Nixon administration or the Military Assistance Command were at the time willing to concede. For by 13 February, the North Vietnamese had begun to counterattack by launching a series of raids against fire bases General Lam had established to guard the northern flank of the force moving along Highway 9. Meanwhile, the armored brigade on the road itself was encountering dense jungle, difficult terrain, and entrenched enemy troops firing from fortifications built months in

[42] Walter Cronkite, CBS Evening News, 12 Feb 71, *Radio-TV-Defense Dialog*; "Toll for 5 Days One of Highest Since April '67," *Washington Star*, 12 Feb 71.

[43] Blumenthal, "Casualty Reports Raise Skepticism," *New York Times*, 16 Feb 71; Memo, Henkin for Doolin, 11 Feb 71.

[44] News Summary, 17 Feb 71, President's Office files, Annotated News Summaries, box 32, Feb 71, Nixon Papers. The print media handled the administration's viewpoint in much the same way as Kalb. See [UPI], "Allies in Laos Repel Attack," *Washington Star*, 17 Feb 71.

North Vietnamese counterattack on Highway 9, using a captured American tank.

advance of the offensive. As a result, although the South Vietnamese had, by 10 February, moved to Ban Dong, some eighteen kilometers into Laos and half the distance to Tchepone, they were becoming increasingly reluctant to proceed farther.[45]

The vigor of the enemy's reaction and the difficulty of the terrain in Laos provided only a partial explanation for the increasing caution that seemed to characterize the South Vietnamese attack. General Lam and his commanders had become concerned about not only the quality of the opposition they were encountering but also the amount of support their American allies were providing. Lam, in particular, was apprehensive about the extent of the damage enemy antiaircraft fire had caused to the American helicopter force and the ability of the United States to replace those losses quickly. He complained to Abrams as early as 13 February that the Military Assistance Command had promised him the support of 130 helicopters but that after only five days no more than half that number were available.[46]

In addition to the problem with combat air support and the lack of confidence it instilled, a major intelligence loss had also occurred. On 10 February, when the helicopter that had carried Burrows, Huet, and the other reporters had crashed in Laos, a second aircraft in the flight had

[45] Msg, Sutherland DNG 443 to Abrams, 14 Feb 71, Abrams Papers, CMH; Hinh, *Lam Son 719*, p. 75.
[46] Msg, Sutherland DNG 443 to Abrams, 14 Feb 71; Msg, Abrams MAC 1554 to Sutherland, 13 Feb 71, Abrams Papers, CMH.

Communist troops counterattack in Laos.

gone down as well. It had contained, in addition to the chief of South Vietnamese Army intelligence for Military Region 1, code books, signal operating instructions, and an operational map of LAM SON 719. Since no trace of either the helicopter or the intelligence material was ever found, a suspicion developed among some South Vietnamese that the enemy had obtained them. Whether that was true or not, it was clear as the operation developed that the North Vietnamese knew, sometimes many hours in advance, of virtually every tactical move the South Vietnamese made.[47]

The compromise of intelligence information was the sort of thing that could have occurred in any battle and apparently had little effect upon the conduct of the operation. Lam's complaints about helicopter support, however, were troublesome. According to the American commander in the region, Lt. Gen. James W. Sutherland, Jr., the Military Assistance Command had somehow neglected to advise the general in advance that the 130 helicopters he expected were to be used to meet all aviation requirements in Military Region 1, rather than just those of the incursion. Sutherland reassured Lam nevertheless that only 95 helicopters had been required to transport six infantry battalions on the first day of the attack and that there would never be any reason to move that many again.[48]

---

[47] Hinh, *Lam Son 719*, p. 69; Msg, Sutherland QTR 306 to Abrams, 10 Mar 71, Abrams Papers, CMH.

[48] Msg, Sutherland DNG 443 to Abrams, 14 Feb 71.

Sutherland's assurances had little effect, especially upon President Thieu, who perceived the increasing vigor of the enemy's counterattack as a major risk. From his perspective, the troops invading Laos represented not only the cream of South Vietnam's armed forces but also the main backing for his government should a coup occur. In that light, although those troops might indeed prove useful in Laos, their destruction by the enemy was unthinkable. Rather than have that happen, therefore, or to learn at the last moment that he would be unable to extract the men from Laos because American airlift resources were deficient, he instructed Lam on 13 February, only five days after the operation had begun, to halt the offensive for the time being at Ban Dong and to refrain from advancing farther into Laos. The Chief of the South Vietnamese Joint General Staff, General Cao Van Vien, assured General Abrams at the time that he envisioned only a three- to five-day delay and that the operation would proceed when Lam had cemented his lines of supply and solidified his flanks. In fact, whatever Thieu's and Lam's intentions, at that moment the South Vietnamese lost the initiative.[49]

The effects of Thieu's decision became almost immediately apparent in the daily operational summaries that the Defense Department transmitted to the White House. As the offensive stalled, reports also began to arrive which seemed to indicate that enemy logisticians were moving supplies along the Ho Chi Minh Trail and its subsidiaries almost at will and that they intended, despite increasing difficulties, to persist in their efforts until at least the end of February. On 14 February, as a result, Admiral Moorer notified Abrams that there was "high-level" interest in Lam's dispositions in Laos and requested the general's opinion on whether the South Vietnamese were "aggressively and vigorously moving out to achieve the objectives we had expected."[50]

Without mentioning Thieu's instructions to Lam—the White House would learn of them from Moorer only on 18 March—Abrams interpreted the decision to hold at Ban Dong as a temporary adjustment to battlefield conditions. Although the South Vietnamese advance had been "somewhat more deliberate than originally envisioned," he told Moorer, Lam's decision to establish adequate security along his flanks seemed prudent. In addition, the roads on the Laotian side of the border were in far worse condition than expected, many with erosion cuts twenty feet deep. Overall, despite poor flying weather in Laos and helicopter losses that were significant but less than anticipated considering the total sorties flown to date, the performance of the South Vietnamese armed forces had been "professional." With a kill ratio on the order of ten to one, Lam's troops had, indeed, blocked at least one important segment of the Ho Chi

[49] Msg, Abrams MAC 1554 to Sutherland, 13 Feb 71.

[50] Memo, Brig Gen Alexander Haig for Kissinger, 13 Feb 71, A. M. Haig Chron file, box 976, Haig Chron, Feb 9–21, 1971 [2 of 2], Nixon Papers; Telephone Extracts: White House View of Laotian Planning. Quote from Msg, Moorer SPECAT 4057 to McCain, Abrams, 14 Feb 71, sub: Lam Son 719.

Minh Trail. They would continue the move toward Tchepone, Abrams concluded, as soon as circumstances permitted, probably within the week.[51]

Henry Kissinger repeated some of Abrams' reasoning the next day, during an informal talk with reporters accompanying Nixon aboard the presidential aircraft. "The reason why the ARVN has been moving more slowly than expected," he told the newsmen, who later summarized the conversation for the rest of the White House press corps, "is that as they go, they have to set up fire bases to cover their advance and to hit the still-uncut trails ahead. The North Viets are being forced to turn west with their supplies to do an end-run [around] . . . the ARVN. We're trying to hit them with our air."[52]

Reassurances of that sort to the contrary, the situation in Laos continued to deteriorate. By 19 February, the enemy had prepared his counterattack and had launched a major assault against Lam's northernmost flank. During the three days of heavy fighting that followed, he inflicted major casualties upon the 39th South Vietnamese Ranger Battalion, forcing it to abandon the fire base it had defended and to regroup farther to the south with a second ranger battalion. In all, the unit suffered 178 killed and missing and 148 wounded. Of the survivors, 107 were still able to fight but most had suffered some sort of wound. According to official estimates, nearly 700 of the enemy died in the action, mainly as the result of air strikes and artillery fire.[53]

Following the battle from afar, the Saigon correspondents received little satisfaction from South Vietnamese briefers, who as late as 21 February were avowing that 23 rangers had been killed and 40 wounded to 639 enemy dead. The reporters nevertheless learned some details by interviewing survivors, returning helicopter pilots, and the American officers stationed at the border who kept in close touch by radio with the units in the field. They combined that information with what they received from official South Vietnamese sources, concluded that the South Vietnamese had suffered a defeat, and put the word on the wire.[54]

The first reports that appeared in the United States had an edge of criticism but concentrated mainly upon the facts as they were known. On 19 February Walter Cronkite thus told his viewers that "The first major battle of the twelve day old Laotian invasion has broken out at . . . [a]

---

[51] Memo, Jon Howe for Kissinger, 24 Mar 71, sub: White House View of Laotian Planning (February 8–March 20), covering Telephone Extracts: White House View of Laotian Planning. Quote from Msg, Abrams SPECAT to Moorer, McCain, 14 Feb 71, Abrams Papers, CMH.

[52] Pool Rpt, Pierson/Kaplow/Tully, Air Force One—Homestead to Andrews, 15 Feb 71, DDI LAM SON II–Laos file.

[53] Hinh, *Lam Son 719*, p. 79.

[54] Memo, Joe Shergalis for General Haig, 21 Feb 71, sub: Morning Cable Summary for 21 Feb 71, and Memo, Dave Clark for Jim Fazio, 21 Feb 71, sub: Afternoon Cable Summary for 21 Feb 71, both in NSC files, Subject files, box 386, Situation Room Cable Summary, 2/1/71–3/31/71, vol. V, Nixon Papers.

Helicopters refueling at Khe Sanh. Their crew members were major sources of information on Laos for reporters.

South Vietnamese artillery post about eight miles inside Laos. Casualties are . . . heavy. . . . Enemy fire today drove away medical helicopters trying to evacuate at least fifty South Vietnamese wounded. . . . Meanwhile, U.S. aircraft flying Laotian support missions took new losses."[55]

Later reports were far more critical. Craig Whitney of the *New York Times,* for one, left little doubt that a disaster had occurred. The rangers, he said, "regarded as one of the best fighting units the South Vietnamese have," had been driven off a mountaintop in Laos after heavy enemy antiaircraft fire had downed American helicopters delivering supplies and reinforcements. Although the rangers had redeemed themselves, according to American advisers, by tying down a full North Vietnamese regiment, the reporter left little doubt that the conduct of at least some of them had been less than commendable. Each time medical evacuation helicopters had landed to remove the wounded, he noted, able-bodied soldiers had rushed to board.[56]

Although Whitney's report and others like it gave a fairly close description of what had occurred, General Abrams did not believe that the battle was a setback. If the ranger battalion had incurred heavy casualties, he told Admiral Moorer, the unit, with the assistance of American tactical, artillery, and B–52 attacks, had rendered two enemy battalions

---

[55] Walter Cronkite, CBS Evening News, 19 Feb 71, *Radio-TV-Defense Dialog.*
[56] Craig Whitney, "Saigon's Rangers Driven From an Outpost in Laos," *New York Times,* 22 Feb 71. Also see [AP], "Hanoi Troops Attack," *Washington Post,* 21 Feb 71; Memo, Dave Clark for Jim Fazio, 21 Feb 71, sub: Afternoon Cable Summary for 21 Feb 71.

ineffective. When the 39th had abandoned its position, he continued, despite press reports that implied some sort of panicked debacle, the unit had withdrawn with all of its weapons and ammunition, hardly the act of a defeated force in full flight. Admiral McCain agreed with Abrams' assessment. "The impression derived from press articles was totally misleading," he later asserted. "The enemy casualties were buried in text. The orderly withdrawal of the 39th was omitted, and figures quoted were inflated in favor of the enemy."[57]

President Nixon appears to have accepted the military's interpretation. Setbacks were bound to occur, he told Moorer and Kissinger at a meeting on 25 February. All that was necessary was that the South Vietnamese fight well. For the rest, the incident involving the 39th seemed, to him, similar to what had occurred at the Battle of Antietam during the American Civil War, when both sides had bled to the advantage of the North.[58]

Nixon was nevertheless clearly unprepared to tolerate many defeats. Repeating a comment he had made the previous December, while still planning the details of the operation, he emphasized that, beyond the need to disrupt enemy logistics, the real stakes in Laos had little to do with the effort to reach Tchepone. In the end, he said, the appearance of success was at least as important as what occurred in the field. He could not allow the South Vietnamese to sustain a serious setback in Laos because that might damage President Thieu's campaign for reelection and handicap the entire effort to Vietnamize the war.[59]

Information Policy Bends

Although few within the Nixon administration expected friendly treatment at the hands of the news media, many had come to recognize by the end of February that they had to do something either to refute the allegations appearing in the press or to improve relations with the Saigon correspondents. Admiral Moorer, for one, was mostly concerned about the effect that rapid, sensational press coverage could have on the attitude of the president and his advisers. The news stories describing the withdrawal of the 39th South Vietnamese Ranger Battalion from its position in Laos had been difficult to refute, he told Abrams, because reassuring reports from the field had arrived in Washington too late to do much

[57] Msg, Abrams SPECAT to Moorer, McCain, 21 Feb 71, Abrams Papers, CMH. Quote from Msg, McCain SPECAT to Abrams, 23 Feb 71, sub: LAM SON 719, Abrams Papers, CMH.

[58] Memo for the President's file, Alexander Haig, 25 Feb 71, sub: The President's Meeting With Admiral Moorer and Henry Kissinger in the President's Oval Office (12:05–1:09 p.m.), NSC files, Jon Howe Chron files, box 1077, Feb 71, Nixon Papers.

[59] Ibid.

good. To remedy that problem in the future, he said, Abrams would have to issue not only the usual weekly reports on the status of the incursion but also special "flash" assessments that evaluated anything unusual that occurred. In that way, the information would be readily available to counteract the pessimism of the press.[60]

Secretary Laird was likewise concerned but believed that the best solution rested with the reestablishment of official credibility in the field. Concerned that complaints about news restrictions had tainted many articles and commentaries that would otherwise have been either neutral or favorable to the official point of view, he told Abrams that newsmen had to be able to see for themselves—the more, the better. Two steps to remedy the situation seemed imperative, he continued. First, reporters in South Vietnam had to become the source for authoritative news of the operation rather than Washington correspondents who had access to high-level briefings but knew little of events firsthand. To achieve that end, Abrams; his deputy, General Frederick C. Weyand; Ambassador Bunker; and other knowledgeable officials whose word carried weight with reporters had to hold regular background briefings to explain what was happening. Secondly, the Military Assistance Command had to remove the major point of contention between itself and the Saigon correspondents by allowing newsmen to fly into Laos on American as well as South Vietnamese helicopters.[61]

The entire U.S. mission in Saigon was already deeply involved in the sort of effort Laird had described. During the previous two weeks, indeed, military and civilian public affairs officers had discreetly but continually provided newsmen they considered reliable with material designed to demonstrate that the incursion was succeeding. Meanwhile, both Abrams and Weyand had held background sessions for reporters and bureau chiefs representing such important periodicals and newspapers as *Time, Newsweek,* the *New Yorker,* and the *Washington Post.* In addition, at American urging, the South Vietnamese had held at least one major backgrounder at MACV headquarters and, on 20 February, had transported the representatives of the Associated Press, the *New York Times,* the *Baltimore Sun,* the *Christian Science Monitor,* and other print and electronic media more than twenty kilometers into Laos to inspect a forward fire base.[62]

Despite those efforts Abrams promised to do more. Overall, he told Laird, the Military Assistance Command had "studiously avoided releasing information on ARVN operations so as not to usurp . . . [South

[60] Msg, Moorer JCS SPECAT 4610 to Abrams, 23 Feb 71, sub: LAM SON 719, Abrams Papers, CMH.

[61] Msg, Laird SPECAT 4539 to Abrams, 22 Feb 71, Abrams Papers, CMH.

[62] Msg, Bunker Saigon 163 to Kissinger, 23 Feb 71, NSC files, Backchannels, box 412, Amb. Bunker, Saigon, 1971, Nixon Papers; Msg, Abrams SPECAT to Secretary of Defense, 23 Feb 71, sub: Public Affairs in Support of RVNAF Operations, Abrams Papers, CMH.

Vietnamese] release authority or inadvertently disclose information the ARVN considers essential to . . . troop security." He would not change that policy, he said, but to quiet speculation he would redouble efforts to advise Lam to make legitimate news available to the press. In the same way, although he was unwilling to give reporters the sort of unrestricted access to helicopter transportation that they enjoyed in South Vietnam, he promised to dedicate a helicopter to their use. With the dimensions of the American effort to assist the South Vietnamese in Laos well known to the enemy, he also agreed to allow the U.S. Seventh Air Force to fly reporters on fixed wing, AC–130 and AC–119 gunship flights and to release damage estimates for bombing missions flown in the area of the fighting.[63]

True to his word, during a meeting with Thieu later that day, Abrams joined with Ambassador Bunker in emphasizing the necessity to improve relations with the news media by quickening the flow of information to the Saigon correspondents. As a result, Thieu's press secretary shortly thereafter agreed to allow his briefers to meet each day with their American counterparts to discuss the handling of the information they released. He also accepted a suggestion that General Lam replace his briefer at Quang Tri, who spoke only hesitant English, with a more sophisticated officer fluent in the language.[64]

The Military Assistance Command, for its part, dedicated a helicopter to the use of the Saigon correspondents on 25 February and began to transport reporters into Laos on a regular basis. By 22 March the aircraft had made over one hundred trips. At the same time, the command also began to announce aircraft losses in Laos and to release statistics on the types of helicopter missions it was flying. On 2 March it went so far as to reveal that the enemy had launched several surface-to-air missiles in an attempt to thwart American air attacks.[65]

As the Saigon correspondents began to move into Laos, their reports became, at least in the eyes of the Military Assistance Command, far more balanced and factual than in the past. Official credibility had fallen so low, however, that nothing the command could have done would have sufficed to improve the attitude of the press. *Time* thus avowed in its 8 March edition that correspondents had been "virtually stymied" in their attempt to cover the incursion and that the Military Assistance Command had, in fact, prevented reporters from interviewing American helicopter pilots at Khe Sanh by surrounding the pilots' operations center with barbed wire and prohibiting entrance to all civilians. Meanwhile, columnist Marquis Childs charged that if the American news media had finally received permission to ride on U.S. helicopters,

[63] Msg, Abrams SPECAT to Secretary of Defense, 23 Feb 71, sub: Public Affairs in Support of RVNAF Operations.

[64] Msg, Bunker Saigon 163 to Kissinger, 23 Feb 71.

[65] Msg, Leonard MAC 2310 to Henkin, 4 Mar 71, DDI Press Support for Lam Son 719 file.

no reporters had entered Laos on the ground because the South Vietnamese command continued to resent the presence of newsmen on the battlefield. What was better, Childs asked: the over-reporting of zealous young correspondents or the sort of censorship that allowed only the official interpretation to pass?[66]

Although there had never been any concerted effort on the part of the Military Assistance Command to cut off contacts between reporters and pilots at Khe Sanh, official spokesmen allowed the allegation in *Time* to pass without comment because it possessed little moral force. As press reports from the field continually demonstrated, reporters were capable of meeting with helicopter pilots at many locations on the base, not only at the air operations center, and did so continually.

The comment by Childs was a different matter. Jerry Friedheim immediately wrote the columnist to inform him that a number of reporters had, in fact, entered Laos by road, among them, a television crew headed by Howard Tuckner of ABC News.[67]

Friedheim's rejoinder was beside the point. Whatever the access of the press to units in the field, if the incursion had been going well its success would have come increasingly to dominate news dispatches. The sources reporters considered most credible—helicopter pilots, friendly South Vietnamese officers, American advisers, and casualties under treatment at medical facilities—would have corroborated the word released in official communiques. Instead, the opposite occurred. A stream of cautiously positive commentary seemed constantly to emanate from official sources while the news circulating privately became darker by the day.

Helicopter Losses and Other Controversies

Throughout the operation, reporters thus complained that the Military Assistance Command had persisted in minimizing helicopter losses in order either to downplay the American role in the fighting or to make the incursion seem more successful than the facts warranted. To that end, they said, the command would admit to the destruction only of those aircraft it failed to recover from Laos while counting as damaged any it could retrieve, whatever their condition. As late as mid-March, when the facts were known to all, official sources were still admitting only to the loss of 50 helicopters while pilots estimated that 119 had gone down during the first week of the attack alone. At the end of the incursion, indeed, Walter Cronkite announced that if official reports acknowledged 103 heli-

---

[66] "Frustration Near the Front," *Time*, 8 May 71. The Childs report appeared in the *Washington Post* on 3 March. A summary is attached to Ltr, Friedheim to Marquis Childs, 3 Mar 71, DDI Press Support for Lam Son 719 file.
[67] Ibid.

449

copters as lost and 500 more as damaged, sources available to CBS News had revealed that at least 200 of the aircraft listed as damaged would never fly again.[68]

The Military Assistance Command attempted to explain the damage criteria it used and even resorted to a backgrounder on the subject by General Abrams to quell the outcry, but the effort had little effect. The clamor continued, if only because, as Col. Perry Stevens later confirmed, reporters had some grounds for their complaint. With helicopter losses exceptionally heavy on many days—more than 111 had been nonoperational for various reasons, Stevens said, after the first day of fighting—the Military Assistance Command had decided, rather than commit an outright lie, simply to allow bureaucracy to take its course. Adhering as closely as possible to the definitions that damage assessment teams used, official spokesmen thus counted as destroyed only those aircraft that were irretrievable. Those that were unflyable fell into the damaged category until mechanics had time either to repair them or to rate them as total losses. Since heavily damaged aircraft were sometimes ferried to overworked repair facilities at Cam Ranh Bay or in the United States for evaluation, the change in determination could take months. By the time it did, so the reasoning went, reporters were bound to have lost interest. Lightly damaged aircraft that could return to duty with minor repairs never entered into official tallies at all. If they had, Colonel Leonard added, their presence "could only have led to sensational reporting of aircraft damage and misleading information on aircraft availability."[69]

Although the policy fit well with the Nixon administration's desire to play down the American role in LAM SON 719 and to depict the South Vietnamese effort as a success, the outcry that accompanied it would almost certainly have led to some compromise approach, but for another, more solid reason. Despite assurances by Abrams and Sutherland to Lam and his generals, the high volume of helicopter losses during the first two weeks of the operation forced the Military Assistance Command to curtail for a time resupply, medical evacuation, and combat assault missions in support of the troops in Laos. Of the 88 AH–1G Cobra and 44 UH–1C Huey gunships programmed to assist the operation, only 25 Cobras and 8 Hueys were in flyable condition on 23 February. The flow of replacement aircraft from elsewhere in South Vietnam was meanwhile so slow that a substantial decline in combat effectiveness had occurred. Although the condition was temporary and both the South Vietnamese and the enemy clearly understood that American helicopter losses had been great, for

[68] This section is based on Research Rpt, Ann David, Helicopters, LAM SON 719 [U.S. Army Center of Military History], CMH files. Also see Harry Reasoner, "ABC Correspondents Discuss Job of Reporting on the War," ABC News, 2 Apr 71, *Radio-TV-Defense Dialog*. "ABC Round Table on Laos," *Nation*, 19 Apr 71, 212:486–88; Walter Cronkite, CBS Evening News, 9 Apr 71, *Radio-TV-Defense Dialog*.

[69] Interv, author with Col Perry Stevens, 25 Apr 89. Some within the press understood the system. See Richard Egan, "Americans Carry a Big Umbrella for Lam Son 719," *National Observer*, 22 Feb 71. Quote from Ltr, Leonard to the author, 17 Oct 90.

military commanders to confirm that fact through news releases would have been unthinkable.[70]

The Deputy Commander of U.S. Army, Vietnam, Lt. Gen. William J. McCaffrey, later explained that in light of the sorties flown—32,000 between 26 February and 4 March alone—helicopter losses in Laos and adjoining areas had been high but hardly unexpected. Considering the damage the more than 700 aircraft involved had caused to the enemy, McCaffrey continued, the record of their service had been "most impressive." In addition to transporting tens of thousands of passengers and untold tons of food and ammunition, they had accounted for a minimum of 1,500 enemy dead in Laos and an unknown but large number of tanks disabled or destroyed. In contrast, by 16 March, the cost in American crew members amounted to 31 killed and 31 missing.[71]

In general, Bunker, Abrams, and the other Americans directly involved in the operation appear to have believed that even with less than perfect assistance from the South Vietnamese the enormous firepower the United States could bring to bear in Laos would swing the advantage to their side. They thus pressed Lam constantly to bring in reinforcements and to take the initiative but in their reports to Washington agencies expressed only optimism for the future of the operation. Citing heavy bomb tonnages, sortie rates, and enemy casualty statistics, they took it for granted that Lam would move back onto the offensive just as soon as the weather improved, the engineers finished filling cuts and ruts in the roadway on Highway 9, or the South Vietnamese overcame some other difficulty. "In operations of this kind," they cautioned, "One cannot be tied to preconceived ideas of what might be thought of as ideal procedures. A posture has to be maintained flexible enough to adapt to fluid conditions which may be governed by weather, terrain or changes in enemy tactics."[72]

Reassurances of that sort to the contrary, it seemed clear to Henry Kissinger by 23 February that the operation in Laos had bogged down and that substantial losses were occurring. Aware that the president was under extreme pressure to continue withdrawals whatever the ability of the South Vietnamese to survive, he spoke of his concerns in a telephone conversation with Admiral Moorer. "I do not understand what Abrams is doing," he said. "I think the units north of . . . [Highway] 9 are just dug in in a static position in the sort of thing the North Vietnamese know how to fight. And I don't see anything aggressive [to the] south of . . . 9 either. If we are getting run out of Laos, which will happen, I promise you the president will collapse on Vietnam." Referring to a 22 February report

---

[70] Msg, Sutherland QTR 135 to McCaffrey, 23 Feb 71, Abrams Papers, CMH.

[71] Msg, Lt Gen McCaffrey, DCG, USARV, ARV 946 to Lt Gen Williams, ACSFOR, 16 Mar 71, McCaffrey Papers, CMH.

[72] Extracts from Backchannel Messages Concerning Outlook for Operation and Future Plans, 21 Mar 71, app. II to Telephone Extracts: White House View of Laotian Planning. Quote from Msg, Bunker 341 to Kissinger, 3 Mar 71, NSC files, Backchannels, box 412, Amb. Bunker, Saigon, 1971, Nixon Papers.

from Abrams, Kissinger continued that "I'm not showing this cable to the president because he'll blow his fuse. This gives statistics on B–52 sorties. . . . It's a tactical report. The president doesn't give a damn. What we want to know is, 'is he cutting the road.' . . . If we are getting our pants beaten off here, we've had it in Vietnam for psychological reasons. . . . I am talking to you as a friend. I have told the president everything is great."[73]

Hearing from Moorer that "Everything is not great, but [the South Vietnamese] . . . are establishing good logistics bases," Kissinger turned to General Westmoreland for an independent perspective on what was happening. What he heard in return only deepened his concern. Hesitant to pass judgment on his successor's actions, Westmoreland nevertheless stated that the number of troops committed to Laos seemed insufficient for so difficult and ambitious a task and suggested that delays in mounting the operation had allowed the enemy time to mass for a counterattack. In reference to a proposal by Thieu that Lam launch the airborne assault on Tchepone whatever the situation along Highway 9, he warned that any attack of the sort would be dangerous, given the clear resolve of the North Vietnamese to oppose the incursion at all costs and the major resources they had devoted to their response. Instead, the South Vietnamese should hold back until they could stabilize the situation along the road and dominate its intersections with the various tributaries of the Ho Chi Minh Trail. In that way they could cut enemy lines of communication to the east of Tchepone, continue to inflict heavy casualties upon enemy units without risking unnecessary losses of their own, and wreak the utmost damage upon Communist supply caches scattered south and east of Tchepone.[74]

To a question about the quality of the officers leading the incursion, Westmoreland affirmed that he had confidence in Lam but noted as well that there had been a time during 1964 when the general had proved "virtually useless." He could hardly predict, he said, how the other South Vietnamese commanders would perform because he had never seen any of them operate under duress, but he knew the commander of the Airborne Division and doubted he could "produce in a pinch." As for the troops, South Vietnamese units had sometimes failed to "behave themselves" when confronted by heavy enemy pressure. Since they would undoubtedly face many difficulties in Laos, Lam should keep ready replacements on hand and prepare to rotate battalions as the need arose.

Apprised of Westmoreland's evaluation, Secretary Laird responded by criticizing the general's timing. He had briefed Westmoreland and the

---

[73] Extracts from Telephone Conversations Between Dr. Kissinger and Defense Department Officers, attachment to Telephone Extracts: White House View of Laotian Planning.

[74] Quote from Ibid. This section is based on MFR, Westmoreland, 25 Feb 71, sub: Meeting With Dr. Kissinger at the White House, 1030 Hours, 23 Feb 71, Westmoreland History, bk. 39, tab 5, CMH files.

other members of the Joint Chiefs on the operation, he told Kissinger on 25 February, and he had expected them to speak up before the program went forward rather than afterwards. Meanwhile, Admiral Moorer attempted to dilute the effect of Westmoreland's candor by reassuring both the president and Kissinger that Lam was an able if cautious performer and that the forces in Laos were largely unshaken despite some reverses.[75]

President Nixon accepted Moorer's explanation but obviously intended to prepare for any eventuality. Upset with television reports that the incursion had stalled, that the South Vietnamese had failed to cut enemy supply lines, and that the White House was putting an optimistic face on it all, he suggested that official

Damaged U.S. helicopter airlifted from Laos.

spokesmen had placed too much emphasis upon Tchepone as a goal and had exaggerated the success of the South Vietnamese in cutting the Ho Chi Minh Trail. Since a backlash would undoubtedly set in if Lam failed to attain those goals, he therefore instructed Moorer to take up the problem at the next meeting of the National Security Council. Given the youth of the Saigon correspondents and what he saw as the radically antiestablishment inclinations of many, he had little confidence that much could be done. He hoped, however, to dilute any problems that arose by reemphasizing that the South Vietnamese were in Laos only to disrupt enemy supply lines and that Tchepone was at best a minor station along the way. Given the imagery that had arisen in the press, he observed, almost as an afterthought, "It would be a great public relations coup if the ARVN actually reached Tchepone, although they should not attempt it purely for that reason."[76]

[75] Telephone Extracts: White House View of Laotian Planning; Memo, Alexander Haig for the President's file, 25 Feb 71, sub: The President's Meeting With Admiral Moorer and Henry Kissinger in the President's Oval Office (12:05–1:09 p.m.), NSC files, Jon Howe Chron files, Feb 71, box 1077, Nixon Papers.

[76] Telephone Extracts: White House View of Laotian Planning. Also see Memo, Jon Howe for Haig, 24 Feb 71, sub: Items of Interest, NSC files, Jon Howe Chron files, box 1077, Feb 71, Nixon Papers. Quote from Memo, Haig for the President's file, 25 Feb 71, sub: The President's Meeting With Admiral Moorer and Henry Kissinger in the President's Oval Office (12:05–1:09 p.m.).

Shortly after Nixon gave his instructions to Moorer, General Abrams stressed in conversations with newsmen that the operation in Laos sought only to destroy enemy stockpiles and that he had never intended for it to seal off the Ho Chi Minh Trail. Nixon himself repeated the theme at a 4 March news conference and other official spokesmen also took it up. Reporters immediately perceived that a change in rhetoric had occurred. A few interpreted the development as an indication that the administration had modified its goals in Laos, but most accepted the new emphasis with little question. During the days that followed, indeed, they made disruption of the trail one of the criteria by which they judged the success of the operation.[77]

If the president and his advisers thus succeeded in emphasizing limited goals, they did little to dilute the optimism that continued to characterize official statements. At a 24 February briefing, for example, Secretary Laird thought nothing of denying that Lam's forces had bogged down in Laos. The troops had paused deliberately, he said, in an attempt to determine the location of the enemy's next attack. In the same way, President Nixon himself avowed at his news conference that General Abrams had assured him "the South Vietnamese by themselves can hack it. And they can give a better account of themselves even than the North Vietnamese." That meant, he said, that "our withdrawal program . . . is a success and we can continue on schedule and we trust even ahead of schedule."[78]

Despite advice from the White House staff cautioning against any attempt to gauge the success of the operation by enumerating the vast quantities of enemy equipment destroyed or captured in Laos, South Vietnamese and American briefers also continued to measure the operation in those terms. One B–52 strike, they thus noted at a 24 February briefing, had exploded more than 500 tons of ammunition. A second, several days later, had ignited 300 tons more. Fixed-wing and helicopter strikes had likewise eliminated 120 supply and weapons caches, 330 vehicles, 115 bunkers, 420 structures, and 35 gun positions. Meanwhile, the troops on the ground had destroyed four enemy oil pipelines running parallel to the Ho Chi Minh Trail. To strengthen the theme while providing human interest, the Military Assistance Command also brought forward Sp4c. Dennis J. Fuji, who had been shot down in Laos during the fighting around the 39th South Vietnamese Ranger Battalion and had stayed with the unit to treat the wounded after several attempts at rescue had failed. A born actor who sensed instinctively that reporters would appreciate youthful enthusiasm, Fuji made a number of positive comments about the work of

[77] "Red Tanks Hit So. Viet Post in Laos," *Chicago Tribune*, 26 Feb 71; "Transcript of President Nixon's News Conference," *New York Times*, 5 Mar 71; White House News Summary, 26 Feb 71, President's Office files, Annotated News Summaries, box 32, Feb 71, Nixon Papers. Also see Clarence Wyatt, "Truth From the Snares of Crisis, The American Press in Vietnam" (M.A. diss., University of Kentucky, 1984), pp. 73f.

[78] Msg, JCS 4851 to Unified and Specified Commands, 25 Feb 71, sub: News Briefing by SECDEF Melvin R. Laird at Pentagon, Wednesday, February 24, 1971, 319–84–051, box 9, WNRC. Quotes from "Transcript of President Nixon's News Conference."

South Vietnamese medics and the hard fighting of the rangers. His remarks received good play in the press.[79]

So many problems nevertheless remained in Laos that newsmen could still hardly contain their doubts. John Scali of ABC, who would shortly join the Nixon administration as a troubleshooter, thus reported on 24 February that a high-level White House source had told him the odds for success in Laos had been calculated at only 53 to 48. Correspondents for NBC underscored the bitter conclusion of some South Vietnamese that they had allowed themselves to become pawns of the United States by entering Laos. Marvin Kalb contended on CBS that U.S. intelligence had seriously underestimated the strength of North Vietnamese artillery and antiaircraft firepower. While those comments were appearing, a whole series of reports also began to arise charging that major combat had erupted around another landing zone in Laos known as Hill 31 and that South Vietnamese forces had once more begun to falter.[80]

The record was not totally unfavorable to the administration's point of view. Crosby Noyes charged in the *Washington Star*, for example, that "reporting on the war gets worse every day," and columnist Kenneth Crawford observed that the youthful correspondents reporting from Saigon were "sometimes wrong in their strategic and tactical judgments and simplistic in their politics." President Nixon was nonetheless so angered by it all that he ordered H. R. Haldeman to begin outlining another assault on the news media for Vice President Agnew to deliver.[81]

The Operation Falters

Whatever the efforts of the Nixon administration to counter the word of its critics, by the end of February a mood of pessimism had clearly begun to spread within American official circles. On 24 February intelligence reports revealed that, despite the best South Vietnamese and American efforts, the enemy's engineers had completed a new spur to the

[79] Henry Kamm, "Main Allied Base of Laos Drive Hit," *New York Times*, 25 Feb 71; Interv, author with Col Perry Stevens, 25 Apr 89. President Nixon received full details on the Fuji story. See Annotated News Summary, 25 Feb 71, President's Office files, Annotated News Summaries, box 32, Feb 71, Nixon Papers.

[80] The television reports are noted in Memo, Mort Allen for Haldeman, 25 Feb 71, sub: Notations for February 25 News Summary, White House Special files, Buchanan, Chron files, box 1, Feb 71, Nixon Papers; White House News Summary for 28 Feb 71, President's Office files, Annotated News Summaries, box 32, Feb 71, Nixon Papers. Also see Marvin Kalb, CBS Evening News, 26 Feb 71, *Radio-TV-Defense Dialog*; Alvin Shuster, "South Vietnamese Base in Laos Reported Under Heavy Attack," *New York Times*, 26 Feb 71.

[81] Crosby S. Noyes, "Reporting on the War Gets Worse Every Day," *Washington Star*, undated clipping, CMH files; Kenneth Crawford, "Washington on the Delaware—With the Media," *Miami Herald*, 27 Feb 71; Handwritten Note on White House News Summary, 28 Feb 71, President's Office files, Annotated News Summaries, box 32, Feb 71, Nixon Papers.

Ho Chi Minh Trail that bypassed the area of the fighting. As a result, although necessarily slowed by the incursion, the flow of enemy supplies appeared to be continuing. The next day, the vigorous commander of the operation's little-noticed Cambodian segment, Lt. Gen. Do Cao Tri, died in a helicopter accident along with veteran correspondent Francois Sully. Shortly thereafter, the effort he had led with considerable success began to slow because his replacement, Lt. Gen. Nguyen Van Minh, proved unprepared to take the slightest risk. The situation at Hill 31 likewise continued to deteriorate. Although General Lam assured reporters that his forces remained in possession of at least a portion of the base, word soon arrived from the Military Assistance Command that the enemy appeared to have overrun the position and that he had captured 2 full colonels, 14 lower ranking officers, and up to 100 enlisted men. The news was hardly more encouraging from areas where the fighting was less intense. Although the performance of the 1st South Vietnamese Infantry Division and its commanders was outstanding, General Abrams told Moorer, that of the Airborne Division and the 1st Armored Task Force was worrisome. The troops fought well but their leaders, who had begun to squabble among themselves, were unimpressive.[82]

As concern mounted, Henry Kissinger complained to Secretary Laird that the briefings he received from the Joint Chiefs were at times uninformative. "I got a briefing this morning," he noted in a telephone conversation on 25 February, "and they didn't mention Hill 31 and I pick it up in the newspapers and if someone asks me I don't know what's going on."[83] Even so, enough information was available for Kissinger's aide W. R. Smyser to comment the next day that

The President's decision to stake much on the success of this program, and thus of his Administration, on two foreign divisions was an example of cool and confident judgment. However, I am appalled to read in the daily reports that only 10,000 ARVN soldiers are actually in Laos. This means that we have engaged ourselves in a critical battle with exactly one percent of our assets—in fact, less than one percent if you count the American forces. I know of no successful commander in history who has ever done that. . . . The resources which have so far been dedicated to this effort are almost disastrously inferior to its significance.[84]

As Smyser had observed, the enemy was indeed capable of massing almost four times as many troops in Laos as the South Vietnamese had

---

[82] Memo, Joe Shergalis for Jim Fazio, 24 Feb 71, sub: Morning Cable Summary for 24 Feb 71, and Memo, McManus for Clark, 25 Feb 71, sub: Morning Cable Summary for 25 Feb 71, both in NSC files, Subject files, box 386, Situation Room Cable Summaries, 2/1/71–3/31/71, Nixon Papers; Msg, Abrams SPECAT to Moorer, 26 Feb 71, sub: LAM SON 719, Abrams Papers, CMH.

[83] Telephone Extracts: White House View of Laotian Planning.

[84] Memo, W. R. Smyser for Dr. Kissinger, 26 Feb 71, sub: Quality of ARVN on Operation Lam Son, NSC files, Vietnam Subject file, box 84, Special Operations file, Feb 9–28, 1971, vol. 5, Nixon Papers.

mustered. That General Abrams and his planners might have missed that fact in preparing for the operation, however, seemed unthinkable at the time. From their standpoint the attack was a raid. As such, it hardly required the huge numbers of troops that would have been necessary if Lam and his commanders had sought to hold the territory they had entered for a long period of time. Instead, as Moorer and Kissinger had avowed during meetings prior to the incursion, the presence of those forces in Laos would threaten the enemy's lifeline to the south and oblige him to respond. When he did, he would expose himself to American fire-power. There was an element of danger in the approach, Ambassador Bunker told Kissinger on 3 March, if only because the enemy needed the Ho Chi Minh Trail to survive and obviously intended to protect it at any cost. Yet President Thieu was just as aware that his own reputation and political future were at stake in Laos and thus seemed resolved to see the attack through to a successful conclusion.[85]

Both Bunker and Abrams blamed the character of the news media's reporting for the credibility problems they were experiencing. Reporters had gotten the impression that Tchepone was the operation's principal objective, Bunker said, and once that fact had become "lodged in their minds," when progress toward Tchepone had stopped, they had concluded much too readily that the attack had bogged down. In fact, the United States and South Vietnam had all along sought only to disrupt the enemy's supply and infiltration network where it converged in the area between Tchepone and the border. Although heavy fighting remained ahead, Bunker concluded, paraphrasing a comment by General Abrams,

We once fought the *NVA 9th Division* around Saigon, and we are now fighting it in Cambodia; we once fought the *NVA 308th* and *320th Divisions* around Hue and Da Nang, and they are now being fought in Laos. The enemy has lost heavily in tanks, weapons, ammunition and other materiel. His POL pipeline has been cut. Friendly casualties reported to date are 393 KIA and may be higher. Enemy casualties are reported as 3,742 KIA. Even discounting this figure by a substantial percentage, it is clear that the enemy has suffered heavily.[86]

Whatever the suffering of the enemy, from the perspective of the Nixon administration, the climate of opinion in the United States was growing increasingly hostile to the incursion. If the operation failed, Smyser thus told Kissinger's military aide, Brig. Gen. Alexander Haig, who was preparing to depart for a fact-finding trip to South Vietnam, the event would destroy the small domestic political base that remained for further campaigns in Indochina and call the entire Vietnamization program into question. "The malaise about the war is spreading wider and deeper," he said. "Domestic opinion is very sensitive to anything

[85] Ibid.
[86] Msg, Bunker 341 to Kissinger, 3 Mar 71, NSC files, Backchannels, box 412, Amb. Bunker, Saigon, 1971, Nixon Papers.

which smacks of a setback or which our TV commentators can so describe."[87]

On 1 March the Gallup poll corroborated Smyser's contention that public support was wearing thin by revealing that, despite the president's statements to the contrary, Americans believed two-to-one that the Laotian incursion would lengthen rather than shorten the war. On the same day, news media analysts at the White House warned the president that if the press continued to give wide play to official statements of optimism, the great bulk of news reporting and commentary also expressed a view that progress had hardly been as great as the administration claimed.[88] That evening, radical antiwar activists in Washington added to the sense of urgency surrounding the issue by setting off a bomb in the Senate wing of the U.S. Capitol.

Word of the atmosphere spreading in the United States made its way to South Vietnam with Haig if by no other means. A handwritten aide memoire that the officer carried to Saigon reminded him to advise Bunker and Abrams that "Pres. is determined to draw down rapidly—Sec. Def. is encouraging and politics impelling."[89]

Adding to the difficulty of the moment, if the Military Assistance Command's background briefings for the press continued to stress enemy losses and the overall success of the operation, word from the field remained mixed. On 2 March, in what appeared a burst of renewed aggressiveness, General Lam thus announced preparations for an airborne assault upon Tchepone and launched a series of moves to consolidate security along Highway 9 and to occupy or reinforce fire support bases to the north and south of the target. The development heartened American commanders, who took it to mean that the South Vietnamese would press forward. Yet on the same day, despite the urging of Abrams and Sutherland, Lam also refused to reinforce his units in Laos with a third division. The withdrawal of a force that large from its duties in South Vietnam, he told Sutherland, could only degrade the country's security and the progress of the pacification program. Soon afterwards, alluding vaguely to "the politics involved with the Airborne Division," he also confirmed a decision by President Thieu to begin withdrawing that unit from Laos within the next ten days.[90]

[87] Memo, Dick Smyser for General Haig, n.d., sub: Your Conversation With Amb. Bunker on Political Initiatives, NSC files, A. M. Haig Special file, box 1013, Haig SEA Trip, Mar 71 [2 of 2], Nixon Papers.

[88] George Gallup, "Americans Feel Invasion of Laos Will Lengthen War," *Baltimore Sun*, 1 Mar 71; Weekend News Review, 1 Mar 71, President's Office files, Annotated News Summaries, box 32, Mar 71, Nixon Papers.

[89] Haig, Handwritten Note, n.d. [Mar 71], sub: Talker: Abrams/Bunker, NSC files, A. M. Haig Special file, box 1012, Haig SEA Trip, Mar 71 [2 of 2], Nixon Papers.

[90] See, for example, Memo, 2 Mar 71, sub: MACV Background Briefing To Up-date the Progress of Operation Lam Son 719 and Operation Toan Thang 01/71 and a Summary of Enemy Reaction to Date, DDI Lam Son II–Laos file. Hinh, *Lam Son 719*, pp. 89–97. Quote from Msg, Sutherland QTR 237 to Abrams, 2 Mar 71, Abrams Papers, CMH.

As if that were not enough, General Sutherland informed Abrams on 2 March that he was concerned about discipline and morale within the Airborne Division. The unit's commanding general had developed a defeatist attitude, he said. In addition, during a recent attempt to resupply Fire Support Base 30 to the north of Highway 9, at that time under heavy enemy attack, helicopters had been able to extract only 10 wounded and 4 dead because 94 soldiers, including the base commander, had forced their way aboard.[91]

As the operation lengthened, news stories tended to reflect the ambiguities Sutherland and Abrams were encountering. Although reports appeared regularly, for example, that the campaign in Laos was faltering and that the South Vietnamese were suffering their most severe losses since the Tet offensive of 1968, editors and producers seemed continually to waver between whether the incursion was going well or poorly. On 27 February Edwin Newman thus noted on the NBC Saturday Evening News that, despite some of the heaviest fighting of the war, South Vietnamese spokesmen had implied that Communist forces were running away. "We would like to see the enemy stand and fight with us, and the enemy is not doing what we expected him to do." Shortly thereafter, on the same program, correspondent George Lewis nevertheless suggested that South Vietnamese officials were of two minds. One had told reporters that the Army had gone as far as it intended to go in Laos, leading to speculation on the part of the newsmen present that Thieu planned an early end to the operation, while others had said their forces were digging in rather than preparing to pull out. In the same way, the Associated Press repeated claims by official American spokesmen that the incursion had disrupted Hanoi's plans for a dry season offensive. The piece, however, also relayed allegations by an unidentified American source that the South Vietnamese Army had hardly improved as much as some American generals were saying and that some of its units had abandoned their wounded and "bugged out."[92]

On 6 March the South Vietnamese appeared to settle the question of whether they were going to stay or depart by launching their air assault into Tchepone. The enemy had received at least thirty-six hours' advance notice of the move, but the preparations for the attack were so skillfully laid that B–52, tactical air, and gunship sorties eliminated most of the opposition. As a result, the first troops to land encountered only sporadic gunfire and almost immediately began to find large numbers of enemy dead. President Nixon was so buoyed by the messages he received from

---

[91] Msg, Sutherland QTR 197 to Abrams, 2 Mar 71, Abrams Papers, CMH.

[92] See, for example, Other Laos Developments, White House News Summary, 27 February–6 March, 8 March 71, President's Office files, Annotated News Summaries, box 32, Mar 71, Nixon Papers; and Iver Peterson, "U.S. Copter Pilots in Laos Invasion Question the Risks," *New York Times*, 7 Mar 71. NBC Saturday Evening News, 27 Feb 71, *Radio-TV-Defense Dialog*; [AP], "Laos, Cambodia Thrusts Seen Foiling Red Plans," *Washington Star*, 2 Mar 71.

Abrams and Bunker the next day that he commended the two for the excellence of their reporting. Passing the compliment to Bunker, Henry Kissinger noted, "The president made the additional comment that our worst enemy seems to be the press."[93]

[93] Msg, Sutherland QTR 306 to Abrams, 10 Mar 71, Abrams Papers, CMH; Handwritten Draft Memo, Haig for Kissinger, n.d. [Apr 71], sub: Lamson 719, NSC files, A. M. Haig Special file, box 1013, Haig SEA Trip, 14–21 Mar 71 [2 of 2], Nixon Papers; Hinh, *Lam Son 719*, pp. 97f. Quote from Msg, Kissinger WHS 1012 to Bunker, 9 Mar 71, NSC files, Backchannels, box 412, Amb. Bunker, Saigon, 1971, Nixon Papers.

19

Saving Face

The assault on Tchepone came at a difficult moment for the U.S. Army and the Nixon administration. The trial of Lieutenant Calley was reaching a climax, giving rise to a swarm of stories in the press on the My Lai massacre and its aftermath. Articles and commentaries were continuing to appear on the illegal activities of former Sergeant Major of the Army Wooldridge. Official spokesmen had also just confirmed that Army investigators had conducted covert surveillance of private American citizens and organizations since 1968 in order to anticipate possibly violent antiwar protests. Meanwhile, both the Nixon administration and the military services were smarting from a stinging documentary by CBS News that criticized the Defense Department's wide-ranging public affairs program. Titled "The Selling of the Pentagon" and broadcast on 23 February 1971, the telecast claimed that the military services were spending up to $190 million per year—more than the annual news budgets of the three television networks combined—on public relations activities that extolled the violence of war, advertised expensive weapon systems, and presented biased opinions as fact.[1]

To make matters worse, Secretary of Defense Laird acknowledged on 4 March that Defense Department spokesmen had used misleading evidence to illustrate contentions that the South Vietnamese were succeeding in Laos. Prodded by inquiries from a congressional committee, Laird affirmed during a briefing that Lt. Gen. John W. Vogt of the U.S. Air Force had allowed newsmen to assume during a press conference that a segment of pipe he displayed had come from an enemy petroleum pipeline severed by Lam's forces in Laos. In fact, the exhibit had no connection

---

[1] Mary McGrory, "A Bad Week for the Army," *Washington Star*, 28 Feb 71. The CBS report appeared on 23 Feb 71. A complete transcript may be found in Marvin Barrett, ed., *A. I. du Pont–Columbia University Survey of Broadcast Journalism, 1970–1971, A State of Siege* (New York: Grosset & Dunlap, Inc., 1972), pp. 151–71. Hereafter cited as Barrett, *Columbia University Survey of Broadcast Journalism, 1970–1971*.

with the incursion. American and South Vietnamese raiders had retrieved it at least six months earlier during a clandestine intelligence-gathering mission. The disclosure provoked ridicule from the press. One sarcastic newsman even commented after a reception for members of the House of Representatives, at which a congressman had performed on a harmonica, that Laird should have come to "play his pipe." Others spoke not only of a credibility gap but of a "pipe gap."[2]

The criticism rising in the press coincided with the sentiments of the American people. On 7 March the Gallup poll reported that public approval for President Nixon's handling of the war had dropped eighteen points and that nearly seven out of ten Americans doubted the president had told them everything they needed to know about events in Southeast Asia. The Harris poll revealed shortly thereafter that most Americans disapproved of the incursion into Laos by a margin of 42 to 39 percent. Despite presidential assurances to the contrary, 41 percent likewise expressed concern that the stepped up fighting in Laos would delay the departure of U.S. troops from South Vietnam, and 51 percent said that they would favor a congressional resolution requiring the completion of all U.S. withdrawals by the end of the year.[3]

There was little anyone could do to transform the discontent of the American people into enthusiasm for the war. Instead, on 16 March, Laird attempted to assuage public opinion by hinting broadly during a televised interview that the president might soon announce the recall of substantially more than 100,000 troops by January 1972. In the same way, as far as the scandals appearing in the press were concerned, neither the Army nor the Defense Department could do much more than concede the obvious. Assistant Secretary of Defense for Administration Robert F. Froehlke emphasized in highly publicized testimony before a Senate subcommittee that the Army considered its attempts at domestic surveillance legal and necessary. Yet he felt constrained to admit, in the next breath, that the effort had been, "at the very minimum, inappropriate."[4]

"The Selling of the Pentagon" was a different matter. Many within the Nixon administration, including both Daniel Henkin and Jerry Friedheim, agreed that the Defense Department's public affairs activities had been, at times, more heavy-handed than necessary. They were quick to point out, however, that CBS had used highly unorthodox methods in editing some of the material it had presented. Henkin, in particular, declared in a wide-

---

[2] George C. Wilson, "Pipe Bares an Earlier Laos Raid," *Washington Post*, 4 Mar 71; Charles W. Corddry, "Press Misled on Section of Pipeline Seized in Laos," *Baltimore Sun*, 5 Mar 71. Quotes from "Laird Bemoans Pipe Gap," *Washington Post*, 5 Mar 71.

[3] George Gallup, "The Gallup Poll," *Washington Post*, 7 Mar 71; Louis Harris, "The Harris Survey," *Washington Post*, 8 Mar 71.

[4] James Wieghart, "Laird Hints Even Faster Viet Pullout," *New York Times*, 17 Mar 71. Quote from [UPI], news clip, 2 Mar 71, CMH files. Also see William Kling, "How Army Viewed Spy Activities," *Chicago Tribune*, 8 Mar 71. Froehlke became secretary of the Army later in the year.

ly reprinted letter to the Chairman of the House Armed Services Committee, Congressman F. Edward Hebert of Louisiana, that the network had changed the meaning of an interview he had given by reducing the size of one of his comments and then inserting two sentences from his response to a different question. Later, he showed that the network's producers had edited the comments of other speakers to make points the originators had never intended.[5]

Researcher Marvin Barrett would afterwards assert that the "rearrangements" CBS had introduced into the program had at most flawed an otherwise admirable piece of investigative journalism. Whether that was so or not, "The Selling of the Pentagon" attracted fewer than ten million viewers out of an audience of fifty-eight million and would probably have disappeared forever from public consciousness but for the Nixon administration's sensitivity to the criticism that continued to accompany the incursion. For in the days that followed the seizure of Tchepone, the operation in Laos began to disintegrate, leading the White House staff to cast about for some means both to discredit its critics in the press and to save face for Thieu and the United States. The president had already issued instructions for Vice President Agnew to begin another assault on the news media.[6] "The Selling of the Pentagon" seemed tailor-made to the purpose. That the subject had nothing to do with Laos, which was already receiving more than its share of attention, only made it more inviting.

Questioning Continues

If the public image of the war was under attack in the United States, circumstances were little better in Southeast Asia, where reporters continued to complain that the Military Assistance Command was impeding their ability to cover the whole story of the incursion. Allegations by Associated Press correspondent Holger Jensen were typical. On 3 March Jensen charged in a long dispatch from Quang Tri that despite some easing of restrictions the situation was little changed from earlier in the operation. Statements by South Vietnamese briefers remained "uncoordinated and often misleading," while MACV itself had yet to reveal the true extent of helicopter losses. Jensen continued that if some officers in the field feared publicity enough to refuse to cooperate even on stories

---

[5] "Pentagon Aide Says CBS Shifted Words," *Washington Post*, 4 Mar 71. Also see Interv, author with Jerry Friedheim, 3 Oct 86, and Interv, author with Daniel Z. Henkin, 10 Oct 86, both in CMH files; Barrett, *Columbia University Survey of Broadcast Journalism, 1970–1971*, p. 37.

[6] Barrett, *Columbia University Survey of Broadcast Journalism, 1970–1971*, p. 37; Handwritten Note on White House News Summary, 28 Feb 71, President's Office files, Annotated News Summaries, box 32, Feb 71, Nixon Papers.

favorable to the armed forces, others abhorred the press. When reporters on one occasion had thus complained that they had waited 7½ hours for what should have been routine access to a flight from Da Nang to Khe Sanh, an American lieutenant colonel had told them, "To be quite frank with you, the reason you are not getting on our planes is because we don't want to be bothered with you. So goodbye. Please leave this office." As for MACV's decision to put a helicopter at the disposal of the press, Jensen said that reporters were uncomfortable with the arrangement. Many appeared to agree with Denis Cameron of *Newsweek*, who saw no reason to endanger the lives of aircrew members just to provide the press with a look at combat. They preferred to ride on helicopters that had legitimate fighting missions and to take their chances with everyone else.[7]

General Sidle would later note with a touch of irony that reporters had used a dedicated helicopter provided by the Military Assistance Command throughout much of 1967 and had protested vigorously, along with the MACV Office of Information, when the command had insisted upon terminating the arrangement. At that time, however, relations between the military and the news media had been relatively even. This was no longer the case in 1971. Reporters were more inclined than ever to value their independence and to resent any encroachment upon what they viewed as their prerogatives.[8]

As the operations in Laos and Cambodia proceeded, events in the field did little to improve the reporters' attitude. With the war at what the *Washington Post* termed a "fierce standstill," reporters continued to hover near the runway at Khe Sanh, where they itemized the complaints of American pilots. The enemy's gunners were "definitely good," one young warrant officer told Iver Peterson of the *New York Times*. "And they're getting better because of all the practice we've given them." Another complained that "I'd rather hand it out for my own people—all of us would. The guys thought they were coming over here to work with Americans and now we get blown away for people who don't even like us."[9] The newsmen also witnessed a steady stream of killed and wounded returning from the battlefield. "Sometimes you don't have to go to Laos to see the evidence of South Vietnamese problems on the other side of the border," correspondent Steve Bell commented on the 3 March edition of the ABC Evening News. "This is just one of many helicopters that have come in . . . bringing back . . . wounded and dead South Vietnamese trapped for days deep inside Laos. It's the kind of story that often fails to show up in the official releases."[10]

---

[7] Holger Jensen, "Journalists Get Little Cooperation Trying To Dig Out Truth About Laos," *Philadelphia Evening Bulletin*, 3 Mar 71.

[8] Ltr, Sidle to the author, 5 Nov 90, CMH files.

[9] Peter A. Jay, "Laos War Is Fierce Standstill," *Washington Post*, 2 Mar 71; Iver Peterson, "U.S. Copter Pilots in Laos Invasion Question the Risks," *New York Times*, 7 Mar 71.

[10] Steve Bell, ABC Evening News, 3 Mar 71, *Radio-TV-Defense Dialog*.

With the death of General Tri in Cambodia, reporters also began to pay more attention to the operation in the Chup Plantation. Craig Whitney of the *New York Times*, for one, gored the Military Assistance Command by suggesting that its public affairs policies had contributed inadvertently to Tri's death. Reflecting in his article an increasing tendency on the part of the Saigon correspondents to question the proficiency of South Vietnamese helicopter crews but also naming an American officer, Col. Robert Montague, as his source in order to establish the credibility of his comment, Whitney noted that Tri had flown usually with only reliable American helicopter crews. On the day he had died, however, he had chosen to employ less skilled South Vietnamese because journalist Francois Sully was to be present and U.S. policy had dictated at the time that reporters were never to cross the border in American aircraft.[11]

Although tied to a source, Whitney's comments about the death of Tri were questionable at best. Since no one had survived the crash, neither Montague nor anyone else had grounds to state that the incompetence of a South Vietnamese pilot had been the cause. Indeed, it was General Sidle's understanding at the time that Tri had chosen to fly in a South Vietnamese helicopter on that particular day to demonstrate the competence of South Vietnamese aircrews to Sully, who had long been a critic of the war.[12]

Whatever their biases, Whitney and other reporters were on stronger grounds when they observed that if the troops in Cambodia had fought with considerable vigor under Tri, the operation had ground to a halt almost as soon as he had died. Whitney attempted to explain the situation by suggesting that the South Vietnamese Army depended inordinately upon the leadership of its generals and had never developed the sort of flexibility at the middle levels of command that could provide continuity from one leader to the next in an emergency. Michael Parks of the *Baltimore Sun* had a more down-to-earth explanation. "General Tri operated in the manner of the old warlord," he said, quoting an American adviser, "and the staff and field officers worked for him out of loyalty rather than duty. . . . Besides, Tri [was] . . . the only one who knew what the battle plan was."[13]

The move into Tchepone provided a brief respite from criticism for both the South Vietnamese armed forces and the Nixon administration. The American television networks were relatively upbeat in their assessments. On the evening of 9 March CBS carried no mention of the war, but Howard K. Smith of ABC repeated claims by MACV spokesmen that the incursion had set the enemy back by at least five months. That break

---

[11] Craig R. Whitney, "Saigon's Cambodia Drive in Confusion After Death of Its Colorful Commander," *New York Times*, 2 Mar 71. Also see Gloria Emerson, "Vietnamese Copter Pilots Criticized," *New York Times*, 5 Mar 71.

[12] Ltr, Sidle to the author, 5 Nov 90.

[13] Michael Parks, "Death of Saigon General Snarls Push Into Cambodia," *Baltimore Sun*, 9 Mar 71.

might stretch to a year, he said, by the time the operation had ended. The "Huntley-Brinkley Report" on NBC was somewhat more cautious, noting with a touch of sarcasm that both U.S. and South Vietnamese officers continued to describe the incursion in "glowing" terms. Even so, the program's anchormen relayed official claims that the South Vietnamese had apparently cut nine branches of the Ho Chi Minh Trail. That achievement had guaranteed a five-month setback to the enemy, they said, a figure that could stretch to nine months if the incursion continued to go as well as it had. The print media were also favorable but much more analytical. Alvin Shuster of the *New York Times* thus observed that the capture of Tchepone had delivered an important psychological boost to the Saigon regime and a blow to Hanoi. That being the case, he continued, any judgment that the South Vietnamese had given a better overall account of themselves than the enemy still seemed premature. For although North Vietnamese forces had suffered far heavier casualties, much of the damage had been done by American bombers, helicopters, and artillery. Michael Parks made the same point, adding that if the South Vietnamese in Laos had proved they were indeed an elite force by fighting well and hard, their dependence upon American air support for both transportation and firepower raised doubts about whether they would ever become totally self-sufficient.[14]

The confidential communications between General Abrams and his superiors in Washington were as upbeat on the surface as those of the press, but they, too, betrayed an undercurrent of doubt. "Morale and confidence of the ARVN commanders has risen appreciably during the past three or four days and I believe they would willingly accept almost any mission assigned," Abrams thus told Moorer on 8 March. "However, the general feeling is that their mission has been accomplished and it is now time to withdraw. They do not concede that there is still much to be done . . . or that there is now the opportunity to exploit initial successes with even more telling results."[15] The observation led General Haig to remark in a note to Henry Kissinger that the message seemed to contain "a slight tone of uncertainty . . . which tends to confirm my suspicion that General Abrams was confronted with a massive problem [with the South Vietnamese] earlier in the operation, the residue of which still remains. On balance, I believe this is a fairly accurate command assessment . . . which tends to provide for ample notice of potential setbacks."[16]

Abrams' message, Haig's oblique warning, and a comment by Thieu that he had already accomplished a year's work in Laos led both Nixon

[14] White House News Summary, 10 Mar 71, Annotated News Summaries, box 32, Mar 71, Nixon Papers; Alvin Shuster, "Laos Battle in Crucial Phase With Outcome Uncertain," *New York Times*, 7 Mar 71; Michael Parks, "It's Up to Saigon's Army (With a Little Help From U.S.)," *Baltimore Sun*, 7 Mar 71.

[15] Msg, Abrams SPECAT to McCain, Moorer, 8 Mar 71, NSC files, A. M. Haig Chron files, box 977, Mar 7–9, 1971 [I of II], Nixon Papers.

[16] Note, Haig to Kissinger, 8 Mar 71, NSC files, A. M. Haig Chron files, box 977, Mar 7–9, 1971 [I of II], Nixon Papers.

and Kissinger to suspect that the South Vietnamese intended to abandon the incursion. From their point of view, it seemed altogether possible that Thieu had staged the attack on Tchepone to avoid the politically disastrous charge that he had subjected the elite of his Army to major casualties without attaining any tangible results. If that was true, so the reasoning went, the attack on Tchepone was a public relations gambit designed to hide a concession of defeat rather than a genuine attempt to deliver a lasting blow to the enemy.[17]

Responding to a suggestion from Abrams that the South Vietnamese might be susceptible to "a good kick in the ass," Kissinger cabled Ambassador Bunker on 9 March to inform him of Nixon's concern and to instruct him to put some starch into Thieu.[18] "We want it clearly understood that in our view this is the last chance that ARVN will have to receive any substantial U.S. support on the scale now provided," Kissinger said. Because of that Bunker was to impress upon Thieu

the need not to allow the potentially significant benefits of this operation to be sacrificed for short lived publicity based on more limited gains achieved thus far. If military conditions permit, we anticipate that Lam Son 719 should run well into the month of April. . . . From our perspective, every week ARVN stays in Laos represents a serious blow to the enemy's offensive capability, not only for this dry season but, more importantly, for the next. We have not gone through all of this agony just for the favorable headlines achieved as a result of recent successes and would hope that President Thieu would view the situation from the same perspective."[19]

Acutely aware that his troops were fatigued after more than thirty days of intense combat but unwilling to reinforce the divisions in Laos with high-quality units comparable to the ones he had first committed to the battle, Thieu temporized. When Abrams and Bunker inquired, he assured them that although he would withdraw his troops from Tchepone within the week he would continue search and destroy operations against the enemy's logistical commands south of the town for at least ten days. After that, he said, he would withdraw his force to Khe Sanh to rest and then strike back into the enemy's Laotian sanctuary through the A Shau Valley.[20]

Henry Kissinger had little understanding of Thieu's dilemmas but recognized that the expedient the president had proposed was at best a

[17] This analysis is based upon the general drift of the backchannel messages, briefing transcripts, and telephone conversation transcripts attached to Telephone Extracts: White House View of Laotian Planning. See, in particular, Telecon, Kissinger with Laird, 9 Mar 71, p. 9.

[18] Telecon, Kissinger with Moorer, 9 Mar 71, quoted in Telephone Extracts: White House View of Laotian Planning.

[19] Msg, Kissinger to Bunker, 9 Mar 71, quoted in Extracts from Backchannel Messages Concerning Outlook for Operation and Future Plans, 21 Mar 71, p. 10, attachment to Telephone Extracts: White House View of Laotian Planning.

[20] Msg, Abrams to Moorer, 11 Mar 71, and Msg, Bunker to Kissinger, 12 Mar 71, both quoted in Extracts from Backchannel Messages Concerning Outlook for Operation and Future Plans, 21 Mar 71, pp. 10–12, attachment to Telephone Extracts: White House View of Laotian Planning.

facade. "Then they're really bugging out in the next ten days," he exclaimed angrily at a private briefing at the White House by a representative of the Joint Chiefs of Staff, Lt. Col. David Martin:

[Kissinger:] Those sons of bitches. It's their country and we can't save it for them if they don't want to. We would never have approved the plan if we thought they were only going to stay for a short time, six to eight weeks. They spent three weeks sitting on [Highway] 9 and [Route] 92 and then as soon as they get to Tchepone they decide to bug out. They have not acted decisively and it won't have a significant impact on the enemy if it is not through the dry season. It is useful, better than nothing, but it could have been much better. Why do they really want to get out?

Martin: It is not clear. The mission now of the first regiment . . . is to get to the Binh Trams [logistical commands to the south of Tchepone] and every indication we have is that the enemy will fight.

Kissinger: If the enemy is going to fight then the ARVN probably won't go in.[21]

Abrams and Bunker also had reservations. They told Thieu that South Vietnamese forces would lose whatever momentum they had built up if they withdrew from Laos to rest and then returned. There were also political and public relations problems having to do with

whether it might not appear that RVNAF forces had been forced to withdraw despite the heavy casualties inflicted on the enemy; how such a move would be interpreted by the South Vietnam, American, and international press; the effect this would have on the political situation in South Vietnam [where Thieu was preparing to run for reelection]; the fact that a return to Laos after withdrawal might be considered a new venture and give critics of the present operation something new to hang on to.[22]

Thieu responded that those considerations also bothered him. As a result, he had decided on yet another approach. Rather than withdraw from Laos, his forces would continue the operation, but various units, beginning with the Airborne Division, would rotate to Khe Sanh for rest and refitting. Once that was done, the troops would begin exploiting enemy base area 611 to the south of Tchepone, which contained a considerable portion of the North Vietnamese supplies stored in the region.[23]

[21] MFR, David R. Young, 11 Mar 71, sub: Briefing, Kissinger, Col. Kennedy, David R. Young, Lt. Col. Martin on Laos (LAM SON 719), Cambodia (TOAN THANG 01–71), NSC files, Backchannels, box 433, Laos & Cambodia Briefings [March 10–20, 1971], Nixon Papers. A representative of the Joint Chiefs of Staff, usually Colonel Martin, briefed Kissinger regularly on the operation. The record of those briefings will be cited hereafter, with the relevant date, as Kissinger Briefing Notes.

[22] Msg, Abrams to Moorer, 11 Mar 71, and Msg, Bunker to Kissinger, 12 Mar 71, both quoted in Extracts from Backchannel Messages Concerning Outlook for Operation and Future Plans, 21 Mar 71, pp. 10–12.

[23] Ibid., pp. 10f.

Abrams and Bunker accepted the plan in the belief that Thieu shared "our perspective of the operation and the public image it must have."[24] Continuing to place great faith in air power, Abrams, in particular, was optimistic. With the plan in place, he told Moorer, Thieu would be able to "reinforce success" and "take full military and political advantage of the current favorable situation" to demolish the enemy's stockpiles and facilities.[25]

Kissinger nevertheless continued to doubt. When Moorer predicted on 13 March that the South Vietnamese would remain in Laos for the full extent of the dry season, the national security adviser could only respond, "Across roads or horsing around?"[26] In the same way, he doubted that General Lam's forces had done much damage to the enemy at Tchepone. Reflecting on the fact that the South Vietnamese had found relatively few enemy caches near Tchepone and noting as well that both a lull had occurred in the fighting around the town and the enemy had just completed an annex to the Ho Chi Minh Trail that bypassed the zone of battle, he told the briefer from the Joint Chiefs on 13 March that the situation reflected enemy strategy. "They have gotten most of their supplies past Tchepone," he said. "They fought like hell while they were trying to get them through, but now that they have gotten them through they don't care."[27]

Official statements to legislators and the press reflected nothing of the turmoil occurring within U.S. official circles. Administration spokesmen in the United States and public affairs officers in South Vietnam continued to speak about the success of the operation and to concentrate upon the huge number of enemy casualties and the losses in trucks, tanks, and heavy weapons that South Vietnamese forces had inflicted. Lam's forces were killing Communists at a very heavy rate, Admiral Moorer thus told a Republican leadership meeting at the White House on 6 March. The United States hardly expected them "to win every battle," but they were "doing very well indeed." Total enemy losses during the operation to date were approximately 7,100, Military Assistance Command spokesmen added in a 10 March backgrounder for the Saigon correspondents. "When compared to friendly losses the . . . ratio is about nine to one in favor of allied forces. . . . It is estimated that at least five [enemy] regiments have suffered casualties equivalent to one or more of their battalions." Meanwhile, truck activity along the enemy's supply routes in the region had declined by 50 percent, and enemy deserters had revealed that North Vietnamese forces might soon begin to face serious food and

[24] Ibid., p. 11.
[25] Msg, Abrams to Moorer, 14 Mar 71, quoted in Extracts from Backchannel Messages Concerning Outlook for Operation and Future Plans, 21 Mar 71, p. 13, attachment to Telephone Extracts: White House View of Laotian Planning.
[26] Telecon, Kissinger with Moorer, 13 Mar 71, quoted in Extracts from Telephone Conversations Between Dr. Kissinger and Defense Department Officers, p. 13, attachment to Telephone Extracts: White House View of Laotian Planning.
[27] Briefings, 12 and 13 Mar 71, Kissinger Briefing Notes.

Enemy transports on the Ho Chi Minh Trail move supplies despite the offensive.

ammunition shortages. In all, they had lost enough rice to feed 159 battalions for 30 days, 800 tons of ammunition, and enough individual and crew-served weapons to equip between eight and nine of their infantry battalions.[28]

Relying on sources of their own, the Saigon correspondents took those assurances with great caution. On 8 March Alvin Shuster thus questioned assertions by the president and others that the incursion had cut enemy traffic on the Ho Chi Minh Trail by 55 percent. In fact, the reporter said, reflecting doubts similar to those that Kissinger had expressed, if any decrease had occurred it had probably been a matter of the enemy's own timetable. According to his contacts, the flow of supplies had returned almost to preinvasion levels in areas seldom touched by the fighting.[29]

Public affairs officers could do little to relieve the doubts of the press. During the question and answer session that followed the 10 March brief-

---

[28] There were usually three infantry battalions in a North Vietnamese regiment. The quote from Moorer is in Memo, Patrick J. Buchanan for the President's file, 9 Mar 71, sub: Notes From GOP Leadership Meeting 8:00 A.M. March 9, 1971, White House Special files, Buchanan, Chron files, Mar 71, Nixon Papers. For the MACV backgrounder, see MACOI, Background Briefing, 10 Mar 71, DDI LAM SON II–Laos file.

[29] Alvin Shuster, "Enemy Supply Traffic Increases North of Saigon's Drive in Laos," *New York Times*, 5 Mar 71. Also see Robert B. Semple, "President Says Laos Aids U.S. Pullout," *New York Times*, 5 Mar 71.

470

ing in Saigon, for example, the newsmen present began to pick at MACV's statistics. "The ARVN claim 90 tanks, you say 50. Why the divergence?" one asked. "Our figures are based on U.S. observations," came the response, ". . . and the figures you get from the ARVN are based on their observations." Another reporter wanted to know whether the enemy's ammunition losses had resulted in decreased antiaircraft fire. "That's very difficult to measure," the briefer replied, "but I don't think so." A reporter then asked, "Since we have just gone in there and blown up the ammunition that we have found, what is your basis for estimates on the amount which has been destroyed?" The briefer could only respond, "Ground observations by the ARVN, and some by secondary explosions reported by pilots."[30]

On 12 March, when U.S. officials announced that the South Vietnamese would shortly begin to move away from Tchepone toward enemy base areas to the south, Murrey Marder and Michael Getler were equally skeptical. Writing a long article for the *Washington Post*, they commented that the Military Assistance Command had justified the redeployment as a strike at a major Communist staging area. In fact, the move served as much to shift South Vietnamese forces out of an area near North Vietnam, where they were most vulnerable to counterattack, and into a region much farther removed from the enemy's source for supplies and manpower. "With the . . . thrust into Laos officially hailed as a major success in Washington and Saigon," the two reporters said, "both capitals now have a vested interest in trying to avoid jeopardizing those claims. This suggests, some sources believe, that the allied operation, privately projected to extend through the dry season in Laos, may be terminated earlier."[31]

Admiral Moorer attempted to refute some of the pessimism during an interview on the ABC news program "Issues and Answers." Avowing that the incursion had presented North Vietnam with "the worst military situation it has been in," he claimed that the success of the operation had been so great it had even raised the chances for a breakthrough in the stalemated Paris peace talks. In the same way, Moorer discounted reports from the field that the South Vietnamese had begun to pull back under strong enemy pressure and suggested that the incursion had so weakened the enemy that the Thieu regime might even decide to launch an invasion of North Vietnam.[32]

Moorer's remarks had little effect on Iver Peterson of the *New York Times*. Administration spokesmen had claimed, the reporter replied, that the success of the incursion had demonstrated the effectiveness of the

[30] MACV Backgrounder, 10 Mar 71, DDI LAM SON II–Laos file.

[31] Murrey Marder and Michael Getler, "S. Viets Expected To Move Southward From Sepone," *Washington Post*, 12 Mar 71.

[32] Transcript, "Interview with Admiral Moorer," ABC News, "Issues and Answers," 14 Mar 71, DDI LAM SON II–Laos file. Also see Frank Van Riper, "Moorer Says N. Viet Faces Worst Danger," *New York News*, 15 Mar 71; [UPI], "Moorer Says Saigon Strike in Laos Is Nearly at Peak," *New York Times*, 15 Mar 71.

Vietnamization program. In fact, the South Vietnamese had conducted the operation from beginning to end with the assistance of massive U.S. air support. "How do you call this an indication that Vietnamization is working?" Peterson asked. "The air is rescuing most of those people." Moorer dismissed the objection. The operation was designed to be a marriage, he said, between an aggressive South Vietnamese forward element and U.S. air power. It had "paid off handsomely."[33]

Withdrawal Begins

Moorer may have made his comment about invading North Vietnam in an attempt to throw the enemy off balance or to prompt him to divert some of his resources to the task of preparing for an attack that would never come. If so, the attempt was unavailing. The enemy increased his pressure in the days that followed, and the South Vietnamese buckled. Confronted by an enemy force that had grown over the preceding weeks to five divisions—over 40,000 men—and suffering heavy casualties from enemy antiaircraft fire and artillery, senior South Vietnamese field commanders lost confidence in Lam and began to use their political connections to appeal his orders directly to Thieu. Harsh words followed when Thieu sided with the commanders, leading to further problems in the field and a decline in the cohesion and coordination of the troops facing the North Vietnamese. By 15 March 1971, all forward motion by the South Vietnamese had stopped, and the first withdrawals from Laos had begun.[34]

Abrams, Sutherland, and Moorer nevertheless all still continued to believe that the South Vietnamese might yet remain in Laos until mid-April. As for the difficulties that Lam and his forces were experiencing, Sutherland, at least, placed part of the blame upon the press. For although a multitude of problems indeed afflicted the South Vietnamese, he told General Haig, who had arrived to assess the situation for Kissinger and the president, "the press reports all engagements as defeats even though enemy casualties are great and ARVN losses are small. Future plans are reported before they happen, causing problems for ARVN." Haig agreed. Without adverting to the enemy's long-standing breach of South Vietnamese security in Laos, he added that it seemed to him as though many of the Saigon correspondents had all along wanted the incursion to fail.[35]

---

[33] Transcript, "Interview with Admiral Moorer," ABC News, "Issues and Answers," 14 Mar 71.

[34] After Action Report (AAR), XXIV Corps, Lam Son 719, 30 Jan–6 Apr 71, RG 334, G–3 Advisor AARs, box 2, WNRC. Also see Msg, Sutherland QTR 308 to Abrams, 10 Mar 71, Abrams Papers, CMH; Hinh, *Lam Son 719*, pp. 100–104.

[35] Msg, Sutherland QTR 843 to Abrams, 18 Mar 71, Abrams Papers, CMH.

Enemy forces counterattack at Fire Support Base LOLO, driving South Vietnamese forces from the position.

Whatever the validity of Sutherland's complaint and Haig's remark, the enemy perceived the ebbing of South Vietnamese resolve and redoubled his efforts. Some of Lam's troops fought back, causing many enemy casualties, but by 19 March, as Haig put it in a memorandum to Kissinger, their withdrawal had become "simultaneous across the entire front."[36]

The Saigon correspondents, for their part, understood what was happening almost immediately. By 18 March all three of the television networks in the United States were reporting that South Vietnamese forces were retreating from Laos and that helicopter pilots had confirmed the serious damage many units had sustained. A report by Phil Brady of NBC News was particularly painful to White House news media analysts. The reporter told of South Vietnamese troops who had called upon gunships to fire into their own positions and who had escaped only after crawling over the bodies of their dead companions. It was South Vietnamese practice to fall back upon completion of an operation, the reporter concluded, "but there was nothing orderly or planned" about what was happening in Laos. All talk to the contrary was "pointless."[37]

Reporters dutifully recorded the rejoinders of Jerry Friedheim at the Pentagon, who declared that everything was "proceeding according to plan" and that the South Vietnamese were only engaged in an airmobile

---

[36] Handwritten Memo, Haig for Kissinger, n.d. [late Mar 71], sub: Lamson 719, Nixon Papers.

[37] White House News Summary, 19 Mar 71, President's Office files, Annotated News Summaries, box 32, Mar 71, Nixon Papers.

473

operation against the enemy, but they continually balanced those assertions against others that came from Americans at the scene who had a different story to tell. "They can talk about helicopter mobility all they want," one helicopter pilot thus told the Associated Press, "but from where I'm flying there's only one way to describe it—retreat, and a bad one."[38]

Henry Kissinger was almost as dismayed as the reporters. The South Vietnamese withdrawal would "kill us domestically," he told Admiral Moorer on 18 March. "If they had told us a week ago they were . . . [going to do] this we could have said we have our victory. Instead they are moving down [Route] 914 and not saying a word to us. Of course, we control the helicopters." Moorer had no doubt about what Kissinger meant. "We can't just leave them in there," he responded. "Why not?" asked Kissinger. "We could," said Moorer, "but [that would] make more political problems."[39]

As the withdrawal proceeded, Kissinger grew even angrier. "What I don't understand is how no one could have known that they were going to pull out this quickly," he told Colonel Martin on 19 March. ". . . When did we know that they were going to move out?" Martin did not answer. "Well then, Colonel Martin," Kissinger continued angrily, "when did you know?" The officer responded, "I would rather have you ask the Chairman that question. It is my impression that you knew at the same time the Chairman did." The response did little to soothe the national security adviser. "What . . . [the South Vietnamese] did was go ahead with the withdrawal plan which they allegedly cancelled," he said. "We can never reconstitute the operation." Kissinger continued that the real tragedy was that the United States and South Vietnam had been within a single division of victory and had lost the chance because Thieu and Lam had refused to commit the troops. "That is true," the briefer replied, "but . . . you should be aware . . . that the real tragedy is going to be the morale of the ARVN units coming out. These are supposed to be some of their best units. . . . The people coming out are coming out with the feeling that they have been beaten. They are scrambling for the helicopters and they are being shot at. The morale of the men in the field is going to be low."[40]

General Abrams was well aware that the morale of South Vietnamese forces might suffer in the face of the withdrawal. To finish the operation on a psychological upswing, he therefore suggested that President Thieu consider a surprise raid by elite units on an enemy supply point about twenty kilometers to the south of Tchepone near the Laotian town of Muong Nong. The operation would involve heavy B–52 attacks prior to

[38] [AP], "Viet Forces in Laos Said To Retreat," *Washington Post*, 18 Mar 71.
[39] Telecon, Kissinger with Moorer, 18 Mar 71, quoted in Extracts from Telephone Conversations Between Dr. Kissinger and Defense Department Officers, p. 13, attachment to Telephone Extracts: White House View of Laotian Planning.
[40] Briefing, 19 Mar 71, Kissinger Briefing Notes.

an air assault of the sort that had occurred in the attack on Tchepone. The troops would stay on the ground for several days to destroy enemy stockpiles but would withdraw before the enemy could respond in force, allowing Thieu to declare publicly and without risk that his troops retained both the initiative and the ability to strike at will in Laos. Thieu saw the logic in the proposition and agreed to the attack but refused to take action until the end of the month, when most of his troops would be out of Laos.[41]

In the interim, Nixon administration spokesmen sought to counter increasing reports of panic among the South Vietnamese in Laos by emphasizing in statements to the press that the incursion continued to be successful and that any withdrawal would be gradual and methodical. Ronald Ziegler at the White House thus told reporters on 18 March that the South Vietnamese had intended to limit the operation in time and place from the very beginning. They were proceeding according to plan and continued to disrupt the flow of enemy supplies through Laos. In the same way, Vice President Agnew insisted at a news conference in Boston that the South Vietnamese had accomplished their objectives in Laos. "This was not a rout. This was an orderly retreat . . . in accordance with plan. They were not forced out."[42]

Assertions of that sort had little effect on many reporters, especially those who tended to see the worst. James McCartney, for one, observed caustically in the *Philadelphia Inquirer* that

The South Vietnamese have invented a new kind of warfare in Laos. They avoid fighting whenever they can, they flee an area when the Communists start showing up on the battlefield, and they consistently claim "victory" or "success" when the operation involved is over. . . . Many U.S. military men used to criticize the South Vietnamese for a tendency to "cut and run" when a battle loomed in Vietnam. Now, when the South Vietnamese flee, Pentagon spokesmen are inclined to praise their "mobility."[43]

Despite their misgivings, a number of reporters nonetheless gave heavy play to the administration's version of what was happening. Alvin Shuster of the *New York Times* devoted considerable attention to official statements that acknowledged the South Vietnamese pullback but stressed that the troops were also consolidating their positions and continuing to disrupt Communist supply lines. If the South Vietnamese were heavily outnumbered in Laos, Shuster said, "the allies feel they are offsetting the numerical superiority of the Communists with intense air

[41] Msg, Haig Saigon 641 to Kissinger, 19 Mar 71, NSC files, A. M. Haig Chron files, box 977, Mar 10–20, 1971 [I of II], Nixon Papers.

[42] Murrey Marder, "Saigon Starts 'Methodical' Laos Pullout," *Washington Post*, 19 Mar 71. Quote from David S. Broder, "Agnew Calls Pullback in Laos 'Orderly Retreat,'" *Washington Post*, 20 Mar 71.

[43] James McCartney, "S. Vietnamese 'Succeed' by Backing Away," *Philadelphia Inquirer*, 18 Mar 71.

assaults." Peter Kann of the *Wall Street Journal* also tended to reflect the official point of view. Commenting on the optimism among the South Vietnamese people that he believed the incursion had produced, he noted that "despite the ARVN retreats of recent days, military officials . . . believe they already have seriously disrupted the North Vietnamese army supply line and thus the enemy's future plans." Peter Jay of the *Washington Post* likewise emphasized in an article on 19 March that accurate information about what was happening in Laos was difficult to come by even in areas near the fighting and that a thorough evaluation of what had happened might take months to complete. "You talk to a wounded soldier and he says its like hell out there," he reported, quoting a high-ranking South Vietnamese officer. "And it was like hell for him. But he doesn't know how many men on the other side were in an even worse hell at the same time." Keyes Beech in the *Chicago Daily News* made much the same point on 20 March. If the incursion appeared to have fallen short of early expectations, the reporter said, "Nobody in his right mind expected the invasion of the Laotian panhandle to be a picnic, and it hasn't been. . . . But to suggest that the operation has been a failure because South Vietnamese forces have, willingly or unwillingly, given up a string of fire bases is both unfair and premature. The jury, in President Nixon's phrase, is still out."[44]

As the withdrawal from Laos gained momentum, confidential reports appearing within official circles were sometimes as caustic as those of the Saigon correspondents. Informed, for example, on 22 March that the enemy had apparently released large quantities of rice wine to his troops to whip them into a suicidal frenzy, Henry Kissinger could only allude to increasing drug abuse in the South Vietnamese armed forces. "This ought to be a great battle," he asserted at a White House meeting, "one army hopped up on drugs and the other . . . on booze."[45]

General Haig was more understanding of South Vietnamese deficiencies but no more reassuring. On 19 March he cabled Kissinger to warn that a new set of circumstances had come into being in Laos. Although the enemy had suffered huge casualties, he said, the "smell of victory is in his nostrils and all-out effort on his part can be anticipated." Throughout the week, Haig continued, Abrams had urged Lam and Thieu to reinforce the operation but they had refused. As a result, the soldiers fighting in Laos had lost stomach for further combat and only wanted out. Although the Nixon administration had instructed Abrams to encourage Thieu to leave his forces in Laos until the begin-

---

[44] Alvin Shuster, "Saigon's Forces Still Move Back in Laos Fighting," *New York Times*, 18 Mar 71; Peter R. Kann, "Paradox of War, Optimism in Vietnam Fear in Laos Point Up Ambiguities of Battle," *Wall Street Journal*, 18 Mar 71; Peter Jay, "Results of Laos Operation Murky Even at the Front," *Washington Post*, 19 Mar 71; Keyes Beech, "Viet Rout in Laos 'Not Decisive,'" *Chicago Daily News*, 20 Mar 71.

[45] The comment about drug and alcohol addiction is in MFR, 22 Mar 71, sub: Briefing of March 22, 1971, Kissinger Briefing Notes.

ning of the rainy season in April, Haig continued, advice of that sort had to cease. With defeat impending, Abrams should attempt to salvage the limited gains the operation had thus far achieved by persuading Thieu and his commanders to conduct an orderly, phased withdrawal rather than allow the retreat to dissolve for lack of direction into some sort of panic.[46]

Although official spokesmen maintained an encouraging tone in their statements to the press during the days that followed, all concerned understood that the enemy intended to attack relentlessly, that heavy fighting was bound to occur, and that anything could happen. Rather than allow false expectations to build, the Defense Department, in particular, thus took pains once the facts became clear to assure the American public that the plan of withdrawal was flexible enough to allow for a rapid pullback if circumstances so required. It was up to President Thieu to decide when Saigon's forces would leave Laos, Jerry Friedheim told reporters. That withdrawal, he implied, might come sooner than expected, if only because it would be imprudent for the South Vietnamese to wait until the last day before the rains came to begin their return.[47]

At a special backgrounder for the Saigon correspondents on 21 March, General Abrams likewise stressed the gains the South Vietnamese had achieved and denied that any sort of catastrophe had occurred. Continuing to concentrate on the large quantities of supplies Lam's forces had destroyed, on kill ratios of ten to one, and on the loss by the enemy of thirteen out of thirty-three maneuver battalions, he conceded in response to hard questioning that the enemy had routed at least one battalion of Airborne troops, whose own commander had deserted his men. Yet the members of the more successful units, he said, would emerge from Laos with confidence higher than they had ever possessed. "In a thing like this it's what . . . [the troops] believe [that counts]. They believe . . . that they handled . . . [an] enemy regiment. . . . I don't know whether they did or not. But that's the way those people . . . are going to believe forever."[48]

Those assurances and others like them continued to receive wide play in the press. On 22 March, for example, George Ashworth of the *Christian Science Monitor* observed that "A valid assessment of the success or failure of the military operations in Laos will not be possible for weeks—even months. Officials here who have followed the war closely for years maintain that there are just too many uncertainties."[49]

[46] Msg, Haig Saigon 641 to Kissinger, 19 Mar 71.

[47] Marder, "Saigon Starts 'Methodical' Laos Pullout."

[48] Questions and Answers Following Background Briefing in Saigon, 21 Mar 71, DDI LAM SON II–Laos file. Also see Memo, Henry Kissinger for the President, 21 Mar 71, sub: General Abrams' Remarks, NSC files, Vietnam Subject files, box 82, Vietnam: Operations in Laos and Cambodia, vol. 6, Nixon Papers.

[49] George W. Ashworth, "Battle Smoke Dims Lao Overview," *Christian Science Monitor*, 22 Mar 71.

South Vietnamese soldiers struggle to board a helicopter leaving Laos.

There remained, nevertheless, a strong undercurrent of questioning, especially on television. On 23 March, for example, Tom Streithorst of NBC News described the evacuation of a regiment of weary troops from Highway 9. "The generals of the ARVN High Command insist the withdrawal is going according to plan," the reporter said,

But many observers believe that the withdrawal timetable has been speeded up because of the heavy North Vietnamese counter attack. Many of the troops seemed desperate to get out. We filmed three separate instances of panicked ARVN soldiers who rode on the skids of helicopters in preference to waiting for another helicopter that might not come. There were more troops flying out on the skids we didn't film.

Streithorst talked to an American airman who had accompanied the flight. "Were the troops very anxious to get out?" he asked. The soldier responded, "Yeah. . . . They were all most scared and I had to kick them off [the skids]. . . . We couldn't move." Changing subjects, the reporter then noted that as the South Vietnamese left Laos, the American units that had braced the operation from the rear would face increasing danger as the enemy followed the retreating troops into South Vietnam. Many of those Americans, he said, already believed that the U.S. Army had failed to provide them with adequate support, and others seemed so exhausted they were on the verge of rebellion.[50]

[50] Tom Streithorst, NBC Nightly News, 22 Mar 71, *Radio-TV-Defense Dialog.*

478

Streithorst's report, especially the part that depicted American soldiers complaining about the support they were receiving, galled Henry Kissinger. He had little confidence left in the South Vietnamese but even less in the press. "I just don't see how we can fight a war like this," he told congressional leaders at a White House briefing. "Interviewing GI's is the worst way to find out what's going on. In the Battle of the Bulge [during World War II] I remember an incident: It seemed like two battalions of Germans but it was only a couple of tanks. The people in the middle of it have the least idea of what is happening." As for the photographs of South Vietnamese troops clinging to the skids of helicopters, Kissinger said, "What's interesting to me is that in the photos these ARVN riding on the helicopters are carrying their weapons and their packs. This is not the sign of troops panicking."[51]

An Attempt at Image Preservation

O ther members of the Nixon administration were equally annoyed, not only at news stories such as the one by Streithorst but also because the Defense Department, by cautiously attempting to prepare the American public for a possible early withdrawal from Laos, had given the appearance of being less than energetic in refuting critics. White House media analyst Mort Allen, for one, told H. R. Haldeman that "The job of getting out a positive—let alone neutral—evaluation of the Laos operation is clearly deserving of high priority attention. The perfunctory DOD statements and listing of statistics simply won't do the job in the face of night after night of panic stricken ARVN."[52]

The president's staff had already taken a number of steps to remedy the situation. As South Vietnamese fortunes in Laos had declined, its members had made effective use of their connections on Capitol Hill to elicit support for the president's policies and to castigate the news media. Senator Clifford P. Hansen of Wyoming, for example, had taken up the cause by issuing a series of highly publicized attacks from the floor of the Senate on television coverage of the operation. On 12 March, indeed, he had held a two-hour screening of television news segments dealing with the incursion that purported to demonstrate the bias of CBS and NBC. Meanwhile, Henry Kissinger and Admiral Moorer held positively oriented briefings on Laos for important members of Congress, and fact sheets on the incursion went out to Republican legislators along with instructions on

[51] The quote on press coverage of LAM SON 719 is from Memo of Conversation, 24 Mar 71, sub: Congressional Briefing on the End of Laotian Operation, NSC files, Presidential/HAK Memcon files, box 1025, Mar 25, 1971, Nixon Papers.

[52] Memo, Mort Allen for H. R. Haldeman, 22 Mar 71, sub: Notations for March 16, 17, 18, 19, 20, 22 News Summaries, White House Special files, Buchanan, Chron files, box 1, Mar 71, Nixon Papers.

how they were to be used in support of the administration's policies in Laos. While they were doing that, the White House staff prevailed upon loyal members of Congress who had met with the families of American prisoners of war to deliver speeches on the floor of the House linking the fate of the prisoners to the incursion. The effort had an effect. On 29 March Charles Colson could report that his staff had tallied thirty-two speeches in Congress supporting the incursion and attacking the news media.[53]

As those efforts proceeded, on 19 March, Vice President Agnew attempted further to discredit television news by issuing a broadly based attack on CBS for its report, "The Selling of the Pentagon." Alleging that the news media seemed "to cloak themselves in a special immunity to criticism," he told Boston's Middlesex Club that, in fact, the networks appeared to believe "freedom of expression is fine so long as it stops before any question is raised or criticism lodged against national media policies and practice." With that, the vice president cited several examples of what he said were efforts by CBS to warp facts to fit its own needs. In one case, he noted, citing a congressional investigation, network personnel had apparently even provided funds for an abortive invasion of Haiti before finally abandoning the documentary they were filming. "My purpose," Agnew noted at a news conference the next day, "was simply to tell the American people and to show them through uncontroverted evidence based on substantial and complete investigation that they cannot rely on CBS documentaries for facts."[54]

Agnew's charges caused an uproar in the press, which paid avid attention to the controversy as it developed. During the days that followed, the president of CBS, Frank Stanton, denied that his network had done something wrong and asserted that CBS had never broadcast the program on Haiti. Agnew replied that the comment was "a typical non-rejoinder." CBS then chose to rebroadcast "The Selling of the Pentagon" on 23 March, along with comments on the program by Agnew, Secretary of Defense Laird, and Congressman F. Edward Hebert. More charges and countercharges followed when CBS, declining to cede editorial judgments to outsiders, refused to allow the vice president's representatives and those of the other commentators to choose which of their remarks would appear on the program.[55]

[53] Memo, Charles Colson for H. R. Haldeman, 22 Mar 71, White House Special files, Action Memoranda 1970–1971, box 8, White House Action Memos 1441 [II of III], Nixon Papers. Also see Memo, Jim Hogue for Chuck Colson, 29 Mar 71, sub: Congressional Support for Laos Operation, White House Special files, Staff Member Office files, Colson, box 120, Nixon Papers; Barrett, *Columbia University Survey of Broadcast Journalism, 1970–1971*, p. 39.

[54] Agnew is quoted in Barrett, *Columbia University Survey of Broadcast Journalism, 1970–1971*, pp. 38–39. Also see [UPI], "Agnew Assails CBS for Show on Pentagon," *Philadelphia Bulletin*, 19 Mar 71.

[55] Barrett, *Columbia University Survey of Broadcast Journalism, 1970–1971*, p. 41; [UPI], "Agnew Assails CBS for Show on Pentagon." Agnew is quoted in [UPI], "CBS-TV Challenged by Agnew," *Boston Herald-Traveler*, 21 Mar 71.

At the height of the controversy, President Nixon himself took the air to criticize the news media and to emphasize that the operation in Laos had achieved many of its goals. On the evening of 22 March, during a special televised interview with ABC newsman Howard K. Smith, he cautioned that it was too soon to judge whether the incursion was a success or a failure but still stressed that the raid had made considerable progress toward ensuring the continuation of American withdrawals and reducing the threat to the American forces that remained in Southeast Asia. Noting that the campaign in Laos had allowed the South Vietnamese to develop "a considerable capability of their own," he went on to emphasize that the impression of panic conveyed by television news films was inaccurate. "What have the pictures shown?" he said. "They've shown only those men in the four ARVN battalions . . . that were in trouble. They haven't shown people in the other 18 battalions. That is not because it's been deliberate. It's because those make news."[56]

As the interview continued, Nixon made criticism of the press a theme. Never raising his voice or showing undue emotion, he avowed that he had received less support from the news media than any president in the century. Rather than dwell upon Laos, he then addressed the performance of the press during the 1970 incursion into Cambodia. "I just saw a summary of two weeks' coverage by the television networks and by the newspapers [of that operation]," he said, ". . . but for two weeks—and there were some notable exceptions that we don't need to go into—but for two weeks the overwhelming majority of the nation's press and television, after Cambodia, carried these themes: one, the Chinese might intervene; two, casualties would soar, the war would be expanded; and third, there was a danger that American withdrawal might be jeopardized." None of those things had happened. "Now, what does this prove: It doesn't prove the press was trying deliberately to make America look bad. That wasn't the point. But naturally they were seeing it from one vantage point; I had to see it from another."[57]

The news media accepted Nixon's claim that the final results of the incursion would become apparent only months in the future, making it a theme in the weeks that followed. They nevertheless questioned a number of the president's other assertions. Fixing on a remark Nixon had attributed to General Abrams, that the South Vietnamese armed forces "by themselves can hack it and they can give a better account of themselves than the North Vietnamese," the *Philadelphia Bulletin*, for one, observed that the judgment appeared overly optimistic. "Without our air cover and without 51 battalions of U.S. troops holding the fort . . . one can only guess at how much worse the situation might have been." The

---

[56] Tad Szulc, "Nixon Says Drive by Saigon Helps Reach Key Goals," *New York Times*, 23 Mar 71.

[57] Nixon is quoted in Barrett, *Columbia University Survey of Broadcast Journalism, 1970–1971*, pp. 40–41. Also see Robert B. Semple, Jr., "Nixon Suggests Press Distorts Policy," *New York Times*, 23 Mar 71.

General Lam (left)

Boston Globe was equally skeptical. "The president . . . should know how well an 'incursion' has succeeded when the troops, who were to continue harassing the North Vietnamese and disrupting their supply lines until the monsoons early in May are fleeing six weeks early with half of them already back in South Vietnam. . . . One does not expect, in this war, the total honesty of the late Gen. Joseph "Vinegar Joe" Stilwell who declared, after Burma in World War II, 'I claim we got a hell of a beating . . . and it is damned humiliating.' But there is no excuse for concealing from Americans and the South Vietnamese peasants the facts known only too well in Hanoi." Meanwhile, the *New York Post* questioned how the press could have told the story of the eighteen successful battalions when its representatives were barred from covering the operation firsthand. "Time and again," the paper continued,

Mr. Nixon reverted to the theme that the Laotian and Cambodian enterprises were justified because, whatever else might be said about them, they had "protected American lives." The validity of that claim is debatable. But even if true, it clearly called for another question that was never asked. How long will Asians relish this rationale for the war—the portrait of mounting Asian deaths in the higher cause of American safety?[58]

[58] "'Hacking' It in Laos," *Philadelphia Bulletin*, 23 Mar 71; "The Withdrawal From Laos," *Boston Globe*, 23 Mar 71; "The Nixon Show (Contd.)," *New York Post*, 23 Mar 71.

482

By 25 March most of the troops in Laos had returned to South Vietnam. The incursion had all but ended. Instead of releasing tensions, however, the withdrawal increased them. Concern began to rise in Washington that the enemy might attack across the border toward Khe Sanh, where he could inflict significant casualties upon American forces. There was also some thought that if American troops tarried too long at the base before pulling back themselves, circumstances might arise that were similar to those that had prevailed during 1968, when Khe Sanh had been under siege by the North Vietnamese. Hoping to avoid a public relations disaster, Kissinger thus took pains to instruct Haig to inform the Defense Department that during the final stages of the withdrawal from Laos South Vietnamese units should hold the border "so that we don't bear the brunt of any attack across." Recommendations also began to surface that General Abrams should remove U.S. troops from Khe Sanh just as soon as that was practical.[59]

The situation at Khe Sanh was, indeed, deteriorating rapidly, but less from enemy action than because the South Vietnamese commanders continued to fight among themselves. General Lam wanted the South Vietnamese Marines to place a force in the Co Roc, a region in Laos just south and west of Khe Sanh that had been the site of the enemy's main artillery batteries during the siege of Khe Sanh in 1968. The marine commander had no intention of doing so, at least on Lam's order. Meanwhile, Lam's deputy indicated that he was not interested in issuing instructions to the rangers and the marines.[60]

As the wrangling continued, American commanders became increasingly concerned. "When it appeared this morning that I Corps was coming apart at the seams," Sutherland told Abrams, "I decided to start removing the airfield matting on 26 March rather than wait until 1 April. I consider this prudent under the circumstances and can slow down or speed up as the situation dictates." Sutherland added, ". . . As you have stated before we can take [the South Vietnamese] . . . only so far; beyond that point they must go on their own. We have reached that point in LAM SON 719. Today I am not sure of how much further we can take them."[61]

Despite the conditions that had prompted Sutherland's disgust, there was little possibility that the Nixon administration would relax its efforts to save face for the South Vietnamese. The force in Laos had lost a large number of men, at least 1,100 by official tally but undoubtedly many more. Over half of the killed in action had been interred where they had

---

[59] Quote from Memo of Briefing, 24 Mar 71, sub: Lam Son 719; Toan Thang 01/71, NSC files, Jon Howe Chron files, box 1077, Mar 71, Nixon Papers. Memo, Jerry Friedheim for Deputy Secretary of Defense, 23 Mar 71, sub: Posture and Plan of U.S. Public Comment on Lamson 719 for the Next Few Months, NSC files, Vietnam Subject files, box 86, Special Operations [Mar 71], Nixon Papers.

[60] Msg, Sutherland QTR 515 to Abrams, 25 Mar 71, Abrams Papers, CMH.

[61] Ibid.

fallen, to the chagrin of the commanders involved, who understood that many of the families of the dead practiced ancestor worship and would object vehemently to a failure by the government to return their relatives for proper burial. In addition, the enemy had embarked on a propaganda campaign to discredit the South Vietnamese government before its own people by demonstrating that a devastating defeat had occurred. If it became clear that the incursion had indeed resulted in disaster, all of those ingredients might combine to undermine the validity of the Thieu regime not only before the world but also in the eyes of the South Vietnamese people. If that occurred, Secretary of State Rogers told Bunker and Abrams, "the consequences could be most unfortunate."[62]

The president's staff was, for a time, uncertain about how best to proceed. "Based on the news summaries of the past two days, we are again getting clobbered on Laos," Charles Colson told H. R. Haldeman on 25 March. ". . . [assistant to the president for congressional relations William E.] Timmons tells me that even our stalwarts on the Hill are afraid to get in right now and mix it up. They are scared of the news reports and Bill believes that he would have little success in trying to get them to start a drumbeat for us next week."[63]

In the end, while insisting that long-term results took precedence over immediate tactical gains, the president appears to have left the main promotional activities to Thieu and to have attempted to direct the American public's attention toward the continuing U.S. withdrawal from South Vietnam. On 7 April, although refusing to set a fixed date for the termination of all American combat involvement in the war, he thus promised to extract 100,000 troops from South Vietnam between May and November.[64]

Jerry Friedheim explained the approach in a memorandum to the deputy secretary of defense on 23 March. The interest of the American public and news media remained centered on U.S. activities, he observed. As a result, while the South Vietnamese would do everything in their power to stress that the campaign in Laos had succeeded by giving speeches, conducting background briefings, presenting awards, and displaying captured enemy weapons, it seemed unlikely that there would be any rush by the American news media to take up those pronouncements of success. Instead, reporters would continue to concentrate on the activities of American forces and would react strongly to any increase in U.S. combat involvement or casualties. The same would

---

[62] Msg, Sutherland QTR 518 to Abrams, 25 Mar 71, sub: ARVN Accounting for KIA and MIA, Abrams Papers, CMH. Quote from Msg, Joint State-Defense 51947 to Bunker, Abrams, 27 Mar 71. Memo, Kissinger for the President, 29 Mar 71, sub: Countering Enemy Propaganda Campaign on Lam Son 719. Both in NSC files, Vietnam Subject files, box 85, Special Operations, March 20 on, Nixon Papers.

[63] Memo, Colson for Haldeman, 25 Mar 71, sub: Coverage on Laos, White House Special files, Buchanan, Staff Memoranda, box 3, Colson 1971 [I of II], Nixon Papers.

[64] Memo, Kissinger for the President, 29 Mar 71, sub: Countering Enemy Propaganda Campaign on Lam Son 719; John S. Carroll, "Nixon Steps Up Pace of Viet Pullout, Sets 100,000-Man Cutback," *Baltimore Sun*, 8 Apr 71.

be true for the rest of the American public. Whether LAM SON 719 was a tactical military success or not, the minds of most Americans would be on U.S. withdrawals and "our determination to shift our strategic attention to other more important world goals."[65]

Too much was involved, however, for administration spokesmen to abandon the attempt to justify the incursion entirely. As the operation in Laos ended, attacks on the press therefore continued, with Admiral Moorer, in particular, asserting on 26 March that the Saigon correspondents had gone into the operation "itching for the South Vietnamese to lose."[66] Vice President Agnew likewise asserted during a speech on 7 April to the Los Angeles Chamber of Commerce that "most knowledgeable people" believed it was too soon to judge the effectiveness of the incursion but that the news media were already pronouncing it a failure. That was, he said, just one example of a growing American "masochism" that might "destroy us as a nation."[67]

Administration spokesmen also attempted to strike back at news stories that displeased them. When Tammy Arbuckle thus alleged in a 25 March Associated Press dispatch from Saigon that South Vietnam had suffered nearly 10,000 killed and wounded in Laos and that government reports had either lagged significantly behind the facts or were deliberately distorted, Secretary of Defense Laird contacted the reporter's employers and succeeded in having the story withdrawn on grounds that it was erroneous.[68]

Even if Arbuckle's figures were exaggerated, however, information available to the Military Assistance Command confirmed the reporter's suspicion that some dissembling had occurred. Overall, the South Vietnamese government later claimed that it had suffered 7,683 killed, wounded, or missing in Laos. Yet, as General Sutherland indicated in a message to Abrams on 28 March, the true figure was higher. The officers of the 1st South Vietnamese Infantry Division, Sutherland said, had confirmed privately in conversations with American officers that they had lost at least 775 of their men in Laos, but official South Vietnamese tallies for the operation to date listed only 491 dead for that division. Similarly, the Airborne Division claimed that it had suffered absolutely no missing in action during the operation but South Vietnamese officers who had served during the campaign attested after the war that they had "first

[65] Memo, Jerry Friedheim for Deputy Secretary of Defense, 23 Mar 71, sub: Posture and Plan of U.S. Public Comment on Lamson 719 for the Next Few Months.

[66] Orr Kelly, "Reporters 'Itched' To Have Viets Lose, Adm. Moorer Feels," *Washington Star*, 26 Mar 71. Also see David Breasted, "Laird & Moorer Plug Laos Drive," *New York Daily News*, 25 Mar 71; "Allies Attained Goal in Laos, Laird Asserts," *Philadelphia Inquirer*, 25 Mar 71.

[67] "Agnew Calls News Media Doubts Over Laos a Sign of Wide U.S. Masochism," *New York Times*, 8 Apr 71.

[68] [AP], Indochina Roundup, 25 Mar 71, CMH files. Also see Memo, Haig for the President's files, 26 Mar 71, sub: Meeting With the President, Secretary of Defense Laird et al., NSC files, A. M. Haig Chron files, box 978, Mar 21–31, 1971, Nixon Papers.

hand information" about "a number of Airborne officers and troops . . . captured by the enemy."[69]

Assessments

As Friedheim had observed, the American news media paid little attention to South Vietnamese avowals of success during the days following the end of the operation. When President Thieu, after canceling the raid on Muong Nong because of potentially heavy enemy resistance, launched a minor but successful attack against a secondary target and then declared that his troops had proved their ability to operate at will in Laos, the development received only fleeting attention in the American press. Most reporters received the declaration as little more than a routine attempt to save face.[70]

Friedheim's comments to the contrary, however, the news media remained intensely interested in the long-term results of the operation, and what they had to say was, at times, hardly as opinionated as Agnew and Moorer seemed to expect. Whether journalists agreed with the decision to enter Laos or not, for example, almost all commentators accepted official assertions that only time would tell whether the attack had achieved its ends. A number also adopted themes that could only have pleased the president and his advisers. The *Omaha World-Herald* thus echoed Moorer in asserting on 27 March that if the campaign in Laos had closed under circumstances of little credit to the South Vietnamese Army, "It might be well to bear in mind, that many who will be passing judgment . . . have a vested interest in having . . . [the operation] adjudged a flop, because they predicted failure even before the South Vietnamese got into trouble." The *National Observer* said much the same thing. Just as the Tet offensive of 1968 had ultimately proved less than the reverse for the South Vietnamese that critics of the war had predicted, the paper's editors avowed, so might the raid into Laos. Meanwhile, without addressing the incursion directly, the influential financial weekly *Barron's Magazine* voiced its firm support for Vice President Agnew's criticism of CBS. Condemning what it considered a continuing pursuit of "distorted and slanted reporting" that seemed well-exemplified in "The Selling of the Pentagon," the magazine even called upon the Federal Communications Commission to revoke the network's access to the nation's airwaves.[71]

---

[69] The official figures may be found in Hinh, *Lam Son 719*, p. 129. Quote from Ibid. Msg, Sutherland QTR 567 to Abrams, 28 Mar 71, Abrams Papers, CMH.

[70] "Fog, Guns Force Allies To Cancel Laos Raid," *Washington Post*, 30 Mar 71; "Viet Troops Enter Laos, Attack Base," *Baltimore Sun*, 7 Apr 71.

[71] "Laos Jury Still Out," *Omaha World-Herald*, 27 Mar 71; Richard Egan, "A Look at the Balance Sheet on the Laos Affair," *National Observer*, 29 Mar 71; "Broadcast License: CBS Has Forfeited Access to the Nation's Airwaves," *Barron's Magazine*, 29 Mar 71.

If a number of journals and commentators sided with the Nixon administration, most nevertheless continued to criticize the incursion and its results. ABC News, for one, interviewed four of its correspondents in Saigon in an attempt to outline the difficulties newsmen had encountered in covering the operation. Summarizing the controversies that had occurred over helicopter losses and restrictions on access to the units fighting in Laos, the four—Jim Giggins, Howard Tuckner, Steve Bell, and Don Farmer—complained bitterly that public affairs officers in both South Vietnam and Washington had attempted to mislead the press by refuting stories about South Vietnamese reverses that had, in fact, been well founded. "Now, I recall in Cambodia," one of the newsman observed, ". . . [the South Vietnamese] never missed an opportunity to set up little displays, even at the most remote outposts, of captured weapons, captured documents. [They would] take you out and show you enemy dead where they'd had a fire fight the night before. They made these tremendous victory claims in Laos and never once were they able to take newsmen to show them what they were talking about." A second reporter added, "We were told by the Americans and by the Vietnamese . . . that this was a great victory. Well, . . . it may have been in some aspects. The ARVN proved themselves to be good fighting men. . . . But when they say things like, 'We have now cut the Ho Chi Minh Trail,' you and I know that that is absurd and that's the kind of statements we were getting and they are so unbelievable that I think sometimes . . . we start looking for lies where maybe they don't even exist."[72]

On 29 March the *Christian Science Monitor* paid little attention to the hindrances newsmen had encountered. Instead, it ran a forthright commentary by correspondent Daniel Southerland that credited the South Vietnamese with some achievements but still called many aspects of the operation into question. If a large portion of the soldiers in Laos had performed bravely and well, Southerland said, the conduct of some of their senior commanders had hardly seemed worthy. In addition, although some American officers remained convinced that the campaign had disrupted the enemy's plans, others clearly believed that its results had cast doubt upon the assumptions that had formed the basis for American withdrawals. "Laos showed that the North Vietnamese are not any less determined to fight now than they were two years ago," Southerland said, quoting an American military observer. "If they're willing to lose a hundred tanks, and more than three of their reserve divisions in a fight like this, they are not about to negotiate and just quit fighting."[73]

Time made much the same point, terming the operation "a costly miscalculation" that would take more than a year of rebuilding to correct. Noting that less than a battalion of regular reserves remained in the

[72] ABC Evening News, 1 Apr 71, *Radio-TV-Defense Dialog*.
[73] Daniel Southerland, "Laos Shortfall Stirs Sticky Queries," *Christian Science Monitor*, 29 Mar 71.

487

Saigon area, the magazine added a quote from an American official who had said, "Quite frankly, it scares me. . . . I wonder whether the other side realizes just how bare the cupboard is."[74]

The *Baltimore Sun* was equally critical but chose to publish an article by correspondent Michael Parks concentrating on the mutual recriminations that had begun to spring up between some of the American and South Vietnamese officers involved in the operation. One South Vietnamese colonel, who had lost much of his regiment in Laos, reflected on comments he had heard on the Voice of America that the campaign had saved many American lives. "Why," he asked, "are American lives so much more valuable than Vietnamese? . . . These comments are insulting and now the Americans have the gall to say we did not fight well and that we panicked. Most of the mistakes that were made were made by Americans but they cost Vietnamese lives." Another officer told the reporter that "we went in with fewer troops than the enemy and counted on American planes to make up the difference. . . . Candidly, I must say, the Americans let us down." For their part, Parks noted, American pilots complained that the South Vietnamese had failed to guide air strikes properly and had often endangered their lives by directing them into antiaircraft fire.[75]

Meanwhile, on 12 April, in a scathing editorial that labeled the incursion "one of the biggest fiascoes of the Vietnam War," the *Cleveland Plain Dealer* noted that American forward air controllers had concluded traffic along the Ho Chi Minh Trail was even heavier than before the invasion. "Rather than the military success President Nixon has acclaimed," the newspaper's editors speculated, "it appears the Laos incursion was a defeat that has bolstered Hanoi's confidence."[76]

General Abrams and his commanders disputed many of the claims appearing in the press. Their attitude appears to have been that of Lt. Gen. Melvin Zais, who remarked in a meeting with Kissinger on 22 March that the morale of the troops coming out of Laos was hardly susceptible to general assessments because the situation was neither all good nor all bad. "War is a kaleidoscope," Zais said. "Some will come back exuberant having really whipped the enemy where they were. Others will come back semi-panicked." In general, most of the military continued to believe that the incursion had harmed the enemy, that the South Vietnamese had fought well, and that the failure of President Thieu to reinforce the attack with another division had made all the difference.[77]

From Henry Kissinger's perspective and that of his staff, however, very little had gone well. Even the Cambodian portion of the operation had bogged down, with the troops doing little more, as reporters alleged, than patrol the roads while avoiding contact with the enemy. During May, indeed, the South Vietnamese would cut off all news of the operation

[74] "Assessing the Laos Invasion," *Time*, 5 Apr 71, p. 25.
[75] Michael Parks, "U.S., Saigon Blame Each Other for Laos," *Baltimore Sun*, 29 Mar 71.
[76] "Hanoi Supplies Still Moving," *Cleveland Plain Dealer*, 12 Apr 71.
[77] Briefing, 22 Mar 71, Kissinger Briefing Notes.

rather than continue to face what they termed the inaccuracies appearing in the press. The move was probably well advised, for shortly thereafter part of the force became trapped at Snuol while withdrawing into South Vietnam and a brigade that arrived to provide relief panicked and ran. Painfully aware of what was happening both in Cambodia and Laos, the national security adviser had little choice in his dealings with the press but to reaffirm President Nixon's assurances that the South Vietnamese were fighting well. Privately, he nevertheless continued to question every aspect of what was going on, from South Vietnamese body counts to the fact that, as he put it, "Throughout this operation no plan has stuck for a week."[78]

Believing that the president had never received information that accurately reflected future planning and that public statements by official spokesmen had diverged too often and too far from realities in the field, Kissinger attempted to clarify the situation by assigning his staff to determine the sequence of events that had occurred in Laos. The answers he received only added to his misgivings. Alexander Haig explained that the operation's planners had badly underestimated the enemy's ability and willingness to reinforce his forces, a fact that had bred a host of complications among the South Vietnamese, from tired, dispirited troops to personality conflicts among the operation's commanders. One of Kissinger's staff experts, Comdr. Jonathan Howe, did an extensive survey of all the messages, telephone conversations, and memorandums on the subject that had passed between the White House and the various agencies responsible for the operation. He reported that the assurances the president had received from all quarters, even from General Abrams, had rarely corresponded with what was actually happening in the field. Instead, from the perspective of the White House, the South Vietnamese had failed to give their American advisers an adequate picture of what was occurring. Meanwhile, General Abrams had been "slow in reporting, in taking the initiative to correct the situation, and in grasping initially the importance of keeping Washington informed of developments," and the Joint Chiefs of Staff had appeared "understandably reluctant" to pass on raw reports from the field while questions remained to be answered. As a result, administration spokesmen had again and again taken positions contrary to subsequent events in the field.[79]

[78] Briefing, 24 Mar 71, Kissinger Briefing Notes; Craig R. Whitney, "Saigon Cuts Off Cambodian News," *New York Times*, 17 May 71; MACV History, 1971, p. E-9. See, for example, Background Briefing at the White House with Dr. Henry A. Kissinger, 7 Apr 71, DDI Backgrounders file. Quote from Telecon, Kissinger with Moorer, 22 Mar 71, quoted in Extracts from Telephone Conversations Between Dr. Kissinger and Defense Department Officers, p. 2, attachment to Telephone Extracts: White House View of Laotian Planning.

[79] Handwritten Memo, Haig for Kissinger, n.d. [late Apr 71], sub: Lamson 719, NSC files, A. M. Haig Special file, box 1013, Haig SEA Trip, 14–21 Mar 71 [2 of 2], Nixon Papers. Quote from Memo, Comdr Jonathan Howe for Kissinger, 24 Mar 71, sub: White House View of Laotian Planning (February 8–March 20), covering Telephone Extracts: White House View of Laotian Planning. The conclusions in this report are considerably more elaborate than this treatment can provide.

Kissinger took up his misgivings with the president. According to Nixon's chief of staff, H. R. Haldeman, both decided they had been misled by Abrams in the original evaluation of what the operation might accomplish and that they should have followed Westmoreland's advice to cut off the Ho Chi Minh Trail to the south rather than drive toward Tchepone. The town had been "a visible objective" but the attempt to take it had turned out to be "basically a disaster." Nixon and Kissinger concluded, Haldeman noted, "that they should pull Abrams out, but then the P made the point that this is the end of the military operations anyway so what difference does it make."[80]

Although Kissinger and the president believed, as Haldeman observed, that the operation was "clearly not a success," Kissinger and his staff put the best face they could on what had happened by noting both privately and in their conversations with reporters that the North Vietnamese had consumed supplies that would normally have found use in South Vietnam.[81] Because of that and because the enemy would need time to restock, the attack into Laos appeared to have eliminated any possibility that the enemy would mount sustained large-unit attacks in South Vietnam during the rest of 1971. "The supplies and units which have been destroyed or damaged would have been available this year and next," Kissinger observed at a meeting with his staff on 23 March, "and you would have had the situation of American forces heading for their ships while the North Vietnamese were cranking up a major offensive."[82] It was better to have undertaken the incursion, the head of Kissinger's systems analysts, Wayne Smith, added at a meeting on 1 April, than to have waited for the North Vietnamese to attack. "This was on our terms rather than the enemy's. We chose the time and place . . . and . . . there were . . . far fewer U.S. casualties."[83]

Those judgments had much to commend them, but they told at best part of the story. For far from seeking to ensure the safety of South Vietnam only during 1971, the incursion's planners had all along expected the enemy's main effort to come in 1972, when they believed the North Vietnamese would attempt to achieve a major victory to capitalize on the continuing American withdrawal and to complicate President Nixon's chances for reelection. From that perspective, Kissinger and his staff readily admitted in private that the future looked grim. Ample opportunity remained for the Communists to recover enough strength to keep to their timetable, and the United States had little ability to stop them. If they did so, as Kissinger staff member Robert Sansom observed

[80] H. R. Haldeman, *The Haldeman Diaries*, entry for 23 Mar 71, p. 259.

[81] Quote from ibid.

[82] MFR, Jeanne W. Davis, 23 Mar 71, sub: Large Staff Meeting, March 23, NSC files, Backchannels, box 433, Laos-Cambodia Briefings, Nixon Papers.

[83] MFR, 1 Apr 71, sub: Meeting Between Dr. Kissinger, Gen. Alexander Haig, Col. Richard Kennedy, Winston Lord, Wayne Smith, W. Richard Smyser, Robert Sansom, Sven Kraemer, NSC files, A. M. Haig Chron files, box 978, Apr 8–12, 1971 [1 of 2], Nixon Papers.

at the meeting on 1 April, it seemed certain that there would be "bad trouble in I Corps next year."[84]

In the end, the controversy that developed over the incursion was probably inevitable. On the American side, the military and the news media had become fatigued, both with the war and one another. As the conflict had lengthened and American withdrawals had continued, the two had sparred incessantly over issues as diverse as combat refusals, the Green Beret Affair, the tiger cages at Con Son, and the drug and morale problems of the American soldier. Coming in that context, on the heels of congressional restrictions prohibiting the introduction of American ground forces and advisers into Cambodia and Laos, the incursion could hardly have produced anything but a major imbroglio.

Although the origins, objectives, and results of the operation were of importance to the press and remained the subject of continual controversy, those issues were only part of the problem. Of equal importance, especially to the Saigon correspondents, was the way in which the American and South Vietnamese commands had handled relations with the news media and the obvious desire of the Nixon administration to control all word of what was happening. Confronted by public affairs policies far more restrictive than ever in the past and already profoundly suspicious of officialdom, reporters reacted with all the outrage they could muster. Their anger came to taint everything that occurred in Laos, whether good or bad. General Abrams and President Nixon contributed to the problem: Abrams by holding to the embargo long after its military usefulness had ended and well after it had become a political liability to the president; Nixon by encouraging the South Vietnamese to assert their prerogatives against the news media and by permitting Agnew to bait the press.

In taking those positions, both men appear to have allowed their anger at the news media to prevail over calmer judgments and to have paid little attention to the work of many influential reporters that was either balanced in tone or, if jaundiced, still a fair approximation of what was happening in the field. A careful analysis will show, indeed, that the president usually had his way with the press. The themes he and his advisers wanted most to convey—that, for example, the South Vietnamese intended only to "disrupt" the Ho Chi Minh Trail and that it would take months to assemble a final appraisal of the operation—appeared time and again in news reports, almost as soon as someone in a position of influence stated them.

Yet even if Nixon, Abrams, and the others had adopted a more accommodating approach to the news media, the campaign in Laos would probably still have played poorly in the press. The South Vietnamese were of necessity taking increasing charge of their own public affairs, and they remained unsophisticated in the handling of correspon-

[84] Ibid.

dents. Add the disdain many within the press felt for South Vietnam's generals and fighting men, and a clash between the two became inevitable. If the campaign in Laos had triumphed, of course, the problems that developed would have meant little. The victory would have shone forth. But instead the operation went sour, and South Vietnamese and American efforts to paint it otherwise served only to reinforce the darkest conclusions.[85]

[85] Laird, for one, termed the operation a fiasco. See MFR, Phil Odeen, 15 Jun 71, sub: Vietnamization Meeting With Secretary Laird, 330–76–197, box 79, Viet 092 (Jun) 1971, Laird Papers, WNRC. Also see Clarence R. Wyatt, *Paper Soldiers: The American Press and the Vietnam War* (New York: W. W. Norton, 1993), pp. 196, 202–04.

20

Holding the Line, 1971

The incursion into Laos was not the only public relations problem confronting the Nixon administration and the military services as 1971 lengthened. Besides continuing bipartisan calls in Congress for accelerated U.S. withdrawals from Southeast Asia, allegations were beginning to arise that the violent manner with which the United States had fought the war to date constituted by its very nature a crime against humanity.[1] All the while, a few disgruntled Army officers created storms of bad publicity by using the news media to air their complaints.

The claim that the war was in itself an atrocity punishable by law was especially distressing. Under criteria established during the trials of German and Japanese war criminals at the end of World War II, Neil Sheehan argued in the 28 March 1971 edition of the *New York Times Book Review*, major figures within the U.S. government, including the president of the United States and General Westmoreland, might be subject to trial.[2]

Sheehan's assertion that, for example, hundreds of thousands of civilians had perished as a result of American combat tactics and that Army commanders had indulged in the wholesale destruction of hospitals set off a flurry of activity within the Pentagon, where teams of researchers began constructing point-by-point rebuttals. The entire subject was nevertheless so nebulous and so open to interpretation that little came of the effort. General Counsel of the Army Robert E. Jordan commented on an obscure public television program that by all precedents "faulty judgment does not constitute a war crime, certainly not in all cases, and . . . the allowable standard is not hindsight," but the Army, for the most part, never made much use of the arguments its researchers developed. Although it prepared an extensive critique justifying the conduct of the war and exonerating Westmoreland of complic-

---

[1] Chalmers Roberts, "GOP Senators Prod Laird on Pullout," *Washington Post*, 7 Apr 71.
[2] Neil Sheehan, "Should We have War Crime Trials?," *New York Times Book Review*, 28 Mar 71, p. 1.

493

(Left to right) *Friedheim, Sidle, and Henkin*

ity in war crimes, it held back the report on the advice of its historians and the Chief of U.S. Army Information, General Sidle.[3] Commending the analysis as "an excellent piece of work" but recognizing that any attempt at rebuttal could only aggravate the issue, Sidle used the study only as "a ready reference" for his action officers. The historians were more ambivalent. Recommending against any sort of public release, Walter Hermes, for one, remarked in a note to his superiors that "much of the material [cited in the critique] could be taken out of context and used to prove the opposite."[4]

The Herbert and Hackworth Affairs

The same reluctance to make more of a problem than necessary prevailed in the case of two officers who resorted to the news media to air their grievances during the latter half of 1971, Lt. Col. Anthony Herbert and Col. David Hackworth. A highly decorated veteran of the Korean War, Herbert had received an unsatisfactory performance

[3] Quote from WETA-TV, Washington, "Nuremberg and Vietnam: Who Is Guilty," 7 Jun 71, *Radio-TV-Defense Dialog,* copy in CMH files. Department of the Army, Final Report of the Research Project: Conduct of the War in Vietnam, May 71, CMH files.
[4] Memo, Sidle for Col R. W. Argo, Jr., OCSA, 17 Aug 71, sub: Study Group Report, CMH files; Memo, Walter Hermes for Brig Gen James L. Collins, Chief of Military History, 7 May 71, CMH files.

appraisal and had been relieved of duty as a battalion commander while serving during 1969 with the 173d Airborne Brigade in South Vietnam. After exhausting all appeals in an attempt to reverse that action, some eighteen months after the event, he pressed formal charges against his commanding officer in Vietnam, alleging that war crimes had occurred during his time with the 173d and that his knowledge of a cover-up within the brigade was the source of his problems with his superiors. The Military Assistance Command began an immediate investigation, but during September, in an obvious attempt to pressure the Army by playing to public concern about the My Lai massacre, Herbert granted interviews to reporters from a large number of news media outlets.

Hackworth was also a discontented officer, but, unlike Herbert, had never been the subject of an adverse personnel action. A highly respected combat veteran who had served more than five years in South Vietnam as an adviser and troop commander, he had written extensively on counterinsurgency warfare. By June 1971, however, he had become so unhappy with what he considered the mistakes of American policy makers in the conduct of the war that he, too, turned to the press by announcing melodramatically in public that he intended to resign from the Army in order to speak his mind.

The Herbert affair made the largest impression in the news media, with a story by James Wooten in the *New York Times Magazine* setting the pace. Entitled "How a Supersoldier Was Fired From His Command," Wooten alleged that Herbert had been discredited and harassed by the Army because he had courageously reported war crimes to his superior officers. The *Times* summarized Wooten's account on its editorial page, adding that "Herbert's allegations are at least as terrifying in their implications as any that have arisen out of the My Lai massacre. Did high-ranking officers deliberately prevent a combat commander of unblemished credentials from putting a stop to the commission of war crimes and order his career destroyed for his efforts?" Sympathetic stories and commentaries followed on the NBC Nightly News and in the *Washington Post*, the *Chicago Sun-Times*, the *Wall Street Journal*, and a host of other news media outlets. In the end, Herbert's story received favorable treatment not only on television and in most newspapers and magazines in the United States but also in Europe and Great Britain.[5]

---

[5] James Wooten, "How a Supersoldier Was Fired From His Command," *New York Times Magazine*, 5 Sep 71. The quote is from "The Army on Trial," *New York Times*, 5 Sep 71. Also see Fact Sheet, 5 Nov 71, sub: Col. Herbert, attachment to Memo, Comdr W. J. Bredbeck, USN, Military Assistant, OSD, for Brig Gen James D. Hughes, Military Assistant to the President, 5 Nov 71, and Memo, SGS for Westmoreland, 12 Nov 71, sub: Herbert Matters—Period of 7–12 November 1971, Herbert Notebooks, vol. 2, both in CMH files; John Chancellor, NBC Nightly News, 8 Sep 71, *Radio-TV-Defense Dialog*; "Col. Herbert Takes Lie Test on Vietnam Atrocity Story," *Washington Post*, 8 Sep 71; "War Hero vs. Pentagon," *Chicago Sun-Times*, 9 Sep 71; "Colonel Herbert's Case," *Wall Street Journal*, 10 Sep 91; Godfrey Hodgson, "Colonel Herbert: The Humiliation of a War Hero," *London Sunday Times*, 21 Nov 71.

As the controversy over Herbert's allegations built, Under Secretary of the Army Kenneth E. Belieu instructed the Army staff to refrain from taking any action against the officer that could be construed as vindictive. The best way to discredit Herbert, he said, would be to review his record and his public statements and quietly to plant seeds of disbelief in the minds of key congressional leaders. In the weeks that followed, Army investigators reviewed Herbert's medical records to substantiate or refute claims the officer had made, for example, about having received three bayonet wounds during the Korean War. The Army also released a statement to the effect that Herbert had raised the war crimes issue for the first time in September 1970, eighteen months after he was relieved of command in Vietnam and only after he had exhausted other means of salvaging his military career. Exonerated by an Army review panel, Herbert's former commander in Vietnam, Maj. Gen. John W. Barnes, also came forward, as did the deputy brigade commander of the 173d Airborne, Col. J. Ross Franklin. Both officers stated that they had come to mistrust Herbert in Vietnam. "He was incapable of telling the truth, even on inconsequential matters," Franklin said. " . . . And after [one combat assault], I realized the man was extremely dangerous. I had doubts even as to his sanity, and I was fearful for what he might do in the future." When reporters noted that Herbert had passed a polygraph examination, Barnes responded angrily, "I suppose that if you live a lie long enough, you can pass a lie test."[6]

Those efforts had much of the effect the Army sought. As early as 6 October 1971, for example, columnist Paul Dean had questioned Herbert's motives in the pages of the *Arizona Republic*. On 12 November, with the Army's campaign to discredit Herbert in full swing, the Associated Press replayed information contained in a second article by Dean, including a comment by a Roman Catholic chaplain to the effect that Herbert had told him, "I have no God damn integrity. I'll lie about anything to get what I want." The news service added that knowledgeable sources had revealed incidents in which Herbert had abused unarmed South Vietnamese villagers and in which he had threatened to seek revenge against Barnes, Franklin, and other officers whom he deemed responsible for his misfortunes. In the same way, on 20 November, the *National Observer* published an evenhanded summary of the controversy between Herbert and the Army. Leaving conclusions up to the reader, it commented nevertheless that if it was difficult to imagine Herbert as a "ruthless, vindictive, overaggressive combat commander," that image of him had emerged, "jarringly, from conversations with fellow officers finally permitted to speak out and from hundreds of pages of sworn testimony, never before publicized, that

---

[6] Belieu's instructions are a paraphrase of his actual words. Memo, SGS for Westmoreland, 12 Nov 71, sub: Herbert Matters—Period of 7–12 November 1971. Also see Morton Kondracke, "Gen. Barnes Lashes Back, Charges Herbert Was Lying," *Washington Star*, 12 Nov 71. Franklin is quoted in Daniel St. Albin Greene, "Colonel Herbert: A Hero or a Liar?," *National Observer*, 20 Nov 71.

the Army made available . . . last week." *Time* repeated many of those charges in a summary of its own on 22 November.[7]

In the end, the Military Assistance Command found some truth in a few of Herbert's allegations but was able to do little. Those that were verifiable were already under adjudication. The rest were impossible to confirm either because too much time had elapsed or because they involved South Vietnamese forces beyond the jurisdiction of the United States. With that, avowing that Herbert's poor efficiency rating might have been an unfortunate exception to an otherwise creditable record of service, Secretary of the Army Robert F. Froehlke revoked the performance appraisal that had caused the trouble and opened the way for the officer to retire. Herbert did so, but once more in a blare of publicity. "I have been shot five times and bayoneted three times," he told reporters dramatically while revealing his decision to leave the Army, "none of which was as painful to me as the decision I must now announce."[8]

The controversy dragged on over the next year, with Herbert appearing on ABC's "Dick Cavett Show" and NBC's "Today Show" during November 1971 and receiving feature treatment in a *Playboy* interview during July of the following year. He then published a best-selling book that recounted his experiences in Vietnam and once more detailed his charge that the Army had retaliated against him for reporting war crimes. The doubts sown by the Army nevertheless had their effect. Shortly after the book appeared, on 4 February 1973, the CBS news magazine "60 Minutes" aired a report produced by Barry Lando and narrated by correspondent Mike Wallace that discredited many of the charges Herbert had levied over the years. The *Atlantic Monthly* then published an article by Lando that made the same points in more detail. The two reports killed whatever lingering credibility Herbert held with the press. From that time on, General Sidle would later recall, "I had very little trouble re[garding] the Herbert allegations." Herbert attempted to salvage his reputation by suing CBS, Lando, and Wallace. Although the Supreme Court found in his favor on a minor point of law, the Federal Appeals Court in New York finally put the issue to rest in 1986 by summarily dismissing his case.[9]

[7] Paul Dean, "My Lai Coverup Claim Called Act of Revenge," *Arizona Republic*, 6 Oct 71; [AP–1014], Herbert, 12 Nov 71, copy in CMH files; Paul Dean, "Countercharges Leveled Against War Hero Herbert," *Arizona Republic*, 12 Nov 71; Greene, "Colonel Herbert: A Hero or a Liar?"; "The Military: Colonel Herbert v. the Army," *Time*, 22 Nov 71.

[8] [AP], "Harassment Claimed, Col. Herbert Sets Army Retirement," *Washington Star*, 8 Nov 71. Also see Msg, Sidle WDC 4218 to Abrams, 11 Mar 71, Abrams Papers, CMH; Memo, Robert Cocklin, Acting Chief of Army Information, for Secretary of the General Staff, 8 Jul 71, CMH files.

[9] Transcript, "The Dick Cavett Show," 19 Nov 71, CMH files; Transcript, Today Show, NBC-TV, "An Interview with Lt. Col. Herbert," 22 Nov 71, CMH files; "*Playboy* Interview: Anthony Herbert," *Playboy*, Jul 72, CMH files; Anthony Herbert with James T. Wooten, *Soldier* (New York: Hold, Rinehart & Winston, 1973); Barry Lando, "The Herbert Affair," *Atlantic Monthly*, May 73, p. 73. Quote from Ltr, Sidle to the author, 5 Sep 91, CMH files. Jeffrey Toobin, "Enduring Insults: Old Lawsuits Never Die," *New Republic*, 10 Mar 86; "No Case, Colonel," *Time*, 27 Jan 86.

Herbert's interviews with the press disturbed the Army, but their potential for embarrassment was small in comparison with the charges leveled by Hackworth. Participating in a series of interviews with ABC correspondent Howard Tuckner and appearing on an edition of the ABC news program "Issues and Answers," Hackworth raised issues that went to the heart of the American effort in South Vietnam. The United States had always possessed the wherewithal to win the war, he said, but the enemy was becoming stronger rather than weaker because managers rather than warriors had taken control of the Army. As a result, U.S. commanders had trained the South Vietnamese to fight as Americans, using enormous volumes of firepower and equipment, when they should have taught them to fight like the Viet Cong, in as spare and efficient a manner as possible. Hackworth continued that the president was not receiving a true picture of the war because the facts were altered and distorted as they moved up the various chains of command in the field, that the body count continued to be exaggerated, that the incursion into Laos had been improperly planned, and that the South Vietnamese government was profoundly corrupt. On the side, he noted that President Nixon's announcement that he would release Lieutenant Calley from the stockade at Fort Benning and personally review whatever final sentence the courts imposed was wrong and that "the due process of law" should continue without political interference.[10]

Secretary of Defense Laird perceived immediately that there was much of substance in Hackworth's allegations and for a time considered inviting the colonel to the Pentagon to speak with the various committees that handled war-related policy. Although inclined to disagree with the assertion that the South Vietnamese were using the wrong tactics, he believed that it made little sense to attack someone with Hackworth's credentials. Instead, he told his staff, "we ought to listen." On those grounds, Laird advised General Westmoreland to avoid any attempt to rebut the officer's allegations publicly and asked the White House to adopt the same approach.[11]

General Abrams nevertheless decided that the MACV inspector general should interview Hackworth. The grounds he gave were that the officer seemed to have made a number of allegations about falsified body counts and other crimes that bore directly upon the proper functioning of his command. In fact, there seems to have been some hope on his part and on that of the Army that the session could be used to determine whether Hackworth had any more "surprises" in store. Also, as the Vice Chief of Staff of the Army, General Bruce Palmer, Jr., observed, the meet-

---

[10] Hackworth's points are summarized in Daniel Southerland, "U.S. Hero Colonel Quitting Over Vietnam," *Christian Science Monitor*, 18 Jun 71; Howard Tuckner, ABC Evening News, 22, 23, 24 Jun 71, *Radio-TV-Defense Dialog*; Transcript, "Issues and Answers," 27 Jun 71, copy in CMH files.

[11] MFR, Phil Odeen, 25 Jun 71, sub: Vietnamization Meeting With Secretary Laird, folder 77, Thayer Papers, CMH files.

ing would serve to remind him "of the standards of conduct expected of a commissioned officer, in particular an experienced senior officer."[12]

Whatever Abrams' intentions, the meeting bore little fruit. Most of the officer's allegations were amorphous or dealt with matters too far in the past to be open to investigation. In addition, Hackworth alleged that in a number of cases the press had altered the meaning of his statements by omitting qualifying phrases and that he had never intended for his remarks to be seen as some sort of attack upon the Army.[13]

There the matter might have rested, but for the inspector general, Colonel Cook, who began to track down leads he had received from some of Hackworth's subordinates, who were stricken in conscience by the disparity between the carefully groomed public persona the colonel had adopted in his interviews and the private activities in which he had indulged during his tours of duty in South Vietnam. Cook shortly found that the officer, if he had indeed performed heroically in combat, had also profited from black market trading, currency manipulation, drug abuse, and organized prostitution. Informed of those findings, the Army sought to bring charges against the officer. "Hackworth represents a unique case for which there are very few precedents in the Army's long history," the USARV Deputy Commander, Lt. Gen. William J. McCaffrey, told Westmoreland. "I don't think we have had his like since George A. Custer."[14]

In the end, the Military Assistance Command dropped its investigation. Although Laird would later defend the move on grounds that the case against the colonel had been weak and had fallen apart upon close examination, Hackworth himself later confirmed many of its findings in a personal memoir. It seems clear, in that light, that, whether the officer would in the end have been found guilty or innocent, he had benefited from the same sort of politically oriented largess that he had so decried in the case of Calley. The desire of the Nixon administration and the Army to avoid anymore controversy than necessary at that late stage in the war had prevailed.[15]

If the Army, where Herbert and Hackworth were concerned, faced its critics reluctantly and with indecision, its approach was hardly different

[12] Msg, Palmer WDC 11298 to Abrams, 25 Jun 71. Also see Msg, Abrams MAC 6410 to Palmer, 25 Jun 71. Both in Abrams Papers, CMH.

[13] Msg, Abrams MAC 6410 to Palmer, 25 Jun 71.

[14] Msg, Abrams MAC 7313 to Westmoreland, 30 Jul 71, Westmoreland Papers, CMH. The Report of Investigation on Hackworth may be found in MACVIG, MIV–67–71, 26 Aug 71, sub: Report of Investigation Concerning Col. David Hackworth, 334–77–0074, box 1, vol. 5, tab T, WNRC. McCaffrey is quoted in Msg, Palmer WDC 16632 to Westmoreland, 10 Sep 71, sub: The Hackworth Case, Westmoreland Papers, CMH.

[15] MFR, Phil Odeen, 22 Sep 71, sub: Vietnamization Meeting With Secretary Laird, 330–76–197, box 79, Viet 092 (Jul–Dec) 1971 file, Laird Papers, WNRC; David Hackworth and Julie Sherman, *About Face: The Odyssey of an American Warrior* (New York: Simon and Schuster, 1989), pp. 803–04; Memo, Larry Higby for Chuck Colson, 25 Jul 71, sub: Col. Hackworth, Papers of John Scali, Subject files, box 1, Colson Action Memos [2 of 7], Nixon Papers.

from that of the rest of the military establishment in the final years of the war. With consensus in the United States in support of the war diminishing, few generals saw much use in fighting losing battles with the press. All concerned looked forward to the moment when a final withdrawal could occur and sought, in the interim, mostly to hold the line. Their attitude appeared to coincide with that of a ranking officer, who told the *Wall Street Journal* during June 1971 that he believed an increase in withdrawal rates for U.S. forces in South Vietnam could only benefit the Army. As American involvement in the war ended, he said, the morale of the troops would increase and officers would be able to reestablish proper discipline. That would revitalize the effort to alleviate racial tensions among the men and eliminate drug abuse.[16]

Deepening Malaise

The heightening awareness that the war was coming to an end produced more than a simple desire to avoid controversy. It seemed to aggravate the decline in morale that was already apparent among the soldiers serving in South Vietnam. As the American role in combat diminished and questions continued to rise in the United States, the various sides in the debate over the war hardened their positions. As they did, the written and unwritten codes that had earlier defined the limits of proper conduct for soldier and civilian official alike began to give way.

Enlisted men had never had much difficulty telling newsmen, for example, that they were unwilling to be the last to die in Southeast Asia, but by 1971 high-level leaks to the press were also beginning to proliferate. During March, April, and May, syndicated columnist Jack Anderson, for one, authored a host of news stories based upon highly classified documents that could only have come from extremely well-connected, inside sources, some of them military. The revelations opened aspects of the war to public scrutiny that had long been hidden: U.S. Air Force efforts to increase rainfall along the Ho Chi Minh Trail by seeding monsoon clouds in Laos, the Pentagon's programs for domestic surveillance, official complaints about the amount and quality of the information supplied to the negotiators in Paris, contingency plans for the bombing of Haiphong, intelligence-gathering raids into Cambodia, the enemy's advance knowledge of the incursion into Laos, and American efforts to spy on the Saigon regime.[17]

Hard upon the leaks to Anderson, the *New York Times* published a secret Defense Department history of war-related decision making during the Johnson administration that became known as the *Pentagon Papers*.

---

[16] "About Face," *Wall Street Journal*, 25 Jun 71.

[17] Rpts of Investigation, 13 Apr 71, 21 Jun 71, sub: Unauthorized Disclosure of Classified Defense Information, Papers of David Young, Subject files, Nixon Papers.

500

The combination of the two sets of leaks convulsed the Nixon administration, which had just learned that the Chairman of the People's Republic of China, Mao Tse-tung, after months of maneuvering, had agreed to receive Henry Kissinger in a secret state visit designed to begin the normalization of relations between the United States and his country. "Our nightmare," Kissinger later observed, commenting on the leaks,

> was that Peking might conclude our government was too unsteady, too harassed, and too insecure to be a useful partner. The massive hemorrhage of state secrets was bound to raise doubts about our reliability . . . and the stability of our political system. [In addition] we had secret talks going on . . . with the North Vietnamese. . . . We were at an important point in the sensitive SALT [Strategic Arms Limitation Talks] . . . [with the Soviet Union]. And we were in the final stages of delicate Berlin negotiations which also depended on secrecy.[18]

In the end, the revelations appear to have had little effect upon the Nixon administration's diplomacy, but the president and his advisers moved immediately to shore up their credibility with friend and foe alike. Attempting to block the publication of the *Pentagon Papers*, they also took what steps they could to establish the identities of those who had leaked sensitive information, whether to the *Times* or to Anderson. Over the next several months, they succeeded in identifying the man who had released the *Pentagon Papers*, former Defense Department analyst Daniel Ellsberg, and one of Anderson's probable sources, a U.S. Navy yeoman on the National Security Council staff, YN1 Charles Radford. In the process, the president's investigators took steps, as Kissinger noted, whose "sordidness, puerility, and ineffectuality . . . eventually led to the downfall of the Nixon administration."[19]

Ellsberg's spectacular revelations drew most of the attention of the press, but they dealt only with the decisions of the Johnson administration. Beyond the questions of diplomacy Kissinger had raised, they thus posed few genuine political concerns for Nixon. Anderson's disclosures were a different matter. They dealt with topics of immediate concern to the administration, and, as official investigators shortly discovered, much more was involved than simple leaks to a reporter. As the inquiry progressed, it became clear that Radford had passed stolen White House documents through his military superiors to Admiral Moorer, who apparently so mistrusted the White House staff that he felt a need to have a clandestine source at the National Security Council to keep him abreast of initiatives that might affect the military. Although a tacit understanding had long existed in official circles that military men serving the president would at times pass word of White House thinking to their superiors at the Pentagon, the case was unique. Radford had appar-

---

[18] Kissinger, *The White House Years*, pp. 729–30.
[19] Ibid. Also see Memo, Fred Malek for Haldeman, 2 Nov 71, sub: Progress Report on Leaks—Month of October, David Young Subject files, box 20, Leak Chronology, Nixon Papers.

ently duplicated classified documents wholesale and even admitted to presidential adviser John Ehrlichman that he had purloined and copied material entrusted to his care in the briefcases of National Security Council staff members. Stricken in conscience by some of the material he had read and already compromised by his services to Moorer, Radford, so the reasoning went, turned to a fellow member of his church, Anderson, for advice, and ended up releasing part of what he knew to the reporter.[20]

Moorer denied that he had any knowledge of Radford's activities, and Radford insisted that he had never given National Security Council materials to Anderson. Nixon himself, however, appears to have been convinced that Moorer was somehow implicated and told his advisers dejectedly, if somewhat disingenuously, that he would have given the admiral any information he wanted, if only he had asked. In the end, Nixon declined to take action against any of the principals involved, but he still became so distrustful of the military that he briefly questioned the advisability of continuing to employ officers in key positions on the National Security Council staff. Although he never took any action on the matter, he noted at a White House meeting on 22 December 1971 that Henry Kissinger seemed surrounded by military subordinates—Haig, Commander Howe, and others. As a result, he said, a danger existed that those officers might so isolate the national security adviser from political reality that they could bend him completely to their own military point of view on the war.[21]

If the Radford case and the Nixon administration's reaction to it exemplified the decline in standards that had set in at the highest level in Washington, a similar breakdown was occurring in South Vietnam, where the war seemed to have become, more than ever before, a bureaucratic exercise. As early as November 1970, for example, the Office of the Secretary of Defense had found that the U.S. Army in South Vietnam was firing more artillery rounds than it had during the Tet offensive of 1968, despite large decreases in U.S. force levels and declines in enemy activity. Since much of the firing came in the morning and evening, just before

[20] Interv, John Ehrlichman with YN1 Charles Radford, 23 Dec 71, White House Special files, Staff Member Office files, Ehrlichman, Special Subject file, Young Project, Nixon Papers. Laird asserted at the time that a channel similar to the one involving Radford had long existed. See Telecon, John Ehrlichman with Secretary Laird, 23 Dec 71, David Young Subject files, box 24, Special Report to the President from David R. Young [folder 5 of 5], Nixon Papers.

[21] Memo, David Young for the President, n.d., sub: Record of Investigation of Classified Information in Jack Anderson Articles, December 14 and 16, 1971, David Young Subject files, box 23, Special Report to the President from David R. Young, Memorandum for the Record, Nixon Papers. This compendium contains a relatively complete record of the Yeoman Radford affair. Nixon's concerns were expressed at a 22 December meeting at the Executive Office Building summarized in the file. Also see Interv, Ehrlichman with Radford, 23 Dec 71; Stephen E. Ambrose, *Nixon, The Triumph of a Politician, 1962–1972* (New York: Simon and Schuster, 1989), pp. 486–88.

changes in shift at artillery batteries, the conclusion seemed inescapable that commanders were judging the performance of their artillery units solely by the number of rounds they fired and that the men were saving their ready ammunition until the ends of their shifts, lest they run short in an emergency.[22]

In the same way, it became clear to Secretary Laird toward the end of 1970 that the U.S. Air Force and Navy were flying attack missions on a routine basis in South Vietnam rather than in response to genuine combat requirements. To his mind, the technique was an attempt on the part of those services to preserve funding for bombs and other munitions that might have evaporated if word had surfaced in Congress that part of the previous year's allocation had gone unused. Defense Department officials took up the matter with Abrams during June 1971. Noting that the general looked as though he were carrying the "weight of the world," they reported that the commander was well aware of the practice but declined to do anything about it because he believed his air assets were his only real reserve in case of trouble. Laird, for his part, beyond advising restraint, also took no action. According to Jerry Friedheim, he understood that he would only add to the demoralization of the military by imposing some sort of Draconian solution from above. In addition, it seemed clear that the military services were less at fault than a system of budgeting adopted by Congress in times of peace that lacked the flexibility war required.[23]

A Single Bad Day of Publicity

Laird's inclination to avoid disturbing the status quo was similar to the approach Nixon had adopted with respect to Anderson, Moorer, and Radford. As 1971 progressed, indeed, the inclination to put off controversy became one of the underpinnings of high-level thinking on the war. Where possible, officials both in the United States and South Vietnam preferred to hold back, even when strong action appeared necessary, rather than provoke an outcry in the press that might somehow damage what was left of official credibility.

Many cases occurred, of course, in which officials had little choice but to admit to disagreeable facts rather than allow reporters to find out for themselves. During February 1971, for example, after maintaining for years that hardly any statistics existed on the causes of civilian war casualties in South Vietnam, the U.S. Agency for International Development discovered that the South Vietnamese Ministry of Health had been keep-

---

[22] MFRs, Phil Odeen, OASD SA, 3 Aug 70 and 10 Aug 70, sub: Vietnamızation Meeting With Secretary Laird, folder 76, Thayer Papers, CMH.

[23] MFR, Phil Odeen, 4 Nov 70, sub: Vietnamization Meeting Wıth Secretary Laird, and MFR, Phil Odeen, 17 Jun 71, sub: Vietnamization Meeting With Secretary Laird. Both in folder 77, Thayer Papers, CMH. Interv, author with Jerry Friedheim, 3 Oct 86, CMH files.

ing rough figures since at least 1967 on whether hospital admissions were caused by friendly or enemy fire. On grounds that a *Newsweek* reporter was closing in on the story, the agency released the figures to the Senate Judiciary Committee's Subcommittee on Refugees, even though it had doubts about their validity.[24]

Occasions of that sort to the contrary, the way the Military Assistance Command handled an announcement revising its tabulation of aircraft losses was much more characteristic of official preferences at the time. Reports to the press on the subject had long classified losses in the air under one of two groupings: Category I, aircraft that crashed as the result of hostile action in North or South Vietnam; and Category II, aircraft lost to nonhostile causes, support aircraft losses, and all other losses in connection with the war. To keep from revealing the extent of American involvement in Cambodia and Laos, the command had lumped all aircraft that went down in those countries from whatever cause into the nonhostile grouping. During March 1970 a presidential directive designed to improve official credibility had required the command to report losses in Laos as they occurred. MACV had complied, including the information in its nightly briefings for the Saigon correspondents, but it had neglected to make the change in the weekly statistical summaries it released to the press. By mid-1971, however, the practice seemed less and less tenable. With American involvement in ground combat tapering off and the Saigon correspondents increasingly preoccupied with the air war, it was clear that reporters would sooner or later begin to compare what they were hearing in the briefings with the written reports they received and conclude that the command was somehow dissembling.[25]

During June the Office of the Assistant Secretary of Defense for Public Affairs, with the concurrence of the White House, began consideration of ways to remedy the problem. The change in reporting procedure posed little difficulty in itself. It was merely a matter of separating aircraft losses by combat or noncombat causes and breaking down the totals by country. Yet as the Chief of the Directorate of Defense Information's Southeast Asia Division, Cdr. Joseph Lorfano, noted in a memorandum to Assistant Secretary Henkin, it seemed certain that the announcement accompanying the revision would spark "a flurry of analysis type news stories probably inferring combat losses previously hidden, finally revealed under pressure of future political impact, etc."[26] MACV public affairs officers proposed a solution. To minimize any adverse reaction that might devel-

[24] Memo, Lars H. Hyde for Mr. Engle, 1 Feb 71, sub: Origin of Civilian War Casualties, DDI Civilian Casualties file. Also see Msg, Saigon 5036 to State, 6 Apr 71, sub: Civilian War Casualties, Pol 27 Viet S file, FAIM/IR.

[25] Draft Memo, OASD PA for Brig Gen Alexander Haig, n.d., sub: Announcement of Aircraft Losses in SEA, attachment to Memo, Comdr Joseph Lorfano for Henkin, 11 Jun 71, sub: Proposed Change in Reporting of U.S. Aircraft Losses in SEA, DDI Air Incidents/Policy file.

[26] Memo, Lorfano for Henkin, 11 Jun 71, sub: Proposed Change in Reporting of U.S. Aircraft Losses in SEA.

op, they noted in a message to the Defense Department, official spokesmen might announce the change during September, at the height of the South Vietnamese election campaign. The Saigon correspondents would be so preoccupied with the rivalries between the principal South Vietnamese candidates, Thieu and Ky, so the reasoning went, that they would undoubtedly pay less than complete attention to a relatively routine announcement about statistical recordkeeping. In the end, according to General Hill, the Defense Department approved the approach, the Military Assistance Command made the announcement, and the press accepted the change as a matter of course, with little untoward comment.[27]

The Army adopted a similar approach in the case of an incident that occurred during March 1971, when enemy sappers attacked a 23d Infantry "Americal" Division fire support base named MARY ANN, located in Quang Tin Province, some eighty kilometers south of Da Nang. After firing hundreds of mortar shells in preparation, a group of between fifty and sixty well-prepared enemy sappers penetrated the base. In the half-hour that followed, they killed or wounded virtually all of the installation's officers by tossing grenades and satchel charges into its tactical operations center. They also destroyed many of the bunkers on the base's perimeter. By the time they were through, they had killed 30 Americans and wounded 82 while losing at most 12 of their own men. Since the toll was the largest incurred by a U.S. force in a single action in over two years, constituting more than one-third of the week's casualties, it was impossible to hide. Public affairs officers had little choice but to allow the press to proceed to the site of the disaster and to fill in accounts of the event with whatever details they had available.[28]

Reporters, for their part, interviewed the survivors and discovered almost immediately that the officers and enlisted men at the base had been lax in their preparations to repel an assault. "In contrast to the Communists' well executed attack, the men at the fire base were caught unaware . . .," Nicholas Proffitt told *Newsweek*.

---

[27] Msg, MACV 71094 to CINCPAC, ASD PA, 9 Aug 71, sub: Proposed Change in Announcement of Aircraft Losses in SEA, CMH files. The exact date of the change is unclear but it almost certainly occurred during September 1971. General Hill, for one, was of that mind and confirmed that MACV had attempted to release word of the development as unobtrusively as possible in order to avoid controversy. See Interv, author with Maj Gen L. Gordon Hill, 23 Aug 89, CMH files.

[28] Casualty figures vary, with initial reports putting them at 33 killed and 76 wounded. See Msg, Maj Gen Baldwin, CG, 23d Inf Div, ACD 421 to Abrams, 28 Mar 71, sub: Attack on FSB Mary Ann, Abrams Papers, CMH. The numbers used here and other details are from later reports. Msg, Abrams MAC 5611 to Westmoreland, 6 Jun 71, sub: 28 Mar 71 Attack on FSB Mary Ann, and Msg, Baldwin ACD 483 to Abrams, 7 Apr 71, sub: Interim Report of Investigation Concerning Attack on FSB Mary Ann, both in Abrams Papers, CMH. The comparison with casualty counts from earlier years is made in U.S. Department of State, Bureau of Intelligence and Research, Intelligence Note, 26 Apr 71, sub: South Vietnam: Intensity Levels of the War for the Month of March, 1971, Pol 27 Viet S file, FAIM/IR.

The Americal Division was cutting down on the number of troops in Quang Tin province (believing the danger there was lessening) and was abandoning Mary Ann in favor of a new base, Mildred. . . . Indeed, so convinced was the command that there would be no more trouble at Mary Ann that it did not send out reconnaissance patrols on the night of the attack. "There was no need for them," Lt. Col. W. B. Doyle, the battalion commander, told me. "Our intelligence had not reported any type of enemy activity in the area." The grunts were as unprepared as the officers. Although a third of Charlie Company was on perimeter guard duty, no one spotted the sappers' approach.

Proffitt added that, in the aftermath of the event, some soldiers had told television crews that the enemy had broken through MARY ANN's defenses because the guards were smoking marijuana. "I took the names of the two men who had recounted the pot stories," he said, "and, upon checking, discovered that neither was listed on the company roster. It is likely that they were not at Mary Ann on the night in question. 'I ain't saying there's no pot up there,' one soldier told me, 'but if we catch anybody doping up heavily we get him quick.'" The reporter concluded that even without slurs such as the marijuana story, it was clear that the Americal Division, in the wake of the controversy over My Lai, had suffered another blow to its reputation. "But it is not the division alone that was stung by Mary Ann," he added. "The attack clearly demonstrated that, despite the recent invasion of Laos, the Communists have not lost their ability to inflict stunning losses on U.S. troops."[29]

Investigators employed by the Americal Division corroborated the reports appearing in the press. They found, for example, that if marijuana had not been a consideration in the debacle, the officers in charge at MARY ANN had indeed failed to follow standard operating procedures that required them to post at least one guard at each entrance of the tactical operations center as well as others at each bunker on the base's perimeter. In addition, it was doubtful that commanders had laid down lines of fire for their men and that they had positioned a satisfactory number of mines, tear gas dispensers, napalm charges, and wire detonated explosives in the perimeter surrounding the base. Commissioned and noncommissioned officers had likewise failed to check the bunker line at least once during each hour of the night, and the unit's officers had neglected to assign a roving guard force to protect open areas such as the base helicopter pad. Although the complex was experiencing a period of reduced visibility, the battalion commander had also failed either to assign a searchlight team to illuminate the perimeter or to warn his men of the need for increased caution by changing the installation's alert status from green to yellow.[30]

[29] Nicholas Proffitt, "The Massacre at Fire Base Mary Ann," *Newsweek*, 12 Apr 71. Jonathan Larson filed a similar report for *Time*. See "The Massacre at Fire Base Mary Ann," *Time*, 12 Apr 71.

[30] Msg, Baldwin ACD 483 to Abrams, 7 Apr 71, sub: Interim Report of Investigation Concerning Attack on FSB Mary Ann.

With questions rising in Congress and the news media, General West-moreland cabled U.S. Army, Vietnam, for its best estimate of when some sort of final report would be ready. In that way, he said, he would be able to coordinate the Army's public position on the incident with that of the Department of Defense. Abrams responded cryptically that although the American's investigators had done an adequate job of assessing blame at the lower levels of command, they had provided little insight into the role brigade and division officers had played. To leave time for MACV's inspector general to do a more thorough study, he recommended that Westmoreland put off questions for at least a month by making some sort of noncommittal statement that an investigation was in progress.[31]

Abrams' final report, when it came on 5 July, was to the point. The event had occurred much as investigators had found, the general observed, and senior officers at brigade and division levels, including the division's commander, Maj. Gen. James L. Baldwin, had been negligent in the attention they paid to deficiencies at the base. Not only had they failed to ensure that the units assigned to MARY ANN adhered to proper defensive procedures, a number of them had dissembled when confront-ed under oath by the inspector general with the fact that five of the enemy's dead had been burned in the base trash dump despite standing regulations that required burial. The infraction was relatively minor, but the commander of the 196th Infantry Brigade (Light), Col. William S. Hathaway, who was high on the Army's list for promotion to brigadier general, had knowingly provided false and misleading information on the incident. The 23d Infantry Division's chief of staff, Col. Alphus R. Clark, had denied under oath that he had known anything about the burning of bodies when he had, in fact, seen photographs provided by Hathaway. Also Baldwin himself had known of what had happened but had failed to report it to his superiors or to take any action to discipline the individuals responsible.[32]

"To put the matter of the attack on Fire Support Base Mary Ann into the proper perspective," MACV's inspector general, Colonel Cook, con-cluded,

consideration should be given to the fact that this incident could very well have happened to other units of the 23d Infantry Division or to like combat units in Vietnam today. The reduced level of combat activity and the increasing publicity by the news media focused upon ending of the war tend to create complacency among both the troops and their commanders. Coupled with this is the effect of anti-Vietnam and anti-military attitudes within the CONUS [continental United States] and the growth of permissiveness within the military establishment. All of these factors confront a commander in Vietnam today with a formidable task

[31] Msg, Westmoreland WDC 9882 to McCaffrey, Dep CG, USARV, 5 Jun 71, and Msg, Abrams MAC 5611 to Westmoreland, 6 Jun 71, sub: 28 Mar 71 Attack on FSB Mary Ann, both in Abrams Papers, CMH.

[32] Msg, Abrams MAC 6497 to Westmoreland, 6 Jul 71, sub: 28 Mar 71 Attack on FSB Mary Ann, Abrams Papers, CMH.

(challenge) of maintaining a high state of discipline and alertness among his troops. Nevertheless, it must be recognized that if this type of situation is allowed to prevail, we can expect that in the months to come, there may occur an even greater disaster. Therefore, the hard facts . . . which have been revealed during this investigation must be recognized and acted upon.[33]

With MACV's findings and Cook's recommendation in hand, General Abrams removed Baldwin from command of the 23d Division and reassigned him to a duty station in Washington, where his presence would expedite any further action the Army decided to take in the case. The move caused a flurry of comment in the press and Congress, but the Army, deeply involved in determining how it should discipline Baldwin and his officers, continued to postpone any substantial revelation of the facts. Although the chairmen of the House and Senate Armed Services Committees received a briefing, in confidence, on the full results of MACV's investigation, anyone else who inquired again received what Westmoreland termed an "interim reply." After delivering a brief description of the incident that omitted any mention of the burned bodies, official spokesmen avowed that most of the officers and noncommissioned officers in charge at MARY ANN had been killed or wounded in the attack. As a result, they continued, although there were indications that a lack of security might have contributed to American losses, the investigation was taking longer than expected. To preclude any prejudice to the rights of individuals who might face disciplinary action, the Army would, for the time being, refrain from releasing further details.[34]

Concerned that some sort of news release was necessary, General McCaffrey attempted to compromise. On 21 July he proposed that the Military Assistance Command issue a communique to the Saigon correspondents that revealed the full extent of its findings about the attack upon MARY ANN but left off the names of the individuals who faced punitive action.[35]

General Westmoreland once more demurred, on grounds that a partial news release during July followed by a complete accounting in August, when all reviews were scheduled to end, would "only serve to create two full cycles of stories on the matter." It seemed best, he said, to reveal no more than that the Army had assigned Baldwin to a duty station in Washington, where he could remain fully available to investigators. If the press became too insistent or a leak occurred, further delay might prove impossible, but otherwise "we would all do better to try to

[33] Inspector General, MACV, Rpt of Investigation, 5 Jul 71, sub: To Assess the Effectiveness of the Functioning of Command Within the 23d Infantry Division as It Pertains to the Attack on FSB Mary Ann, Reports of Investigations and Inquiries, 1971–1972, vol. 5, tab W, p. 6, 334–77–0074, box 1, WNRC.

[34] Msg, McCaffrey ARV 2455 to Westmoreland, 21 Jul 71, 319–81–051, box 9, WNRC; Msg, Westmoreland WDC 12471 to Abrams, 13 Jul 71, sub: Attack on FSB Mary Ann, Abrams Papers, CMH.

[35] Msg, McCaffrey ARV 2245 to Westmoreland, 21 Jul 71, Abrams Papers, CMH.

condense the story into just one major overall bad story." McCaffrey yielded to Westmoreland's reasoning. Since the Saigon correspondents appeared for the time being to have lost interest in the subject, he canceled his announcement and agreed to wait.[36]

In the days that followed, McCaffrey, in consultation with General Abrams and his deputy, General Frederick C. Weyand, decided to punish almost all of the officers involved in the incident. He recommended a reprimand and reduction in rank for Baldwin, removal from the list for promotion to brigadier general and reprimand for Hathaway, and reductions in rank for the rest. At that time, McCaffrey once more submitted a draft press release that outlined MACV's findings in the case but left out details of the punishments the command proposed to inflict upon Baldwin and his officers.[37]

Westmoreland again held off. The release, he reasoned, would have little value as news if it failed to include the actions McCaffrey had recommended against Baldwin and the others. Yet since those moves were all administrative rather than criminal in nature, they would have to be evaluated and approved by the Department of the Army in Washington. A premature official statement on the subject thus risked unfair damage to the reputations of the individuals involved if the Army declined to certify the steps McCaffrey had suggested. In addition, since more news releases would become necessary once the Army's review was complete, the communique "would not," as Westmoreland put it in a message to McCaffrey, "wind up the entire case with a single bad day of publicity as we had hoped. . . . As you can divine . . . the secretary [of the Army] and I want to do our best to reduce the number of self-inflicted wounds which the Army is receiving." As an alternative, Westmoreland once more authorized McCaffrey to inform only those reporters who inquired that the matter remained under review and that any further comment would be inappropriate.[38]

The instruction stood for almost a year, until 21 April 1972, when Secretary Froehlke finally disclosed in public that he had issued a letter of admonition to Baldwin, reprimanded Hathaway and one other officer, and removed Hathaway from the promotion list to brigadier general, all for substandard performance of duty. Brief notices followed in many papers. Relying on the Associated Press, the *New York Times* observed that a reprimand, in Army parlance, was a stronger administrative penalty than an admonition. The *Washington Post* printed a United Press International dispatch that linked Baldwin's fate to that of his predecessor at the American Division, General Koster, who had likewise been censured. Yet little more was said. The Army had released the story at the height of

---

[36] Quotes from Msg, Westmoreland WDC 13090 to McCaffrey, 22 Jul 71. Msg, McCaffrey ARV 2479 to Westmoreland, 23 Jul 71. Both in Abrams Papers, CMH.

[37] Msg, McCaffrey ARV 2638 to Westmoreland, 5 Aug 71, sub: 28 Mar 71 Attack on FSB Mary Ann, 319–81–051, box 9, FSB Mary Ann file, WNRC.

[38] Msg, Westmoreland WDC 14227 to McCaffrey, 9 Aug 71, Westmoreland Papers, CMH.

the enemy's Easter offensive of 1972, the most serious threat to the life of South Vietnam since the Tet offensive of 1968. The news media were so preoccupied that they failed completely to summon up the "overall bad story" Westmoreland had worked so long to postpone.[39]

Face-Off in Vietnam

I f General Westmoreland and other officials in Washington were interested in minimizing controversy in the press, some of their counterparts in South Vietnam were seething with animosity toward the news media. During the weeks that followed the incursion into Laos, indeed, the Saigon correspondents began to complain bitterly that American unit commanders in the field were doing everything they could to blackout reporting of the war. The charge was hardly new. Reporters had for some time protested that the MACV staff was cutting back on the information it released to the press, but public affairs officers had in the past always been able to respond that the American role in the war was changing and hardly anything of major interest was happening on the battlefield. In this case, arguments of that sort were unavailing because the reporters could see for themselves that commanders had taken steps to leash those members of the press who decided to visit units in the field.[40]

In some cases, reporters found that their reputations had preceded them. During a brief visit to South Vietnam at the beginning of April 1971, for example, Morley Safer of CBS News discovered that the sometimes critical reports he had filed early in the war but also his network's documentary on "The Selling of the Pentagon" had aroused the suspicions of some officers about his intentions. In a memorandum that later fell into the hands of the press, a public affairs officer near Pleiku even warned officers in the area to be cautious with Safer because he was obviously in search of an expose. Colonel Leonard apologized for the lapse on 7 April and dispatched a circular message to all commanders that reemphasized MACV's commitment to cooperation with reporters, but the incident led to yet another series of stories in the press on military suspicion of the news media. The *San Francisco Chronicle* even charged that the Army was "ringing the leper's bell" everywhere that Safer went.[41]

---

[39] Msg, Westmoreland WDC 20046 to Abrams, 2 Nov 71, 319–81–051, box 9, WNRC; [UPI], "General and Two Other Officers Reprimanded in Vietnam Incident," *Washington Post*, 22 Apr 72; [AP], "Three Rebuked in GI Deaths," *New York Times*, 22 Apr 72.

[40] See, for example, "Newsmen Say U.S. Reduces Viet Reports," *Baltimore Sun*, 17 Jan 71.

[41] Msg, Leonard MAC 3990 to Comdr Joseph Lorfano, OASD PA, 19 Apr 71, DDI Backchannel Messages file; Walter Cronkite, CBS Evening News, 8 Aug 71, *Radio-TV-Defense Dialog*; [AP], "Warn Viet Yanks on CBS Reporter," *Chicago Tribune*, 8 Apr 71; "The Army Rings a Leper's Bell," *San Francisco Chronicle*, 9 Apr 71.

The operation that followed the incursion into Laos, LAM SON 720, provided another example of the increasing irritability of Army officers. A major attack against formidable enemy strongholds in the A Shau Valley involving the 1st South Vietnamese Infantry Division and portions of the U.S. 101st Airborne Division, the deployment seemed dangerous enough to commanders to justify restraining the press on grounds of military security. The Saigon correspondents nevertheless had little doubt that an attempt at repression was under way. Walter Cronkite felt so strongly, indeed, that he prefaced a special report on the subject by commenting, "When newsmen complain that they face obstruction in covering . . . a military operation in Vietnam, there are some who accuse them of special pleading [or] of a cry baby attitude. But . . . those charged under a democratic system with keeping the public informed feel that it is important that the public know the restrictions that are put upon them." During the report that followed, correspondent Ed Rabel claimed that public affairs officers for the 101st Airborne Division had refused to reveal anything more than generalizations about the operation and that the division's commander had even placed military police guards at the doors of his forward command post to keep newsmen out. In the same way, the U.S. Army pilots of the helicopters supporting the attack had strict instructions to keep newsmen off. Rabel interviewed a lieutenant about the situation. The officer confirmed the rules, adding that reporters were allowed to ride on helicopters only if they had a public affairs officer with them and that he and the other officers of the division had been told to "watch what we say" any time the press was present. Noting that, in addition to his current tour of duty as a lieutenant, he had spent nineteen months in South Vietnam during 1966 and 1967 as an enlisted man, the officer then observed that in all of his years of experience with the war he had never seen restrictions on the press similar to the ones in effect. Rides into the field had always been available to newsmen, he said, and soldiers had always been able to speak freely with reporters.[42]

When word of the restrictions arrived in Washington, public affairs officers at the Pentagon were as concerned as the press. On the day before Cronkite aired Rabel's report, the chief of the Defense Department's Directorate of Defense Information, Col. L. Gordon Hill, cabled the MACV Office of Information in Saigon to inform Colonel Leonard that, judging from the tenor of the complaints appearing thus far, U.S. commanders had obviously taken it upon themselves to deny reporters access to American units in the field. A feeling was developing in Washington, Hill said, that some senior officers had dedicated helicopters to the sole use of the press, rather than allow reporters to travel on the usual space-available basis, in order to prevent newsmen from moving freely about the combat zone. If that was true,

[42] Msg, MACV 75862 to OASD PA, 29 Apr 71, sub: Press Support for LAM SON 720, White House Special files, Staff Member Office files, Scali, box 8, Subject files, Vietnam [4 of 4], Nixon Papers. Quote from Walter Cronkite, CBS Evening News, 23 Apr 71, *Radio-TV-Defense Dialog.*

although bona fide restrictions might at times be necessary, the potential for public relations disaster was so great that the Military Assistance Command should consider keeping careful records on every attempt to control the press to ensure that each was "justifiable after the fact."[43]

Hill's remonstrance had little effect. Leonard responded that the local American commander, Brig. Gen. Paul E. Smith, was well within his rights in imposing restraints on the press because he thought them necessary for the safety of his troops. Leonard added that public affairs officers at the scene were releasing all significant information on the operation and had, in fact, escorted a number of newsmen into the combat zone. For the rest, Smith believed that the regulations governing the release of information of value to the enemy took precedence over the wishes of reporters. On the side, Leonard informed the Saigon correspondents that a local commander had the authority to assign escorts to accompany them if he so desired. Whatever the inhibiting effect the policy might have had upon interviews with individual soldiers, he said, he "could not and would not" order officers to give up their right to protect their troops as they saw fit. From his own standpoint, Leonard later recalled, the practice of escorting reporters had been well established both in the United States and overseas and seemed reasonable. "The major complaint in Vietnam seemed to revolve around the escort officer 'intimidating' soldiers' responses to reporters' questions. Like it or not, the escort officer could bring balance to some soldiers' remarks."[44]

Confronted by Smith's unquestionable right to restrict the press when he felt it necessary and Leonard's unwillingness to push emphatically for a change in approach, Hill could only watch during the weeks that followed as a stream of news reports emanated from the A Shau Valley criticizing the Army's unwillingness to be candid about the operation. The *New York Times* asserted that the secrecy surrounding LAM SON 720 had led some observers to doubt the campaign's success. The *Philadelphia Bulletin* reprinted a comment by the South Vietnamese commander of the operation, Brig. Gen. Vu Van Giai, contrasting his own attitude toward the press with that of Smith. "I do not understand," Giai said. "You are Americans. Gen. Smith is an American. It should be easier for you to talk to him than for me. Why doesn't he want to tell you anything?" As late as 22 May, a month after Hill had sent his message, Donald Kirk reported in the *San Francisco Chronicle* that news from the A Shau Valley remained in short supply and that the "information war" between the military and the media in South Vietnam had obviously escalated to new levels of hostility.[45]

---

[43] Msg, Defense 4444 to MACV, L. Gordon Hill to IO, 22 Apr 71, DDI Lam Son 719 Press Support file.

[44] Msg, MACV 75862 to OASD PA, 29 Apr 71, sub: Press Support for LAM SON 720; Msg, Leonard MAC 3990 to Lorfano, 19 Apr 71. Quote from Ltr, Leonard to the author, 17 Oct 90, CMH files.

[45] [AP], "Several Attacks by Foe Reported in South Vietnam," *New York Times*, 26 Apr 71; [AP], "U.S. Officers Stall Press at A Shau, Allies Don't," *Philadelphia Bulletin*, 26 Apr 71; Donald Kirk, "The War News Blackout," *San Francisco Chronicle*, 22 May 71.

Distressed by the angry tone of the press coverage coming out of South Vietnam, Assistant Secretary Henkin instructed General Sidle to make a quick trip to Saigon to assess the situation. Serving, in effect, as an inspector general but under instructions to pass off the trip as a fact-finding mission, Sidle was to arrive with the least possible advance announcement in order to cut off any attempt by officers at the scene to hide the results of their bad decisions or to put a good face on their actions.[46]

Upon arrival, Sidle spoke with trusted contacts among the Saigon correspondents even before consulting with the Military Assistance Command. He found that if the majority of public affairs officers remained responsive to the press, the officers in charge of paperwork at the command, especially the generals who set policy for the military agencies that coordinated responses to queries from the Saigon correspondents, had come to dislike reporters with an intensity bordering on hatred. As a result, beginning in 1970 but continuing into 1971, the time it took for the command to reply to a legitimate query from the press had increased markedly, much to the detriment of correspondents who sought to construct a balanced picture of events. A reporter might thus make a reasonable request for background information but encounter so many delays and obfuscations that he received his answer hours or even days after his deadline had passed. In the same way, Sidle confirmed that there had been no attempt in months to provide reporters with regular intelligence briefings, a fact that he believed had cut them off from material they needed to put the situation in South Vietnam into context and that had inevitably become a major point of contention in the developing controversy between the military and the news media. Strong leadership at the MACV Office of Information might have served to arrest those problems, Sidle concluded, but the individuals in charge by 1971 seemed incapable of producing the sort of strong impact on the MACV staff that circumstances clearly required. Under the circumstances, given the problems the press was experiencing and the difficulties confronting the Military Assistance Command in South Vietnam, it seemed inevitable that news coverage of the war would become increasingly nearsighted and unpleasant.

With Sidle's observations in hand, the question became how best to reverse the trend. In a meeting with Abrams, Sidle urged the general to push those members of his staff who were strongly against the press to cooperate with the Office of Information's efforts. He also told the general, according to Leonard, who spoke to Abrams afterwards, that he could have a replacement chief of public affairs on station within forty-eight hours. When Abrams signified that he still had confidence in Leonard, Sidle dropped the matter. Later, in a meeting with Henkin in Washington, Sidle nevertheless suggested that it might be wise to end Leonard's tour of duty early and to put a more forceful officer in his place. Since

[46] This section is based on Interv, author with Maj Gen Winant Sidle, 15 Sep 89, CMH files.

Leonard's term at the command would expire shortly anyway and the officer retained Abrams' trust, Henkin took no action on the suggestion, but he did, in conjunction with Sidle, restructure the assignment of the next chief of MACV information, Col. Phillip H. Stevens. That officer would go to South Vietnam as planned, but would serve initially as deputy to Colonel Hill, who would travel with him and function as chief of information for a period of from three to six months. Since both Hill and Stevens were strong personalities, there seemed some hope that the two, working together, might be able to restore a balance between the requirements of the press and those of the military. Because Stevens was particularly adept at working with reporters, he would seek to improve relations with the Saigon correspondents. Hill, who would be a brigadier general by the time he departed, would meanwhile encourage his fellow generals to keep communications with the press open. "Between them," Sidle told General Abrams, the two officers ". . . could give you immediate assistance at a time when you have potentially formidable press problems as a result of a changing situation."[47]

The White House staff and some within the other agencies concerned with the war immediately began to look upon Hill as some sort of savior who would not only reverse the negative attitude of the Saigon correspondents but also promote a number of other causes. John Scali, who had just been appointed as a special consultant to the president, told Charles Colson, for example, that one of Hill's duties would be to promote more extensive news coverage of the withdrawal of American forces and equipment from South Vietnam. In addition, since the president had recently told the American public that he was doing everything he could to remedy the drug problem among American forces, Hill would also push the attention of the press toward the enormous effort the Military Assistance Command was making to identify and treat drug abusers before they returned to the United States.[48]

The State Department and the U.S. Information Agency also had ideas about what Hill should do. Since the South Vietnamese would have to take responsibility for many of MACV's traditional public affairs activities as the American role in the war declined, both agencies wanted the general to keep reporters from concluding that the transition somehow represented an attempt to cut off information about the war.

---

[47] There is some disagreement between Sidle and Leonard on the course of events. Sidle does not remember suggesting a replacement for Leonard in his meeting with Abrams but does say he brought the issue up with Henkin. Leonard, however, insists that Abrams called him to his office after Sidle's visit and informed him of Sidle's suggestion. Since the episode would have been easier for Sidle to forget than Leonard, I have followed Leonard's recollection. See Ltr, Leonard to the author, 17 Oct 90; Interv, author with Sidle, 30 Nov 90, CMH files. Quote from Msg, Sidle WDC 9874 to Abrams, 5 Jun 71, sub: TDY of Col. (P) Gordon Hill and Assignment of Col. Phil Stevens, Sidle Sends for Mr. Daniel Z. Henkin, ASD (PA) OSD, Abrams Papers, CMH.

[48] Memo, John A. Scali for Charles W. Colson, 4 Jun 71, sub: Troop Withdrawal Coverage, White House Special files, Scali, box 8, Vietnam Withdrawal Rate 6/71, Nixon Papers.

The need to turn the nightly briefing for the press, the "Five O'Clock Follies," over to the South Vietnamese was of particular concern. The director of the State Department's Office of Press Relations, Charles W. Bray III, for one, suggested that the Military Assistance Command time the change to coincide with the end of the American role in ground combat, projected to occur toward the end of 1971. In that way, the move could underscore South Vietnam's growing self-reliance at a moment when President Thieu's attempt to win reelection was at its peak. Exposing the Saigon correspondents to the full vigor of an Asian nation's presidential campaign without the interference of American intermediaries, it would also "serve indirectly," as Bray put it, "to reinforce our posture toward the elections, that we are not committed to President Thieu as the sole possible democratic leader. . . . It will also further . . . remove 'the war'—as opposed to 'Viet-Nam'—from center stage for American correspondents."[49]

Hill doubted his ability to have much effect even before he left for South Vietnam. When he learned that Washington agencies were planning to end the American role in the nightly briefing, for example, he objected vigorously that any arbitrary move in that direction would serve only to inflame the anger of the Saigon correspondents. In the past, he observed, even minor changes in wording, let alone policy, had triggered outbursts from the press. The same would occur in the future. Reporters would never accept the decreased significance of the U.S. effort in South Vietnam as sufficient reason to end the sessions. A single U.S. casualty, aircraft loss, or installation under attack would spark their interest. Lacking the information that the briefings provided, they would almost certainly conclude that the Military Assistance Command was hiding facts, suppressing the news, and attempting to play down the American role in the war. The claim would then reappear in the press that the credibility gap was alive and well in Saigon; pressure would mount for a reevaluation of the policy; and the command, despite the loss of face involved, would have little choice but to back down and reinstate the briefing.[50]

Hill preferred a less emphatic approach. When the time came, he told his superiors, the chief of MACV information would have to sit down with the bureau chiefs in Saigon to explain that reductions at the Military Assistance Command had necessitated certain changes in the public affairs program. At that time, he would propose that on certain rare occa-

---

[49] Memo, B. McGurn for Mr. Bray, 25 Jun 71, sub: Vietnam Information Policy, attachment to Memo, Frank Shakespeare for Henry Kissinger, 30 Jun 71. Quote from Memo, Charles W. Bray III, Director, Office of Public Relations, for Mr. McCloskey, 21 May 71, attachment to Memo, Shakespeare for Kissinger, 30 Jun 71. Both in White House Special files, Scali, box 8, Vietnam [3 of 4], Nixon Papers.

[50] Hill's position is closely paraphrased in Memo, Comdr Joseph Lorfano for Lt Col Robert Burke, 11 Jun 71, sub: Phase Out of Military Briefings, DDI MACOI Correspondence 36a. A copy of the memorandum went to the White House. See White House Special files, Staff Member Office files, Scali, box 8, Subject files, Vietnam [3 of 4], Nixon Papers.

sions, "when absolutely no significant action involving U.S. forces" had occurred, the American military briefer would leave the podium entirely to the South Vietnamese briefers but remain available to answer questions by telephone. In that way, the command would be able to phase out the briefings without giving rise to recriminations. Even so, when it did finally succeed in ending the sessions, it would have to give something to the press in exchange, perhaps a weekly briefing that dealt only with military developments involving the remnant of American forces, still numbering some 225,000 men but declining rapidly.[51]

When Hill arrived in South Vietnam toward the end of July, he confirmed Sidle's impression that circumstances had changed considerably from those that had prevailed during 1969 and 1970, when he had served his tour as the chief of MACV information. Although a number of highly experienced correspondents remained among the 335 accredited newsmen in South Vietnam, he said in an interview, the television networks in particular had begun to rotate reporters in and out of the country with such frequency that it seemed to him as though they were operating a system of "ticket punching" similar to the one the press habitually accused the military of indulging. A reporter would arrive in South Vietnam, he observed, stay just three months, long enough to enhance his job resume with the term *war correspondent*, and then rotate to another assignment before learning much of substance about what was going on. In addition, with American forces less and less involved in the fighting, fewer reporters than ever were following combat action in the field.[52]

On the military side, the situation seemed almost as bad. Hill was dismayed to learn that many of the programs Sidle had instituted earlier in the war to keep the press informed and to serve as an outlet for discontent had ceased. The chief of information, for example, had maintained a villa in Saigon during 1969 and 1970 where he and his officers had met with the press in an unhurried environment. General Abrams had often used the facility to host quiet dinners for selected correspondents. Both practices had faded away. Although the house remained a residence for some on the MACV Office of Information's staff, it appeared run down and lacked furniture. As for the dinners, they ended on Abrams' own initiative because the general had become convinced that they had deteriorated into an opportunity to air complaints.[53] In the same way, Hill confirmed that MACV's chief of intelligence had long before ended direct intelligence briefings for selected members of the press and that reporters continued to resent the omission.

It was likewise clear to Hill that the MACV Office of Information had staffing problems similar to those afflicting the press. Although the

[51] Ibid.
[52] This section is based on Interv, author with Maj Gen L. Gordon Hill, USA (Ret.), 6 Mar 89, 8 Aug 89, CMH files.
[53] Ltr, Leonard to the author, 17 Oct 90.

amount of work to be done by public affairs officers remained much the same as ever, the office had lost more than 300 officers and enlisted men throughout South Vietnam and additional reductions were in the offing. The twelve-month rotation policy instituted at the beginning of the war was also having an effect. Besides continuing to destroy the institutional memory of the organization, it removed men from duty at just the moment when they seemed fully trained and effective. Meanwhile, the public affairs officers arriving as replacements lacked experience with the war, and those who remained with the requisite time in place continued to be too few to make up for the deficiency.[54]

The press perceived that Hill was in South Vietnam to improve relations between the military and the news media and for a time appears to have expected conditions to improve. "Although late in the game," the *Army Times* thus reported, on 1 September "[the] Army has one of its top press officers in Vietnam trying to sell senior officers on the wisdom of talking (when possible) to reporters. . . . Washington officials are known to believe that some flaps in Vietnam could have been avoided if senior commanders were more receptive to reporters. A major example is the alleged lack of cooperation with Vietnam newsmen during the Laotian invasion."[55] There was little, nevertheless, that the general could do to improve the attitude of either the generals or the Saigon correspondents, short of a wholesale change of personnel on both sides. Officers with real or imagined grievances against newsmen remained hostile to the press, and those reporters who had experienced frustration at the hands of the military were not inclined to forgive or forget.

Since the Military Assistance Command was already pushing hard to publicize withdrawals and the steps it was taking to curb drug abuse, Hill wasted little effort in those directions. He did, however, attempt to cut back on MACV's evening briefings for the press by terminating the Sunday session. The grounds he cited—that all briefings of the sort involving American spokesmen would have to end sooner or later anyway and that reporters were so little interested in the Sunday meeting that they rarely asked questions—made sense to many newsmen. Although the change prompted a brief flurry of complaints from Joseph Fried of the *New York Daily News* and a few others, most of the Saigon correspondents, according to Hill, went along with the move.[56]

On the side, Hill also drafted a contingency plan for the gradual but orderly elimination of the MACV Office of Information. The document avoided mentioning dates beyond July 1972, when the office was expected to consist of fewer than seventeen people, but Hill understood that

---

[54] For more on the fading of institutional memory, see Chapter 15.

[55] "Cooperation With Reporters Backed," *Army Times*, 1 Sep 71.

[56] The plan apparently no longer exists. Hill described his actions in Interv, author with Maj Gen L. Gordon Hill, 23 Aug 89, CMH files. Sidle refers to the figure seventeen in Memo, Sidle for ASD PA, 24 Jan 72, sub: U.S. Public Affairs in SEA, DDI Correspondence with MACV IO 36a.

assignments and requests for replacements had to be made long in advance of requirements and that some sort of plan would have to be in place if the program was to end on anything more than a haphazard basis. Overall, as was the case with Westmoreland in Washington, Hill felt that public affairs officers at MACV could do little more than hold the line by keeping the Pentagon informed of developments in the field and by attempting, within their ability, to head off problems with the press before they damaged official credibility.[57]

The South Vietnamese Election of 1971

H ill remained in South Vietnam until December, when he returned to Washington to become the Defense Department's director of defense information. His successor, Colonel Stevens, carried on with the policies he had set in place, but, despite all efforts to the contrary, proved unable to restrain the sort of controversies with the press that Hill had hoped to avoid. Events in South Vietnam were taking their own direction. The line that Hill, Westmoreland, and the others had hoped to hold was beginning to come undone.

A case in point was the fate of the Nixon administration's desire, as expressed by Bray, subtly to underscore South Vietnam's presidential election as an indication that the nation was well on its way to becoming a democracy. If Thieu could gain a second term in a reasonably honest election involving at least one other major candidate, so the reasoning went, that result would sustain support for his regime among the South Vietnamese people and perhaps tip the enemy's calculations toward a negotiated settlement. At the least, it would help to shore up support for the war in the United States by demonstrating that the Thieu regime was a viable entity and indeed worth saving.[58]

Profound doubts existed in the United States that Thieu was equal to the task. As early as April 1971, proposals had surfaced in Congress to cut off all aid to South Vietnam if he sought unfair advantages over his opponents or if the Nixon administration attempted somehow to prejudice the election in his favor. So vehement were the opinions rising in Congress that Henry Kissinger decided the administration would probably face a major political battle as Thieu's campaign progressed. "It goes without saying," he told Ambassador Bunker, "that at least some of these congressional groups will trumpet even the most minute suggestion of unfair play (such as the government having more loud-speakers than its opponents) and will try to claim any support we give to any

---

[57] Ibid.

[58] Draft Memo, Kissinger for the President, 17 Sep 71, sub: Vietnam, NSC files, A. M. Haig Special file, box 1013, Gen Haig's Trip to Vietnam, Sept 71 [I of II], Nixon Papers; Msg, Saigon 1391 to State, Bunker to the President, 28 Jan 71, Bunker Papers, FAIM/IR.

South Vietnamese program in the next six months is intended to help Thieu."[59]

The doubts circulating in Congress notwithstanding, Ambassador Bunker believed that Thieu could win honestly in a two- or three-man race and told him so on a number of occasions. So confident was the Nixon administration in that result that it even considered dispatching a nonpartisan group of American observers to Saigon to monitor the election, just as President Lyndon Johnson had done in 1967. Discussions also began in the White House on how best to promote the election as an indication that peace was coming and that American forces would be returning home with honor.[60]

Nguyen Cao Ky

Those plans and expectations came to nothing because Thieu himself lacked confidence in his own ability to win a clear victory in the election. Convinced that he faced serious risks if he ran a fair race and yearning for the sort of success that would put all doubt to rest that the South Vietnamese people backed his regime, he laid plans well in advance to cut his most serious opponent, Vice President Ky, out of the running. To that end, he drafted an election law that forced presidential candidates to be endorsed by at least 40 members of the National Assembly or 100 members of South Vietnam's various provincial councils. He then overrode the South Vietnamese Senate's objections and bribed the lower house of the National Assembly into enacting the bill. That done, he proceeded to coerce or purchase 452 out of a possible 550 signatures in the local councils and gathered a majority of signatures in the assembly. Even as he did, he sent secret writ-

[59] Msg, Kissinger WHS 1037 to Bunker, 12 Apr 71, NSC files, Backchannels, box 412, Amb. Bunker, Saigon, 1971, Nixon Papers.

[60] This section is based on Msg, Bunker Saigon 198 to Kissinger, 18 Sep 71, NSC files, Backchannels, box 412, Amb. Bunker, Saigon, 1971, Nixon Papers. Discussion of how best to promote the election began with Memo, DeVan L. Shumway for Mr. Baukol, 17 May 71, attachment to Memo, W. Richard Howard for John Scali, 24 May 71, White House Special files, Scali, Subject files, box 1, Nixon Papers. For general background on the election, see Memo, Scali for Kissinger, 12 May 71, and Memo, Scali for Kissinger, 8 Jun 71, both in White House Special files, Staff Member Office files, Scali, Subject files, box 5, Kissinger, Nixon Papers. Msg, Saigon 11162 to State, 15 Jul 71, sub: Meeting With President Thieu, 15 July 1971; Msg, Saigon 11670 to State, 23 Jul 71; and Msg, Saigon 12885 to State, 12 Aug 72, sub: Meeting With Minh. All in General Abrams' Personal file 40, CMH.

ten instructions to his supporters among the nation's province chiefs to do whatever was necessary to assure his victory. The letter leaked to his opponents, who caused an angry outcry in the press.[61]

In the weeks that followed, Ky scrambled to gather endorsements from provincial counselors and succeeded in gathering 102. The South Vietnamese Supreme Court nevertheless disqualified forty, on grounds that the signatories had already committed their names to Thieu. That left only one other credible candidate, Maj. Gen. Duong Van Minh, who had enough signatures in the National Assembly but withdrew his name from consideration because, as he put it, Thieu's "sharp practices" had led him and his supporters to believe that the election was "not honest right from the beginning."[62]

Thieu, for his part, had apparently never sought to disqualify anyone but Ky, believing that Minh's presence on the ballot would give the election more than enough credibility and that the general would prove easy to defeat. Forced to run unopposed, he attempted to save face by turning the election into a plebiscite on his regime's performance in office. Voters had only to tear or deface their ballots, he thus announced, to register their disapproval with his policies. The expedient became a magnet for criticism in the American news media, which had described Thieu's machinations from the beginning and had long before concluded with Minh that the entire election was a sham.[63]

As with Thieu, President Nixon attempted to put the best face he could on what had happened. Addressing the issue at a 16 September news conference, he avowed that he would have preferred to have had a contested election but that "we . . . cannot get people to run when they do not want to run." In fairness to the democratic process and how it was working in South Vietnam, he added, those who criticized South Vietnam's presidential election might well pay more attention to how well the country's recent election for the National Assembly had worked. Eighty percent of the nation's people had participated, in comparison with the 60 percent in the United States who had voted during the 1970 congressional election. The situation was, indeed, "infinitely better in South Vietnam, where they at least have some elections, than in North Vietnam where they have none."[64]

Nixon's confident remarks became the keystone in the administration's effort to allay public criticism of Thieu during the weeks that followed but they had little effect upon Laird, Bunker, and Kissinger, all of whom were somber. Reflecting upon Thieu's one-sided campaign at a meeting during August 1971, Laird, for one, observed that the United

[61] For a description of Thieu's maneuvers, see "No Ky and a Big Win?," *Newsweek*, 16 Aug 71.

[62] Ibid.

[63] Ibid.; "Saigon's Election Fraud (Cont'd)," *New York Post*, 21 Sep 71.

[64] Msg, State 171045 to Saigon et al., 17 Sep 71, sub: President's Comments to Press on Vietnam Election, Pol 14 Viet S file, FAIM/IR.

Nixon and Kissinger

States had given the South Vietnamese government sufficient means to protect its interests but that the will and desire of the nation's people to bend to the task was in the end all that mattered. Bunker responded that Laird had cut "right to the crux of the problem." There was nothing more the United States could do to assist the South Vietnamese. The rest was up to them. There was no way to know whether they had the will and desire to survive until after American forces had departed.[65]

Kissinger was similarly preoccupied. Concerned about the implications of Thieu's activities, he composed a long memorandum to President Nixon in September in which he noted that "recent events" had forced him to take "a dispassionate look at where we are on Vietnam, the likely prospects, and the policy options as we head into the terminal phase of our involvement."[66] The conclusions he reached were unattractive. The manner in which the United States ended the war, or at least its participation, he said, was "crucial for America's global position and for the fabric of our society." A swift collapse in South Vietnam traced to precipitate American withdrawal would leave deep scars in the United States, fuel impulses for recrimination, create a crisis of authority, and impair the president's efforts to shape a new foreign policy.

[65] Memo of Conversation, 10 Aug 71, sub: Meeting With Ambassador Bunker, 330–76–197, box 79, Vietnam 091.112, 1971, Laird Papers, WNRC.

[66] Draft Memo, Kissinger for the President, 17 Sep 71, sub: Vietnam. It is unclear whether Kissinger ever sent the memo, but the thoughts it contains are worth the telling.

521

Kissinger continued that from the outset of Nixon's term in office the administration had consistently followed the two strands of Vietnamization and negotiation. Even so, the president and his advisers had always understood that the South Vietnamese might fail and had always preferred a negotiated settlement to the pursuit of a military victory that risked the crumbling of South Vietnam while American forces remained. A successful negotiation would end the war with a graceful "act of policy" that would help to heal the wounds in the United States. Leaving South Vietnam "to the historical process," it would likewise divorce that country's fortunes from the actions of the United States by providing for "a healthy interval" between the American withdrawal and the culmination of whatever South Vietnam's fate would be.[67]

To date, Kissinger continued, the United States had navigated that "precarious course quite well, balancing off the demands of the negotiating process, stability in South Vietnam and our domestic scene." Even so, U.S. assets were wasting. Rising domestic pressures for a total American pullout had left the enemy with little disposition to pay for what he knew would probably fall into his lap, and Thieu's intemperance during the recent election had only furthered the process by weakening his credentials before the American public while feeding his opposition within South Vietnam. As a result, the enemy continued to have "every incentive to wait for the interreacting [*sic*] combination of unrest in South Vietnam and an American domestic squeeze to topple [Thieu's government] . . . and pave the way for their eventual control." The problem was already making its appearance. Momentum for a rapid disengagement was rising in the United States, "and we now face the real danger of Congressional legislation setting a date for our withdrawals and perhaps limiting our assistance to South Vietnam." Meanwhile, in South Vietnam, the currents of political unrest were stirring as members of the non-Communist opposition burnished their credentials for a compromise with the Viet Cong, members of the Thieu administration and the army prepared to hedge their bets, and the Communists demonstrated their continuing ability to strike at will by conducting terrorist attacks in Saigon and other cities.[68]

Under the circumstances, Kissinger said, few alternatives remained. The United States might negotiate agreement with North Vietnam that traded fixed withdrawals for the American prisoners of war, but that could only weaken South Vietnam and spur its demise. More attractive would be a policy of playing out the Vietnamization program, announcing reductions in the American presence down to a residual force, and bombing the North Vietnamese panhandle. Yet that approach, too, was flawed because of domestic American political considerations. Besides the pressures already mounting for restrictive legislation on troops and aid, debate in the United States would inevitably focus on Thieu, "and we

[67] Ibid.
[68] Ibid.

522

could probably not sustain our position given the uncontested election." For the same reasons, a policy of escalation was impossible, despite the fact that a series of severe jolts to North Vietnam might produce a negotiating breakthrough in Paris. "We could never sustain this policy here at home," Kissinger avowed. "The public and Congressional outcry would be deafening, and governmental discipline would break down. . . . [The] Peking and Moscow summits would almost certainly be sunk, and with them probably the fruits of various outstanding negotiations."[69]

The only alternative left, Kissinger concluded, was a policy of more of the same. Do everything possible to limit criticism of Thieu to shore up his regime while directing a new negotiating initiative to North Vietnam. Laden with enough concessions to be attractive but too few to destroy South Vietnam's ability to bargain with the enemy after a cease-fire, the move would be designed to lead either to an American disengagement from the war or, if it failed, to the sort of reduced profile that would allow the United States to maintain a small residual force in South Vietnam until all American prisoners were released. "Even the most dovish opponent," the national security adviser said, "could hardly claim he would offer more for a negotiated settlement."[70]

Whatever the merits of Kissinger's negotiating strategy, his remarks on the status of the American consensus supporting the war were to the point. Even as Westmoreland, Sidle, Henkin, Hill, and all the agencies involved with the war fought to hold the line, support in the United States was slipping away, and the country was becoming increasingly divided against itself. The mounting calls for war crimes trials, the leaks to Anderson, the Hackworth and Herbert affairs, Admiral Moorer's use of Yeoman Radford in an attempt to divine the intentions of the Nixon administration, and even the loss of heart that was apparent just beneath the surface of Kissinger's memorandum showed it clearly. So, too, did the anger of military commanders in the field at the reporting of the press and attempts by those officers to restrain the Saigon correspondents. Although American involvement in the war would continue for another year, the line was breaking. The war was spinning toward its conclusion with a momentum all its own.

[69] Ibid.
[70] Ibid.

523

21

The Easter Offensive

LAM SON 719 was the last time major U.S. Army units encountered sustained combat in South Vietnam. Although American platoons, battalions, and brigades continued to keep the enemy off balance during the months that followed by patrolling in force near their bases and logistical complexes, few saw heavy fighting. Instead, the number of American servicemen assigned to South Vietnam continued to decline, dwindling from a high of 554,000 in March and April 1969 to fewer than 141,000 in the first months of 1972, a reduction of more than 400,000 men. The sum of the correspondents covering the war also diminished, going from 468 during January 1969 to less than 200 at the start of 1972. Of those, 117 were American.[1]

Although the statistical summaries released to correspondents showed that during some weeks fewer than ten American casualties of any sort occurred, the reporters who remained in South Vietnam still had to justify the heavy expenses their employers incurred in order to provide on-the-spot coverage of the war. Largely ignoring South Vietnamese operations to vie for the few stories that remained of interest to the American public, they did little to remedy the turmoil that had long characterized relations between the military and the news media in South Vietnam.

The evolving nature of the conflict in Southeast Asia complicated matters. For if the U.S. Army's efforts in South Vietnam were ending, U.S. air operations were continuing with a vigor that was bound to prove irresistible to correspondents increasingly bereft of opportunities. In addition, by January 1972 the enemy had begun to speed preparations for the massive offensive that American intelligence analysts had long expected to

---

[1] Ltr, Jerry Friedheim to Honorable Charles S. Gubser, 20 Jun 72, 330–77–0094, box 75, Viet 000.1–Viet 381, 1972, Laird Papers, WNRC; MS, Joel Meyerson, Logistics in the Vietnam Conflict [U.S. Army Center of Military History], CMH files; [UPI], Arthur Higbee, "Vietnam News Sources Dry Up as War Wanes," *Editor and Publisher*, 29 Jan 72.

occur during the early months of the year. That attack, when it came, would provide President Nixon and Henry Kissinger with the excuse they sought to pound Hanoi toward a peace agreement that would save face for the United States, but it would also provoke major new problems with the press at a moment when the credibility of the Military Assistance Command was probably as low as it had ever been in the history of the war.

Covering a Backwater War

As the number of reporters present in South Vietnam had diminished, the composition of the corps of correspondents had also continued to change. A few of the newsmen who remained in South Vietnam had covered the war for many years: George McArthur, who had started with the *Los Angeles Times* in 1966 but had switched to the Associated Press in 1969; Wendell Merick of *U.S. News & World Report*, present almost continuously from 1965 onward; Howard Tuckner, who had reported the war intermittently since 1967, first for NBC and then for ABC; George Esper of the Associated Press, a 1965 arrival; and Joseph Fried, who had worked in South Vietnam since 1963 for the *New York Daily News* and the Mutual Radio Network. Some of the others had arrived during 1970 or 1971 but by 1972 were relatively well-experienced with the war: Craig Whitney, a former Navy officer who had produced a number of perceptive reports on Lam Son 719 for the *New York Times*; Holger Jensen, who had done the same for the Associated Press; and Alexander Shimkin, who had worked in the countryside for two years with a private volunteer service organization before joining the staff of *Newsweek* in 1971. Unlike many of his colleagues, Shimkin was fluent in the Vietnamese language.[2] A number of correspondents were also present who were well on their way to prominence as reporters: Fox Butterfield of the *New York Times*, Henry Bradsher of the *Washington Star*, Bob Simon and Phil Jones of CBS, Garrick Utley of NBC, and Peter Osnos of the *Washington Post*. Many of the rest, however, were new to Southeast Asia, and a few were still cutting their teeth as journalists.

Hardly an enemy of the press, General Sidle had little good to say about many of the newsmen he met during a two-week trip to Saigon in January 1972. Reporting to the assistant secretary of defense for public affairs upon returning to Washington, he characterized the majority of correspondents as lethargic and inept. "The quality is down considerably from my time in MACV," he said, "and there are only a few mature, reliable reporters on the scene. The remainder are either inexperienced, lazy, trying to make a reputation, or some combination of the three. Most seem

---

[2] Database of Vietnam War Correspondents, Abbreviated Master List, CMH files.

unwilling to make any real effort to expand their reportorial efforts beyond the old standards of stressing the fighting, the politics, or something negative."[3]

Sidle's opinion corresponded to a belief prevalent in official circles that the press continued to fail to cover positive aspects of the situation in South Vietnam. Among the untold stories the general noted were what he considered the long strides the South Vietnamese armed forces had made in providing their own logistical support, the establishment of a new 3d South Vietnamese Infantry Division and the rapid gains the unit had made in preparing for combat, and the "solid" success of General Abrams' program to achieve racial harmony among the American troops remaining in South Vietnam.[4]

The Saigon correspondents had their own view of the situation. Some were willing to concede, as *New York Times* reporter Sydney Schanberg observed in a long article on official credibility, that at least a few reporters were indeed suffering from "a sense of weary *deja vu* about Vietnam and maybe a hardening of viewpoint." They nevertheless denied that they were lacking in energy or prejudiced against positive aspects of the effort to bring the war to a conclusion. If the press often adopted a negative point of view, Schanberg said, that was because many of the Saigon correspondents had traveled into the field and had "used their eyes and ears and common sense to paint an accurate picture of Vietnam over the years." A single news story hardly ever represented the whole truth, he concluded, but over time a pattern of truth almost inevitably emerged if a newsman was conscientious in what he had to say.[5]

As with so much else that occurred in South Vietnam, neither Sidle nor Schanberg was wrong. The circumstances were so contradictory by that moment in the war that reasonable observers could interpret the same events in entirely different ways. As a result, reporters and officials could both sometimes mount considerable evidence in support of widely divergent claims.

Sidle's contention, for example, that many correspondents were either inexperienced or sensation-seeking was well exemplified during February 1972 by an altercation that broke out between the Military Assistance Command and UPI over an announcement broadcast by Radio Hanoi that North Vietnamese gunners had just downed seven U.S. fighter bombers. The MACV Office of Information, following routine procedure, immediately advised reporters that the claim was exaggerated and provided the true figures. In doing so, the briefing officer

[3] Memo, Sidle for ASD PA, 24 Jan 72, sub: U.S. Public Affairs in Southeast Asia, DDI Correspondence with MACV IO 36a. Sidle's trip to South Vietnam occurred between 7 and 21 January 1972.

[4] Ibid.

[5] Sydney H. Schanberg, "The Saigon Follies: or Trying To Head Them Off at Credibility Gap," *New York Times Magazine*, 12 Nov 72, p. 38.

assumed that all of the reporters present would, as stipulated by the MACV guidelines for the press, delay any release of the figures until an official communique announced that search-and-rescue operations for lost airmen were complete. Although all of the reporters who had attended the command's briefing held back as required, Kim Willenson of UPI nonetheless dispatched a story shortly thereafter, informing the world that a loss had occurred and that a rescue attempt was in progress. Adding insult to the injury, when instructed by MACV to cancel the story, the reporter filed a retraction, but in a manner that made it appear as though the command was attempting to cover up errors rather than safeguarding the lives of aircrewmen in danger. As a result, the cancellation had little effect, and the original story received wide play around the world.[6]

Public affairs officers were incensed, as were most of the reporters who had observed MACV's rule. When Willenson excused himself by contending that the briefing officer had failed to note any embargo on the information, the chief of MACV information, Colonel Stevens, wrote a memorandum to the reporter's bureau chief, Arthur Higbee. "I am willing to concede," he said, "that the MACOI duty officer may have assumed too much in the belief that all [news] agencies understood the basic rule that no information on downed aircraft is releasable until the SAR [Search and Rescue] is terminated. It is my contention, however, that Mr. Willenson deliberately took advantage of the duty officer's naivete in order to move the item before any other agency."[7]

In the end, since some doubt existed about how the briefing officer had phrased the announcement, Stevens declined to discipline Willenson. Instead, he moved to avoid incidents of the sort in the future by ending his command's practice of advising the news media of aircraft losses prior to the completion of search-and-rescue operations. Although the move was bound to harm relations with the press by ensuring that reporters would at times fall victim to Hanoi's exaggerated claims, "Our desire to be helpful," Stevens said, "cannot be stretched far enough to rationalize the risk involved."[8]

If the episode involving Willenson demonstrated that some reporters were dedicated to the search for sensations, it took little experience with war for others to discern that official claims of progress were often of questionable value. General Sidle's conclusion that the Saigon correspondents had done little to cover the gains achieved by the newly organized 3d South Vietnamese Division and the improvements achieved in the South Vietnamese logistical system was a case in point. At the very moment when the general was visiting South Vietnam and making his observations about the press, CBS correspondent Phil Jones

---

[6] Ltr, Col Phillip H. Stevens, Chief of Information, MACV, to Arthur L. Higbee, Bureau Chief, United Press International, Saigon, 19 Feb 72, DDI Aircraft Statistics file.
[7] Ibid.
[8] Ibid.

was visiting 3d Division positions along the Demilitarized Zone and observing South Vietnam's logisticians at work. The reporter acknowledged that American advisers had devoted considerable attention to the division, but where Sidle saw progress, Jones perceived major problems. To the reporter's mind, the South Vietnamese were straining against time to comprehend sophisticated American tactics and equipment but seemed woefully inadequate to the task. Compounding those difficulties, the South Vietnamese logistical system had failed to provide necessary supplies and maintenance, organization at all levels seemed deficient, morale among the troops was low, and commanders in far away Saigon appeared disinterested. "Some soldiers haven't been paid in two months," Jones avowed in a report that aired on 14 January, "and the apparent lack of support from the Saigon command is appalling." In the end, Jones appeared to have been more perceptive where the 3d was concerned than the general. When the division came up against the invading North Vietnamese during March and April, it was virtually destroyed in the early fighting.[9]

In the same way, the improvements in American morale that Sidle was able to see, if perhaps real, were often difficult to demonstrate on a practical level. While interracial animosities may have declined, probably as the result of the American drawdown, drug abuse continued on a broad scale and far too many soldiers appeared detached from the military realities that supposedly governed their lives. The problem of discipline within the ranks seemed so intractable, indeed, that even the strongest of American commanders in the field at times expressed frustration.

Many generals attempted to counter the trend by issuing strict instructions on conduct to the members of their commands, but the lower ranking officers who enforced those rules were themselves hardly immune to the malaise. Although rarely expressing their concern by wearing peace symbols and beads, they increasingly regarded duty in South Vietnam as unattractive. As Secretary of the Army Froehlke noted in a report to Laird, captains and lieutenants, in particular, saw little further benefit to their careers from service in the war, and even the carefully selected career officers who served as advisers to the South Vietnamese armed forces were growing disenchanted. All concerned were preoccupied with the diminishing American role in the conflict, the almost certain reductions in force that would follow, and the lack of future promotion potential within the Army.[10] Under the circumstances, given the condition of American morale in the field, it was likely that

---

[9] Phil Jones, CBS Evening News, 14 Jan 72, *Radio-TV-Defense Dialog.* For appraisals of the 3d Division's performance, see Clarke, *Advice and Support: The Final Years,* p. 467; and Lt. Gen. Ngo Quang Truong, *The Easter Offensive of 1972,* Indochina Monographs (Washington, D.C.: U.S. Army Center of Military History, 1980), pp. 15–41.

[10] Memo, Robert F. Froehlke for Secretary Laird, 27 Jan 72, sub: East Asia and Pacific Trip, 330–77–0095, box 8, Viet 333, Froehlke, 1972, Laird Papers, WNRC.

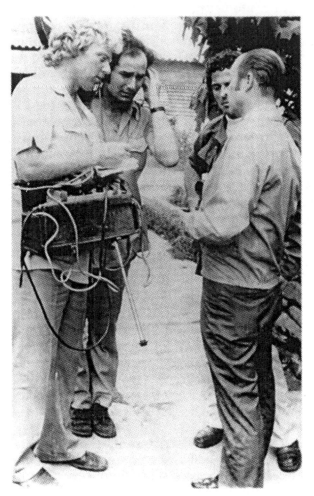

An American adviser talks to reporters. Advisers were important sources for the press throughout the war.

the Saigon correspondents would pay little attention to positive aspects of the situation.

The declining American role in public affairs complicated matters further. With American troops hardly ever involved in major combat, information officers for the South Vietnamese armed forces were increasingly the main sources for news of the ground war. Ill-disposed to candor and disinclined to do anything more than what was absolutely necessary for reporters, they became a source of constant friction between the Military Assistance Command and the Saigon correspondents.

The guidelines for the press that the South Vietnamese inaugurated in December 1971 were part of the problem. While resembling those that the MACV Office of Information had employed almost from the beginning of the war, they were designed, as the spokesman for the high command, Lt. Col. Le Trung Hien, candidly admitted, to "very much restrict reporting on military operations." The rules thus barred disclosure of troop movements smaller than those of divisions and the revelation of the exact location of military units of any sort until authorized officials had released the information. In the same way, reporters might use details obtained from the commanders of regiments and other large-size units, all of whom were well attuned to political realities in South Vietnam, but they were obliged to check with official spokesmen before dispatching material they had obtained from battalion commanders and below. The penalties for infractions were severe. A minor violation of the rules might result in the suspension of a reporter's press credentials for up to sixty days. Repeated or serious offenses could lead to permanent disaccreditation and expulsion from the country.[11]

The U.S. mission in Saigon considered the new guidelines "a move in the right direction," if only because they were, as one embassy officer put it, "an attempt to create order out of . . . chaos" where South Vietnamese handling of the press was concerned. Even so, the mistakes the South Vietnamese armed forces had made in dealing with the Saigon correspondents earlier in the war and the mistrust that the Thieu regime had always displayed toward reporters led few responsible American public affairs officers to place much faith in the new procedures. Instead, they attempted to fend off future complaints from the press by drafting a bland statement to the effect that the rules had been "formulated in keeping with security requirements in the RVN [Republic of Vietnam], and to protect lives and safety of correspondents who cover combat operations."[12]

Disavowals of that sort, of course, had little effect upon the Saigon correspondents. Although the South Vietnamese could be extremely effective in dealing with the press when their forces had won a victory, reporters complained bitterly that confusion and crossed lines of communication were inhibiting their ability to cover the news. Arthur Higbee, for one, protested that the information he was receiving was "more fragmented, conjectural, and undetailed" than at any time in his experience. A reporter from Reuters agreed. Citing "a succession of official and semiofficial reports" and subsequent "firm official denials" by South Vietnamese spokesmen, the newsman asserted that such ineptitude had forced reporters to resort to the lowest and least reliable level of sources for a considerable portion of the information they used. "Today's military briefing was an example [of the confusion that often resulted] . . .," the reporter said. "It contained no less than three denials of reports—all of which [had] originated from the amorphous structure of South Vietnamese military officers, Government officials, and official and semi-official radio and television stations and news agencies . . . [that] have now become the main source of information for foreign correspondents and other journalists."[13]

The anger of the Saigon correspondents at what seemed unjustified and arbitrary restrictions inevitably rebounded upon the already damaged credibility of the Military Assistance Command. Constrained to follow South Vietnamese conceptions of military security, for example, U.S.

[11] Quote from [Reuters], "Saigon Will Tighten Its Rules on Press Coverage of War," *New York Times*, 22 Jul 71. Msg, Saigon 18880 to State, 2 Dec 71, sub: SVN Rules for Press Coverage of Military Operations, Pol 27 Viet S file, FAIM/IR. Also see [UPI], "Rules on War News Tightened by Saigon," *New York Times*, 1 Dec 71.

[12] Msg, Saigon 18880 to State, 2 Dec 71, sub: SVN Rules for Press Coverage of Military Operations.

[13] For an example of a well-coordinated South Vietnamese attempt to move the press to the scene of a victory, see Peter Osnos, "Press Trip Undergoes Vietnamization," *Washington Post*, 21 Mar 71. Higbee, "Vietnam News Sources Dry Up as War Wanes"; [Reuters], "Reports, Then Denials, Befog Vietnam News," *New York Times*, 30 Jan 72.

spokesmen were sometimes unable to confirm that American helicopters and logistical units were assisting important ground operations until after long delays had elapsed. Higbee was thus able to complain on one occasion that when the South Vietnamese had launched a drive into the enemy's Cambodian sanctuaries during December 1971, the Military Assistance Command had declined for three days to verify that American helicopters were flying sorties in support of the operation. Recounting a long string of what appeared to be additional attempts by the command to minimize the extent of American involvement in the war, the reporter then observed that "The word has gone down the line in somewhat garbled form: the war is over, we in the military are doing nothing but going home, its an all-Vietnamese war now, so don't write about us Americans."[14]

Higbee's conclusion was understandable, but the conditions he described were often more the result of the situation that had evolved in South Vietnam than of official policy. Many American officers who still commanded combat units or who advised South Vietnamese forces in the field, for example, persisted in the belief that the press was somehow an enemy. Because of that, they attempted to exclude reporters from their areas of operation or instructed their subordinates to say as little as possible in the presence of newsmen. On those occasions, public affairs officers could do little more than make rejoinders, most of which had little effect.[15]

In the same way, with the negotiations proceeding in Paris and the war approaching some sort of climax, Washington agencies were playing a heavier role than ever before in the coordination of information released to the press. As a result, MACV information officers sometimes received instructions to refrain from answering questions on sensitive topics, only to find later that higher ups, for reasons of state or because they had failed to comprehend the problems of information officers in the field, had released the information themselves at background briefings and press conferences at the White House or the Pentagon. When that occurred, a storm of recriminations from angry reporters inevitably broke upon public affairs officers in Saigon.[16]

There were times, as well, when the United States even lacked control over what appeared to be its own property. When the State Department decided during April 1972, for example, to allow reporters to accompany AC–130 gunship missions originating from air bases in Thailand, it encountered opposition from the Thai government, which had long contended that the United States had leased only the bases and that decisions on access for newsmen to those facilities remained a Thai prerogative. The U.S. ambassador to Thailand argued that visits to the bases by groups

[14] Higbee, "Vietnam News Sources Dry Up as War Wanes."
[15] Ibid.
[16] For examples, see Ibid. Sydney Schanberg reflected on the problem in "The Saigon Follies: or Trying To Head Them Off at Credibility Gap," p. 38.

532

of reporters would cause little harm and would deter negative news stories on the subject, but Thai military leaders refused to take immediate action on the request. The American news media had continually criticized Thailand for its role in supporting the war, they said, and reporters would undoubtedly compose even worse stories if Thailand allowed them to visit the bases. They relented later in the year, but little changed. Reporters visited the bases, but only under carefully controlled conditions and never received the sort of wholesale access that they had grown accustomed to in South Vietnam.[17]

The requirement that the Military Assistance Command should continue to close down some of the functions of the MACV Office of Information also affected military credibility. During March Colonel Stevens attempted to bar television cameras from the evening briefing unless he received notice twenty-four hours in advance that the equipment would be present. He justified his announcement as an attempt to assist his briefers, who he said were line officers rather than public affairs specialists and frequently camera shy, but the change seems to have been, as well, an attempt to wean reporters away from reliance upon the sessions. The Saigon correspondents refused to accept Stevens' excuse and questioned his need to close down the Office of Information. Interpreting the move as an attack, they protested so vehemently that the command had little choice but to abandon the innovation within a week.[18]

In the same way, as the enemy buildup for the coming spring offensive continued and the United States flew an increasing number of air strikes against enemy installations in North Vietnam that had begun to fire upon American reconnaissance aircraft, Stevens ended a practice that had grown up within his office of disclosing the number of fighters and bombers involved in such attacks. The grounds he cited, that the procedure was useful to the enemy and endangered the lives of American pilots, sat poorly with reporters, who immediately objected that the Military Assistance Command was attempting to hide an escalation of the air war. "It is more than obvious to us—as it should be to Colonel Stevens—" the *Chicago Sun-Times* avowed, "that the number of American aircraft being exposed to destruction is 'information which properly belongs to the public.' What is 'useful to the enemy' (and destructive of

[17] Memo, Friedheim for Secretary of the Air Force, 26 Apr 72, sub: AC–130 Gunship Media Coverage, DDI 1972 Press Coverage file; Msg, Bangkok 9150 to Secretary of State, 29 Jun 72, sub: Congressional Interest in Press Access to Thai Bases, DDI Thailand Base Visits 1972 file. Also see Msg, Commander, U.S. Military Assistance Command, Thailand (COMUSMACTHAI), 27365 to CINCPAC PAO, 17 May 72, DDI Thailand Base Visits file. The conditions under which the press operated at the bases are detailed in Msg, Bangkok 4457 to State, 18 Apr 72, sub: Guidelines for News Media Visits to RTG Air Bases, DDI Thailand Base Visits 1972 file.

[18] [UPI–46], "Viet Briefing," 9 Mar 72, copy in CMH files; Nelson Benton, "CBS News Banned from News Conference in VN," CBS Morning News, 9 Mar 72, *Radio-TV-Defense Dialog*; [AP], "TV Banned at U.S. Viet War Briefing," *Chicago Tribune*, 10 Mar 72; [AP], "TV Men Get OK To Film Viet War Briefings," *Washington Star*, 10 Mar 72.

our strength) is the erosion of trust that . . . is caused by an overzealous security system."[19]

Although there may indeed have been an inclination on the part of some in official circles to say as little as possible about the strength of air attacks on North Vietnam, Stevens' ruling would, in fact, have hardly deterred opponents of the war from making the issue a subject of comment. The truth of the matter was simpler. From the beginning of the war, the Military Assistance Command had never authorized the release of sortie statistics where air strikes in North Vietnam were concerned, on grounds that there was little reason to fill gaps in the enemy's intelligence or to improve his knowledge of American tactics. Over time, a few public affairs officers had nevertheless grown accustomed to releasing the statistics on their own, as a favor to reporters but also to relieve some of the pressure they experienced from the press. Far from seeking to hide anything, Stevens was thus merely attempting to reassert a long-standing rule and to abolish a practice within his command that he considered detrimental both to legitimate military security and to proper discipline. On those grounds, despite the objections of the press and the storm of criticism that ensued, both he and the Department of Defense refused to make any change.[20]

Warnings of a Spring Offensive

Although sometimes justified in their complaints, reporters were less bereft of opportunities than they sometimes made it appear. Enterprising correspondents received great volumes of information, both from the private contacts that they cultivated and from official American sources sympathetic to them. In addition, the imminence of the enemy's offensive had caused considerable apprehension within the Nixon administration. It, too, worked to the advantage of the press.

Expecting the North Vietnamese to commit all but one of their reserve divisions and to wage an attack on at least the scale of the Viet Cong's 1968 Tet offensive, the president and his advisers were determined to avoid the sort of reaction in the news media that had occurred during 1968, when reporters had interpreted initial but transitory enemy gains as a major defeat for the United States. If that occurred again, so the reasoning went, especially if U.S. casualties were high, it would obviously reinforce the antiwar mood in the United States and

---

[19] "Camouflage and Credibility," *Chicago Sun-Times*, 11 Mar 72. Also see Larry Green, "A Wall of Secrecy Rings U.S. Air War," *Chicago Daily News*, 10 Mar 72.

[20] See, for example, John S. Knight, "U.S. Compounds Errors by Escalating Air War," *Philadelphia Inquirer*, 14 Nov 71; "Escalation of New Air Raids Inadequate To Ease Concern," *Denver Post*, 29 Dec 71; "We Can't Bomb Our Way Out," *Los Angeles Times*, 28 Dec 71; Ltr, Laird to Congressman John B. Anderson, 28 Mar 72, DDI Policy file (1972).

534

might even prompt Congress to mandate a total withdrawal of U.S. forces within an unacceptably short period of time. Meanwhile, the enemy would reap considerable propaganda advantages by disproving American claims that Vietnamization was succeeding and by embarrassing President Nixon just prior to his ground-breaking visit to China, slated to begin on 11 February 1972. It was "important to note," Secretary Laird warned as early as June 1971, "how [the news] media, especially in U.S., can be expected to report local or regional DRV [Democratic Republic of Vietnam] successes, even if they are temporary or short lived."[21]

To avoid those effects, the president and his advisers took pains to prepare the American public and press for the possibility that an offensive would occur and that the fighting would be heavy. Reasoning, as Kissinger told White House speechwriter William Safire, that it would pay "to be very conciliatory" so that "if we have to counterattack, then we'll be attacking a truculent enemy who chose to make war and not peace," President Nixon announced during mid-January that he would withdraw 70,000 American troops from South Vietnam by 1 May. Then, to undercut contentions by his Democratic opponents that he had failed to offer the North Vietnamese a fixed date for complete withdrawal in return for the repatriation of American prisoners of war, he revealed in a nationally broadcast speech on 25 January that Kissinger had in fact met secretly with North Vietnamese negotiators on twelve different occasions and had indeed made an offer of that sort, only to be refused.[22]

While those activities were progressing, administration spokesmen dealt directly with selected reporters to emphasize the imminence of an offensive. "I am personally responsible for two stories by Stu Hensley of UPI warning of how the North Vietnamese are building up more forces in an effort to undermine the president's China trip," John Scali thus reported to Charles Colson on 25 January; "one story by Bill Gill and another by Tom Jarriel, warning of the same; a similar piece by Lou Gulick of AP; several radio reports and a piece by Bob Pierpoint of CBS; and guidance to two of the three other reporters whose output I have not yet seen."[23]

In the same way, when the president decided during December to launch reinforced protective reaction strikes against North Vietnam's increasingly aggressive air defenses, the Defense Department moved

[21] Msg, Bunker Saigon 0017 to Kissinger, 17 Jan 72, NSC files, Backchannels, box 414, Bunker, 1972 [part II], Nixon Papers; Msg, Abrams MAC 948 to Moorer, 1 Feb 72, sub: Unnumbered COSVN Resolution, Abrams Papers, CMH. Quote from Laird, Handwritten Comment on Draft Memo for the President, n.d. [Jun 71], sub: South Vietnamese Capabilities and U.S. Force Levels, 330–76–207, box 14, Viet 320.2, 1971 file, Laird Papers, WNRC.

[22] Kissinger is quoted in Ambrose, *Nixon, The Triumph of a Politician*, pp. 508–09.

[23] Memo, John Scali for Chuck Colson, 25 Jan 72, sub: Your News Summary Attached, White House Special files, John Scali, Subject files, box 1, Colson Action Memos [VII of VII], Nixon Papers.

North Vietnamese surface-to-air missile strikes an American aircraft.

immediately to release as many particulars as it could. "One of my bosses asked me to suggest . . . that you initiate a message requesting authority to release details about the strikes beyond those already authorized," General Hill cabled Stevens. "Specifically, you should ask for authority to generally describe the targets and types of targets hit, as well as a general rundown on the BDA [bomb damage assessments]. He feels this latter is necessary because the operation has run several days and a comment along the line that 'we don't have BDA yet' won't hold water. In other words, ask for authority on all generalized details that you need." In the month that followed, while withholding specific sortie numbers for air attacks in countries other than South Vietnam and information on aircrew losses until search-and-rescue operations were completed, the Military Assistance Command routinely announced air operations in Laos and Cambodia and all protective reaction strikes against North Vietnam. Regular announcements of munitions expenditures also occurred, as well as weekly summaries of aircraft and casualty losses.[24]

During February and early March 1972, when the anticipated enemy offensive failed to materialize and the press began to speculate that the

---

[24] Quotes from Msg, Defense 13451 to Saigon, Hill to Stevens, 28 Dec 71, sub: Authority for Release of Details, DDI Protective Reaction file. Ltr, Dennis J. Doolin, Dep ASD ISA, to Congressman Michael J. Harrington, 30 Mar 72, 330–77–0094, box 81, Viet 385.1 (Feb–Mar) 1972, Laird Papers, WNRC.

danger had passed, unidentified South Vietnamese and American sources likewise took pains to inform reporters that the enemy had merely postponed the attack to complete logistical preparations. The Communists would move up to 80,000 men into South Vietnam during the first four months of 1972, those sources warned, more than in all the months of the previous year. They had already increased their anti-aircraft defenses in the southern portion of North Vietnam by at least 25 percent and had doubled them in the region surrounding the Ho Chi Minh Trail in Laos. In addition, North Vietnam had stationed surface-to-air missile units near the Demilitarized Zone, where, for the first time in the war, they had begun to threaten American aircraft flying in South Vietnam.[25]

The effort produced the desired results. Although Nixon's announcement of Kissinger's meetings had little effect upon the administration's critics—a headline in the *Washington Post* termed the offer to the North Vietnamese "The Same Old Shell Game"—a long succession of news stories detailed the movement of American aircraft and ships into Southeast Asia to counter the enemy threat and relayed predictions from official sources that the enemy would launch his attack toward the end of March. Some reports even passed along speculation from within the administration that the enemy intended to use the attack to create damaging headlines in the United States.[26]

Although many of those reports seem routine and even banal in hindsight, a few carried important information about the war. The Hearst papers, for example, printed a remarkable if little-noticed interview with General Abrams in which the commander disclosed, in just a few words, his own thinking on the importance of American air power in the coming offensive and the abilities of his ally. Describing the continuing overreliance of the South Vietnamese armed forces upon American firepower, Abrams observed to reporters Kingsbury Smith and Bob Considine that the enemy could never prevail in any offensive as long as American fighters and bombers dominated the battlefield. But if the United States withdrew those resources too quickly, he said, "the psychological effect on South Vietnamese commanders in the field could be 'catastrophic.'"[27]

[25] See, for example, Joseph Treaster, "Officers Near DMZ See Enemy Offensive as Unlikely," *New York Times*, 6 Feb 72. Craig Whitney, "Bombing Is Linked to High Infiltration Rate," *New York Times*, 16 Feb 72; Larry Green, "Hanoi Strengthens Aerial Defenses," *Chicago Daily News*, 15 Mar 72.

[26] "The Same Old Shell Game," *Washington Post*, 27 Jan 72. Also see Kissinger, *The White House Years*, pp. 1044–45; "Ahead: An Acid Test for South Vietnam's Army," *U.S. News & World Report*, 21 Feb 72; Charles W. Corddry, "Enemy Offensive Still Expected by Most Vietnam War Analysts," *Baltimore Sun*, 27 Feb 72; Henry S. Bradsher, "Big Hanoi Attack Predicted," *Washington Star*, 21 Mar 72; George W. Ashworth, "Hanoi Aim: Damaging Headlines," *Christian Science Monitor*, 21 Jan 72.

[27] Kingsbury Smith and Bob Considine, "Abrams Says S. Vietnam Needs U.S. Air Power," *Baltimore News-American*, 17 Mar 72.

The Offensive Begins, April 1972

By the end of the first week in March, North Vietnam's preparations were almost complete. It was manifest, General Haig told Kissinger, that the enemy intended to launch strong attacks in Military Regions 1 and 2 while conducting supporting actions in Military Regions 3 and 4 designed both to freeze South Vietnamese reserves in place and to sow confusion in densely populated areas. Haig continued that North Vietnam had established a strong political posture by canceling forthcoming private meetings in Paris with Kissinger and by publicly protesting American air attacks against North Vietnam. Meanwhile, enemy forces had moved heavy artillery and even tanks into the Laotian panhandle and continued to stockpile supplies in areas of Cambodia and Laos that provided easy access to targets in South Vietnam.[28]

President Nixon responded by assigning two extra aircraft carriers to Southeast Asian waters; deploying additional B–52 and tactical aircraft variously to Guam, Thailand, and South Vietnam; allowing ship and airborne antiaircraft missiles to fire upon targets near Hanoi and Haiphong if enemy aircraft became hostile; and authorizing higher sortie rates for bombers flying missions in South Vietnam. Those efforts apparently disrupted Communist plans enough to force the enemy to postpone the offensive. Even so, his preparations were so far advanced and his posture so militant by the first week in March that General Abrams had little choice but to conclude that the attack had, for all practical purposes, begun. Citing National Security Decision Memorandum 149, which had promised authorization for limited air strikes against targets in North Vietnam when the invasion started, he requested permission to launch sorties against a number of particularly dangerous antiaircraft missile sites in the North Vietnamese panhandle.[29]

Although as concerned as Abrams, President Nixon refused. Convinced that he would gain a freer hand in responding to the offensive if he waited for Hanoi to make the first move, he instructed Abrams' supe-

[28] Memo for Henry Kissinger, unsigned [Haig], 10 Mar 72, and Memo, Moorer CM–1625–72 for Secretary of Defense, 9 Mar 72, sub: Urgent Request for Air Authorities, both in NSC files, A. M. Haig Chron files, box 992, Haig Chron, Mar 7–15, 1972, Nixon Papers.

[29] Memo, Laird for the President, 8 Mar 72, sub: Actions Relative to the North Vietnamese Dry Season Offensive, NSC files, A. M. Haig Chron files, box 992, Haig Chron, Mar 7–15, 1972, Nixon Papers. Admiral Moorer presented Abrams' assessment of the situation to Laird in Memo, Moorer CM–1625–72 for Secretary of Defense, 9 Mar 72, sub: Urgent Request for Air Authorities. Laird passed Abrams' request to the president in Memo, Laird for the President, 8 Mar 72, sub: Actions Relative to the North Vietnamese Dry Season Offensive. NSDM 149 specified that as soon as the enemy offensive began, but not prior to 1 March, the secretary of defense should authorize, after receiving final clearance from the president, tactical air strikes against occupied SAM sites and associated equipment in an area of North Vietnam running as far north as nineteen nautical miles above the Mu Gia Pass.

riors to resubmit the request as soon as it became obvious a major attack upon South Vietnamese territory had begun.[30]

The assault finally came on 30 March, when North Vietnamese forces struck across the Demilitarized Zone into South Vietnam's Quang Tri Province. During the two days that followed, they also launched major attacks upon South Vietnamese positions in the hills west of Hue, around Kontum in Military Region 2, and at Loc Ninh and An Loc in Military Region 3. A number of assaults also occurred in Military Region 4, where enemy forces reentered areas they had abandoned under heavy pressure earlier in the war. *(Map 5)*

As the offensive developed, little went well for the South Vietnamese, especially in Quang Tri. The 3d Division's commanders had expected the enemy to attack from the west out of Laos rather than across the relatively flat and open Demilitarized Zone. Caught unprepared, while exchanging two of their regiments between positions, they nevertheless managed to withdraw their forces to a line of defense behind the Cua Viet and Cam Lo Rivers, slightly to the south of their original position along the edge of the zone. There they stood until 2 April, when members of the division's 57th Regiment near Highway 1 panicked and joined a stream of refugees fleeing down the road toward the provincial capital, Quang Tri City. The division's commander, Brig. Gen. Vu Van Giai, arrived on the scene in time to stem the rout, but he could do little for another of his regiments, the 56th, which had become surrounded during fighting at Camp Carroll, on the western flank of the 3d Division's position. Under heavy attack and lacking effective air and artillery support because of poorly planned fire support coordination, the regiment's commander had become increasingly despondent. Concluding that all was lost despite the presence of a powerful force of artillery at his disposal and more than 1,500 men, he decided to save what he could and needlessly surrendered a considerable portion of his command to the enemy. By so doing, he yielded up, on only the fourth day of the offensive, nearly half of his men and the largest accumulation of artillery in the entire region—more than twenty-two heavy weapons, including a battery of 175-mm. guns. Despite that setback and a continuing lack of extensive American air support because of poor flying weather, the South Vietnamese still managed to hold their positions south of the Cua Viet until 9 April, when the enemy exhausted his supplies and withdrew temporarily to regroup.[31]

The assault on Kontum opened more slowly but also produced demoralizing defeats. To the north of the city at Tan Canh, North Vietnamese artillery hit and destroyed the command post of the 22d

---

[30] Memo, Nixon for Secretary of Defense, 18 Mar 72, NSC files, A. M. Haig Chron files, box 992, Haig Chron, Mar 16–31, 1972, Nixon Papers.

[31] For a complete description of all aspects of the offensive, see Truong, *The Easter Offensive of 1972.* For a more concise account, see Lt. Gen. Phillip B. Davidson, USA (Ret.), *Vietnam at War* (Novato, Calif.: Presidio Press, 1988), pp. 673–713.

MAP 5

South Vietnamese Infantry Division. Overcome by fright, the division's commander refused to abandon the position, even though American advisers had established a second command post close by. Because of deficiencies in command and control that resulted, the regiment holding the base disintegrated the next morning, when North Vietnamese tanks struck the unit in force. The same thing occurred during an attack on a nearby base at Dak To. The installation's demoralized defenders abandoned the position and fled into the surrounding jungle. By 4 May Kontum itself lay open to attack. Meanwhile, to the east in the coastal lowlands, enemy forces cut Highway 1, drove most of the South Vietnamese units guarding the area from their bases, and, by so doing, gained control of almost all of Binh Dinh Province.

Perhaps the most important attack, from the enemy's point of view, came in Military Region 3 on the morning of 2 April, when Communist forces threw a feint at South Vietnamese bases in Tay Ninh Province and then launched a major drive farther to the east in Binh Long, to block Highway 13 below An Loc and to capture that city and its neighbor to the north, Loc Ninh. An Loc made an inviting target at the time because its defenses appeared weak. In addition, it was important enough and far enough to the south to serve as a credible capital for the Communist government the North Vietnamese intended to install in South Vietnam as soon as they had captured enough territory.

In the end, although Loc Ninh fell within days, the North Vietnamese division assigned to take An Loc made several errors. For one, it gave the defenders time to prepare by delaying its assault for almost a week to resupply. During the interim, the senior American adviser to the South Vietnamese forces in Military Region 3, General Hollingsworth, cajoled South Vietnamese commanders, coordinated air resupply missions, and plotted B–52 strikes. When the attack finally came, the South Vietnamese were ready and beat it back again and again. In the same way, the enemy failed to leave some avenue of escape for the town's defenders. Had he done so, according to Hollingsworth, they would probably have fled, whatever the impact of the B–52s. Instead, the attackers blocked Highway 13, forced their opponents to stand and fight, and exhausted their own resources. By 28 April, as a result, their assault had stalled, and they had little choice but to stand down to regroup and resupply.[32]

As the offensive evolved, President Nixon concluded that the United States had nothing to gain from a South Vietnamese defeat. Balancing the political consequences of a vigorous American response against those that would occur if he adopted a policy of restraint, he decided that few would blame him for responding vigorously but that he would receive little praise for his moderation if he allowed the enemy to prevail. On those

---

[32] Hollingsworth made the point in Interv, Dale Andrade with Maj Gen James F. Hollingsworth, USA (Ret.), 6 Nov 89, CMH files. Also see Kissinger, *The White House Years,* p. 1169.

Above, *Destruction at Kontum City;* below, *North Vietnamese troops attack a fire base near Quang Tri City.*

grounds, he instructed General Abrams to do whatever was necessary to defeat the attack.[33]

Handling the Press

If the president was willing to support strong measures to thwart the offensive, however, he and his advisers were keenly aware that the situation posed special public relations problems. "How this offensive plays in the American press may be the actual ultimate test of the success of Vietnamization—" Henry Kissinger's assistant Les Janka told General Haig, "since it is our own people we must convince."[34]

The press guidance that came from the White House reflected that concern. To avoid creating an atmosphere of crisis and to shield the president and his staff from unfortunate developments that might occur in the field, those instructions stipulated that only the Department of Defense and the Military Assistance Command were to issue detailed comments on the tactical situation in the field. Meanwhile, to keep the press from concentrating on the deficiencies of the South Vietnamese armed forces and to deflect questions about how much the United States would have to contribute to salvage the situation, White House spokesmen were to blast Hanoi for its aggression but otherwise to adopt the reassuring line that the president was keeping a close watch on events, that General Abrams continued to report regularly, and that all concerned believed the South Vietnamese would prevail. "Above all," the author of the instructions, Les Janka, noted, "we should let the bad news come from elsewhere."[35]

Following those instructions, the State Department's spokesman, Robert J. McCloskey, made it a point to term the offensive "a flagrant violation" of both the 1954 Geneva Agreements and the 1968 "understanding" that had led to the cessation of American bombing in North Vietnam. Jerry Friedheim at the Defense Department did the same, adding that the North Vietnamese had carried out the attack with Soviet-manufactured equipment and weapons.[36]

The press picked up the theme, but not without noting that the State Department's reaction, in particular, seemed much stronger than that of the White House and that officials in both Saigon and Washington were obvi-

[33] Msg, Kissinger to Bunker, 14 Apr 72, NSC files, A. M. Haig Chron files, box 992, Haig Chron, Apr 1–21, 1972, Nixon Papers.

[34] Memo, Les Janka for Alexander Haig, 3 Apr 72, sub: Press Handling of Vietnam Offensive, Jon Howe Vietnam Chron files, box 1082, 4–2–72, Nixon Papers.

[35] Ibid.

[36] McCloskey's comment is noted in Memo for Director of Defense Information, 3 Apr 72, sub: State Department Briefing, April 3, DDI Spring Offensive file. Also see [UPI–90], 3 Apr 72, in Jon Howe Vietnam Chron files, box 1082, 4–2–72, Nixon Papers. Friedheim made his observations in an interview with ABC News. See Transcript, n.d. [3 Apr 72], sub: ABC Interview, DDI Spring Offensive file.

ously seeking to avoid any appearance that a crisis was in progress.[37] "The Nixon administration in public is expressing confidence that South Vietnam can turn back the North Vietnamese offensive. . .," Ron Nessen observed on the 1 April edition of the NBC Saturday Night News. "That is about all the administration can say. . . . There are not enough American troops left in Vietnam to have any effect on ground combat." In the same way, on 4 April, the Associated Press noted that the Pentagon had begun to refer all questions about tactical aspects of the offensive to the South Vietnamese. "The attitude reflects what has now become U.S. policy—" the news service noted, "that it's South Vietnam's war despite the continued heavy U.S. air involvement. And, with the Nixon administration trying to defuse the war as a political issue at home, it's talking less about it."[38]

For their own part, reporters both within the United States and South Vietnam never had any doubt that a major emergency existed. As the offensive broadened, they and their editors used such words as *rout, disarray,* and *crushing* to describe what was happening, especially the retreat from the Demilitarized Zone toward Quang Tri. The *New York Daily News* termed the attack the first real baptism by fire for Vietnamization, and UPI quoted the opinions of American servicemen at the scene who believed that there was little possibility the South Vietnamese could hold the line along the Cua Viet River for long.[39]

The authors of a 4 April White House news summary gave the president a vivid description of press coverage to that date. "U.S. readies one of its biggest air armadas of the war in effort to help ARVN stop the NVA's 'flagrant invasion' of the South," they noted, paraphrasing selected news leaders and headlines from around the country. "With weather improving, B–52's pound NVA [North Vietnamese Army] concentrations near Quang Tri. Lengthy leads on all net[work]s with reports on urgent WSAG [Washington Special Actions Group] session—'all options open'—and the 'river of refugees' joined by the 'overwhelmed' ARVN troops heading for besieged Quang Tri City. Discouraging picture of situation altho [sic] NVA reported temporarily bogged down north of Quang Tri." The analysts continued that both CBS and ABC had run film of American advisers evacuating a base near Quang Tri and that neither network had apparently accepted a conclusion adopted by United Press International and the Associated Press that an air of normalcy pervaded the White House. Instead, network news commentators had tended to underscore

---

[37] [UPI–140], 3 Apr 72, in Jon Howe Vietnam Chron files, box 1082, 4–2–72. AP comments along those lines are noted in White House News Summary, 4 Apr 72, President's Office files, box 401, Apr 1–11, 1970 [I of II], Nixon Papers. Also see Fox Butterfield, "U.S. Aides in Saigon Calm in Face of North's Drive," *New York Times*, 3 Apr 72; Lawrence H. O'Rourke, "Reds Test Vietnamization Idea," *Philadelphia Inquirer*, 5 Apr 72.

[38] Ron Nessen, NBC Saturday Evening News, 1 Apr 72, *Radio-TV-Defense Dialog*; [AP], "Pentagon Ducks Viet Queries," *Baltimore News-American*, 4 Apr 72.

[39] Memo, Bruce Kehrli for Henry Kissinger, 3 Apr 71, White House Special files, Scali, Subject files, box 8, Vietnam [II of IV], Nixon Papers. Also see "Vietnamization Gets First Trial by Fire," *New York Daily News*, 2 Apr 72.

544

the pervading gloom that they sensed was present in South Vietnam and the concern of policy makers in Washington.[40]

In composing the analysis, the president's staff concentrated on news coverage that conflicted with the Nixon administration's views and ends. In fact, although newspapers and commentators who had long opposed the war were indeed hostile to the South Vietnamese and to any increase in American involvement in Southeast Asia, the press as a whole gave considerable coverage to themes that the administration considered desirable.

Editorials in many newspapers were forthrightly negative. Terming the renewed air war against North Vietnam a "reescalation," the *New York Times* called upon Congress to assert its constitutional prerogatives, presumably to restrict or cut off funds for the war. The *New York Post* was similarly critical. Referring to the president's decision to renew bombing of North Vietnam as "a desperate prescription," the newspaper asserted that the "vicious malignancy" present in South Vietnam had begun to spread again. *Long Island Newsday* questioned whether the South Vietnamese could ever survive and termed the whole process of Vietnamization a myth. Meanwhile, the front-running candidate for the Democratic presidential nomination, Senator George McGovern, asserted that the offensive and the South Vietnamese reaction to it had convinced him the Vietnam War was a "hopeless venture." The United States should conclude an agreement with North Vietnam, he said, that exchanged the release of American prisoners of war for a firm timetable of American withdrawals.[41]

Many other newspapers and commentators, however, were supportive of administration policy. If somewhat doubtful about South Vietnam's ability, in the end, to overcome the enemy, the *Washington Daily News*, for example, wished the country well and observed that "Not too much should be made of the South Vietnamese Army's failure to hold the bases [along the Demilitarized Zone]. The northerners attacked in bad weather, which inhibited allied air strikes. They also had the advantage of short supply lines, tank support, and cover from long-range artillery emplaced just north of the buffer zone. As they move farther from their bases, Hanoi's troops and their supply lines should become more vulnerable to . . . air power." The *Washington Star* was even more reassuring. Observing that the enemy's aims were as much political as military, the newspaper accused McGovern of playing into enemy hands with his comment and warned that it was hardly the time "to push the panic button." Jerry Greene of the *New York Daily News* was likewise positive. Conceding that

---

[40] White House News Summary, 4 Apr 72. Also see Garrick Utley, "SVNese Retreat in Quang Tri," NBC News, 2 Apr 72, *Radio-TV-Defense Dialog.*

[41] "Reescalation," *New York Times*, 9 Apr 72; "A Desperate Prescription," *New York Post*, 7 Apr 72; "Fourteen Months Later," *Long Island Newsday*, 5 Apr 72. McGovern is quoted in Bernard Gwertzman, "U.S. Officials Say Hanoi Drive Violates 1968 Accord," *New York Times*, 3 Apr 72.

a critical test of the president's policies in Indochina had begun, the columnist emphasized that "So far as can be determined by reports to the White House's War Room, the South Vietnamese troops . . . have withdrawn in orderly manner; no unit has been decimated and none has surrendered." The *Kansas City Star* and the *Denver Post*, for their part, while clearly opposed to the reintroduction of American ground forces into South Vietnam, refused to question the president's decision to increase American air attacks on North Vietnam. It was, they said, too soon to make a realistic assessment of what was happening in the field.[42]

As the offensive evolved and the South Vietnamese gave the appearance of holding their ground, the pessimistic stories continued but so did the favorable accounts. Long convinced that the war was hopeless, *Newsweek*, on the one hand, stressed that the "staggering armada of ships and planes" President Nixon had dispatched to the war zone in response to the attack "only underscored the frailty of the Vietnamization program." South Vietnam's most pressing problem, the magazine said, was one that had plagued it from the beginning of the conflict: "the simple lack of a will to fight on the part of the average peasant soldier."[43] More supportive, *Time*, on the other hand, cited the opinion of unidentified American experts who believed that most South Vietnamese military units would be able to withstand the enemy's offensive unless overwhelmed by vast numbers of North Vietnamese regulars. The magazine told of a hard fighting Popular Forces unit that had murdered a wounded enemy prisoner, but countered that story with another about how the tanks of a South Vietnamese armored squadron had successfully thwarted a North Vietnamese spearhead until U.S. bombers could arrive to destroy it. Henry Bradsher of the *Washington Star* and Henry S. Hayward of the *Christian Science Monitor* were also positive. Bradsher observed on 13 April that the first phase of the enemy's offensive had ground to a halt after achieving only limited successes. Hayward reported on the eighteenth that "what Saigon's forces have done wrong in some cases has received quicker notoriety than what they have done right. . . . Now the Army of the Republic of Vietnam has settled down somewhat and demonstrated an ability to respond to furious enemy onslaughts with stubborn, hard fighting of its own."[44]

If the reaction of the press in the United States was heavily dependent upon the various commentators' opinions of the war, reports from the

---

[42] "On Hacking It in Vietnam," *Washington Daily News*, 4 Apr 72; "Tet Revisited," *Washington Star*, 4 Apr 72; Jerry Greene, "Capitol Stuff," *New York Daily News*, 5 Apr 72; "Vietnamization's Biggest Combat Test Is Under Way," *Kansas City Star*, 4 Apr 72; "Crucial Test for Vietnamese: Must Do Without Our Troops," *Denver Post*, 7 Apr 72.

[43] First quote from "The War That Won't Go Away," *Newsweek*, 17 Apr 72, p. 16. Second quote from "Vietnamization: A Policy Put to the Test," *Newsweek*, 17 Apr 72, p. 18.

[44] "Vietnamization: A Policy Under the Gun," *Time*, 17 Apr 72, p. 30; "Escalation in the Air, Ordeal on the Ground," *Time*, 24 Apr 72; Henry S. Bradsher, "Red Drive Enters Phase 2," *Washington Star*, 13 Apr 72; Henry S. Hayward, "ARVN Puts Mistakes Behind," *Christian Science Monitor*, 18 Apr 72.

field were much less alarmist than they might have been, especially in comparison with those that had accompanied the Tet offensive of 1968, when reporters had concluded that the United States and South Vietnam had experienced a sharp setback. During the first days of the attack, as South Vietnamese fortunes wavered, the Saigon correspondents were understandably critical. Later, as the situation stabilized, they were nevertheless also quick to point out that the enemy's effort appeared to have stalled in Quang Tri and that the confidence of the South Vietnamese force in An Loc had increased immeasurably once the troops had received and learned to use American antitank weapons. As for the morale of the enemy, freelance Canadian photographer Gerard Herbert reported that he had personally viewed the remains of a North Vietnamese soldier who had been chained to his station inside a tank to keep him from fleeing under fire.[45]

That being the case, most correspondents still had little choice but to conclude, as Arthur Higbee put it, that the overall performance of the South Vietnamese had been "mixed." Some described scenes in which demoralized infantrymen attempted to escape the fighting at An Loc by clinging to the skids of departing helicopters. Others criticized the South Vietnamese armed forces for the indolent manner in which some of their units had responded to the attack—"Try to get [tactical or medical evacuation assistance from] any VNAF [Vietnamese Air Force] chopper at night," UPI correspondent Alan Dawson charged. "It can't be done." All concluded early that American air power had provided the critical margin of strength necessary to allow the South Vietnamese to withstand the attack.[46]

The reporters' assessments were different only in emphasis from those of high officials of the U.S. government. Ambassador Bunker and General Abrams, for example, were much more optimistic than much of the press but equally concerned. "I believe the [South Vietnamese] government under Thieu's excellent leadership has displayed a steady hand and remarkable effectiveness since the enemy offensive began," Bunker reported to Henry Kissinger on 12 April, relaying his own estimate of the situation and that of Abrams. ". . . I find a startling and encouraging difference between the way orders are being given and obeyed today and the chaos that characterized Tet 1968." Given Thieu's leadership, however, and the heroic efforts of some South Vietnamese military units, Bunker still felt compelled to add that South Vietnamese performance had been "mixed" and that "the fabric [of the nation] would not have held without U.S. air

[45] Peter Braestrup makes this point. See Peter Braestrup, *Battle Lines, Report of the Twentieth Century Fund Task Force on the Military and the Media* (New York: Priority Press Publications, 1985). Gerard Herbert, "Communist Crewmen Chained to Their Tanks," UPI clipping, 17 Apr 72, CMH files; Arthur Higbee, "The ARVN: A Mixed Performance," *Stars & Stripes*, 28 Apr 72.

[46] For a picture of wounded South Vietnamese soldiers clinging to the skids of a helicopter, see *Time*, 8 May 72, p. 29. Also see Don Tate, "Frantic Arvns Dangled From Chopper," *Washington Daily News*, 22 Apr 72. Dawson is quoted in Arthur Higbee, "The ARVN: A Mixed Performance," *Stars & Stripes*, 28 Apr 72.

power."[47] Secretary Laird was equally cautious. Cabling Abrams toward the end of April, he declined to criticize the sometimes negative reporting of the press, which he described as "generally balanced," even though he would have preferred an approach more supportive of the South Vietnamese. The Saigon correspondents had "dramatized those SVN actions that have been less than inspiring," he said, but both he and the president had themselves been "disappointed" by some aspects of the South Vietnamese effort.[48]

Problems With the Saigon Correspondents

If the Saigon correspondents' coverage of the offensive had been accurate and fair, as Colonel Stevens observed during an interview with reporter Peter Braestrup in 1972, problems still occurred.[49] Some were brought on by the inevitable confusion and perplexity that accompany any war, others by the inexperience of some of the young reporters stationed in Saigon. Occasionally, as well, they were the result of the friction that continued to spark between the military and the news media in South Vietnam.

Almost as soon as the offensive began, for example, the MACV Office of Information announced that it would refrain as usual from providing details on operational matters until commanders in the field had given them leave to do so. Despite that precaution and standard guidelines for the press that embargoed troop movements of any sort until official spokesmen issued a formal communique, UPI reporter Alan Dawson revealed almost immediately that U.S. helicopter units had begun to move into Military Region 1. Dawson contended later that MACV's guidelines had little application to his report because the troops in question had reinforced a base rather than entered combat, but his excuse was unpersuasive. Ascribing the infraction to inexperience brought on by a heavy turnover in news correspondents but disinclined to be lenient in the case of so flagrant a violation, the MACV Office of Information announced on 12 April that it had resolved to disaccredit the reporter. "We want to provide as much information as possible concerning the activities of U.S. forces," Daniel Henkin told Colonel Stevens at the time, "but only (repeat only) when this can be done without endangering lives."[50]

Although George Esper of the Associated Press and Veronique Decondu of Agence France Presse were later disaccredited briefly for sup-

---

[47] Msg, Bunker Saigon 0061 to Kissinger, 12 Apr 72, sub: Current Situation in South Vietnam, NSC files, Backchannels, box 414, Bunker, 1972 [part II], Nixon Papers.

[48] Msg, Laird OSD 4215 to Abrams, 30 Apr 72, Abrams Papers, CMH.

[49] Braestrup, *Battle Lines*, p. 73.

[50] Msg, Defense 7806 to MACV, 4 Apr 72, sub: Premature Disclosure of News Information, DDI Policy file. Also see "U.S. Command Plans To Bar a Newsman From War Zone," *New York Times*, 13 Apr 72.

posedly announcing troop movements in advance, the move against Dawson appears to have inhibited any inclination on the part of most reporters to make premature disclosures of sensitive information.[51] Even so, the Saigon correspondents remained difficult to manage, and fewer than ever seemed much inclined to cooperate with the military.

In the same way, officers in the field were just as willing as ever to believe the worst of the press. A case in point occurred during April, shortly after the announcement about Dawson, when a number of officers from the 2d Battalion, 1st Infantry, 196th Infantry Brigade (Light), operating near Da Nang, alleged in signed affidavits to the Military Assistance Command that newsmen had nearly caused a combat refusal in their unit. Learning that a planned airlift had been canceled and that men from the battalion would be moving overland by truck, the reporters had allegedly passed rumors to the troops that the area they were to traverse was booby-trapped and that an enemy ambush was likely. Then they had asked "leading questions" about whether the men intended to obey their orders. In a widely reported remark, the commander of the unit, Lt. Col. Frederick P. Mitchell, declared at the time, "All you press are bastards. I blame you for this and you can quote me on it."[52]

It seems clear from the officers' statements that the reporters present, by obstinately pursuing the story, had made themselves unwelcome. Whether any had actively promoted a combat refusal was nevertheless difficult to determine. Was the newsman who purportedly asked, "Do you think it's right that they send you into a booby-trapped area by trucks?" attempting to incite disobedience, or aggressively seeking a reaction from a soldier who already understood that mines were probably present and obviously had doubts? Did the reporters' actions actually contribute to the incident or were they a response to a problem that had already developed? The answers to those questions were impossible to determine because few of the officers who complained had been present personally when the reporters had interviewed the troops. By the same token, the officer assigned to accompany the newsmen had never learned the names of the reporters he was escorting, and other officers who might have had some direct knowledge of what had happened were unable to identify individual newsmen by name. Under the circumstances, given the predisposition of both the military and the media to believe the worst of one another and the confusion that had prevailed at the time of the incident, public affairs officers issued a cautionary note to the Saigon correspondents but declined to take punitive action against any of them.[53]

---

[51] Esper and Decondu both protested their innocence. See [UPI], "Saigon Dropping Action Against Two Reporters," *New York Times*, 30 Apr 72.

[52] [AP], "GI Unit Balks," *Washington Star*, 11 Apr 72; "Colonel Assails Newsmen," *New York Times*, 13 Apr 72.

[53] Memo, with attachments, Information Officer, HQ, FRAC, for Chief, IAAD, MACOI, 28 Apr 72, sub: 12 Apr 72 Phu Bai Incident, 334–74–593, box 14, Bad Guy List, WNRC.

Burning enemy tanks on the road to Quang Tri

As the offensive continued, even well-intentioned efforts by the press seemed to cause difficulties for the military. On one occasion, CBS News played a taped interview with General Hollingsworth. The officer noted candidly that he would never entertain a proposal by the Red Cross that the two sides should declare a temporary cease-fire at An Loc to treat the wounded. On another occasion, speaking of An Loc's attackers, he told reporters he intended to "kill them all before they get back to Cambodia." In each case it was clear that Hollingsworth considered himself the effective commander at An Loc, even though a South Vietnamese officer was technically in charge.[54]

Although true, Hollingsworth's comments contradicted long-standing U.S. assertions that the South Vietnamese were in total control of their own affairs. Soon after the interview appeared, Jerry Friedheim thus cabled Stevens to emphasize that MACV's briefers "should continue to point out that U.S. advisors are not in command of South Vietnamese units." General Abrams meanwhile reportedly instructed Hollingsworth to "shut his mouth," and the South Vietnamese issued a wrathful statement disavowing the general and his comment. "No Vietnamese general

[54] Msg, Friedheim Defense 9791 to Stevens, 24 Apr 72, sub: CBS TV Interview with MG Hollingsworth, DDI Spring Offensive file; "In Furious Battle," *Newsweek*, 24 Apr 72.

550

needs any foreign general to help him command his own troops," a spokesman for the high command observed heatedly at the time. "To say that he does, is the same as saying Vietnamese generals are not capable of doing their job . . . and it only helps the Communists."[55]

On the same day that the comment appeared, the *New York Times* published word that South Vietnamese civilian and military policemen had set up checkpoints along Highway 13 below An Loc, where they were allowing most of the traffic to pass but barring without explanation anyone bearing press credentials. Alluding to Dawson's disaccreditation and the other disputes that had occurred between the American military and the news media, the author of the report could only conclude that everything seemed connected. "Relations between Saigon and foreign correspondents have never been smooth," he said. "Now United States officials generally appear to regard the situation with neither sympathy nor special interest and some confess that they share Saigon's antipathy."[56]

The observation was accurate, in some respects, but American officials in positions of responsibility were still more concerned with opening up information than with closing it off. Although Ambassador Bunker himself agreed with a decision Thieu had made to seize fourteen out of the twenty-four Vietnamese-language daily newspapers based in Saigon because they had published lurid and overly dramatized accounts of the fighting, he also clearly believed that the ability of President Thieu to survive politically during the troubled times ahead depended upon much more than the brute force his regime could muster. In that regard, he told Henry Kissinger, for the sake of credibility, Thieu and his government had to do more to improve the way they dealt with the news media both of South Vietnam and the world. If recent, highly publicized military successes such as the ones that had blunted the enemy's attack in Quang Tri had done much to avert the growth of a sense of discouragement among the South Vietnamese people, he said, the facts reporters were gathering at the scene of the fighting still conflicted with the news released by government briefers. The Army's casualty reports, in particular, had so distorted reality that they had created a credibility gap.[57]

Neither Thieu nor his generals were much inclined to the task but their lack of interest appears to have had little effect. Thieu made a number of well-timed speeches during April that increased the confidence of the South Vietnamese people in his leadership by conveying an impres-

[55] Friedheim quote from Msg, Friedheim Defense 9791 to Stevens, 24 Apr 72, sub: CBS TV Interview with MG Hollingsworth. Abrams is quoted in "In Furious Battle," p. 31. Hollingsworth confirmed the thrust of the quotation if not the actual words in Interv, Andrade with Hollingsworth, 6 Nov 89. The South Vietnamese disavowal is from "Saigon Says It Needs No U.S. General," *Baltimore Sun*, 16 Apr 72.

[56] "Saigon Making Moves To Curb Bad-News Coverage of the War," *New York Times*, 16 Apr 72.

[57] Msg, Saigon 4672 to State, 5 Apr 72, sub: Reaction to NVA Offensive, DDI Spring Offensive file; Msg, Bunker Saigon 0061 to Kissinger, 12 Apr 72, sub: Current Situation in South Vietnam, Nixon Papers.

sion that he was firmly in control of events in the field. By mid-April, as well, the Saigon correspondents were preoccupied with a new subject. With the enemy pulling back in Quang Tri to regroup and South Vietnamese forces holding their own at An Loc, President Nixon had chosen the moment to begin the bombing campaign in North Vietnam that he and Kissinger had long considered necessary to jar the enemy toward a breakthrough in the Paris negotiations.[58]

The Air War Escalates

From a purely military standpoint, Nixon's decision seemed questionable, especially to Secretary Laird. In early April, shortly after Admiral Moorer presented the president with draft contingency plans to mine Haiphong Harbor and to use B–52s to bomb targets near Hanoi on a one-time basis, Laird outlined his reservations in a memorandum to Henry Kissinger. The enemy's sources of production were centered in the Soviet Union and the People's Republic of China, he said, beyond the reach of American bombers. The targets that did exist in North Vietnam were meanwhile part of a "diverse and diffused distribution system" that could take many shapes. Throughout the war, the enemy had consistently demonstrated his ability to adopt new logistical approaches when the old ones proved vulnerable. Although there was a certain value in threatening the relatively small industrial base that North Vietnam had developed since the bombing halt of 1968, the significance of the threat would diminish once that base was gone. Of more importance was the political impact the attack would have in the United States and throughout the rest of the world, where the bombing had become a negative symbol and a rallying point for antiwar activists. As for the plan to mine Haiphong, Laird continued that there was a basic inconsistency between the end the president sought and the effort he proposed to expend. Nixon wanted to close Haiphong Harbor to block the importation of war materiel into North Vietnam, but mining alone would hardly achieve that end. An intense air campaign would also be necessary to block North Vietnam's border with China and to seal off the rest of the nation's coastline. Laird concluded his memorandum with a handwritten note: "Henry—" he wrote, "The political impact of these plans may be what is wanted by the President. If the Russians want an excuse to stop their present major (80% supplies) contribution to North Vietnam, mining might have that political impact but I would doubt it."[59]

---

[58] See, for example, Draft Memo, Kissinger for the President, 17 Sep 71, sub: Vietnam, Nixon Papers.

[59] Memo, Laird for Assistant to the President for National Security Affairs, 6 Apr 72, sub: Contingency Plans for Operations Against North Vietnam, NSC files, Jon Howe Chron files, box 1079, Feb, Mar, Apr 72, Nixon Papers. Laird's handwritten note is on the final page of the memorandum.

Laird's reasoning had little apparent influence upon either Kissinger or the president, both of whom were already thinking in terms far larger than the limited attacks Moorer had plotted. As General Haig noted in passing Laird's memorandum to the national security adviser, if the secretary was correct in observing that the political and military impact of the strikes hardly justified the domestic and international costs, the president already had a program "of much greater scope" under consideration.[60]

Sorely aware of South Vietnam's dependence upon American air power, General Abrams was also disturbed. When the president decided to postpone any decision on the mining but to go ahead on 16 and 17 April with air attacks on logistical targets in the vicinity of Hanoi and Haiphong, the general immediately requested a delay. A major battle of great significance was developing at An Loc, he said. In addition, the commander of Military Region 1 was beginning an offensive to expand and improve defensive positions around Quang Tri. Since the battle for An Loc alone had generated a requirement for up to 160 tactical air and 30 B–52 sorties per day, the raid on North Vietnam would obviously impair the air support available for both of those endeavors. Twenty-four hours prior to the attack, the aircraft carriers stationed off the coast of South Vietnam would have to terminate their operations to reposition themselves farther north. Following the strikes, another 24-hour delay would occur while the carriers steamed back into their old positions and performed necessary maintenance on their aircraft. A further lag would occur if bad weather postponed the operation.[61]

Intent upon demonstrating American determination at a time when Henry Kissinger was slated to begin secret negotiations in Moscow on a possible Soviet-American summit, President Nixon denied Abrams' request. He nevertheless sent General Haig to Saigon to evaluate the situation and to explain his decision to Abrams. Haig later informed Kissinger that he had engaged in a "long and fruitful exchange with General Abrams," who "understands completely the necessity for escalation of air effort to North." Haig continued that Abrams had compensated somewhat for the absence of the carriers by refueling Thailand-based aircraft in the Saigon area but that the general was under "severe pressure" to husband his air assets. "I spent the afternoon in III Corps with General Hollingsworth, who together with his deputy, [Brigadier] General [John R.] McGiffert, has been holding together a most tenuous situation [at An Loc]. . . . The only factor which has prevented a major debacle has been U.S. air, especially B–52's. Three enemy main force units reinforced by tanks and artillery have been deployed against one of ARVN's weakest

[60] Memo, Haig for Kissinger, n.d. [Apr 72], sub: Contingency Planning, NSC files, Jon Howe Chron files, box 1079, Feb, Mar, Apr 72, Nixon Papers.

[61] The instructions are contained in Msg, Moorer JCS SPECAT Exclusive 8374 to McCain, info Abrams et al., 13 Apr 72, sub: Freedom Porch, and Msg, Abrams SPECAT Exclusive to Moorer and McCain, 14 Apr 72, sub: Freedom Porch, both in NSC files, Jon Howe Chron files, box 1079, Feb, Mar, Apr 72, Nixon Papers.

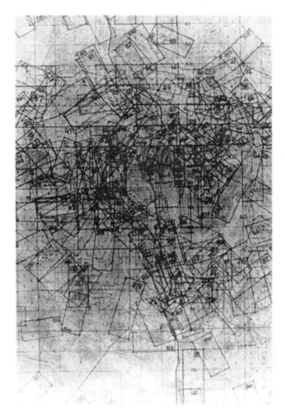

General Abrams placed great reliance on the B–52 bomber during the Easter offensive. On this map of An Loc, barely visible, each overlapping box represents the target for a single strike.

divisions along a route leading directly to Saigon."[62]

The public affairs handling for the raids was straightforward. Shortly after the attacks began on 16 April, the MACV Office of Information introduced reporters at Da Nang to pilots who had participated. The officers gave vivid descriptions of the billowing flames and columns of smoke that had risen above the targets and that had remained visible from a distance of over one hundred miles as the striking aircraft returned home. One noted that "there were more SAM's [surface-to-air missiles] than I have ever seen in my life." Another, who had flown in North Vietnam during 1968, observed that "It was the most satisfying mission I've ever been on. I don't think when I was here before we ever had a target that was quite that lucrative." To counter any possible enemy attempt to distort the results of the attacks, public affairs officers also revealed that preliminary damage assessments indicated the raids had caused major damage to antiaircraft, warehouse, oil storage, and railroad facilities near Hanoi and Haiphong.[63]

As those efforts were continuing in South Vietnam, the Nixon administration was preparing the ground for the larger program of air attacks it had under consideration. On the day after the raids, in testimony before the Senate Foreign Relations Committee, Secretary of State Rogers thus observed quietly that the president intended to take "whatever action is necessary to halt the enemy drive." Secretary of Defense

[62] Kissinger, *The White House Years*, p. 1121. Quotes from Msg, Haig Saigon 0064 to Kissinger, 16 Apr 72, NSC files, Backchannels, Bunker, 1972 [part II], Nixon Papers.

[63] [UPI–033A], 17 Apr 72, CMH files. Also see [AP], "Hanoi Raid a Success, U.S. Says," *Baltimore Sun*, 23 Apr 72; Bill Brannigan, ABC Evening News, 21 Apr 71, *Radio-TV-Defense Dialog*.

Laird was more emphatic. Meeting with the committee on 18 April, he remarked that U.S. commanders in South Vietnam had received authority to use both tactical fighter bombers and B–52 aircraft anywhere in North Vietnam, as the situation in the field warranted. He added that all of North Vietnam would be subject to American attack for as long as the offensive continued and that there was a possibility "the United States might even blockade or mine the harbor of Haiphong." Questioned on Laird's comments, Pentagon spokesmen emphasized that everything the secretary had said was to be taken at face value. Admiral McCain and General Abrams, they continued, had received authority to employ the full range of American air power in North Vietnam, as they and their commanders saw fit.[64]

The raids generated considerable comment in the United States, especially in Congress. On 20 April the House Democratic Caucus rejected by a narrow margin of 105 to 97 a resolution demanding an end to all American involvement in the war within thirty days. Meanwhile, in a five-hour Senate debate, Republican Senator Barry M. Goldwater of Arizona called for more bombing, but his Democratic opponents asserted vigorously that the president was risking endless war in South Vietnam, possible collapse of promising nuclear arms limitation talks with the Soviet Union, and disruption of newly established relations with China for the sake of a discredited regime in South Vietnam that was of little genuine value to the United States. Republican Senators Robert J. Dole of Kansas and Howard H. Baker, Jr., of Tennessee attempted to moderate the debate by denying that the bombing was part of a long-term plan to defend Thieu and by insisting that the president was moving resolutely to put an end to American involvement in the war. Democratic Senator Thomas F. Eagleton of Missouri nevertheless countered that "we cannot bomb North Vietnam into submission. Time and again, our experience has shown that, if anything, their resolve will be strengthened."[65]

Commentaries in the news media resembled the debate in Congress, with columnists and newscasters on both sides of the question drawn inevitably to the parallel between President Nixon's decision to renew attacks on North Vietnam and the earlier decision by President Johnson to begin bombing in the first place. In general, the differences between the conclusions each group reached seemed as marked as they had been during the 1960s. Editorials in the *New York Times* termed the bombing "an

[64] Laird and Rogers are quoted in John W. Finney, "Laird Says Raids Can Continue Until Enemy Calls Off Invasion," *New York Times*, 19 Apr 72. Also see [UPI], "Rogers Rushes to House To Counter Doves," *Washington Daily News*, 19 Apr 72; Charles W. Corddry, "Laird Hints Possibility of Shutting Off Haiphong," *Baltimore Sun*, 19 Apr 72; Edward Rohrbach, "N. Viet Bomb Strikes Continue; U.S. Lifts All Target Limits," *Chicago Tribune*, 19 Apr 72; Orr Kelly, "Commanders Pick Targets: New Policy on Viet Bombing," *Washington Star*, 19 Apr 72.

[65] Spencer Rich and Mary Russell, "Debate Over Bombing Rages on Capitol Hill," *Washington Post*, 20 Apr 72.

exercise in folly and futility" while the *San Diego Union* considered it "a courageous, non-political act"; the *Los Angeles Times* asserted that "B–52's cannot buy victory," but the *Arizona Republic* avowed that "bombs should continue to fall north of the Red River." Even so, the contrast between the two sides was probably less than it had ever been. For if so-called doves within the press clearly sought to be done with the war and worried that the bombing might hinder good relations with the Soviet Union, even hawkish editors themselves, as *Time* noted, tended to see the bombing more as a step hastening a final American withdrawal than as a means toward some sort of military victory.[66]

The American public, for its part, despite considerable ambivalence, appears to have sided with the president. Although Louis Harris observed that by May 1972 a massive 76 percent of all Americans wanted U.S. troops home by the end of the year and that 60 percent were willing to sacrifice Thieu as the price of a cease-fire, a poll by the Sidlinger organization during April revealed that support for the president himself had increased noticeably, going from 35.4 percent prior to the bombing of Hanoi and Haiphong to 46.4 afterwards. A Gallup poll released on 25 April noted that the public was almost evenly divided on the question, with 47 percent of respondents favoring the bombing, 44 percent opposed, and 9 percent undecided, but a poll released by the Opinion Research Corporation at the same time appeared much more favorable to the administration. When asked whether they agreed with the statement, "our air and naval attacks on military targets in North Vietnam will be continued until the North Vietnamese stop their offensive in South Vietnam," 69 percent of those who responded in that case agreed, 24 percent disagreed, and 7 percent had no opinion.[67]

Public support for any president tends to rise in times of international crisis, but informal man-on-the-street interviews in a number of journals suggested at the time that support for the bombing ran much deeper than the ambivalence revealed in some polls might have indicated. Most of the people reporters interviewed, *Newsweek* thus observed, believed North Vietnam deserved to be bombed because it had committed a clear act of aggression. Similarly, the *Philadelphia Inquirer* reported that if a number of the people it had contacted had asserted that it was wrong "to kill innocent people to save a corrupt government," others had spoken adamantly of the need to stop the escalation of the war by the North even if that required the use of nuclear weapons.[68]

---

[66] See, for example, Henry Bradsher, "Is It an Entirely New War?," *Washington Star*, 19 Apr 72; Orr Kelly, "U.S. Following 'Classic' Script in Escalation," *Washington Star*, 23 Apr 72; "Escalation in the Air, Ordeal on the Ground," p. 20. The newspapers are quoted in "The Bombing Blues," *Time*, 1 May 72.

[67] [UPI–151], 24 Apr 72, copy in CMH files. The Gallup poll is cited in JCS History, 1971–1973, p. 376. Memo, Alexander P. Butterfield, Deputy Assistant to the President, for Members of the Cabinet, 1 May 72, sub: Americans Strongly Support the President's Vietnam Stand, 330–77–0094, box 81, Viet 385.1 (1 May–3 May) 1972, Laird Papers, WNRC.

[68] "The War on Two Fronts," *Newsweek*, 1 May 72, p. 22; "The Public Speaks," *Philadelphia Inquirer*, 20 Apr 72.

If the American public harbored little sympathy for North Vietnam, the mood on the nation's college campuses, supposedly hotbeds of anti-war ferment, seemed muted and even apathetic. A call by Ivy League newspaper editors summoning college students to a general strike to protest the attacks fell flat. Although a number of demonstrations occurred around the country and North Vietnamese spokesmen even addressed a rally in San Francisco by telephone, most of the protests, according to *Newsweek*, had been planned long in advance of the raids. For the rest, if the president of Columbia University canceled classes because of a threatened student boycott and Governor Marvin Mandel of Maryland declared a state of emergency after three days of violence at his state's College Park campus, most of the demonstrations that occurred were orderly, and the majority of students appear to have gone about their business with little regard for either the protesters or the bombing. It was examination time for many, *Newsweek*'s editors later suggested, and the chances of being drafted at that late stage in the war seemed remote for most.[69]

President Nixon understood nevertheless that the situation could change dramatically in a short period of time. As Alexander Haig observed in a message to Ambassador Bunker on 23 April, the president believed it was essential to continue to "(1) confuse and muffle residual dove sentiment here in the United States, especially in the Congress; (2) assure U.S. Right [wing] that the president is determined to do everything necessary to succeed in his program; (3) balance (1) and (2) above in such a way that maximum military and psychological pressure can be placed on Hanoi at this critical juncture."[70]

In pursuit of those ends, Haig continued, the president intended to address the nation on 26 April. Since the United States' ability to withdraw ground forces even in the face of an all-out offensive by the North Vietnamese would "contribute immeasurably to public confidence in the Vietnamization program," he said, Nixon intended at that time to announce that he was withdrawing another 20,000 men from Vietnam. He would also play upon Henry Kissinger's secret trip to Moscow. The fact that Soviet leaders would meet with the national security adviser at a time when the United States was bombing their ally would inevitably disconcert North Vietnamese leaders and might add to the president's flexibility in continuing air operations against the North.

To make the speech as up-to-date as possible, Haig continued, the president wanted General Abrams to send him a personal estimate of the situation in South Vietnam. Addressing the nature and scope of U.S. air

[69] Memo, 25 Apr 72, sub: Vietnam Situation Report, NSC files, Subject files, box 388, Summaries, 3/1/72–4/30/72, vol. XI, Nixon Papers. Also see "The War on Two Fronts," p. 22; Greg Jackson, "Anti-war Demonstrations Held," ABC Evening News, 21 Apr 72, *Radio-TV-Defense Dialog*.

[70] Unless otherwise indicated, this section is based on Msg, Haig to Bunker, 23 Apr 72, NSC files, A. M. Haig Chron files, box 992, Haig Chron, Apr 22–30, 1972, Nixon Papers.

operations "in the context of the need to protect U.S. lives as our troops are withdrawn," it was to be short and general in nature and "as optimistic as the situation legitimately permits." Recalling President Nixon's use during LAM SON 719 of a comment Abrams had made to the effect that the South Vietnamese could "hack it," Haig added that "Perhaps some colorful terminology of this kind would be helpful."

For the rest, he said, the planned return of U.S. negotiators to the plenary sessions of the Paris peace talks on 27 April and subsequent U.S. participation in a secret negotiating session on 2 May would also further the president's ends by presenting "irrefutable evidence of U.S. and GVN reasonableness in the face of the most flagrant enemy violations of past understandings." If the 2 May session, in particular, proved unfruitful, "we will have then established the base for a most intense increase in air activity in North Vietnam, including additional strikes in the Haiphong area."

General Abrams provided the president with the assessment he had requested but neglected to deliver any of the turns of phrase Haig had sought. He stressed instead the quiet dignity of the South Vietnamese and their determination to repel the enemy's attack. The president, for his part, followed Abrams' approach during the speech, emphasizing the general's judgment that the South Vietnamese were bearing up well but that hard fighting would continue. For the rest, he pursued the themes Haig had laid down in the message to Bunker. Declaring his intention to draw down American troop strength in South Vietnam to 49,000 men by 1 July, he emphasized his support for the Thieu regime and his own determination to continue the bombing until Hanoi renounced its offensive. He then observed, alluding to Kissinger's secret trip to Moscow, that he hoped to travel to the Soviet capital himself within the next month, just as he had to Peking during February. Although he would never yield to demands that he make unilateral concessions in Paris to achieve detente with the Soviet Union, he added, he had already instructed the American negotiators in Paris to attempt once more to inaugurate discussions that could lead to substantive progress toward peace.[71]

The speech seemed "more of the same" to *Newsweek*, which had looked for Nixon to unveil "some dramatic new turn in U.S. policy toward Vietnam." In fact, despite contentions of that sort, it seems clear in hindsight that the president had indeed grimly embarked upon the only course he believed would produce a viable peace for the United States in Southeast Asia. His intentions are evident in a talk Henry

---

[71] Abrams' appraisal is in Msg, Abrams MAC 3810 to Laird, 26 Apr 72, sub: Personal Assessment of the Situation in RVN as of 26 April 1972, Abrams Papers, CMH. Also see Kissinger, *The White House Years*, p. 1163; "And the War Goes On," *Newsweek*, 8 May 72, p. 19. The president's speech is in "A Report on the Military Situation in Vietnam and the Role of the United States: An Address by President Nixon," Department of State *Bulletin*, 15 May 72, p. 683.

Kissinger gave to the White House staff on 26 April, shortly before the address to the nation. Outlining the general posture the White House would adopt toward the press during the weeks that followed, Kissinger observed that

We do not want the White House to protest our undying devotion to peace. We do not want the White House to proclaim that we are really in league with the peace marchers but have just a minor tactical disagreement with them. . . . We cannot afford any breast feeding or any flinching. We are now engaged on a course in which the other side has put all the chips into the pot and in which we have put our chips into the pot and the only way we are going to make it and the only reason we have made it go up to now is that we have convinced our opponents that this time, for once, against all probability, we mean business and therefore, we are not interested in giving the impression that we are just on the verge of backing off, that really all we want is to surrender with grace. . . . We have the possibility now, better than at any time in the Administration, . . . of getting perhaps some serious talks started . . . because the president made [the North Vietnamese] . . . believe they might lose everything and because they have adopted a strategy that if they do not win, they will lose everything.[72]

---

[72] "And the War Goes On," p. 19; Briefing by Dr. Henry Kissinger to Members of White House Staff, Roosevelt Room, 26 Apr 72, White House Special files, Haig, box 44, General Speech Material [II of V], Nixon Papers.

22

Ultimatum: "Settle or Else!"

Although disappointed with some aspects of the South Vietnamese effort to oppose the offensive, President Nixon, Secretary Laird, and General Abrams all believed that their ally had fought well under difficult circumstances and that Thieu and his generals would in the end prevail. As Laird observed in a 25 April 1972 memorandum to the president, American B–52s might have played an important role in blocking the first wave of the Communist attack, but they would never have achieved that effect if South Vietnam's soldiers had failed to stand their ground.[1]

All concerned nevertheless agreed that the enemy had pushed the South Vietnamese to the limit and that hard fighting would continue. In the field, the senior American adviser in Military Region 2, John Paul Vann, told reporters that he expected Kontum to have a few more days of quiet but then "the tide will come rolling in." Analysts at the State Department's Bureau of Intelligence and Research were of much the same mind. Although Hanoi had experienced some setbacks, they observed in a late April report, it retained a solid claim to success in the offensive. If its forces had failed to destroy South Vietnam's divisions, they had still proved that they could maul significant portions of the nation's army. Meanwhile, the North Vietnamese had compelled a graphic demonstration of South Vietnam's dependence on heavy American air support and had scrambled the country's defenses. Despite considerable losses, they still possessed the means to sustain the offensive over many months and clearly intended to fight on well into the summer.[2]

---

[1] Memo, Laird for the President, 26 Apr 72, sub: Personal Assessment of the Situation in RVN as of 26 April 1972, 330–77–0094, box 79, Viet 385 (16–30 Apr) 1972, Laird Papers, WNRC. Abrams agreed. See Msg, Abrams MAC 3757 to Laird, 24 Apr 72, sub: Personal Assessment of the Situation in RVN as of 24 April 1972, Abrams Papers, CMH.

[2] Quote from [AP–83], 26 Apr 72, NSC files, Jon Howe Vietnam Chron files, box 1085, Apr 72, Nixon Papers. Msg, State 70195 to All Diplomatic Posts, 22 Apr 72, sub: South Vietnam. Hanoi Maintains Its Options, DDI Spring Offensive file.

The prospect of a prolonged enemy offensive was hardly daunting to President Nixon and Henry Kissinger. As Kissinger's talk to the White House staff on 26 April had indicated, both viewed the attack as an opportunity rather than a threat. With the B–52s on station in Southeast Asia, there seemed little chance that the enemy would prevail over the short term. In the meantime, Nixon's overtures to China and the increasing likelihood of an American summit with the Soviet Union had tended to isolate North Vietnam from its main supporters. All that remained was to pound the Communists toward a peace agreement acceptable to the United States. The offensive provided the occasion.

Nixon's predilections were vividly apparent in a 30 April 1972 memorandum to Henry Kissinger. Referring to a meeting between the national security adviser and North Vietnamese negotiators slated for 2 May, he instructed Kissinger to inform Hanoi's representatives that "they have violated all understandings, they stepped up the war, they have refused to negotiate seriously. As a result, the President has had enough and now you have only one message to give them—Settle or else!"[3]

Nixon continued that he considered it essential for the United States to launch a major air strike against Hanoi and Haiphong within days of the meeting, unless the North Vietnamese agreed to make immediate, major concessions in the peace talks. Commencing about 5 May, that attack would run for three days and involve at least 100 B–52s and as many tactical aircraft as General Abrams could spare. The approach, Nixon implied, would bleed the enemy enough to give the South Vietnamese a reasonable chance to repel attacks that might occur within the next two years, "when we no longer will be able to help them with major air strikes." It might also spur the North Vietnamese to faster action on the negotiations and might bolster public opinion in the United States.

Timing, Nixon suggested, was all-important.

We have to recognize the hard fact—unless we hit the Hanoi Haiphong complex this weekend, we probably are not going to be able to hit it at all before the election. After this weekend, it will be too close to the Russian Summit. During the summit and for a couple of weeks afterwards, our hands will be tied for the very same good reasons that they were tied during and after the Chinese summit. Then we will be in the middle of June with the Democratic Convention only three to four weeks away and it would be a mistake to have the strike at that time. Another factor is that the more time that passes there is a possibility that the Congress will act to tie our hands. Finally, support for taking a hard line, while relatively strong now, will erode day by day, particularly as the news from the battle area is so viciously distorted by the press so that people get a sense of hopelessness, and then would assume that we were only striking out of desperation.

Avowing that he would sacrifice even the summit in Moscow to deliver the blow he intended, Nixon told Kissinger to "Forget the domestic reac-

[3] This section is based on Memo, the President for Henry Kissinger, 30 Apr 72, NSC files, President's Office files, box 3, Memos, Apr 72, Nixon Papers.

tion. Now is the best time to hit them. Every day we delay reduces support for such strong action."

In the weeks and months that followed, Nixon's injunction carried heavy weight but public relations was still never far from the minds of the president and his advisers. As Nixon and Kissinger pursued the high stakes they had set for themselves, the need to maintain appearances became essential. It turned the MACV Office of Information into little more than an outlet for the carefully tuned pronouncements of Washington agencies and forced even the legitimate concerns of soldiers in the field into second place.

General Abrams Intervenes

As Nixon's memorandum to Kissinger showed, the president intended to do whatever was necessary to achieve his ends but he also understood that the diminishing consensus in the United States could only inhibit his flexibility. To postpone that effect for as long as possible and to shore up support for the actions he intended to take, he thus instructed Laird to request that Abrams or his deputy hold a background briefing for the press to put the situation in the field into perspective. The Saigon correspondents had dramatized less-than-inspiring aspects of the South Vietnamese Army's performance. The commanders at the scene, so the reasoning went, were the ones best suited to assert the opposite point of view.[4]

Abrams was open to the idea but circumstances had begun to change. On 28 April the town of Dong Ha, north of Quang Tri in Military Region 1, had fallen to the enemy. Over the next two days, Communist forces had renewed their attack on the South Vietnamese line of defense along the Cua Viet River, and General Lam had withdrawn his forces to the south. By the time the backgrounder was to have occurred, the worst had happened. Panic had set in among the units guarding the approaches to Quang Tri, and they had abandoned the city. Joining a swarm of refugees moving south down Highway 1 toward Hue, the fleeing troops provided an inviting target for North Vietnamese gunners, who were already attempting to provoke mass confusion by firing at the refugees on the road, mostly civilian noncombatants, the elderly, women, and children. Enemy pressure also increased in Military Region 2, where the South Vietnamese forces guarding bases along the approaches to Kontum began to buckle and pull back.[5]

Although Thieu immediately replaced Lam with one of the few truly skilled commanders he possessed, the impeccably honest Lt. Gen. Ngo

[4] Msg, Laird OSD 4215 to Abrams, 30 Apr 72, Abrams Papers, CMH.
[5] Msg, Abrams MAC 4021 to Laird, 1 May 72, sub: Personal Assessment of the Situation in RVN as of 1 May 72, Abrams Papers, CMH.

Destruction along Highway 1, south of Quang Tri City

Quang Truong, Abrams had little choice but to cable Laird that South Vietnam's senior military leadership "has begun to bend and in some cases to break. In adversity it is losing its will and cannot be depended on to take the measures necessary to stand and fight. . . . In light of this, there is no basis for confidence that Hue or Kontum will be held. . . . I recommend I not have a backgrounder."[6]

The decision was probably fortunate, for little that Abrams could have said would have made much difference to the Saigon correspondents, who were already in the field and well aware of what was happening. Some never made it back to Saigon to tell their stories. Alexander Shimkin of *Newsweek* disappeared during June in a hail of enemy grenades on the outskirts of Quang Tri City, and James D. Gill, a photographer stringing for the *London Daily Telegraph*, was captured, bound hand and foot, and then murdered by the North Vietnamese during the fighting north of Da Nang. Those that did, however, had little good to say about the way South Vietnamese forces were conducting themselves.[7]

The reporters based many of their accounts on the testimony of American advisers. In relating the fall of Tan Canh, twenty kilometers north of Kontum, for example, a correspondent for *Time* magazine quoted one of five American officers who had survived the disaster. "Tan Canh

[6] Ibid. Truong's character is discussed in Msg, Saigon 6463 to State, 4 May 72, sub: LTG Truong Named MR 1 Commander; Other ARVN Personnel Changes, DDI Spring Offensive file.

[7] [Reuters–PMS 36], Photographer, 31 Jul 72.

The enemy took this artillery base near Cua Viet with its guns intact.

fell," the adviser said, "because ARVN never got off its ass and fought." Describing the fighting at Bong Son, a town on the seacoast to the east of Kontum, *New York Times* reporter Craig Whitney quoted the senior American adviser in the area, Maj. George H. Watkins, Jr. "There was a lot of valor by some individuals," that officer noted as he told of the collapse of the South Vietnamese forces in the town and of his own escape at the last moment, "and there was a lot of cowardice. . . . The troops' morale was just broken. Some broke and ran, just ran and didn't know where to go. Some deserted to the VC. They just didn't know what to do, and that was because of their lack of leadership in any depth." Whitney's colleague, Sydney Schanberg, sketched the shambles the enemy had made of the refugee column along Highway 1. "Please understand," one American officer had told the reporter delicately. "Quang Tri is not cut off. We're just not going there today."[8]

It was perhaps natural that most reporters would blame the South Vietnamese for what was happening. As the *Washington Star*'s correspondent in South Vietnam, Henry Bradsher, noted, if instances of bravery had indeed occurred, impartial observers had little choice but to conclude that lethargy and military incompetence had too often been the rule among the South Vietnamese. The performance of the forces attempting to move

[8] "Setting in for the Third Indochina War," *Time*, 8 May 72, p. 28; Craig R. Whitney, "As Town Falls, American Sees Valor and Cowardice," *New York Times*, 30 Apr 72; Sydney H. Schanberg, "Convoys to Quangtri Blocked; Refugees Crowd Hue," *New York Times*, 30 Apr 72.

up Highway 13 to relieve the siege at An Loc was a case in point. It hardly seemed, Bradsher said, that the units involved wanted to win. Recently returned from a trip to South Vietnam, Richard Levine of the *Wall Street Journal* agreed with Bradsher. Assessing the performance of the South Vietnamese over the previous week, he noted on 8 May that many Americans had become disillusioned with their ally. "You can't give a man guts," he observed, quoting a U.S. Army general with long experience in Vietnam. Meanwhile, the *New York Times* introduced an article by Craig Whitney on South Vietnamese performance during the offensive with the headline, "Where There's No Will, There's No Way."[9]

Newsweek's Pentagon correspondent Lloyd Norman nevertheless placed the blame squarely upon the United States. American intelligence had failed to predict the attack across the Demilitarized Zone and the appearance of massive numbers of enemy tanks on South Vietnamese territory. The sobering spectacle of those tanks and heavy enemy artillery operating deep inside South Vietnam raised serious questions about the ultimate effectiveness of American air power and seemed to suggest that much of America's bombing over the years had been in vain. Although the president and his spokesmen had continually asserted that Vietnamization was a success, South Vietnamese performance thus far in the offensive suggested the opposite. "Technically, the White House has been correct in saying that the ARVN has the capability to stand alone," the reporter concluded.

The South Vietnamese armed forces both outnumber and outgun their Communist adversaries—and enjoy the luxury of almost unlimited air support. . . . Perhaps the fatal flaw . . . has been the inability of the United States to instill in the South Vietnamese soldier the esprit and determination necessary to take on Hanoi's highly motivated and tightly disciplined troops. It was relatively easy for the United States to hand out the rifles, the artillery, the attack planes and the tanks that the ARVN lacked. . . . But last week, when more U.S. tanks arrived in South Vietnam to replace those lost to the Communists, one U.S. official in Saigon snapped, "For Christ's sake, they don't need more damn equipment. They need some guts."[10]

Although the North Vietnamese generally fought only when conditions heavily favored their side and when they outgunned their opponent, events in the days that followed tended to confirm many of the judgments appearing in the press. For as enemy pressure increased in Military Region 1 and around Kontum, the performance of the South Vietnamese armed forces continued to lag. "The collapse of the defenses of Kontum Province, the retreat from Quang Tri and the slowness with

---

[9] Henry S. Bradsher, "Painful Conclusions on War," *Washington Star*, 30 Apr 72; Richard J. Levine, "South Vietnam Army Causes Rising Concern for U.S. Military Men," *Wall Street Journal*, 8 May 72; Craig Whitney, "Where There's No Will, There's No Way," *New York Times*, 7 May 72.

[10] "What Went Wrong in Vietnam: The Fallacies in U.S. Policy," *Newsweek*, 15 May 72, p. 24.

which ARVN has moved up Route 13 to relieve the siege of An Loc have introduced new and sobering aspects to the situation here," Ambassador Bunker thus told Kissinger on 6 May. Although Kontum City might fall, he continued, the loss would be of little consequence. What mattered was Hue. If the old capital came under enemy control in a manner that further reduced public confidence in the army or the Thieu regime, the government of South Vietnam might be in jeopardy.[11]

Bunker felt certain that Truong would hold Hue, but the situation still seemed so grave that General Abrams decided to assert his rights as commander in the field and to postpone the massive B–52 strike against Hanoi and Haiphong that the president had ordered for the weekend of 6 May. Convinced that the president's show of force would have little effect on the battlefield in the South and that Nixon was sending B–52s "away hunting rabbits while the backyard was filled with lions," he told Admiral Moorer on 4 May that he considered the will to fight of South Vietnam's military leaders the most critical problem confronting his command. With major enemy attacks at Kontum and Hue imminent and with Truong in the midst of moving fresh troops into Military Region 1, it was essential for the United States to pour its air power into the South, both to sustain Truong's morale and to buy time while the general regained control. "In this situation," Abrams said, " . . . any interruption in our support to the key RVNAF commanders [will be] . . . reflected in their will and determination. We must stay with them at this critical time and apply the air power where the immediate effect is greatest."[12]

Although Nixon acceded to Abrams' wishes, Kissinger told Ambassador Bunker shortly thereafter, he was "nearing the end of his patience with the general." Abrams had to understand that "we are playing the most complex game with the Soviets involving matters which extend far beyond the battle in Vietnam as crucial as it is." In fact, General Haig had been sent to Saigon "for the specific purpose of making these broader political considerations clear" to the commander.[13]

Abrams, for his part, was equally adamant. Meeting briefly with Vice President Agnew at Tan Son Nhut Airport on 17 May, he observed that if the South Vietnamese rank and file had fought well when properly led, there were, to his mind, only ten generals in the entire country who were earning their pay. Under those circumstances, the presence of American

---

[11] Msg, Bunker Saigon 87 to Kissinger, 6 May 72, NSC files, Backchannels, box 414, Backchannel Msgs, Bunker, 1972 [part II], Nixon Papers.

[12] Abrams made the comment about lions and rabbits in a conversation with Lt. Gen. Donald Cowles See BDM Corporation, Vietnam: A Study of Strategic Lessons Learned, vol. 6, Conduct of the War, pp. 4–90, CMH files. Abrams' request for a postponement and his comment to Moorer is in Msg, Abrams SPECAT to Moorer and McCain, 4 May 72, sub: Frame Glory, NSC files, Jon Howe Chron files, box 1086, May 4, 1972, Nixon Papers. Also see Msg, Abrams MAC 4039 to Laird, 2 May 72, 330–77–0095, box 8, Viet 385, 1972, Laird Papers, WNRC.

[13] Msg, Kissinger WHS 2063 to Bunker, 4 May 72, NSC files, Backchannels, box 414, Backchannel Msgs, Bunker, 1972 [part II], Nixon Papers.

General Weyand

advisers on the battlefield and the application of unrestricted American air power had been critical in the days following the enemy's offensive. Indeed, if South Vietnam had survived to date, the B–52 bombers were the reason. Available twenty-four hours a day in all weather, they had been, as the summary of the general's briefing for the vice president noted, "the principal factor that had maintained the morale of the ARVN as well as the integrity of the delicate fabric of the GVN system and its will to resist."[14]

Concentrating on larger goals, President Nixon nevertheless had the final say. Already dissatisfied with the general's performance during LAM SON 719, he had debated for some time whether to recall Abrams. On the evening of 4 May, a few hours after agreeing reluctantly to cancel the strike on Hanoi and Haiphong, he resolved to take the step. In so doing, he told Haig, he would appoint the general to a two-year term as chief of staff of the Army, if Kissinger concurred and Abrams himself agreed to abide by certain unspecified conditions. Infighting in Washington appears to have delayed public announcement of the decision until 20 June, when the White House finally revealed the change and disclosed that Abrams' former deputy, General Frederick Weyand, would assume charge of the Military Assistance Command.[15]

[14] Msg, Abrams MAC 4600 to Vice President Agnew, 17 May 72, sub: MEMCON of Meeting at Tan Son Nhut Base Operations VIP Lounge, Abrams Papers, CMH

[15] Memo, Haig for Kissinger, 5 May 72, sub: Talking Points for Your Breakfast Meeting With Secretary Laird, 8:00 a.m., Saturday, May 6, 1972, NSC files, A. M. Haig Chron files, box 993, Haig Chron, May 1–20, 1972 [II of II], Nixon Papers. Nixon's unhappiness with the performance of the military in general during this period appears briefly in Kissinger's memoirs. See Kissinger, *The White House Years*, p. 1200. Nixon had wanted a complete reorganization of the command structure in South Vietnam, with General Bruce Palmer becoming the supreme commander of a new Southeast Asian theater while General William DePuy took charge of whatever U.S. Army forces remained in South Vietnam. He apparently yielded to arguments by Laird and the Joint Chiefs that, given the critical tactical situation, a minimum of disruption within the Military Assistance Command was essential. Since Weyand had been on the scene for years and had developed close ties to the South Vietnamese, he became the one to succeed Abrams. See Memo, Laird for the President, with attached Memos, Moorer for Laird, 10 May 72, sub: Command Structure in the Pacific/Southeast Asia Area, NSC files, Kissinger Office files, box 146, FY 73–74 Defense Budget, Nixon Papers.

Mining and Bombing North Vietnam

In the interim, the president continued to pursue his ends. On 6 May, Henry Kissinger thus informed Ambassador Bunker that Nixon tentatively planned to announce during a speech to the nation two days later a sharp increase in air attacks on North Vietnam, intensified naval bombardment of the country's coastal regions, and the mining of its ports. "To put it in the bluntest terms," he said, "we are not interested in half-measures; we want to demonstrate to Hanoi that we really mean business; and we want to strike in a fashion that maximizes their difficulties." Kissinger added that the president wanted to highlight the enemy's abuse of the South Vietnamese people in the speech and requested that Bunker provide the necessary statistics on civilian casualties. "Do not hesitate to give us ball-park figures," he said, "and we will not object if they incline towards the high side."[16]

Bunker complied and Nixon made the speech on 8 May. Avowing that the enemy had inflicted over 20,000 casualties upon the civilian population of South Vietnam "in wanton disregard of human life," he reviewed the events of the offensive and recent U.S. peace initiatives. Only two issues remained, he said. "First, in the face of a massive invasion, do we stand by, jeopardize the lives of 60,000 Americans, and leave the South Vietnamese to a long night of terror? . . . Second, in the face of complete intransigence at the conference table, do we join with our enemy to install a Communist government in South Vietnam?" Since neither alternative was possible, "We shall do whatever is required to safeguard American lives and American honor. . . . We will not cross the line from generosity to treachery." To that end, because the enemy had rejected all offers and abandoned all restraints, he had ordered the mining of North Vietnam's ports and had instructed U.S. forces to continue air and naval strikes to cut the country's lines of internal communication. The mines were timed to activate within three days to give foreign vessels an opportunity to vacate the ports. They would remain in service and the air and naval attacks would continue until the enemy had returned all American prisoners of war and had agreed to an internationally supervised cease-fire throughout Indochina.[17]

---

[16] Msg, Kissinger WHS 2066 to Bunker, 6 May 72, NSC files, Backchannels, box 414, Backchannel Msgs, Bunker, 1972 [part II], Nixon Papers. Also see Memo, Brig Gen Robert E. Pursley for Haig, 6 May 72, Nixon Papers; Kissinger, *The White House Years*, pp. 1180f. According to Lewis Sorley, Abrams was not informed until the last moment that Nixon had issued orders to mine North Vietnam's harbors Sorley quotes Laird to the effect that the omission was an oversight. Even if that was the case, given the central role Abrams had played in the war, the fact clearly indicates the depths to which Abrams had fallen in the eyes of the Nixon administration. See Sorley, *Thunderbolt*, pp. 324f.

[17] News Release, Office of the White House Press Secretary, "Address by the President on National Radio and Television," 8 May 72, White House Special files, Staff Member Office files, Colson, Vietnam Speech, 5/8/72 [I of IV], Nixon Papers.

The announcement provoked a flurry of antiwar demonstrations across the United States. Most were peaceful but some were marred by violence. Several policemen were shot at the University of Wisconsin, Madison, when they attempted to arrest a group of students accused of arson. The president of the University of New Mexico meanwhile declared a state of emergency on his campus, after police had wounded fourteen demonstrators. Despite the disruptions, however, it was clear within days that the protests had failed to gather momentum. Almost "ritualistic" and pro forma, *Newsweek* noted later, they appeared to have attracted mainly veteran demonstrators while recruiting few new ones from the public at large.[18]

In the same way, the reaction of the news media was hardly unanimous. Many newspaper and television commentators expressed outrage at the attacks and voiced concern that the president's moves might impede prospects for the summit with the Soviet Union scheduled to begin on 22 May. Others questioned Nixon's good judgment. Columnist Joseph Kraft, for example, claimed that the president had risked almost everything for what would be at most a "fig leaf for defeat." Rowland Evans and Robert Novak termed the president's moves "dangerously high-risk poker." Keyes Beech of the *Chicago Daily News* asserted that the decision to impose a naval blockade on North Vietnam was "the act of an angry and desperate man." The *Denver Post* charged that the decision to mine Haiphong Harbor involved "a risk to the United States and the peace of the world which should not have been taken." And the *New York Times* called upon Congress to save the nation from disaster by putting the power of the executive branch under leash.[19]

If opinions of that sort gained the most attention, especially at the White House, a swell of support for the president nevertheless also developed in the news media. The *Washington Star* declared that since "the Rubicon is crossed . . . the place of this newspaper is behind the President of the United States." The *Detroit News* praised Nixon's "guts." The *Richmond News Leader* asserted that every American could take pride in the president's decision to take a stand. The often critical *Seattle Post-Intelligencer* voiced its support for Nixon's "response to Communist

[18] "Clamor and Caution," *Newsweek*, 22 May 72, p. 24. Also see "Upsurge of War Protests, but Support for Nixon Policy, Too," *U S. News & World Report*, 22 May 72, p. 35.

[19] See, for example, ". . . And Where It Leaves Us With Moscow," *Washington Post*, 10 May 72, and Hobart Rowen, "The President's Forays," *Washington Post*, 11 May 72. Joseph Kraft, "Fig Leaf for Defeat," *Washington Post*, 11 May 72; Rowland Evans and Robert Novak, "Doubling the U.S. Bet," *Washington Post*, 11 May 72; "Mr. Nixon's Brinkmanship," *New York Times*, 11 May 72. The news media's reactions were well documented at the time, both by official observers and in the press. White House media analysts summarized it in MFR, n.d., sub: The President's Vietnam Initiatives and the Media: A Case of Unrestrained Coverage and Commentary, White House Special files, Staff Member Office files, Colson, Vietnam Speech, 5/8/72 [III of IV], Nixon Papers. Henry Kissinger did the same in *The White House Years*, pp 1190–91. Among news media outlets, *Time* published one of the most comprehensive surveys. See "Thunder All Around," *Time*, 22 May 72, p. 39.

aggression." Of them all, the *New York Daily News* was particularly point-ed. The paper avowed that 90 percent of the American people would back the president's moves. As for the remaining 10 percent, it would include "kooks, would-be presidents, Nixon-hating politicians, com-mentators and columnists, domestic Reds and others who have sabo-taged the war effort for years and still have a right to freedom of the speech and press."[20]

Although perhaps too broad in its characterization, the *Daily News* was near the mark in its prediction of what public support for the presi-dent would be. During the week after Nixon made his announcement, a telephone poll by Sidlinger & Company revealed that, whatever the opposition of the news media to the mining, up to three-quarters of the American people—76.2 percent—supported the president. A poll by the Opinion Research Corporation confirmed the finding. Up to 74 percent of the Americans queried by the organization backed the decision to mine North Vietnam's ports. Polls by ABC and Louis Harris put the number at a more modest 59 percent, but even at that lower level the figures were heartening to an administration that viewed itself as increasingly under siege. "This support is particularly important," Herbert Klein observed at the time, "because it is clear that the enemy is carefully monitoring U.S. public opinion. Their reason is twofold: nega-tive reaction will aid in their bargaining position at the negotiation table, and it will also enable them to generate internal propaganda in North Vietnam."[21]

President Nixon did everything he could to take advantage of the public mood while it lasted. To emphasize the firmness of American resolve, he instructed official spokesmen on all levels to play down any implication that the United States might restrain its attacks in some man-ner. Instead, he wanted to apply maximum pressure to North Vietnam by hitting targets such as power plants, that would have a profound psycho-logical effect on the morale of the enemy population. "Remember," he told Kissinger, "that we will [never] have more support than we will in the days ahead. As each day goes by criticism will reduce support for our action and also the failure to get results will reduce the enthusiasm of our supporters." He added that the United States had tended in the past, dur-ing the Johnson presidency, "to talk big and act little." The enemy, he con-tinued, "has now gone over the brink *and so have we.* We have the power to destroy his war making capacity. The only question is whether we have the will to use that power. What distinguishes me from [Lyndon] Johnson is that I have the *will* in spades."[22]

[20] MFR, n.d., sub: The President's Vietnam Initiatives and the Media: A Case of Unrestrained Coverage and Commentary; "Thunder All Around," p. 39.

[21] Memo, Bill Rhatican for Chuck Colson, 25 May 72, sub: Commentators. Quote from Ltr, Herbert G. Klein to an unknown addressee, 16 May 72. Both in White House Special files, Staff Member Office files, Colson, Vietnam Speech, 5/8/72 [I of IV], Nixon Papers.

[22] Memo, Nixon for Henry Kissinger, 9 May 72, White House Special files, President's Office files, box 4, May 72, Nixon Papers.

During the days that followed, administration spokesmen used every forum in the news media to maintain as much flexibility as possible for the president. Emphasizing the enemy's aggression, they urged Americans to consider that the North Vietnamese outnumbered their opponents in the South in each major battle zone and that the forces invading South Vietnam were armed with a new generation of modern weapons characterized by such recent innovations as mobile antiaircraft guns and the latest heat-seeking missiles—all supplied by the Soviet Union through the ports under blockade. Secretary Laird meanwhile stressed American willingness to negotiate and to follow through on the president's promise to withdraw completely from the war. He also made it a point to underscore in news releases that General Abrams intended to reduce American troop levels in South Vietnam to 49,000 men by 1 July. "The American people always have supported our president when Americans are endangered and the cause of freedom has been threatened," he asserted. "This is no time for quitters or for a lot of talk about 'instant surrender.'" When the effect of those initiatives began to wear off, on 28 June, Nixon reinvigorated the campaign by revealing that he had instructed the Army to refrain from sending draftees to Vietnam unless they volunteered.[23]

Controversy With the Press Continues

As the mining began and air attacks on North Vietnam intensified, the military commands responsible for operations in the field attempted to open what information they could to the press. Newsmen were intensely interested in the tactics and equipment the United States was using to mine North Vietnam's harbors and sought a broad range of information on those subjects. The Associated Press, for example, requested permission to observe the loading of mines onto the ships of the Seventh Fleet and to photograph actual mining operations. Concerned lest the enemy glean too much information from press reports, the chief of naval operations responded by warning "all hands, military and civilian" to hold classified material close and to refrain from saying anything "through any channel directly or indirectly that might reach unauthorized recipients concerning mines, mining, or mine countermeasures."[24]

[23] Talking Paper, Key Points in the Vietnam Debate, 15 May 72, attachment to Memo, Bill Rhatican for Chuck Colson, 25 May 72, sub: Commentators. Quotes from Memo for Correspondents, 10 May 72. Both in White House Special files, Staff Member Office files, Colson, Vietnam Speech, 5/8/72 [I of IV] and [II of IV], respectively, Nixon Papers. Kissinger, *The White House Years*, p. 1305.

[24] Msg, Commander, U.S. Navy, Philippines (COMUSNAVPHIL), to Commander in Chief, Pacific Fleet (CINCPACFLT), 9 May 72, sub: News Media Request for Permission to Photograph Ship Loading Ops and Embark Photog. Quote from Msg, CNO to Naval Operations (NAVOP), 9 May 72, sub: Mine and Mine Countermeasures Information. Both in DDI Mining Haiphong 1972.

The press was undeterred. Combining what it could sift from official sources with word from unofficial contacts, *Newsweek*, for one, was able to report in its 22 May issue that the Mark–53 and –55 mines employed in the operation were the most technically advanced in the American arsenal and that fewer than a dozen carrier-based aircraft flying at 10,000 feet had taken less than an hour to deploy them in North Vietnam's major waterways. "These sophisticated, modern mines usually contain a variety of sensors to detect a ship's magnetic field, the noise given off by its turbines and screws, the pressure of its displacement or any combination of these," the magazine continued. "In fact, it is believed that most of the mines dropped by the U.S. last week were programmed to go off only when all three characteristics registered simultaneously in the mines' minicomputers—thus blocking attempts to trigger them with dummy ships."[25] The security violation, if it was one, probably worked to the advantage of the United States by underscoring the seriousness of the president's intentions and by warning the enemy that it would be futile to attempt to disarm the mines.

The MACV Office of Information, for its part, was concerned with giving the press as much perspective as possible and with countering any propaganda the enemy might make. In the case of the war on the ground, it thus released sanitized intelligence information to the Saigon correspondents to stress topics such as North Vietnamese abuse of civilians in captured areas that might otherwise have gone unnoticed by reporters.[26]

It also attempted to liberalize the rules governing the release of information on the air war. Noting that prior to the 1968 bombing halt, public affairs officers had informed the press of U.S. air operations in North Vietnam on a daily basis rather than yield the initiative to Hanoi, the chief of MACV information, Colonel Stevens, for example, requested permission to do much the same thing again and to include general descriptions of the targets under attack, their locations, and assessments of the damage inflicted. The Defense Department authorized a loosening of some information but at first permitted the release of bomb damage assessments only after two or three days had elapsed. It relented on 22 May, when the effectiveness of the bombing began to come into question in the press, to advise "the American and free world public on a more timely basis about the determination . . . with which we are carrying out the president's policies." The Office of the Assistant Secretary of Defense

---

[25] "How the Mines Work," *Newsweek*, 22 May 72, p. 21. On 22 May the Commander of the U.S. Seventh Fleet, Admiral William Mack, mistakenly revealed some protected information in an interview with United Press International. See Msg, Jerry Friedheim OASD PA 5483 to Col Al Lynn, USAF, CINCPAC IO, 23 May 72, sub: 7th Fleet Change of Command Press Interview, DDI Mining Haiphong 1972.

[26] See, for example, Joseph B. Treaster, "Enemy Is Said To Execute Hundreds in South Vietnam," *New York Times*, 4 Aug 72; Msg, State 142261 to Saigon, 5 Aug 72, sub: Release of Sanitized Intelligence to Media, DDI Press Coverage, 1972.

for Public Affairs also instructed the Military Assistance Command to accelerate release to the Saigon correspondents of photographs depicting bomb damage and to expedite the transmission of those pictures to Washington. Shortly thereafter, the Defense Department also began work on large charts to illustrate for the benefit of reporters the locations where important cuts in North Vietnam's railroad system had occurred and key points where air strikes had destroyed enemy petroleum transmission and storage facilities. The effort had its effect. *U.S. News & World Report*, for one, published a map illustrating the major targets of U.S. attacks in its 5 June issue, along with pictures of the effects of American pinpoint bombing. Those materials appeared in the context of an extensive treatment of how television and laser-guided "smart bombs" were "squeezing" North Vietnam.[27]

Less advantageous to military credibility were revelations that surfaced in the news media during May and June that on at least twenty-eight occasions between 7 November 1971 and 9 March 1972 armed escorts accompanying U.S. reconnaissance aircraft in North Vietnam had exceeded their authority by attacking targets without provocation. The missions had been preplanned to strike the enemy's transportation facilities, airfields, and petroleum supplies with the knowledge of the Commander of the U.S. Seventh Air Force in South Vietnam, General John Lavelle, at a time when severe restrictions on bombing in the North had prevailed. When the aircraft had returned to base, again on Lavelle's instructions, aircrews and debriefing teams had falsified their reports to indicate that the attacks had been legitimate "protective reactions" carried on to suppress enemy antiaircraft fire against unarmed reconnaissance aircraft.[28]

The attacks came to the attention of the Senate in early March, when a young Air Force sergeant involved in the cover-up wrote to Senator Harold E. Hughes of Iowa to complain that his superiors had required him to falsify official reports. Hughes sent the letter to Senator Stuart Symington, a former secretary of the Air Force, who in turn passed it to the Chief of Staff of the Air Force, General John D. Ryan. Ryan investigated, determined that the sergeant had told the truth, and relieved Lavelle of command. At that time, to avoid embarrassment and to keep discussion of the subject from spreading to other cross-border operations such as the secret bombing of Cambodia, the Defense Department apparently decided to refrain from making a full disclosure of the reasons behind Lavelle's

[27] Msg, MACV 14464 to JCS/Secretary of Defense, 11 May 72, sub: Public Affairs Reporting of Air War North, DDI Policy file. Quote from MFR, Jerry Friedheim, 22 May 72, sub. Actions Accomplished Per Monday's Discussion, 330–77–0094, box 75, Viet 000.1–Viet 381, 1972, Laird Papers, WNRC. "How 'Smart Bombs' Are Squeezing North Vietnam," *U.S. News & World Report*, 5 Jun 72, p. 23.

[28] See Jim Adams, [AP–244], 24 May 72, in 330–77–0094, box 77, Viet 322, 1972, Laird Papers, WNRC; Memo, Laird for the President, 16 Jun 72, sub: Circumstances Surrounding the Replacement of Gen. John D. Lavelle as Commander of 7th Air Force, 330–77–0094, box 77, Laird Papers, WNRC.

relief to the press.[29] The news release that announced the general's retirement thus avowed blandly that Lavelle had seen fit to relinquish his command and to retire for reasons of health. In the same way, on the day the retirement took effect, the Air Force adhered to custom and requested that the president honor Lavelle's years of exemplary service by advancing the general one rank on the list of retirees.[30] With Congress involved, Nixon could do nothing of the sort. Although he allowed the Air Force to retire Lavelle on a disability, he demoted the general.

By 15 May the attempt to give the episode a low profile had begun to fall apart. With both the Senate and the House Armed Services Committees planning hearings on the subject and leaks almost certain to appear in the press, General Ryan found he had no choice but to amend the earlier announcement to specify that Lavelle had been relieved of command because of "irregularities" in the conduct of his responsibilities. With little information coming from the Military Assistance Command, which refused to answer questions on the subject because the matter was still technically under investigation, nothing of consequence appeared in the press until the twenty-fourth. On that date, a ranking member of the House Armed Services Committee, Congressman Otis G. Pike of New York, told the Associated Press that Lavelle had detected the enemy buildup that preceded the Easter offensive and had apparently conducted raids to deter it on his own, despite orders to the contrary. Pike noted that once the offensive had begun, the president had gone forward with exactly the sort of air strikes Lavelle had conducted. Shortly thereafter, at Pike's

[29] During interviews both Daniel Henkin and Jerry Friedheim insisted that there was a National Security Council dimension to Lavelle's actions. Lavelle was too professional an officer to have taken them on his own, they asserted, without some intimation from higher ups that the attacks were in the best interests of the nation. Official visitors from the White House arrived continually in South Vietnam, Friedheim observed. It would have taken no more than an oblique reference to the president's wishes for Lavelle to get the message. Henkin suggested that the Nixon Papers should say something on the subject, but the national security files available to the author failed to address the issue. Laird appears initially to have wanted to deal severely with Lavelle. He backed away from that alternative either because of intimations from Lavelle that he would be very candid if court-martialed or because the trial of so high an officer for failing to obey rules that Air Force officers believed had caused needless American casualties would inevitably do severe damage to what was left of military morale. As it was, Lavelle insisted in testimony before Congress that Generals Ryan and Abrams understood the outlines of what he was doing. See Interv, author with Daniel Z Henkin, 10 Oct 86; Interv, author with Jerry Friedheim, 3 Oct 86. Both in CMH files. Lavelle's retirement is covered in MFR, 7 Jun 72, sub: Lavelle, 330–77–0094, box 77, Laird Papers, WNRC. Material pertinent to the subject may be found in 330–77–0094, box 77, Laird Papers, WNRC. An oral history interview with Lavelle exists. At the request of the general's family, it remains sealed within the files of the Office of Air Force History.

[30] Seymour M. Hersh, *The Price of Power* (New York: Summit Books, 1983), p. 507. As documentation of the desire to keep a low profile, see MFR, R Adm Daniel J. Murphy, Military Assistant to the Secretary of Defense, 7 Jun 72, sub: Lavelle, 330–77–0094, box 77, Laird Papers, WNRC. The desire to restrict knowledge of other operations is implied in Talking Paper, 17 Oct 72, sub: Impact of Lavelle Investigation, 330–77–0094, box 77, Viet 322, Laird Papers, WNRC; Memo for the President, 7 Apr 72, sub: Air Force General Officer Action, 330–77–0094, box 77, Viet 322, 1972, Laird Papers, WNRC.

urging, Seymour Hersh published a major story in the *New York Times* outlining what had occurred and suggesting that Lavelle's superiors in Saigon and Washington might have known what was happening.[31]

On the day that Hersh's story appeared, Lavelle made the same point in secret testimony before the Senate Armed Services Committee. Soon after, leaks from the session prompted speculation in the press that General Abrams was somehow involved. Having no authority over air strikes in North Vietnam, which remained under the control of the commander in chief, Pacific, throughout the war, Abrams denied the accusation, but to little effect. Although there was considerable sympathy for Lavelle on the part of some in the press and few within the news media were willing to deny Abrams promotion to chief of staff of the Army, the charge surfaced again and again over the weeks that followed. Allegations also appeared that other officers had taken the war into their own hands and that civilian control of the military in the American society seemed in jeopardy. "Anyone reading the details of the story is bound to feel sympathy for the general and the things he did," the *Christian Science Monitor* observed on 16 June, ". . . [but] independent decision making by soldiers in the field is—dangerous."[32]

In response, Admiral Moorer moved to reassure Congress and the press that surveillance of military operations in North and South Vietnam had become so stringent after the revelations about Lavelle that a repeat of the affair was unlikely. Laird meanwhile told the Chairman of the Senate Armed Services Committee, Senator John Stennis, that he was doing all he could to improve the effectiveness of the headquarters staffs that controlled military operations. Declining to excuse any of the deficiencies that had occurred, he illustrated the broad dimensions of the problem facing the military by noting that the 137 illicit strike sorties Lavelle had conducted were almost invisible in the context of the more than 25,000 legitimate sorties the Seventh Air Force had coordinated during the period when the attacks were taking place.[33]

While not altogether successful in relieving pressure on the Pentagon (*Newsweek*, for one, asserted on 25 September that "Somebody was lying—maybe somebody high up"), official efforts to clarify what had happened and to put it into context at least kept attention on Lavelle.

[31] Memo for Correspondents, 15 May 72, DDI Aircraft Statistics file. MACV's handling of the incident may be seen in Msg, Lt Col Donald J. Peterson, USAF, Acting CINFO, MACV, to Lorfano, 15 Sep 72, sub: *Time-Life* Correspondent Barry Hillenbrand, DDI Aircraft Statistics file. Also see Jim Adams, [AP–244], 24 May 72. Hersh recounts how he came to write his story in Hersh, *The Price of Power*, p. 507.

[32] Msg, Laird OSD 6406 to Abrams, 14 Jun 72. Msg, Abrams to Secretary of Defense, 15 Jun 72. Both in Abrams Papers, CMH. See, for example, "Laird Clears Abrams on Lavelle's Bombing," *Washington Post*, 22 Jun 72; "The Private War of General Lavelle," *Newsweek*, 26 Jun 72; "Was Lavelle Alone?," *Newsweek*, 25 Sep 72; "The Lavelle Case," *Christian Science Monitor*, 16 Jun 72.

[33] Press Interview, Moorer, 19 Sep 72, 330–77–0094, box 77, Viet 210, 1972, Laird Papers, WNRC. Ltr, Laird to Honorable John C Stennis, 18 Oct 72, DDI Protective Reactions file.

Earlier operations of a similar nature by a fighter wing stationed in Thailand never came under scrutiny. Neither did the fact that Laird—for all his protestations about the difficulty involved in recognizing illicit air strikes—had himself recognized that something was amiss as early as February and had queried the chairman of the Joint Chiefs on the high number of protective reactions occurring in North Vietnam. Nothing surfaced, as well, on the bombing of Cambodia, which would take another year to become public.[34]

If the Lavelle affair gained considerable attention in the press, it was hardly the only issue confronting public affairs officers as the Easter offensive lengthened. The enemy and his allies had no intention of allowing the Nixon administration to mine and bomb North Vietnam with impunity and began to search for flaws in the U.S. position that would make for credible anti-American propaganda.

The Communist Chinese were the first to come forward. Shortly after the mining and bombing began, the People's Republic charged that American bombers had hit several Chinese cargo ships anchored in North Vietnamese ports. In early June it also complained that the United States had allowed its aircraft to intrude upon Chinese air space during raids in the northernmost portions of North Vietnam.[35]

While those charges were circulating, the government of North Vietnam settled upon an issue of its own. Asserting that it had succeeded in managing the problems caused by the air campaign without undue stress, it avowed that American aircraft had deliberately struck civilian habitations and the system of dikes that protected the homes of its people from flooding during the rainy season. To substantiate those claims, it then permitted American newspaper correspondents and celebrities known for their antiwar sympathies to travel to Hanoi to view the damage.[36]

The United States passed off China's charge that American aircraft had bombed its ships by noting simply that there was no information in American files to confirm the claim. In fact, if something of the sort occurred, at that time or later, it was an act of inadvertence rather than policy. As the blockade lengthened, Chinese merchant ships achieved enough success unloading supplies across North Vietnam's beaches to tie up four American aircraft with attacks on the lighters moving the materiel for twenty-four hours a day. The ships themselves, however, were never targets, if only because the Nixon administration had long before decided to foster good relations with the People's Republic of China and had little wish to reverse the progress it had made.[37]

---

[34] "Was Lavelle Alone?," p. 64; Talking Paper, 17 Oct 72, sub: Impact of Lavelle Investigation.

[35] Memo for the Director of Defense Information, 9 May 72, sub: State Department Briefing, 9 May, DDI Mining Haiphong 1972.

[36] Craig R. Whitney, "Hanoi Says Raids Struck at Dikes," *New York Times*, 9 May 72.

[37] Ibid. Also see Msg, John Lehman Saigon 109 to Haig, 10 Jul 72, NSC files, Backchannels, box 414, Backchannel Msgs, Bunker, 1972 [part II], Nixon Papers.

As for purported intrusions upon Chinese air space, no evidence existed that anything had occurred because the United States had long kept its aircraft from entering a buffer zone it had established along North Vietnam's border with China. In hopes of diverting the press from the issue, the commander in chief, Pacific, nevertheless instructed official spokesmen on 14 June to substitute Hanoi for China as a point of reference when describing the location of bombing attacks in North Vietnam.[38]

The news stories that resulted from visits to North Vietnam by reporters and celebrities were more of a problem because they challenged U.S. claims that the bombing had targeted only military installations. When Anthony Lewis of the *New York Times* thus visited North Vietnam and began to assert that the mining and bombing had caused considerable damage to civilian lives and property, the president and his advisers were enraged. Considering the stories a calculated attempt by the North Vietnamese to influence American public opinion through, as the president himself put it, "our left-wing friends," they defended themselves with vigor.[39]

Lewis himself refused to accept North Vietnamese contentions that the damage was intentional. He believed it was the result of mistakes and said so. That being the case, he still questioned whether American strategists truly understood the human cost of the bombing. Describing damage apparent at Phuc Loc in the Red River delta, where villagers described an attack by American bombers that had supposedly killed or wounded more than 120 civilians, he noted that "death is always less painful in the abstract. I was critical of the means used by the United States in this war before coming here. But tallying the numbers of bomb craters is not the same as seeing Phuc Loc."[40]

Lewis' assertions were by that time almost the standard fare of the antiwar movement and drew far less attention from the president and his advisers than claims the reporter passed on from the North Vietnamese that they were clearing American mines from their harbors. An independent source, Lewis said, had confirmed that, as a result, at least one East German ship had entered Haiphong after the United States had supposedly closed the port. What particularly galled the president was that the *New York Times* appeared to have slighted Pentagon denials that anything of the sort had occurred by including them, between brackets, as a third paragraph in Lewis' dispatch. Worse, the front page headline introducing

---

[38] Ibid. Also see Msg, John Lehman Saigon 109 to Haig, 10 Jul 72; Msg, CINCPAC to CINCPACAF et al., 15 Jul 72, DDI Policy file; JCS History, 1971–1973, p. 415.

[39] Memo, the President for Henry Kissinger, 6 Jun 72, NSC files, Subject files, box 341, HAK/President Memos, 1971, Nixon Papers. Also see Msg, Saigon 8776 to State, 13 Jun 72, sub: Current DRV/VC Propaganda, NSC files, Jon Howe Chron files, box 1091, Jun 13, 1972, Nixon Papers. American policy stipulated that every possible precaution was to be taken to minimize damage to the dike system if attacks on valid military targets occurred. See Memo, Laird for the President, 31 Jul 72, sub: Targeting in North Vietnam, NSC files, Jon Howe Chron files, box 1080, Jul–Aug 72, Nixon Papers.

[40] Anthony Lewis, "Death in Phuc Loc," *New York Times*, 22 May 72.

the item had stressed that "Communists Report Mines at Haiphong Swept, Ships Sailing."[41]

The article, along with another by Benjamin Welles to the effect that the mines sown in Haiphong and six other North Vietnamese harbors were designed to deactivate themselves before President Nixon's planned trip to Moscow on 22 May, thus prompted an immediate official reaction. On the day after it appeared, in a widely reprinted comment, the deputy director of White House communications, Kenneth W. Clawson, charged that the *Times*, by failing to give official denials the proper weight, had become, in effect, a conduit of enemy propaganda to the American people.[42]

The paper defended itself editorially by alleging that the Nixon administration wanted the American news media to "suppress all statements by the North Vietnamese government as inherently false and to accept all statements by the U.S. government as the beginning and end of truth." Even so, its handling of the story was criticized by other members of the news media. Long a critic of the war itself, *Newsweek*, for example, noted that if the Nixon administration's record of "miscalculation, lack of candor and self-serving pronouncements on Vietnam" merited little trust, "the *Times* had some questions to ponder, too. Had its treatment of conflicting claims really been evenhanded or responsible? And when a journalist, however brilliant he may be, is permitted to take sides as a columnist, what happens to his credibility as a reporter?" Lewis, for his part, backed away from his story in a subsequent article. Observing that "direct evidence is extremely difficult to obtain" in North Vietnam, he noted that most international observers on the scene were convinced that the Port of Haiphong was closed and that the North Vietnamese themselves had all but conceded the fact.[43]

If President Nixon was incensed by Lewis' article, Welles' allegation was also a source of concern to him. Referring to it in a memorandum to General Haig on 20 May, he avowed that there should be no letup in air strikes on North Vietnam during his trip to Moscow and that both the Military Assistance Command and the Defense Department should counter "instantly" stories in the press to the contrary. "There is nothing that could hurt us more in the minds of public opinion," he said, "than some suggestion that we made a deal with the Russians to cool it in Vietnam while trying to negotiate agreements with them in Moscow." On comments by Lewis that the resumption of the bombing had yet to cause

[41] Anthony Lewis "Communists Report Mines at Haiphong Swept, Ships Sailing," *New York Times*, 18 May 72; "Conflict of Interest," *Newsweek*, 29 May 72.

[42] Benjamin Welles, "Mines Said To Hold Device for Shut Off Before Nixon Trip," *New York Times*, 14 May 72; Welles, "Last Two Soviet Ships Bound for Haiphong Said To Veer Away, *New York Times*, 19 May 72, [UPI–327A], 19 May 72, copy in CMH files. Also see "Conflict of Interest."

[43] "White House Repeats Criticism of the Times, Which Responds," *New York Times*, 20 May 72; "Conflict of Interest"; Anthony Lewis, "Closing of Ports Conceded by Hanoi," *New York Times*, 23 May 72.

much disruption in the lives of the North Vietnamese people, Nixon continued that he wanted Abrams and Bunker to put out more information on morale problems in North Vietnam. Recognizing, as had Lewis, that absolute evidence was often hard to come by in Vietnam, he concluded that "If they say they don't want to get out on a limb, ask them what they think I have done."[44]

Haig took it upon himself to carry out the president's instructions. In a "deep background, off the record" briefing that included correspondents from the major television networks and a number of prominent newspapers but pointedly excluded representatives of the *New York Times*, he revealed that, according to intelligence reports in his possession, North Vietnam had begun to experience severe dislocations as a result of the bombing and mining. Estimating tentatively that the enemy had suffered between 75,000 and 100,000 casualties since the start of the Easter offensive, he said that the country's social system, in particular, was beginning to show signs of strain. The cut off of supplies from China was putting a much greater demand on the local production of food and diverting manpower to agricultural pursuits that could have been used in support of the war. Meanwhile, Radio Hanoi had begun to warn against saboteurs and hooligans; reliable reports had surfaced indicating that Hanoi authorities had executed black market profiteers; and, contrary to reports by Lewis, prostitution was on the rise in Hanoi due to the impact of inflation upon fixed income families. The problem extended even into the countryside, where young women were having difficulty finding males of marriageable age and had disrupted community social structures by consorting with older, married men.[45]

Haig had some grounds for his claims. Reports from Hanoi by a variety of foreign observers, some of them sympathetic to the North Vietnamese, had confirmed that extreme dislocations were occurring. The evacuation of families from Hanoi and Haiphong to rural areas, the dispersion of government agencies, shortages of food, price inflation, and the worries and mourning brought on by heavy casualties in the South, all had fostered discontent among the people.[46] Even so, Haig's clumsy handling of the *New York Times* ensured that his role in the interview would ultimately leak into the press and throw his points into doubt.

On 24 May, as a result, Henry Bradsher of the *Washington Star* disputed the general's claims. Citing "Hanoi watchers" at the U.S. mission in Saigon who contended that the disruptions occurring in North Vietnam hardly indicated any essential weakening of the state, the reporter assert-

---

[44] Memo, the President for Haig, 20 May 72, NSC files, A. M. Haig Chron file, box 992, Haig Chron, May 1–20, 1972 [I of II], Nixon Papers.

[45] Memo of Conversation, Haig With Selected Correspondents, 22 May 72, NSC files, A M. Haig Chron files, box 993, Haig Chron, May 21–31, 1972 [II of II], Nixon Papers. Also see "White House Aide Says Morale Is Low in Hanoi," *New York Times*, 23 May 72.

[46] Msg, Saigon 7919 to State, 27 May 72, sub: Situation in North Vietnam, NSC files, Jon Howe Chron files, box 1089, May 27, 1972, Nixon Papers.

ed that many of the effects Haig had underlined had existed long before the renewal of the bombing campaign and the mining.[47]

The State Department contested Bradsher's story on the morning after it appeared. Several days later, the Military Assistance Command in Saigon likewise held a background briefing dealing with the effectiveness of the interdiction effort. A wide variety of news stories followed quoting U.S. intelligence sources on the success of the bombing and mining and Hanoi's inability to move supplies southward. The effect of the effort was nevertheless at best mixed. Although most reporters accepted the effectiveness of the bombing, a few began to worry that noncombatants would be the ones to suffer the most. Orr Kelly of the *Washington Star*, for one, reported on 30 May that if North Vietnam was being dismantled by the cumulative effect of U.S. mining, bombing, and shelling, another month of attacks at the current rate would almost certainly assure a human disaster in that country by cutting off food and other necessities to the innocent.[48]

Whatever the hopes of the Nixon administration and the concerns of the press, if the bombing produced dislocations in North Vietnam, it appears, at least in some reports by knowledgeable observers, to have had little if any effect upon the morale of the country's people. As one discerning traveler noted upon returning from a mission to Hanoi, the civilian population of the city acknowledged the precision of American bombing by making little attempt to hide when U.S. aircraft arrived. Instead, people stood in the streets and cheered when surface-to-air missiles or antiaircraft fire succeeded in downing a bomber.[49]

If Lewis' allegations were troublesome, they were at least open to question. North Vietnam's charges about the dikes were more difficult to handle. Although the United States had never made it a policy to destroy the enemy's flood control system and had attempted as far as possible to avoid striking it, American pilots had, in fact, hit the dikes from time to time, either with bombs that overshot their true targets or out of self-defense to silence antiaircraft batteries mounted upon them. Since there was thus a grain of truth in the assertion that the United States had bombed dikes, the matter constituted a made-to-order propaganda theme for the enemy. He repeated it again and again in every international forum possible and added credence to his claims by squiring visiting reporters and antiwar celebrities such as actress Jane Fonda, former U.S. Attorney

[47] Memo, Situation Room for Kissinger, 11 Jun 72, sub: Morning Cable Summary, NSC files, Jon Howe Chron files, box 1091, Jun 11, 1972, Nixon Papers; Henry Bradsher, "U.S. Reports of Foe's Distress Called Old, Out of Context," *Washington Star*, 24 May 72. Also see "Speak Out Openly, Gen. Haig," *Philadelphia Inquirer*, 5 Jun 72.

[48] Memo, Les Janka for Ron Ziegler, 24 May 72, sub: Daily Press Items, and Msg, Janka to Ziegler, 30 May 72, sub: Wrap-up of Daily Press Items, both in HAK Administrative & Staff files, Janka, box 18, Janka Press Guidance, Jan–Jul 72 [I of II], Nixon Papers. Also see Michael Prentice, [Reuters–1345], 26 May 72, copy in CMH files; Barney Sieber, [UPI–256A], 5 Jun 72, copy in CMH files.

[49] Msg, Vientiane 6291 to State, 21 Aug 72, sub: Impressions of Hanoi, DDI Enemy Activities, 1972.

Enemy antiaircraft guns atop a dike near Hanoi fire on U.S. aircraft.

General Ramsey Clark, and Nevin Scrimshaw of the Senate Subcommittee on Refugees to sites where attacks had supposedly occurred. American intelligence analysts speculated at the time that propaganda was only part of the reason for the campaign. Severe flooding the year before had caused considerable damage to North Vietnam's dikes. Lacking time and the resources to make proper repairs, so the reasoning went, the country's officials were attempting to deflect to the United States criticism that might fall upon them if the facilities failed during the coming rainy season.[50]

American official spokesmen handled the charges when they first arose by denying that American bombers had ever followed a systematic policy of bombing dikes, but they were none too forward in affirming that mistakes might have occurred. "Anything is possible," one Air Force general told reporters when queried on the subject, "but I think it's highly improbable."[51] When the enemy's campaign continued and intensified, the State Department instructed its foreign posts to label the effort an instance of "the big lie technique," and President Nixon himself addressed the issue at a 29 June news conference. "The United States has used great restraint in its bombing policy," he said, "and I think properly so. . . . We have had orders out not to hit dikes because the results in terms of civil casualties would be extraordinary. . . . I do not intend to allow any orders to go out which would involve civilian casualties if it can be avoided.

[50] Msg, Saigon 8776 to State, 13 Jun 72, sub: Current DRV/VC Propaganda, NSC files, Jon Howe Chron files, box 1091, Jun 13, 1972, Nixon Papers. Also see Memo, Laird for the President, 31 Jul 72, sub: Targeting in North Vietnam.

[51] Seymour M. Hersh, "Dikes in Hanoi Area Represent 2000-Year Effort To Tame Rivers," *New York Times*, 14 Jul 72.

Military targets only will be allowed."[52] Those efforts notwithstanding, reports from Hanoi, especially by the resident correspondent for Agence France Presse, Jean Thoraval, continued to buttress North Vietnamese claims that U.S. bombers had hit dikes. As a result, Secretary of Defense Laird decided to go on record with a clear statement of what was, in fact, happening. Alluding to the possibility that North Vietnamese were attempting to cover up their own failure to repair the dikes, he admitted at a 6 July news conference that American aircraft at times struck North Vietnam's flood control system, for very good reasons. "Some of the dikes and dams may be on roadways that are being used or they may be in a position where antiaircraft weaponry is placed,

Jane Fonda poses while looking through the sights of an antiaircraft gun in North Vietnam.

and, of course, our pilots are given the opportunity and they should have this capability to attack North Vietnamese gun emplacements."[53]

The question of the dikes nevertheless remained an issue. Jane Fonda reemphasized it during her visit to the North. Films by a Swedish television crew purporting to show damage to the dikes played on the American television networks. Agence France Presse reported that a group of foreign journalists visiting North Vietnam had narrowly escaped death when American bombers had attacked a dike they were visiting. The Secretary General of the United Nations, Kurt Waldheim, accused the president of deliberately bombing dams and levees. And Ramsey Clark, after visiting North Vietnam, claimed to have seen damaged dikes with his own eyes. Senator Edward Kennedy professed himself shocked by Clark's revelation and promised an investigation in the Senate.[54]

In hopes of settling the controversy over the dikes once and for all, the Office of the Assistant Secretary of Defense for Public Affairs

[52] Msg, State Circular 125205 to All Diplomatic Posts, 11 Jul 72, sub: Charges of Bombing North Vietnamese Dikes, DDI Dikes, NVN.

[53] Hersh, "Dikes in Hanoi Area Represent 2000-Year Effort To Tame Rivers."

[54] Msg, Belgrade 126 to State, 13 Jul 72, sub: Media on Bombing NVN Dikes, and Talking Paper, n.d., sub: Stories Concerning Strikes Against Dikes in Nam Sach District, Hai Duong Province, North Vietnam, both in DDI Dikes, NVN. Unattributed AP clipping, 5 Aug 72, in 330–77–0094, box 81, Viet 385.1 (Aug) 72, Laird Papers, WNRC. Also see Ambrose, *Nixon, The Triumph of a Politician,* p. 589.

released an intelligence study containing photographs that detailed the damage stray bombs had caused to dikes but demonstrated that the harm had been minor and easily repaired. At that time, public affairs officers in Saigon and elsewhere also made the point that a policy of bombing dikes would have little effect on North Vietnam's transportation system because there were too many alternative dry routes. The worst effects would occur only during the rainy season and would require a large-scale coordinated bombing effort because key components of the system (locks and water runoff chutes) were widely dispersed. In all, the officials said, only twelve dikes had been damaged rather than the forty North Vietnam claimed, and none were in the Hanoi area, the most lucrative target if dikes were to be bombed. President Nixon himself probably made the best rebuttal at a 27 July news conference. Underscoring the thousands of South Vietnamese made homeless by North Vietnam's offensive, he pointed out that, although accidents had inevitably occurred, if the United States had wanted to destroy the dikes it could have done so in less than a day.[55]

Those comments and others like them laid much of the controversy over the dikes to rest, but doubts nevertheless remained, in part because of the Lavelle affair. Although most commentators within the news media were willing to accept that the United States had not deliberately targeted dikes, a suspicion remained among a few that pilots and their officers might have taken it upon themselves to attack the facilities. As a result, the *Washington Star* advised President Nixon on 3 August to make it "perfectly clear" to U.S. military commanders that dikes were never to be targeted or attacked except in cases of the utmost provocation.[56]

Misdirected bombs and the accidental damage they caused remained a source of embarrassment for the Nixon administration and public affairs officers in South Vietnam until the very end of the war. On 11 October, for example, radio reports from North Vietnam indicated that U.S. aircraft had bombed the French legation in downtown Hanoi, killing the charge d'affaires. Following a superficial preliminary investigation by the Seventh Fleet, whose aircraft had struck Hanoi at about the time the damage occurred, the MACV Office of Information accepted the Navy's assurances that all bombs had been on target. But, since France was a major American ally, official U.S. spokesmen also very cautiously conceded that if an accident had indeed occurred they regretted any personal injury or damage. It was well that they did. For although MACV's comments at the time cast doubt upon the enemy's claim by suggesting that falling North Vietnamese surface-to-air missiles might have hit the lega-

---

[55] Talking Paper, North Vietnam: The Dike Bombing Issue, covered by Memo, OASD PA for Henkin et al., 28 Jul 72, 330–77–0094, box 81, Viet 385.1 (Jul) 1972, Laird Papers, WNRC; "The President's News Conference of July 27, 1972," *Public Papers of the Presidents· Richard M Nixon, 1972* (Washington, D.C.: Government Printing Office, 1974), p. 752.

[56] The *Washington Star* is quoted in Msg, State 141620 to Saigon, 4 Aug 72, sub: August 4 Indochina Press Summary, DDI 1972 Press Coverage file.

tion, a more thorough investigation later confirmed that a bomb from an American aircraft had done the damage. On 20 October, for the sake of official credibility, the United States thus had no choice but to clarify the record by taking full responsibility for the incident.[57]

The Situation in South Vietnam

Although wrangling over the dikes, the extent of civilian casualties in North and South Vietnam, the effectiveness of the bombing and mining, and the Lavelle affair continued to cause problems for public affairs officers, circumstances in South Vietnam slowly began to improve. As the result of South Vietnamese efforts to reorganize and Abrams' massive air attacks, the enemy's offensive slowed by the beginning of June. Although the Communists continued their hold on Binh Dinh Province, General Truong managed to consolidate his forces at Hue, and another well-qualified professional, Col. Ly Tong Ba, took charge at Kontum. An Loc also held firm, although the town remained cutoff by road until the beginning of July. As early as 19 May Ambassador Bunker thus felt justified in reporting that the enemy was clearly experiencing difficulties and had failed to achieve his main objectives.[58]

On 28 June Truong launched a counteroffensive northward to retake Quang Tri. Within the month his forces had advanced to the northeast wall of the city's citadel, but it took until 14 September for them to take that strongpoint itself and to declare the city in friendly hands. The delay was a source of some criticism in the press, but Truong considered Quang Tri a ruin with little remaining military value and was disinclined to waste manpower on its recapture. He agreed reluctantly to do so only when Thieu himself insisted that the entrance of South Vietnamese forces into the city was an important symbol to the South Vietnamese people.[59]

If the advance of Truong's forces seemed labored to some, the performance of the South Vietnamese in other areas was erratic, especially at An Loc, where during June the 21st Infantry Division made hardly any progress in breaking the enemy's hold on the only road leading to the town. Considering the impasse an extreme embarrassment, President Nixon pressured Abrams to do something to prevail on Thieu to push his

[57] Msg, CTG Seven Seven Pt Zero/CTG Seven Seven Pt Three to NMCC, 11 Oct 72, sub: Alleged Bombing of French Mission, Hanoi, DDI Incident file; MACV Statement to the Press, 11 Oct 72, 330–77–094, box 80, Viet 381.5, Oct 72, Laird Papers, WNRC; Ltr, Col Robert Burke to the author, 27 Jun 90, CMH files; Memo, Moorer CM–2258–72 for Secretary of Defense, 19 Oct 72, 330–77–0095, box 9, Viet 385.1 (Aug–Nov) 1972, Laird Papers, WNRC; Memo for Correspondents, OASD PA, 20 Oct 72, Staff Member Office files, Ziegler, box 43, Foreign Policy Guidance, Aug–Oct 72 [I of III], Nixon Papers.
[58] Msg, Bunker Saigon 0094 to Kissinger, 19 May 72, sub: Vietnam: Assessment of Present Situation, NSC files, Jon Howe Chron files, box 1088, May 19, 1972, Nixon Papers.
[59] Interv, Dale Andrade with Lt Gen Ngo Quang Truong, 1990, CMH files.

South Vietnamese forces recapture Quang Tri.

troops harder, if only to deny critics in the press access to the issue.[60] The general was able to do little. Although enemy fire slackened enough around the town toward mid-June to allow helicopters to reinforce and resupply the troops inside, correspondents were still reporting at the end of the month that the American aircrews involved in the process were "furious" and "bitter" because of the failure of the South Vietnamese armed forces to play any significant role in the operation. Comments by American advisers also continued to appear in the press, paying grudging tribute to the capabilities of the North Vietnamese around An Loc while criticizing the lack of discipline and leadership of the South Vietnamese force that remained stranded on the road into the town. "They (the Communists) monitor ARVN all the time," one told Laurence Stern of the *Washington Post*, "and the ARVN invariably give away everything before it happens."[61]

Despite disappointments of that sort, by July it seemed clear to both U.S. intelligence analysts and the news media that North Vietnam's offensive had failed. Although the quality of the leadership within the South Vietnamese armed forces remained uneven and South Vietnamese coun-

[60] Msg, Kissinger WHS 2068 to Bunker, 10 May 72, NSC files, Haig Chron file, box 993, Haig Chron, May 1–20, 1972, Nixon Papers; Msg, Haig to Abrams, n.d., NSC files, Haig Chron file, box 993, Haig Chron, Jun 13–30, 1972, Nixon Papers; Memo, Bruce Kehrli for Haig, 23 Jun 72, sub: ARVN Relief Unit, and Memo, Les Janka for Haig, 24 Jun 72, sub: Kehrligram on ARVN Ineffectiveness, both in NSC files, Kissinger Office files, Administrative and Staff files, Janka Chron, box 18, Jan–Jul, 1972, Nixon Papers.

[61] Malcolm W Browne, "Copters Ferry More Saigon Troops Into Anloc as Enemy Fire Ebbs," *New York Times*, 15 Jun 72. Also see White House Weekend News Review, 26 Jun 72, NSC files, box 994, Nixon Papers. The weakness of enemy fire may have been the result of B–52 strikes based upon intelligence from agents situated within the enemy's higher headquarters at Kontum. See Orrin DeForest and David Chanoff, *Slow Burn: The Rise and Bitter Fall of American Intelligence in Vietnam* (New York: Simon and Schuster, 1990). Laurence Stern, "Lifting the Siege of Anloc: 'A Grunt Will Think Twice,'" *Washington Post*, 15 Jun 72.

This picture of a girl hit by napalm during the Easter offensive became a symbol of the cruelty of war.

teroffensives in Military Regions 2 and 3 had been disappointing, *Newsweek* observed on 24 July that the enemy had exposed his men and his tanks too readily to American air power and had taken a heavy beating as a result. According to reports that reached the White House from the field, civilian casualties had been a problem in Quang Tri because of the heavy use of B–52 bombers. There was evidence that enemy forces were being resupplied across the beaches of the region despite the efforts of the U.S. Navy. Yet, as General Haig observed after a brief visit to South Vietnam at the time, "In terms relative to ARVN, the NVA are now extremely weak. Although they continue to infiltrate replacements, the quality of their infantry has declined sharply and ARVN is no longer intimidated by their armor. Many recently captured NVA are young and inexperienced with reports that some have only had rudimentary training. . . . Saigon has been given a new lease on life."[62]

As early as 1 July, indeed, the situation seemed so promising that a high-level Air Force briefer at the Military Assistance Command, overcome by enthusiasm, went out of his way to predict the recapture of Quang Tri City "pretty darn fast." He added that enemy strength in Military Region 1 had been "cut in half," that the United States had "photographic evidence of everything," and that the plan to reopen Quang Tri had been largely of American origin. The session proved such an egre-

---

[62] "A Balance Sheet," *Newsweek*, 24 Jul 72, p. 42; Msg, Lehman Saigon 109 to Haig, 10 Jul 72, NSC files, Backchannels, box 414, Backchannel Msgs, Bunker, 1972 [part II], Nixon Papers. Quote from Trip Rpt, Jul 1–3, 1972, Vietnam and Cambodia, NSC files, A. M. Haig Special file, box 1015, Gen. Haig's Trip to Vietnam (Jul 1–3, 1972), Nixon Papers, copy in CMH files.

587

gious violation of standing procedures that it prompted an immediate cable from Friedheim to the new chief of MACV information, Col. Robert L. Burke, who had succeeded Stevens on 1 July. Reminding Burke that for the previous three years the command had been under instructions to refrain from making predictions and setting timetables on possible future actions and accomplishments, the assistant secretary of defense for public affairs cautioned that spokesmen for the Military Assistance Command had no choice but to hew to the policy. Friedheim continued that "photographic evidence should not be touted unless it has been approved for release . . . under our normal procedures to safeguard intelligence matters," and "care must be taken not to issue contradictory assessments of intelligence particularly as it relates to enemy strengths. We had too much of that in the early years of this war."[63]

If success in the South, however marginal, proved exhilarating to some, hardly anyone, either in official circles or the news media, doubted the enemy's ability to continue the war into the indefinite future. As one Radio Hanoi broadcast put it in June, virtually paraphrasing American intelligence reports, "Our people can walk, can use torchlights, can eat diluted congee [water rice gruel]. . . . Even if the enemy succeeds in the bomb destruction of our cities and our large industrial installations, they can never paralyze our economy to the point of preventing our survival and our ability to supply the South."[64]

Yet, if the bombing and mining by themselves could never totally abolish Hanoi's war-making potential, they had increased the price of continuing the war enormously for the enemy by complicating his efforts in South Vietnam. Since the Easter offensive was a largely conventional campaign, North Vietnam's supply requirements in the South were much higher than earlier in the war. That raised the volume of men and materiel moving down the Ho Chi Minh Trail and made enemy attempts at resupply much more vulnerable to air attack than in the past. In the same way, although North Vietnam could replace its petroleum supplies through hidden pipelines coming from China and could rely indefinitely on imports arriving by road and provisions and equipment it had stored up in earlier years, the presence of mines in Haiphong meant the end of supply, over the long run, for most of the heavy equipment that the nation received from the Soviet Union.[65]

Understanding the enemy's predicament and sensing the grief the North Vietnamese must have felt when the Soviet Union went through

---

[63] Msg, Friedheim to Col Robert L. Burke, 1 Jul 72, sub: Press Briefing Guidance, DDI Spring Offensive file.

[64] [AP], "North Admits War Toll," *Baltimore Sun*, 6 Jun 72. Also see Memo, Moorer CM–1951–72 for Secretary of Defense, 15 Jun 72, sub: The Air Campaign in North Vietnam, 330–77–0094, box 81, Viet 385 1 (Jun) 1972, Laird Papers, WNRC; Tad Szulc, "Hanoi Held Able To Fight 2 Years at Present Rate," *New York Times*, 13 Sep 72

[65] Memo, Phil Odeen for Kissinger, 12 Aug 72, sub: CIA Assessment of the Bombing and Mining, NSC files, Vietnam Subject files, box 96, Air Activity in Southeast Asia, Jan–Aug 1972, vol. III, Nixon Papers.

with the summit despite the mines and bombing, President Nixon refused to allow any letup in the attack on North Vietnam. When he became aware at the end of July of a gradual reduction in air sorties against the northernmost portions of North Vietnam brought on by bad weather, he urged the Air Force to redouble its efforts. If all constraints with regard to civilian casualties and buffer zone restrictions for the area between North Vietnam and China were of necessity to remain fully in force, Henry Kissinger informed Ambassador Bunker on 30 July, the president refused to tolerate any additional restraints designed to meet fiscal or ordnance expenditure ceilings. "In the period ahead," Kissinger said, "our best hope for success in the negotiations is the maintenance of a steady and effective level of military pressure against the North." On 29 August President Nixon said the same thing in public by warning North Vietnam at a news conference that the bombing would continue without stint until substantial progress in the negotiations had occurred.[66]

[66] Quote from Msg, Kissinger WHS 2093 to Bunker, 30 Jul 72, NSC files, Backchannels, box 414, Backchannel Message file, 1972, to Amb. Bunker, Saigon, Nixon Papers. "The President's News Conference of August 29, 1972," *Public Papers of the Presidents Richard M. Nixon, 1972,* pp. 827–31.

23

The Realities of Power

By the end of August 1972 even Hanoi's leaders seemed prepared to admit that compromise was in order. Not only had they sustained a heavy bloodletting in South Vietnam, their allies, the Soviet Union and the People's Republic of China, appeared little disposed to take their interests to heart. Meanwhile, whatever their losses, their forces in the South had attained as good a tactical position as they were likely to achieve in the foreseeable future. Besides threatening important lines of communication in South Vietnam, they had greatly increased the Communist presence in areas near Saigon, held strong positions in Military Regions 1 and 2, and had succeeded in reversing South Vietnamese gains in some parts of the Mekong Delta. As a result, they were well positioned to claim large amounts of additional territory, provided the negotiators in Paris could succeed in winning a peace agreement that permitted the Americans to disengage gracefully while leaving Communist forces in place in the South.[1] On the political front, public opinion polls in the United States indicated that Nixon would win the coming presidential election by impressive margins. In that sense, it seemed better for North Vietnam to bargain with Nixon immediately, while he was still campaigning and uncertain, than to delay until a time when he might be stronger politically and much less inclined to deal.

A Peace Offensive

On 8 May 1972, the United States had laid out three conditions for peace: a cease-fire, the return of American prisoners of war with an

[1] Memo, Phil Odeen for Dr. Kissinger, 6 Oct 72, sub: Vietnam Trip Report, NSC files, A. M. Haig Special file, box 1017, Gen Haig's SEA Visit (29 Sep–3 Oct 72), Nixon Papers. This is the conclusion of intelligence estimates in Saigon toward the end of the year. Msg, Haig Saigon 305 to Kissinger, 20 Dec 72, NSC files, For the President's files, Lord, Vietnam Negotiations, box 870, Camp David Cables, Dec 72, Nixon Papers.

accounting of those still missing in action, and assurances that the people of South Vietnam would have the right to determine their own future without the interposition by force of either a Communist government or a coalition involving Communists. North Vietnam's representatives in Paris made their first move toward agreement on those points on 1 August, by dropping their demand for the dismemberment of the government of South Vietnam. From that moment, the negotiations progressed rapidly. "Both sides recognized that the pursuit of a settlement . . . involved taking chances," Kissinger's aide, John D. Negroponte, wrote during December,

and it seemed . . . that U.S. and DRV interests had converged sufficiently to form the basis for a settlement. This is to say that we were prepared to disengage from South Vietnam in exchange for which Hanoi was willing to forego accomplishment of all its objectives in the South immediately. Among the essential elements of this negotiating framework were Hanoi's apparent willingness to leave the political process in the South to a reasonable period of evolution, to restrict its right to intervene militarily in the South by accepting a prohibition on further infiltration, and their agreement to withdraw forces from Laos and Cambodia.[2]

By 11 October the two sides had reached substantial agreement. As a humane gesture, the United States proposed to contribute to the economic reconstruction of North Vietnam and to withdraw all of its forces from the South. It specified, however, that it would continue, subject to certain limitations, to supply the South Vietnamese armed forces with arms and equipment. The Thieu regime would meanwhile remain in place in Saigon, but so would North Vietnamese forces in the countryside. A National Council of National Reconciliation and Concord with Viet Cong representation would come into being, but it would have jurisdiction over little more than elections, to which the South Vietnamese government would have to agree.[3]

Neither the Nixon administration nor the Hanoi regime had any illusions about the arrangement. By leaving North Vietnamese forces in position in South Vietnam, it provided Hanoi with, as Negroponte observed in his message to Kissinger, "a better than equal chance of ultimately achieving its objectives." Kissinger nevertheless believed that it was the best agreement possible under the circumstances and won the president's support for quick ratification. After some last-minute jockeying in Paris, the national security adviser thus traveled to Saigon on 18 October to inform Thieu of the treaty's provisions and to win his agreement. If all went well, the United States would stop bombing North Vietnam on 21

[2] Memo of Conversation, 30 Nov 72, sub: President's Meeting With the Joint Chiefs of Staff, NSC files, Jon Howe Chron files, box 1081, Nov–Dec 72, Nixon Papers. Quote from Msg, John D. Negroponte to Kissinger, 14 Dec 72, sub: Hanoi's Behavior in the Negotiations, NSC files, Vietnam Negotiations, box 870, Camp David files, Dec 72, Nixon Papers.

[3] For a more thorough discussion of the October agreement and its background, see Kissinger, *The White House Years*, pp. 1341–59.

Thieu argues against the peace agreement.

October; Kissinger would initial the accord the next day in Hanoi; and formal signing of the treaty would occur on the thirty-first, at a meeting in Paris between Secretary of State Rogers and the foreign ministers of North and South Vietnam.[4]

Kissinger's expectations to the contrary, nothing went as planned. Thieu understood clearly that the treaty put South Vietnam at extreme risk. Considering the proposed National Council little more than a thinly veiled coalition government, he refused emphatically to approve the projected agreement.

While Kissinger was in Saigon, the United States began Operation ENHANCE PLUS, a massive airlift of supplies and materiel to South Vietnam designed to provide Thieu's forces with as much equipment as possible before treaty provisions limiting resupply efforts went into effect. When that failed to reassure Thieu and he insisted on both a total withdrawal of North Vietnamese forces from his country and elimination of the National Council from the settlement, Kissinger had no choice but to cancel his trip to Hanoi and to return home.[5]

By that time, speculation was rising in the press that a treaty was at hand, and both *Time* and *Newsweek* were carrying stories that purported

---

[4] Quote from Msg, Negroponte to Kissinger, 14 Dec 72, sub: Hanoi's Behavior in the Negotiations. Kissinger describes the proposed treaty in *The White House Years*, pp. 1341–59.

[5] Ambrose, *Nixon, The Triumph of a Politician*, pp. 627–35.

to contain drafts of the peace formula. Those accounts were wide of the mark, but President Nixon and his advisers understood clearly that time was running out. North Vietnamese Prime Minister Pham Van Dong had already given an interview to *Newsweek* editor Arnaud de Borchgrave. If the United States hesitated for too long, there seemed every likelihood that the North Vietnamese would release the provisions of the treaty to the press. Once that happened and the American people realized that the enemy had essentially fulfilled the 8 May conditions, a backlash might develop in Congress and the public that would tie the president's hands but fall most heavily upon the South Vietnamese. Thieu had to be made to understand, Kissinger thus told Bunker on 24 October, "that his alternatives really revolve around accepting what is good in the offer or in persisting in an intransigent position which will surely result in a cut-off of U.S. funds through congressional action if not from us. . . . [He] must remember that everything he gains in South Vietnam as a result of these tactics he loses here in the United States where he needs continued military and economic support."[6]

Thieu remained adamant. Turning to the press, he avowed in the presence of reporters that if the North Vietnamese stayed in South Vietnam after an accord "the war will have proved to be only a U.S. war of aggression and the GI and ARVN sacrifices will have proven unnecessary and a betrayal."[7]

Concerned that continued disagreement could only lead to a bruising showdown with Thieu at a moment when the U.S. presidential election was imminent, and unable to implement the treaty to any practical extent without Thieu's cooperation and that of the South Vietnamese bureaucracy, President Nixon had no choice but to inform the North Vietnamese on 25 October that a "brief delay" had become necessary. Hanoi had to realize, he said, that it was impossible for the United States to sign a document implying the consent of one of the parties when that party had not concurred.[8] The North Vietnamese government responded the next evening by broadcasting the terms of the agreement to the world.

With speculation rising everywhere, Nixon and Kissinger moved immediately to guarantee that the American version of what had happened received greater play in the press than the enemy's maneuver. On the morning after the announcement, Kissinger went on television with a

---

[6] Arnaud de Borchgrave, "Exclusive From Hanoi," *Newsweek*, 30 Oct 72; Msg, Haig WH 29646 to Kissinger, 23 Oct 72, NSC files, Kissinger Office files, Country files, box 104, HAK's Saigon Trip, Oct 16–Oct 23, 1972, Nixon Papers; Kissinger, *The White House Years*, p. 1348. Quote from Msg, Kissinger WHS 2293 to Bunker, 24 Oct 72, NSC files, Vietnam Negotiations, box 870, Camp David files, Oct 72, Nixon Papers.

[7] Bernard Kalb, CBS Radio, 24 Oct 72, as quoted in News Summary, 25 Oct 72, Nixon Papers.

[8] Msg, Haig WH 0081 to Col Guay, Paris, 25 Oct 72, NSC files, For the President's file, Lord, Vietnam Negotiations, box 870, Camp David Cables, Oct 72, Nixon Papers. Also see Walter Scott Dillard, *Sixty Days to Peace* (Washington, D.C.: National Defense University, 1982), p. 6.

live briefing—the first of his career—to declare that peace is at hand but that minor details remained to be worked out. Editors and producers around the world seized upon the catchphrase "peace is at hand," and paid scant attention to Kissinger's caveat. As a result, a wave of euphoria swept the United States, with both Republicans and Democrats praising the development.[9]

The next day, nevertheless, Thieu declared publicly from Saigon that he would not be bound by a peace agreement that he had never signed and repeated his objections to the National Council and the presence of North Vietnamese troops on his country's soil. Hanoi meanwhile announced that it had no intention of meeting with Kissinger to settle the minor details he had mentioned and that peace could be found only "at the end of a pen." Shortly thereafter, Democratic presidential candidate George McGovern and other critics of the war began to compare the treaty's provisions with demands the enemy had made at the start of the negotiations. What, they asked, had the president achieved in return for the four years of blood and sacrifice that had intervened?[10]

Nixon responded on 2 November, in his first major, televised speech of the political campaign. Confirming that a breakthrough had occurred in the negotiations, he avowed that minor technicalities had delayed a final settlement but that they were too important to be handled carelessly, as had occurred in 1968, when Lyndon Johnson had rushed the bombing-halt agreement to completion prior to that year's election without clarifying all the details. There would be no misunderstandings this time, he declared. "We aren't going to allow an election deadline or any other kind of deadline to force us into an agreement which would be only a temporary truce and not a lasting peace. We are going to sign the agreement when the agreement is right, not one day before; and when the agreement is right, we are going to sign, without one day's delay."[11]

The speech, along with the confirmation ENHANCE PLUS provided that the United States was continuing fully to support South Vietnam, appears to have had the sort of effect in the United States that Nixon sought. Harris polls during August had revealed that a majority of Americans were unhappy with the president's failure to fulfill his 1968 promise to end the war.[12] The speech made it appear that he had taken major steps in that direction and that he was doing so in a way that would preserve American honor. Although the *New York Times* endorsed McGovern and the *Washington Post* hammered away at the Watergate affair, Nixon won the next week's election by the sort of very wide margin that everyone

[9] Richard M. Nixon, *RN, The Memoirs of Richard Nixon* (New York: Grosset & Dunlap, Inc., 1978), p. 705. The reaction to the announcement is described in Ambrose, *Nixon, The Triumph of a Politician*, pp. 644–45.

[10] Ambrose, *Nixon, The Triumph of a Politician*, pp. 644–45.

[11] Excerpt from President Nixon's speech, "A Look to the Future," 2 November 1972, Department of State *Bulletin*, 20 Nov 72, p. 605.

[12] The poll is cited in Msg, State 156860 to Saigon, 28 Aug 72, sub: August 28 Indochina Press Summary, DDI Press Coverage 1972 file.

had expected. Despite his continual complaints about the news media and their tendentious coverage of both the war and his administration, 1,807 (89 percent) of the 2,144 daily newspapers in existence in the United States at that time had endorsed his candidacy.[13] Of more importance for the future of the war, however, was the performance of the president's party in the election. The Republicans gained twelve seats in the House of Representatives but remained more than fifty short of the majority they needed. They meanwhile lost two seats in the Senate, leaving the Democrats in control of that body by a margin of 58 to 42.

The Negotiations Break Down

Although Nixon had won a second term in office, his problems with the negotiations increased almost immediately. If the North Vietnamese had seemed open to compromise before the election, they drew back afterwards, either because their tactical position in South Vietnam had suddenly deteriorated or, more likely, because they believed they might be able to achieve additional advantages. When the negotiations reconvened on 20 November, the United States sought to insert language into the treaty to clarify that the National Council lacked governmental functions and to establish the principle, however indirectly, that North Vietnam had no unequivocal right to intervene militarily in the South. It succeeded mainly in removing the term *administrative structure* from the description of the National Council, an important stumbling block to Thieu. For the rest, Hanoi attempted to delay the proceedings in every way possible by seeking to renegotiate portions of the treaty that had seemed all but settled before.[14]

Thieu, for his part, was hardly more forthcoming. Aware that enemy commanders in the South had told their troops the cease-fire would be "very profitable to us because it allows us to maintain a tooth comb or leopard skin posture in South Vietnam," he continued to object strenuously to the agreement. He was willing to negotiate directly with the National Liberation Front (the Viet Cong), he avowed, if that organization were released from Hanoi's domination. Since the treaty compelled his American ally to withdraw from the war, it seemed only just and correct for the North Vietnamese, who had invaded his country, to do the same.[15]

---

[13] Memo, Herbert G. Klein for the President, 8 Nov 72, sub: Editorial Endorsements, White House Special files, Klein, Memoranda 71–72, Nixon Papers.

[14] Msg, Negroponte to Kissinger, 14 Dec 72, sub: Hanoi's Behavior in the Negotiations.

[15] Quote from Msg, Bunker Saigon 239 to Kissinger, 28 Oct 72, NSC files, Backchannels, box 413, Backchannel Messages, Sep 72, From Bunker. Msg, Bunker Saigon 267 to Kissinger, 13 Nov 72, NSC files, Backchannels, box 413, Backchannel Messages, Nov 72, From Bunker. Both in Nixon Papers.

General Haig traveled to South Vietnam on 9 November with emphatic instructions from the president to tell Thieu that "We will not stand still" if South Vietnam continued to obstruct the treaty. "Given the complexion of the new Congress, we simply will not be able to hold congressional support. This Congress is more liberal than the last. The only useful thing to discuss now is joint planning."[16]

Convinced that his options were sorely limited and that the 8 October principles were the best obtainable, Nixon wrote Thieu directly on 15 November. Observing that it was "unrealistic to assume that we will be able to secure the absolute assurances which you would hope to have on the troop issue," he stressed that the United States would meet continued North Vietnamese aggression with "swift and severe retaliatory action." He continued, however, that his authority to strike in that manner depended upon the support of Congress and the American people. Indeed, if Thieu appeared to be an "obstacle to a peace which American public opinion universally desires, I would, with great reluctance, be forced to consider other [unilateral] measures."[17] A week later, with Thieu still holding fast, Nixon instructed Ambassador Bunker to tell him in the strongest terms that "even with [the] massive mandate I personally received in the election," Congress would no longer support continuation of the war in the light of Hanoi's peace offers. The leading supporters of the war in the Senate "were not only unanimous but vehement in stating their conclusion that, if Saigon is the only roadblock for reaching agreement on this basis, they will personally lead the fight when the new Congress reconvenes on January 3 to cut off all military and economic assistance to Saigon." Continuation of the war was thus impossible. "The door has been slammed shut hard and fast by the long time supporters of my policies in Vietnam in the House and Senate who control the purse strings." Further delays were dangerous. "The fat is on the fire" and "it is time to fish or cut bait."[18]

On the side, Ambassador Bunker reinforced the president's arguments by telling Thieu that, compared with the enemy, he had the preponderance of numbers and resources on his side and should have little difficulty handling a political contest with the Communists. "It seems to me [that] we have reached that point where we have given the Vietnamese the resources to do the job," the ambassador later told Henry Kissinger. "The draft agreement you have worked out gives them the opportunity, and . . . we have discharged fully our responsibilities. It is up to them now to make it possible for us to support them."[19]

---

[16] Msg, Kissinger WHS 2331 to Haig, 10 Nov 72, NSC files, A. M. Haig Special files, box 1019, Gen. Haig's Saigon Trip, 9–13 Nov 72, ToHaig/HaigTo & Misc [I of III], Nixon Papers.

[17] Msg, Kennedy WHP 141 to Haig for Kissinger, 24 Nov 72, NSC files, Jon Howe Chron files, box 1107, 11/24/72, Nixon Papers. Quote from Ltr, Nixon to Thieu, 15 Nov 72, Bunker Papers, FAIM/IR.

[18] Msg, Kissinger WHS 2257 to Bunker, 26 Nov 72, Bunker Papers, FAIM/IR.

[19] Msg, Bunker Saigon 282 to Kissinger, 27 Nov 72, NSC files, Backchannels, box 413, Backchannel Messages, Nov 72, From Bunker, Nixon Papers.

If President Nixon was meeting resistance from Thieu, he also faced reservations on the part of the American military. Shortly after stepping down as chief of staff of the Army in August 1972, General Westmoreland had urged him to continue bombing the North and blockading Haiphong until the enemy had no choice but to make the sort of concessions that would give South Vietnam a chance at survival.[20] General Abrams himself had long agonized over the issue.

To put those doubts to rest, the president and Kissinger met with the Joint Chiefs on 30 November to explain the treaty and to request their public support. Whatever the objections of those who favored continuation of the war, Nixon asserted at the meeting, the United States had stayed one step ahead of the sheriff, just missing fund cutoffs in Congress. The North Vietnamese had conceded all of the conditions for peace announced on 8 May, even though the Saigon regime argued that this was not enough. In fact, if the American people knew all the details of what North Vietnam had offered, they would never support further prolongation of the war. As it was, Congress controlled the purse strings. It would cut off all aid for South Vietnam within two weeks if the agreement failed.[21]

Nixon continued that the American military had to express pride in the settlement because anything else would feed contentions on the left that the war itself had been useless. As for Thieu's objections, all concerned had to understand that words on paper meant little and that a contract was only as good as the will of the parties. What mattered in the case of the treaty was that the United States would support Saigon by enforcing the paper commitments. The true settlement was thus not just the pact itself, but a series of "interlocking understandings" with other powers that reflected strategic realities. Thieu was hung up on words. The realities of power were what counted.

Reassured by the president that they should begin contingency planning for retaliatory strikes against North Vietnam in case the agreement either failed or was violated, the Joint Chiefs went along. Neither Thieu nor the North Vietnamese were as compliant. On 12 December Thieu went before South Vietnam's National Assembly to register his objections to the treaty in a manner that would undoubtedly be seen around the world as a firm rejection of the draft settlement. Hanoi's negotiators in Paris, meanwhile, continued to back and fill, so much so that, as early as 5 December, a break-off in the negotiations had become a strong possibility.[22]

[20] William C. Westmoreland, *A Soldier Reports* (Garden City, N.Y.: Doubleday, 1976), p. 393.

[21] The account of the meeting is a close paraphrase. See Memo, Haig for the President's files, 30 Nov 72, sub: The President's Meeting With the Joint Chiefs of Staff, 30 Nov 72, NSC files, Jon Howe Chron files box 1081, Nov–Dec 72, Nixon Papers.

[22] Ibid.; Memo, Haig for the President, 12 Dec 72, sub: Vietnam Negotiations, NSC files, Kissinger Office files, HAK Trip files, box 27, HAKTO & Memos to Pres, etc. [I of II], Nixon Papers; Msg, Kissinger HAKTO 13 to the President, 5 Dec 72, NSC files, Jon Howe Chron files, box 1109, 12/5/72, Nixon Papers.

Henry Kissinger had no doubt about what the president should do. Assuming that the negotiations in fact failed, he told Nixon,

We will have to take the initiative both on the military front, by drastically step-ping up the bombing, and on the public relations front, by seizing the initiative with respect to explaining the negotiations. . . . Precisely because we are at a critical juncture we will need a personal address by you to the American people. We obvi-ously face a major domestic problem and we should start out strongly in order to get on top of it—especially as we can expect Hanoi to launch a broadside. . . . Your appeal should not be melodramatic and should make clear that we are nearing the end of our involvement. . . . It would be clear that we made a maximum effort to arrange a comprehensive settlement among all the parties but that this was impos-sible. Having failed in this effort, and having bought enough time and given enough strength to our allies, the only remaining task is to pursue a firm policy until we get our men back and can disengage with honor. I believe you could con-vey this message in clear and simple terms in a 10 to 15 minute speech.[23]

Nixon was hardly as certain. It would be unwise for the United States to deliver any sort of ultimatum, he told Kissinger, or to demand conces-sions, such as the withdrawal of all North Vietnamese forces from the South, that it knew in advance the enemy would never accept. If the talks broke off, the North Vietnamese "must manifestly be the ones to do it." As for a presidential speech,

I realize that you think that if I go on television that I can rally the American peo-ple to support an indefinite continuation of the war simply for the purpose of getting our prisoners back. I agree that this is a possibility at this time. But that can wear very thin within a matter of weeks—particularly as the propaganda organs—not only from North Vietnam, but in this country—begin to hammer away at the fact that we had a much better deal in hand, and then because of Sai-gon's intransigence we were unable to complete it.

The choices he had to make, Nixon continued, were becoming increas-ingly bleak. He had to weigh the criticism he would receive for a massive-ly increased bombing campaign of up to eight months in duration—along with the attendant possibility that South Vietnam would collapse during that time because Congress had cut off all funds for the war—against

a course of action in which at its worst we would simply decide what was neces-sary to offer the North Vietnamese to get our prisoners back now and take the risk of the collapse of Saigon occurring now, rather than waiting until later. This is something we will of course do everything to prevent. Whether continuing the bombing for the sole purpose of getting our prisoners back is going to be worth the cost in terms of what it will do to our relations with the Congress, to our sup-port in the country, domestically, and to our relations with the Chinese and the Russians are also factors that we have to consider.[24]

[23] Msg, Kissinger HAKTO 13 to the President, 5 Dec 72.

[24] Msg, the President to Kissinger, TOHAK 71, 6 Dec 72, NSC files, Kissinger Office files, HAK Trip files, box 27, HAK Paris Trip, 3–13 Dec 72, TOHAK 1–100, Nixon Papers.

Nixon concluded that if the next meeting with the North Vietnamese failed to produce a settlement he would quietly "embark on a very heavy bombing of the North." Even so, he appears to have questioned whether military action would have much effect and to have preferred a policy of upgrading the mining and extending reconnaissance missions to gauge the enemy's reaction. Thus, when no progress occurred at the next day's meeting but the North Vietnamese continued to talk, he failed to authorize the heavy additional attacks he had threatened. The possibility of a bombing campaign nevertheless weighed heavily upon his mind. On the day after he sent his message to Kissinger, Deputy Secretary of Defense Kenneth Rush informed him that contingency planning was well advanced for a series of attacks on North Vietnam that would inflict a mass psychological shock upon that country's people and government.[25]

The situation reached its climax on 12 December, when North Vietnam's chief negotiator, Le Duc Tho, announced that he would leave for Hanoi on the fourteenth and that all remaining issues could be resolved by message. Both Nixon and Kissinger concluded that Hanoi was playing for time in hopes of exploiting the split that had occurred between Thieu and the United States once Congress reconvened on 3 January. Kissinger and Haig appear to have favored massive bombing as a response—"a turn to the right," as Haig put it—but Secretary of Defense Laird opposed the idea because of the severe political risks and his own judgment that South Vietnam was the main arena of the war. Nixon himself seems to have continued to waver. He favored bombing, but he also doubted that the American people would understand. Whatever the rationalizations the United States could bring to bear, he told Haig, the reality was that the United States rather than Hanoi had backed away from the agreement because it had, in effect, placed additional demands on North Vietnam. There thus seemed every likelihood that antiwar elements in Congress and the press would respond to the bombing by beginning a mammoth effort to prove that the administration was little more than a tool of the South Vietnamese.[26]

In the end, Nixon decided on 14 December that a massive bombing campaign was his only alternative. A program of limited attacks, he seems to have reasoned, would only deceive North Vietnam into believing that the United States was unwilling any longer to assert itself with vigor. Meanwhile, he would "take the same heat" before Congress and in the

---

[25] Quote from Ibid. This conclusion can be drawn from Msg, Haig WH 29895 to Kissinger, 13 Dec 72, NSC files, Jon Howe Chron files, box 1110, 12/14/72, Nixon Papers. Memo, Kenneth Rush for the President, 7 Dec 72, sub: North Vietnam Contingency Plan, NSC files, Jon Howe Vietnam Subject files, box 1133, Project folder re: Vietnam, Nixon Papers. Also see Kissinger, *The White House Years*, pp. 1437–42.

[26] Nixon, handwritten comment on Memo, Haig for the President, 12 Dec 72, NSC files, Kissinger Office files, HAK Trip files, box 27, HAKTO & Memos to Pres, etc. [I of II], Nixon Papers. Quoted phrase from Msg, Haig WH 29896 to Kissinger TOHAK 191, 13 Dec 72, Kissinger Office files, HAK Trip files, box 27, HAK Paris Trip, 3–13 Dec 72, TOHAK 100–192, Nixon Papers.

press, whether he chose a carefully measured military campaign or moved abruptly with his B–52s to shock enemy leaders into making peace.[27]

The Christmas Bombing

In line with his desire to avoid giving even the semblance of an ultimatum to the North Vietnamese, Nixon refused to explain his decision in public. Instead, he instructed Kissinger to hold a press conference on 16 December 1972 to describe the reasons for the breakdown in the negotiations and to place the onus squarely upon North Vietnam. At that time, the national security adviser hinted that the president might react to the enemy's intransigence with stern measures of some sort, but he studiously avoided any comment that might have jeopardized continuation of the negotiations by making the North Vietnamese lose face.[28] It was the only explanation of the bombing even remotely touching the facts to come from administration sources until much later.

The attacks commenced two days later, when waves of B–52s struck the Kinh No storage complex, the Yen Vien rail yard, and a series of airfields near Hanoi. Over the days that followed, more aircraft struck the Thai Nguyen thermal power plant and the Kinh No and Hanoi oil storage areas. By the end of the third day of attacks, the bombers had done severe damage to their targets but the North Vietnamese had themselves scored, inflicting a loss rate of 6 percent upon their attackers by bringing down nine B–52s and damaging three more.[29]

The operation slackened over the five days that followed. When the enemy brought down two more B–52s on the twenty-first, American commanders prohibited attacks in the vicinity of Hanoi and began to strike at the enemy's missile storage areas. On the twenty-second, President Nixon cabled Hanoi to promise a halt to the bombing above the 20th Parallel beginning on 31 December, if North Vietnam would agree to resume the talks in Paris by 3 January 1973.

When the enemy failed to respond, on 26 December Nixon launched the heaviest attack to that date. One hundred and twenty bombers

[27] Msg, Haig to Col Guay, 14 Dec 72, NSC files, Vietnam Negotiations, box 870, Camp David files, Dec 72, Nixon Papers. Nixon was thinking along these lines on the day before he made his final decision. The quotation is Haig's paraphrase. See Memo, Haig for Kissinger, 13 Dec 72, sub: Items To Discuss With the President's Meeting at 10:00 A.M., December 14, NSC files, Kissinger Office files, HAK Trip files, box 27, HAK Paris Trip, 3–13 Dec 72, Nixon Papers.

[28] Kissinger, *The White House Years*, pp. 1448–49; Msg, State 227604 to Saigon, 16 Dec 72, Jon Howe Vietnam Chron files, box 1110, 12/16/72, Nixon Papers.

[29] This section is based on James R. McCarthy and George B. Allison, *Linebacker II: A View from the Rock* (Maxwell Air Force Base, Ala.: Air War College, 1979). For a brief description of the attacks, see Mark Clodfelter, *The Limits of Air Power* (New York: Free Press, 1989), pp. 184–202.

B–52s did heavy damage to the outskirts of Hanoi.

struck ten targets in Hanoi and Haiphong over only a fifteen-minute period. The enemy launched large numbers of missiles in response but brought down only two bombers. Shortly thereafter, the Hanoi regime informed Nixon that it would be willing to resume negotiating but set 8 January as the date. The president responded that he would accept the change but stipulated that talks between Kissinger and North Vietnam's technical staff in Paris should commence on 2 January and that North Vietnam should agree to refrain from bringing up matters already covered by the basic agreement. If Hanoi accepted those terms, Nixon said, he would stop bombing north of the 20th Parallel within thirty-six hours.

While the enemy deliberated, the bombing continued. Communist gunners brought down two more B–52s between 27 and 29 December 1972, but by the tenth day of the attacks they had run out of missiles and could muster hardly any resistance at all. On the twenty-eighth, the Hanoi regime signaled Nixon that it would accept his conditions, and the president ordered an end to all attacks above the 20th Parallel the next day.

Although Nixon thus achieved his ends, he conducted the bombing in an environment heavy with secrecy and so left the propaganda initiative to the enemy. Radio Hanoi and the Soviet news agency TASS were thus the first to reveal that an escalation of the bombing had occurred. The White House was ready with a statement of its own, but it was almost a total fabrication. In delivering it, the president's spokesman, Ron Ziegler,

602

Kinh No after bombing

avoided mentioning the peace talks and instead linked the attacks to the possibility of an enemy offensive in the South.[30]

"Top Pentagon officials" later denied in off-the-record interviews with the press that any sort of enemy offensive was building in South Vietnam, but, adhering to administration policy, they remained publicly as uncommunicative as the White House. Secretary Laird, for one, was tight-lipped. On the morning after the raids, he spoke with reporters briefly, but only to confirm that "air operations are being conducted throughout North Vietnam at the present time. I do not care to discuss any other matters in relation to these operations because of my desire to protect the safety and the security of the men involved in these present operations."[31]

In Saigon the MACV Office of Information was equally uncommunicative. With the Defense Department already scripting many of the statements and announcements it delivered to the press and under instructions, especially in the case of the mining, to avoid expanding upon or deviating from the approved texts, it followed the official line by refusing at first to confirm that attacks on Hanoi and Haiphong had begun. After acknowledging that American aircraft had struck "military

[30] [AP–48] and [AP–68], 18 Dec 72, Jon Howe Chron files, box 1111, 12/18/72, Nixon Papers.

[31] George C. Wilson, "Officials Split on Bombing," *Washington Post*, 21 Dec 72. Laird's quote is from Rudy Abramson, "Bombing of North Resumed by U.S.," *Los Angeles Times*, 19 Dec 72. Also see Draft News Release, 18 Dec 72, Staff Member Office files, Ziegler, box 43, Foreign Policy Guidance, Nov–Dec 72 [I of II], Nixon Papers.

targets from which North Vietnam is supporting continued infiltration . . . into South Vietnam," the command's spokesmen thus routinely announced the number of American fighters and bombers lost but refused to reveal what the Saigon correspondents wanted most, the targets of the attacks and the damage the bombing had caused.[32]

Denied high-level information on what was happening, the press had little choice but to reach its own conclusions. Despite the Nixon administration's attempts to save face for the North Vietnamese, for example, few reporters doubted that the bombing was anything more than the product of a breakdown in the negotiations. The president's news summary for 19 December noted the result. "All net[work]s dominated by the renewed heavy U.S. bombing above 20th parallel as U.S. apparently seeks to show NVN that delay in the talks won't help Hanoi," the document's authors noted.

A CBS source at DOD says there are fewer bombing restrictions than at any time in war. And NBC noted new targets are available w/possibly heaviest bombing of the war now being carried out. "RN took off the kid gloves," said Cronkite in lead. . . . Technical talks in Paris broken off by NVN to protest raids. . . . Reasoner, w/a very harsh commentary, accuses RN of breaking HAK's word and breaking faith with the U.S. public. . . . Sevareid, w/less harshness, told of the "depression" in Washington and the "astonishing" fact, if true, that the real sticking point is the same one that's long been the key to the war—SVN's claim to be a separate nation. . . . AP's Freed [*sic*] leads: "The futility of the private talks has been underlined by RN's decision to use bombs where diplomacy has failed." The Admin. couched its announcement in terms of protecting U.S. pilots, but it's apparent that RN intends to show Hanoi it can't escape military retaliation. AP says even tho HAK talked of a settlement "99% complete," it was clear the missing 1% dealt w/ "the central issue of the war"—political control of SVN.[33]

Newspaper editorials commenting on Nixon's decision were divided in their assessments. Having concluded from the resumption of the negotiations in November that peace was indeed at hand, many journals in the United States and around the world were disappointed. They questioned Hanoi's responsibility for the breakdown of the negotiations and the effectiveness of bombing as a means of achieving a peace agreement and launched a vehement attack. Others, less critical of the war, endorsed the president's action. "How did we get in a few short weeks from a prospect for peace that 'you can bank on,'" the *Washington Post* thus asked rhetorically in a 28 December editorial, "to the most savage and senseless act of war ever visited, over a scant ten days, by one sovereign people upon another?" The *Chicago Sun-Times* was equally distressed.

[32] Msg, Defense 3055 to CINCPAC et al., 6 Dec 72, sub: Possible Media Queries, DDI Mining Haiphong, 1972. Quote from Joseph Fried, "New Raids on Hanoi Called 'Devastating' by Red Radio," *New York Daily News*, 19 Dec 72.

[33] News Summary, 19 Dec 72, President's Office files, box 46, Dec 72 [III of III], Nixon Papers. The quotation refers to correspondent Joseph Fried, who worked for the *New York Daily News*.

604

"The American public wants an end of its involvement in Vietnam and it wants it now," the paper's editors claimed. "If peace was at hand two months ago, it should be at hand now. Only a momentous foul-up would justify a resumption of bombing." The *New York Times* was also indignant. "The best hope for peace in Indochina since 1954 has been severely shaken by a hail of American bombs. . . . [The bombing] is not likely to hasten—and could indefinitely postpone—the 'just and fair' agreement that Henry Kissinger has said is the president's objective." The *Minneapolis Tribune* agreed. "We find it hard to see how Hanoi will be made more amenable by a U.S. air offensive. Mr. Nixon has often spoken of the importance of giving the Thieu Government a 'chance.' How great, how certain, how long and at what cost does he intend that chance to be." In the meantime, the *London Times* questioned whether Nixon's actions were those of a man who wanted peace very badly and Hamburg's *Die Zeit* termed the attacks "a crime against humanity."[34]

Despite the criticism, the president had defenders in the news media. Balancing the *Times*, the *New York Daily News* asserted that "The way to peace and permanent relief from bombing is open to North Vietnam any time it is ready for a real peace effort. Until that day comes, the enemy shouldn't expect immunity from attack while prolonging the conflict." The *Honolulu Star-Bulletin* was equally supportive. "Even though this seems likely to open a new round of recrimination in America and in the Congress, the evidence since last May suggests that the American public will support the bombing of the North and the mining of its harbors rather than simply surrender." The editors of the *Detroit News* meanwhile observed that "Unless he is willing to sign a meaningless settlement in order to wash his hands of a bad situation, the president has no alternative but to resume . . . the kind of military pressure which brought Hanoi to the peace table in the first place."[35]

The response of Congress, especially among the Democrats, was heavily negative, but the president, as with the press, also had supporters. Senate Democratic Leader Mike Mansfield termed the bombing "a stone age tactic." Senator George McGovern called upon Congress to force an end to the war because Nixon had failed to do so. Senator Stuart Symington challenged Kissinger to explain the breakdown of the negotiations to the Senate and warned that key Democrats who had kept silent while the negotiations had showed some hope of progress were preparing to renew their criticism. Even so, Congressman F. Edward Hebert, long a supporter of the war, called for an intensification of the bombing. "We

[34] Martin F. Herz describes the reaction of the so-called Prestige Press in Martin F. Herz, *The Prestige Press and the Christmas Bombing, 1972: Images and Reality in Vietnam* (Washington, D.C.: Ethics and Public Policy Center, 1980). Initial reactions are summarized in [AP], Bombing Decision Roundup, 19 Dec 72, copy in CMH files. Also see "Terror Bombing in the Name of Peace," *Washington Post*, 28 Dec 72; "A Reply to Stalling," *Detroit News*, 20 Dec 72; "Outrage and Relief," *Time*, 8 Jan 73, p. 14.

[35] [AP], Bombing Decision Roundup, 19 Dec 72.

would never have got them to the peace table in the first place if we hadn't bombed them," he told United Press International in a telephone interview. "Mine Haiphong! Bomb Hanoi! Bomb them all!"[36]

With much of the American news media and the Congress clearly opposed to the bombing and the Nixon administration saying little of substance on the subject, the North Vietnamese took every opportunity to present themselves as innocent victims. In an attempt to save civilian lives, the B–52s had struck only on the outskirts of Hanoi and had left targets within the city to bombs delivered by more accurate tactical aircraft. Mistakes nevertheless inevitably occurred, and the enemy publicized each one. On 21 December North Vietnam thus claimed that bombs had hit the jail containing most of the American prisoners of war, the so-called Hanoi Hilton, and brought the American singer and antiwar activist Joan Baez to the scene. Baez and other visitors also charged that bombs had hit the civilian air terminal at Hanoi's Gia Lam Airport. On the twenty-third North Vietnam likewise declared that American bombers had destroyed the Bach Mai Hospital, the largest medical center in North Vietnam. They took more visiting Americans to see the damage—including the famous jurist Telford Taylor, the chief prosecutor of German war criminals at the Nuremberg trials following World War II, and Nevin Scrimshaw, who was visiting North Vietnam at that time on behalf of the Senate Subcommittee on Refugees. The visitors returned to the United States with pictures. Meanwhile, foreign governments such as Egypt, Poland, and India complained that the attacks had damaged their legations in Hanoi.

President Nixon was incensed by those claims. Avowing emphatically at a 4 January meeting that "if anyone is punished for hitting that hospital, I'll fire someone," he was strongly tempted to respond with a propaganda campaign of his own that emphasized Communist depredations in the South. Kissinger's belief nonetheless continued to prevail that if the United States pressed the issue too far the North Vietnamese might attempt to save face by adopting a hard line in the negotiations. As a result, the State Department extended tentative expressions of regret to the nations that had sustained damage to their diplomatic missions but remained, as one UPI report noted, "studiously silent" where the bombing was concerned. The White House likewise worked quietly among its supporters in the House and Senate, releasing fact sheets and conducting private briefings, but held itself to the barest details in public.[37]

---

[36] Shirley Elder, "Raids Draw Usual Protest From Congress," *Washington Star*, 20 Dec 72; [UPI–140], 18 Dec 72, Jon Howe Vietnam Chron files, box 1111, 12/18/72, Nixon Papers.

[37] Nixon is quoted in Memo of Conversation, Nixon, Rogers, et al., 4 Jan 73, NSC files, Presidential/HAK Memcons, box 1026, Memcons, Jan–Mar 73, Nixon Papers. Kissinger's concerns are apparent in that memo but also in Msg, Kissinger WHS 2298 to Bunker, 30 Dec 72, Jon Howe Chron files, box 1112, 12/30/72, Nixon Papers. [UPI–094] (Viet Bombing), copy in CMH files; Memo, Les Janka for Ronald Ziegler, 22 Dec 72, sub: Janka Guidance for Thursday, Staff Member Office files, Ziegler, box 43, Foreign Policy Guidance, Nov–Dec 72 [I of II], Nixon Papers; Msg, Richard T. Kennedy WH 29944 to

The Pentagon carried most of the burden of dealing with the press and experienced the greatest damage. Denying at first that American bombs had "hit" the Bach Mai Hospital and insisting that it was Hanoi's obligation under the Geneva Convention to keep prisoners of war out of danger areas, Jerry Friedheim conceded that civilian structures in Hanoi might have experienced some collateral damage but emphasized that the United States had struck only military targets.[38] Under instructions to say nothing more of substance, he could not release the sort of evidence that might have carried some weight with the press.

As the attacks progressed and the controversy over the bombing continued, Friedheim and the reporters he briefed seemed to go into a dance each time the subject arose. The reporters pressed for details, if only so they could tell their editors they had asked, while the deputy assistant secretary used every rhetorical means at his disposal to sidestep the issue. Urged repeatedly to comment on reports of heavy damage and casualties in nonmilitary sections of Hanoi, Friedheim on one occasion thus responded vaguely, "You have to judge the sources of that information." The reporters then asked him to say something about North Vietnamese allegations that the B–52s were "carpet bombing" civilian areas. The deputy assistant secretary would do nothing of the sort and restated his government's position: "The adjectives you'll have to choose for yourselves. If the implication of your question is that we are bombing civilian areas, the answer is no." Calling an end to the duet, one reporter finally asked, "Is it your position that you don't want to discuss the topic, and that any comment is that the North Vietnamese often use such situations for propaganda purposes?" Friedheim responded with obvious relief, "I'll accept that summation."[39]

In the end, on 27 December, in an attempt to counteract some of the bad publicity, the Defense Department released a list of targets and a preliminary assessment of damage. It nevertheless took until 2 January for the agency to acknowledge that the Bach Mai Hospital had sustained "limited, accidental" damage. Although conceding that the facility stood less than 1,100 meters from a prime target for the B–52s, a military air base, and some 300 meters from a major oil storage area, the department's spokesmen even then attempted to play down the possibility that the bombers had been entirely to blame by observing that falling surface-to-air missiles might have been responsible. There appears to have been some justice to the claim, given the huge volume of missiles and antiaircraft shells that the enemy had fired at the attacking aircraft, but the argument had been discre-

Haig, 21 Dec 72, Jon Howe Chron files, box 1111, 12/22/72, Nixon Papers; Memo, Situation Room for Kissinger, 2 Jan 73, NSC files, Subject files, box 345, HAK's Noon and Evening Notes, 12/1/72–2/28/73, Nixon Papers.

[38] See, for example, Bob Schieffer, CBS Evening News, 27 Dec 72, *Radio-TV-Defense Dialog.*

[39] *New York Times,* 30 Dec 72, as quoted by Herz, *The Prestige Press and the Christmas Bombing,* p. 25.

dited only a short time before, in the case of the French embassy bombing, and appears to have had little effect.[40]

Lacking an adequate explanation from the U.S. government, the news media, especially those journals that opposed the bombing, gave North Vietnam's claims far more prominence than they might have had otherwise. Since the B–52s had dropped at least 20,000 tons of explosives—"the equivalent of the Hiroshima bomb"—on targets that abutted civilian areas, an editorial in the *New York Times* asked the paper's readers to imagine what would happen if a comparable enemy force were unleashed to bomb railheads, shipyards, truck parks, and command and control facilities in their city. "It requires no horror stories from Hanoi radio," the newspaper said, "to deduce that the destruction and human suffering [in North Vietnam] must be very extensive indeed." The *Boston Globe* meanwhile implied that the bombing was little more than a form of "mass murder" and accused President Nixon of a callous disregard for genuine human feeling when he renewed the attack on North Vietnam after the Christmas stand-down. "One would expect [that] the President of the United States might have been moved by news accounts and news pictures of the all but incredible charnel house which American bombers are making of both North and South Vietnam."[41]

When the Defense Department finally released its target list and estimates of preliminary bomb damage, columnist David Lawrence attempted to introduce some perspective into the discussion. Although civilians had presumably suffered, he said, the effect had been unintentional. The Pentagon's list was so extensive and the damage to the targets so clear that it was obvious North Vietnam's war-making potential had been the bombers' objective rather than the country's civilian population.[42]

Rejoinders of that sort notwithstanding, in the absence of an effective campaign to counter the enemy's propaganda, the issues were hardly as clear as Lawrence made them seem. The war had already taken a heavy toll of civilians, both in the North and the South. In that light, pictures and eyewitness accounts of damage to civilians in Hanoi carried heavier weight in the eyes of the press than the diffident communiques issued by official sources. Columnist Harriet Van Horne thus observed vividly in the 3 January issue of the *New York Post* that "We are fortunate this week in having the Pentagon's transparent lies set alongside eye-witness accounts of travellers just back from Hanoi, plus film showing how a city looks after wall to wall, street to street, carpet bombing. . . . No government ever tried to censor the news unless it had reason to fear the truth."

[40] Dana Adams Schmidt, "'Terror Raids' by U.S. Denied," *Christian Science Monitor*, 28 Dec 72; [UPI–075] and [UPI–076], 2 Jan 72, copy in CMH files; Louis A. Wiesner, *Victims and Survivors, Displaced Persons and Other War Victims in Viet-Nam, 1954–1975* (New York: Greenwood Press, 1988), p. 305.

[41] "Terror From the Skies," *New York Times*, 22 Dec 72; "The Slaughter Resumed," *Boston Globe*, 27 Dec 72.

[42] "David Lawrence," *Washington Star*, 29 Dec 72.

The next day, the *Philadelphia Inquirer* compared Friedheim's terse acknowledgment that limited damage might have occurred to the hospital at Bach Mai with Telford Taylor's graphic descriptions of "huge fresh craters" and "buildings . . . shattered by blasts." It headlined the piece, "Why Can't the United States Be Truthful About Bombing?" Citing "a multitude of eyewitness press reports and diplomatic dispatches" as at least partial corroboration, the 8 January issue of *Newsweek* also persisted in claiming that "there was so much civilian damage in Hanoi and Haiphong that the relentless raids seemed to amount to a campaign of terror against North Vietnam." As late as 15 January, I. F. Stone, in a *Washington Star* article titled "Blitzkrieg in Southeast Asia," described the bombing as a moral and military defeat for the United States and asserted that he found it difficult to decide which was worse, "the . . . cruelty of the air raids or the lies told to excuse them."[43]

In the end, a few of the so-called eyewitnesses and some within the press backed away from the charges they had levied. Traveling to Hanoi for a second time during January, Telford Taylor, for one, refused to concede that bombing for the sake of terrorizing civilians was permissible but nonetheless concluded that the United States could have destroyed Hanoi in two or three nights if it had so desired. He also noted the proximity of the air base to the hospital at Bach Mai and observed that the damage to civilian areas within the city had obviously been an unintentional by-product of attacks on legitimate military targets. During March and April 1973, reporters such as Malcolm Browne of the *New York Times*, Peter Arnett of the Associated Press, and Peter Ward of the *Baltimore Sun* also traveled to Hanoi. They discovered, as Browne put it, that the city had suffered remarkably little damage in comparison with the allegations that had circulated during the bombing. "The damage . . . was grossly overstated by North Vietnamese propaganda. . . . Hanoi remains a beautiful and bustling city." The enemy inadvertently reinforced those conclusions on 4 January by revealing that 1,318 civilians had been killed in Hanoi during the attacks and 1,261 wounded, substantial numbers, but far fewer than would have been the case if the United States had pursued a policy of indiscriminate bombing. The disclosure prompted Orr Kelly of the *Washington Star* to conclude that the attack on North Vietnam had been cheap in terms of human lives.[44]

On 4 April the Defense Department produced photographs of Hanoi that might have gone a long way toward refuting the charge that the U.S.

[43] Harriet Van Horne, "Pentagon Spokesman," *New York Post*, 3 Jan 73; "Why Can't the United States Be Truthful About Bombing," *Philadelphia Inquirer*, 4 Jan 73; "What the Bombing Did," *Newsweek*, 8 Jan 73, p. 11; "Diplomacy by Terror," *Newsweek*, 8 Jan 73; I. F. Stone, "Blitzkrieg in Southeast Asia," *Washington Star*, 15 Jan 73.

[44] Herz, *The Prestige Press and the Christmas Bombing*, pp. 54–59, 68; Malcolm Browne, "Hanoi's People Still Curious and Likable," *New York Times*, 31 Mar 73. Also see Peter Ward, "In Hanoi There Is an Air of a City in Victory," *Baltimore Sun*, 25 Mar 73. Kelly's report is noted in Memo, Situation Room for Kissinger, 9 Jan 73, NSC files, Subject files, box 345, HAK's Noon and Evening Notes, 12/1/72–2/28/73, Nixon Papers.

Air Force had targeted civilians, but the action was too late to have much effect. Not only were newspapers that had attacked the bombing as cruel and inhumane clearly disinclined to make much point of the development, the story was old news by the time it appeared. Accounts of the final peace treaty with North Vietnam, the withdrawal of the last American military units from the South, the return of the prisoners of war, and the unfolding of the Watergate affair had long before supplanted it. Although the *New York Times* thus reported the release of the pictures in an article by Drew Middleton headlined "Hanoi Films Show No 'Carpet Bombing,'" it waited until 2 May to do so and made no editorial comment. The *Washington Post* was more punctual, reporting the story on 5 April—but only briefly, on page 24, at the end of an article on Cambodia. The national news magazines *Time* and *Newsweek* said nothing about it at all.[45]

Whatever the failure of the press to correct itself, the news media's heavy reporting of civilian casualties and the destruction of North Vietnam appears to have made little impression upon the people of the United States. In earlier years, Nixon and his predecessors could have counted on at least a small surge in public support whenever they made a difficult decision involving the war. This time, according to the Harris poll, the opposite occurred. The public opposed the bombing by a margin of 51 to 37 percent. The reaction had little to do with qualms about the morality of the attacks or the other concerns that had appeared so forcefully in the news stories and commentaries surrounding the raids. Fewer than 50 percent of those interviewed agreed that "it was inhuman and immoral for the U.S. to have bombed Hanoi's civilian centers." Instead, 67 percent rejected North Vietnam's claims that hospitals and residential areas had been destroyed and an impressive 71 percent said they believed "what we did in bombing Hanoi was no worse than what the Communists have done in the Vietnam War." A plurality even contended that "the only language Hanoi will listen to is force, such as our bombing their cities." What turned the public against the raids was the issue of American losses, which had received some coverage in the press, but far less than the supposed brutality of the attacks. Unwilling to tolerate further attrition, whether in aircraft or men, a majority agreed by 55 to 30 percent that "we lost many American lives and B–52s unnecessarily in the bombing raids."[46]

The End of American Involvement

As President Nixon had predicted, the House Democratic Caucus revealed the direction the new Congress would take by voting 154 to

---

[45] Drew Middleton, "Hanoi Films Show No 'Carpet-Bombing,'" *New York Times*, 2 May 72; "Cambodian Peril Is Discounted by Pentagon," *Washington Post*, 5 Apr 72. Also see Herz, *The Prestige Press and the Christmas Bombing*, pp. 59–60.

[46] Harris, *The Anguish of Change*, p. 78.

74 on 3 January 1973 to work to cut off funds for further U.S. operations in Indochina. Spurred by that development and by his own perception that time was indeed running out, the president pressed ahead with both the negotiations and his efforts to bring Thieu into line. On the day after the Democrats met, while preliminary meetings began in Paris, he therefore cabled Thieu to warn, as he had during December, that he fully intended to initial an agreement as soon as North Vietnam's negotiators settled the final issues holding up the accord. If South Vietnam failed to go along at that time, he continued, "the unity of our two countries . . . would be gravely jeopardized. . . . The actions of our Congress since its return have clearly borne out the many warnings we have made."[47]

Helicopter deactivates mines in Ha Long Bay north of Haiphong.

By 13 January the draft agreement was complete. Among other provisions, the North Vietnamese had agreed to drop the term *administrative structure* from the description of the National Council, to respect both sides of the Demilitarized Zone, and to expand the provisions governing support for the South to allow for the continuation of almost unrestricted American military assistance to the Saigon regime. In return, to Thieu's chagrin, they had retained the right to leave their forces in place in South Vietnam.[48]

The next day, with South Vietnam's leaders still refusing to cooperate, Nixon informed Thieu that, in view of the "significant progress" that had

[47] Msg, Kissinger WHS 3001 to Bunker relaying a message from the President to Thieu, 4 Jan 73, NSC files, Backchannels, box 415, Backchannel Messages, to Bunker, 1973 [part I], Nixon Papers.

[48] Nixon explained the changes to Thieu in Msg, Kissinger WHS 3050 to Bunker relaying a letter to Thieu carried by Haig, 17 Jan 73, NSC files, Backchannels, box 415, Backchannel Messages, to Bunker, 1973 [part I], Nixon Papers. Also see Kissinger, *The White House Years*, p. 1466.

Kissinger and North Vietnamese negotiator Le Duc Tho (foreground) *initial peace agreement.*

occurred, he was directing the suspension of all bombing and mining in North Vietnam. When that had no effect on Thieu and he continued to request revisions, Nixon sent a second message to reassure him that the United States had never recognized the right of foreign troops to remain on South Vietnamese soil and would "react vigorously to violations of the agreement." Even so, Nixon continued, the time for delay had passed. He had "decided irrevocably" on his present course. Rather than suffer a total cutoff of funds to assist South Vietnam, he would initial the agreement on 23 January and sign it on the twenty-seventh. "We have only one decision before us," he concluded, "whether or not to continue in peacetime the close partnership that has served us so well in war."[49]

In support of the president's warning, apparently at the suggestion of Kissinger's staff, Senators Barry Goldwater and John Stennis, who in the past had consistently backed U.S. assistance to South Vietnam, went on record in interviews with the press to warn Thieu that he should do noth-

[49] Msg, Kissinger WHS 3050 to Bunker relaying a letter to Thieu carried by Haig, 17 Jan 73.

612

ing further to impede the agreement. If he did, Goldwater declared, "it would imperil any future help which South Vietnam might obtain from this country." Stennis added that "The South Vietnamese government must realize that there are limits to what the American people are willing to do." Shortly thereafter, Henry Kissinger instructed Ambassador Bunker to show Thieu news reports on the senators' comments and to make the point that South Vietnam's strongest friends in Congress believed the agreement was sound and that further obstruction would be a disaster.[50]

With that, Thieu relented. He had told Haig during December that he believed the enemy might never resort to the sort of aggression that would prompt the massive American retaliation Nixon had promised but that the agreement would at least guarantee continued American support for South Vietnam during the struggle that seemed certain to follow the American withdrawal. On those grounds, bowing to the inevitable, he notified Nixon on 20 January that he would send Foreign Minister Tran Van Lam to Paris to represent his country at the signing.[51] Kissinger initialed the agreement three days later.

Syndicated columnist Marquis Childs broke first word of the development in the press, but Kissinger declined to confirm the story when reporters inquired.[52] Instead, the president made a formal announcement that evening, in a brief speech to the nation. According to the treaty he described, all American prisoners of war were to be returned within the next sixty days, and all American combat forces were to vacate South Vietnam. Bombing would continue in Cambodia and Laos until settlements ended the conflict in those countries, and civilian contractors would continue to provide essential technical and engineering support for the South Vietnamese, but the role of American combat forces in South Vietnam had come to an end.

Over the days that followed, the MACV Office of Information slowly went out of existence. Although it provided public affairs support for the American team participating in the military commission that was to monitor implementation of the treaty, it held the final session of the famous Five O'Clock Follies on 27 January, the day the accord went into effect. There were over 385 correspondents in South Vietnam at that time. The command continued briefly to coordinate their activities but ceded that responsibility progressively to the South Vietnamese and to JUSPAO's successor, the U.S. embassy's Office of the Special Assistant for Press Affairs. As the last American military units departed, public affairs officers shut down the command's troop information newspaper, the *MACV*

[50] Msg, Kissinger WHS 3068 to Bunker, 18 Jan 73, NSC files, Backchannels, box 415, Backchannel Messages, to Bunker, 1973 [part I], Nixon Papers. Also see Kissinger, *The White House Years*, p. 1470.

[51] Msg, Haig 301 to Kissinger, 19 Dec 72, NSC files, A. M. Haig Special file, box 1020, Gen Haig's Vietnam Trip, 17–22 Dec 1972, ToHaig/HaigTo & Misc Memos, etc. [II of III], Nixon Papers.

[52] Msg, Scowcroft TOHAK 45 to Kissinger, 23 Jan 73, NSC files, For the President's files, Lord, Vietnam Negotiations, box 871, Camp David Cables, Jan 17–23, 1973, Nixon Papers.

Last session of the Five O'Clock Follies

Observer, and closed all of the Armed Forces Radio and Television Service stations that remained in South Vietnam, except for the one in Saigon, which continued to operate under the embassy's supervision.[53]

A few big stories remained. Although American participation in the war ceased with the treaty, incidents continued to occur between the South Vietnamese, the Viet Cong, and the North Vietnamese as all sides pushed to consolidate their positions. By 31 January enemy forces had cut all major roads in South Vietnam's Military Region 2 and were moving to intersect the country's main north-south road, Highway 1, to the south of Da Nang. Meanwhile, enemy tanks were reported to be moving along the Ho Chi Minh Trail in Laos, American bombing continued in Cambodia, and the enemy's Central Office for South Vietnam proclaimed "a new era of political struggle" to its adherents in the South.[54]

Portions of those stories found their way into the press, along with the efforts of the South Vietnamese armed forces to curb the energies of the hitherto freewheeling Saigon correspondents. They nevertheless gained little attention in comparison with the return of the prisoners of war, which played in the news media for weeks. Some reporters grumbled at the time that the Military Assistance Command and the Defense

[53] Ltr, Col Robert L. Burke to the author, 27 Jun 90, CMH files; Msg, Saigon 17433 to State, 12 Dec 72, sub: Ceasefire Planning: Press Affairs, Jon Howe Chron files, box 1110, 12/12/72 (323), Nixon Papers.

[54] Memo, Situation Room for Kissinger, 31 Jan 73, NSC files, Subject files, box 345, HAK's Noon and Evening Notes, 12/1/72–2/28/73, Nixon Papers.

Department were attempting to retaliate for years of criticism by keeping reporters at a distance from the prisoners, but, as the Deputy Assistant Secretary of Defense for Health and Environment, Maj. Gen. George Hayes, explained afterward, that was not the case. The Army had learned from its experience following the Korean War that former prisoners sometimes had difficulty adapting to normal living patterns. In that sense, premature exposure to even the most carefully controlled media interviews might have harmed the men. A different approach might have prevailed during the earlier years of the war, when the president had needed the cooperation of the press. But the war was over in the eyes of the American military; there was nothing left to sell. Preoccupied with the need to regroup and rebuild, they were already closing in upon themselves.[55]

Jerry Friedheim's first decision upon succeeding Daniel Henkin as assistant secretary of defense for public affairs shortly after the signing of the treaty symbolized the change in attitude. Entering his new office for the first time, he noticed a map of Vietnam that had hung prominently on one wall during all the years of the war. Turning to his secretary, he instructed her to have it removed.[56]

[55] Interv, author with Maj Gen George Hayes, 21 Apr 74, CMH files.
[56] Interv, author with Jerry Friedheim, 3 Oct 86, CMH files.

24

Conclusion

What happened between the military and the news media in Vietnam? During World War II and most of the Korean War, relations between the two had been relatively even and temperate. Both sides worked on the assumption that if disagreements and frictions were bound to occur because one needed to close off information while the other existed to open it, all concerned could benefit from a cooperative relationship. By the end of the Vietnam War hardly a vestige of that earlier attitude remained. With some exceptions, the military and the news media were enemies.

The effect was unexpected, for reporters and soldiers alike went into the war with much of the old spirit intact. At the beginning, correspondents such as Neil Sheehan, Malcolm Browne, and David Halberstam displayed a strong sense of solidarity with Americans in the field, especially the advisers to the South Vietnamese armed forces. If they disagreed with official policy, it was not to question the ends of the war but to argue in favor of more effective tactics and less official obfuscation. The military, for their part, reciprocated. When censorship of the press became an issue, they rejected the expedient, on grounds that it was impractical and that the South Vietnamese, culturally insensitive to the requirements of a free press, would have to be involved. Instead, they advocated a system of voluntary guidelines that showed great respect for the willingness of reporters to refrain voluntarily from publishing information of value to the enemy.

The policies that evolved from that decision succeeded in preserving both military security and the rights of the news media. Although critics of the press would later cite instances when reporters violated the guidelines, those episodes pale in the context of the tens of thousands of news reports emanating from South Vietnam during the conflict that adhered to the rules. In addition, as one of the Army's most experienced public affairs officers during the war, Maj. Gen. Winant Sidle, would later attest, despite some notable lapses, most of the reporting was either advantageous to the U.S. government and its policies or, given the errors of fact that often accompany the transmission of fast-breaking news, a reasonably neutral approximation of what was happening in the field.[1] Meanwhile, if critics of the military within the press complained that MACV's briefings and news releases were at times incomplete, uninformative, or self-serving, few would have denied that the system the military put into place gave reporters ample means to do their jobs, even when the results were embarrassing to the government. As correspondent Peter Braestrup observed in 1969, newsmen had little difficulty getting at the reality of the war. "They had to be willing to take dawn airplanes, spend a few nights a month with ARVN and American troops, tour key districts with veteran U.S. advisers, dine with political specialists, and ask intelligent questions of generals, sergeants and province chiefs. There were always knowledgeable U.S. Old Hands, ready to offer a viewpoint which conflicted with the White House line . . . [and] always truths to be had at battalion level."[2]

With so much that was right, what went wrong? The answer lies beyond the relationship between the news media and the military in Vietnam. It rests in the conceptions and complexities that underlay the war itself. For the conflict was born in contradiction and grounded in ambiguity. The seeds of controversy existed at its root, from the very beginning.

The many parallels between Lyndon Johnson's approach to the war and the policies of his successor, Richard Nixon, show what happened. Johnson believed that major American involvement might be necessary to save South Vietnam, but thought it critical to increase the commitment slowly, to avoid confrontation with the Soviet Union and the People's Republic of China and to retain a solid base of support for his domestic policies. Nixon sought to pull out of the war Johnson and his predecessors had created. Like Johnson, however, he had a larger agenda. Seeking to build a new world order with the United States in the lead by creating openings to China and the Soviet Union, he adopted a policy of gradual withdrawal designed to extract the United States from the war without triggering the sort of collapse in South Vietnam that would inevitably weaken American influence worldwide.

In pursuit of their goals, both Johnson and Nixon sought to enlist the military as spokesmen for their points of view. Where in earlier wars the president and his party had conducted most of the public relations, in Vietnam the military rather than the political sector came to bear heavy responsibility for the effort. Johnson relied on Westmoreland and his public affairs officers to justify his efforts and to endorse his claims of progress. Nixon likewise pushed Abrams and his staff for statements in support of his policies, especially the success of the Vietnamization program.

[1] Ltr, Sidle to the author, 5 Nov 90, CMH files.
[2] Peter Braestrup, "Covering the Vietnam War," *Nieman Reports*, 23 Jan 70.

Johnson found his task easier than Nixon did. After some resistance, Westmoreland went along with the president's desire for optimism. Abrams was more grudging. Unable always to escape requests for information "which can be used," as Wheeler observed during the incursion into Cambodia, "to validate the impression we wish to convey," he nevertheless attempted to keep his command clear of politics by taking refuge whenever he could in the principle that the war should speak for itself.

In the end, of course, Nixon prevailed. Continuing a process that had begun under Johnson, he concentrated public affairs policy making in Washington, where he and his staff could tune it to the politics of the moment. Although he attempted to divorce the White House from the dirt and blood that controversial operations such as LAM SON 719 entailed—leaving the burden of relations with the press in those cases to the Defense Department and the Military Assistance Command—he saw to it that his staff closely monitored almost all aspects of the public affairs process. By the time of the Christmas bombing in 1972, as a result, many substantive news releases emanating from the Military Assistance Command were drafted for the most part in Washington, with only perfunctory input from agencies in the field. It was a far cry from the early days, when, for example, General Westmoreland's command, in conjunction with the U.S. mission in Saigon, had played a major role in the development of guidelines for the press.[3]

As the war progressed, time grew short for both Johnson and Nixon. By 1967 Johnson was preoccupied with his failure to produce on his promises of success in Vietnam and with the possibility that he would face severe questioning on the subject during his coming campaign for reelection. Nixon confronted much the same dilemma toward the end of 1971. In response, both presidents resorted to the press to communicate their views to the American public and both sought to shape the perceptions of reporters and editors. Playing upon the credibility of the armed forces by using military spokesmen as his intermediaries, Johnson launched powerful public relations campaigns to demonstrate that his policies were working and that the United States was winning the war. Nixon resorted to public relations campaigns as well, but used the military less, in part because of the resistance mounted by Laird and others within the Department of Defense and in part because the credibility of the armed forces had declined as opposition to the war had increased in the United States. Embittered by what he considered biased news coverage of his administration and increasingly suspicious of his political opponents, he indulged those journalists who were predisposed to his point of view but used Vice President Spiro Agnew to wage verbal war on his enemies. If he could not gain their submission, so the theory went, he might at least pound them into silence.

In the end neither strategy worked. Neither Johnson nor Nixon succeeded in their attempts to manage news coverage of the war. Culti-

[3] Interv, author with Col Phillip Stevens, 26 Apr 73, CMH files.

vating the appearance that the war was going well despite many indications that he had achieved at best a stalemate, Johnson peppered the public record with so many inconsistencies that when the Tet offensive of 1968 occurred much of the press and many within the administration itself questioned General Westmoreland's accurate avowals that the enemy had suffered a costly setback. Increasingly ambivalent about the war, Johnson declined to run again for office and began the effort to achieve a negotiated settlement.

That decision had a profound effect upon Nixon by cutting off his ability to escalate the war as he might have liked. Nixon responded by using every public affairs outlet at his disposal to gain the leverage he believed he needed either to avert an outright South Vietnamese collapse, or, failing that, to create a healthy interval between a final American withdrawal and the disintegration of his ally. By 1972, nevertheless, time had run out for him just as it had for Johnson. With the American public and Congress increasingly restive and with Thieu unwilling or unable to accomplish reforms that might have made his government attractive to Congress, the president decided it was time to "cut bait." Proclaiming the ultimate success of Vietnamization, he concluded an unfavorable treaty with North Vietnam and withdrew American forces from the war.

"Our worst enemy seems to be the press!" Nixon had exclaimed during the 1971 incursion into Laos, but his comment oversimplified a matter of the greatest complexity. So many contradictions existed, indeed, within his administration's effort to bring the war to a satisfactory conclusion that the opposition of many within the news media was almost guaranteed. Nixon had no choice, for example, but to reduce the size of the American force in South Vietnam, but he also sought to pursue an appearance of resolution in hopes of convincing the enemy to negotiate a peace favorable to American ends. The disparity between the two approaches, while perhaps necessary to preserve American standing before the world, set up ambiguities that led inevitably to criticism. Whatever the explanations of the president and his spokesmen, many in Congress and the press were bound to ask how it could be that the United States was withdrawing from South Vietnam while also sponsoring a major escalation by sending troops into Cambodia. Stories from the field pointing up the disparity between the administration's claims and the reality of what the troops were achieving were the inevitable result. In the same way, Nixon time and again proclaimed the success of Vietnamization, yet astute observers within the press could see that American advisers and B–52s had a more important bearing upon South Vietnam's ability to beat back its enemy than the sometimes valiant but often inept efforts of that nation's armed forces.

A vicious circle developed. When Nixon began the process of withdrawal, the American public, Congress, and news media viewed the event as an indication that their role in the war would end within a reasonable period of time. Hope soared, only to be dashed when Nixon

620

approved the attack into Cambodia. The news media, with some exceptions, reacted with anger. Closely attuned to their sources within both Congress and the president's sharply divided administration, reporters and editors raised arguments against the attack that mirrored those arising within the president's own closest councils. Whether the charges and the countercharges that followed had any influence on public opinion is difficult to tell. What is clear is that the administration's credibility fell, especially in Congress, which moved to restrict the president's power ever again to employ American forces in Cambodia. The president and his advisers, in turn, hardened their own position. Asserting that the incursion had been a thorough success despite indications that less had been achieved than hoped, they continued the American withdrawal in order to shore up public morale but were still disposed, when an opportunity presented itself in Laos, to duplicate what they considered their earlier achievement. When that operation collapsed, more recriminations followed, especially from the Saigon correspondents. Under the lash, the president and his advisers drew themselves into a tighter ring and resolved to forge ahead.

By the time of the Christmas bombing in 1972, the press had lost much of its confidence in official sources. Bereft by Nixon's order of the on-the-record official comments and communiques from which they routinely took their leads and ready to believe the worst anyway, a number of reporters and columnists gave the enemy's claims heavier weight than they deserved. Exaggerated news stories on the bombing of dikes, the destruction of the Bach Mai Hospital, and the carpet bombing of Hanoi resulted.

The condition of American forces in South Vietnam complicated the situation. As drawdowns proceeded and the effort to reduce American casualties took effect, the soldiers who remained behind spent less and less time in combat and fell into make-work routines that had little to do with the original purpose of their presence in South Vietnam. Morale declined, and with it the self-respect of some of the troops. Drug abuse flourished, interracial tensions multiplied, the incidence of fragging and combat refusals increased, and too many officers responded as had those involved with the incident at Fire Support Base MARY ANN, by attempting to insulate their careers from the effects of the malaise. Lacking a strong market for Vietnam stories at home because of the cutback in coverage after 1968, an increasingly adversarial corps of correspondents in Saigon reported the crisis of morale, sometimes with painful accuracy, but often with flourishes that galled the many within the military who had maintained their integrity.

More was involved in the response of the press, however, than mere insensitivity. With public support for the war declining and with the president mainly pursuing political rather than military goals, a clash of cultures had come into being that increasingly separated the military from civilians at all levels of the war. The problem could be seen in the leaks surrounding the Yeoman Radford affair; in President Nixon's comment that he would have supplied Admiral Moorer with whatever information he had needed, if only the admiral had asked; and in General Abrams' decision to retain the news embargo on LAM SON 719 long after the political damage it caused to the president's policies exceeded the threat to American and South Vietnamese forces. It was apparent in Henry Kissinger's explosive reaction when events in the field during LAM SON 719 rarely seemed to go as Abrams and his officers had predicted. It could also be seen in Nixon's anger at Abrams when the general canceled the president's carefully fashioned air strike against North Vietnam to maintain unstinting support for South Vietnamese forces fighting to repel the enemy's Easter offensive. In many of those cases, there was no right or wrong, only differing points of view and a failure on all sides to communicate.

The press might, at times, have provided some relief. During the May 1968 enemy offensive, critical but well-founded news stories had helped to link opposing military and civilian perspectives and had forced Clifford and Abrams to come to terms. During the final years of the war, however, minds were too closed and the rhetoric too thick for that. Continuing to take their themes from sources in Washington that sought to be done with the war, reporters interpreted events from that perspective, questioned aspects of the conflict that officers took for granted, and by so doing drove a powerful wedge between themselves and the military. Neil Sheehan's call for war crimes trials was an extreme example, but far more characteristic was Jack Laurence's story of Charlie Company. No one disputed the facts in that case, but where the reporter had perceived a budding mutiny, officers saw the normal give-and-take that sometimes occurred between soldiers and commanders in combat. It was all a matter of interpretation. The reporter saw the bad while the officers—almost of necessity, given their position—preferred an optimistic appraisal. In the same way at Con Son, Don Luce perceived violations of basic human rights and turned them into an international sensation. Without disputing the substance of his reporting, military officers tended to see a fundamental human dilemma. For how, they reasoned, could the South Vietnamese provide amenities to prisoners who were their enemies while feeding their own loyal soldiers less? The reporters, in all those cases, may have jumped to easy conclusions without sufficient reflection, but they were already sensitive to the American public's desire to end the war and to their realization that few of the American soldiers present any longer believed South Vietnam was worth dying for. Although most reporters remained straightforward and largely nonjudgmental in their work, those disposed to criticize, in particular, became less inclined than ever to give the military the benefit of a doubt.

The contradictions afflicting the United States in South Vietnam only made matters worse by providing those reporters with the evidence they needed to contend that their points were, in fact, close to the truth.

622

Focusing upon those within the press who obviously violated accepted journalistic standards, the military for its part responded much as the Nixon administration had, by withdrawing into a shell. "There were some fine people in the Saigon press corps," Colonel Leonard thus avowed, years after the war had ended, "but there were also some whose principal concern was self-advancement." It was difficult, Leonard continued, for the military

to understand how the press could support some of the people who were correspondents in name only. The Luce case is an example of a part-time correspondent who apparently engaged in anti-war activities in a combat zone in defiance of his own and the host government. The protection afforded by the press who saw his ouster as an infringement on their rights kept him in country regardless of his questionable activities. This was incomprehensible to me.[4]

Leonard and the other public affairs officers at the Military Assistance Command were caught hard between the concerns and point of view of the institution they served and the fact that both military leaders and civilian administrators required an unfettered press to communicate their views credibly to the American public and Congress. Serving as brokers between two increasingly embittered antagonists, they advanced the ends of each with considerable success but ended up satisfying neither.

After 1968 at the Tet offensive, for example, many within the military would have been pleased to exclude reporters from combat operations, but public affairs officers understood that any attempt to do so would have a devastating effect upon what was left of official credibility. Although they refused to contest the prerogative of commanders to restrain the press on grounds of military security, they opposed whenever possible attempts by officers in the field to invoke unjustifiable restrictions. "As had happened with Don Luce," Leonard emphasized, "any attempt by MACV to limit . . . [the number or access of reporters] would have resulted in a public outcry. Hence we supported everybody as best we could."[5] Unable to see much of what the public affairs officers had accomplished on their behalf, many reporters concluded that the MACV Office of Information opposed their interests. Interpreting every attempt by the command to discipline errant correspondents or to protect security requirements as evidence of ill-will, they complained continuously in print and on the air that the Military Assistance Command was attempting to manipulate the truth.

Blinded by institutional loyalties every bit as strong as the attitudes of the press, influential members of the military meanwhile took the opposite approach. When the MACV Office of Information declined to discipline reporters such as the ones who had allegedly attempted to provoke a combat refusal during the Easter offensive, MACV's inspector general, Colonel Cook, for one, decided the command's public affairs offi-

---

[4] Ltr, Col Robert Leonard to the author, 17 Oct 90, CMH files.
[5] Ibid.

cers were "great pushovers for the press" and little more than reporters themselves.[6] A thorough professional, Cook buried his anger, as did most of his fellow officers. A few, however, were less conscientious. Failing to provide routine transportation for the press in combat areas, delaying the release of information, and declining to provide timely briefings, they caused damage to official credibility out of all proportion to their number.

Throughout the war, but never more than in its final years, appearances carried heavy weight. Compelled by domestic opinion to extract American forces from the conflict on a schedule that threw into extreme doubt the already questionable ability of South Vietnam to survive, Richard Nixon had no choice, for reasons of state, but to accomplish the task in a manner that would confer the opposite impression. As a result, despite deficiencies at every level and distressingly inadequate leadership, the South Vietnamese armed forces had to appear to improve as their former protectors departed. In the same way, the sorely corrupt and autocratic Thieu regime had to appear to represent the legitimate aspirations of its people; the incursion into Cambodia had to be made to appear a major setback for the enemy, whatever its true results; and the South Vietnamese force fighting in Laos could not be allowed to withdraw, refit, and attack again because that would have given an appearance of defeat.

Appearances became, perhaps, even more important after the peace treaty and the final departure of American forces. The need to "convey an impression of firmness and resolve" for the sake of the healthy interval the United States hoped to foster seemed more important than ever, yet the political situation in the United States made it difficult for the Nixon administration to deliver on its promises of support for South Vietnam in an emergency. Because of that, Kissinger avowed in a 9 April 1973 message to Haig that it might become necessary for him at times to be "over-explicit with regard to promises of future action should the situation out there deteriorate."[7]

With so many ambiguities, what was real? For some, it may be comforting to think that the news media pierced the mist, threw everything into focus, and brought the war to an end by forcing the American people to confront reality. Yet, if press coverage between 1969 and 1973 conveyed more truth than did official pronouncements on subjects such as drug abuse, race relations, the state of military morale, the incursions into Cambodia and Laos, and the conditions within the South Vietnamese government and armed forces, it was still highly circumscribed by the nature of journalism as it is practiced in the United States.

Reporters and editors, for example, tended to hew to the sources that gave their work the most weight—the president, the vice president, and other high officials of the executive and legislative branches of the gov-

---

[6] Interv, author with Col Robert Cook, 22 May 87, CMH files.

[7] Msg, Kissinger to Haig, 9 Apr 73, NSC files, A. M. Haig Special file, box 1020, Gen Haig's SEA Trip, Apr 7–11, 1973 [I of III], Nixon Papers.

ernment. During the war, the tendency sometimes harmed official credibility. When President Nixon announced during the incursion into Cambodia that he had targeted COSVN headquarters, the comment had such an effect that the press picked it up and clung to it, despite later efforts by public affairs officers to issue a clarification. More often, however, it worked to the advantage of the official point of view. Every presidential and vice presidential news conference and speech of any importance, especially those that were critical of the press, received heavy publicity in print and on the television networks, even in those segments of the news media that opposed the president and the war. In that way, Vice President Agnew was able to score heavily against the press, using the very news media he was criticizing. The reverse was also true. If the administration sought to lessen the impact of some aspect of the war, it could eliminate or significantly delay press coverage by keeping silent, or, if it had to comment, by moving the story away from Washington. The bombing of Cambodia provides a case in point. Despite William Beecher's early account of the attacks and despite the ability of reporters to stand at South Vietnam's border and hear the unmistakable sound of B–52 strikes in Cambodia, the silence of official sources on all sides— whether in the United States, Cambodia, or North Vietnam—ensured that the subject died an early death in the press. In the same manner, the Defense Department was able to postpone the initial reaction of the news media to the My Lai massacre by using low-level sources to announce the trial of Lieutenant Calley and by issuing the communique in a location far from Washington. In that case, however, a storm was inevitable. Official efforts to play down the event only made matters worse by feeding the suspicions of the press.

The routines reporters followed also tended to dilute news coverage of the war. Adhering to deadlines, constrained to write on subjects that producers and editors believed readers and viewers would want, and subject to increasing pressure because of cutbacks in personnel, the Saigon correspondents spent considerably less time covering events in the field during the years after 1968 than they had earlier in the war. Even when they did, there was no guarantee that what they wrote would see print. Sometimes—as was the case when Peter Arnett submitted his account of the sacking of Snuol—editors preferred to hold back, either to avoid controversy or, as Wes Gallagher noted with regard to Arnett's report, to keep from contributing to the chaos that seemed about to descend on all sides.

Time was also a problem, especially in the case of television news, as an episode related by former ABC News correspondent Don North indicates. Years after the war, while preparing a documentary on the conflict, North received permission from his old network to review the archived reels of filmed reports he and other members of the ABC bureau in Saigon had filed during the war. As his work progressed, it became apparent from the unplayed condition of much of the film and the heavily edited nature of the scripts that harried producers in New York, working against sometimes extreme deadlines, had often reviewed just enough of the material to put together a coherent story. With that in hand, especially in the case of dated material, they had hardly ever bothered to go on into the deeper recesses of a reel, where, North contended, some of his best and most pointed reporting often rested. The record was better where pieces that could be played at any time were concerned, the reporter continued, because producers and editors could work with them at their leisure. Even so, it was clear to him that much of the work he and his colleagues had submitted over the years had never been seen. It remained, tightly wound, just as it had come from the developer's lab.[8]

Yet official manipulation and journalistic failures are relatively superficial aspects of the story. The question can legitimately be raised whether either the press coverage of the conflict or the government's efforts to marshal public opinion had much effect upon the people of the United States. There is evidence that from the beginning of the war, whatever the efforts of the government or the press, the American public had gone its own way. As early as March 1966, for example, a carefully balanced survey of public opinion revealed deep ambivalence on the part of many Americans, despite the efforts of the Johnson administration to mold a public consensus in favor of the conflict and the acquiescence of large portions of the press in the process. Although it approved of the president's handling of the war, a majority of those interviewed favored deescalation and was willing to support free elections in South Vietnam, even if the Viet Cong should win. Fifty-two percent were, indeed, willing to accept a coalition government that included Communists, a position anathema to the Johnson administration at that stage in the fighting.[9] In the same way, during the Nixon years, many members of the American public supported Vice President Agnew's contention that television presented the news in a biased fashion, but a large majority nonetheless believed that the news media should continue to criticize government. Although Americans almost invariably rallied to the president's side during times of crisis and were clearly unwilling to abandon the conflict without the return of the prisoners of war, their regret that they had ever become involved increased steadily as American losses mounted.[10]

Richard Nixon understood the tenuous nature of public opinion and bought time for his policies to work by curtailing American combat casualties during the final years of the war. Yet by the beginning of his second term in office, despite a victory in the 1972 elections that approached the dimensions of a landslide, he had still lost most of his

[8] Interv, author with Don North, 15 Nov 90, CMH files.

[9] Hammond, *Public Affairs: The Military and the Media, 1962–1968*, pp. 227–29.

[10] Mark Lorell, *Casualties, Public Opinion, and Presidential Policy During the Vietnam War* (Santa Monica, Calif.: Rand Corporation, 1985), summarized by Richard Morin, "How Much War Will Americans Support?," *Washington Post*, 2 Sep 90.

leverage. Failing to rise to his support, the public rejected his Christmas bombing campaign by a wide margin.

It would be tempting to conclude that distorted news coverage of the attacks in the press had wrought that effect, or that enemy propaganda designed to depict North Vietnam as the victim of an American terror campaign had succeeded. But in fact, if the news media through its coverage of Communist claims had inevitably highlighted the issues, telling people, in effect, what to think about, Americans continued to think for themselves. By a margin of almost two to one, they disavowed the claims of both the Communists and the press, to side instead, very simply, with the conclusion that "we lost many American lives and B–52's . . . in the raids."[11] The reaction had nothing to do with softness, moral laxity, lack of will, or an inability to face the necessary frustrations of a long war. It was simple common sense. If more men, more bombs, and more killing had proved earlier to be of no avail and if South Vietnam itself showed few of the traits necessary for survival, why prolong the struggle? The American people had had enough. At the end of the war as at the beginning, they had followed their own, third course, marked by independence of judgment and a substantial measure of contempt for all those who sought to manipulate the public mind.

What happened in Vietnam between the military and the news media was thus symptomatic of what had occurred in the United States as a whole. At the beginning of the conflict, the country had acquiesced as the Johnson administration had moved to contain Chinese and Soviet ambitions in Southeast Asia by going to war in South Vietnam. Although professedly suspicious of government as a matter of principle, the American news media had both reflected and reinforced the trend, replaying official statements on the value of the war and supporting the soldier in the field if not always his generals. With time, under the influence of many deaths and contradictions, society moved to repudiate that earlier decision. The press followed along, taking its lead from an increasingly divided American elite and becoming ever more critical as the conflict lost whatever meaning it had held for the American people. The military, for its part, lacked the independence to do the same. Remaining in Vietnam to retrieve the nation's honor, many of its members fixed their anger upon the most visible element of the society that appeared to have rejected them, the press, rather than upon the failed policies that had brought them to that point. When reporters took up the challenge, anger and recrimination on all sides were the inevitable result. Whether time and circumstance would heal the ensuing rift remained to be seen.[12]

---

[11] Harris, *The Anguish of Change*, p. 78.

[12] The author first examined this theme in an essay for *Reviews in American History*. William Hammond, "The Press in Vietnam as Agent of Defeat: A Critical Examination," *Reviews in American History* (June 1989): 312–23.

Bibliographical Note

This book builds upon its predecessor, *Public Affairs: The Military and the Media, 1962–1968*, but the documentation it uses branches off into new directions. Volume 1 relied heavily upon the Defense Department's history of decision making during the early years of the Vietnam War, *The Senator Gravel Edition of the Pentagon Papers*; the State Department's central files; and the voluminous records amassed by General William C. Westmoreland while he was commander of the U.S. Military Assistance Command in Vietnam. To a lesser extent, it also used the records of the Southeast Asia Desk of the Defense Department's Directorate of Defense Information.

For a number of reasons, none of those sources were adequate for volume 2. The *Pentagon Papers*, for example, dealt in detail with the Kennedy and Johnson administrations but were of no value for the second half of the war. Meanwhile, although useful, the State Department's files were thin for the years after 1968, reportedly because harried administrators had never taken the time to retire working records. Westmoreland's papers remained important, especially those dealing with morale and personnel issues and those covering the few periods when the general served as acting chairman of the Joint Chiefs of Staff. On the whole, however, they provided little day-to-day information on events in the field because the general ceased to play a significant role in war-related policy making after becoming chief of staff of the Army in 1968.

As for the records of the Directorate of Defense Information, they contained a vast amount of information of enormous value to both volumes but were thinned progressively by administrators more interested in the space they occupied than in the unique historical resource they represented. From six large filing cabinets filled with records, the collection shrank to the equivalent of one. Although what remained was of use, much of the perspective it might have provided disappeared with the documents that were gone—among them, important backchannel messages; highly classified policy papers; policy critiques; telephone conversation summaries; commentaries, directives, and draft memorandums, some handwritten on scratch paper; and a broad range of news clippings and press summaries.

Official Records

Since the extensive archives of the MACV Office of Information were apparently abandoned during the fall of Saigon in 1975, the author had to rely, as in the case of volume 1, upon the bureaucracy's habit of making copies. The public record was thus reconstructed by drawing upon the documentation left by those agencies and individuals in the federal government that had some say over public affairs.

The papers of Westmoreland's successor, General Creighton Abrams, on file at the U.S. Army Center of Military History in Washington, D.C., provided a starting point. Composed of the backchannel messages Abrams sent and received, that collection is very informative for the years 1968, 1969, and 1970 but incomplete for the final years of the war. The Center never received a large number of messages from the years 1971 and 1972. The whereabouts of that portion of the collection remains unclear. A file of microfilmed special category (SPECAT) messages composed of cables Abrams sent after 1971 filled in some details for those years, as did General Abrams' Personal file, a collection composed of the information copies Abrams received of messages transmitted by the U.S. embassy in Saigon to the State Department in Washington. Housed at the Center, those records detail the handling of controversies such as the Con Son tiger cages affair but say little about the origins of public affairs policy in Vietnam during the final years of the war. The papers of the Deputy Commander, U.S. Army, Vietnam, during 1970 and 1971, Lt. Gen. William J. McCaffrey, also on file in the Center, likewise provide background on the morale problems that plagued that period.

A scattering of policy documents pertaining to the Military Assistance Command's public affairs program were retired under accession 72A4722 by the Office of the MACV Historian to the Washington National Records Center at Suitland, Maryland. At the time of publication, those materials were about to be moved to the National Archives and Records Administration's facility in College Park, Maryland. Insights are also available from the records retired by the U.S. Army, Vietnam's Office of Information (USARVIO), filed at Suitland under accession 72A6694. Those sources have considerable value in the context of the other records collections consulted in this study, but they are so fragmentary and disjointed that they have little meaning on their own.

Similarly, the papers of Ambassador Ellsworth Bunker, housed in Washington, D.C., at the State Department's Foreign Affairs Information Management, Bureau of Intelligence and Research (FAIM/IR), are sometimes revealing but hardly constitute a complete collection. The White House maintained a direct, private channel to Bunker during the final years of the war. It bypassed all agencies, including the State Department. The messages it produced constitute a much better record of Bunker's dealings and his opinions of men and events. They are also pertinent to General Abrams, who sometimes used Bunker's secure line when dealing with the president. Contained in the National Security Council (NSC) files of the Nixon administration under the title "Backchannels," those records were in the possession of the Nixon Materials Project at the National Archives' federal records center in Alexandria, Virginia, but are also to be moved to the National Archives at College Park. They are, for the time being, closed to most researchers, even those affiliated with government agencies.

The papers of Clark Clifford and of George Christian, on file in the Lyndon Baines Johnson Library in Austin, Texas, are much more open to academic researchers. They contain considerable information on policy making during Lyndon Johnson's final year in office. Clifford's handwritten meeting notes are particularly revealing and shed great light on Clifford's opinion of the Thieu regime and his decision to push for a negotiated settlement. The papers of Nixon's Secretary of Defense Melvin Laird pertaining to the Vietnam War, particularly Phil Odeen's notes of Laird's meetings with his Vietnamization Committee, are similarly candid. The collection is huge. Its Vietnam holdings alone comprise 108 large archive boxes that contain well-organized files on every subject from Vietnamization to problems with morale and discipline. Although still classified, they were on file in Record Group 330 at the Washington National Records Center in Suitland but will also shortly move to the National Archives at College Park. More complete citations can be found in the footnotes of this volume. A collection of the Vietnamization Committee meeting notes has been retained at the Center of Military History, as part of the papers of Thomas Thayer, who served as director of the Southeast Asia Intelligence and Force Effectiveness Division of the Southeast Asia Programs Office under the assistant secretary of defense for systems analysis for most of the period between 1967 and 1975.

A number of the record groups on file at the U.S. Army's Military History Research Collection in Carlisle, Pennsylvania, proved important. The papers of the commander of XXIV Corps during LAM SON 719, Lt. Gen. James W. Sutherland, were valuable in reconstructing aspects of that operation. The papers of John Paul Vann detail some aspects of U.S. relations with the South Vietnamese. The Military History Institute also houses a vast oral history collection. The interviews with Lt. Gen. Arthur Collins and General Bruce Palmer, in particular, contained a number of insights.

Few of the records consulted in the course of this study, however, were as valuable as the collection of the papers of Richard M. Nixon administered by the Nixon Materials Project. For the researcher who has the time to go through the hundreds of boxes of material that bear upon the Vietnam War, they not only illuminate the relationship between the military and the news media during the Nixon administration, they also constitute the most broadly based record of the war's final years in existence. If the Abrams and Bunker Papers are fragmented and those of Melvin Laird view the conflict mainly from the perspective of the Department of Defense, the motivations for public affairs policy directives that often arrived unexplained in the field become clear at the White House level.

The Nixon Papers are split into two parts, one open to researchers, the other closed. Among the open files, H. R. Haldeman's handwritten notes proved useful, as did the office files of such staff members as John Ehrlichman, Charles Colson, and John Scali. Since Nixon and his lawyers had final say over what is released to the public, however, and since security classifications remain intact on many documents, the closed portions of the collection are of much more value to researchers, especially the NSC files. The author gained admittance to the portions of those files dealing with the Vietnam War through the efforts of the Center of Military History and former Secretary of the Army John O. Marsh, Jr., on grounds that a thorough understanding of what happened between the military and the news media in Vietnam would be essential if the United States ever went to war again.

Much that is missing from the Bunker and Abrams Papers funneled into the White House for the use of the president's analysts and advisers. The Backchannels mentioned in relation to Ambassador Bunker, for example, contain not only messages from and to the president by Kissinger, Bunker, and Abrams but also considerable correspondence between Kissinger, Alexander Haig, and other members of the National Security Council staff. The Vietnam Country and Vietnam Subject files duplicate messages and memorandums from a number of government agencies and cover all aspects of the war. The Chronological file collected by Comdr. Jonathan Howe on Kissinger's staff contains much of the Kissinger-Haig correspondence and a wealth of other documents detailing the inside stories of occurrences in the field. The Staff Member Office files are telling, especially the papers of Herbert Klein, John Ehrlichman, Charles Colson, John Scali, Ron Ziegler, and Les Janka. Janka sometimes issued day-by-day public affairs guidance on issues important to the White House. John Ehrlichman's Special Subject file contains much on the Yeoman Radford affair.

The files pertaining to the president himself are especially valuable. The various speech files contain considerable background on the talks the president gave and the public affairs initiatives that surrounded them. The Annotated News Summaries file holds those of the president's daily news summaries that contain the president's own handwritten marginal comments. Some are very revealing. Memorandums of conversations between Nixon and Kissinger are in the Presidential/HAK Memcon files. Formal memorandums from various staff members are in the President's Office files. The President's Personal file contains whatever documents Nixon's secretary found on his desk at the end of the day.

Messages, memorandums, and other documents from and to Henry Kissinger are scattered throughout the Nixon Papers, but they are also present in Kissinger's Office files. Kissinger's Trip and Country files on Vietnam were particularly useful. Alexander Haig's Special and Chronological files constitute a separate category of records, but they are intimately related to Kissinger's papers and sometimes add new insights into what was happening. The Vietnam Negotiations file, of course, contains much Kissinger and Haig material.

News Media Sources

As mentioned in the preface, the book relies heavily upon the newspaper, magazine, and television news reports and summaries collected by the Air Force News Clipping and Analysis Service in the Pentagon. Some of that material, but by no means all of it, was published either in the *Early Bird*, a daily survey of the print media's coverage of military issues, or in the *Radio-TV-Defense Dialog*, which paraphrases radio and television news reports on important military topics. Both are on file at the News Clipping and Analysis Service. Back issues of the *Early Bird* are retained at the Office of Air Force History at Bolling Air Force Base in Washington, D.C.

The author also made extensive use of the *New York Times*, the *Wall Street Journal*, the *Washington Post, Time, Life, Newsweek, U.S. News & World Report*, and the *Congressional Record*, all of which are on file either in the Pentagon Library, the Newspaper Reading Room of the Library of Congress, or various public libraries in the vicinity of Washington, D.C. News summaries compiled by the Defense and State Departments and the White House were useful in backing up those sources on the few occasions when a very broad view of press coverage seemed necessary to give the flavor of what the media had to say, either in the United States or around the world.

Official Histories

Several official histories provided important material for this work. All remain unavailable to the general public at this time. Henry F. Ackerman's work, He Was Always There: The U.S. Army Chaplain Ministry in the Vietnam Conflict [U.S. Army, Office of the Chief of Chaplains, 1988], contains a wealth of interview material on the morale problems that afflicted U.S. forces in South Vietnam as the war lengthened. The U.S. Military Assistance Command, Vietnam, produced a history for each year in which the American military participated in the war. Cited here as the MACV History, it provides a general view of the war's technical aspects and is sometimes valuable in reconstructing controversies with the news media that are poorly documented in other sources. In the same way, the Office of the Joint Chiefs of Staff has written periodic histories of that agency's involvement in the war. Referred to here as JCS History, that source is very candid. It sometimes supplements the materials present in the Laird and Nixon Papers.

A number of limited edition official works are, however, open to the public. At the end of the war, for example, the United States Army attempted to record the reminiscences of important South Vietnamese colonels and generals who had fled their country when it fell to the North. Collected in a series titled Indochina Monographs and published by the U.S. Army Center of Military History, those works provided useful background for this study. Maj. Gen. Nguyen Duy Hinh's *Lam Son 719* (Washington, D.C.: U.S. Army Center of Military History, 1979) tells the South Vietnamese side of that operation and contains important intelligence information. Hinh also authored a monograph entitled *Vietnamization and the Cease-Fire* (1980). Brig. Gen. Tran Dinh Tho's *The Cambodian Incursion* (1984) also proved useful, as did General Cao Van Vien's and Lt. Gen. Dong Van Khuyen's *Reflections on the Vietnam War* (1980); Col. Hoang Ngoc Lung's *The General Offensives of 1968–69* (1981); Col. Hoang Ngoc Lung's *Intelligence* (1981); and Lt. Gen. Ngo Quang Truong's *The Easter Offensive of 1972* (1979).

Interviews

During the course of this study, interviews of many of the men responsible for the conduct of public affairs during the final years of the war were used to supplement documentary sources. Jerry Friedheim and Daniel Henkin offered a broad range of insights into public affairs policy making at the Defense Department. Maj. Gens. Winant Sidle and L. Gordon Hill covered some of the same ground but were able to include the role of the Military Assistance Command, Vietnam, where they served lengthy tours of duty. Brig. Gen. Joseph Cutrona covered his year as chief of public affairs at MACV, as did Cols. Phillip Stevens and Robert Burke. Col. Robert Leonard, who could not be located until late in the study, nevertheless contributed important new insights in several lengthy telephone conversations and a long letter. Col. Perry Stevens was most candid in describing the handling of the press during LAM SON 719. Comdr. Joseph Lorfano, who served as a public affairs officer in the Pentagon throughout the final years of the war, retiring in 1973 as the last special assistant for Southeast Asia, also contributed his recollections. Henkin, Hill, and Phillip Stevens have since passed away.

General Abrams' Inspector General, Col. Robert Cook, contributed important background on the Military Assistance Command's problems with morale and discipline. A former chief of the Histories Division at the Center of Military History, Col. Robert Sholly, who for a time served on Cook's staff in Vietnam and participated in many investigations, also provided major insights.

Since it was not the place of the U.S. Army to write a history of the press or press coverage or to pry into reporters' sources and methods, the Saigon correspondents were allowed to speak mostly through the work they published. Even so, to gain essential background, the author conducted a number of conversations with former *Washington Post* Saigon bureau chief Peter Braestrup; with *U.S. News & World Report*'s long-time correspondent in South Vietnam, Wendell "Bud" Merick; and with Associated Press veteran Peter Arnett. Arnett has since published his memoirs, *Live From the Battlefield, From Vietnam to Baghdad, 35 Years in the World's War Zones* (New York: Simon and Schuster, 1994). They shed significant light on his career to date.

Some Significant Secondary Works

Books and articles by many authors contributed heavily to this work as it progressed. Herbert J. Gans' *Deciding What's News* (New York: Vintage Books, 1979); Leon V. Sigal's *Reporters and Officials: The Organization and Politics of Newsmaking* (Lexington, Mass.: D.C. Heath and Company, 1973); Chalmers Roberts' *The Washington Post, The First 100 Years* (Boston: Houghton Mifflin, 1977); Harrison E. Salisbury's *Without Fear or Favor* (New York: Times Books, 1980); and Chris Argyris' *Behind the Front Page* (San Francisco: Jossy-Bass Publishers, 1974) deal at length with the organization of the news business in the print media during the final years of the war. Their insights are essential for understanding the move the news media made away from support for the war and toward a more questioning approach. Marvin Barrett describes some aspects of decision making at the television networks in the *A. I. du Pont–Columbia University Surveys of Broadcast Journalism for 1969–1970, 1970–1971,* and *1971–1972* (New York: Grosset & Dunlap, Inc., 1971 and 1972; Thomas Y. Crowell Co., 1973).

In "Truth From the Snares of Crisis, The American Press in Vietnam" (M.A. diss., University of Kentucky, 1984) and *Paper Soldiers: The American Press and the Vietnam War* (New York: W. W. Norton, 1993), Clarence Wyatt documents the news media's shift away from support for the war by describing how the press covered events in South Vietnam at critical junctures. George A. Bailey's dissertation, *The Vietnam War According to Chet, David, Walter, Harry, Peter, Bob, Howard, and Frank: A Content Analysis of Journalistic Performance by the Network Television Evening News Anchormen* (Ann Arbor, Mich.: University Microfilms, 1973), describes the process and how it worked in the case of television and television anchormen. Daniel C. Hallin's *The Uncensored War: The Media and Vietnam* (New York: Oxford University Press, 1986) uses content analyses to define what happened and to assert that the news media's turn against the war mirrored changes that were occurring within the leadership of the United States.

For the views of a Nixon administration stalwart, see James Keogh's *President Nixon and the Press* (New York: Funk & Wagnells, 1972). The media were criticized by a prominent member of the antiwar movement in Todd Gitlin's *The Whole World Is Watching: Mass Media in the Making and Unmaking of the New Left* (Berkeley: University of California Press, 1980) because they failed to give that cause the sort of hearing its proponents felt it deserved. Edward Jay Epstein's *News From Nowhere* (New York: Random House, 1973) suggests that the politics and economics of the news-gathering process during the final years of the war was partly the reason for the news media's less than perfect performance. As Dennis T. Lowry suggests in "Agnew and the Network TV News, A Before/After Content Analysis," *Journalism Quarterly* 48 (Summer 1971): 205–10, however, the problem afflicted all sides of the debate over the war, not just the New Left. President Nixon apparently also failed to have much effect on the way the news media reported. The most recent study on the subject, Melvin Small's *Covering Dissent, The Media and the Anti-Vietnam War Movement* (New Brunswick, N.J.: Rutgers University Press, 1994), appeared as this book was going to press. It asserts that the American news media tended to reflect middle-class, moderate values and thus did not present a particularly fair picture of the antiwar movement between 1965 and 1971. Indeed, the media's caricature of the movement's activities and objectives during that time fed the American public's distrust of those who fail to reflect generally accepted standards of conduct and belief and slowed the growth of antiwar sentiment in the United States.

Whether press coverage of the war had much influence on public opinion is difficult to tell. This work relied upon the Gallup, Harris, and Sidlinger polls but also used a number of studies to sketch the outlines of what the public felt. Prominent among those were Louis Harris' *The Anguish of Change* (New York: W. W. Norton, 1973), and Hazel Erskine's "The Polls: Is War a Mistake," *Public Opinion Quarterly* 34 (Spring 1970): 134. Michael Wheeler's book questioning the polls and the entire process of public opinion sampling, *Lies, Damn Lies, and Statistics: The Manipulation of Public Opinion in America* (New York: Liveright, 1976), posed a counterweight.

Richard A. Lau, Thad A. Brown, and David O. Sears observe in "Self-Interest and Civilians' Attitudes Toward the Vietnam War," *Public Opinion Quarterly* 42 (Winter 1978): 464 that many factors influenced the American public's opinion of the war, not only the news. Indeed, John E. Mueller's *War, Presidents and Public Opinion* (New York: Wiley, 1973) links the decline of public opinion of the war to casualties in the field. Mark Lorell and Charles Kelley, Jr., confirm and augment Mueller's research in *Casualties, Public Opinion, and Presidential Policy During the Vietnam War*, Project Air Force Report R–3060–AF (Santa Monica, Calif.: Rand Corporation, 1985). The various essays presented in Peter Braestrup, ed., *Vietnam as History* (Washington, D.C.: Woodrow Wilson International

Center for Scholars, 1984), especially the appendixes by Mueller and Lawrence Lichty also bear upon the issue. The *Journal of Communication* devoted considerable space in its Autumn 1975 issue to Alden Williams' "TV's First War: Unbiased Study of Television News Bias," which examined television's approach to the war. The author addressed these issues and many of the myths surrounding the war in "The Press in Vietnam as Agent of Defeat: A Critical Examination," *Reviews in American History* (June 1989): 312.

With the Nixon Papers largely unavailable, most studies of the Vietnam War slight the conflict's final years or base their analyses of that period upon newspaper files, personal reminiscences, and interviews. Some are, nevertheless, very well documented and have been exceedingly useful to this study. Ronald H. Spector's *After Tet* (New York: Free Press, 1992) provides an excellent introduction to the period by documenting the last year of Lyndon Johnson's presidency. Although subjective in its point of view, Henry Kissinger's memoir, *The White House Years* (Boston: Little, Brown and Co., 1979), bears many resemblances to the official documents that are at its core. Walter Isaacson's *Kissinger, A Biography* (New York: Simon and Schuster, 1992) contains much new material and sheds important light on the Nixon presidency. Jeffrey Clarke's *Advice and Support: The Final Years, 1965–1973*, United States Army in Vietnam (Washington, D.C.: U.S. Army Center of Military History, Government Printing Office, 1988), defines and clarifies U.S. relations with the South Vietnamese. Stephen E. Ambrose's political history, *Nixon, The Triumph of a Politician, 1962–1972* (New York: Simon and Schuster, 1989), places the war solidly into the context of the national and international concerns that preoccupied Nixon during his years as president. Lewis Sorley's biography of Abrams, *Thunderbolt: General Creighton Abrams and the Army of His Times* (New York: Simon and Schuster, 1992), is overly sympathetic to its subject and lacks complete references but still contains many insights. Guenter Lewy's *America in Vietnam* (Oxford: Oxford University Press, 1978) and Graham A. Cosmas' and USMC Lt. Col. Terrence P. Murray's *U.S. Marines in Vietnam: Vietnamization and Redeployment, 1970–1971* (Washington, D.C.: History and Museums Division, Headquarters, U.S. Marine Corps, 1986), draw upon many heretofore obscure official sources to sketch the uncertainties and moral ambiguities that afflicted the American force in South Vietnam.

A number of well-documented studies have covered the Green Beret affair. Among the most useful were Jeff Stein's *A Murder in Wartime: The Untold Spy Story That Changed the Course of the Vietnam War* (New York: St. Martin's Press, 1992) and John Stevens Berry's *Those Gallant Men: On Trial in Vietnam* (Novato, Calif.: Presidio Press, 1984).

Bui Diem's memoir with David Chanoff of his years as South Vietnamese Ambassador to the United States, *In the Jaws of History* (Boston: Houghton Mifflin, 1987), adds much to our perception of the South Vietnamese leadership and its problems. The bitterness that many

South Vietnamese continue to feel at what they consider the betrayal of their country by the United States is readily apparent in Jerrold L. Schecter and Nguyen Tien Hung's collection and analysis of President Nixon's letters and messages to Thieu, *The Palace File* (New York: Harper and Row, 1986).

Photo Credits

Illustrations courtesy of the following sources:

White House files, p. 10
Department of Defense files, pp. 24, 29, 35, 50, 57, 66, 109, 118, 131, 175, 202, 213, 325, 328, 330, 338, 383, 412, 445, 536, 568, 582, 586, 602, 603, 611
Sp4c. Robert Hodierne/Department of Defense files, p. 94
UPI/Bettmann, pp. 27, 44, 86, 92, 166, 183, 221, 229, 372, 593
Fred Mayer/Magnum Photos, p. 47
Nixon Papers, National Archives, pp. 58, 112, 126, 156, 161, 257, 282, 295, 415
Courtesy of the Hill family, p. 74
AP/Wide World Photos, pp. 87, 141, 152, 162, 178, 195, 222, 234, 252, 270, 304, 356, 428, 478, 587
Life Magazine © Time Inc., p. 105
U.S. Army Center of Military History files, pp. 133, 264, 278, 390, 402, 441, 470, 473, 519, 521, 550, 554, 565
Reni Photos/courtesy of Ambassador Bui Diem, p. 136
Ennio Iacobucci/*Time* Magazine © Time Warner Inc., p. 208
Ron Haeberle/*Life* Magazine © Time Inc., p. 225
S. L. A. Marshall Collection, U.S. Army Military History Institute, p. 244
Courtesy of Jerry Friedheim, pp. 268, 418, 494
Stars and Stripes Collection, U.S. Army Military History Institute, p. 300
Courtesy of Col. Joseph F. H. Cutrona, p. 312
John Filo, p. 317
Courtesy of Col. Robert Leonard, p. 351
Courtesy of Senator Thomas Harkin, p. 360
Courtesy of M. Sgt. Wolfgang Scherp, p. 432
Keystone Press Agency, p. 442
Archive Photos/Express Newspapers, p. 453
Zais Collection/U.S. Army Military History Institute, p. 482
Finch Collection/U.S. Army Military History Institute, pp. 530, 542
MTI/Eastfoto, pp. 542, 583
Black Star, p. 564
Indochina Archives, Berkeley, p. 612
Le Minh/*Time* Magazine © Time Warner Inc., p. 614

Index

LaVergne, TN USA
10 February 2010
172675LV00001B/16/A

9 780898 756043